The Bristol and Gloucestershire Archaeological Society
Gloucestershire Record Series

Hon. General Editor
C. R. Elrington, M.A., F.S.A., F.R.Hist.S.
formerly General Editor of the
Victoria History of the Counties of England

Volume 14

Calendar of Gloucester Apprenticeship Registers, 1595–1700

A CALENDAR OF THE REGISTERS OF APPRENTICES OF THE CITY OF GLOUCESTER 1595–1700

Edited by Jill Barlow, M.A.

The Bristol and Gloucestershire Archaeological Society

2001

The Bristol and Gloucestershire Archaeological Society
Gloucestershire Record Series

© The Bristol and Gloucestershire Archaeological Society 2001

ISBN 0 900197 54 4

British Library Cataloguing in Publication Data.
A catalogue record for this book is available from the British Library.

Printed in Great Britain by J. W. Arrowsmith Ltd., Winterstoke Road, Bristol BS3 2NT

CONTENTS

Acknowledgements	vii
List of Abbreviations	ix
Introduction	
Historical Background	xi
Gloucester Apprentices	xiii
Conditions of Apprenticeship	xvii
Apprenticing Charities	xx
Apprentices for Virginia and Barbados	xxiii
The Registers as Historical Evidence	xxiii
The Registers	xxix
Editorial Method	xxxii
Calendar	
1595–1646	1
1645–1668	107
Apprentices for Virginia and Barbados 1659–60	181
1668–1700	183
Appendixes	
I. Specimen Apprenticeship Indentures	261
II. Apprenticing Charities	263
III. Agreement to discharge a Tewkesbury apprentice	264
IV. Admissions of Freemen, 1595–1641	265
V. Apprentices possibly bound more than once	274
Index of Persons	277
Index of Places	321
Index of Trades, Occupations and Ranks	332
Index of Subjects	341

ACKNOWLEDGEMENTS

The Society acknowledges the cooperation of the City of Gloucester in granting permission for the publication of copyright material in its possession.

Transcription of the Gloucester apprenticeship registers was started some twenty years ago by volunteers working in the Gloucestershire Record Office, and I have been able to make use of the work done by the late Mrs. Joyce Popplewell.

I should like to thank the former County and Diocesan Archivist, David J. H. Smith (the Society's general secretary), for suggesting the project to me in the first place and for supporting me with his encouragement and good advice to ensure that the task was brought to fruition. I am grateful to the staff of the Gloucestershire Record Office for producing quantities of increasingly heavy volumes and to all those, especially Brian Frith, who cheerfully answered my endless stream of questions. The general editor of the Gloucestershire Record Series, Christopher Elrington, has coped patiently with my apparent belief that I could reply to his questions by thought transference rather than by letter, and I am very grateful for his wise guidance.

This book is dedicated to the memory of my late father, Bill Reed, who died on 21 June 2001, shortly before it was to go to press.

Cheltenham, July 2001   Jill Barlow

ABBREVIATIONS

Ben Amos, *Adolescence and Youth*	I. K. Ben Amos, *Adolescence and Youth in Early Modern England* (Yale University Press, 1994)
Dunlop, *Apprenticeship and Child Labour*	O. J. Dunlop, *Apprenticeship and Child Labour* (London, 1912)
Fosbrooke, *City of Gloucester*	T. D. Fosbrooke, *An Original History of the City of Gloucester almost wholly compiled from new materials . . . including also the Original Papers of Ralph Bigland* (London, 1819)
Freemen	*A Calendar of the Registers of the Freemen of the City of Gloucester, 1641–1838*, ed. John Juřica (Bristol and Gloucestershire Archaeological Society, Gloucestershire Record Series vol. 4, 1991)
GBR	Gloucester Borough Records, in the Gloucestershire Record Office
GRO	Gloucestershire Record Office, Gloucester
Lane, *Apprenticeship in England*	Joan Lane, *Apprenticeship in England, 1600–1914* (London UCL Press, 1996)
PRO	Public Record Office, Kew, London
VCH Glos iv	*Victoria History of the Counties of England: Gloucestershire*, volume IV, The City of Gloucester, ed. N. M. Herbert (Oxford University Press, 1988)

INTRODUCTION

Historical Background

'Another species of servants are called apprentices (from *apprendre*, to learn) and are usually bound for a term of years, by deed indented or indentures, to serve their masters, and be maintained and instructed by them. This is usually done to persons of trade, in order to learn their art and mystery.'[1] Apprenticeship as a method of training can be traced back to the 13th century and although much altered it still exists today.

The apprenticeship system[2] was set up and administered by the medieval craft guilds who each formulated their individual rules, though some basic conditions were common to all. The apprentice had to be bound by written indenture for a period of at least seven years. He had to live with his master and mistress and promised to serve them faithfully, to keep their secrets and not to indulge in drink, dice or matrimony. In exchange the master would provide food and clothing and teach the craft to the best of his ability. Some guilds imposed terms of service longer than seven years or required a 'proof piece' to demonstrate that the apprentice had reached the necessary standard of skill.

At the end of his term the apprentice was entitled to the freedom of his guild. By controlling training the guilds were able to maintain standards of workmanship and to restrict competition. By serving an apprenticeship a boy (and very rarely a girl) learned a skill and earned the right to trade in the town where he could hope to learn a respectable living. Bristol, in 1344, was one of the earliest towns to grant municipal freedom to apprentices who had served their term.[3]

The Statute of Artificers, 1563,[4] introduced standardised rules for the whole country, based on the customs of London. It specified that the apprentice had to be under 21 when bound, that the apprenticeship had to last at least seven years and could not end until the apprentice was at least 24. Only householders could take apprentices and no-one could set up in trade without serving an apprenticeship. Masters in some trades, including goldsmiths, mercers, clothiers and ironmongers, could take as apprentice only their own sons or the sons of fathers with property worth 40*s.* a year in boroughs or 60*s.* a year in market towns which were not boroughs. Weavers, tailors and shoemakers among other trades were required to employ a journeyman if they had more than three

---

[1] Sir William Blackstone, *Commentaries on the Laws of England*, vol. i (1770), p. 426.
[2] Much of the information on the historical background to apprenticeship is drawn from O. J. Dunlop, *Apprenticeship and Child Labour* (1912), and Joan Lane, *Apprenticeship in England, 1600–1914* (1996).
[3] *Little Red Book of Bristol*, ed. F. B. Bickley (Bristol, 1900), i, p. 36.
[4] 5 Eliz. I, cap. 4.

apprentices at a time. The indentures were legally enforceable even though the apprentice was under 21, and neither master nor apprentice could break the contract without showing good reason. It is not clear how strictly the provisions of the Statute of Artificers were enforced, since as mentioned below there was no national supervision.

Apprenticeship, providing as it did both a home and training, was seen as a means of coping with poverty and vagrancy. The Poor Law Act, 1601,[1] gave churchwardens and overseers of the poor, with the agreement of two justices of the peace, the power to bind poor children apprentice. The Settlement Act, 1691,[2] allowed overseers to fine reluctant masters if they refused to accept a parish child.

Wealthy philanthropists sometimes left land or money specifically to provide funds for apprenticing poor children. An Act of 1610 was intended to ensure that such charity funds were properly administered.[3] A master receiving money from an apprenticing charity had to provide one or two sureties and sign a bond for double the sum received to the corporation which awarded the money. The money had to be repaid at the end of seven years or if the apprentice died. Poor apprentices were to be no older than 15. Although the charity money was intended to save children from 'idleness and disordered kinds of life', by no means all the recipients were paupers.

The Statute of Artificers did not establish any central authority to oversee its implementation and it was administered locally by the guilds, which by the 17th century were more generally known as companies or fraternities. As the influence of the companies waned with the growing belief in freedom of trade, the requirements of the Statute of Artificers were more leniently interpreted in the law courts and made less stringent by further legislation. Among the many Acts governing apprenticeship was one which allowed an apprentice to gain his freedom by securing the conviction of two offenders guilty of coining.[4] In 1768[5] the age for completing an apprenticeship was reduced from 24 to 21. New industries were introduced into the country and it was argued that the restrictions in the Act applied only to trades which existed in 1563. An 18th-century jurist described some of its directions as 'entirely obsolete and of no use',[6] but the Act was not repealed until 1814.

The wording of indentures changed very little over the centuries. A Norwich indenture of 1291[7] uses the same terms as the one dated 300 years later which is transcribed first in Appendix I below. The English indenture in Appendix I, dated 25 September 1604, while not an exact translation of the Latin, imposes the same conditions and is written with the same rhythmic, almost sing-song, phrasing.

[1] 43 Eliz. I, cap. 2.
[2] 3 Wm. & Mary, cap. 11.
[3] 7 Jas. I, cap. 3.
[4] 6 & 7 Wm. & Mary, cap. 17.
[5] 8 Geo. III, cap. 28.
[6] R. Burns, *The Justice of the Peace and Parish Officer* (12th edn., 1772), p. 57.
[7] Dunlop, *Apprenticeship and Child Labour*, p. 351.

The indentures of non-poor apprentices say that the boy 'hath put himself apprentice' whereas those of pauper children placed by the parish state that he was placed by the churchwardens or the overseers.

The indenture was a contract, originally in the standard form, where the agreement was written out twice on a single piece of parchment. The two halves were then cut apart along a jagged line so that each of the parties could keep one and the halves could if necessary be fitted together as evidence of their authenticity. The Statute of Artificers specified that the contract of apprenticeship should be 'by deed indented', but printed forms were used long before 1757, the year in which indentures ceased to be legally necessary and were replaced by a stamped deed. The English indenture in Appendix I, dated 1604, is a printed form with the apprentice's details filled in later.

Gloucester Apprentices

In Gloucester apprenticeship was accepted as a route to municipal freedom from 1454 or earlier.[1] By the early 17th century apprentices to trades governed by the companies of mercers, weavers, bakers, tanners, haberdashers, innkeepers, tailors, butchers, shearmen, glovers, shoemakers, barbers, metalmen and joiners were entitled to the freedom.[2] The companies could add their own conditions to the provisions of the Statute of Artificers: the metalmen's rules of 1606[3] forbade the teaching of the craft to a son or servant for more than six months unless he was bound apprentice for at least seven years and the indentures were enrolled both with the clerk of the company and the clerk of the city; the bakers' company rules of 1636[4] had the same provisions but allowed only two months' teaching.

The mayor, the aldermen and the members of the common council (the governing body of the city) were all freemen and were naturally concerned to protect their privileges. These included the right to vote in parliamentary elections and the right, exclusive except at the time of fairs, to trade within the city. These trading rights were increasingly under threat from unregulated traders setting up their own businesses. The common council minute books throughout the 17th century contain references to attempts to regulate the enrolment of apprenticeship indentures and ensure that only apprentices who had served their proper term were admitted as freemen. The earliest existing register was begun in June 1595, just as a new town clerk took up his post, perhaps with the enthusiasm of a new arrival for doing things properly. It opens with a statement that the 'roll' (i.e. the register) was made in accordance with a decision taken in 1554,[5] but if there was an earlier register it has been lost.

---

[1] VCH *Glos* iv. 57 n.
[2] *Freemen*, p. xvi.
[3] GBR B1/4
[4] GBR B1/6
[5] Below, p. 1.

The son of a freeman was entitled to admission by patrimony only if he was born after his father was admitted to the freedom. Many freemen's sons therefore served a term of apprenticeship in order to gain the freedom of the city. The fees for becoming a freeman by patrimony, as set out by the common council in 1646, were 12*d*. to the mayor, 6*d*. apiece to the sheriffs, 4*d*. to the steward and 2*s*. 8*d*. for a bucket (a contribution towards fire fighting).[1] An apprentice had to pay a 4*s*. fine, in addition to all the other fees, so there was some financial advantage in claiming by patrimony if possible.

To gain the municipal freedom by apprenticeship a man had to have been bound to a freeman and to have served for at least seven years. In 1613 the common council tried to prevent the practice of antedating indentures to shorten the term by decreeing that 'henceforth no apprentice shall be bound to serve any man within this city but before the mayor of this city and in his presence, and that for that purpose a book or register shall be kept in the custody of the said mayor for the time being wherein the true dates and terms of all indentures of apprentices shall be entered and registered'.[2]

There were clearly difficulties in applying the decree and in 1617 the council found that 'the mayor being busied many times with matters of greater consequence' was not always able to supervise the enrolment of apprentices. Freemen were therefore required to pay the town clerk or his deputy 2*s*. to make the indentures and to enter them in the book kept for the purpose. A heavy fine of 5*s*. was imposed for every month's delay between the making and the enrolling of the indentures.[3] In fact the register was particularly badly kept during these years, perhaps because the town clerk, William Guise, was so often absent in London[4] that he too was unavailable to supervise enrolments.

In 1652 another complaint that indentures were not being properly enrolled[5] coincided with the appearance in the apprenticeship register of several indentures enrolled years after they were made. Some were enrolled only when the apprentice was reassigned and the omission came to the attention of the town clerk (below, **2**/110 and **2**/151).

Fraudulent apprenticeships were a continual problem. John Bosley was discharged from his apprenticeship after four months in 1636 when it was realised that he was aged more than 27 and a married man (**1**/481). In 1677 Thomas Croker was disfranchised for taking two apprentices 'merely as a deceit to obtain the privilege of being a burgess'.[6] John Sowdley procured the freedom for his son by falsely swearing that he had served him as an apprentice for seven years.[7]

---

[1] GBR B3/2 p 371.
[2] GBR B3/1 f. 249.
[3] Ibid. f. 443.
[4] Ibid. f. 449.
[5] GBR B3/2 p. 660.
[6] GBR B3/3 pp. 674–5.
[7] Ibid. p. 890.

By 1680 the right of burgesses to vote in parliamentary elections was becoming increasingly important and the council made yet another attempt to prevent burgesses taking apprentices 'not to teach them their trade but to let them in to the freedom of this city'.[1] It ruled that before anyone could claim the freedom by apprenticeship, the chamberlain was to inspect the book of enrolments to make sure that the indentures had been duly registered.

The rules were occasionally set aside and it was possible for an apprentice to be made free despite losing his indenture[2] or despite never having had indentures at all if his master was prepared to swear that he had served as an apprentice.[3] An apprentice could be made to serve extra years before becoming free if his master was not a freeman at the start of his apprenticeship.[4] The freedom could be given as a reward to a man prepared to take a poor child as an apprentice.[5]

In theory only apprentices in the 'composition trades' (those governed by one of the trade companies listed above) were entitled to the freedom of Gloucester.[6] The companies were becoming less influential, however, and between 1641 and 1700 men from at least 75 separately described trades claimed the freedom by right of apprenticeship (see Table I, overleaf). It seems unlikely that all the trades included were regarded as being under the control of one of the composition trades, and in 1732 the common council noted that the privilege of the freedom had been awarded 'without due regard and distinction' to many who were not entitled to it.[7] Yet again the council decreed that indentures were to be enrolled only if the master belonged to a composition company, this time adding the requirement that he should live within the city. Not until 1787 was the freedom officially opened to the apprentices of all resident freemen.[8]

Despite the concern with excluding those who were not properly qualified, in Gloucester as in Bristol[9] and elsewhere, a high proportion of apprentices failed to become freemen. On average 41 apprentices were enrolled in Gloucester each year, but in the 60 years between 1641 and 1700 only about a quarter of them can be identified in the registers of freemen admitted by right of apprenticeship. Each year there were also a few admissions by apprenticeship, in the register of freemen, of men who do not appear in the register of apprentices. Some of these may have served an apprenticeship outside Gloucester, but most discrepancies are probably due to defects in registration. Some may not have been identified because the time between enrolment as an apprentice and enrolment as a freeman was so long. For example, Thomas Billamy, apprentice of Edward Key,

---

[1] GBR B3/3 p. 778.
[2] GBR B3/1 f. 522.
[3] GBR B3/3 p. 890.
[4] GBR C10/1 p. 162.
[5] GBR B3/2 pp. 370, 399.
[6] *Freemen*, p. xvi.
[7] GBR B3/9 f. 317.
[8] *Freemen*, p. xvi.
[9] I. K. Ben Amos, 'Failure to become freemen', *Social History*, vol. 16 no. 2 (May 1991), p. 155.

glover (**1**/198), seems to have waited 41 years before claiming the freedom in 1653[1] and Phoenix Badger, apprentice of Thomas Baily, pinmaker (**2**/333), waited 36.[2] Almost half, however were admitted to the freedom as soon as their apprenticeship was over and three quarters were admitted within 10 years of the apprenticeship being enrolled. Only a tiny percentage waited more than 20 years.

TABLE I: *Trades of men claiming the freedom by apprenticeship, 1641–1700*

apothecary	cutler	milliner & hosier
baker	draper	pewterer
barber	farrier	physician
barber & periwig maker	feltmaker	pinmaker
barber surgeon	furrier	ropier
bell founder	gardener	saddler
blacksmith	garter weaver	scrivener
bodice maker	glazier	serge weaver
brazier	glover	sievemaker
brewer	glover & fellmonger	silkweaver
bricklayer	grocer	skinner
broadweaver	gunsmith	stationer
butcher	haberdasher	stone carver
button maker	haberdasher of hats	stone cutter
cardmaker	horner	tailor
carpenter	innholder	tanner
carrier	ironmonger	tiler & plasterer
chandler	jersey comber	tobacco-pipe maker
chandler & soap boiler	joiner	tobacconist
clothier	lantern maker	turner
collar maker	maltster	upholsterer
comb maker	mason	vintner
cook	mercer	wiredrawer
cooper	merchant	woolcomber
cordwainer/currier	milliner	woollen draper

Some of those admitted by right of patrimony were also enrolled as apprentices, frequently bound to masters in quite different trades from their father. Half were admitted as soon as they had finished their apprenticeship but a quarter were admitted before the end of their term. Most of these were apprenticed in their father's trade, if not to their fathers, and it seems unlikely that many of them bothered to complete their apprenticeship. Daniel Bryan, however, a cordwainer's son, was apprenticed to an apothecary (**3**/365) and despite becoming a freeman by patrimony after only four years of apprenticeship later traded as an apothecary.[3] Perhaps the change of trade was seen as a means of improving his social status.

[1] *Freemen*, p. 11.
[2] Ibid. p. 56.
[3] Ibid. pp. 53, 100.

By the end of the century admissions by apprenticeship were becoming fewer. In the 1650s, on average 20 men were admitted by apprenticeship and 15 by patrimony each year; in the 1690s an average of 17 were admitted by apprenticeship and 24 by patrimony.

Conditions of Apprenticeship

Premium

The apprenticeship was usually arranged by the boy's father or a kinsman. Although the property qualifications of the Statute of Artificers applied only to certain trades, sureties had to be provided to indemnify the master against damage caused by the boy or against his running away. The Cirencester weavers' rules of 1558[1] also required sureties to be given to the warden of the company that the apprentice would be able to pay his dues to the company at the end of his term. By the 17th century it was common practice for a premium to be paid to the master when the boy was apprenticed.[2] This was originally a private arrangement and did not need to be recorded in indentures until 1709 when stamp duty was imposed on premiums. London mercers could charge hundreds of pounds for apprenticeships, but fees paid to tradesmen in Bristol were far more modest,[3] as presumably they were in Gloucester. The trustees of William Holliday's charity (see below) reduced the payment from £7 10s. to £5, which was regarded as adequate. In 1638 when Richard Sparkes, the son of a labourer, was apprenticed to a cooper, his kinsman gave 40s. (**1/505**).

Term

At the end of the 16th century, seven years was the most usual length of apprenticeship, but there were many of eight, nine and even ten years. By the end of the 17th century, seven years was almost universal.

By law the term should have been long enough to ensure that the apprentice was bound until he reached the age of 24. In an attempt to see how strictly this was enforced, the baptisms of 100 Gloucestershire apprentices who were aged between 12 and 19 at the time of binding have been identified with some degree of confidence. The average age of apprentices at the start of their service was between 15 and 16, 27% being aged 16 and 30% aged 14 or 15. This stayed much the same throughout the 17th century, but because the terms served were becoming shorter the likelihood of an apprentice having to serve until he was at least 24 decreased: the percentage fell from 45% in the first half of the century to 27% in the second half. Of the 100 apprentices in the sample, 50% were aged 16 or over when they were indentured. Although they were required to live with the master and his wife and be subject to social control and punishment, they were

---

[1] GRO D4590 1/1.
[2] Dunlop, *Apprenticeship and Child Labour*, p. 53.
[3] Ben Amos, *Adolescence and Youth*, p. 91.

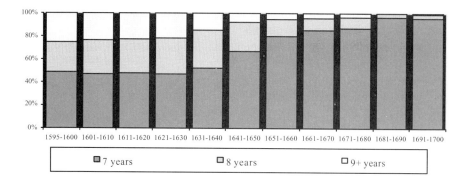

Figure 1. Number of years for which apprentices were bound

already young men and likely to find the strictures against drinking, gambling and fornication very irksome.

The master was normally expected to provide all 'necessaries' – food, drink and clothing – but this was occasionally varied and the parents agreed to find clothes or food for at least part of the term (see for example **1**/246 and **1**/271) or the apprentice found them for himself (**2**/9). The pinmaker William Powell gave his apprentice 4s. a week during the last year and was excused from finding meat, drink and apparel (**2**/155).

Payment

At the end of their apprenticeship boys were normally given two suits of clothes, one for work and one for holidays, and a sum of money. The sum of

TABLE II: *Age of apprentices at the end of the term* (*years from baptism*)

Age	All apprentices	Apprenticed 1595–1649	Apprenticed 1650–1700
19	5	1	4
20	6	3	3
21	13	5	8
22	17	4	13
23	23	10	13
24	16	9	7
25	8	5	3
26	12	7	5
TOTAL	100	44	56

money is recorded in the registers until 1680 when it becomes less frequent and eventually ceases to appear. Whether it was no longer paid or whether the clerk simply failed to include it is not clear. In Bristol the number of apprentices recorded as receiving a sum of money at the end of their term was less than 50% in the first decade of the 17th century and had shrunk to 8% by 1641–5.[1]

The amounts vary from 6*d.* to £10 and seem to bear no relation to the provenance of the boy, the trade which he learned or the length of the term which he served. Of the 400 apprentices bound between 1595 and 1605 about 50% were to receive 5*s.* or less, 17% had 1*s.* or less. The most generous master was the brewer John Thorne who agreed to pay each of his four apprentices £5. In a similar sample taken from between 1668 and 1676 there was far less variation in the amounts to be paid: 43% were to receive 2*s.* 6*d.*, 35% to receive 5*s.* and only 13% more than 5*s.*; of the 18 boys who were to receive 20*s.*, 13 were apprenticed to their fathers and the two sums of £5 were to be paid by joiners to their sons.

Some of the clerks specified the two suits of clothes in the register but most seem to have regarded them as a normal part of the contract and did not bother to mention them. Occasionally more detail is given, as for Giles Churches, the son of a clothier, who was to have two suits 'whereof one is to consist of five yards of broad cloth of the price of 10*s.* at the least' (**2/256**).

Once he had served three or four years, the apprentice would be sufficiently proficient to be useful. His master could regard him as a marketable property and 'sell' him.[2] For a cordwainer's apprentice who was put over to a new master after five years the former master was paid 20*s.* 'in full discharge of his service' (**1/212**).

There are several instances of a boy appearing before the justices to be 'turned over' to another master in the same trade. It was usually done with the consent of the boy, his father, and his master (or his master's widow). Where a reason is given, it is because the master had died or 'gone off'. When Thomas Horsington went away in 1654 he left his children and apprentice in the charge of his wife, Margery (**2/131**). They were thought likely to become chargeable to the parish of St Mary de Lode and the apprentice, John Alday, was turned over to a new master. Horsington had taken on two other apprentices in the previous three years (**2/71**, **2/121**) but no mention is made of them. Either they had already left his service or John Alday was subject to greater supervision because he had been apprenticed with money from Sarah Browne's charity. More mysteriously, in 1659 Thomas and Margery Horsington appear to have taken on another apprentice (**2/239**). Several apprentices served three masters: e.g. Thomas Elridge served Robert Porter (**1/346**), John Hopkins and Thomas Cooke (**1/401**); Samuel Manning served William Preedie, Augustine Gwyn (**1/348**) and Henry Selwin (**1/418**); and at least one was assigned to a second master and then returned to the first (**1/330**).

---

[1] Ben Amos, *Adolescence and Youth*, p. 300.
[2] Paul Griffiths, *Youth and Authority, Formative Experiences in England 1560–1640* (1996), p. 332.

There are also examples of boys being officially discharged from their apprenticeship, sometimes with the indentures being burned to emphasise the end of the relationship. No reason is given, though towards the end of the century some are discharged 'by order of the sessions', which suggests some irregularity or complaint.

A surprising number of boys appear to have been indentured twice with no reference to the cancellation of the first indenture. The phenomenon was also noted in the introduction to the Bristol apprenticeship registers for the 16th century.[1] Some instances may be a coincidence of name, but surely there was only one Jeremiah Hodgshon and only one Theophilus Meysey. A list of boys apparently indentured more than once is given below as Appendix V. Certainly some boys did serve more than one apprenticeship. Humphrey Long was indentured to a weaver for 11 years in 1621 (**1**/304) and after 6¾ years entered into a new indenture with the same master for 8 years. The amount he was to be paid at the end of his term rose from 6s. 8d. to £4.

Some apprentices having successfully completed their term reappear in the registers as masters. Of 522 apprentice cordwainers who were bound before 1690, 79 (15%) went on to take apprentices of their own. A few more are likely to have taken apprentices after 1700 and so are not recorded in this calendar. Of those taking apprentices, 25% did so within two years of the end of their own apprenticeship, 34% did so within 8 to 12 years while 41% waited up to 22 years. The percentages for weavers were virtually identical.

Apprenticing Charities

Alderman Holliday

A number of apprenticeship charities were established in Gloucester during the 17th century. The most substantial was the bequest of the Gloucester-born London alderman William Holliday, a former master of the Mercers' Company and governor of the East India Company. When he died in 1624 Alderman Holliday's holdings in Gloucestershire included the manor of Pucklechurch and the 'house called Gray Friers' in Gloucester. He left £500 to the city of Gloucester which was to provide £30 a year interest to apprentice 'four boys who have had an honest education . . . and whose parents do want means thereunto'.[2]

The first four boys to benefit from the charity were apprenticed in 1625. In July 1627 the common council laid down the rules for a master taking an apprentice with Alderman Holliday's money.[3] He was 'to be bound in a bond of £15 to the mayor and burgesses with the condition that he shall instruct the boy

---

[1] *Calendar of the Bristol Apprentice Book, Part I 1532–42*, ed. D. Hollis (Bristol Record Society, vol. xiv, 1948), p. 15.
[2] PRO PROB 11/143 (PCC 21 Byrd).
[3] GBR B3/3 f. 518v.

INTRODUCTION

in his art or trade, maintain him with all necessaries sufficiently and at the end of the term pay back to his apprentice the sum of 50*s*., parcel of the £7 10*s*., towards a stock to set up his trade. And if he should die or fall into decay the boy [is] to be turned over to some other sufficient burgess in the same trade and 50*s*. to be paid back.' This order was repealed almost immediately 'by common consent', but the charity was probably administered under similar rules. When the payment for each boy was reduced from £7 10*s*. to £5, the amount of the bond was reduced to £10.

Two of the boys apprenticed under the bequest in 1627, John Cugley and Richard Bradgate, were said to be kin to Alderman Holliday. Richard Bradgate seems to have kept the money in the family by apprenticing his two sons to himself and obtaining a grant from the charity with each (**2**/63 and **2**/244).

In January 1629 William Holliday's widow, who had married the earl of Warwick, was asked to give permission for the money to be divided among six boys each year with a reduced premium of £5 for each. Thereafter the common council agreed the names on or about 21 July. In 1654 the nominations could not be dealt with until 28 July because the assizes were scheduled to begin on 21 July.[1] Anything up to 14 names were put before the council for a vote. When necessary, the mayor had the casting vote.[2] In 1655 the common council decided that it would not consider a petition on behalf of any boy to have Mr Holliday's £5 unless a certificate was given or an oath made that he was aged over 14.[3]

Of the 360 recipients of Holliday's charity money who can be identified in the registers, 98 had fathers who were recorded as deceased. There were, however, four sons of gentlemen and twelve sons of mercers, clothiers or drapers who may not have been entirely wanting in means. Eight were the sons of yeomen. The masters covered the whole spectrum of Gloucester trades and included a clothier (who took two apprentices) and three mercers (one of whom also took two). Several masters took two or even three apprentices with Holliday's money. Although the money was nominally awarded to a boy, it would be given only if the master was approved and it seems on occasion to have been paid directly to the masters. Of the boys identified, 98 were apprenticed to their fathers (including eight of the ten blacksmiths' apprentices) and one to his mother. Parents were thus being paid to train their own children rather than give an opportunity to a less privileged child. The common council felt this to be an abuse of the system and complained in 1682 that 'parents procure their children to be bound to themselves and by that means get the money into their hands'.[4] In future no charity money was to be paid to apprentices bound to their father or mother. The prohibition seems to have been observed for about six years before the practice was resumed.

[1] GBR B3/2 p. 773.
[2] Ibid. p. 774.
[3] Ibid. p. 821.
[4] GBR B3/3 p. 824.

In the early years of the charity, most of the recipients were noted in the apprenticeship registers. When that was not done, it can be difficult to identify the boys because the council minutes give sometimes the name of the boy, sometimes that of a parent and sometimes just a surname. In addition, the date of the indenture may be several months before or after the date of the award. Where the indenture was later than the award the gap in time is understandable, but it is harder to understand why a boy who had already succeeded in finding an apprenticeship and presumably in agreeing the financial arrangements should then be awarded £5. Occasionally an explanation is given for the money not being accepted (in 1660 Thomas Yearnold's son was 'beyond the sea'[1]) and it was sometimes reallocated. If the following entry from the minutes of 1660 reflects the sort of manoeuvring that went on all the time but was not usually recorded, it is not surprising that there are discrepancies between the registers and the minutes: 'Whereas the son of Henry Bradley had £5 of the gift of Mr Hollidaye granted to him but was not 14 years old at the time, the £5 is to be granted to Robert Cowdell who is already bound apprentice and was to have £5 of the gift of Alderman Clutterbuck but could not receive it.'[2]

Sarah Browne

Mrs Sarah Browne, the widow of a city alderman, gave land to provide income for apprenticing poor boys aged between 14 and 16 to be chosen by the mayor and burgesses on the Feast of the Annunciation (25 March) each year.[3] From 1647 three boys each year received £4. From 1664 to 1667 sums that seem to be Mrs Browne's gift are recorded in the register as the gift of the mayor and burgesses.

Sir Thomas Rich

From 1669 six boys each year received £10 of the gift of Sir Thomas Rich for clothing and for apprenticing them to masters approved by the mayor and aldermen. Under the terms of his gift preference was to be given to boys from his Bluecoat school and only three boys each year were to be bound in the city of Gloucester.[4] This explains in part why so few of the boys apprenticed with Sir Thomas Rich's bequest appear in the registers.

Alderman Powell

Alderman John Powell left £100 'being money due to him upon the account of the Irish adventure' to be used to give £5 a year to apprentice a poor boy, to be paid on the feast of St James (25 July). The first recipient was to be Henry Wintle, nominated by the town clerk, in 1681.[5]

---

[1] GBR B3/3 p. 140.
[2] Ibid. p. 149.
[3] [*14th*] *Report of the Commissioners for Inquiring Concerning Charities*, p. 33; *VCH Glos* iv. 356.
[4] GBR B3/3 p. 823.
[5] Ibid. p. 785. Wintle is not named, however, in the register.

Other charities

A number of other gifts or bequests are mentioned in the registers or in the minutes. In 1640 six boys each received £5 bequeathed by Alderman Blackleech (**1**/520–2, 530); two boys were enrolled in 1660 with money given by Alderman Jasper Clutterbuck (mayor of Gloucester in 1646 and brother-in-law of William Holliday) (**2**/253); in 1662 Serjeant Seys expressed the wish that the fee due to him as Recorder should be used to bind boys apprentice and two boys were nominated to receive £3 6s. 8d.;[1] in 1682 one boy received £6 described as the gift of Baron Gregory.[2]

Apprentices for Virginia and Barbados

At the end of the second volume of the register there is a list of twenty women and nine men who were to go to Barbados or Virginia in 1659–60. The five for Virginia were bound to James Bridger or William Jennings, both described as merchants of the city of Bristol. Those for Barbados were bound to John Woodward, merchant. All except the three bound to James Bridger were to receive £10 at the end of four years. The men were almost all husbandmen and the women were described as spinsters. Most came from Gloucester or Herefordshire and South Wales. A search for baptisms yielded only three probable matches; those three suggested that William Powell, Thomas Lawrence and Elizabeth Drinkwater were all aged 20 or 21. Only two of the entries make reference to a father. It seems likely that the men and women were not true apprentices but indentured servants setting off for the sugar plantations in Barbados and the tobacco plantations in Virginia.

The Registers as Historical Evidence

Most entries give the date of indenture, the name of the apprentice, the father's name, trade and place of residence, the name of the master and mistress to whom the apprentice was bound, the trade which he was to learn, the number of years for which he was to serve and the sum of money which he was to receive at the end of the term.

The indentures of some 4,280 apprentices were enrolled in the Gloucester registers[3] between October 1595 and the end of the mayoral year in October 1700, an average of 41 each year. Multiplying the average by a little more than seven (the average number of years to be served), and assuming that the number of apprentices who died, absconded or changed masters is balanced by the number whose indentures were not registered, gives a very approximate average of 300 apprentices in the city at one time. That number represents about 6% of

---

[1] GBR B3/3 p. 221.
[2] Ibid. p. 814.
[3] The following account excludes consideration of the apprentices for Virginia and Barbados.

Gloucester's population of 5,000.[1] The comparable figure for Bristol was 10% and for smaller country towns about 5%.[2] Numbers in Gloucester were highest during the 1660s and 1670s when an average of 57 each year were enrolled, with a peak of 94 in 1669. During the siege year of 1643 only eight apprentice indentures were enrolled and six of them were for charity apprentices.

Only three girls are mentioned in the registers up to 1700: Alice Drinkwater, the daughter of a Hatherley yeoman, apprenticed to Elizabeth Purlewent, spinster sempstress, for seven years in 1615 (**1/248**); Mary Rogers of the Leigh, apprenticed to John Bulbricke, garter weaver, for five years in 1621 to learn bone lace weaving (**1/305**); and Joan Bodman, daughter of a Gloucester baker, apprenticed to Henry and Joan Thomas for eight years in 1647 (**2/26**). No trade is given for Henry Thomas and he does not appear to have taken any other apprentices.

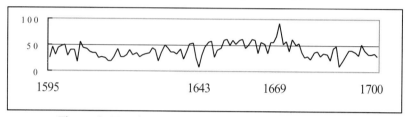

Figure 2. Total number of apprentices (by year)

Place of origin

In the course of the 17th century there was a general decrease in migration to Gloucester[3] and in apprenticeship migration throughout the country,[4] a trend which is reflected in the registers. The proportion of apprentices whose father's place of residence was given as the city of Gloucester increased from 23% in the first ten years of the 17th century to 53% in the last ten while the proportion coming from more than 25 miles away shrank from 13% to 5%. Some boys travelled very long distances – two came from Ireland, three from Cornwall and two from Westmorland. There were several from Wales, some still using their father's first name as a surname (for example, **1/159** – the son of William Jones from Monmouthshire called himself Morgan Williams). Most apprentices came from the villages of Gloucestershire and neighbouring counties, but a few arrived from big cities (16 from Bristol and 18 from London). One boy who had been apprenticed to a draper in London was sent home to be apprenticed to a blacksmith in Gloucester, which must have caused a reappraisal of his future (**2/284**). Except between 1640 and 1650, when the political situation presumably kept them away, apprentices came to Gloucester from neighbouring towns, 53 from Cheltenham, 43 from Tewkesbury and 25 from Stroud. Of nine boys

---

[1] *VCH Glos* iv. 102.
[2] Ben Amos, *Adolescence and Youth*, p. 84.
[3] *VCH Glos* iv. 102.
[4] Ben Amos, *Adolescence and Youth*, p. 86.

coming from Stroud after the Civil War, six were apprenticed to silkweavers. Four of them were bound to John Beard, probably the John Beard who himself came from Stroud as an apprentice in 1637 and evidently kept contacts in his home town.

TABLE III: *Place of origin of apprentices*

		1595–1600	1601–10	1611–20	1621–30	1631–40	1641–50	1651–60	1661–70	1671–80	1681–90	1691–1700
Number of apprentices	4280	248	380	274	342	394	392	567	569	420	316	378
Gloucester	1742	32%	23%	24%	35%	43%	46%	38%	46%	47%	52%	53%
0–4.9 miles	683	16%	15%	17%	18%	16%	13%	21%	17%	14%	11%	15%
5–9.9 miles	765	16%	16%	15%	22%	19%	17%	18%	19%	23%	16%	16%
10–24.9 miles	634	20%	19%	12%	15%	14%	18%	16%	13%	11%	16%	10%
25–40 miles	136	5%	7%	4%	4%	5%	3%	3%	2%	0%	2%	2%
Over 40 miles	140	8%	6%	3%	4%	3%	2%	2%	3%	1%	2%	3%
no information	180	3%	14%	26%	2%	1%	2%	2%	1%	3%	0%	1%

Fathers' occupations

Just over half the boys who came from outside the city were the sons either of yeomen (32%), or of farmers and husbandmen (21%). Among the others were the sons of trowmen, fishermen and coalminers. Of the dozen sons of fullers or tuckers, most were from the south of the county and none arrived after 1668. The making of caps had once been an important industry in Gloucester but it had almost disappeared by the start of the 17th century. Only two sons of Gloucester cappers appear in the register, both apprenticed before 1600.

There were 209 fathers described as gentleman, five as esquire and one as knight. There were also nine city aldermen and 87 clerics. Unsurprisingly they chose to apprentice their sons to the profitable trades of mercer, draper and grocer, with a higher than average number learning to become apothecaries, barber surgeons and merchants. In England at large the number of gentry sons apprenticed increased after the Civil War.[1] In Gloucester although there was a rise it was only slight.

Almost a quarter of all fathers (including 41% of the gentlemen) were recorded as deceased. That proportion has to be regarded as a minimum since there is no guarantee that the clerk recorded the fact that the father was no longer

---

[1] Lane, *Apprenticeship in England*, p. 13.

TABLE IV: *Trades to which the sons of gentlemen (including aldermen and clergy) were apprenticed*

Trade	Number	Percent
mercer	66	21%
cordwainer	25	8%
grocer/chandler	22	7%
draper	21	7%
baker	19	6%
weaver	16	5%
metal work	16	5%
apothecary	16	5%
tailor	16	5%
haberdasher	13	4%
tanner	11	4%
glover	11	4%
barber surgeon	9	3%
merchant	8	3%
clothier	6	2%
brewer	4	1%
other trades	32	10%
TOTAL	311	100%

alive. Figure 3 shows the number of fatherless apprentices as a percentage of the total number enrolled in each decade. The percentage rose significantly in the years after the Civil War and reached a peak in 1653 when 56% of the apprentices enrolled were fatherless.

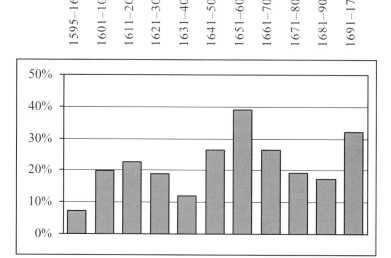

Figure 3. Fatherless apprentices (by decade)

Some 300 boys were apprenticed to their fathers, almost a third of them with money from William Holliday's charity. If his father was dead a boy could be apprenticed to his mother or brother. About 225 were apprenticed to masters in the same trade as their father.

Widows who had helped their husbands in their trade for seven years were admitted to the freedom of their company. The list of metalmen who were to be 'free of their trade' in Gloucester in 1607[1] included Joan Hill, widow. Some boys were reassigned when their master died, but some doubtless stayed on with his widow and many widows took on apprentices in their own right. Bakers' widows were the most likely to take on apprentices (sacks of flour were very heavy) but boys were also bound to widows in the trades of barber surgeon, butcher, chandler, cooper, cordwainer, cutler, farrier, feltmaker, glover, grocer, innholder, joiner, mercer, pewterer, pinmaker, silkweaver, tailor, and tanner. Bakers' widows seem to have enjoyed remarkably long working lives. Anne and John Hayes took on five apprentices between 1601 and 1618 and Anne took a further seven between 1626 and 1641; Margaret Parker, as wife and widow, took nine between 1646 and 1679; Alice Jennings took five after her husband's death.

Only three pauper children placed by the parish appear in the registers: one in 1597 placed by the churchwardens of St Oswald's (**1/51**) and two in 1698 placed by the overseers of St Aldate's (**3/381**) and St Catherine's (**3/382**), both of whom were apprenticed to the same pinmaker. The first boys apprenticed with money from Alderman Holliday's charity were described as paupers, as were a further nine between 1621 and 1641. In most cases the word is added in the margin of the register. Apart from one, the son of a spinster from Down Hatherley (**1/500**), they were the sons of Gloucester tradesmen and most of their fathers were dead. Three were placed by the mayor. The entry for the son of a labourer in 1647 is marked 'pauper' and deleted (**2/20**).

Trade learned

Almost a quarter (1,000) of the apprentices enrolled in the registers calendared here were bound to leather workers – 214 to tanners and 564 to cordwainers or curriers. The term currier seems to have replaced cordwainer in the register from about 1650 to 1675, with the same men being described variously as currier, cordwainer and shoemaker. Between 1600 and 1690, 55 of the master shoemakers had only one apprentice, 60 had two or three and 57 took on at least four. Several had nine or more. The apprentices were spread over a master's working life of 20 or 30 years and may well not have served their full term. Even so, if there were any rules restricting the number of apprentices who could be taken on at one time they do not seem to have been enforced. Francis

---

[1] GBR B1/4.

Yeate, cordwainer, had seven apprentices at the time of his death in 1699. Six carried him to his grave and the seventh preached his funeral sermon.[1]

The largest group of metalworkers were the pinmakers. Pinmaking was introduced into Gloucester in the 1620s[2] and became a flourishing industry and major employer. John Tilsley was said to employ 80 boys and girls in the 1630s,[3] but none of them was enrolled in the register. Seventy-one pinmakers took apprentices during the century, most of them having several at once. Philip and Anne Tilsley had 16 in the space of seven years, Samuel and Eleanor Pitt 13 in fourteen years and Stephen and Elizabeth Doughton 10 in sixteen years.

TABLE V: *Apprenticeship by occupational groups and decades*

		1595–1600	1601–10	1611–20	1621–30	1631–40	1641–50	1651–60	1661–70	1671–80	1681–90	1691–1700
Number of apprentices	(100%)4246	248	378	268	341	390	390	566	567	415	314	369
leather	24%(1000)	21%	26%	33%	30%	28%	28%	22%	19%	19%	23%	15%
metal	16% (672)	13%	13%	7%	12%	15%	17%	20%	18%	17%	22%	14%
food	13% (556)	12%	12%	13%	15%	10%	12%	12%	13%	12%	15%	19%
distribution	13% (547)	21%	20%	19%	21%	17%	15%	10%	7%	7%	5%	9%
textiles	11% (474)	13%	12%	9%	7%	11%	7%	11%	18%	16%	8%	6%
clothing	10% (420)	9%	6%	5%	5%	9%	10%	13%	11%	11%	11%	15%
wood	6% (244)	5%	6%	9%	5%	5%	5%	5%	5%	7%	6%	7%
professional	3% (136)	2%	3%	2%	1%	3%	3%	4%	4%	3%	4%	5%
building	1% (48)	0%	0%	0%	1%	0%	1%	1%	1%	1%	1%	5%
other	4% (149)	2%	3%	2%	3%	3%	2%	2%	4%	7%	5%	4%

Note. The table excludes 34 apprentices whose trade is not stated in the registers.

Although the numbers apprenticed in the textile trade apparently remained fairly constant throughout the period, the nature of their employment changed radically. In the first half of the 17th century 15 master broadweavers and 18 masters described only as weavers had just one apprentice each. By the second half the broadweavers had disappeared and most boys were bound to silkweavers, who each had at least two and sometimes many more apprentices: Thomas and Bridget Onyon had 14. Serge weaving appeared only in the second half of the century.

---

[1] Epitaph in the church of St John the Baptist, Gloucester, quoted in Fosbrooke, *City of Gloucester*, p. 157.

[2] Fosbrooke, *City of Gloucester*, p. 24.

[3] *VCH Glos* iv. 76.

The shearmen's company was defunct by 1634[1] and no shearmen are recorded after Thomas White was apprenticed to his father in 1626. No dyers are mentioned after 1610.

TABLE VI: *Apprentices in the textile trade*

	Number of masters (and widows)	
	1595–1649	1650–1700
Weavers (*unspecified*)		
1 apprentice	18	2
2 or 3 apprentices	2	1
4+ apprentices	2	
Broadweavers		
1 apprentice	15	
2 or 3 apprentices	7	
4+ apprentices	3	
Silkweavers		
1 apprentice	4	7
2 or 3 apprentices	6	10
4 to 7 apprentices		7
8+ apprentices	1	6
Narrow/garter weavers		
1 apprentice	2	
2 or 3 apprentices	1	2
4+ apprentices		2
Serge weavers		
1 apprentice		3
2 or 3 apprentices		2

The Registers

The registers of Gloucester apprentices are in four volumes, covering the years 1595 to 1742 and 1765 to 1834. They are held among the Gloucester borough records in the Gloucestershire Record Office as GBR C10/1–4. This calendar summarises the contents of the first two volumes and the first part of the third, stopping at 1700. Stevenson's printed catalogue of borough records of 1892 confusingly lists only the second volume. It is catalogued as number 1458 'a register of apprentices 1645–1659' and is described as being stamped with the number 1583. The volumes are of paper and seem to have been originally

---

[1] *VCH Glos* iv. 80.

purchased as bound blank books. They were rebound, probably in the late 19th century, in dark brown leather and have 'RESTORED BY MALTBY, OXFORD' stamped inside the front cover.

The first register, C10/1, contains entries for 1595–1646. It has 1595–1647 stamped in gold on the upper part of the spine and 1458 at the foot. The page size is approximately 295mm x 190mm. At the front are five leaves repaired with paper which are blank except for some blots and several attempts by a Thomas to write his name. There are six leaves after the last of the apprenticeship enrolments on page 588. On page 589, upside down to the rest of the volume, is the release of a Tewkesbury apprentice, included below as Appendix III. On the very back page, also upside down, is a record of the sale of a grey mare and some brown cows in 1624. The volume has been damaged by damp and the corners of the pages have been repaired. The foot of page 87 is missing and a pencilled note records that it had gone by July 1847. Otherwise virtually no text has been lost. The pages have been numbered twice in pencil, the second pagination presumably correcting the first.

The second register, C10/2, contains entries for 1645–68. It has 1645–1659 stamped in gold on the upper part of the spine and 1458A/1583 at the foot. The page size is approximately 295mm x 190mm. There are two blank leaves before the start of the text. The first page is stamped 1583. The top of page 139 is missing and the page has been repaired with paper. The last three pages contain the entries for Virginia and Barbados dated 1659–60, presumably giving rise to the confusion about the terminal date in Stevenson's catalogue and in the stamp on the spine. Pagination is in ink and appears to be contemporary.

The third register, C10/3, contains entries for 1668–1742. It has those dates stamped in gold on the upper part of the spine and 1458B at the foot. The page size is approximately 310mm x 200mm. Pagination is in pencil and pages 1 to 8 are blank.

Text

The registers are the work of many clerks and the legibility of their hands varies greatly.

For four of the first six mayoral years the first entry gives the full text of the indenture. The other entries are in a standardised abbreviated form with the name of the apprentice written in the margin:

> *Thomas Terret the son of Samuel Terret of Stroud in the county of Gloucester, husbandman, hath put himself apprentice to Henry Knight of the City of Gloucester, innholder, and Prudence his wife by indenture bearing date the ninth day of May 1651 for the term of eight years and they give him in the end of his term one shilling.*

INTRODUCTION

With a few exceptions the entries are in Latin up to 1649 and after 1660; between those dates they are in English. Marginal notes, most of which record the reassignment or discharge of apprentices, are usually in English but some are in Latin.

The date given is the date of the indenture. While some indentures were enrolled immediately, others were delayed by many months and the early entries are in far from chronological order. The names of the new mayor and sheriffs were usually written at the top of a page at the start of the mayoral year which began, as laid down in the charter of 1483, on the first Monday after Michaelmas (29 September). An attempt was made to keep entries within the correct year: some which strayed into the wrong year had the correct mayoral year written in the margin (**1/190**) or were even declared void (**1/312**). Nevertheless many entries, especially the early ones, remain uncorrected in the wrong year. At some periods (for example 1601–4 and 1610–17) the registers were particularly badly kept and full of repetitions and cancellations.

Not all the entries give all the relevant information. From 1611 to 1613 very few occupations of fathers are given; the father's place of residence is missing in many entries from 1606 to 1616; more than 800 entries, especially those late in the period, do not give the name of the master's wife, many of them leaving a gap in the text for it to be filled in; after 1680 very few entries give the sum payable at the end of the term and it is not possible to tell whether this is an omission on the part of the clerk or whether the sum was not promised. Between 1653 and 1662 and occasionally elsewhere a date is given for the start of the apprenticeship. This can be several months earlier or later than the date of the indenture.

There is evidence of under-registration: many of the boys who were awarded money from a charity do not appear in the register, nor do many of those who appear in the register of freemen as claiming the freedom by apprenticeship. Some who do appear in both registers are shown with different masters. They must have been reassigned but the fact was not recorded.

It is possible, however, to trace some families over several generations and to follow the careers of some apprentices as they became masters themselves. For example, Denis Wise, the mayor of Gloucester at the time of the siege in 1643, was the son of Robert, a gentleman of Gloucester. He was apprenticed first to a mercer's widow for nine years in 1598 and almost immediately reassigned for a term of seven years (**1/31**); he took the first of his ten apprentices in 1607 (**1/160**). His wife was called Hephzibah and his two sons, Urian and Denis, were apprenticed to him in 1647 and 1654 (**2/31** and **131**).

Some names familiar to Gloucester historians appear in the registers, including Abraham Rudhall the bellfounder, apprenticed to his father in 1694 (**3/346**), and those of members of the families of Lysons (**3/216**) and Wantner (**3/308** and **379**).

Editorial Method

The text of the registers has been calendared in a standard format. The volume-number and the number of the page within the volume are given at the left-hand margin, followed by the date of the indenture with the year and the day and month in separate columns. For the substance of each entry the calendar has on the first line the apprentice's surname, his first name and his father's name, place of residence, and occupation or rank; on a new line are the master's surname, first name and wife's name, the term to be served, the trade to be learned and the sum of money to be given at the end of the term. The surname of the apprentice and his father frequently appears twice in the register entry but it is not repeated in the calendar unless the spelling (or the surname) is different. The county has been omitted for places in Gloucestershire and for county towns elsewhere. Notes which appear in the MS as additions to the entries as first registered are set in the calendar in italic. Text supplied to fill omissions in the MS is enclosed in square brackets. Editorial notes are given in italic and enclosed in square brackets.

Footnotes referring to decisions about the use of charity money for more than one apprentice are appended to the entry for the apprentice who is named earliest in the register.

The calendar uses '[*blank*]' to show that a space has been left in the register, whereas an em-dash (—) is used in the calendar to indicate a simple omission in the MS.

Dates are given according to the Julian calendar in use in England throughout the relevant period, but the year is treated in the calendar as beginning on 1 January. Dates expressed in the MSS as festivals are rendered in the calendar as days of the months. Roman numerals have been converted to arabic.

The spelling (other than that of personal surnames), the punctuation and the use of initial capitals has been modernised. A spelling of a place-name that is notably different from the modern form is given in brackets after the modern form. Place-names that have not been identified are enclosed in quotation marks.

CALENDAR OF GLOUCESTER APPRENTICESHIP REGISTERS, 1595–1700

GBR C10/1   **1595–1646**

Roll of all the apprentices bound in the city of Gloucester made in accordance with the order of common council, 5 Oct 1554

1/1   **Henry Hazarde, mayor [1594–5]**
         Christopher Capell and John Brewster, sheriffs and bailiffs

Richard Baker, town clerk, took up his post on 21 June 1595 and died 7 Oct 1598 at Abergavenny

1595   24 Jun   Greninge, Jasper son of John, husbandman, of Moreton Valence
                  Gwilliam, John & Joan   8 yrs   silkweaver   3s 4d and 2 suits of clothes
                  [*Text of indenture given in full. See Appendix I*]

          25 Jul   Bikenell, Theophilus son of John, dec'd, of Gloucester
                  Clebery, John & Alice   12 yrs   haberdasher   3s 4d

1/2   8 Sep   Johnson, William son of William, husbandman, of Tewkesbury
                  Gotheridge, William   8 yrs   apothecary   3s 4d

          29 Sep   Butler, Thomas son of Thomas, cordwainer, of Gloucester
                  Cuglie, Richard & Elizabeth   7 yrs   cardmaker   3s 4d

                 Skinner, William son of Robert, victualler, of Gloucester
                  Edwardes, Richard & [*blank*] 7 yrs   glover   10s

                 Thorne, Richard [son of John *deleted*], of Gloucester
                  Thorne, John, gentleman, & Joan   9 yrs   maltster & brewer   £5

                 Frewen, John son of [*blank*]
                  Thorne, John, gentleman, & Joan   7 yrs   maltster & brewer   £5

1/3   Messinger, Christopher son of John, husbandman, of Cricklade, Wilts
                  Thorne, John, gentleman, & Joan   7 yrs   brewer   £5

                 Holiday, Samuel son of Lawrence, mercer, of Gloucester
                  Wilshier, Lawrence, clothier, & Sarah   7 yrs   weaver   7s

                 Webb, John son of Nicholas, tucker [MS. kucker], of Kingswood, Wilts
                  Wilshier, Lawrence, clothier, & Sarah   7 yrs   weaver   13s 4d

                 Richard Webb, mayor [1595–6]
                 Thomas Rich and John Paine, sheriffs

1595   7 Oct   Langford, Nicholas son of Nicholas, stationer, of Gloucester
                  Baugh, John & Margaret   9 yrs   mercer   10s

          15 Oct   Morgan, Thomas son of Thomas, gentleman, of Gloucester
                  Fleminge, Richard & Tabitha   8 yrs   barber   3s

1/4	1595	18 Oct	Lane, Samuel son of Thomas, cordwainer, of Tetbury Lane, Richard & Joan 7 yrs saddler 3s 4d
		1 Nov	Drinkwater, Edmund son of William, yeoman, of Withy Bridge Elbridge, John, cordwainer, & Joan 7 yrs shoemaker 12d
			Wadley, Richard son of Thomas, husbandman, of Auberrow, Herefs Houlder, Thomas & Cather[ine] 8 yrs broadweaver 10s
			Woodward, Walter son of James, labourer, of Sandhurst Fleshall, Robert & Agnes 9 yrs fletcher 5s
		9 Dec	Dowtonne, Richard son of Arnold, capper, of Gloucester Dowtonne, Arnold, his father, & Eleanor 7 yrs capper 12d
1/5		29 Dec	Barrett, Roger son of Thomas, yeoman, of Berkeley Tomsonne, William 8 yrs tailor 12d
		31 Dec	Arkell, Edward son of Nicholas, clerk, of Leonard Stanley Batt, Edmund & Anne 7 yrs hosier 10s *5 Feb 1601, assigned to Hill, Geoffrey & Anne*
	1596	3 Jan	Tikle, Samuel son of Walter, yeoman, of Longney Greene, John & Margery 11 yrs ropemaker 13s 4d
		23 Jan	Cotton, Thomas son of Samuel, of Tewkesbury Mason, Thomas & Mary 8 yrs butcher 40s
1/6		20 Jan	Tricke, Walter son of John, of Longhope Thorne, John & Joan 7 yrs brewer £5
	1595	25 Jul	Durin, Derias son of Paul Duryn, brewer, of Gloucester Blisse, Thomas & Anne 9 yrs turner 40s
		25 Dec	Moore, John son of John, fletcher, of Gloucester Sandes, Henry & Margaret 8 yrs cutler 6s 8d
		29 Sep	Horne, Henry son of Nicholas, tanner, of Gloucester Guye, Thomas & Elizabeth 8 yrs cutler 12d
1/7	1596	24 Feb	Pearse, Thomas son of Thomas, yeoman, of Kingsholm Jones, Thomas & Margaret 10 yrs capper 3s 4d
		12 Mar	Arnold, Thomas son of Thomas, husbandman, of Minsterworth Arnold, Francis & Eleanor 7 yrs glover 3s 4d
	1595	1 Nov	Thomas, Walter son of Thomas Prichardes, yeoman, of Talgarth, Brecon Lightfoote, William & Joan 7 yrs pewterer 10s
1/8	1596	25 Mar	Atkinson, Edward son of William, butcher, of Gloucester Barnes, John & Anne 7 yrs butcher 20s
			Bevis, Richard son of Lawrence, glover, of Gloucester Cosens, Thomas 8 yrs wiredrawer 10s
		21 Apr	Rowles, Robert son of Philip, yeoman, of St. Briavels Whittington, Robert 8 yrs apothecary 12s
		25 Mar	Bande, Henry son of Thomas, husbandman, of Norton Hamons, John, clothier, & Martha 9 yrs broadweaver 20s

1/9	1596	30 May	Greene, Thomas son of Robert, husbandman, of Minsterworth Owram, Richard 8 yrs salter 12d
		23 Jun	Hawkins, Giles son of William, husbandman, of Sandhurst Elbridge, John & Joan 7 yrs cordwainer 12d
		24 Jun	Jefferis, Richard son of Richard Geffreys, yeoman, of Longdon, Worcs Hill, William 10 yrs mercer 12d
		1 Aug	Moore, William son of William, yeoman, of Mitcheldean Key, Edward & Grace 7 yrs glover 6s 8d
1/10		11 Jun	Scriven, Nicholas son of William, labourer, of Tewkesbury Scriven, Thomas & Jane 10 yrs blacksmith 6s 8d
		23 Jun	Andros, Thomas son of Christopher, husbandman, of 'Pitchersoken' [Peterchurch?], Herefs Bridges, William & Isobel 7 yrs broadweaver 13s 4d
		30 May	Halford, Robert son of Stephen, yeoman, of Halford, Worcs [*recte* Warws?] Caple, Christopher & Grace 9 yrs mercer 3s 4d
		11 Apr	Hayward, Richard son of Edmund, husbandman, of Garsdon, Wilts Beale, Geoffrey & Joan 9 yrs mercer 12d
1/11		1 Aug	Simons, Thomas son of Nicholas, barber, of Birmingham, Warws Howe, Charles & Mary 8 yrs saddler 12d
		25 Jul	Bushop, Richard son of William, husbandman, of Kingsholm Woodward, Thomas & Elizabeth 7 yrs broadweaver 20s
		24 Jun	Kirby, John son of John, husbandman, of Badgeworth Gwilliam, John & Joan 7 yrs silkweaver 12d
			Yonge, William son of John, dec'd, sailor, of Gloucester Whitefield, Richard & Alice 12 yrs cordwainer 3s 4d
		25 Mar	Hitchman, Thomas son of Anthony, dec'd, yeoman, of Down Ampney Holman, Humphrey, merchant, & Mary 9 yrs vintner 20s
1/12		2 Feb	Martin, Henry son of Richard, dec'd, yeoman, of Tortworth Dowsing, John & Sybil 7 yrs smith 10s
		16 Sep	Barnewood, Henry son of William Barnwood, weaver Oram, Richard 7 yrs salter 12d
		25 Mar	Grime, Richard son of Richard, husbandman, of Cherington Petifer, Robert, gentleman, & Margaret 7 yrs saddler 20s
		8 Sep	Coxe, John son of John, husbandman, of Longford Ockey, William & Margaret 7 yrs baker 3s 4d
1/13		24 Jun	David, William son of David, dec'd, carpenter, of Gloucester Blowmer, Thomas 7 yrs sailor 40s
		29 Sep	Yonge, William son of William, of Barton Street, Gloucester Sandie, John & Margery 9 yrs smith 10s
			Sturmy, Thomas son of Thomas, yeoman, of Cheltenham Webbe, Thomas 10 yrs mercer 12d

	1595	25 Dec	Ladde, William son of John, husbandman, of Gloucester
			Woolley, Thomas & Agnes 7 yrs weaver 16s
1/14	1596	24 Aug	Gorway, John son of Humphrey, weaver, of Gloucester
			Gorway, Humphrey & Anne, his parents, 10 yrs weaver 6s 8d
		29 Sep	Howell, Meredith son of Meredith, husbandman, of Llanyre, Radnor
			Dowsing, William & Margaret 10 yrs smith 3s 4d
		1 Nov	Adams, Richard son of John, husbandman, of Matson
			Tolson, John & Anne 7 yrs smith 6s 8d
		2 Feb	Geste, William son of Alan, husbandman, of Swindon
			Wattes, Robert & Anne 7 yrs smith 6s 8d
1/15		25 Mar	Byforde, George son of Hugh, dec'd, butcher, of Slimbridge
			Lothingham, John & Joan 9 yrs mercer & glover 5s
		29 Sep	Atkins, Francis son of Richard, husbandman, of Upton
			Browne, John jr 10 yrs mercer 12d
	1595	25 Dec	Hunte, John son of John, husbandman, of Gloucester
			Tirry, William & Mary 9 yrs shoemaker 12d
	1596	30 May	Sanford, Henry son of Ancell, yeoman, of Stonehouse
			Willshire, Lawrence & Sarah, 8 yrs weaver 40s
1/16		29 Sep	Boilson, Thomas son of Thomas, tanner, of Bewdley, Worcs
			Browne, John jr & Eleanor 10 yrs mercer £3
			Liddiat *alias* Brewer, Thomas son of Thomas, tucker, of King's Stanley
			Carpenter, Henry & Dorothy 7 yrs broadweaver 40s
		24 Jun	Hill, Henry son of John, sievemaker, of Upper Arley [MS Overarle], Staffs
			Browne, Francis & Elizabeth 7 yrs sievemaker 3s 4d
			Jones, Robert son of Richard, dec'd, surgeon, of Gloucester
			Marshall, John & Joan 7 yrs butcher 40s
1/17		29 Sep	Bishopp, Peter son of Peter, dec'd, of Evesham, Worcs
			Elbridge, John & Joan 8 yrs cordwainer 12d

1/19			**Grimbald Hitchins, mayor [1596–7]**
			John Baughe and Nicholas Langford, sheriffs and bailiffs
	1596	30 Nov	Wickes, William son of Thomas, tanner, of Gloucester
			Lugge, William & Margaret, 7 yrs tanner 10s as a stipend and 2 suits of clothes
1/20		25 Dec	Dobbes, Thomas son of John, baker, of Gloucester
			Lothingham, John & Joan 8 yrs mercer & glover 2s 6d
			Becke, Christopher son of Richard, carpenter, of Newent
			Cicill, David & Eleanor 8 yrs cooper 13s 4d
	1597	2 Feb	Scriven, Richard son of John, husbandman, of Longhope
			Scriven, Thomas & Jane 12 yrs blacksmith 6s 8d

	1596	18 Oct	Harrys, Thomas son of Humphrey sr, husbandman, of Whaddon Fletcher, Edward & Margery 7 yrs gunmaker 6s 8d
1/21		25 Dec	Carpenter, John son of Richard, gentleman, of Quedgeley Hitchins, Grimbald & Eleanor 7 yrs draper 26s 8d
	1597	24 Feb	Stallard, Robert son of Robert, weaver, of Harescombe Keare, John & Elizabeth 7 yrs weaver 13s 4d
			Venn, Richard son of Richard, yeoman, of Staverton Kay, Thomas & Joan 9 yrs glover 6s 8d
			Nashe, Richard son of Richard, dec'd, yeoman, of Elmore Price, Matthew & Joan 7 yrs tanner 5s
		1 Mar	Phillipps, John son of Richard, yeoman, of Dore, Herefs Weale, Thomas & Elizabeth 7 yrs glover 12d
1/22		4 Apr	Asteman, Thomas son of Thomas, husbandman, of Tibberton Freame, Richard & Mary 10 yrs woollen draper 12d
		27 Mar	Lincecome, John son of William, yeoman, of Twyning Browne, Nicholas & Margery 7 yrs glover 12d
		7 Apr	Weaver, Thomas son of Thomas, butcher, of Tewkesbury Teinton, Thomas 10 yrs butcher 20s
		25 Apr	Cooke, Jeremy son of Thomas, carpenter, of Gloucester Taylor, John & Elizabeth 7 yrs vintner 20s
1/23		1 May	Webbe, Richard son of Thomas, gentleman, of Ampney Crucis Price, Albert & Sybil 10 yrs hosier 3s 4d
		18 Jun	Price, Walter son of Richard ap Gwillim, yeoman, of Brilley, Herefs Moore, John & Margaret 7 yrs tailor 12d & a new cloak
		1 May	Woodd, Richard son of John, dec'd, mercer, of Gloucester Elbridg, William & Alice 10 yrs apothecary 10s
		24 Jun	Venn, Thomas son of Richard, yeoman, of Staverton Smith, Thomas & Anne 10 yrs tailor 5s
		24 Aug	Cugley, Henry son of Thomas, woollen draper, of Gloucester Browne, Henry 9 yrs woollen draper 20s [*cf Appendix V*]
1/24			Prichard, Thomas son of Anthony, sailor, of Elmore Atkins, John & Sybil 8 yrs baker 3s 4d
		19 Sep	Wiett, Thomas son of John, dec'd, hatmaker, of Gloucester Jones, John 7 yrs blacksmith 6s 8d
		29 Sep	Hanman, Thomas son of John, yeoman, of Monmouth, Mon Freame, Richard & Mary 9 yrs woollen draper £40
			Sedgewicke, John son of William, gentleman, of Colwall, Herefs Kiste, Edward & Juliana 8 yrs saddler 2s 6d
			Langford, Robert son of Ralph, tailor, of Gloucester Sparkes, Abel & Eleanor 8 yrs hosier 3s 4d

1/25	1597	29 Sep	Tailor, Richard son of Thomas, glover, of Monmouth, Mon Lane, Richard & Joan 7 yrs saddler 40s
	1596	25 Dec	Clemence, Thomas son of Thomas, husbandman, of Barton Street Flemynge, Richard & Tabitha 7 yrs barber 3s 4d
	1597	24 Jun	Teynton, Walter son of Tainton, John, husbandman, of Churchdown Rich, Thomas & Anne 9 yrs mercer 3s 4d
		29 Sep	Wilkins, John son of Thomas, tailor, of Arlingham Adams, Thomas, clothier, & Jane 8 yrs weaver 6s 8d
			Shingleton, Lawrence son of William, yeoman, of Taynton Madocke, John, draper, & Margaret 9 yrs woollen draper 5s
1/26		4 Jul	Parker, Thomas son of Thomas, weaver, of Westbury Crumpe, William 7 yrs cordwainer 6s 8d
1/27		29 Sep	Eliotts, Edward son of Edward, tailor, of Gloucester Eliotts, Edward, his father, 7 yrs tailor 6s 8d

1/29 **John Jones, mayor [1597–8]**
Henry Darbie and Lawrence Wilshire, sheriffs and bailiffs

	1597	18 Oct	Edge, Thomas son of John, tanner, of Mitcheldean Tailor, Humphrey & Frances 9 yrs wiredrawer 3s 4d and 2 suits of clothes [*Text of indenture given in full.*]
1/30		1 Nov	Wattson, Richard son of Matthew, husbandman, of 'Scopby' [Sotby?], Lincoln Kiste, Edward & Juliana 7 yrs saddler £10 *On 2 Mar 1602, Thomas Semys, John Taylor and Henry Hassard, aldermen and justices came* [*Incomplete*]
		31 Oct	Cosby, John son of Richard, tailor, of Gloucester Nutte, William & Margery 10 yrs cordwainer 3s 4d
		26 Nov	Sedgwicke, William son of William, gentleman, of Colwall, Worcs [*recte* Herefs] Cox, Thomas & Eleanor 7 yrs baker 6s 8d
		30 Nov	Birchley, Thomas son of John, labourer, of Birtsmorton, Worcs Baughe, Francis & Eleanor 10 yrs cordwainer 12d
1/31		25 Dec	Walle, William son of William, dec'd, of 'Crable' [Cradley?], Worcs Shingleton, Thomas & Dorothy 7 yrs woollen draper 10s
	1598	6 Jan	Davies, John son of John, tailor, of Langford Budville, Somerset Guy, Thomas & Elizabeth 7 yrs cutler £3
			Cowdall, Thomas son of John, alderman, of Gloucester Robins, Edward *alias* Owen & Alice 7 yrs feltmaker 20s
		14 Mar	Wise, Denis son of Robert, gentleman, of Gloucester Snead, Alice, widow, 9 yrs mercer *20 Oct 1598, to be put over to Thomas Ceely, mercer from 29 Sep 1598 to 29 Sep 1605 then to be made free and the rest of the years remitted. Before Christopher Caple, mayor, and Edmund Clemence, master of the Mercers*

1/32	1598	1 Apr	Barrett, Robert son of Robert, tailor, of Gloucester Moore, John & Margaret 7 yrs tailor 13s 4d [*cf Appendix V*]
		16 Apr	Varney, Edward son of Timothy, dec'd, gent, of Hartwell, Northants Snead, William & Anne 10 yrs mercer 3s 4d
		22 Apr	Wilson, Samuel son of Willson, Richard, dec'd, clerk, of Staverton Smith, John & Anne 9 yrs tailor 12d
		2 Feb	Heyward, Walter son of John, labourer, of Hartpury Price, Richard & Anne 8 yrs barber 3s 4d
		1 May	Russell, John son of Henry, clothier, of Cirencester Price, William 8 yrs mercer 5s
		1 Nov	Etheridge, George son of John, dec'd Bromley, John & Anne 12 yrs glover 3s 4d
1/33		16 Apr	Madock, William son of John Madocke, draper, of Gloucester Tiler, Walter 8 yrs draper 10s
		4 Jun	Brooke, John son of Roger, husbandman, of 'Collwey' [Colwall?], Herefs Farmer, Richard & Margaret 7 yrs tailor
		24 Jun	Purlewent, William son of Roger, broadweaver, of Gloucester Adams, Albert & Anne 7 yrs broadweaver 13s 4d
		21 Jul	Clutterbuck, Robert son of Sapience, shearman, of Gloucester Bowland, Thomas & Jane 7 yrs mercer 10s
1/34		25 May	Sturmy, Robert son of Thomas, husbandman, of Cheltenham Symkins, John & Eleanor 7 yrs glover 26s 8d
	1597	24 Dec	Blisse, William son of John, dec'd, carpenter, of Gloucester Webley, Thomas & Catherine 7 yrs hosier 3s 4d
	1598	25 May	Vaughan, Richard son of James, glass carrier, of Gloucester Bubbe, Thomas jr & Cecily 9 yrs joiner 30s
		2 Feb	Launder, William son of William, dec'd, gardener, of Gloucester Sandie, John & Margery 9 yrs blacksmith 13s 4d
		24 Jun	Shingleton, William son of William, yeoman, of Taynton Stevens, George 8 yrs haberdasher 5s
1/35		1 Aug	Fawkener, John son of Robert, gentleman, of Gloucester Woodward, Thomas & Elizabeth 8 yrs broadweaver 26s 8d
		25 Jul	Madock, Lewis son of John, dec'd, draper, of Gloucester Mason, John & Alice 9 yrs mason 12d
		24 Jun	Lindsecom, Samuel son of William, gentleman, of Twyning Knowles, John & Mary 9 yrs broadweaver 40s
		15 Aug	Heyward, Walter son of William, dec'd, of Sandhurst Lane, William & Cecily 7 yrs tailor 3s 4d
1/36		1 Sep	Seaman, Richard son of Thomas, smith, of Gloucester Ardwaie, John & Catherine 8 yrs butcher 3s 4d

	1598	25 July	Dobbes, John son of John, baker, of Gloucester
			Dobbes, John, his father, & Anne 8 yrs baker 3s 4d
		25 Mar	Plaister, Thomas son of John, husbandman, of Westbury
			Smalman, Richard 8 yrs baker 5s
		29 Sep	Jones, Nicholas son of Richard, clerk, of Gloucester
			Cordell, Jane, widow, 10 yrs glover 3s 4d
		2 Feb	Craker, John son of Giles, pewterer, of Lancaster, Lancs
			White, John & Margaret 7 yrs merchant 40s [*Repeated, with a different year date, at 1/45*]
1/37		29 Sep	Bellinger, Christopher son of John, dec'd, of Gloucester
			Tailor, Humphrey 7 yrs wiredrawer 12d
			Bellinger, Thomas son of John, dec'd, of Gloucester
			Tailor, Humphrey 8 yrs wiredrawer 12d
		4 June	Camme, John son of Francis, broadweaver, of Westend
			Walshe, Robert & Anne 7 yrs broadweaver 20s
1/38		25 Mar	Cartwright, Edmund son of Edmund, husbandman, of Charlton Kings
			Micklewright, Walter & Joan 7 yrs shearman 3s 4d
		29 Sep	Caple, William son of Christopher, mercer, of Gloucester
			Caple, Christopher & Grace 7 yrs mercer 3s 4d
			[*Repeated, altered, at 1/40*]

1/39

Christopher Caple, mayor [1598–9]
John Brewster and John Little, sheriffs
Thomas Atkins clerk (*who died 17 April 1603*)

	1598	29 Sep	Taylor, Burall son of John, alderman, of Gloucester
			Caple, Christopher & Grace 9 yrs mercer 6s 8d [*Text of indenture given in full. Entry repeated, altered, at 1/40*]
1/40			Taylor, Burall son of John, gentleman, of Gloucester
			Caple, Christopher & Grace 9 yrs mercer 6s 8d [*Repeating entry at 1/39*]
		18 Oct	Pitt, Henry son of Henry, yeoman, of Hempsted
			Whitfeilde, Richard & Alice 10 yrs shoemaker 12d
		1 Nov	Blanche, John son of Miles, fuller, of Eastnor, Herefs [MS Estnor, Glos]
			Yarnar, Francis & Eleanor 7 yrs glover 3s 4d
1/41			Evans, Thomas son of Anne, widow, of Gloucester
			Tuncks, John & Katharine 9 yrs pewterer 12d
		25 Dec	Clissolde, Giles son of John, yeoman, of Ashton
			Barrett, Christopher & Alice 8 yrs barber surgeon 12d
		21 Dec	Hoare, Charles son of Charles, saddler, of Gloucester
			Hoare, Charles, his father, & Margery 8 yrs saddler 40s
1/42		1 Nov	Beedell, James son of William Beedle, yeoman, of Evesham, Worcs
			Bishopp, Nathaniel & Isobel 8 yrs woollen draper 6s 8d

	1598	30 Nov	Parker, Edward son of Robert, dec'd, carpenter, of Bishampton, Worcs Greene, John & Margery 7 yrs ropemaker 10s
	1599	29 Sep	Hawlinge, Francis son of William, husbandman, of Churchdown Beale, Geoffrey & Joan 9 yrs mercer 3s 4d
1/43	1598	1 Nov	Edwardes, Robert son of Thomas, carpenter, of Welsh Newton, Herefs Jeninge, Christopher & Anne 7 yrs baker 12d
	1599	24 Feb	Sawcome, Edmund son of Thomas, husbandman, of Norton Farre, John & Agnes 9 yrs smith 3s 4d
	1598	29 Sep	Cosby, Thomas son of Richard, innholder, of Gloucester Shurvington, Thomas & Isobel 7 yrs tailor 6s 8d
1/44		25 Dec	Merrett, Thomas son of Richard, wiredrawer, of Gloucester Sandes, Ralph & Catherine 8 yrs wiredrawer 3s 4d
	1599	2 Feb	Cooke, William son of Thomas, fisherman, of Hempsted Ryce, John 8 yrs cordwainer 12d
		24 Feb	Harbert, William son of John, dec'd, yeoman, of Twigworth Morse, Thomas 7 yrs tanner 20s
1/45		2 Feb	Yonge, Walter son of William, blacksmith, of the Hermitage [MS Armitage] Barnes, Thomas & Elizabeth 8 yrs blacksmith 3s 4d
			Craker, John son of Giles, pewterer, of Lancaster, Lancs White, John & Margaret 7 yrs merchant 40s [*Replacing, with a different year date, the entry at 1/36*]
		25 Mar	Hill, John son of James, dec'd, tucker, of Cradley, Herefs Hawkins, John & Joan 7 yrs mercer 12d
		29 Sep	Cooke, Thomas son of Richard, dec'd, of Gloucester Hawkins, John & Joan 8 yrs mercer 20s
1/46		25 Mar	Rea, John son of Richard, clerk, of Badgeworth Evans, John & Joan 9 yrs glover 20d
		8 Apr	Barrett, Robert son of Robert, tailor, formerly of Gloucester Higginson, William & Eleanor 7 yrs tailor 12d [*cf Appendix V*]
	1598	29 Sep	Longe, Henry son of Edmund, husbandman, of Ruardean Reynolds, John & Alice 7 yrs cordwainer 6s 8d
1/47	1599	25 Mar	Stacie, John son of John, mercer, of Cirencester Riche, Thomas & Anne 8 yrs mercer £2
			Daves, Thomas son of Hugh Davis, of Marden, Herefs Lukas, Robert & Katharine 7 yrs blacksmith 20s
		18 Oct	Farmer, William son of Richard, tailor, of Gloucester Hoare, Charles & Margery 8 yrs saddler 3s 4d
1/48		25 Mar	Hillarie, Simon son of John, dec'd, of Gloucester Guylliam, John & Joan 10 yrs silkweaver 20s
		24 Jun	Croes, Jasper son of William, broadweaver, of Longney Greene, Richard & Margaret 9 yrs broadweaver 6s 8d
		25 Jul	Thoare, John son of Thomas, husbandman, of Undy, Mon Rawlynge, Edward *alias* Gybson & Elizabeth 8 yrs joiner 12d

1/49	—	1 May	Weale, Thomas son of Walter, dec'd, of Farmington
			Tirry, William & Mary 12 yrs cordwainer 3s 4d
	1599	20 Aug	Wyman, Henry son of Arthur, dyer, of Gloucester
			Coxe, John & Elizabeth 9 yrs cordwainer 3s 4d
		25 Mar	Langford, Henry son of Nicholas, gentleman, of Gloucester
			Busshope, Nathaniel & Isobel 9 yrs woollen draper 6s 8d
1/50		29 Sep	Snowe, John son of John, shearman, of Gloucester
			Houlder, Thomas & Katharine 7 yrs weaver 5s
		14 Sep	Dowle, William son of William, fletcher, of Gloucester
			Sparkes, Abel & Eleanor 8 yrs hosier 2s 6d
		24 Aug	Tyler, William son of William, mercer, of Bisley
			Payne, Giles & Joan 9 yrs mercer 20s
1/51		21 Sep	Dower, Robert, by the churchwardens of St Oswald's parish, [Gloucester]:
			William Bridges, John Carpenter, Gabriel Woodward, Thomas Lane
			Shurvington, Thomas & Isobel 8 yrs tailor 10s
		29 Sep	Hawkes, William son of John, tailor, of Cheltenham
			Moore, John & Margaret 7 yrs tailor 40s
			Warde, Anthony son of Thomas, dec'd, of Bushley [MS Bushey], Worcs
			Gardner, William & Elizabeth 8 yrs dyer 20s
	1598	25 Dec	Capener, William son of John, husbandman, of Longford
			Browne, John & Eleanor 8 yrs brewer 3s 4d[1]
1/52	1599	29 Sep	Merrick, Humphrey Lewis son of Lewis, of 'Tarracleeve', Mon
			Dowsinge, William & Margaret 7 yrs [smith] nil
			Agreed that Humphrey should serve one year after his term as a covenanted servant for a stipend of 26s 8d
			Mason, Robert son of William, dec'd, of Gloucester
			Mason, William & Margaret 9 yrs cutler 6s 8d
		25 Mar	Baker, Luke son of William, broadweaver, of Gloucester
			Gorway, John & Anne 7 yrs broadweaver 6s 8d
1/53			Horsley, Francis son of William, weaver, of Gloucester
			Staynar, Richard 7 yrs cutler 3s 4d
		29 Sep	Battie, Richard son of John, dec'd, of Gloucester
			Hoare, Charles & Margery 8 yrs saddler 10s
			Farrington, Thomas son of Edmund, husbandman, of Cheltenham
			Carter, Giles & Mary 9 yrs skinner 6s
1/54		25 Mar	Joones, John son of David Johnes, of Abergavenny
			Smyth, Richard & Sarah 8 yrs tanner 12d
		29 Sep	Johnsons, William son of William, of Tewkesbury
			Holman, Humphrey and Mary 7 yrs merchant 3s 4d

---

[1] Entry inserted at the foot of the page.

	1598	25 Dec	Lewes, John son of John, tiler, of Gloucester Wood, John 7 yrs tanner 12d *5 Oct 1600: assigned to Thomas Clarke, tanner*
1/55	—	24 Jun	Wilshere, William son of Robert, husbandman, of Oakley, Beds Wilsheere, Lawrence, clothier, & Sarah 7 yrs weaver [*blank*]
	—	24 Jun	Nurse, Luke son of Walter, of Gloucester Nurse, Walter, his father, & Margaret 7 yrs mercer 46s 8d
	—	30 Nov	Crowdy, Thomas son of Nicholas, dec'd, of Longford Browne, John & Eleanor 7 yrs brewer 2s
1/61			**Thomas Semys, mayor [1599–1600]** **Thomas Barnes and John Maddock, sheriffs**
	1599	1 Nov	Hawlinge, Walter son of John, husbandman, of Parton in Churchdown parish Clibery, John & Anne 8 yrs haberdasher 3s 4d as a stipend and 2 suits of clothes viz for feast days and for work [*Text of indenture given in full.*]
1/62		30 Nov	Flouke, Edward son of Edward Flowke, yeoman, of Apperley Tirrey, William & Mary 11 yrs cordwainer 12d
		25 Dec	Carpinter, John son of John, dec'd, husbandman of Upton St Leonards Porter, Robert & Joan 7 yrs joiner 12d
	1600	6 Jan	Molgrave, Walter son of John, baker, of Westbury Saunders, John & Joan 7 yrs haberdasher 5s
1/63	1599	25 Dec	Goade, Thomas son of John, husbandman, of Sandhurst Paine, Giles & Joan 10 yrs mercer 20s
			Vaughan, John son of John, tailor, of Cirencester Wittar, John & Anne 7 yrs tailor £2
	1600	2 Feb	Litle, William son of William, mason, of Leckhampton Paine, Giles & Joan 8 yrs mercer 20s
	1599	25 Dec	Ap Rice, Powell son of Richard, joiner, of parish of St Michael [Mitchel Troy?], Mon Marshall, Thomas & Sybil 7 yrs butcher 40s
1/64			Edwardes, William son of David, cooper, of English Bicknor Guye, Thomas & Elizabeth 10 yrs cutler 12d
		1 Nov	Clark, Henry son of Roger, of Wotton near Gloucester White, Henry & Alice 8 yrs haberdasher 3s 4d
		21 Dec	Odie, Wm son of Odye, Thomas, husbandman, of Brinkworth, Wilts Johns, William & Joan 7 yrs baker 12d and 2 suits of clothes
1/65	—	2 Feb	Woodwarde, William son of Woodward, John, dec'd, of Gloucester Cooke, Peter & Katharine 10 yrs broadweaver 20s
	—	25 Dec	Venn, John son of William, capper, of Gloucester Endall, William & Anne 8 yrs shearman 3s 4d

	1599	25 Dec	Watkine, Richard son of Henry, yeoman, of Llanwenarth, Mon Smithe, Richard & Sarah 7 yrs tanner 12d
	1600	27 May	Milton, Robert son of Reginald, husbandman, of Arle Cowcher, John & Kathleen 9 yrs cordwainer 12d
		2 Feb	Cowell, John son of William, woollen draper, of Winchcombe Hawkins, John & Joan 8 yrs mercer £5
1/66		25 Mar	Cooke, John son of Thomas, dec'd, clothier, of Gloucester Cooke, Stephen & Joan 9 yrs woollen draper 20s
	1599	25 Dec	Massock, John son of John Massocke, dec'd, glover, of Gloucester Bramley, John & Anne 7 yrs glover 12d
	—	25 Mar	Barnelme, William, son of the people Marckle, John sr & Margaret 10 yrs turner 10s
1/67	—	25 Mar	Sandforde, Thomas son of Edward, yeoman, of Stonehouse Holforde, Stephen 10 yrs mercer 12d
	1600	20 Apr	Lambert, John son of John, dec'd, baker, of Stow [on the Wold] Gamnon, John 7 yrs baker 20s
		25 Mar	Whitthorne, John son of John, dec'd, yeoman, of Charlton Kings Pitt, Thomas 7 yrs baker 2s 6d
		1 May	Monnsloe, Thomas son of Thomas, yeoman, of English Bicknor Clarke, John & Margery 8 yrs tanner 13s 4d
1/68		25 Apr	Smithe, Thomas son of John, dec'd, yeoman, of Lassington Smith, Richard 7 yrs cordwainer 12d
		25 Mar	Hardinge, Thomas son of John, husbandman, of Brookthorpe Whitter, John 7 yrs tailor 20s
			Cugley, Henry son of Thomas, dec'd, draper, of Gloucester Baugh, John 7 yrs mercer 6s 8d [cf Appendix V]
		25 Apr	Simons, William son of James, dec'd, capper, of Wellington, Herefs Porter, Robert 8 yrs joiner 12d
1/69		25 Mar	Searche, George son of John, dec'd, merchant, of Bristol More, Thomas 8 yrs tanner 6s 8d
		24 Jun	Barnarde, William son of William, husbandman, of Boddington Coxe, John & Elizabeth 8 yrs cordwainer 10s
		25 Jul	Lustie, James son of Richard, broadweaver, of Berkeley Tailor, John, alderman, and John, his son 7 yrs to begin on 29 Sep maltster 40s
1/70		24 Jun	Deymonte, William son of Roger, gentleman, of Tiverton, Devon Hamons, John & Martha 8 yrs clothier 5s
		25 Jul	Hues, Henry son of Heues, William, gentleman, of Llantrissant, Mon Tarne, Leonard & Margaret 8 yrs glover 10s

	1599	30 Nov	Sawcombe, John son of Thomas, husbandman, of Norton Farre, John & Anne 7 yrs smith 2s 6d
	1600	1 Aug	Cleeveley, John son of Thomas Madocke, John & Juliana 7 yrs tanner 26s 8d
1/71		25 Jul	Pate, Thomas son of John, yeoman, of Maisemore Price, Matthew & Joan 7 yrs tanner 13s 4d
			Purse, Robert son of Edward, dec'd, of Quorndon [MS Quarden], Leics Saunders, John & Joan 8 yrs haberdasher 20s
		29 Sep	Williams, Thomas son of William Jones, of Pendoylan, Glam Thorne, John & Joan 7 yrs brewer £2
		24 Jun	Hagburne, Richard son of William, smith, of Churchdown Riche, Thomas & Anne 10 yrs mercer 10s
1/72	—	—	Hitchman, John son of Anthony, dec'd, husbandman, of Glos Meringe, Richard & Joan 7 yrs tailor 20s
	—	—	Springe, Lewis son of Henry, husbandman, of Gloucester Bubbe, Thomas sr & Bridget 8 yrs joiner 40s
	—	—	Watkins, Simon son of William, yeoman, of Newchurch, Radnor Bennett, Thomas & Anne 7 yrs shearman 5s
	1600	29 Sep	Roache, Thomas son of Charles, yeoman, of Gloucester Woode, John & Elizabeth 7 yrs tanner 3s 4d
1/73		25 Mar	Comminge, Thomas son of Thomas, formerly of parish of Pauntley Langforde, Nicholas & Anne 11 yrs stationer or any other art or mystery which the said Nicholas now practises 5s
		29 Sep	Charleton, Michael son of Roger, husbandman, of Gloucester Cugley, Robert & Joan 7 yrs wiredrawer 6s 8d
			Whithe, John son of Withie, husbandman, of Wormsley, Herefs [*Incomplete: see 1/ 79*]
			Emmett, John son of Bennet Emmotte, husbandman, of Padstow, Cornwall Mericke, Henry 8 yrs merchant 12d
1/74	1599	18 Oct	Whoper, John son of John, shoemaker, of Gloucester Smythe, Richard 7 yrs shoemaker 3s
		29 Sep	Hall, Roger son of James, miller, of the Leigh Hall, Richard 7 yrs cooper 10s
		25 Jul	Redfin, Henry son of Thomas, glover, of Gloucester Dickinson, Edward and Margaret 7 yrs salter £5 [*Repeated in part at 1/83*]
1/75		29 Sep	Harbert, Richard son of John Harberte, yeoman, of Twigworth Coxe, Richard and Isobel 7 yrs maltmaker 40s [*Repeated in part at 1/83*]

	1600	1 Nov	Shingleton, Thomas son of William, of Southampton, Southampton
			Shingleton, William & Frances 7 yrs woollen draper 3s 4d and 2 suits of clothes [*Repeated at 1/84*]
		29 Sep	Bennett, John son of John, of Mells, Somerset
			Prior, Henry & Anne 7 yrs brazier 20s
		25 Mar	Currye, Thomas son of Arthur, dec'd, of Crowan [MS Crewen], Cornwall
			Hill, William & Margaret 7 yrs [mercer] 2s 6d
1/76		29 Sep	Elliots, Thomas son of Elliotts, Thomas, clerk, of Gloucester
			Thorne, John & Joan 8 yrs beer brewer 40s
		25 Jul	Parler, William son of William, yeoman, of English Bicknor
			Jorden, Thomas & Anne 9 yrs cutler
		1 Nov	Cowarne, James son of Walter, yeoman, of Cleeve, Herefs
			Ceely, Thomas & Joan 8 yrs mercer 3s 4d
			[*Repeated & cancelled at 1/101*]
		29 Sep	Pomec, John son of Thomas, husbandman, of Over
			Pitt, John & Margaret 7 yrs hooper 20s and 2 suits of clothes
1/77		24 Aug	Garbrande, Edward son of Richard *alias* Harkes, stationer, of Oxford, Oxon
			Wilshere, Lawrence & Sarah 8 yrs clothier 13s 4d

1/79			**Luke Garnons, esq, mayor [1600–1]**
			John Thorne & William Hill, sheriffs
	1600	1 Nov	Whithie, John son of John, husbandman, of Wormsley, Herefs
			Gardner, William & Elizabeth 7 yrs shearman 3s
			[*Replacing incomplete entry at 1/73*]
		25 Dec	Hyde, Francis son of John, tanner, of Minchinhampton [MS Hampton]
			Micklewright, Walter & Joan 7 yrs dyer 12d
	—	25 Mar	Paine, William son of Mark, tucker, formerly of Cirencester
			Shurvington, Thomas & Isobel 7 yrs tailor 26s 8d
1/80	1601	12 Apr	Webbe, Nicholas son of Thomas, husbandman, of Frocester
			Bowar, John & Anne 8 yrs apothecary 6s 8d
	—	1 Nov	Bradwell, Richard son of Thomas, husbandman, of the Leigh
			Hawlinge, John & Katharine 8 yrs locksmith 3s 4d
	1601	6 Jan	Roache, Richard son of Charles, yeoman, of Gloucester
			Phelpes, Richard & Eleanor 7 yrs glover 3s 4d
			Before Henry Darby, Justice, 23 Apr 1605, with his master's consent put over to Joan Key, widow
1/81		12 Apr	Bagott, John son of Thomas, yeoman, of Frampton Mansell
			Baughe, John & Margaret 7 yrs mercer 10s
		25 Mar	Tirrett, John son of Richard, yeoman, of Gupshill
			Okaye, William & Margaret 7 yrs baker 6s 8d

| | 1601 | 20 May | Dutton, Henry son of Thomas, gentleman, of Northleach |
| | | | Paine, Giles & Joan 9 yrs mercer 10s |

| 1/82 | | 1 May | Weale, Thomas son of Henry, husbandman, of Maisemore |
| | | | Haies, John & Anne 8 yrs baker 3s |

| | 1600 | 25 Dec | Tremeare, Anthony son of Stephen, glover, of Stroud |
| | | | Watkins, Maurice & Anne 7 yrs hosier 3s 4d |

| | 1601 | 25 Jul | Bennett, Henry son of Thomas |
| | | | Strawford, Alice, widow, 8 yrs butcher 3s 4d |

| 1/83 | | 24 Jun | Cooke, John son of Thomas, yeoman, of Hempsted |
| | | | Morse, Thomas 7 yrs tanner 20s |

Redfin, Henry son of Thomas, of Gloucester [*Deleted: see 1/74*]

Harbert, Richard son of John, of Twigworth
Cancelled, entered previously   [*See 1/75*]

21 May Farmar, Richard son of Robert, yeoman, of Norton
Simpkins, John & Eleanor 7 yrs glover 6s 8d

26 Sep Cissell, James son of Philip, yeoman, of parish of St Devereux, Herefs
Smith, Richard, tanner, & Sarah 7 yrs glover 12d

| 1/84 | | 29 Sep | Sandie, Randolph son of William, yeoman, of Eldersfield, Worcs |
| | | | Smith, Richard & Sarah 8 yrs tanner 5s |

	1600	1 Nov	Shingleton, Thomas son of William
			Shingleton, William & Frances 7 yrs woollen draper 3s 4d
			[*Repeating entry at 1/75*]

	1601	24 Jun	Mayor, William son of William, husbandman, of Great [MS Broad] Somerford, Wilts
			Beale, Geoffrey & Joan 10 yrs mercer 12d
			[*Repeated in part at 1/92*]

| | — | 25 Mar | Coulstons, John son of Colstons, George, pewterer, of Gloucester |
| | | | Colstons, George, his father, 7 yrs pewterer 3s 4d |

| 1/85 | 1601 | 29 Sep | Brushe, William son of Thomas, yeoman, of Brockworth |
| | | | Snead, William & Anne 8 yrs mercer 3s 4d |

21 May Phillippe, Thomas son of George Phillippes, yeoman, of Westoning, Beds
Saunders, William 7 yrs haberdasher 2s 6d
[*Repeated in part and cancelled at 1/94*]
12 Apr 1605: The apprentice came before Mr Nurse, Justice, and by his own consent is put over to serve the residue of his years with Peter Lugg, haberdasher

31 May Webbe, Sergeant son of John, tailor, of Gloucester
Webbe, John, his father, & Isobel 7 yrs tailor 10s

2 Feb Wytherley, Thomas son of Thomas, miller,
Butt, Thomas & Alice 7 yrs cooper 12d

1/86	1601	24 Aug	Davis, William son of Edward, yeoman, of Sandhurst Baughe, Francis, cordwainer, & Eleanor 8 yrs shoemaker 3s 4d
		29 Sep	Tylsley, John son of Philip Tilsley, chapman, of Mitcheldean Taylor, Humphrey & Frances 8 yrs wiredrawer 3s 4d
			Robartes, Henry son of Robert, weaver, of Berkeley Horne, Thomas & Elizabeth 7 yrs pewterer 10s
	—	25 Jul	Bardle, William son of William, labourer, of Maisemore Cugley, Robert & Joan 9 yrs wiredrawer 6s 8d [*Repeated in part & deleted at 1/104*]
1/87	—	25 Dec	Lugg, Toby son of Thomas, tanner, of Gloucester Russell, Thomas & Alice 7 yrs skinner 3s 4d
	1601	12 Apr	Thorne, Giles son of John, smith, of Brockworth Kible, Thomas & Agnes 7 yrs weaver 20s
	1600	25 Dec	Deighton, Samuel son of Thomas, dec'd, of Cirencester Deighton, John & Anne, 7 yrs surgeon 6s 8d
			Rogers, John son of Richard, clerk, of Lassington Pitt, John & Margaret 7 yrs hooper 2s 6d and 2 suits of clothes[1]
1/88	1601	24 Aug	Phelpes, William son of Nicholas Phelepes, yeoman, formerly of Minsterworth Rice, John 8 yrs cordwainer 12d
		25 Mar	Thorne, Roger son of John, [smith], of Brockworth Brewster, John & Katharine 8 yrs skinner 13s 4d

1/91 **Thomas Machen, mayor [1601–2]**
Henry Darbie and Lawrence Wilshire, sheriffs

	1601	1 Nov	Davis, Arnold son of John, of Gloucester Endall, William & Anne 8 yrs shearman 12d and 2 suits of clothes
			Teinton, Humphrey son of John, of Churchdown Stephens, George & Olive 9 yrs haberdasher 3s 4d
		30 Nov	Robartes, Hugh son of Percy, of 'Scheviock', Flints Browne, Nicholas & Margery 7 yrs glover £7
1/92		25 Dec	Bushop, Thomas son of Bushoppe, John, clerk, of Gloucester Whitfeild, Richard & Alice 9 yrs cordwainer 12d
			Mayor, William [*Incomplete: see 1/84*]
	1602	3 Feb	Martimer, Giles son of Thomas, dec'd, of Todenham Cissell, David, hooper, & Eleanor 9 yrs cooper 10s
		4 Mar	Lanckford, John son of Ralph Langford, tailor, of Gloucester Guy, Hugh & Eleanor 9 yrs cutler 2s 6d after 8 yrs and for the 9th year 10d per week

---

[1] The foot of the page (possibly 1 entry) has been cut off. A pencil note: *'Bottom gone, July 5th 1847'* has been added.

1/93	1602	25 Mar	Smithe, Richard son of John, dec'd, of Lassington
			Coxe, John & Elizabeth 8 yrs cordwainer 6s 8d
			Ardwaye, William son of John, butcher, of Gloucester
			Graye, Alice, widow, 7 yrs butcher 20s
		2 Feb	Pitt, Richard son of Edward, husbandman, of Sutton Freen [i.e. Freen Court; MS Sutton Freance], Herefs
			Scriven, Thomas & Jane 8 yrs smith 10s
1/94		4 Apr	Evans, Thomas son of Matthew, dec'd, of Gloucester
			Carpenter, Henry & Dorothy 9 yrs weaver 13s 4d
			Phillippe, Thomas, son of George Phillippes, yeoman, of Westoning [MS Weston], Beds *Cancelled, entered previously. [See 1/85]*
		1 Nov	Keene, John son of Anthony, yeoman, of Rendcomb
			Kene, Miles, draper, & Joan 7 yrs woollen draper 6s 8d
			Abbottes, Richard son of Richard, yeoman, of Haughton, Lancs
			Abbottes, William & Elizabeth [*no term*] tailor 10s
1/95		28 May	Yemans, William son of Thomas, husbandman, of Churchdown
			Lugge, Richard & Joan 7 yrs glover 12d
		23 Jul	Tunckes, William son of Edward Tunkes, husbandman, of Lower Drayton in the parish of Penkridge, Staffs
			Davis, Humphrey 10 yrs mercer 3s 4d
		24 Jun	Bubbe, William son of William, yeoman, of Brockworth
			Bubbe, Walter 10 yrs mercer 30s
1/96		1 May	Brooke, John son of William, yeoman, of Quedgeley
			Thomas, John & Joan 7 yrs cordwainer 10s
		23 May	Slaughter, William, of Tirley
			Wantner, William & Margaret 8 yrs smith 20s
		3 May	Jorden, Thomas son of Thomas, yeoman, of Ashchurch
			Price, Matthew & Joan 7 yrs tanner 5s
		25 Mar	Heyward, William son of James, yeoman, of Hartpury
			Evan, Richard & Anne 8 yrs clothier 5s
1/97		4 Apr	Butt, Walter son of John But, yeoman, of Marden, Herefs
			Bennet, Thomas & Anne 8 yrs shearman 12d
		24 Jun	Robertes, Thomas son of Thomas, gentleman, of the parish of Llandysilio, Mont
			Elbridge, John & Joan 7 yrs cordwainer 2s
		23 May	Davis, Roger son of Thomas, weaver, of Gloucester
			Elbridge, John & Joan 8 yrs cordwainer 12d
		24 Jun	Owen, John son of John, yeoman, of Gloucester
			Kiste, Edward & Juliana 10 yrs saddler 10d
		29 Sep	Warde, William son of William, husbandman, of Hook Norton, Oxon
			Wager, Richard 7 yrs glazier 40s

1/98	1602	2 Feb	Tyll, Richard son of Robert, husbandman, of Whitgreave [MS Whitgrove], Staffs Tyll, John & Alice 8 yrs cutler 40s
		1 Aug	Perckes, Richard son of George, yeoman, of Leominster, Herefs Bennet, Thomas & Anne 7 yrs shearman 10s
		4 Apr	Browne, Francis son of John, yeoman, of Whaddon Battye, John & Elizabeth 7 yrs baker 12d
		24 Jun	Tayler, Thomas son of Thomas, yeoman, of Kings Pyon, Herefs Tayler, William & Katharine [*no term*] shearman 12d *Cancelled, entered later* [*See 1/100*]
		29 Sep	Lane, John son of John, tailor, of Gloucester Shervington, Thomas & Isobel 7 yrs tailor 5s *13 Feb 1604, John Lane came before Mr Nurse and prayed to be put over for the residue of his term to Thomas Smith, tailor*
1/99		23 May	Gybbes, Richard son of Richard, shoemaker, of Gloucester Colstance, George 7 yrs pewterer 2s
		25 Jul	Cromwall, Henry son of Thomas, weaver, of Gloucester Cooke, Peter & Juliana 11 yrs weaver 5s
		1 Aug	Hearynge, Thomas son of Richard, gentleman, of Tillington, Herefs Brown, Henry & Isobel 9 yrs woollen draper 10s
			Baker, William son of John, yeoman, of 'Buston' [Old Bishton?] Thorne, John & Joan 7 yrs beer brewer 20s
1/100		24 June	Tayler, Thomas son of Thomas, yeoman, of Kings Pyon, Herefs Tayler, William & Katharine 8 yrs shearman 30s [*Replacing entry at 1/98*]
		4 Apr	Varentur, Edmund son of Edmund, bagger, of Cheltenham Bruster, John & Catherine 12 yrs skinner 20s
		8 Apr	Aspden, John son of Guy, tailor, of Leigh Hall, Richard 11 yrs hooper 20s
		4 Apr	Wood, Giles son of Richard, yeoman, of Gloucester B[l]isse, Thomas & Anne 12 yrs turner 3s 4d
		29 Sep	Jones, David son of John, dec'd, of Dore, Herefs Strawford, Alice, widow, 7 yrs butcher £7
1/101		21 Sep	Chatterton, Howell son of Edward, yeoman, of Southgate Street, Gloucester Field, Thomas 8 yrs hosier 5s
		1 May	Bennett, James son of John, dec'd, labourer, of Gloucester Jones, John 7 yrs smith 12d
	—	25 Mar	Lysence, Christopher son of Edmund, haberdasher, of Gloucester [*Deleted: see 1/105*]
	1602	1 Nov	Cowarne, James son of Walter, yeoman, of Cleeve, Herefs Ceely, Thomas & Joan 8 yrs mercer 3s 4d *Cancelled, entered previously* [*See 1/76*]

1/103		**Richard Coxe, mayor** **Nicholas Langford & Thomas Adams, sheriffs, 1602–3**
	1602 30 Nov	Watkins, Walter son of John, yeoman, of Brockworth Clements, Edward & Anne 9 yrs mercer 3s 4d
	1 Nov	Tayler, William son of William, smith, of Ledbury, Herefs Dowsinge, John & Sybil 8 yrs [smith] 20s
	30 Nov	Thorne, John son of John *alias* Prentice, yeoman, of Brockworth Thorne, John & Sybil 9 yrs ropemaker 40s
	1603 13 May	Carpenter, Thomas son of William, labourer, of Tirley Cissell, David & Eleanor 8 yrs cooper 10s
	24 June	Williams, John son of Henry, cordwainer, of Gloucester Grene, John & Isobel 9 yrs ropemaker 13s 4d
1/104 —	1 May	Vyler, Henry son of John, husbandman, formerly of [Upper] Sapey, Herefs Pincke, William & Joan 7 yrs baker 5s
—	24 June	Restell, John son of Richard, yeoman, of Gloucester Berrowe, George & Catherine 7 yrs tailor 2s 6d
—	24 Apr	Peacocke, Henry son of John, cordwainer, of Malmesbury, Wilts Marshall, Thomas & Sybil 8 yrs butcher 20s
—	—	Bardle, William son of William, of Maisemore [*Deleted: see 1/86*]
	1603 24 Apr	Niccolls, Charles son of Walter, broadweaver, of Lypiatt Taylor, John, merchant, 7 yrs malt maker 3s 4d
	24 Mar	Heare, William son of Richard, husbandman, of Norton Deveris, John & Margery 8 yrs haberdasher 10s
1/105	24 Feb	Niccolls, John son of William, smith, of Longhope Younge, John & Margaret 8 yrs cooper 3s 4d
	24 Jun	Jeninges, Roland son of John, dec'd, of Gloucester Elbridge, John & Joan 9 yrs cordwainer 2s
	25 Mar	Lysence, Christopher son of Edward, haberdasher, of Gloucester Kirbie, Thomas sr & Margaret 7 yrs butcher 6s 8d [*Replacing incomplete entry at 1/101*]
	24 Jun	Langforde, John son of Nicholas, gentleman Addames, Thomas & Jane 7 yrs weaver 13s 4d
1/106	24 Jun	Beard, George son of Thomas, dec'd, of Gloucester Tailor, William & Catherine 7 yrs dyer 10s
	25 Jul	Rix, Samuel son of Humphrey, cooper, of Gloucester Wayte, James & Alice 8 yrs cooper 26s 8d
	15 Sep	Knowles, Richard son of Richard, dec'd Mercer, Robert & Mary 8 yrs fishmonger 2s 6d
	24 Jun	Heynes, John son of John, dec'd, of Gloucester Steyner, Robert & Cecily 9 yrs vintner 20s

1/107 1603 25 Mar Tailor, John son of John, waterman, of Bankside, Surrey
Tailor, Humphrey & Frances 9 yrs wiredrawer 3s 4d

Sare, Ralph son of John, clothworker, of Kington [MS Keynton], Herefs
Tailor, Humphrey & Frances 8 yrs wiredrawer 3s 4d

24 Apr Knipe, John son of Edward, cordwainer, of Over Kellet, Lancs
Tarne, Leonard & Margaret 8 yrs glover 6s 8d

29 Sep Wager, Richard son of Richard, glazier, of Gloucester
Wager, Richard, his father, 7 yrs glazier 6s 8d

24 Jun Payne, Roger son of Richard, dec'd, of Golden Valley, Herefs
Heath, Richard & Matilda 8 yrs pewterer 5s

25 Mar Cooke, Thomas son of William, husbandman, of Minsterworth
Barnewood, Thomas & Elizabeth 8 yrs joiner 13s 4d

1/108 Lewes, Humphrey son of Thomas, dec'd, of Longney
Greene, John & Isobel 7 yrs ropemaker 13s 4d

Ockwell, Arnold son of John Okewell, dec'd, of Lassington
Tayler, Timothy & Joan 9 yrs cordwainer 10s

25 July Jones, John son of John, dec'd, cordwainer, of Gloucester
Pakington, Thomas & [*blank*] 7 yrs cobbler 10s

12 Jun Warne, John son of Henry, dec'd, scrivener, of Ross, Herefs
Brookehowse, John & Joan 7 yrs feltmaker 5s

1/109 25 Mar Palmer, Edward son of Thos, dec'd, husbandman, of Eckington, Worcs
Angell, Abel & Mary 7 yrs baker 3s 4d

24 Jun Beard, Thomas son of John, dec'd, yeoman, of Wanstead, Essex
Beard, Richard & Anne 7 yrs mercer 6s 8d

1602 1 Nov Mason, Edward son of William, dec'd, of Gloucester
Pettefer, Robert & Margaret 7 yrs saddler 10s

1603 25 Jul Walker, John son of Thomas, husbandman, of Westend
Partredge, Robert & Anne 7 yrs weaver 20s

24 Apr Wilkins, Richard son of Thomas, husbandman, of Notgrove
Browne, Richard & Jane 7 yrs wiredrawer 3s 4d & 2 suits of clothes

1/110 25 Mar Ockford, Giles son of John, dec'd, weaver
Owen, John & Elizabeth 7 yrs weaver 6s 8d & 2 suits of clothes

29 Sep Sandforde, Thomas son of Edward Sandford
Angell, Robert & Anne 8 yrs mercer 10s

25 Dec Fletcher, Francis
Fletcher, Edward & Margery 7 yrs gunmaker 6s 8d

1 Aug Selwyn, Thomas son of Robert, cordwainer, of Malmesbury, Wilts
Baughe, Francis & Eleanor 7 yrs cordwainer 12d

25 Mar Woodward, John son of James, husbandman, of Hatherley
Darby, Henry sr & Margaret 7 yrs baker 13s 4d

1/111			**Thomas Riche, mayor [1603–4]** **John Browne and Thomas Kerby, sheriffs**
	1604	2 Feb	Hickes, Miles son of William, dec'd, weaver, of Bristol Willes, Leonard & Martha 7 yrs haberdasher £5
	1603	1 Nov	Greene, Simon son of William, dec'd, of Churcham Cissell, David & Eleanor 7 yrs cooper 3s 4d
		30 Nov	Lloyde, John son of John, tailor, formerly of Weston, Herefs Hallinge, William & Joan 7 yrs dyer 6s 8d
		1 Nov	Rodman, Francis son of Francis, dec'd, of Hillsley Clibery, John & Alice 8 yrs haberdasher 5s
1/112		25 Mar	Sowtherne, Thomas son of William, glover, of Tewkesbury Cox, John & Elizabeth 8 yrs cordwainer 10s
		30 Nov	Evans, Edward son of David, dec'd, of Gloucester Clibery, John & Alice 8 yrs haberdasher 3s 4d
		25 Mar	Hale, John son of William, husbandman, of Leigh Beale, Humphrey & [blank] 8 yrs mercer 10s
		25 Apr	Ball, Nathaniel son of Robert, clerk, of Eastington Price, William & Joan 8 yrs mercer 2s 6d
1/113	1604	29 Sep	Watts, Thomas son of Thomas, husbandman, of Highnam Price, Matthew & Joan 7 yrs tanner 6s 8d
		24 Jun	Carpinter, Guy son of Thomas, dec'd, of Tuffley Carpinter, Lawrence & Joan 7 yrs cordwainer 2s 6d and 2 suits of clothes
			Smith, Michael son of John, weaver, of King's Stanley Rutter, Luke & Joan 7 yrs weaver 6d and 2 suits of clothes
		17 Mar	Jones, Emanuel son of Samuel, clerk, of Hole, Devon Atkins, Jane, widow, 7 yrs apothecary 40s and 2 suits of clothes
1/114		24 Aug	Heyward, Edward, son of John Hayward, basket maker, late of Gloucester Pitt, John & Margaret 7 yrs cooper 20s and 2 suits of clothes
		25 Mar	Atwood, Maurice son of William, dec'd, of Berkeley Riche, Thomas, gentleman, & Anne 8 yrs mercer 10s
1/116	1603	30 Nov	Ryman, John son of Edward, yeoman, of Hungerford, Berks Lane, Richard 7 yrs saddler at the end, nothing, but throughout the term, all necessaries, food and clothes, linen and wool
1/117			**Henry Hazarde, mayor [1604–5]** **Edmund Clemence and Robert Pettifer, sheriffs**
	—	1 Nov	Nurse, John son of John, husbandman, of Twyning Browne, Nicholas 7 yrs glover 3s 4d
	—	30 Nov	Ashbie, Samuel son of John, clerk, of Hardwicke Went, John & Katherine 7 yrs weaver 20s

		1 Nov	Jeyne, William son of William, maltster, of Marshfield
			Smith, Richard & Sarah 9 yrs tanner 5s [*Repeated at 1/118*]
	1604	1 Nov	Read, David son of John
			Read, John & Elizabeth 7 yrs maltster 6s 8d [*Repeated at 1/123*]

1/118   18 Oct Whittingam, Henry son of Richard, dec'd, trowman, of Gloucester
                    Sands, John & Margery 8 yrs smith 3s 4d

             1 Nov Jeyne, William son of William, dec'd, malt maker, of Marshfield
                    Smith, Richard & Sarah 9 yrs tanner 5s
                    [*Repeating entry at 1/117*]

     1605   2 Feb Woodward, Thomas son of William, dec'd, husbandman, of Gloucester
                    Farr, John & Anne 7 yrs smith 6s 8d

             2 Mar Whithead, William son of Thomas, yeoman, of Southrop
                    Cosbie, John & Elizabeth 8 yrs turner 23s 4d

            25 Mar Pritchard, Philip son of John Prichard, clerk, of North Cerney
                    Caple, Christopher & Grace 9 yrs mercer 3s 4d

1/119 1604 25 Dec Persivall, John son of William, dec'd, haberdasher, of Gloucester
                    Kempe, Thomas & Jane 7 yrs capper 2s 6d

                    Allen, Richard son of Edward, husbandman, of Sutton, Herefs
                    Dowson, John & Sybil 8 yrs smith 40s

     1605   2 Feb Dappin, John son of John, husbandman, of Frampton on Severn
                    Taylor, Thomas & Ursula 8 yrs clothier 10s

            25 Apr Nicollson, John son of Anthony, husbandman, of Quedgeley
                    Woodward, Gabriel & Joan 9 yrs weaver 3s 4d

            17 May Eaton, Robert son of Peter, husbandman, of Elkstone
                    Nutte, William & Margery 8 yrs cordwainer 2s 8d

            24 June Elliottes, Henry son of Thomas, clerk, of Gloucester
                    Mayo, Abraham & Alice 7 yrs clothier 12d

            29 Sep Tompkins, Nicholas son of Thomas, clerk,
                    Vaughan, Roland & Margaret 11 yrs [*no trade*] 26s 8d

1/120 — 21 Sep Copner, Robert son of Richard, dec'd, of Upton
                    Scriven, Thomas 9 yrs smith 6s 8d

         — 24 Jun Linnet, Richard son of John, husbandman, dec'd, of Milbourne, Wilts
                    Evans, John & Joan 11 yrs glover 2s 6d

         — 31 Mar Hodshon, Richard son of Marmaduke, gentleman, of Gloucester
                    Gwillim, John & Cecily 10 yrs silkweaver 3s 4d

         —   Bridges, Thomas son of John, joiner, of Newent
                    Key, Edward & Grisegan 7 yrs glover 12d

         — 24 Jun Hitche, Thomas son of John, barber, of Wotton under Edge
                    Symons, Francis & Jane 8 yrs barber 3s 4d

1/121	1605		Nurse, John son of John, husbandman, of Hempsted Hawle, Richard & Anne 9 yrs cooper 23s 4d
			James, John son of Lewis, dec'd, of Ross, Herefs Browninge, John & Catherine 7 yrs wiredrawer 3s 4d
		25 Jul	Baylie, John son of William, dec'd, clerk Yarnolde, Francis & Eleanor 8 yrs glover 3s 4d
	1604	25 Dec	Weblye, Thomas son of Thomas Webly, draper, of Gloucester Bishoppe, Robert & Mary 9 yrs draper 10s
			Shere, Thomas son of Thomas, labourer, of Blaisdon Wager, Robert & [*blank*] 7 yrs glazier 33s 4d
1/122	1605	30 Mar	Heane, Walter son of Roland, tanner, of Littledean Smith, Richard, gentleman, & Sarah 8 yrs tanner 12d
		21 Sep	Jelfe, Thomas son of John, husbandman, of Hartpury Langford, Toby & [*blank*] 8 yrs stationer 20s
			Cowley, Richard son of Thomas, farmer, of Hempsted Tomkins, John & Elizabeth 7 yrs smith 2s
		19 May	Crowdy, Edward son of Richard, broadweaver, of city of Bath Weale, Thomas & Elizabeth 7 yrs glover 3s 4d
		9 May	Michell, Robert son of Roger, dec'd, gardener, of Gloucester Addames, Thomas & Jane 10 yrs clothier 13s 4d
1/123		19 May	Fowle, William son of Richard, joiner, of Blakeney Kiste, Edward & Elizabeth 8 yrs joiner 40s
		24 Jun	Barrett, Thomas son of Thomas, dec'd, of Hucclecote Weekes, William & Margaret 7 yrs tanner 20s
		25 Jul	Terry, Richard son of William, cordwainer, of Gloucester Terry, William & Mary 7 yrs [cordwainer] 6s 8d
			Terry, William son of William, cordwainer, of Gloucester Terry, William, his father, & Mary 10 yrs cordwainer 6s 8d
			Collericke, John son of Thomas, clerk, of Churchdown [MS Chursdon] Tyler, Walter & [*blank*] 9 yrs draper 10s
	1604	1 Nov	Read, David son of John Read, John 7 yrs maltster 6s 8d [*Later insertion at bottom of page. Repeating entry at 1/117*]
1/124	1605	24 Aug	Hazarde, Arthur son of Arthur, clerk, of Sandhurst Lane, William & Anne 7 yrs tailor 12d
		29 Sep	Hayward, Thomas son of Richard, dec'd, of Sandhurst Crumpe, William & Joan 8 yrs cordwainer 2s
		24 Jun	Clements, Thomas son of Edward, mercer of Gloucester [Clements], Edward, his father, & Anne 7 yrs mercer 6s 8d
			Merewether, Samuel son of Richard, gentleman, of Burford, Oxon Madocke, John & Margaret 9 yrs draper 10s & 2 suits of clothes

	1605	25 Mar	Swayne, William son of Edward, carpenter Blisse, Thomas & Anne 12 yrs turner 6s 8d & 2 suits of clothes
1/125		25 Jul	Jones, Lewis son of John [Jones *deleted*] Harry, husbandman, of Llanwenarth, Mon Clarke, John & Margery 7 yrs tanner 20s & 2 suits of clothes
			Clarke, John son of Thomas, dec'd, husbandman, of Withy Bridge Baugh, Francis & Eleanor 7 yrs cordwainer 20s & 2 suits of clothes
	1604	25 Dec	Showell, William son of Hugh Showle, weaver, of Barton Street, Gloucester Sandes, Ralph & Catherine 7 yrs wiredrawer 3s 4d & 2 suits of clothes
	1605	25 Mar	Charleton, Edward son of Richard, husbandman, of Gloucester Cugley, Robert & Joan 7 yrs wiredrawer 6s 8d & 2 suits of clothes
			Howlet, Thomas son of Richard, dec'd, of Gloucester Browninge, John & Catherine 7 yrs wiredrawer 3s & 2 suits of clothes
1/126		29 Sep	Smarte, John son of John, yeoman, of Througham Morse, Thomas & Elizabeth 8 yrs tanner 20s & 2 suits of clothes [*Repeated on same page*]
		25 Mar	Phelpes, William son of Henry, dec'd, of Gloucester Horner, Brian 8 yrs coverlet weaver 2s 6d & 2 suits of clothes
		29 Sep	Done, Arthur son of Robert, yeoman, of Weston under Penyard, Herefs Guye, Thomas & Elizabeth 9 yrs cutler 6s 8d & 2 suits of clothes
			Hunt, Richard son of John, husbandman, of Gloucester Bub, John & Eleanor 9 yrs cordwainer 6s 8d & 2 suits of clothes
			Smart, John son of John Smarte, yeoman, of Througham Morse, Thomas & Elizabeth 8 yrs tanner 20s & 2 suits of clothes *Cancelled* [*Repeating first entry at 1/126*]
1/127			Shewen, John son of John, miller, of Cranham [MS Cram] Smaleman, Richard & Joan 7 yrs baker 6s 8d
			Bradford, Arnold son of Thomas, yeoman, of Linton Hamons, John & [*blank*] 7 yrs clothier 7d
1/129			**Henry Darby, mayor [1605–6]** **Matthew Price and Nathaniel Bishopp, sheriffs**
	1605	1 Nov	Dobbes, Lawrence son of John, baker, of Gloucester Sturmey, Robert & [*blank*] 7 yrs glover 10s & 2 suits of clothes [*cf Appendix V*]
			Badger, Brian son of Giles, dec'd, of Barnwood Sandford, Henry & Sybil 7 yrs[1] broadweaver 6s 8d & 2 suits of clothes

---

[1] MS *pro termino septem librorum annorum* (literally, 'for term of seven books of years'); the meaning is not clear, and the wording may be a mistake.

| | 1605 | 1 Nov | Clarke, Daniel son of Robert, dec'd, of Gloucester |
| | | | Dimocke, Thomas & Jane 8 yrs cooper 10s & 2 suits of clothes |

           30 Nov Lane, William son of John, tailor, of Gloucester
                     Browninge, John & Catherine 7 yrs wiredrawer 12d & 2 suits of clothes

1/130   25 Dec Bromley, John son of John, dec'd, of Gloucester
                           Yarnold, Francis & Eleanor 8 yrs glover 12d & 2 suits of clothes

        1606 2 Feb Showe, Roger son of Roger, formerly of Upleadon
                       Gwilliam, John & Cecily 8 yrs silkweaver 6s 8d & 2 suits of clothes

                         Clarvo, Thomas son of Thomas, dec'd, of the Leigh
                         Shingleton, William & Frances 9 yrs draper 3s 4d & 2 suits of clothes [*Repeated in part at 1/131*]

        1605 25 Mar Clutterbucke, Thomas son of John, broadweaver, of Gloucester
                       Holder, Thomas & Anne 8 yrs weaver 13s 4d & 2 suits of clothes

1/131   2 Feb Watkins, George son of Thomas, smith, of Littledean
                       Heathe, Richard & Matilda 7 yrs pewterer 2s & 2 suits of clothes

             25 Mar Nelme, John son of John, yeoman, of Berkeley
                       Beard, Richard & [*blank*] 10 yrs mercer 2s 6d & 2 suits of clothes

                       Havard, Peter son of John, gentleman, of New Radnor, Radnor
                       Greeninge, Jasper & [*blank*] 12 yrs silkweaver 2s & 2 suits of clothes

             1 Nov Plomer, Giles son of John, butcher, of Gloucester
                       Weaver, Francis & Joan 8 yrs butcher 10s & 2 suits of clothes

        1606 2 Feb Clarvo, Thomas son of Thomas, dec'd, of the Leigh
                       [*Incomplete and cancelled: see 1/130*]

1/132 1605 1 May Overton, Richard son of Humphrey, butcher, of Gloucester
                       Webbe, William & Anne 7 yrs butcher 20s & 2 suits of clothes
                       Cancelled

                     Casye, Richard son of Richard, dec'd, glover
                     Smith, Richard & Sarah 12 yrs tanner 20s & 2 suits of clothes

            31 Mar Clinch, Richard son of Thomas, miller, of Gloucester
                     Woodward, Thomas & Elizabeth 10 yrs weaver 10s & 2 suits of clothes

             1 Nov Hitchins, Thomas son of Thomas, husbandman, of Comberton, Worcs
                     Daunce, Richard & Joan 7 yrs cordwainer 3s 4d & 2 suits of clothes

         —   24 Jun Nelme, Thomas son of John, yeoman, of Berkeley
                     Webb, John 10 yrs mercer 2s 6d & 2 suits of clothes

1/133 1606 25 Mar Pirry, Thomas son of Robert, weaver, of Kempley
                     Pirry, Henry & Katharine 7 yrs cordwainer 10s & 2 suits of clothes

             1 Jun Clarvoe, George son of John, husbandman, of Didbrook
                     Caple, Christopher & Grace 9 yrs mercer 3s 4d & 2 suits of clothes

1606 20 Apr Clarke, Henry son of William, yeoman, of Chaddesley [Corbett], Worcs
Elbridge, John & Joan 8 yrs cordwainer 12d & 2 suits of clothes

1 Jun Pearce, Thomas son of Edward, labourer, of Twyning
Bowle, Henry & Tacy 10 yrs vintner 20s & 2 suits of clothes

20 Apr Raynoldes, Robert son of Henry, dec'd, of Gloucester
Clarke, John & Margery 7 yrs tanner 20s & 2 suits of clothes

24 Jun Stookes, William son of Walter, dec'd, of Ashleworth
Hayward, John & Joan 7 yrs chandler 10s & 2 suits of clothes

1/134 Lugge, John son of Thomas, tanner, of Gloucester
Lugge, Peter & [*blank*] 9 yrs haberdasher 10s & 2 suits of clothes

25 Jul Wilcox, John son of William Willcox, yeoman, of Hartpury
Sandford, Henry & Sybil 7 yrs clothier 6s 8d & 2 suits of clothes

Smith, William son of Roger, yeoman, of Twyning
Atkins, John & Mathea 7 yrs baker 5s & 2 suits of clothes

Pirry, Thomas son of Walter, dec'd, clothier, of Gloucester
Wilsheire, Lawrence & Sarah 8 yrs clothier 10s & 2 suits of clothes

Holman, Henry son of Humphrey, merchant
Addames, Albert & Anne 7 yrs clothier 13s 4d & 2 suits of clothes

Hall, Elias son of John Halle, cordwainer, of Ledbury, Herefs
Whitfeild, Richard & [*blank*] 10 yrs cordwainer 3s 4d & 2 suits of clothes

1/135 17 Sep Price, Henry son of Matthew, gentleman, of Gloucester
Raynoldes, John & Mary 8 yrs draper 5s & 2 suits of clothes

29 Sep Longe, Richard son of Giles, yeoman, of Bentham
Ceely, Thomas & Joan 10 yrs mercer 3s 4d & 2 suits of clothes

Egby, William son of Robert, dec'd, of Stroud
Clarke, John & Margery 7 yrs tanner 20s & 2 suits of clothes

Keyse, John jr son of John, tailor, of Barton Street, Gloucester
Shervington, Thomas & [*blank*] 7 yrs tailor 2s 6d & 2 suits of clothes

21 Sep Kerry, John son of William, weaver, of Minchinhampton [MS Michell Hampton]
Good, Thomas sr & Isobel 7 yrs sievemaker [MS seavegar] 2s 6d & 2 suits of clothes

29 Sep Moore, Alexander son of Thomas, husbandman, of Hughley, Salop
Carpenter, John & Dorothy 7 yrs joiner 6s 8d & 2 suits of clothes

1/136 25 Mar Smith, Thomas son of John, yeoman, of Deerhurst Walton
Langford, Nicholas & [*blank*] 9 yrs mercer 5s & 2 suits of clothes

Nelme, Anthony son of Jeremy, yeoman, of Berkeley
Hoare, Charles & Margery 8 yrs saddler 12d & 2 suits of clothes

	1606 25 Mar	Clarke, Martin son of Richard, dec'd, of Rudford
		Lugge, William & Margaret 8 yrs tanner 40s & 2 suits of clothes
	29 Sep	Itheridge, John son of Robert, dec'd, of Prior's Norton
		Crumpe, Giles & Anne 9 yrs cordwainer 3s 4d & 2 suits of clothes
	30 Nov	Garner, John son of William
		Addames, Albert & Anne 7 yrs clothier 3s 4d
1/137	29 Sep	Hassard, John son of Arthur, clerk, of Sandhurst
		Greninge, Jasper & Tacy 9 yrs silkweaver 5s & 2 suits of clothes
	24 Jun	Hayes, Thomas son of Thomas Haies, dec'd, of Stanley
		Bennett, Thomas & Mary 9 yrs shearman 5s
	1 Nov	Batt, Daniel son of William
		Thomas, John & Joan 8 yrs cordwainer 3s 4d
	1 Aug	Gamon, Edward son of Thomas
		Kiddon, Robert & Eleanor 9 yrs milliner 6d
	24 Jun	Pullin, Francis son of Robert, dec'd, of Down Ampney
		Smithe, Richard & Sarah 8 yrs tanner 12d
	29 Sep	Evans, Robert son of Robert, smith, of Hardwicke
		Seaman, Thomas & Margaret 7 yrs smith 10s
1/138	8 Jun	Dobbes, Lawrence son of John, baker, of Gloucester
		Dobbes, Richard & Welthian 7 yrs cordwainer 2s 6d
		[cf Appendix V]
	1605 25 Dec	Pincke, John son of William, baker, of Gloucester
		Pincke, William, his father, & Joan 7 yrs baker 6s 8d
		[Repeated in part and deleted at 1/180]
	1606 26 Mar	Deighton, Richard son of William, of city of London
		Deighton, John & Jane 8 yrs surgeon 10s
	20 Apr	Churche, Richard son of Thomas Church, miller, of Gloucester
		Woodward, Thomas & Elizabeth 10 yrs weaver 10s
	25 Jul	Bennett, Anthony son of Arthur
		Cooke, Peter 7 yrs weaver 2 suits of clothes
	29 Sep	Niccolson, William son of Anthony
		Cooke, Stephen & Joan 9 yrs draper 2s 6d

1/141 **Lawrence Wilsheire, mayor [1606–7]**
Richard Smith and Geoffrey Beale, sheriffs

	—	Veysie, James son of Nicholas, husbandman, of Shipton Sollers [MS West Shipton]
		Lucas, Robert & Katharine 7 yrs smith 40s & 2 suits of clothes
	1606 18 Oct	Richards, Henry son of Ferdinand, husbandman, of Gloucester
		Biglin, Edward & Sybil 8 yrs smith 10s & 2 suits of clothes
	1 Nov	Gilbert, Nicholas son of Simon, gentleman, of Garway, Herefs
		Dimocke, Thomas & Jane 8 yrs cooper 10s & 2 suits of clothes

	1606	1 Nov	Waples, John son of Henry, of Brize Norton, Oxon
			Meredith *alias* Younge, William & Margaret 8 yrs vintner 3s 4d & 2 suits of clothes
1/142	1607	2 Feb	Beck, Anthony son of Anthony, chapman, of 'Kerby Kendall' [Kirkby Lonsdale?], Westmld
			Kiste, Edward & Juliana 8 yrs saddler 3s 4d & what has been agreed
	1606	1 Nov	Cowles, Walter, husbandman, of Bisley
			Dowsinge, William & Margaret 7 yrs smith 2s
		30 Nov	Englea, John son of William
			Tailor, James & Edith 8 yrs cutler 2s 6d
	1607	25 Mar	Whoper, Jesse son of John, cordwainer
			Woodcock, Thomas 7 yrs cordwainer 12d
		2 Feb	Williams, Hugh son of James, of Abergavenny, Mon
			Deveris, John & Margery 7 yrs haberdasher 10s
		5 Apr	Hewson, Thomas son of Yewen, dec'd, of Tewkesbury
			Barrett, Christopher & Alice 7 yrs barber 3s 4d
1/143		24 Jun	Lysence, Edward son of Edward
			Smith, John & Eleanor 7 yrs butcher 6s 8d
		25 Jul	Savage, Anthony son of John
			Browninge, John & Catherine 8 yrs wiredrawer 3s 4d
		29 Sep	Newman, William son of William, husbandman, of Prestbury
			Sturmy, Thomas & [*blank*] 10 yrs mercer 2s 6d
		24 Jun	Barkesdale, Giles son of John, tanner, of Winchcombe
			Cooke, Thomas & [*blank*] 7 yrs chandler 2s 6d
		29 Sep	Whitmay, Thomas son of George, husbandman, of Over
			Hore, Richard, clothier, & Anne 7 yrs weaver 10s
1/144		25 Mar	Brookehowse, John son of John, feltmaker, of Gloucester
			Brookehowse, John, his father, & Joan 7 yrs feltmaker 10s & what has been agreed
			Brookehowse, Thomas son of John, feltmaker, of Gloucester
			Brookehowse, John, his father, & Joan 7 yrs feltmaker 10s
			Rawlins, Hugh son of William, clerk, of Newnham
			Brookehowse, John & Joan 7 yrs feltmaker 10s
		24 Aug	Bleeke, Arthur son of Richard, yeoman, formerly of Charlton Kings
			Beale, Geoffrey & Joan 7 yrs mercer 2s 6d
		25 Mar	Bennett, John son of John, broadweaver, of Gloucester
			Gwilliam, John & Cecily 10 yrs silkweaver 6s 8d
		1 May	Davis, James son of Christopher, yeoman, of Bridstow, Herefs
			Hurte, John & Elizabeth 7 yrs clothier 13s 4d
1/145		24 Jun	Poyner, Edward son of John, yeoman, of Whitchurch, Mon
			Warde, William & Elizabeth 8 yrs cordwainer 3s 4d

	1607	26 May	Hawlinge, Henry son of Giles, husbandman, of Swindon
			Bubb, John & Eleanor 7 yrs cordwainer 12d
		21 Sep	Evans, Richard son of Matthew, labourer, of [Gloucester]
			Kynner, William & Joan 9 yrs glover 5s
	—	2 Feb	Merrie, Richard son of Thomas Mirrie, husbandman, of Sandhurst
			Rice, George John & Elizabeth 8 yrs cordwainer 2s 6d
	—	6 Jan	Dutton, Richard son of Thomas, dec'd, of Northleach
			Stevens, George & Olive 9 yrs haberdasher 10s
	1607	24 Jun	Wallis, John son of Ralph, yeoman, of Elmley [MS Elineth] Castle, Worcs
			Bower, John & Anne 8 yrs apothecary 3s 4d
1/146		25 Mar	Warner, Richard son of Henry, dec'd, of Ross, Herefs
			Dobbes, Richard & Welthian [MS Wealthinque] 8 yrs cordwainer 3s 4d
		24 Jun	Burte, Robert son of Robert, dec'd, of Haresfield
			Elliottes, Edward & Elizabeth 7 yrs tailor 2s 6d
		29 Sep	Wyndow, Edward son of [blank], dec'd, butcher, of Stanley
			Hayes, John & Anne 9 yrs baker 13s 4d
	—	25 Mar	Hornedge, Thomas son of William, husbandman, of Hempsted
			Mayoe, Abraham & Alice 7 yrs clothier 5s
	1607	29 Sep	Evans, Morgan son of John, shearman, formerly of Gloucester
			Strawford, Walter & [blank] 7 yrs butcher 5s
		24 Jun	Knipe [MS Knighte. See 1/107] William son of Edward, dec'd, of Over Kellet, Lancs
			Cosby, John & Elizabeth 7 yrs turner 3s 4d
1/147			Farmer, John son of William, labourer, of Gloucester
			Addames, Francis & Elizabeth 9 yrs clothier 12d
		24 Aug	Grigg, William son of William, yeoman, of Gloucester
			Price, Matthew & Joan 7 yrs tanner 10s
		25 Jul	Howe, Stephen son of James, of Hope Mansell, Herefs
			Nurse, Walter & Elizabeth 8 yrs currier 2s 6d
		29 Sep	Russell, William son of William, dec'd, tailor, of Barton Street, Gloucester
			Shervington, Thomas & [blank] 7 yrs tailor 5s
			Bridgges, John son of Thomas, labourer, of Southgate Street, Gloucester
			Browne, Richard & Jane 8 yrs wiredrawer 3s 4d
		25 Jul	Lewes, Richard son of Lewis Jones, dec'd, of Penmaen, Merioneth
			Wheeler, John & [blank] 9 yrs mercer 20s
		26 May	Williams, David son of William James, husbandman, of Llanwenarth, Mon
			Watkins, Richard & Mary 7 yrs tanner 2s 6d
1/148		25 Mar	Angell, Edward son of Richard, dec'd, of Ashton Keynes, Wilts
			Endall, William & Anne 8 yrs shearman 20s
			Hore, Thomas son of Charles, saddler, of Gloucester
			Hore, Charles, his father, & Margery 7 yrs saddler 6s 8d

1607 1 May Allen, Lawrence son of Edward, cordwainer, of Gloucester
Dance, Richard & Joan 8 yrs cordwainer 2s 6d

1606 30 Nov Kinges, James son of Thomas, dec'd, of Eldersfield, Worcs
Cox, John & Elizabeth 7 yrs cordwainer 3s 4d

25 Dec Keene, William son of John, husbandman, of Great Witcombe
Whitter, John & Anne 7 yrs tailor 6s 8d

1/157

John Baughe, mayor [1607–8]
Thomas Addames and William Locksmith, sheriffs, 1607 & 1608

1608 25 Jul Smale, Edward son of Edward, cordwainer, of Cirencester
Batty, Richard 7 yrs saddler 10s

29 Sep Lane, Edward son of Michael, husbandman, of Bushley, Worcs
Fowler, Ferdinand & [blank] 7 yrs mercer 20s

25 Mar Rea, Nicholas son of Thomas, gentleman, of Hill Croome, Worcs
Cugley, Richard & Anne 9 yrs mercer 6s 8d

15 May Twyninge, Richard son of James, husbandman
Ockey, William & Mary 8 yrs baker 3s 4d

Taylor, Henry son of Henry, dec'd
Edge, Thomas 8 yrs pinner 5s

1/158 25 Mar Nelme, William son of John, husbandman, of Berkeley
Cooke, John & [blank] 10 yrs draper 3s 4d

1607 30 Nov Allen, Richard son of Robert, gentleman, of Evesham, Worcs
Smith, Richard & Sarah 7 yrs tanner 12d

1608 15 May Davis, Thomas son of Samuel, cordwainer
Wilshere, William & [blank] 8 yrs clothier 13s 4d

24 Jun Woode, James son of Charles, dec'd, of Alstone [MS Alscon], Worcs
Wilshere, Lawrence & Sarah 7 yrs clothier 13s 4d

24 Aug Webbe, John son of John, butcher, of Southgate Street, Gloucester
Endall, John & Alice 7 yrs butcher 2s 6d

29 Sep Rice, William son of Henry, labourer
Rice, John & Elizabeth 7 yrs cordwainer 5s

25 Jul Hardwicke, Walter son of John, husbandman, of Arlingham
Thorne, John sr & Joan 9 yrs brewer £4

1/159 25 Mar Marten, George son of John, husbandman, of Apperley
Browne, John, gentleman, & [blank] 7 yrs brewer 3s 4d

25 Jul Frewen, Thomas son of Thomas, tailor, of Gloucester
Craddocke, Richard & Mary 9 yrs tailor 3s 4d

25 Mar Bennett, Robert son of Robert, labourer, of Bulley
Batten, John & Elizabeth 9 yrs baker 12d

1607 1 Nov Sandye, George son of William, dec'd, of Aston, Herefs
Pitt, John & Margaret 8 yrs cooper 23s 4d

| | 1607 30 Nov | Cosby, Jasper son of Richard, tailor, formerly of Gloucester |
| | | Jeninges, Brian & Alice 7 yrs baker 26s 8d |

    1608 29 Sep Hewes, Edward son of Thomas, dec'd
                    Hayes, Richard & Margery 8 yrs cutler 5s

           25 Apr Williams, Morgan son of William Jones, dec'd, of Tredunnock, Mon
                   Lugg, William & Margaret 7 yrs tanner 20s

1/160   24 Jun Collyer, John son of William, vintner, of Aston, Herefs
                   Hawle, Roger & [*blank*] 9 yrs cooper 16s

   1607 25 Dec Davys, Samuel son of Thomas, dec'd, yeoman, of Nailsworth in parish
                 of Minchinhampton
                 Wyse, Denis 9 yrs mercer etc

   1608 29 Sep Gwyn, Augustine son of Thomas, yeoman, of Hempsted
                 Crompe, William & Joan 10 yrs cordwainer 6s 8d

                 Haynes, William son of John, innkeeper, of Gloucester
                 Pitt, Thomas & Joan 7 yrs baker 20s

          25 Jul Maysey, Theophilus son of Ralph, clerk
                 Whittington, Robert & Anne 10 yrs apothecary 6s 8d
                 [*cf Appendix V*]

         29 Sep Emott, John son of William, gardener
                 Guy, Thomas & Elizabeth 10 yrs cutler 26s 8d

         24 Aug Clevely, William son of Adam, husbandman, of Over
                 Bishoppe, Robert & Mary 8 yrs draper 6s 8d

1/161   24 Jun Minchyn, Richard son of Michael Mynchin, dec'd, husbandman, of
                 Ilmington, Warws
                 Jans, William & Joan 8 yrs baker 3s 8d

   1607 1 Nov Beale, Thomas son of Joan, of county of Worcs
                 Price, William & Elizabeth 9 yrs mercer 2s 6d

   1608 29 Sep Witcome, Thomas son of William, dec'd
                 Whittern, John & Anne 7 yrs tailor 20s

                 Vaughen, Richard son of William, mason
                 Gwilliam, John & Cecily 8 yrs silkweaver 3s 4d

          25 Jul Pearce, Giles son of William, dec'd, of Newland
                 Addames, Albert, clothier, & Anne 7 yrs weaver 6s 8d

   1607 25 Dec Wodley, John son of William, cordwainer, of Northleach
                 Morse, Thomas & Elizabeth 8 yrs tanner 6s 8d

1/162 1609 25 Apr Willins, Nicholas son of William Jones, farmer, of Pendoylan, Glam
                 Wheeler, Henry & Margaret [*no term*] carpenter
                 19 Jun 1615 Before John Thorne and Thomas Adammes, justices
                 Whereas the said master was not [a freeman] at the time of the
                 binding of the apprentice that therefore the apprentice shall
                 continue to abide with his said master as his apprentice until the
                 25th day of April 1617 which maketh up the full number of seven
                 years thereby to receive his freedom of this city

1608 24 Jun Griffith, Francis son of Robert
　　　　　　　Lug, William & Margaret 7 yrs tanner what is specified in the indentures

　　　　　　Powell, John
　　　　　　　Browne, John 7 yrs brewer 5s

　　25 Jul Thomas, Arnold son of Griffith, dec'd, of St Brides, Glam
　　　　　　　Sparkes, Abel & Eleanor 9 yrs hosier 10s

1/167 **John Brewster, mayor [1608–9]**
Edward Clements and Robert Pettefer, sheriffs, 1608 & 1609

1608 1 Nov Clements, Toby son of Edward, gentleman, of Gloucester
　　　　　　　Clements, Edward, his father, & Anne 9 yrs mercer 13s 4d

　　25 Dec Cowper, Walter son of John, dyer, of Gloucester
　　　　　　　Morgan, William & Elizabeth 10 yrs glazier 12d

　　30 Nov Birde, Ferdinand son of Richard, dyer, of Stroud
　　　　　　　Greene, Margaret, widow, 7 yrs upholsterer 6s 8d

1609 2 Feb Bodnam, Richard son of John, dec'd, yeoman, of Upton St Leonards
　　　　　　　Pincke, Walter & Margery 8 yrs baker 2 suits of clothes

1/168 1608 25 Dec Evans, Nathaniel son of John, dec'd, shearman
　　　　　　　Prior, Henry & Anne 8 yrs brazier 3s 4d

　　30 Nov Smithe, Thomas son of Edward, husbandman, of Bishop's Cleeve
　　　　　　　Hallinge, John & Catherine 7 yrs smith 10s

1609 1 May Worgan, John son of Robert, yeoman, of Gloucester
　　　　　　　Stevens, George & Olive 9 yrs haberdasher 40s

　　20 Apr Skyllarne, William son of John, dec'd
　　　　　　　Morse, Thomas & Elizabeth 7 yrs tanner 6s 8d

　　2 Feb Frewen, Richard son of Thomas, glover, of Gloucester
　　　　　　　Ven, Richard & [blank] 11 yrs glover 6s 8d

　　25 Mar Butler, Robert son of Thomas, dec'd, of Stroud
　　　　　　　Warde, William & Elizabeth 8 yrs cordwainer 3s 4d

1/169 25 May Hawcome, Henry son of John, shepherd, of Lea, Wilts
　　　　　　　Howlett, Anthony & Anne 7 yrs butcher 2s 6d

1608 8 Oct Yealfe, Thomas son of Richard, dec'd, of Longney
　　　　　　　Smithe, Richard & Sarah 7 yrs tanner 2s 6d

1609 24 Jun Grymes, Thomas son of Thomas, dec'd, of Lambeth, Surrey
　　　　　　　Sturmy, Robert & Eleanor 7 yrs glover 12d

　　4 Jun Keylocke, William son of James, husbandman, of Hardwicke
　　　　　　　Angell, Abell & Mary 8 yrs baker 3s 4d

1608 25 Dec Davis, Robert son of Richard, labourer, of Gloucester
　　　　　　　Mason, William & Margaret 10 yrs cutler 6s 8d

1/170	1609	24 Jun	Price, Ralph son of William, dec'd, of Aston, Herefs Woodwarde, Gabriel, clothier, & Joan 8 yrs weaver 3s 4d
		6 Jan	Handes, Alexander son of John, yeoman, of Burford, Oxon Walbridge, John & Elizabeth 8 yrs barber surgeon 10s
		25 Jul	Hogg, Peter son of Peter, clerk, of Harescombe Meringe, Richard & Joan 8 yrs tailor 10s
		2 Feb	Hewes, Richard son of Richard, dec'd, of Tewkesbury Taynton, Thomas & Joan 7 yrs butcher £3
		25 Jul	Fowle, William son of Thomas, husbandman, of Huntley Haule, Roger & [blank] 9 yrs cooper 26s 8d
			Byrde, John son of William, husbandman, of Great Malvern, Worcs Craker, John & Margaret 8 yrs salter 13s 4d
1/171		24 Aug	Man, Thomas son of Francis, weaver, of Painswick Batten, John & Elizabeth 9 yrs baker 12d
		25 Mar	Woodward, Henry son of John, husbandman, of Southgate Street, Gloucester Packington, Thomas & Joan 8 yrs cobbler 13s 4d & what is agreed according to the customs of the city of Gloucester
			Whittington, William son of Richard, gentleman, of Linton Hamons, John & [blank] 8 yrs clothier 20s
	1608	30 Nov	Hodges, William son of Robert, cordwainer, of Gloucester Taylor, Timothy & Joan 7 yrs cordwainer 10s
	1609	29 Sep	Travell, William son of Robert, yeoman, of Ledbury, Herefs Price, Matthew & Joan 7 yrs tanner 5s
		6 Jan	Walbridg, Richard son of John, barber surgeon, of Gloucester Walbridg, John, his father, & Elizabeth 7 yrs barber surgeon 10s
1/172		29 Sep	Bosley, Thomas son of Thomas, tailor, of Cheltenham Yarnold, Francis & Eleanor 11 yrs glover 3s 4d
			Moore, Thomas jr son of Thomas, yeoman, of Gloucester Atkins, John & Martha 7 yrs baker 2s 6d
			Mace, Ferdinand son of John, husbandman, of Gloucester Taylor, William & Catherine 7 yrs shearman & dyer 12d
			Garrett, William son of Walter, dec'd, of Narberth, Pembs Midlewrighte, Walter & Joan 8 yrs dyer 3s 4d
		25 Mar	Beaven, Lewis son of Lewis Bevan, husbandman, of Garway, Herefs Midlewrighte, Walter & Joan 7 yrs dyer 3s 4d
1/173		24 Jun	Carne, Hugh son of Henry, dec'd, glover Gwilliam, John & Cecily 7 yrs silkweaver 6s 8d
		29 Sep	Drinkwater, Richard son of Edmund Drinkewater, dec'd Palmer, John & [blank] 7 yrs cooper 6s 8d
		24 Jun	Harriattes, Anthony son of John, labourer, of Gloucester Woodcocke, Thomas & Anne 9 yrs cordwainer 12d

	1608	25 Dec	Berry, Richard son of John, yeoman, of Brookthorpe Meringe, Richard & Joan 7 yrs tailor 10s
	1609	29 Sep	Rixe, Richard son of Anthony, dec'd, husbandman, of Upton Addames, Thomas, clothier, & Jane 8 yrs broadweaver 6s 8d
		16 Apr	Addames, Thomas son of Thomas Sawle, William & Sarah 7 yrs mercer [blank]

1/177

John Thorne, mayor [1609–10]
Toby Bullock and Humphrey Holman, sheriffs 1609 & 1610

  1609 1 Nov Copland, Richard son of John Coplande, dec'd
        Cox, John & Elizabeth 8 yrs cordwainer 3s 4d

     25 Dec Freame, John son of Thomas, tailor, of Cirencester
        Whitter, John & Anne 7 yrs tailor 2s 6d

     1 Nov Jones, Nathaniel son of Samuel, clerk, of Hole, Devon
        Snead, William & Bridget 9 yrs mercer 3s 4d

  1610 2 Feb Addis, William son of John, dec'd, of Frampton
        Pincke, Walter & Margery 7 yrs baker 3s 4d

     21 Sep Piperd, Thomas son of Thomas, husbandman, of Linton, Herefs
        Edge, Thomas & [blank] 9 yrs pinner 6s 8d

1/178   2 Feb Greene, Samuel son of John, yeoman, of Churcham
        Johns, William & Joan 7 yrs baker 2s 6d

     1 May Kircome, John son of Thomas, labourer, of Gloucester
        Scryven, Thomas & Alice 9 yrs smith 6s 8d

        Edwardes, John son of William, glover,
        Lugg, Peter & Margaret 10 yrs haberdasher 10s

     24 Jun Gardner, William son of William, dyer, of Gloucester
        Singer, John & Felix 7 yrs dyer 20s

  1609 25 Dec Jenninges, John son of John, yeoman, of Gloucester
        Mason, Robert & Deenes 9 yrs cutler 13s 4d

  1610 8 Apr Stephens, Henry son of Robert, husbandman, of Corse
        Hyron, Humphrey & Audrey 9 yrs chandler 5s

1/179   25 Mar Clotterbooke, Samuel son of Daniel, dec'd, tucker, of North Nibley
        Porter, Robert & Elizabeth 9 yrs joiner 2s

     2 Feb Hopkins, Benedick son of Ralph, of Walford, Herefs
        Watkins, Richard & Mary 7 yrs tanner 5s

     25 Jul Bennett, Arthur son of Thomas, dyer, of Gloucester
        Bennett, Thomas, his father, & Mary shearman & dyer 10s

     24 Aug Sturmy, Edward son of George Sturmye, cordwainer, of Painswick
        Whitfield, Richard & Alice 7 yrs cordwainer 7s

        Cotterell, Henry son of Henry, clerk, of Donnington, Herefs
        Seaman, Thomas 7 yrs smith 2s 6d

	1610	25 Jul	Meysey, Theophilus son of Ralph, clerk, of Randwick
			Langeford, Toby & Eleanor 8 yrs stationer 6s 8d [*cf Appendix V*]
		29 Sep	Lovelock, Zacheus son of William, tailor
			Whoper, John & [*blank*] 7 yrs vintner £5
1/180		25 Jul	Abrahall, Thomas son of Simon, dec'd, of Snodhill, Herefs
			Whitter, John & Anne 9 yrs tailor 12d
	1609	25 Dec	Pincke, John son of William, baker, of Gloucester
			Pincke, William, his father, & Joan baker [*Deleted: see 1/138*]
	1610	29 Sep	Evans, John son of John, dec'd, of Gloucester
			Ven, John & Elizabeth 7 yrs feltmaker 2s 6d
		25 Jul	Jones, Moses son of David, labourer
			Abbottes, Richard & Anne 8 yrs tailor 5s
		29 Sep	Willis, James son of Richard, yeoman, of Tredington
			Price, Matthew and Joan 7 yrs tanner 6s 8d
			Lawrence, Thomas son of Thomas, dec'd, of Withington
			Bennett, Thomas & Mary 8 yrs dyer & shearman 2s 6d
			[*Repeated at 1/181*]
1/181			Hayes, Christopher son of Thomas, dec'd, of Leonard Stanley
			Wager, Robert & Ursula 7 yrs glazier 5s
		28 Oct	Heyward, Thomas son of John, dec'd, of Sandhurst
			Elbridge, John & Joan 8 yrs cordwainer 12d [*Deleted: see 1/187*]
		29 Sep	Jones, John son of Thomas, butcher, of Gloucester
			Greeneberry, John & [*blank*] 7 yrs weaver 5s
		24 Jun	Marson, Edward son of Ralph, dec'd
			Whitington, Robert & Anne 8 yrs apothecary 6s 8d
		29 Sep	Lawrence, Thomas son of Thomas
			Bennett, Thomas & Mary 8 yrs shearman & dyer 2s 6d
			[*Repeating entry at 1/180*]
			Hilman, John son of John, husbandman, of Miserden
			Morse, Thomas 7 yrs tanner 6s 8d
			Feild, Nathaniel son of Thomas Fild, of Stroud
			Nurth, William 7 yrs woollen draper 40s
1/182		25 Mar	Bliss, Thomas son of William Blisse, dec'd
			Edwardes, William & [*blank*] 7 yrs clothier 6s 8d
	1609	25 Dec	Drinkewater, Richard son of Edward
			Sturmy, Robert & Eleanor 7 yrs glover 3s 4d
	1611	2 Feb	Fleminge, John son of John
			Walbridge, John 7 yrs barber surgeon 20s [*Repeated at 1/191*]
	1610	29 Sep	Lawrence, Henry son of Thomas, dec'd, of Eastcott [MS Escott], Wilts
			Dowseinge, John & Sybil 7 yrs smith 30s

1/187			**John Browne, mayor [1610–11]** **Richard Smithe and Henry Browne, sheriffs**

1/187

John Browne, mayor [1610–11]
Richard Smithe and Henry Browne, sheriffs

    1610 28 Oct Heyward, Thomas son of John, dec'd, of Sandhurst
                   Elbridge, John & Joan 8 yrs cordwainer 12d
                   [*Replacing entry at 1/181*]

         1 Nov Tomlingson, Charles son of Nicholas
                   Clarke, John & Margery 7 yrs tanner 3s 4d

    1611 25 Mar Henlock, Godfrey son of Roger, dec'd, of Skegby, Notts
                   Bishopp, Alexander & Bridget 7 yrs cordwainer 6s 8d

         2 Feb Powell, Jeremiah son of James, gentleman
                   Batten, John & Elizabeth 10 yrs baker 10s 10d

    1610 25 Dec Chewe, Thomas son of Michael
                   Hamons, John & Anne 8 yrs clothier 10s

    1611 1 May Brooke, William son of Giles
                   Wantner, William & Margaret 10 yrs smith 12d
                   [*Repeated in part and deleted at 1/189*]

1/188 1610 1 Nov Niccolls, John son of John, tanner, of Longhope
                   Cleevely, John & Joan 8 yrs tanner 2s 6d

    1611 24 Jun Porter, John son of Walter
                   Elliottes, Edward & Elizabeth 8 yrs tailor 2s 6d

        12 May Itheridg, Walter son of Walter, dec'd, of Maisemore
                   Price, Matthew & Joan 8 yrs tanner 5s

        25 Mar Machen, Thomas son of John Machien, yeoman, of Pedington
                   Wickes, William & Margaret 7 yrs tanner 20s [*Repeated at 1/189*]

    1610 25 Dec Wayt, Henry son of Richard Wayte dec'd, yeoman, of Colethrop
                   Bearde, Thomas 8 yrs mercer 3s 4d

    1611 25 Jul Fitche, Thomas son of Francis
                   Hore, Charles jr & Joan 9 yrs saddler 2s 6d

    1610 1 Nov Crompe, John son of Henry
                   Crompe, Giles 7 yrs cordwainer 6s 8d

1/189 1611 25 Mar Machen, Thomas son of John, yeoman, of Pedington in parish of
                   Berkeley
                   Wickes, William & Margaret 7 yrs tanner 20s [*Repeating entry at
                   1/188*]

         1 May Note, Henry son of Richard
                   Venn, John & Elizabeth 7 yrs feltmaker 2s 6d

        24 Jun Hampton, William son of Richard
                   Greene, Richard & [*blank*] 8 yrs glover 3s 4d

        24 Aug Clutterbooke, Daniel son of Walter
                   Russell, Thomas & Alice 8 yrs skinner 40s

         1 May Brooke, William son of Giles, dec'd
                   William [*Incomplete & deleted: see 1/187*]

	1611 12 May	Wytherley, Richard son of Thomas
		Wytherley, Thomas jr & Elizabeth 7 yrs cooper 40s
	29 Sep	Gale, John son of William, dec'd,
		Crompe, William & Joan 12 yrs cordwainer 5s
		[*Cancelled*; *cf Appendix V*]
1/190	1610 25 Dec	Hagborne, Thomas, son of William, smith
		Hore, Richard, clothier, & Anne [*no term*] broadweaver 2s 6d
	1611 25 Dec	Thomas, Thomas son of Lewis, hive maker
		Tayler, John & Anne [*no term*] malt maker 10s *In the time of William Hill, mayor, 1611*
	1610 1 Nov	[Wilshere], Lawrence son of Lawrence, gentleman
		Wilshere, Lawrence, his father, & Sarah [*no term*] clothier 20s
	25 Dec	Shingleton, Lawrence son of William [draper]
		Shingleton, William & Frances [*no term*] his father's art 3s 4d
	1612 25 Mar	Witcome, William son of Thomas, dec'd
		Hore, Richard & Anne 7 yrs clothier £5
1/191	1611 24 Jun	Crompe, Robert son of John, husbandman
		Smith, Richard & Hester [*no term*] tanner 2s 6d *In the time of John Browne, mayor, 1611*
	29 Sep	Thorne, William son of John, dec'd
		Thorne, John & Elizabeth 7 yrs ropemaker 53s
	2 Feb	Flemminge, John son of John, dec'd
		Walburge, John 7 yrs barber surgeon 20s [*Deleted: see 1/182*]

1/197		**William Hill, mayor [1611–12]**
		Thomas Fild and William Price, sheriffs
	1611 18 Oct	Webster, William son of John, dec'd
		Palmer, John & Margaret 7 yrs cooper 6s 8d
	20 Sep	Edwardes, Thomas son of William, of West Hatch, Som
		Jones, John, alderman & diocesan registrar, 7 yrs public notary
	25 Dec	Atkins, Thomas son of Thomas, of Upton
		Bishopp, Alexander & Bridget 8 yrs cordwainer 12d
	1612 2 Feb	Harris, Robert son of William, dec'd
		Price, Matthew & Joan 7 yrs tanner 40s
	1611 29 Sep	Butt, Richard son of Walter, clothier
		Smith, Richard & Hester 8 yrs tanner 2s 6d
1/198	1612 1 May	Wattes, Herbert son of Edward
		Tarne, Thomas & Margaret 8 yrs glover 6s 8d
	24 Aug	Billamy, Thomas son of William
		Key, Edward & Grisgard 7 yrs glover 2s 6d
	25 Mar	Thomas, William son of John, dec'd
		Hardinge, Thomas & Margaret 8 yrs tailor 13s 4d

	1611	25 Dec	Haynes, Thomas son of Edward, dec'd
			Wedge, Anne, widow, 8 yrs weaver 2s 6d
	1612	2 Feb	Bullock, Robert son of Anthony
			Dowsinge, William & Margaret 7 yrs smith 3s 4d
1/199		29 Sep	Hazard, Thomas son of Thomas
			Nutt, William & Margery [no term] cordwainer 2s 8d
		25 Jul	Surman, Thomas son of William
			Lane, William [no term] tailor 12d
		25 Mar	Hooper, William son of John
			Heyford, John & Anne [no term] baker 20s
			Hopton, William son of Ferdinand
			Morse, Thomas [no term] tanner £5 6s 8d
		24 Aug	Evans, Robert son of Richard
			Smalman, Richard & Jonicy [no term] baker 6s 8d
		29 Sep	Keele, Robert son of Nicholas
			Crumpe, Giles & Anne [no term] cordwainer 3s 4d
1/200		30 Nov	Kinge, Henry son of Simon
			Cowcher, John & Joan [no term] cordwainer 3s 4d *In the tenth year of the king. In the time of Thomas Addams, mayor*
		25 Mar	Hawsteed, William son of John
			Marshall, Henry & Catherine [no term] butcher 20s
		1 Nov	Browne, William son of John
			Hurte, John & Elizabeth [no term] broadweaver 2s 6d *In the tenth year of King James. In the time of Thomas Addams, mayor*
		31 May	Blisse, Richard son of William
			Garbrande, Edward & Margaret [no term] clothier 7s
	1611	21 Dec	Collet, Edward son of John
			Weekes, William & Margaret [no term] tanner 10s
1/201	1612	2 Feb	Gale, John son of William
			Baughe, Francis & Eleanor [no term] shoemaker 5s [cf Appendix V]
	1611	25 Dec	Webbe, Geoffrey son of Richard
			Porter, Robert & Elizabeth [no term] joiner 6s 8d
		18 Oct	Hodges, Thomas son of Robert
			Dobbes, Richard & Welthiane [no term] cordwainer 3s 4d
	1612	6 Jan	Mayoe, Guy son of Gregory, of Taynton
			Thorne, John sr, gentleman, & Joan 7 yrs [brewer] £4
			Butler, Thomas son of John, dec'd
			Robinson, Anthony, gentleman, & Hester [merchant] 11 yrs 26s 8d
1/202		25 Mar	Clarke, William son of Thomas, dec'd
			Baughe, Francis & Eleanor 8 yrs [shoemaker] 20s
	1611	1 Nov	Barber, James son of Joan
			Sheyle, Christopher & Elizabeth 7 yrs butcher 6s 8d

| | 1611 | 25 Dec | Pace, John son of Thomas, dec'd, of Ashleworth |
| | | | Porter, Robert & Elizabeth 7 yrs joiner 2s 6d |

	1612	2 Feb	Hopkins, John son of William, of Brickhampton [MS Brickington]
			Carpinter, John & Dorothy 7 yrs joiner 2s 6d
		25 Mar	Walle, Thomas son of John, yeoman, of Gloucester
			Craddocke, Richard & Mary 9 yrs tailor 2s 6d

1/203 1613 6 Jan Clarke, William son of Thomas, husbandman, of Hartpury
                    Bubb, William & Joan 9 yrs mercer 6s 8d

1/207   **Thomas Addames, mayor [1612–13]**
                John Webbe and John Brewster, sheriffs

       1612 21 Sept Davis, William son of Robert
                     Pitt, John & Margaret [*no term*] cooper 20s

       1613 25 Mar   Blowmer, William son of Thomas, dec'd
                     Gryme, Richard & Joan [*no term*] saddler 10s

            13 May   Kirke, Richard son of Thomas, merchant tailor, of Newnham
                     Heath, Richard & Matilda 8 yrs pewterer 6s 8d

             1 May   Blanchflower, Edmund son of Edward, dec'd
                     White, Henry & Alice 9 yrs haberdasher 2s 6d

1/208   4 Apr Heynes, Robert son of Robert
                     White, David & Edith 9 yrs shearman 12d

       1612 30 Nov   Bosley, Richard son of William
                     Bishopp, Thomas & Anne 8 yrs cordwainer £4

       1613 2 Feb   Barkesdale, Nicholas son of John
                     Cooke, Stephen & Joan 7 yrs woollen draper 2s 6d

            23 May   Randle, Richard son of William
                     Wheeler, Henry & Anne 7 yrs carpenter 5s

            25 Mar   Merrett, Thomas son of John
                     Elbridge, John & Joan 7 yrs cordwainer 12d
                         They will find for the said Thomas food, tools, shoes and bedding

1/209   24 Jun Pearce, Robert son of Thomas
                     Bishopp, Thomas & Anne 7 yrs cordwainer 2s 6d

                     Willetts, George son of Robert
                     Charleton, Edward & Alice 8 yrs wiredrawer 10s

       1612 25 Dec   Tomes, Christopher son of William
                     Sherington, Thomas 7 yrs tailor 5s

       1613 2 Feb   Farmer, Edward son of Richard
                     Elizabeth Venn, widow, 7 yrs feltmaker [*deleted*]
                     Ballenger, Christopher 8 yrs wiredrawer 2s 6d

            21 Sep   Holder, Walter son of Henry
                     Seaman, Thomas & Margaret 8 yrs smith 6s

	1613	24 Jun	Niblett, John son of Thomas Venn, Elizabeth, widow, 7 yrs feltmaker 5s
1/210			Clarke, Edward son of Josiah Bradford, Thomas 7 yrs haberdasher 13s 4d
			Morris, Henry son of David Davis, Roger & Elizabeth 9 yrs cordwainer 6s 8d
			Heyward, Edward son of Edward Birde, Ferdinand & Joan 7 yrs upholsterer 40s
		25 Jul	Cosby, Thomas son of John Duringe, Darius & Elizabeth 7 yrs turner 20s
		1 Aug	Hall, Thomas son of Edward Cowlstons, George 7 yrs [upholsterer *deleted*] pewterer 12d
		25 Mar	Jones, Giles son of Evan Graye, William 7 yrs [pewterer *deleted*] butcher 6s 8d
1/211		23 May	Uley, John son of Arthur Witherley, Thomas 7 yrs cooper 20s
	1612	25 Dec	Booth, Thomas son of Anthony Bothe Walbeurge, John & Elizabeth 7 yrs barber surgeon an instrument called a 'sithorne'[1]
	1613	25 Mar	Walker, Anthony son of Richard, broadweaver Addames, John & Margery 7 yrs weaver 20s
		29 Sep	Hatton, John son of William, of Gloucester Hatton, William, his father, & Anne 7 yrs his father's art
	1612	25 Dec	Jones, John son of Thomas, butcher, of Gloucester Browne, Richard & Jane 7 yrs wiredrawer 3s 4d
1/212	1613	29 Sep	Langford, Edward son of Nicholas, gentleman, of Gloucester Terry, Richard & [*blank*] 8 yrs cordwainer 10s
	1612	25 Dec	Collett, Edward son of John, dec'd, of Naunton Weekes, William & Margaret 7 yrs tanner 10s
	1613	24 Jun	Maio, Lawrence son of Robert, clothier, of Gloucester Maio, Abraham & Alice 7 yrs clothier 10s
			Merser, William son of Robert Bisshopp, Alexander & Bridget 7 yrs cordwainer *8 Feb 1618 Before Edward [recte Edmund?] Clements and Matthew Price, justices, William Merser with his consent was put over to serve John Tomas, cordwainer, from 8 Feb to 29 Sep next. John Tomas has paid 20s to Alexander Bisshopp in full discharge of his service*

1/227 **John Taylor, mayor [1613–14]**
John Walton and Richard Beard, sheriffs

	1614	2 Feb	Sire, John son of William, husbandman, of Bullinghope, Herefs Lugg, Thomas & Juliana 8 yrs tanner 20s

---

[1] Presumably not a barber surgeon's instrument but a musical instrument, a citherne.

	1614	12 Jun	Shingleton, Lawrence son of Dorothea, widow, of Gloucester
			Bishopp, Nathaniel, gentleman, & Isobel 8 yrs woollen draper
			15 Oct 1619: assigned to Nathaniel Bishopp, son of the said Nathaniel, for the rest of his term. Before Geoffrey Beale, Justice
		23 May	Smith, William son of Richard, dec'd, of Wootton Bassett [Wilts]
			Massinger, Arthur & Eleanor 12 years cutler 5s
	1613	25 Dec	Davis, Richard son of John, husbandman, of Westbury
			Yarnold, Francis & Eleanor 8 yrs glover 12d
1/228	1614	25 Jul	White, Thomas son of Thomas, yeoman, of Tewkesbury
			Bayly, John & Abigail 8 yrs glover 3s 4d
			Willis, Thomas son of Richard, dec'd, of Tewkesbury
			Baylie, John & Abigail 7 yrs glover 3s 4d
		2 Feb	Kirby, Robert son of Edward, dec'd
			Woodward, Gabriel & Joan 9 yrs clothier [*blank*]
		25 Mar	Godfree, Richard son of Thomas, smith, of Bushley, Worcs
			Johns, William & Joan 8 yrs baker 10s
		25 Jul	Taylor, Richard
			Thomas, John & Joan 10 yrs cordwainer 3s 4d
		29 Sep	Dowle, William son of John, husbandman, of Clearwell
			Heyward, John & Mary 8 yrs chandler 12d
1/229			Smith, Thomas son of Robert, husbandman, of Badsey, Worcs
			Haies, John & Anne 7 yrs baker 2s 6d
		24 Jun	Pitt, William son of Thomas, broadweaver
			Clarck, John & Margery 8 yrs tanner 30s
		18 Oct	Stratford, Anthony son of Thomas, dec'd, of Bisley
			Sandye, Walter & Anne 7 yrs joiner 2s 6d
		8 May	Watkins, George son of William, yeoman, of Dodderhill [MS Dotherhill], Worcs
			Smythe, Richard & Hester 7 yrs tanner 6s 8d
		28 Oct	Jefferis, Richard son of Thomas, dec'd, baker
			Browne, Richard & Jane 7 yrs wiredrawer 10s
1/230		25 Mar	Broade, William son of Edmund Broad, husbandman
			Ockey, William & Mary 8 yrs baker 13s 4d
		29 Sep	Watkins, George son of Robert, yeoman, of Kempsford
			Reynoldes, John & Mary 7 yrs draper 5s

1/237			**Edmund Clements, mayor [1614–15]**
			Thomas Russell and Richard Hore, sheriffs
	1615	6 Jan	Addames, Robert son of Thomas, husbandman, of Minsterworth
			Haies, John & Anne 7 yrs baker 12d [*cf Appendix V*]
	1614	29 Sep	Watkins, John son of Harry, yeoman, of Llanwenarth, Mon
			Dobbes, Richard & Welthian 7 yrs cordwainer 3s 4d

| | 1615 | 24 Apr | Niblett, William son of Richard, farmer, of Brookthorpe
Crompe, Giles 8 yrs cordwainer 6s 8d |
|---|---|---|---|

        1614 25 Dec Hathwaye, Anthony
                              Singleton, William & Frances 9 yrs draper 3s 4d

1/238 1615 25 Mar Thomas ap Thomas, son of Thomas Price, dec'd
                              Gwilliam, John & Cecily 7 yrs silkweaver 10s

                29 Sep Fowler, Samuel son of Daniel, gentleman, of Stonehouse
                              Caple, Christopher, gentleman, & Grace [mercer] 3s 4d

                         Davis, Giles son of Giles, clothier, of the parish of Stroud
                              Beale, Humphrey & Joan 8 yrs mercer 2s 6d

                         Owbery, John son of Thomas, of 'Elumbery' [Clunbury?], Salop
                              Lloyde, John & Cecily 7 yrs vintner 6s 8d

                         Gyll, Thomas son of Thomas, dec'd, husbandman, of Upton St
                            Leonards
                            Elbridge, John & Joan 8 yrs cordwainer 12d

1/239 1614 1 Nov Randle, Edmund son of William, yeoman, of Cheltenham
                            Robinson, Anthony & Hester 7 yrs merchant 6s 8d

        1615 9 Apr Jorden, William son of Thomas, cutler, of Gloucester
                            Gwilliam, John & Cecily 7 yrs silkweaver 3s 4d

                24 Jun Payte, William son of John, yeoman, of Gloucester
                            Cugley, Richard & Anne 7 yrs mercer 6s 8d

                18 May Moore, Ferdinand son of Thomas, of Hughley, Salop
                            Hayward, Edward & Joan 7 yrs cooper [*blank*]

1/245   **Richard Smith, mayor [1615–16]**
                         Thomas Fyld and John Reynoldes, sheriffs

      —   —   Gwilliam, William son of George, gentleman, of Dixton, Mon
                            Barton, William & Eleanor 10 yrs glover 3s 4d

      —   25 Mar Pettefer, Timothy son of Thomas, dec'd
                            Elbridge, John & Joan 8 yrs cordwainer 12d

     1615 29 Sep Pettefer, Joseph
                            Wyndowe, Richard & Anne 8 yrs chandler nil
                                Mr Clements, mayor

              25 Dec Prydye, William jr
                            Prydye, William, his father, 7 yrs cordwainer 10s

     1616 28 Sep Wood, John son of William, husbandman, of Tuffley
                            Price, Matthew & his wife 7 yrs tanner 10s

1/246   24 Jun Greene, Richard son of Hercules, upholsterer, formerly of Gloucester
                            Carpenter, Lawrence 8 yrs cordwainer 3s
                                Father & mother of Richard to find clothes of linen & wool during
                                his term and suitable footwear

| | 1616 31 Aug | Milton, John son of William, dec'd, husbandman, of Maisemore
Tomes, John & Margaret 7 yrs cordwainer 3s 4d |
| | 1615 1 Nov | Robertes, Giles son of Thomas, yeoman, of Harescombe
Cooke, John & Dina 8 yrs [*no trade*] 40s [*cf Appendix V*] |
| | 1616 2 Feb | Woodwarde, John son of John, dec'd
Bennett, Thomas & Mary 9 yrs shearman 5s
18 Dec 1617: Before Geoffrey Beale, mayor, assigned to William Endal, shearman, & Anne for the next 5 yrs 40s & 2 suits of clothes |
| 1/247 | 25 Jul | Jefferyes, John son of Robert Jefferies, yeoman, of Gloucester
Tremere, Anthony & Margaret 9 yrs tailor 3s 4d |
| | 1 Aug | Jones, Thomas son of Thomas, butcher, of Gloucester
Edwards, Alice 8 yrs glover 12d |
| | 1615 1 Nov | Hawkes, John son of John, tailor, of Newland
Shervington, Thomas & [*blank*] 8 yrs tailor 20s |
| | | Madocke, John son of Thomas, of Woolhope [Herefs]
Reynoldes, John & Mary 9 yrs draper 5s |
| | 1616 19 May | Bishoppe, John son of Anthony, dec'd
Greene, Simon & Elizabeth 7 yrs cooper 40s |
| 1/248 | | Bullock, James son of Thomas, dec'd
Wilcox, John & Jane 7 yrs clothier 6s 8d |
| | 24 Jun | Payne, Robert son of Robert, dec'd, yeoman, of Standish
Beard, Richard & his wife 8 yrs mercer 3s 4d |
| | 1615 25 Dec | Drinkwater, Alice daughter of Edward, yeoman, dec'd, of Hatherley
Purlewent, Elizabeth 7 yrs spinster sempstress 5s |
| | 1616 29 Sep | Banckes, Philip son of Henry, yeoman, of Chippenham, Wilts
Button, Richard & Bridget 7 yrs saddler 10s |
| 1/249 | 1617 25 Mar | Mardey, John son of William, yeoman, of Maisemore
Cooke, Thomas & Margaret 7 yrs chandler 2s 6d |
| | 1615 1 Nov | Robertes, William son of Daniel, husbandman, Teddington, Worcs [*recte* Glos]
Woode, James, clothier, & Elizabeth 7 yrs broadweaver 6s 8d |
| | 1616 24 Jun | Banister, Giles son of William, yeoman, of Gloucester
Scudamore, William & Elizabeth 8 yrs woollen draper 3s 4d
Before Alderman Clements, Justice, 25 Mar 1619, assigned to George Clarvoe, mercer, with the consent of his master and his friends |
| | 29 Sep | Singleton, William son of William, woollen draper, of Gloucester
Singleton, William & Frances 9 yrs [woollen draper] 3s 4d |
| 1/250 | 1615 1 Nov | Cadell, William son of William, yeoman, of Miserden
Keene, Miles and Joan 7 yrs woollen draper 3s 4d |

1/255
Matthew Price, mayor 29 Sep 1616 to 29 Sep 1617
John Bullock and Anthony Robinson, sheriffs

1616 30 Nov Stone, Nicholas son of Henry, butcher, of Berkeley
 Warde, William 7 yrs cordwainer 2s 6d

29 Sep Stone, Robert son of Thomas, gentleman, of Cirencester
 Lugg, William 8 yrs tanner 10s

28 Oct Smart, Richard son of John, yeoman, of Over
 Phelpes, William 8 yrs cordwainer 3s 4d

1 Nov Cosby, John jr son of John, lantern maker, formerly of Gloucester
 Baylie, John 12 yrs glover 5s

Cosby, Toby son of John, lantern maker, formerly of Gloucester
 Barnelme, William 7 yrs lantern maker 10s

1/256
25 Mar Hazard, Henry son of Thomas, yeoman, of Over
 Whoper, John 8 yrs vintner 12d

24 Aug Clarke, William son of John, husbandman, of Upleadon
 Abbottes, Richard & Anne 7 yrs tailor 5s

21 Dec Steevens, Oliver son of John, yeoman, of Penrhos [MS Penrouse], Mon
 Hore, Charles & Margery 8 yrs saddler 5s

1 May Hall, John son of John, cordwainer, of Cheltenham
 French, Walter & Elizabeth 7 yrs cordwainer 3s 4d

1 Nov Vaughan, Richard son of Richard, joiner, of Gloucester
 Vaughan, Richard, his father 9 yrs joiner 20s

1/257
Lewes, William son of William, dec'd, of Talgarth, Brecon
 Yong, Walter & Catherine 7 yrs brewer 10s

Townesende, Lawrence son of William, husbandman, of Barton Street
 Yong, Walter & Catherine 8 yrs brewer 2s 6d

1617 6 Jan Tuffley, Nathaniel son of Walter, yeoman, of Down Hatherley
 Hiron, Humphrey & Blanche 7 yrs mercer 5s

1616 25 Dec Browne, Edward son of Richard, yeoman, of Gloucester
 Bishopp, Thomas & Anne 8 yrs cordwainer 10s

Abbottes, Edward son of Ralph, yeoman, of Charlton Kings
 Hazard, Arthur & Alice 7 yrs tailor 5s

1/258
1616 25 Mar Hannys, Richard son of Thomas Hannis, smith, of Gloucester
 Shipway, Richard & Eleanor 14 yrs narrow weaver 5s

1617 6 Mar Stedman, Giles son of William, clerk, of Badgeworth
 Jones, Emmanuel & Elizabeth 7 yrs apothecary etc

1 May Howlett, John son of William, musician, of Gloucester
 Hayward, Edward & Joan 8 yrs cooper etc

Lane, Walter son of Walter, dec'd, husbandman, of Cheltenham
 Heyford, John & [blank] 7 yrs baker etc

1/259	1617	8 June	Butter, William son of William, dec'd, yeoman, of Maisemore Bubb, John & Eleanor 9 yrs cordwainer 2s 6d
		20 Apr	Lea, Francis son of Henry, translater [i.e. shoe mender] Davis, Roger & Elizabeth 7 yrs cordwainer 12d
		25 Mar	Harris, William son of John, dec'd, yeoman, of Whitminster Barkesdale, Giles & [*blank*] 9 yrs chandler 20s
		2 Feb	Addames, Robert son of Thomas, husbandman, of Minsterworth Johns, William & Jane 7 yrs baker 12d [*cf Appendix V*]
1/260		24 Jun	Houlton, John son of George, yeoman, of Hidcote Boyce Hiron, Humphrey & Blanche 10 yrs mercer 5s
		25 Jul	Gretton, William son of William, dec'd, feltmaker, of Gloucester Cosby, Thomas & Alice 9 yrs lantern maker 3s 4d [*cf Appendix V*]
		8 Jun	Harriettes, Giles son of John, dec'd, of Gloucester Haule, Roger & his wife 8 yrs cooper 20s
		29 Sep	Adams, John son of Francis, broadweaver, of Gloucester Edge, Thomas & Barbara 10 yrs pinmaker 10s
			Guylden, George son of Richard, of Haresfield Cooke, Thomas & Anne 8 yrs joiner 3s 4d
1/261		21 Sep	Arundell, Thomas son of James, of Upton St Leonards Besall, Thomas *alias* Tackley & Elizabeth 7 yrs feltmaker etc
		29 Sep	Merricke, Humphrey son of Thomas, glover, formerly of Ross, Herefs Caple, Christopher & Grace 8 yrs mercer 3s 4d
		24 Aug	Pricharde, Walter son of William, labourer, of Gloucester Pitt, John & Margaret 8 yrs cooper 10s *18 Mar 1623: assigned to serve the rest of his term with Simon Greene, cooper, with the consent of John Pitt. Before Geoffrey Beale*
		24 Jul	Dymocke, William son of William, husbandman, of 'East Harkeein' [East Harptree?], Som Wagstaffe, Edward & Katharine 7 yrs brewer 10s
1/262		25 Mar	Jeanes, Thomas son of Richard, mercer, of Carmarthen, Carms Wager, Robert & Ursula 8 yrs glazier 20s
		24 Aug	Lane, John son of William, tailor, formerly of Gloucester Browne, Richard & Jane 11 yrs wiredrawer 10s
		29 Sep	Roberts, George son of Thomas, gentleman, of Wotton, Gloucester Janes, Matthew & Elizabeth 8 yrs [*blank*] 5s
		1 May	Dyer, Humphrey son of Thomas, labourer, formerly of Gloucester Fielde, Thomas & Isobel 7 yrs brewer 6s 8d
1/263		29 Sep	Robins, Nathaniel son of George, butcher, of Painswick Lugge, William & Eleanor 8 yrs tanner 10s
			Angell, William son of Abel, baker, of Gloucester Angell, Abel, his father, & Mary 7 yrs [baker] 10s

1/267 **Geoffrey Beale, mayor, Michaelmas 1617 to Michaelmas 1618**
John Brewster and William Lugge, sheriffs

1617 29 Sep Doppinge, Samuel son of Giles, cordwainer, of Gloucester
 Whitfielde, Richard & Alice 8 yrs cordwainer 2s 6d

8 Jun Tayler, Richard son of John, yeoman, of Slimbridge
 Nelme, John & his wife 9 yrs mercer 2s 6d

18 Oct Archard, John son of William, yeoman, of Down Ampney
 Heyford, John & Joan 7 yrs baker 5s [*cf Appendix V*]

1 Nov Hawkes, John son of John, tailor, of Gloucester
 Stratford, Arthur & Margaret 7 yrs tailor 3s 4d [*Repeated at 1/269*]

1/268 Hitchman, Anthony son of John, gentleman, of Bisley
 Sturmey, Robert & Eleanor 7 yrs glover 5s

Aspin, William son of William, tailor, formerly of Gloucester
 Ocford, Giles & Joan 9 yrs broadweaver 3s 4d [*Repeated at 1/269*]

Arthur, Robert son of Giles, dyer, of Painswick
 Gray, Brice & Joan 9 yrs butcher 20s

29 Sep Purlwent, John son of Roger, weaver, formerly of Gloucester
 Haines, William & Katharine 7 yrs baker 10s

1621 25 Dec Morrall, John son of William, yeoman, formerly of Badsey, Worcs
 Hewes, Richard & Joan 9 yrs butcher 2s 6d

1/269 1617 2 Feb Robertes, Giles son of Thomas, yeoman, of Harescombe
 Byshop, Nathaniel & Isobel 8 yrs draper 6s 8d [*cf Appendix V*]
  15 Oct 1619: assigned to Nathaniel Bisshoppe jr, son of Nathaniel Byshopp, with the consent of Nathaniel & Isobel. Before Geoffrey Beale [*See 1/227*]

1 Nov Aspin, William son of William, tailor, formerly of Gloucester
 Oxford, Giles & Joan 9 yrs broadweaver 3s 4d
  Void entered twice [*See 1/268*]

Hawkes, John son of John, tailor, of Gloucester
 Stratford, Arthur & Margaret 7 yrs tailor 3s 4d
  [*Repeating entry at 1/267*]

25 Dec Solly, William son of Edward, vintner, of the city of Worcester
 Cleevly, William & [*blank*] 8 yrs woollen draper 10s

1/270 29 Sep Clutterbucke, Richard son of Arthur, clothier, of King's Stanley
 Morse, Thomas & Margaret 7 yrs tanner 6s 8d

25 Dec Paine, John son of Robert Payne, dec'd, pewterer, of Gloucester
 Cugly, Richard & Anne 7 yrs mercer 3s 4d

24 Jun Payle, William son of John, yeoman, of Gloucester
 Cugley, Richard & Anne 7 yrs mercer 6s 8d

— — Senmigs,[*blank*] son of William Semigs, innholder, of Gloucester
 [*Incomplete*]

1/271	1618	2 Feb	Farley, John son of John, dec'd, of Gloucester Davis, Thomas & Margaret 7 yrs cordwainer 40s *under the condition that John's mother shall find him apparel, meat, drink, washing and lodging for 3 years and apparel for the rest of the term. Before Jasper James*
		25 Mar	Randell, William son of Giles, clerk, of Cranham Bubb, Thomas & Beatrice 7 yrs weaver £4
	1617	1 Nov	Weaver, Francis son of Francis, butcher, dec'd, of Gloucester Hedges, Robert & Sybil 9 yrs cordwainer 2s 6d [*cf Appendix V*]
1/272		29 Sep	Granger, Joseph son of John, yeoman, of Elmore Webbe, John & his wife 9 yrs mercer 6s 8d
		30 Nov	Elbridge, William son of James, yeoman, of Bentham in parish of Badgeworth Nashe, Richard & Blanche 7 yrs tanner 2s 6d
		25 Dec	Mercer, Robert son of Robert, fishmonger, of Gloucester Reynoldes, Robert & Elizabeth 7 yrs tanner 5s *Michaelmas Sessions 1620: assigned to Walter Etheridge for the residue of his term*
		29 Sep	Drinkwater, Thomas son of William, yeoman, of Withy Bridge Clarke, John & [*blank*] 8 yrs cordwainer 2s 6d
1/273		25 Dec	Jonson, William son of John, yeoman, of Sedgeberrow, Worcs Hayward, John & Mary 8 yrs chandler 5s
	1618	24 Jun	Parker, Nathaniel son of Thomas, yeoman, formerly of Barnwood Adams, John & [*blank*] 7 yrs broadweaver 10s
		3 May	Clutterbok, Stephen son of Fabian Clutterbooke, yeoman, of Eastington Hooper, Nathaniel & [*blank*] 8 yrs woollen draper 10s
1/274		24 Jun	Wantener, Abel son of William Wantner, smith, of Gloucester Preedy, William & [*blank*] 9 yrs cordwainer 10s
		29 Jun	Rogers, William son of Francis, yeoman, dec'd, of the Leigh Palmer, Edmund & [*blank*] 9 yrs baker 12d
		24 Jun	Gibbs, Robert son of James, yeoman, dec'd, of Twigworth Nutt, William & Margery 8 yrs cordwainer 6s 8d
		29 Sep	Roberts, Arthur son of Thomas, gentleman, of Wotton, Gloucester Singleton, Lawrence & [*blank*] 9 yrs draper 5s
1/275		29 Jun	Symons, Robert son of Richard, husbandman, of Hasfield Yarnold, Francis & Eleanor 8 yrs glover 10s
		24 Aug	Symonds, John son of Richard, husbandman, of Hasfield Tomas, John & Margaret 9 yrs cordwainer 10s
		24 Jun	Rogers, Francis son of Francis, dec'd Harris, Thomas 9 yrs gunsmith 5s

	1618	29 Sep	Coxe, John son of Roger, husbandman, dec'd, of Maisemore Bezell *alias* Tacly, Thomas & Elizabeth 9 yrs feltmaker 10s
1/276			Greene, Augustine son of John, yeoman, of Churcham Porter, Robert & Elizabeth 9 yrs joiner 12d
		24 Aug	Nelme, Nicholas son of John, yeoman, formerly of Berkeley Smith, Richard & Hester 7 yrs tanner 12d
		29 Sep	Archard, John son of William, yeoman, of Down Ampney Coxe, John & Elizabeth 7 yrs cordwainer 12d [*cf Appendix V*]
		24 May	Tayler, John son of John, farmer, of Hardwicke Wise, Denis & Eleanor 9 yrs mercer 5s
1/277		29 Sep	Jennings, Thomas son of Henry, yeoman, of Hempsted Cowly, Richard & Eleanor 7 yrs smith 5s
			Sturmy, Daniel son of Henry, tanner, of Aston Redvin, Henry & Isobel 9 yrs upholsterer 40s
		25 Mar	Millards, John son of Richard, yeoman, of Frocester Hyron, Humphrey & Blanche 9 yrs mercer 5s
		24 Aug	Beale, Matthew son of William, clerk, of Hankerton, Wilts Mayo, William 9 yrs mercer 12d
1/278		29 Sep	Marten, Thomas son of William, yeoman, dec'd, of the Leigh Marten, George & Margaret 7 yrs brewer 3s 4d

1/279 **John Jones, mayor [1618–19]**
Robert Bishop and William Singleton, sheriffs
Michaelmas 1618 [MS 1617] to Michaelmas [1619]

	1618	29 Sep	Lacye, John son of William, butcher, formerly of Barton Street, Gloucester Hayes, John & Anne 13 yrs baker 5s [*Repeated at 1/281*]
	1619	24 Feb	Hookam, Nathaniel son of John, tailor, of Lea, Wilts Hookam, Henry & Anne 7 yrs butcher 5s
	1618	25 Dec	Ashmeade, William son of John, yeoman, dec'd, of Cheltenham Purrocke, Thomas & Jane 7 yrs baker 3s 4d [*Repeated at 1/283*]
1/280	1619	1 Jul	Cooke, William son of Richard, dec'd, of Harford [MS Hartford] Webster, William 7 yrs to begin on 21 Dec cooper 6d *1 Oct 1619: assigned to John Daliner, cooper, for the residue of his term. Before John Tailer & Edmund Clements, justices*
	1618	1 Nov	Symondes, Lawrence son of Edward, feltmaker, of Gloucester Symondes, Edward, his father, & Elizabeth 7 yrs feltmaker 20s
		21 Dec	Masters, William son of William, tanner, of city of Bristol Tailor, Humphrey & [*blank*] 8 yrs pinner 6s 8d

	1619 28 Mar	Maddock, Thomas son of William, tailor, of Gloucester
		Pury, Thomas & Elizabeth 8 yrs cordwainer 2s
	2 Feb	Elbridge, Richard son of James, of Badgeworth
		Baughe, John & Margaret 7 yrs mercer 3s 4d
		16 Aug 1625: assigned to Thomas Trippett, mercer. Before Edmund Clemence, justice
1/281	25 Mar	Hickes, Thomas son of William, husbandman, dec'd, of Longford
		Bennet, Anthony & Elizabeth 7 yrs clothier 10s
—	29 Sep	Lacye, John son of William, butcher, dec'd, of Barton Street, Gloucester
		Haies, John & Anne 13 yrs baker 5s [*Repeating entry at 1/279*]
—	25 Dec	Fletcher, Thomas son of John, yeoman, of Maisemore
		Nashe, Richard & Blanche 7 yrs tanner 12d
—	6 Jan	Burt, Thomas son of Richard, miller, of Cirencester
		Crompe, Giles & Anne 7 yrs cordwainer 6s 8d
1/282	— 1 May	Garlicke, Thomas son of Thomas, of Hempsted
		Smith, Richard & Hester 10 yrs tanner 2s
—		Stevens, Matthew son of Edward, yeoman, of Minsterworth
		[*blank*] & Elizabeth 9 yrs [*no trade*] 3s 4d
	1619 16 May	Allen, Edward son of Edmund, cordwainer, of Gloucester
		Walker, John & [*blank*] 8 yrs chandler 2s 6d
	—	Joyner, Giles son of Thomas, weaver, of Gloucester
		Wheeler, Henry & Anne 8 yrs carpenter 10s
1/283	28 Mar	Rogers, Nicholas son of Francis, dec'd, of the Leigh
		Raynoldes, Robert & Elizabeth 7 yrs tanner 5s
	1618 25 Dec	Ashmeade, William son of John, yeoman, dec'd, of Cheltenham
		Purrocke, Thomas & Jane 7 yrs baker 3s 4d
		[*Repeating entry at 1/279*]
	1 Nov	Bonde, John son of John, yeoman, of Upton St Leonards
		Hedges, William 8 yrs cordwainer 5s
1/284	1619 24 Jun	Webb, Peter son of Leonard, yeoman, of Redmarley, Worcs
		Yarnold, Francis & Eleanor 7 yrs glover 12d
	25 Jul	Beale, John son of John, gentleman, of Ross, Herefs
		Caple, Christopher & Grace 9 yrs mercer 3s 4d
	29 Sep	Pearce, William son of William, yeoman, dec'd, of Ashleworth
		Lugge, William & Eleanor 7 yrs tanner 6s 8d
1/285	—	Griffin, Richard son of David, husbandman, of Whitney, Herefs
		Burte, Robert & Joan 9 yrs tailor 18d
	25 Jul	Merret, Edmund son of Richard, clothier, of Rodborough
		Lugge, William & Eleanor 8 yrs tanner 3s 4d
	24 Jun	Witcombe, Thomas son of Thomas, yeoman, of Hempsted
		Witcombe, William 7 yrs clothier no money

1/287 **Christopher Caple, mayor [1619–20]**
William Bubb and William Caple, sheriffs
Michaelmas 1619 to Michaelmas 1620

1620 2 Feb Tailer, John son of Richard, husbandman, of Over
Rixe, Richard & Eleanor 7 yrs broadweaver 5s

25 Mar Baker, Thomas son of Thomas, broadweaver, of Gloucester
Wilcox, John & Jane 8 yrs broadweaver 2s 6d

1/288 1619 25 Dec Bennet, Charles son of William, of 'Spurddone', Notts
Freame, John & Dorothy 8 yrs tailor 5s

Webbe, Richard son of Anthony, formerly of Gotherington
Nelme, William & his wife 7 yrs woollen draper 2s 6d

Hagburne, Abraham son of William Hagborne, yeoman, formerly of Churchdown
Burrowes, Nathaniel & [blank] 7 yrs cordwainer 6s 8d

1/289 1 Nov Clutterbook, Amity son of Walter Clutterbooke, tucker, of Stanley
Elliot, Edward & Russell 9 yrs tailor 6s 8d

Pitt, Nicholas son of Thomas, weaver, dec'd, of Cirencester
Marston, Edward & his wife 8 yrs apothecary 6s

Manns, Robert son of Francis, weaver, dec'd, of Gloucester
Craker, John & Margaret 10 yrs weaver 10s

1/290 — 2 Feb Randell, Abel son of William, carpenter, dec'd, of Gloucester
Abbots, Richard & Anne 7 yrs tailor 5s

1619 1 Nov Stevens, Christopher son of John, gentleman, of Penrhos [MS Penrose], Mon
Nutt, William & Margery 9 yrs cordwainer 3s

25 Dec Carpenter, Henry son of Richard, husbandman, of Tuffley
Taylor, Thomas & Ursula 7 yrs clothier 3s 4d

1/291 Ecoat, Thomas son of William, husbandman, of North Cerney
Gwilliam, John, gentleman, & Cecily 7 yrs silk weaver 3s 4d & 2 suits of clothes

1620 1 May Hill, Richard son of Robert, miller, of Over
Hitchins, William & Margery 9 yrs beer brewer 3s 4d

1619 1 Nov Humfreyes, John son of Thomas, yeoman, of Moreton Valence
Jeninges, Brian & Alice 7 yrs baker 3s 4d

1/292 — 28 Oct Elridge, William son of William, hosier, dec'd, of Gloucester
Hitchins, William & Margery 8 yrs silk weaver £5

1620 16 Apr Roadway, Thomas son of William, yeoman, of Badgeworth
Beard, Richard 9 yrs weaver 6s 8d

1 May Hodghson, Jeremiah son of Marmaduke Hodgshon, dec'd, of Gloucester
Clarke, William & Eleanor 9 yrs cordwainer 3s 4d
[cf Appendix V]

	1620	4 Jun	Yates, William son of Francis, cordwainer, of Gloucester
			Bishop, Thomas & Anne 8 yrs cordwainer 3s 4d
1/293		24 Jun	Masfield, Giles son of John, yeoman, of Churchdown
			White, David & Edith 9 yrs shearman 12d
		25 Mar	Lugg, Thomas son of William, gentleman, of Gloucester
			Lugg, Peter, gentleman, & Margaret 10 yrs haberdasher 10s
		24 Jun	Best, John son of John, yeoman, of Twyning
			Morse, Thomas & Margaret 8 yrs tanner 5s
		25 Mar	Baker, Henry son of William, weaver, of parish of St Catherines, Gloucester
			Morse, Thomas & Margaret 12 yrs tanner 6s 8d
1/294		25 Jul	Walter, John son of John, yeoman, of Adlestrop
			Price, John & Anne 7 yrs tanner 6s 8d
		24 Aug	Butter, Richard son of William, husbandman, dec'd, of Maisemore
			Greene, Simon & Elizabeth 9 yrs cooper 2s 6d
		29 Sep	Thayer, Giles son of Giles
			Dobbs, John & Joan 7 yrs baker 12d
			White, Anthony son of Anthony, broadweaver, dec'd, of Acton
			Nurse, John & Anne 7 yrs cooper 6s 8d
1/295			Cornewall, John son of Richard, saddler, dec'd, of Leonard Stanley
			Kifte, Edward & Juliana 7 yrs saddler 3s 4d
			Bullock, Edward son of Thomas, dec'd, of Highleadon
			Witcombe, Thomas 9 yrs mercer 3s 4d [*cf Appendix V*]
		10 Oct	Leavon, John son of Anthony, labourer, formerly of Gloucester
			Murrey, Richard 7 yrs feltmaker 10s
			29 Jul 1622: assigned to James Freeman, feltmaker, for the residue of his term. With the consent of his master and friends

1/297			**John Baugh, mayor [1620–1]**
			John Deighton and John Gwilliam, sheriffs
			Michaelmas 1620 – 1621
	1620	18 Oct	Woodward, John son of William, of Gloucester
			Woodward, Thomas & Elizabeth 8 yrs [*no trade*] 3s 4d
		1 Nov	Machen, James son of Henry, gentleman, dec'd, of Crickley
			Nurse, Luke & Margaret 8 yrs [mercer] 3s 4d
			Hornedge, Henry son of William, husbandman, of Upton
			Beard, Andrew & Mary 7 yrs [tailor] 12d
1/298		25 Dec	Walburge, John son of Simon, barber, formerly of Burford, Oxon
			Walburge, Richard 8 yrs barber surgeon 3s 4d
		1 Nov	Hedges, William son of Thomas, husbandman, of Noke
			Coutcher, William & Joan 9 yrs haberdasher 5s

	1620 25 Dec	Greene, Richard son of Robert, dec'd, of Minsterworth Whittingham, Thomas & Joan 7 yrs baker 3s 4d
		Gilberte, John son of John, tailor, of Ruardean Edge, Thomas & Barbara 7 yrs pinmaker 2s
1/299	1 Nov	Terrett, Henry son of John, dec'd, of Gloucester Charlton, Edward & Alice 8 yrs wiredrawer 3s 4d
	25 Dec	Hill, Charles son of Thomas, gentleman, of Gloucester Hill, Thomas & Joan 7 yrs goldsmith 6s 8d

Mr Caple, mayor[1]

	1621 24 Feb	Capenor, Giles son of John, yeoman, of Badgeworth Hayward, John & Mary 8 yrs chandler 20s
	4 Jan	Reeve, William son of Thomas, of Todenham Gray, Brice & Joan 9 yrs butcher 40s

1/300		**Roll of apprentices in time of Christopher Caple, mayor**
	2 Feb	Howlett, Anthony son of Anthony, dec'd, of Gloucester Kirke, Richard 8 yrs pewterer 6s 8d
	6 Jan	Hemminge, Arnold son of Henry, yeoman, of Gloucester Heyward, John & Mary 8 yrs chandler 20s
	1620 25 Mar	Browninge, Thomas son of Richard Browneinge, clothier, of Dursley Morse, Thomas & Margaret 7 yrs tanner 10s
1/301		Sparke, Richard son of Thomas, broadweaver, of Barton Street, Gloucester Nurse, John & Anne 10 yrs cooper 6s 8d
	1621 21 Sep	Gardner, Thomas son of John, labourer, of Wotton, Gloucester Springe, Lewis & Isobel 11 yrs joiner 5s
	25 Mar	Leader, Henry son of Henry, chapman, dec'd, of Gloucester Jayne, William & Elizabeth 10 yrs tanner 10s
1/302	24 Jun	Fowler, William son of Anselm, yeoman, dec'd, of Moreton Valence Price, William & Elizabeth 10 yrs mercer 5s
	20 May	Medhopp, John son of Roger, gentleman, formerly of Aston, Oxon Bennett, Anthony & Elizabeth 7 yrs clothier 3s 4d

Time of John Baugh

	1620 1 Nov	Goslinge, Thomas son of Arthur, sievemaker, of Gloucester Dobbs, Richard & Welthian 7 yrs cordwainer [blank]
1/303	1621	*Time of Christopher Caple, mayor*
	24 Jun	Coale, Humphrey, son of John, labourer, formerly of Gloucester Smyth, Richard & Alice 9 yrs gardener 5s

---

[1] Christopher Caple appears as mayor in Jan 1621: GBR B3/1.

1621 20 May Tyler, James son of James, yeoman, formerly of Hasfield
  Ockold, Arnold & [blank] 7 yrs [cordwainer] 2s 6d

 Greene, Thomas son of Richard, gentleman, of Gloucester
  Beard, Richard & Isobel 9 yrs mercer 6s 8d

1/304 1 Apr Johnson, Timothy son of Harman, gentleman, of Eaton Hastings [MS Eaton Haskings], Oxon [recte Berks]
  Price, Henry & Alice 8 yrs woollen draper 6s 8d

 24 Jun Payne, John son of Robert, pewterer, formerly of Gloucester
  Symonds, Edward & Elizabeth 8 yrs feltmaker 20s

 29 Jun Long, Humphrey son of Robert, weaver, dec'd, of Gloucester
  Craker, John & Margaret 11 yrs weaver 6s 8d
   2 Feb 1629: Humphrey Long entered into a new indenture for 8 yrs to John Craker for the sum of £4 to be paid at the end of the term [cf 1/379]

1/305 1 May Stubbs, [son not named] son of Thomas, husbandman, dec'd, of Haydon
  Burrowes, Nathaniel & [blank] 8 yrs cordwainer 5s

 14 Apr Rogers, Mary daughter of Francis, dec'd, of the Leigh [MS Ladye]
  Bulbrick, John, garter weaver, & Anne 5 yrs bone lace weaving

 24 Jun Simonds, Nathaniel son of Thomas, blacksmith, dec'd, of Tirley
  Brookes, William & Alice 7 yrs farrier 3s 4d

1/306 25 Jul Tewe, John son of Francis, pewterer, of Gloucester
  Kerke, Richard & Joan 8 yrs pewterer 10s

 10 May Pearse, John son of Richard, yeoman, of Haydon
  Edwards, John & [blank] 10 yrs haberdasher 3s 4d

 25 Jul Griffith, Henry son of Henry Griffeth, yeoman, dec'd, of Kings Caple, Herefs
  Mason, Edward & [blank] 7 yrs saddler 10s

 Drackett, Giles son of John, yeoman, deceased, of Churchdown
  Hall, Thomas & Eleanor 8 yrs pewterer 3s 4d

1/307 Bishopp, William son of Maurice, dec'd, of Kingsholm
  Thorne, John & Joan 7 yrs brewer 40s

 29 Sep Barbour, John son of Thomas, yeoman, formerly of Upton St Leonards
  Terry, John & [blank] 9 yrs cordwainer 40s

 25 Jul Allen, Arnold son of Arnold, husbandman, of Quedgeley
  Lane, John & Elizabeth 7 yrs baker 10s

1/308 25 Mar Woodward, William son of William, dec'd, of Gloucester
  Sawcombe, John & Joan 7 yrs smith 2s 6d

 25 Jul Lane, Henry son of John, yeoman, formerly of Tirley
  Lane, John & Elizabeth 7 yrs baker 12d

 25 Mar Portman, Robert son of Richard, ironmonger, of Gloucester
  Phellpe, William & Margaret 10 yrs cordwainer 3s 4d

1/310	1621	25 Jul	Sanford, Thomas son of Thomas, gentleman, of Leonard Stanley Cope, Richard & [*blank*] 9 yrs mercer 2s 6d
		29 Sep	Merrett, Richard son of Thomas, dec'd, of Stroud Crompe, Giles & Anne 8 yrs cordwainer 2s 6d
			Merrett, Thomas son of John, tucker, of Stroud Crompe, Giles & Anne 7 yrs cordwainer 2s 6d

1/311

John Brown, mayor [1621–2]
John Heyward and James Powell, sheriffs
Michaelmas 1621 – 1622

	1621	24 Oct	Hayers, Thomas son of John, husbandman, of Cirencester Wantnor, William & Margaret 7 yrs smith 3s 4d
		25 Dec	Deane, Thomas son of John, yeoman, of Badgeworth Lugg, Richard & [*blank*] 7 yrs tanner 5s
		30 Nov	Lawrence, George son of George Lawrrance, yeoman, of Cirencester Jefferies, Richard & [*blank*] 8 yrs mercer 5s
1/312		25 Dec	Redven, Thomas son of Samuel, dec'd, of Gloucester Clarke, William & Eleanor 7 yrs cordwainer 2s 6d
		24 Aug	Phillippes, John son of Thomas, of Gloucester Murrowe, Richard & Alice 7 yrs [*no trade*] 3s 4d *Void because in Mr Caple's year* [*Entry deleted*]
		29 Jun	Willins, Thomas son of Philip, of Cardiff, Glam Clarke, Edward & Eleanor 8 yrs haberdasher 2s 6d *Void because in Mr Caple's year* [*Entry deleted*]
		27 Dec	Murrowe, John son of Richard, feltmaker, of Gloucester Murrowe, Richard, his father, & Alice 7 yrs [*feltmaker*] 3s 4d
1/313		25 Mar	Robinson, [*no name*] son of Thomas, cordwainer, of Gloucester *pauper* Pridaye, William 9 yrs cordwainer 3s 4d
		21 Sep	Moore, Gilbert son of Evan, yeoman, of Stow, Salop Freame, John & Dorothy 7 yrs tailor 5s
	1622	25 Mar	Weaver, Thomas son of Francis, butcher, formerly of Gloucester Anstee, Ralph & Joan 8 yrs butcher 5s
			Horward, Henry son of Edward, yeoman, of Slimbridge Beard, Andrew & Mary 8 yrs tailor 12d
1/314			Yong, John son of Thomas, yeoman, of Westbury Nurse, John & Anne 9 yrs cooper 20s
		21 Apr	Hawlins, Richard son of Robert Hawlings, husbandman, dec'd, of Haydon Wilkins, Richard & Elizabeth 7 yrs wiredrawer 5s
		1 May	Morse, Lewis son of John, maltster, dec'd, of Gloucester Rice, John & Elizabeth 7 yrs cordwainer 5s

	1622	9 Jun	Wrench, Elias son of Elias, clerk, of Gloucester Badger, Richard 8 yrs chandler 5s
1/315	1621	18 Oct	Sole, Andrew son of Andrew, husbandman, of Brookthorpe [MS Bruckropp] Prichards, Thomas & Katharine [*no term*] painter 5s
	1622	1 May	Edwards, John son of Henry, cordwainer, formerly of Gloucester Kent, William & Alice 8 yrs cordwainer 3s
		9 Jun	Best, Thomas son of John, husbandman, of Twyning Collett, Edmund & Hester [*no term*] tanner 6s 8d
			Wintle, Richard son of John, yeoman, dec'd, of Longhope Whooper, Jesse & [*blank*] 7 yrs cordwainer 2s 6d
		1 May	Mayden, John son of Humphrey, husbandman, of Astley, Salop Davis, William & Martha 8 yrs cooper 3s 4d
1/316		24 Jun	Tyther, Robert son of Anthony, gentleman, formerly of Gloucester Lugg, William & Eleanor 7 yrs tanner 10s
			Long, Giles son of Giles, yeoman, of Bentham Davyes, Roger & Elizabeth 7 yrs cordwainer 5s
			River, John son of Robert, yeoman, dec'd, of Maisemore Thomas, John & Margaret 7 yrs cordwainer 3s 4d
1/317	1621	1 Nov	Linkenholt, John son of Thomas, yeoman, of Barnwood Charleton, Edward 7 yrs wiredrawer 5s
	1622	24 Jun	Hardwicke, William son of John, tailor, of Upton Bishop, Herefs Whitton, John & Anne 7 yrs tailor 5s
			Latton, Francis son of John, esquire, formerly of city of London Horwood, Richard 9 yrs woollen draper 5s
			Davyes, Thomas son of John Davies, Richard & [*blank*] 8 yrs glover 12d
1/318		9 Jun	Williams, Richard son of William, clothier, of Wotton under Edge Nashe, Richard & Blanche 8 yrs tanner 20s
		24 Jun	Witts, William son of Thomas, tiler, of Stroud Brinkwell, George & [*blank*] 10 yrs bricklayer £3
			Taylor, William son of William, glover, of Ross, Herefs Dutton, Richard & Margaret 7 yrs haberdasher 5s
		25 Jul	Paynter, Thomas son of Giles, butcher, dec'd, of Severn Stoke, Worcs Smyth, John & Eleanor 7 yrs butcher 20s [*Repeated in part and deleted at 1/323*]
1/319		29 Sep	Cowles, Robert son of John, husbandman, of Gloucester Kerby, Margaret, widow, 7 yrs [*no trade*] 5s
			Wyman, John son of John, husbandman, dec'd, of Maisemore Price, John & [*blank*] 8 yrs smith 5s

	1622 29 Sep	Russell, Thomas son of John, husbandman, of Painswick
		Lugge, William & Eleanor 8 yrs tanner 20s
	1620 24 Dec	Heath, Thomas son of John, yeoman, of Bloxwich, Staffs
		Heath, Richard 8 yrs pewterer [blank]

1/321 **William Hill, mayor [1622–3]**
Thomas Morse and John Scriven, sheriffs 1622

	1622 1 Nov	Browne, William son of William, dec'd, of parish of St Owen's, [Gloucester]
		Hall, Thomas & Eleanor 11 yrs pewterer 5s
		Townshend, Perian son of Edward, cordwainer, of Bisley
		Lugg, Thomas & Anne 8 yrs tanner 5s
		Clarke, James son of Thomas, yeoman, dec'd, of Hartpury
		Bishopp, Nathaniel & Anne 8 yrs woollen draper 5s

1/322 Skett, Benjamin son of Roland, yeoman, of parish of Harley, Salop
Hayward, Edward & Joan 7 yrs cooper 6s 8d

25 Dec Howlett, John son of Anthony, butcher, dec'd, of Gloucester
Hoockam, Henry & Anne 8 yrs butcher 5s

Cooke, John son of Stephen, gentleman, of Gloucester
Lugge, John & [blank] 9 yrs haberdasher [blank]

2 Dec Moreton, John son of Edward, husbandman, of parish of Deerhurst
Heyford, John & Joan 7 yrs baker 12d

1/323 1623 24 Feb Crowday, John son of John Crowdey, carpenter, dec'd, of Gloucester
Cowley, Richard & Eleanor 9 yrs smith 10s

Toney, Thomas son of Thomas, maltster, of Gloucester
Gale, John & Alice 8 yrs cordwainer 12d

1622 25 Mar Townshend, Richard son of Thomas, husbandman, of Great Shurdington
Cugley, Richard & Anne 8 yrs cook 12d

— — Paynter, Thomas son of Giles, formerly of Severn Stoke
[*Incomplete & deleted: see 1/318*]

1/324 — 25 Apr Simmes, John son of William Symmes, carpenter, of Standish
Smyth, Richard sr 7 yrs tanner 2s 6d

1623 13 Apr Pedlingham, Thomas son of Richard, tailor, of Tibberton
Batten, Richard & Bridget 7 yrs saddler 12d

25 Mar Knight, Nathaniel son of Edward, clothier, of Eastington
Cooke, Thomas & Margaret 7 yrs chandler 3s

1622 25 Dec Yonge, John son of Robert, mercer, of Blakeney
Trippett, Thomas & [blank] 10 yrs mercer 3s

1/325 1623 25 Jul Warde, Philip son of William, cordwainer, of Gloucester
Purlewent, Michael 7 yrs cordwainer 3s 4d

| | 1623 | 21 Sep | Ufford, Daniel son of James, of city of Bristol |
| | | | Taylor, Thomas & Anne 8 yrs wiredrawer 10s |

        24 Aug Bennet, William son of William, victualler, of Ross, Herefs
                       Lugg, Thomas & Anne 7 yrs tanner 5s

        25 Jul Erro, John son of Thomas, carrier, of Tewkesbury
                       Hayward, Edward & Joan 7 yrs cooper 3s 4d

1/326   25 Dec Harris, Thomas son of John, husbandman, of Gloucester
                       Simonds, Edward & Elizabeth 7 yrs feltmaker 5s

         1 Jun Clarke, Anthony son of William, husbandman, dec'd, of Whittington
                       Tackey, Thomas & Elizabeth 7 yrs feltmaker £6 13s 4d

        29 Sep Payte, Nathaniel son of John Paite, pinmaker, of Gloucester
                       Freeman, James & Alice 8 yrs feltmaker 10s

                 Pingery, Thomas son of John, yeoman, of Lea, Herefs
                       Woodward, John & Alice 7 yrs innholder 20s
                       [*cf Appendix V*]

                 Cosby, John son of Thomas, baker, dec'd, of Gloucester
                       Pauper, by the mayor
                       Bodnam, Richard & Margaret 11 yrs baker 12d

        24 Jun Jones, Henry son of Francis, yeoman, of Sherborne
                       Paine, Giles 7 yrs chandler 10s

1/327   **Edmund Clements, mayor [1623–4]**
                 Henry Redven and Peter Lugg, sheriffs
                 Michaelmas 1623 to the same feast 1624

      1623 29 Sep Gresham, Thomas son of Henry, haberdasher, of London
                       Window, Richard & Anne 9 yrs chandler 2s 6d

        24 Jun Robyns, James son of John, yeoman, of Matson
                       Beard, Richard & Anne 8 yrs mercer 3s 4d
                       23 Jun 1630: James placed himself with Thomas Green, mercer.
                       Before William Hill & John Brewster, aldermen

        29 Sep Garlicke, James son of Thomas, husbandman, dec'd, Hempsted
                       Brewster, John & Elizabeth 8 yrs skinner 6s 8d

        25 Dec Fletcher, Henry son of Thomas, dec'd, of Painswick
                       Nelme, John & Rachel 9 yrs mercer 2s 6d

         1 Nov Poole, Thomas son of Henry, innholder, dec'd, of Cirencester
                       Fleming, Richard & Tabitha 7 yrs barber 2s

1/328   29 Sep Younge, Abel son of Walter Young, smith, formerly of Gloucester
                       Grimes, Richard & Joan 10 yrs saddler 3s 4d

         1 Nov Hillaker, John son of Robert, cardmaker, of Gloucester
                       Pitt, Samuel & Eleanor 7 yrs pinner 12d

                 Little, Robert son of Robert, yeoman, formerly of Highnam
                       Woods, John 7 yrs tanner 5s

	1623 30 Nov	Hayward, Thomas son of Richard, farmer, of Ryeford Dobbes, Lawrence 7 yrs cordwainer 10s
	21 Dec	Packer, William son of Richard, yeoman, of Painswick Price, John 8 yrs tanner 6s 8d *4 Oct 1626: by the consent of John Price assigned to serve James Steevens tanner for the residue of the term of 7 yrs [sic] specified in the indenture and then to be free. John Price and James Steevens to pay him 40s. Before Matthew Price, mayor, John Jones & Edmund Clements, justices*
1/329	30 Nov	Payne, Richard son of Richard Paine, sawyer, of Gloucester Pytt, Samuel & Eleanor 7 yrs pinmaker 2s
	21 Dec	Loader, John son of Henry, chapman, of Gloucester Evans, Samuel & Elizabeth 10 yrs pinmaker 3s 4d *Pauper, by the mayor and aldermen*
	29 Sep	Mathews, John son of John, husbandman, of Upleadon Mathewes, Thomas & Elizabeth 7 yrs smith 2s 6d
	25 Dec	Grivell, Giles son of Giles, gentleman, of Charlton Kings Beard, Richard jr & Isobel 8 yrs mercer 3s 4d
1/330		Harris, John son of William, yeoman, of Whaddon Bubb, William & Joan 10 yrs mercer 6s 8d
		Ackley, John son of Richard, yeoman, of Great Shurdington in parish of Badgeworth Johns, William 7 yrs baker 12d
	1624 2 Feb	Young, John son of Walter, cook, of Gloucester Younge, Walter & Katharine 7 yrs cook 5s
	1623 25 Dec	Tither, Thomas son of Anthony, gentleman, of Gloucester Shingleton, Lawrence 9 yrs woollen draper 40s
	1624 2 Feb	Leavens, Thomas son of Anthony, labourer, of Gloucester Mero, Richard 7 yrs feltmaker 3s 4d *19 Jan 1630: Thomas Levens being heretofore turned over by Richard Mero to Edward Simonds is now discharged from him and assigned to serve the residue of his term with Richard Mero. Before Anthony Robinson, mayor*
1/331		Smith, John son of Thomas, tailor, dec'd, of Gloucester Whoopper, John & Anne 8 yrs vintner 5s
		Weaver, Francis son of Francis, butcher, dec'd, of Gloucester Whoppere, John & Anne 7 yrs vintner 5s [*cf Appendix V*]
	1623 25 Dec	Ley, William son of Thomas, tailor, of Gloucester Taylor, Thomas & Anne 8 yrs pinmaker 20s
	13 Apr	Garne, Henry son of William, miller, of Coberley Crompe, Giles & Anne 9 yrs cordwainer 3s 4d

	1624	25 Apr	Chapman *alias* Willmetts, Arthur son of Arthur Willmetts, yeoman, of Minsterworth Taylor, Thomas & Anne 8 yrs wiredrawer 5s
1/332	1623	29 Sep	Harris, Walter son of John, yeoman, of Whaddon Ockold, Arnold & Sybil 7 yrs cordwainer 6s 8d
	1624	1 May	Ellis, Godfrey son of John, yeoman, of Longford Hayes, Anne, widow, 7 yrs baker 5s
		6 May	Saule, William son of William, mercer, dec'd, of Gloucester Thomas, John & Margaret 8 yrs cordwainer 3s 4d
		1 May	Bowen, James son of Edward, yeoman, of Usk, Mon Collett, Edmund & Hester 7 yrs tanner 10s
		28 Mar	Webb, Richard son of William, beer brewer, dec'd of Gloucester Hooper, Jesse & Sarah 7 yrs cordwainer 12d
1/333		24 Jun	Partridge, Thomas son of Arthur, yeoman, dec'd, of Malmesbury, Wilts Jennings, Brian & Alice 7 yrs baker 5s
	1623	29 Sep	Browne, James son of William, labourer, of Gloucester Endall, Anne, widow, 7 yrs [shearman] 12d
	1624	16 May	Eckley, Richard son of Robert, yeoman, of Cheltenham Willcoxe, John & Jane 7 yrs clothier 3s 4d
		24 Jun	Taylor, John son of Richard, yeoman, of Eckington, Worcs Whittington, Robert 8 yrs apothecary 6s 8d
		25 Jul	Yates, Francis son of Francis, cordwainer, of Gloucester Byshopp, Alexander 8 yrs cordwainer 4s
1/334			*Mr Clemence mayor* Hyam, Barnabas son of Nicholas, broadweaver, of Tibberton Bennett, Anthony & Elizabeth 7 yrs clothier 5s
		28 Mar	Bankes, John son of Henry Banks, butcher, of Bewdley, Worcs Cooke, Thomas & Margaret 7 yrs chandler 5s
			Bullock, Edward son of Thomas, yeoman, dec'd, of Highleadon Bullock, James 7 yrs clothier 6s 8d [*cf Appendix V*]
		24 Aug	Jorden, John son of Edward, yeoman, dec'd, of English Bicknor Lane, Walter & Isobel 7 yrs baker 2s 6d
1/335	1623	1 Nov	Powell, Thomas son of John, clothier, of Cheltenham Wilcoxe, John & Jane 7 yrs clothier 2s 6d
	1624	25 Jul	Theyer, Hugh son of Robert, yeoman, dec'd, of Ubley, Som Merro, Richard & Alice 7 yrs feltmaker 5s
		29 Sep	Evans, William son of Hugh, gentleman, dec'd, of Llangattock, Mon Bayley, John & Abigail 7 yrs glover 5s
		24 Jun	Masfeild, Thomas son of Thomas, labourer, of Badgeworth Newman, William & Alice 10 yrs mercer 2s

1/337   **Richard Smyth, mayor [1624–5]**
                 John Deighton and Edmund Michell sheriffs

1624   29 Sep   Robyns, Richard son of Richard, gentleman, of Haresfield
                   Caple, William & Mary   9 yrs   mercer   10s
                   Time of Edmund Clements mayor and Henry Redven & Peter Lugg sheriffs. Wrongly entered

               Witcombe, John son of John, husbandman, of Hempsted
                   Gwynn, Augustine & Alice   9 yrs   shoemaker   12d   [*cf Appendix V*]
                   Time of Edmund Clements mayor and Henry Redven & Peter Lugg sheriffs. Wrongly entered

        1 May   Newman, John son of Richard, labourer, of Prestbury
                   Ticklee, Samuel   8 yrs   ropemaker   10s
                   Time of Edmund Clements mayor and Henry Redven & Peter Lugg sheriffs. Wrongly entered

        25 Dec   Comelin, James son of Daniel
                   Whittington, Robert & Hephzibah   8 yrs   apothecary   6s 8d

1/338   1 Nov   Hooke, Edward son of John, yeoman, of Taynton
                   Haynes, William & Katharine   7 yrs   butcher   12d

     1625   2 Feb   Birche, John son of John, smith, dec'd, of Badgeworth
                   Newman, William & Alice   8 yrs   mercer   2s 6d

               Dallome, Robert son of Robert, feltmaker, of Burford, Oxon
                   Symons, Edward & Elizabeth   7 yrs   feltmaker   40s

               Payne, Thomas son of Thomas, wiredrawer, dec'd, of Gloucester
                   Wilkins, Richard & Elizabeth   9 yrs   wiredrawer   3s 4d

1/339   25 Mar   Pettifer, Thomas son of Thomas, clerk, of Shenington
                   [MS Shunington]
                   Pettifer, Joseph   9 yrs   chandler   12d

               Hoare, Alexander son of Richard, gentleman, formerly of Gloucester
                   Lugg, William & Eleanor   7 yrs   tanner   10s

               Wyniat, Joseph son of John, gentleman, of Dymock
                   Fowler, Samuel   7 yrs   mercer   12d

               Hiron, Humphrey son of Humphrey, chandler, of Gloucester
                   Hiron, Humphrey, his father, & Blanche   7 yrs   chandler   10s

1/340   Partridge, Robert son of Robert, yeoman, of Stanley
                   Purlewent, John   7 yrs   baker   2s 6d

        5 Jun   Heynes, Robert son of Richard, husbandman, of South Cerney
                   Wagstaffe, Edward & Katharine   7 yrs   brewer   40s

        24 Jun   Walker, William son of William, tailor, dec'd, of Gloucester
                   Copner, Robert & Anne   9 yrs   lockyer   12d   *pauper*

        25 Jul   Barrett, William son of William, tailor, of Gloucester
                   Freame, John & Dorothy   7 yrs   tailor   5s

1/341	1625	24 Jul	Merrett, George son of Christopher, mercer, dec'd, of Winchcombe Webb, John 9 yrs mercer 2s 6d
		21 Jul	Cordell, William son of Richard, glover, of Gloucester Cordell, Richard, his father, & Margery 8 yrs glover £5 *Pauper. Mr Holliday's money*[1]
			Cater, Giles son of Richard, gentleman, of Gloucester Tailor, Thomas 8 yrs clothier [*blank*] *Pauper. Mr Hollidaie's money*
			Dobbes, Richard son of Richard, cordwainer, of Gloucester [Dobbes, Richard] his father 7 yrs [cordwainer] £5 *Pauper. Mr Hollidaie's money*
		25 Jul	Bird, William son of Andrew, tailor, of Gloucester [Bird], Andrew, his father, & Mary 8 yrs [tailor] 2s
1/342		21 Jul	Jones, John son of David, maltster, of Gloucester Johns, William & Jane 7 yrs baker 40s
	1624	25 Dec	Harris, Francis son of Thomas, gunsmith, of Gloucester Harris, Thomas, his father, & Mary 7 yrs gunsmith 5s
	1625	5 Jun	Edwardes, Humphrey son of William, cooper, of Bromsgrove, Worcs Hockham, Henry & Anne 7 yrs butcher 40s
		24 Jun	Blomer, Giles son of Mary, widow, of Cowley Beard, Richard & Anne 9 yrs mercer 3s 4d *23 Jun 1630: placed with James Machen & Katharine for the* *residue of his term. Before William Hill & John Brewster, aldermen*
1/343		29 Sep	License, Miles son of Henry, gentleman, of Gloucester Purlewent, Michael & Sybil 7 yrs cordwainer 12d
		24 Jun	Armitage, Henry son of Richard, labourer, of Barton Street, Gloucester Hancox, Henry & Anne 7 yrs cordwainer 2s 6d
		29 Sep	Abrahell, James son of Hugh, miller, formerly of Stretton Grandison, Herefs Tickle, Samuel 7 yrs ropemaker 5s
		25 Jul	Gatherne, Richard son of Richard, yeoman, of Hutton, Westmld Tarne, Thomas & Margaret 9 yrs glover 40s
1/344		2 Feb	Carpenter, Toby son of Richard, yeoman, of Tuffley Pitt, Thomas 7 yrs baker 12d
		5 Jun	Brooke, Martin son of Richard, husbandman, dec'd, of Ledbury, Herefs Yearnold, Francis & Joan 8 yrs glover 3s 4d
		25 Mar	Gretton, William son of William, feltmaker, dec'd, of Gloucester Lugg, William & Eleanor 10 yrs tanner 5s [*cf Appendix V*]

---

[1] GBR B3/1 f 507 6 Sep 1625: The £30 appointed to be paid to Richard Dobbs, Richard Cordell, Thomas Taylor and William Johns for the placing of their apprentices according to the gift of alderman Holliday shall be paid to them by alderman Caple.

For William Holliday's apprenticing charity, see above, pp xx–xxii.

1625 24 Jun Dewxell, John son of Thomas, gentleman, dec'd, of Ashleworth
           Webb, John 8 yrs mercer 6s 8d

     29 Sep Sawyer, James son of John, weaver, of Gloucester
           Bennett, Anthony & Elizabeth 7 yrs broadweaver 3s 4d

1/345   **John Jones, mayor [1625–6]**
           John Gwilliam and John Reade, sheriffs and bailiffs

1625 30 Nov Keble, Bernard son of William Keeble, gentleman, of Coates
           Payne, Robert 8 yrs mercer 3s 4d

1626 2 Feb Davis, Robert son of Robert Davys, yeoman, of Quedgeley
           Lane, John & Elizabeth 7 yrs baker 12d

     25 Mar Dun, Edward son of Edward, yeoman, of Hempsted
           Newman, William & Alice 9 yrs mercer 2s 6d

      9 Apr Mills, Humphrey son of Edward, weaver, of Barton Street, Gloucester
           Yarnold, Francis & Joan 8 yrs glover 12d

1/346 1625 25 Dec Poole, Charles son of Thomas, saddler, dec'd, of Tetbury
           Hoare, Charles & Margery 8 yrs saddler 3s 4d

     29 Jun Mathewes, Thomas son of Thomas, yeoman, of 'Awsen' [Alstone?]
           Edwardes, Anthony & Anne 9 yrs mercer 3s 4d

1626 25 Mar Elridge, Thomas son of Thomas, yeoman, of Ashleworth
           Porter, Robert & Elizabeth 9 yrs joiner 12d

     28 May Symons, John son of William, yeoman, of Hucclecote
           Warde, William & Elizabeth 7 yrs cordwainer 6s 8d

      2 Feb Hoare, Thomas son of Charles, brewer, of Gloucester
           Hoare, Charles, his father, 12 yrs brewer 2 suits of clothes
           Time of John Jones 1625

1/347 28 May Tomkins, William son of William, weaver, of Gloucester
           Cugley, Arthur & Elizabeth 8 yrs wiredrawer 12d

           Chomlyn, Thomas son of Thomas, carrier, of Lew, Oxon
           Kinge, Christopher 8 yrs sealmaker 12d

     25 Jul Grymes, Richard son of Richard, saddler, of Gloucester
           Grymes, Richard, his father, & Joan 7 yrs saddler 2s 6d

     [blank] Hagborne, Richard son of Richard, husbandman, of Rockhampton
           Elbridge, John & Joan 8 yrs cordwainer 12d

     28 May White, Thomas son of Richard, yeoman, of Hardwicke
           Payne, Robert 7 yrs mercer 3s 4d

1/348 25 Jul Manninge, Samuel son of Toby, weaver, of Gloucester
           Preedie, William 8 yrs weaver 12d
             4 Nov 1628: turned over to Augustine Gwyn & Alice for the term of 5 yrs

1626 21 Jul Hughes, Giles son of Thomas, cook, dec'd, of Gloucester
Carpenter, John & Bridget 8 yrs cordwainer 6s 8d
Mr Hollidaie's money[1]

Wager, John son of Robert, glazier, of Gloucester
Haies, Christopher & Joan 7 yrs glazier 40s
Mr Hollidaie's money

Tomkins, Abel son of John, smith, of Gloucester
Rice, John & Elizabeth 8 yrs cordwainer 3s 4d
Mr Hollidaie's money

25 Mar Rixe, Richard son of John, yeoman, of Upton
Bennet, Anthony & Elizabeth 7 yrs clothier 6s 8d

1/349

24 Jun Hitchman, Robert son of Edward, yeoman, of Great Witcombe
Mero, Richard & Alice 7 yrs feltmaker 5s

25 Jul Price, John son of James, yeoman, dec'd, of Minsterworth
Taylor, Richard & Joan 8 yrs cordwainer 2s

24 Aug Dun, Nathaniel son of Gabriel, clerk, of Moreton Valence
Bird, Andrew & Mary 8 yrs tailor 12d

25 Jul Gide, Robert son of Richard, clothier, of Stroud
Price, William, alderman, & Elizabeth 9 yrs merchant 12d

29 Sep White, John son of Thomas, husbandman, dec'd, of Minsterworth
Ockold, Arnold & Sybil 7 yrs cordwainer 2s 6d

1/350

Coke, William son of James, husbandman, dec'd, of Corse
Haies, Anne, widow, 7 yrs baker 5s

1625 1 Nov Phelpes, William son of James, baker, of Gloucester
Burrowes, Nathaniel & Dorothy 9 yrs cordwainer 3s 4d

1626 29 Sep Prytchette, Simon son of Gabriel, turner, of Bewdley, Worcs
Davies, William & Martha 8 yrs cooper 2s 6d

25 Mar Prichard, Robert son of William, maltster, dec'd, of Gloucester
Bubb, John & Eleanor 8 yrs cordwainer 5s

6 Dec Townesend, Christopher son of Edward, yeoman, of Bisley
Walbridge, Richard & Anne 8 yrs barber 3s 4d

1/351

Matthew Price, mayor [1626–7]
Thomas Hill and Thomas Pury, sheriffs and bailiffs

1626 17 Oct Brookebanke, Giles son of Elizabeth, widow, of Gloucester
Kyste, Edward 8 yrs saddler 1s

17 Nov Swayne, Kenelm, pauper of the city, apprenticed with the agreement of the mayor & burgesses
Kydon, Robert 10 yrs milliner 2s 6d

---

[1] GBR B3/1 f 512 22 Jun 1626: Agreed that 4 boys shall each have £7 10s of Mr Holliday's money to place them apprentice: Giles Hughes, John Wager, [Abel] Tomkins, John Browne.

	1626 30 Nov	Browne, John son of John, mercer, of Gloucester Newman, William 9 yrs mercer 30s with the agreement of the mayor and burgesses
	21 Dec	Sparhawke, Robert son of Thomas, yeoman, of Hailey in parish of Witney, Oxon Craker, John 7 yrs weaver [blank]
	1627 27 Jan	Hale, Thomas son of Thomas, yeoman, dec'd, of Ashleworth Freeman, James & Alice 7 yrs to start on 2 Feb feltmaker 12d
1/352	2 Feb	Francombe, Henry son of William, yeoman, dec'd, of Tirley Hedges, Nathaniel & Margaret 8 yrs woollen draper 3s 4d
	22 Jan	Higgyns, Edward son of Richard Higgins, yeoman, of St Briavels Wise, Denis, 9 yrs from 13 May mercer 12d
	1626 30 Nov	Crowes, John son of John, husbandman, formerly of Berkeley Bayley, John & Abigail 8 yrs glover 2s 6d
	1627 5 Feb	Gilbert, Henry son of Henry, gentleman, formerly of Whaddon Crompe, Giles & Anne 7 yrs cordwainer 3s 4d
	22 Feb	James, Leigh son of Joan, widow, formerly of Didbrook Jennings, Brian & Alice 9 yrs from 25 Dec 1626 baker 6s 8d
1/353	29 Mar	Symmons, Richard son of Richard, husbandman, of Tirley Symons, Robert 7 yrs glover 2s 6d
	1626 25 Dec	Whyte, Thomas son of David White, shearman, of Gloucester White, David, his father & Edith, 8 yrs shearman 12d
	1627 25 Mar	Baughe, John son of John, husbandman, of Pensham, Worcs Nicolls, John 8 yrs tanner 10s
	3 May	Coopy, Edward son of Thomas, husbandman, of Kingsholm Greene, Simon 9 yrs cooper 1s
1/354	2 May	Hayes, Thomas son of John, baker, dec'd, of Gloucester Hayes, Anne, widow, his mother, 10 yrs baker 10s
	14 May	Hillie, John son of Thomas Hilly, maltster, of Tewkesbury Pryce, Henry & Alice 7 yrs woollen draper 10s
	19 May	Atkings, Henry son of Thomas Atkins, of Cheltenham Moore, Thomas & Mary 8 yrs baker 1s
1/355	20 May	Perkes, John son of Daniel, baker, dec'd, of Gloucester Thayer, Giles & Anne 7 yrs baker 3s 4d & 2 suits
	7 Jun	Harris, John son of John, husbandman, of Norton, Worcs Pynke, John jr 7 yrs baker 3s 4d & 2 suits
	2 Feb	Bishoppe, William son of Anthony, husbandman, of Highnam Bishop, John 8 yrs baker 2s 6d
1/356	14 Jul	Powell, Charles son of Thomas, of Howton, Herefs Hopkins, John 8 yrs joiner 3s 4d & 2 suits
	24 Jun	Smith, William son of Maurice, yeoman, of Hill Crumpe, Giles & Anne 8 yrs cordwainer 5s & 2 suits

| | 1627 29 Jun | Nicholson, Knowles *alias* Knolles son of Christopher, clerk, of Fairford |
| | | Caple, William & Mary 9 yrs mercer 5s |

1/357   13 Aug Hall, Robert son of Henry, dec'd, of Gloucester
                 Amphlett, Richard & Joan 7 yrs ropemaker 5s & 2 suits

         25 Jul Cugley, John son of Robert, yeoman, of Gloucester
                 Harris, Edward & Mary [*no term*] tailor 10s & 2 suits
                 Alderman Holliday's bequest[1]

         —   Collins, Roland son of William, pewterer, of Gloucester
                 Collins, William & [*blank*] 12 yrs pewterer [*Entry incomplete*]
                 Alderman Holliday's bequest

1/358   29 Sep Broadgate, Richard son of Richard, clerk, of Gloucester
                 Fleminge, Richard 8 yrs barber surgeon 50s
                 Alderman Holliday's bequest

         1626 29 Sep Witcombe, John son of John, yeoman, dec'd, of Hempsted
                 Carpenter, John & Bridget 7 yrs cordwainer 3s 4d and 2 suits
                 [*cf Appendix V*]
                 Made in the time of John Jones, mayor, by me George Stephens
                 This indenture was made by Thomas Bullocke 12 months ago and
                 we have enrolled it without fee

         1627 25 Mar Cooke, Richard son of Walter, dec'd, of Quedgeley
                 Whitterne, John & Anne 7 yrs tailor 10s
                 [*Repeated, altered, at 1/362*]

1/359   17 Sep Coxe, Toby son of Thomas, yeoman, of Gloucester
                 Paine, John & Margaret 9 yrs tailor 1s
                 Alderman Holliday's bequest

         24 Aug Middlewright, Leonard son of John, dec'd, of Over
                 Dawes, Richard & Katharine 8 yrs glover 12d

         —   Jefferies, John son of John, of 'Elsfeild' [Eldersfield, Worcs?]
                 Dowsinge, John & [*blank*] 7 yrs [*deleted*] farrier [*blank*]

         24 Jun Millechep, Thomas son of Richard, gentleman, dec'd, of Ludlow, Salop
                 Hyron, Humphrey sr & Blanche 8 yrs chandler 6s 8d

1/360   **Richard Beard, mayor [1627–8]**
                 Richard Keylock and Denis Wise, sheriffs and bailiffs

         1627 29 Sep Bishoppe, John son of Alan, clerk, of Ashton Keynes, Wilts
                 Nelmes, John & Rachel 9 yrs mercer 5s

         27 Oct Toney, John son of Henry Tony, weaver, of Tewkesbury
                 Pettifer, Joseph & Juliana 8 yrs chandler 12d

         1628 1 Apr Humfries, Richard son of Thomas Humphreys, husbandman, of Epney
                 Baker, James & Joan 7 yrs butcher

---

[1] GBR B3/1 f 518 20 Jul 1627: John Cugley son of Robert and Richard Broadgate son of Richard, because they are kin to alderman Holliday, to have £7 10s for their placing as apprentices. Thomas Cox and William Collins to have £7 10s apiece.

1/361	1627	5 Nov	Paine, Robert son of Richard, husbandman, of Harescombe Witcombe, William & Edith 7 yrs clothier 2s 6d
		15 Nov	Greene, Richard son of Richard, gentleman, of Gloucester Price, Henry & Alice 7 yrs woollen draper 6s 8d
		1 Nov	Harris, Humphrey son of Thomas, gunsmith, of Gloucester Lane, John & Elizabeth 7 yrs baker 10s [*cf Appendix V*]
1/362	1628	2 Feb	Good, Thomas son of Richard Goode, labourer, of Gloucester Hopkins, John & Jane 9 yrs joiner 3s 4d
		—	Cooke, Richard son of Walter, yeoman, dec'd, of Quedgeley Whitterne, John tailor [*Incomplete: see 1/358*]
		—	Lugge, John son of Peter, haberdasher, of Gloucester Lugge, Peter, his father, haberdasher [*Entry incomplete*]
1/363	1628	2 Feb	Lisney, Richard son of Richard, fishmonger, dec'd, of London Lane, John & Elizabeth 7 yrs baker 12d
		26 Jan	Frankis, Henry son of William Frankys, yeoman, of Barnwood Bodenham, Richard & Margaret 7 yrs baker 2 suits *This indenture was made by Richard Bodnam himself in English but enrolled*
	1627	21 Dec	Sulicer, Edward son of Edward Slicer, husbandman, of Longhope Lugge, William & Eleanor 8 yrs tanner 5s
1/364	1628	18 Feb	Slicer, James son of Edward, glover, of Longhope Lugge, William & Eleanor 8 yrs tanner 5s
		25 Mar	Harris, Humphrey son of Thomas, gunsmith, of Gloucester Whittingham, Thomas & Joan 7 yrs baker 10s [*cf Appendix V*]
	1627	25 Dec	Smith, Robert son of Robert, dec'd, of Hempsted Nursse, John & Anne 14 yrs cooper 5s
	1628	1 May	Chedworth, Thomas son of Thomas, dec'd, of Ashleworth Dowsinge, William & Elizabeth 8 yrs farrier 2s and 2 suits
1/365		17 May	Lewes, Thomas son of Nathaniel, tanner, of Cirencester Steevens, James & Anne 9 yrs tanner 12d
		22 May	Nelme, Richard son of Richard, husbandman, of Highleadon Pitt, Robert & Elizabeth 9 yrs pinmaker 12d & 2 suits
			Watkins, Thomas son of Thomas, yeoman, of Hasfield Sawcombe, John & Joan 7 yrs blacksmith 3s 4d & 2 suits
1/366	1627	30 Nov	Cowles, William son of John, labourer, of Gloucester Hoockam, Nathaniel 7 yrs butcher 5s
	1628	9 Jun	Rowles, John son of John, butcher, of Frampton Mills, Richard & Hannah 7 yrs broadweaver 6s 8d & 2 suits
		—	Thorne, William son of William, of [*blank*], Glos Gwynne, Augustine & [*blank*] cordwainer [*Entry incomplete*]

1/367	1628	25 Jul	Middlewright, Humphrey son of Thomas, tanner, of Gloucester Stephens, James & Anne 8 yrs tanner £3 & 2 suits
		2 Aug	Daye, William son of Richard, clerk, of Stroud Tither, Robert & Margaret 7 yrs tanner 3s 4d
			Gosling, John son of Thomas Goslinge, husbandman, of Longney Kiddon, Charles & Mary 8 yrs milliner 12d
1/368		24 Jun	Hodges, Christopher son of Thomas, esquire, of Shipton Wise, Denis & Hephzibah 8 yrs mercer 6s 8d
		25 Jul	Price, Richard son of James, yeoman, of Minsterworth Heath, Thomas 8 yrs pewterer 40s
			Feild, Thomas son of Thomas, tailor, of Gloucester Clutterbooke, Daniel & Miriam 8 yrs skinner 5s *Alderman Hollidaie's gift*[1]
1/369			Crumpe, Edward son of Giles, cordwainer, of Gloucester Gwynne, Augustine 9 yrs cordwainer 5s *Alderman Hollidaie's gift*
		– Sep	Sare, John son of Ralph, pinner, of Gloucester Gray, Brice & Joan 10 yrs butcher 5s *Alderman Hollidaie's gift*
		19 Sep	Carter, William son of William, husbandman, of Maisemore Stallard, Anselm & Dorothy 8 yrs cooper 10s
1/370		—	Cooke, Thomas son of Thomas, fisherman, formerly of Hempsted Gregory, Henry & Joan butcher [*Entry incomplete*]
	1627	21 Dec	Barker, Thomas son of John, cordwainer, of Gloucester Tilsley, Philip & Anne 7 yrs pinmaker
	1628	31 Mar	Maddock, Richard son of William Maddocke, yeoman, of Minsterworth Cooke, Thomas & Anne 8 yrs joiner 10s
1/372			**Henry Browne, mayor [1628–9]** **Abel Angell and John Price, sheriffs**
	1628	7 Oct	Powell, Ralph son of John, yeoman, formerly of Cheltenham Nursse, Luke 8 yrs mercer 3s 4d
		18 Oct	Neale, James son of John, husbandman, of Highleadon Gale, John & Alice 8 yrs cordwainer 12d
		7 Oct	Symes, Francis son of Thomas Symmes, gentleman, of Hempsted Taylor, John 9 yrs mercer 5s
1/373			Savage, Giles son of Richard, dec'd, of Gloucester Elles, Henry & Margaret 8 yrs broadweaver 5s and 2 suits

---

[1] GBR B3/1 f 523 1 Jul 1628: Edward Crumpe son of Giles, cordwainer, John Sare son of Ralph, wiredrawer, Thomas Field son of Thomas, tailor, [*blank*] Handes son of Isaac, yeoman, being poor boys of this city, to have £7 10s apiece for placing them apprentice.

	1628	25 Dec	Pester, Alexander son of Christopher, gentleman, dec'd, of [*blank*] Som Window, Richard & Anne 8 yrs chandler 12d
		1 Nov	Stephens, Robert son of William, husbandman, dec'd, of Longney Pitt, Robert & Elizabeth 8 yrs pinmaker 12d
		7 Oct	Lord, Henry son of Henry, yeoman, of Brockhampton Davis, Roger & Elizabeth [*no term*] cordwainer 20s
1/374		18 Nov	Mathewes, Henry son of Richard, weaver, of Gloucester Thomas, William & Katherine 7 yrs tailor 6s 8d and 2 suits
		1 Nov	Jones, Thomas son of William, carpenter, of Gloucester Smith, John & Anne 7 yrs carpenter 3s 4d
			Smith, William son of John, carpenter, of Gloucester Smith, John, his father, & Anne 7 yrs carpenter 20s
1/375			Hodgshon, Jeremiah son of Marmaduke, dec'd, of Gloucester Niccolls, John & Joan 7 yrs tanner 5s and 2 suits [*Repeated at 1/388; cf Appendix V*]
		25 Dec	Broade, Samuel son of Thomas, clerk, of Rendcomb Ockold, Arnold & Sybil 7 yrs cordwainer 3s 4d and 2 suits
		29 Nov	Humfreyes, Samuel son of Thomas Humfryes, yeoman, of Epney Burd, Andrew & Mary [*no term*] tailor 12d
1/376		25 Dec	Cue, John son of John, husbandman, of Dymock Tilsley, Philip & Anne 8 yrs pinmaker 12d
			Walker, Richard son of Nicholas, dec'd, of Gloucester Etheridge, John & Margery 7 yrs cordwainer 12d and 2 suits
		30 Nov	Jones, William son of John, husbandman, dec'd, of Hasfield Jones, John & Rebecca 7 yrs cook 10s and 2 suits
1/377		25 Dec	Hyam, John son of John, husbandman, of Cirencester Willetts, George & Anne 9 yrs wiredrawer 5s
	1629	6 Jan	Jones, John son of David, maltster, formerly of Gloucester Tilsley, Philip & Anne 7 yrs pinmaker 5s and 2 suits
	—	8 Sep	*Baggott, John, allowed over by his own consent and the consent of his master Jesse Whooper to Alexander Bishopp & Bridget* *Before John Jones, William Hill and Toby Bullock*
1/378	1629	6 Jan	Viner, Henry son of William, broadweaver, of Gloucester Loggins, John & Anne 7 yrs broadweaver 5s
	1628	1 Nov	Loggins, Lawrence son of John, freemason, of Gloucester Loggins, John, his father, & Anne 7 yrs freemason 5s
	1629	2 Feb	Randle, Thomas son of George, yeoman, formerly of Haresfield Wilkins, Richard & Elizabeth 7 yrs wiredrawer 6s 8d
1/379			Long, Humphrey son of Robert, weaver, dec'd, of Gloucester Craker, John & Margaret 8 yrs weaver £4 [*cf 1/304*]
			Tailor, Thomas son of Anthony Taylor, husbandman, of Turkdean Pinke, John & Alice 7 yrs baker 12d

| | | | Cleeadly, William son of William, husbandman, of Charleton |
| | | | Hathway, Anthony [*Incomplete*] |

| | 1629 | 24 Feb | Carpenter, William son of James, clothier, dec'd, of Gloucester |
| | | | Tailor, Richard & Joan 7 yrs cordwainer 3s 4d |

| *1/380* | 1628 | 25 Dec | Price, James son of James, husbandman, formerly of Minsterworth |
| | | | Angell, Abel 8 yrs baker 3s 4d |

| | 1629 | 25 Feb | Tainton, Michael son of Richard, husbandman, of Bisley |
| | | | Tither, Robert & Margaret 7 yrs tanner 3s 4d |

1/381		25 Mar	Baker, William son of Thomas, weaver, of Gloucester
			Lucas, Robert & Elizabeth 8 yrs farrier 12d
			Alye, Giles Cancelled [*Incomplete*]

| | 1628 | 12 Oct | Smith, Thomas son of [*blank*], labourer, dec'd, of Hempsted |
| | | | Pinke, Walter & Margery [*no term*] baker [*blank*] |

| | 1629 | 1 May | Welstead, Daniel son of Thomas Welstedd, husbandman, dec'd, of Haresfield |
| | | | Tither, Robert & Margaret [*no term*] tanner 10s |

| *1/382* | | 30 Apr | Kempe, John son of John, mercer, of Gloucester |
| | | | Mason, Edward & Alice 7 yrs saddler 3s 4d [*See 1/405*] |

| | | 15 May | Goodinge, Thomas son of Thomas, husbandman, of Purston, Northants |
| | | | Breethers, Thomas & Blanche 7 yrs keeping accounts [MS. 'bene scribendi et numerandi'] 3s 4d |

	1628	29 Sep	Hankes, Richard son of John, tailor, of Gloucester
			Hickman, John & Mary 9 yrs sievemaker 10s
			Holland registered it in the time of Richard Beard, mayor

| | 1629 | 24 May | Webb, Thomas son of William, yeoman, dec'd, of Hartpury |
| | | | Taylor, John 8 yrs mercer 2s 6d |

| *1/383* | | | Rickettes, James son of John, yeoman, of Hardwicke |
| | | | Wood, John & Elizabeth 8 yrs tanner 12d |

| | | 24 Jun | Webb, William son of John, husbandman, of Longford |
| | | | Lugg, Thomas 9 yrs tanner 5s |

| | | | Gibson, John son of Paul, yeoman, of Hanslope, Bucks |
| | | | Thomas, William & Christiane 7 yrs cook 5s |

| | | 2 Jun | Cluffe, Henry son of John, husbandman, formerly of Compton Wynyates [MS Compton in the Hole], Warws |
| | | | Lugge, Richard & Joan 7 yrs tanner 5s |

| *1/384* | — | — | [*blank*] son of [*blank*], yeoman, of the city of Bristol |
| | | | Tilsley, Philip & Anne pinmaker [*Entry incomplete*] |

| | 1629 | 24 Jun | Eckley, Walter son of Robert, husbandman, of Cheltenham |
| | | | Eckley, Thomas 7 yrs chandler 2s 6d |

| | | | Eckley, William son of Robert, husbandman, of Cheltenham |
| | | | Greene, Edward & Eleanor 7 yrs cordwainer 3s 4d |

1/385	1629	1 Jun	Halsey, Thomas son of William, yeoman, of Eldersfield, Worcs Window, Richard & Anne 8 yrs chandler 2s 6d
		24 Jun	Little, Thomas son of John, yeoman, dec'd, of Maisemore Cooke, Thomas & Margaret 7 yrs chandler 5s
		25 Jul	Toney, John son of Thomas Tony, yeoman, of Gloucester Simondes, Robert 7 yrs glover [blank]
1/386			Palmer, John son of John, cooper, of Gloucester Palmer, John, his father, & Margaret 8 yrs cooper 6s 8d *Alderman Holliday*[1]
			Moore, John son of Alexander, joiner, of Gloucester Moore, Alexander, his father, & Joan 9 yrs joiner 6s 8d *Alderman Holliday*
			Shotford, John son of John, cordwainer, of Gloucester Shotford, John, his father, & Anne 7 yrs cordwainer 6s 8d *Alderman Holliday*
			Mower, Richard son of Thomas, husbandman, dec'd, of Painswick Haines, William & Anne 8 yrs baker [blank]
1/387			West, Richard son of Richard, broadweaver, of Tetbury Heard, Charles [blank] brewer £4
		24 Jun	Higges, Richard son of Richard, yeoman, of the Leigh Whitterne, John & Elizabeth 7 yrs merchant £10
		29 Sep	Wildboare, John son of John, musician, of Ledbury, Herefs Howlett, William & Margery 7 yrs musician 30s
		25 Jul	Anstick, Henry son of Randall, butcher, of Gloucester Anstick, Randall, his father, & Joan 9 yrs butcher 6s 8d
1/388	1628	1 Nov	Hodgshon, Jeremiah son of Marmaduke, dec'd, of Gloucester Niccolls, John & Joan 7 yrs tanner 5s *Alderman Holliday* [*Repeating entry at 1/375 with ref to Alderman Holliday added; cf Appendix V*]
	1629	29 Jun	Chapman, Thomas son of Thomas, smith, dec'd, of Whaddon Beard, Andrew & Mary 8 yrs tailor 2s
		25 Jul	Paite, Walter son of John, hook maker, of Gloucester Paite, John, his father, 7 yrs hook maker 6s 8d *Alderman Holliday*
1/389		29 Jun	Hunt, John son of Thomas, brew[er], of Gloucester Mills, Richard & Hannah 10 yrs weaver 6s 8d
		1 May	Davis, John son of Walter, of Westbury Lugge, Lawrence & Anne 8 yrs tanner £4

---

[1] GBR B3/1 f 532 1 Jul 1629: Poor boys to be given alderman Holliday's money: Henry Anstick son of Randall, Walter Paite son of John, John Palmer son of John, John Shotford son of John, Alexander Moore son of Alexander, Jeremiah Hodgshon son of Marmaduke, gentleman, the Countess of Warwick, widow of alderman Holliday, having agreed that the annual grant of £30 should be divided between 6 poor boys instead of 4.

| | 1629 | 5 Apr | Beard, John son of Thomas, yeoman, of Framilode
Beard, Richard & Anne 9 yrs mercer 3s 4d
23 Jun 1620: transferred with consent of said John to Thomas Greene. Before William Hill & John Brewster, aldermen |

1/391 **Anthony Robinson, mayor [1629–30]**
Richard Greene and Nicholas Webb, sheriffs

| | 1629 | 7 Oct | Howford, Anthony son of Anne, of Inglesham [MS Englesham], Berks
Williams, Richard 9 yrs tanner 12d |
| | | [blank] | Browne, John son of Henry sr, alderman, of Gloucester
Pearce, Thomas & Taylor, Richard 8 yrs mercer 5s |
| | | 5 Nov | Dowers, Richard son of Richard, husbandman, of Harnhill [MS Harnell]
Nurse, Luke & Mary 11 yrs maltster 3s 4d |

1/392 1 Nov Piddinge, Thomas son of William, cordwainer, of Marlborough, Wilts
Hooper, Jesse & Sarah 7 yrs cordwainer 2s 6d

Cooke, William son of Richard, yeoman, of Uckington
Edwardes, Anthony & Anne 9 yrs mercer 5s

Smith, John son of John [*Incomplete*]

1630 22 Feb Raynoldes, Henry son of John, cordwainer, of Barton Street, Gloucester
Llewellin, John & Alice 7 yrs cordwainer 12d

1/393 1629 1 Nov White, Sergeant son of David, shearman, of Gloucester
Burrowes, Nathaniel & Dorothy 9 yrs cordwainer 3s 4d & 2 suits

25 Dec Llewellyn, John son of John, cordwainer, of Gloucester
Tyler, James 9 yrs cordwainer 3s 4d

1630 2 Feb White, Thomas son of Thomas, husbandman, of Minsterworth
Joyner, Giles & [*blank*] 7 yrs carpenter 2s 6d

— — Hill, Thomas son of John, labourer, of Gloucester
Cugley, John [*Incomplete; repeated, altered, at 1/408*]

1/394 25 Mar Elliottes, Walter son of Walter, sailor, of Gloucester
Cugley, John & Elizabeth 10 yrs cardmaker 5s & 2 suits

1 May Cugley, Walter son of Walter, labourer, of Badgeworth
Willottes, George & Anne 8 yrs wiredrawer 18d

29 Jun Yates, John son of Francis, cordwainer, of Gloucester
Bishopp, Alexander 7 yrs cordwainer 2s 6d

1/395 1629 30 Nov Pingrey, Thomas son of John, clothier, of Lea [MS Leigh], Herefs
Craker, John & Margaret 7 yrs clothier 10s & 2 suits [*cf Appendix V*]

1630 16 May Harward, Anthony son of Richard, draper, of Gloucester
Harwood, Richard, his father, & Alice 10 yrs draper 5s

24 Jun Hathwaie, George son of Richard Hathwaye, clerk, of Frocester
Tacklin, Thomas & Elizabeth 7 yrs feltmaker 2s 6d

He was not then a freeman
Thomas Surman, John Surman of Tirley, H Hassington 10 yrs 5s
[Notes added in another hand]

1/396	1630	1 Apr	Rogers, Richard son of Thomas, yeoman, of Gloucester
			Wolley, Henry & Elizabeth 7 yrs barber surgeon 5s
		—	Mercer, William son of William, maltster, dec'd
			Mager, Giles & Mary 8 yrs cordwainer 6s 8d
			Alderman Holliday[1]
		29 Sep	Prichard, George son of William, yeoman, of Penrhos, Mon
			Freame, John & Elizabeth 7 yrs tailor 5s
	—	—	Williams, Isaac son of Michael
			Addams tailor *Addams is not a Freeman and therefore it was not entered* [*Incomplete*]
1/397	1630	5 Aug	Messinger, Witherstone son of Robert, dec'd
			Craker, John & Margaret 10 yrs weaver 10s *Alderman Holliday*
		22 July	Bishopp, John son of Thomas, cordwainer, of Gloucester
			Bishopp, Thomas, his father, & Anne 7 yrs cordwainer 5s
			Alderman Holliday
		25 Mar	Ellis, John son of John, of Gloucester
			Hall, Thomas & Eleanor 8 yrs pewterer 3s 4d *Alderman Holliday*
1/398	1630	16 May	Yearnold, Thomas son of Thomas, glover, of Gloucester
			Yearnold, Thomas, his father, & Sybil 7 yrs glover 3s 4d
	—	—	Webley, Giles son of Giles, yeoman, of Lassington
			Payne, Robert & Elizabeth mercer [*Entry incomplete*]

1/399   **William Price, mayor [1630–1]**
          Luke Nurse and Leonard Tarne, sheriffs 1630

	1630	10 Nov	Simondes, Thomas son of Nathaniel, husbandman, of Dursley
			Lugge, Thomas & Anne 7 yrs tanner 2s 6d
		– Nov	Sparkes, Thomas son of Thomas, weaver, dec'd, of Gloucester
			Sarson, Humphrey & Eleanor [*blank*] sievemaker [*blank*]
	1631	25 Mar	Davis, John son of Roger, cordwainer, of Gloucester
			Nelme, John & Rachel 10 yrs mercer 5s
		17 Jan	Russell, William son of John, clerk, of Painswick
			Lane, William & Katharine 7 yrs feltmaker 40s
1/400	1630	25 Dec	Beard, Richard son of Andrew, tailor, of Gloucester
			Beard, Andrew, his father, & Mary 7 yrs tailor 1s

[*Four names, apparently of apprentices, are set out as though each was to begin an entry:*]
Cooke, William; Roberts, John; Gilbert, Roger; Hodgskins, William
[*In the margin beside the first three are the names of masters:*]
Teekell, Samuel, ropier; Lugg, William, tanner; Crumpe, Giles

---

[1] GBR B3/1 f 543 21 Jul 1630: Poor boys of the city to have £5 to bind them apprentice: John Ellis to Thomas Hall, pewterer, Witherstone Messinger to John Craker, John Rice to John Hopkins, joiner, John Bishopp to his father, cordwainer, John Tutley to John Mutley, pinmaker, William Mercer to Giles Mager, cordwainer.

	1631	9 Mar	Freeman, John son of James, feltmaker, of Gloucester
			Knight, Nathaniel & Joan 9 yrs chandler 12d
1/401		2 Mar	Rickettes, James son of James, yeoman, of Hardwicke
			Pedlingham, Thomas & Susannah 7 yrs saddler 2s 6d
		7 Apr	Badger, Giles son of Brian, cutler, of Gloucester
			Hayes, Richard & Eleanor 7 yrs from 10 Apr cutler 12d
		2 Apr	Faireley, William son of William, miller, dec'd, of Gloucester
			Sparkes, William 8 yrs from 25 Mar last [*no trade*]
		20 Apr	Bubb, William son of William, mercer, formerly of Gloucester
			Rowles, Robert 7 yrs from 25 Mar last apothecary
		2 May	*Thomas Elridge, late the apprentice of Robert Porter, dec'd, was today turned over to John Hopkins, joiner, for 2 years from 25 Mar last past and the rest of his term was forgiven him by Mrs Porter [See 1/346]*
			2 Jul 1631 It is recorded elsewhere that he was transferred to serve with Thomas Cooke for 2 years from 25 Mar last past
1/402		4 May	Gravestock, John son of George, weaver, dec'd, of Hempsted
			Hookham, Nathaniel & Elizabeth 7 yrs from 10 Apr last butcher 10s
		6 May	Frankis, Richard son of William, yeoman, of Barnwood
			Galle, John & Alice 8 yrs from 1 May last cordwainer 12d
		13 May	Pope, John son of Richard, yeoman, of Evington in parish of the Leigh
			Greene, Thomas 9 yrs from 29 May next mercer 3s 4d
		21 May	Harbert, Peter son of Peter, glover, of Oddington
			Collet, Edmund & Hester 7 yrs from 29 May next tanner 2s
		13 May	Collett, John son of Anthony, yeoman, of Slaughter
			Collett, Edmund & Hester 7 yrs from 25 Mar 1630 tanner 12d
1/403		31 Mar	Hill, Robert son of Thomas, goldsmith, of Gloucester
			Hill, Thomas, his father, 7 yrs from 25 Mar last goldsmith 2s 6d
		25 Mar	Walker, John son of William, tailor, dec'd, of Gloucester
			Cugley, Arthur & Elizabeth 8 yrs from 25 Mar 1631 wiredrawer 1s *pauper*
		28 Jun	Blackborne, Richard son of Henry, clerk, of Kempsford
			Ellis, Godfrey & Margaret 7 yrs from 24 Jun last baker 2s 6d
		4 Jul	Pace, Walter son of John, husbandman, of Maisemore
			Bishopp, Alexander 7 yrs from date of indenture cordwainer 2s 6d
		12 Jul	Longe, Thomas son of James, cordwainer, of Mitcheldean
			Tilsley, Philip & Anne 7 yrs from date of indenture [pinmaker] 12d
1/404		14 Jul	Mills, Thomas son of William, glover, of Purton, Wilts
			Stevens, James & Anne 7 yrs from 24 Jun last tanner £6 13s 4d
		4 Aug	Longden, Robert son of Thomas, yeoman, of Hawkesbury
			Scryven, John sr 8 yrs from 25 Jul last ironmonger 3s 4d

			Williams, John son of John, ropemaker, of Gloucester
			Williams, John, his father, & Joan 7 yrs from 3 Aug ropemaker 10s
			Holliday's money[1]
	—	—	Hayward, John son of Edward, hooper, of Gloucester
			Hayward, Edward, his father, & Joan 7 yrs from 3 Aug hooper 10s
	1631	5 Aug	Cuffe, Thomas son of John, cordwainer, dec'd, of Gloucester
			Beale, Geoffrey 9 yrs mercer 2s 6d
1/405		6 Aug	Elliottes, John son of Edward, tailor, of Gloucester
			Elliottes, Edward, his father, & Elizabeth 8 yrs from date of indenture tailor 10s
		12 Aug	Abbottes, Richard son of William, tailor, of Gloucester
			Freeme, John & Dorothy 7 yrs from date of indenture tailor 2s
	—	—	Kemp, John *as above bound to Edward Mason [See 1/382] was drowned 14 Aug 1631*
			Holliday's money
	1631	12 Aug	Williams, James son of Philip, husbandman, of Cwmyoy, Mon
			Clutterbook, Amity & Margaret 8 yrs from date of indenture tailor 12d
		17 Aug	Williams, John son of John, clerk, of Sevenhampton
			Lea, Francis & Isobel 8 yrs from 25 Jul cordwainer 2s
		29 May	Greene, William son of John, yeoman, of Churcham
			Greene, Augustine 7 yrs from date of indenture joiner 3s 4d
1/406		3 Sep	Wagstaffe, John son of Edward, brewer, of Gloucester
			Wagstaffe, Edward, his father, & Katharine 8 yrs brewer 10s
		25 Jul	Longe, John son of James, cordwainer, of Mitcheldean
			Tilsley, Philip & Anne 7 yrs pinmaker £5
		29 Sep	Irish, Roger
			Kiddon, Robert & Eleanor 12 yrs milliner 12d
			Placed by the mayor and burgesses
		1 Nov	Okey, Aaron son of John
			Lugg, John & Jane 9 yrs haberdasher 2s 6d
1/407			**Toby Bullock, mayor [1631–2]**
			Richard Window and Jasper Clutterbuck, sheriffs
	—	—	Robertes, William son of William, yeoman, of Harescombe
			Gwinne, Augustine & Alice 7 yrs cordwainer 2s 6d
			[*cf Appendix V*]
	1631	5 Nov	Hodgshon, Thomas son of Richard, victualler, formerly of Gloucester
			Keeble, Toby 8 yrs bodicemaker 2s 6d [*Holliday*][2]

---

[1] GBR B3/1 f 551 21 Jul 1631: To have £5 of Mr Holliday's money: John Kempe, [John] Williams, John Elliottes, [Thomas] Cuffe, [Richard] Abbottes. Henceforth none under the age of 14 to have alderman Holliday's money. Widow Crowdyer's son to have alderman Holiday's money next year.

[2] GBR B3/1 f 559 21 Jul 1632: To have £5 of Mr Holliday's money: John Crowdy, Thomas Hodgson, Thomas Morse, William Greene, William Stratford, — Blisse.

	1631	8 Oct	Clayfeild, Edward son of Samuel, clothier, dec'd, of Bisley Lugge, William & Eleanor 8 yrs tanner 5s
		8 Dec	Williams, Robert son of David, yeoman, of Monmouth, Mon Davis, William & Martha 8 yrs from 20 May last cooper 12d
1/408	—	25 Mar	Hill, Thomas son of John, labourer, of Gloucester Bulbricke, John & Anne 7 yrs from 23 Jan garter weaver 1s [*Repeating entry at 1/393*]
	1632	2 Feb	Smith, Thomas son of John, yeoman, dec'd, of Morville [MS Morfeild], Salop Lugg, William & Eleanor 9 yrs tanner 10s
		24 Feb	Hooke, Richard son of James, husbandman, of Sneedham in parish of Upton St Leonards Lane, William & Katharine 8 yrs feltmaker 1s
1/409		7 Mar	Helpe, Thomas son of John, tailor, of Worle, Som Taklinge, Thomas & Elizabeth 7 yrs feltmaker 5s
		12 Mar	Foanes, John son of Alice, widow, of Rudford Evens, William 7 yrs glover 16d
		10 Mar	Osborne, Thomas son of Thomas, husbandman, of Newent Tyther, Robert & Margaret 7 yrs tanner 20s
1/410		14 Mar	Wonnes, John son of Thomas, of Gloucester Pynke, John & Eleanor 10 yrs silkweaver 3s
		13 Mar	Smarte, John son of Eleanor, widow, of Gloucester Palmer, Edmund & Hester 7 yrs baker [*blank*] [*Repeated, with sum, at 1/413*]
		29 Mar	Colechester, Thomas son of Richard, husbandman, of Gloucester Edwards, John & Elizabeth 10 yrs haberdasher 1s and 2 suits
1/411		25 Mar	Tyler, Richard son of Richard, husbandman, of Bosbury, Herefs Eldridge, William & Hester 9 yrs silkweaver 3s 4d
		24 Apr	Baughe, John son of William, brewer, of Gloucester Hall, Roger & Margery 8 yrs cooper 10s and 2 suits
		20 Apr	Hye, Richard [*no mention of father*] labourer, of parish of Much Marcle, Herefs Deighton, John 7 yrs master surgeon 2 suits and 2 tunics
		1 May	Bryan, Robert son of Robert, smith, of Haresfield Carpenter, John & Bridget 7 yrs from 20 May next cordwainer 2s
1/412	1633	25 Mar	Hunt, John son of Thomas, husbandman, of Southgate Street, Gloucester Craker, John & Margaret 8 yrs weaver 5s
	1632	1 May	Chestro, George son of George, wheeler, of Cheltenham Bubb, Eleanor, widow, 7 yrs cordwainer 2s *1 May 1632: George Chestro put over by his own consent to serve his time with Toby Bubb, son of the said Eleanor, as appears by the endorsement on the back of the indenture. Before William Hill, alderman*

1/413	1632	13 Mar	Smarte, John son of Eleanor, widow, of Gloucester Palmer, Edmund & Hester 7 yrs baker 2s 6d [*Repeating entry at 1/410 with sum added*]
		10 May	Scudamore, William son of William, woollen draper, of Gloucester Grevill, Giles 8 yrs from 25 Mar last past mercer 5s
		9 Jun	Weale, Richard son of John Barrowe, Henry 7 yrs from 24 Jun next tailor 1s [*Crossed out & repeated at 1/414*]
1/414			Weale, Richard son of John, yeoman, of Highleadon Barrow, Henry & Anne 7 yrs from 24 Jun next tailor 12d [*Replacing entry at 1/413*]
		11 Jun	Falkner, Robert son of John, broadweaver, of Gloucester Tilsley, Philip & Anne 7 yrs from 24 Jun next [pinmaker] 3s 4d
		[*blank*]	Tomes, John son of John, [*blank*], dec'd, of Westbury Tayler, Richard & Eleanor 8 yrs from 29 Sep next mercer 2s 6d *Cancelled* [*Repeated, altered, at 1/415 & 416*]
1/415		4 Jul	Pace, Thomas son of Thomas, baker, formerly of Bulley Stallard, Anselm & Dorothy 7 yrs from 29 Sep next cooper 2s [*Repeated at 1/416*]
		23 Jul	Tomes, John son of John, yeoman, dec'd, of Westbury Taylor, Richard & Eleanor 8 yrs mercer *Cancelled* [*Repeating entry at 1/414. Repeated, altered, at 1/416*]
1/416		23 Jun	Tomes, John son of John, yeoman, formerly of Westbury Taylor, Richard & Eleanor 8 yrs from 29 Sep next mercer 2s 6d [*Replacing entries at 1/414 & 415*]
		4 Jul	Pace, Thomas son of Thomas, baker, dec'd, of Bulley Stallard, Anselm & Dorothy 7 yrs from 29 Sep next cooper 2s [*Repeating entry at 1/415*]
		25 Jul	House, John son of Charles, brewer, of Gloucester House, Charles, his father, & Joan 10 yrs brewer 5s
1/417		3 Jul	Osgood, Gabriel son of William, of Shipton Bellinger [MS Shipton], Hants Tailor, John & Mary 8 yrs mercer 2s 6d
		17 Jul	Gitto *alias* Jones, William son of John Gitto, dec'd, of Longtown in parish of Clodock [MS Cluttocke], Herefs Yarnold, Francis & Joan 7 yrs from 29 Jun last glover 2s
		21 Jul	Baker, Thomas son of William, husbandman, of Hasfield Hickman, John & Mary 9 yrs sievemaker 1s
1/418		25 Jul	Townesend, George son of Edward, yeoman, of Bisley Woodward, John 7 yrs blacksmith 3s 4d
		27 July	*Manning, Samuel, put over with his own consent to serve Henry Selwin of Gloucester, cordwainer, and Isobel for one whole year from 27 July 1632* [*See 1/348*]

	1632	23 Jul	Greene, William son of Simon, cooper, of Gloucester Greene, Simon, his father, & Elizabeth 8 yrs from 29 Jun last cooper 2s 6d *Holiday's money*
1/419			Stratford, William son of Arthur, tailor, of Gloucester Stratford, Arthur, his father, & Margaret 8 yrs from 24 Jun last tailor 2s 6d *Holidaye's money*
	1628	25 Dec	Crowdy, John son of John, carpenter, dec'd, of Gloucester Woodward, Thomas & Elizabeth 7 yrs blacksmith 3s 4d *Mr Holidaye's money in the time of Henry Browne, mayor*
	1632	10 Aug	Dowdswell *alias* Whiller, Henry son of Henry, dec'd, carpenter, of Gloucester Selwin, Henry & Isobel 7 yrs from 25 Jul last cordwainer 5s
1/420		24 Aug	Nelme, Richard son of Richard, husbandman, of Newent Nickolls, John & Joan 8 yrs tanner 5s
		24 Jun	Baker, William son of Richard, beilfounder, dec'd, of Gloucester Edwardes, Urian & Mary 7 yrs [*no trade*] 12d
		4 Sep	Thomas, Thomas son of Henry Hopkins, John 8 yrs 3s 4d [*Repeated & expanded at 1/421*]
1/421			Thomas, Thomas son of Henry Hopkins, John & Jane 8 yrs from 25 Dec next joiner 3s 4d [*Replacing entry at 1/420*]
		24 Jun	Packer, Daniel son of Richard Fletcher, Henry & Margery 9 yrs mercer 5s
		29 Sep	Grace, John son of William, cook, of Gloucester Hayse, John & Anne 7 yrs cordwainer 5s [*Repeated at 1/422*]
1/422			Grace, John son of William, cook, of Gloucester Hayes, John & Anne 7 yrs cordwainer 5s [*Repeating entry at 1/421*]
			Bubb, Thomas son of Thomas, mercer, of Stroud Fletcher, Henry & Margery 10 yrs mercer 5s
		24 Jun	Dobbes, John son of Lawrence, cordwainer, dec'd, of Gloucester Meroe, Richard & Joan 7 yrs feltmaker 3s 4d
1/423	1631	25 Dec	Gibbins, Thomas son of William, clerk, of Upton St Leonards Wilkins, Richard & Elizabeth 7 yrs wiredrawer 3s 4d
	1632	1 Apr	Devis, Thomas son of Richard, wiredrawer Wilkins, Richard & Elizabeth 7 yrs wiredrawer 12d
		29 Sep	Morse, Thomas son of John, yeoman, formerly of Twigworth Bishop, Thomas & Anne 8 yrs cordwainer 4s *Holyday*
		1 Nov	Garnsum, John son of Nicholas Gransum, of Painswick Lugg, Thomas & Anne 9 yrs tanner 10s [*Cancelled: see 1/425*]
1/424		29 Sep	Williams, Richard son of Richard, carpenter, of Gloucester Coke, Thomas & Katharine 7 yrs joiner 3s 4d

1/425			**John Brewster, mayor [1632–3]** **John Woodward and Henry Price, sheriffs 1632**

	1632	1 Nov	Gransum, John son of Nicholas, husbandman, of Painswick
			    Lugg, Thomas & Anne 9 yrs tanner 10s
			    [*Replacing entry at 1/423*]

			Mills, John son of William, glover, of Purton, Wilts Lugge, Lawrence & Mary 9 yrs tanner 40s
1/426		2 Nov	Moore, Jonathan son of Alexander, joiner, of Gloucester Tilsley, Philip & Anne 7 yrs from 24 Aug last pinmaker 6s 8d
		25 Dec	Hilli, Philip son of Thomas, maltster, of Tewkesbury Singleton, Lawrence & Joan 8 yrs woollen draper 10s
1/427		29 Sep	Hayward, John son of Thomas, cordwainer, of Sandhurst Sturmy, Robert & Eleanor 8 yrs glover 3s 4d
		25 Dec	White, Richard son of Richard, yeoman, dec'd, of Gloucester Mayer, Giles & Mary 8 yrs cordwainer 17s
		1 Nov	Crease, William son of John, labourer, dec'd, of Berkeley Gwynne, Augustine & Alice 10 yrs cordwainer 2s 6d
1/428			Robertes, William son of William, yeoman, of Harescombe Purlewent, John & Bridget 7 yrs baker 2s 6d [*cf Appendix V*]
		29 Sep	Blisse, John son of William, hosier, of Gloucester Keeble, Toby & [Mary] 7 yrs bodicemaker 20s
1/429	1633	1 Jan	Stoneum, Thomas son of Nicholas, yeoman, of Parton Wood, John & Elizabeth 10 yrs tanner 12d
	1632	25 Dec	Edwardes, William son of William, clothier, of Gloucester Phillips, John & Jane 7 yrs feltmaker 3s 4d
	1633	2 Feb	Coopie, John son of John, labourer, of Gloucester Tilsley, Philip & Anne 10 yrs pinmaker 2s
1/430			Coopie, Richard son of John, labourer, of Gloucester Tilsley, Philip & Anne 10 yrs pinmaker 2s
			Moris, John son of John, yeoman, of Hartpury Mason, Edward & Alice 8 yrs saddler 3s 4d
	1632	25 Dec	Sutor, Samuel son of John, yeoman, of Evesham [Worcs] Hill, John & Eleanor 7 yrs barber surgeon 5s
1/431	1633	16 Feb	Hobson, John son of Samuel, husbandman, of Brockworth Fowler, William & Abigail 9 yrs from 25 Mar next mercer 5s
		24 Feb	Boulton, Thomas son of William, yeoman, of Hannington, Wilts Poole, Thomas & Sarah 7 yrs barber surgeon 6s 8d
		11 Mar	Watters, John son of John, salter, of Gloucester Kinge, Christopher & Joan 8 yrs sealmaker 12d
1/432		6 Mar	Tully, Thomas son of Richard, cordwainer, of Gloucester Greene, Edward & Eleanor 7 yrs cordwainer 12d

	1633	25 Mar	Jones, Iorwerth son of Lewis, tanner, of Abergavenny, Mon
			Wood, John & Elizabeth 7 yrs tanner 5s
			Cole, Jasper son of Thomas, yeoman, of Bentham
			Davis, Roger & Elizabeth 7 yrs cordwainer 12d
1/433	1632	25 Dec	Goslin, Thomas son of John, dec'd, of Longney
			Thayre, Giles, gentleman 9 yrs [baker] 3s 4d
	1633	25 Mar	Browning, Edward son of Richard Browninge, gentleman, of Dursley
			Davis, Roger & Elizabeth 8 yrs cordwainer 2s 6d
		21 Apr	Taylor, Samuel son of Richard, tailor, of Over
			Jennings, William & Martha 9 yrs barber 10s
1/434	—	—	Fones, John son of John, clerk, dec'd, of Kemerton
			Sturmy, Edward & Blanche 7 yrs glover 6s 8d
	1633	25 Mar	Duglas, William son of William, joiner, of Gloucester
			Pincke, John & Alice 9 yrs baker 3s 4d
		24 Jun	Ferris, George son of George, yeoman, of Ashton Keynes, Wilts
			Gresham, Thomas & [blank] 9 yrs chandler 2s 6d
1/435		21 Apr	Smith, Thomas son of Robert, husbandman, of Hempsted
			Plummer, Robert & Christiane 9 yrs plumber 5s
		24 Jun	Hall, Walter son of Henry, beer brewer, dec'd, of Gloucester
			Kydden, Robert & Eleanor 7 yrs milliner 2s 6d
			Kemble, William son of John, husbandman, of Tirley
			Miles, Richard & Hannah 8 yrs weaver 10s
1/436		25 Jul	Elliotts, Henry son of Henry, tailor, of Gloucester
			Greene, Augustine & Alice 8 yrs joiner 40s *Mr Hollydaye*[1]
			Bramley, Leonard son of John, glover, of Gloucester
			Bramley, John, his father, & Sarah 8 yrs glover 5s
			Mr Holidayes money
			Harris, Edward son of Edward, tailor, of Gloucester
			Harris, Edward, his father, & Mary 7 yrs tailor 12d
			Mr Holidayes money
1/437			Hilliard, John son of Simon, silkweaver, of Gloucester
			Hilliard, Simon, his father, & Sybil 7 yrs silkweaver 12d
			Mr Hollidayes money
		24 Aug	Baggot, William son of John, gentleman, of Gloucester
			Till, William 7 yrs cutler 13s 4d *Mr Holidayes money*
		25 Jul	Hartland, Edward son of Thomas, carpenter, of Westbury
			Davis, Richard & Katharine 8 yrs glover 12d
1/438			Etkins, Robert son of John Atkins, baker, of Gloucester
			Paynter, Thomas & Jane 7 yrs butcher 10s *Mr Holidayes money*

---

[1] GBR B3/2 p 11 22 Jul 1633: To have £5 of Mr Holliday's money: William Baggot son of John, gentleman, Edward Harris son of Edward, tailor, Leonard Bromley son of John, glover, John Hillary son of Simon, silkweaver, Henry Elliottes son of Henry, tailor, Robert Atkins son of John, baker.

	1633 24 Aug	Greene, John son of Richard, tailor, of the Leigh
		Lea, Francis & Isobel 7 yrs cordwainer 2s
	1632 25 Dec	Evans, Thomas son of Augustine, yeoman, of Tirley
		Bishoppe, Robert & Mary 7 yrs beer brewer 5s
1/439	1633 29 Sep	Thomas, William son of Morgan, feltmaker, of Haverfordwest, Pembs
		Busell *alias* Tackley, Thomas & Elizabeth 7 yrs feltmaker 20s
		Barnes, William son of William, dec'd, of Gloucester
		Okey, Anne, widow, 7 yrs baker 5s
1/440	21 Apr	Rickes, John son of Richard, weaver, of Gloucester
		Tarne, Miles & Sarah 9 yrs glover 5s

| 1/441 | | **John Webb, mayor [1633–4]** |
| | | **Nathaniel Hedges and Richard Harward, sheriffs** |

	1633 30 Nov	Knowles, Richard son of John, broadweaver, dec'd, of Newent
		Hooper, John & Anne 7 yrs vintner 2s 6d
	25 Dec	Steephens, James son of James Stephens, yeoman, dec'd, of Corse
		Sawcombe, John & Joan 9 yrs blacksmith 2s 6d
1/442		Bennet, Jesse son of Anthony, broadweaver, of Gloucester
		Russell, William & Elizabeth [*no term*] tailor 2s 6d
	1 Nov	Knight, Henry son of Henry, innholder, of Gloucester
		Mathewes, Thomas [*no term*] mercer 2s 6d
	25 Dec	Owen, Gabriel son of John, gentleman, dec'd, of Cardiff, Glam
		Taylor, Richard & Joan 8 yrs cordwainer 12d
1/443	1 Nov	Fewterel, William son of William, tailor, of Gloucester
		Fewterel, William, his father, & Margaret 7 yrs tailor 2s 6d
		Clifford, Richard son of Richard, gentleman, of Arlingham
		Heath, Thomas & Anne [*no term*] pewterer 10s
	1630 21 Sep	Woodward, Richard son of John, blacksmith, of Mathon, Worcs
		Wills, James 7 yrs tanner 40s and 2 suits of apparel [*Written in English*]
1/444	1633 21 Jul	Taylor, John son of Roger, yeoman, of Westbury
		Hiron, Humphrey jr & Margaret 7 yrs chandler 2s 6d
	1634 2 Feb	Grymes, Thomas son of Thomas, cordwainer, of Shenington
		Pettipher, Timothy & Anne 8 yrs cordwainer 3s 4d
	1633 21 Sep	Dunn, Richard son of Edward Dunne, yeoman, of Hempsted
		Gale, John & Alice 7 yrs cordwainer 2s 6d
1/445	1634 25 Mar	Wyer, Francis son of Leonard, labourer, of Saul
		Nich[ols] John & Joan 8 yrs tanner 40s
	1633 30 Nov	Barker, John son of John, cordwainer, of Gloucester
		Tilsley, [Philip] & Anne 7 yrs pinmaker 2s 6d

| | 1633 25 Dec | Beeke, John son of Thomas, yeoman, of Gloucester |
| | | Tilsley, [Philip] & Anne 8 yrs pinmaker 2s 6d |

1/446 1634 24 Feb Clarver, Matthew son of Richard, butcher, of Corse
                    Kinge, John & Anne 8 yrs glover 18d

       25 Mar Ellietts, Jasper son of Richard, yeoman, of Badgeworth
               Porter, Robert & Mary 9 yrs mercer 3s 4d

               Taylor, William son of Nicholas, yeoman, of Farmington
               Bearde, Andrew & Mary 8 yrs tailor 2s 6d

1/447   6 Apr Michell, George son of Richard, painter, of Gloucester
               Sparrowhawke, Robert & Joan 8 yrs garter weaver 5s [*cf Appendix V*]

       1633 29 Sep Carpenter, William son of Richard, farmer, of Eldersfield, Worcs
                    Dowsing, John & Sybil 7 yrs blacksmith 12d

1/448   25 Dec Stowell, William son of William, clothier, of Mitcheldean
                Tilsley, Philip & Anne 7 yrs pinmaker 5s

       1634 25 Mar Symondes, John son of John, brewer, of Gloucester
                    Tilsley, Philip & Anne 7 yrs pinmaker 2s 6d

1/449   6 Apr Elsmore, Joseph son of Robert, cordwainer, of Longhope
               Tilsley, Philip & Anne 7 yrs pinmaker 10s

       25 May Harris, James son of William, yeoman, of Whaddon
               Burrowes, Nathaniel 8 yrs cordwainer 3s 4d

       24 Jun Robertes, Henry son of Henry, brazier, of Berkeley
               Surman, John 8 yrs glover 2s 6d

1/450   Mathewes, Nicholas son of Richard, labourer, of Mitcheldean
               Tilsley, Philip & Anne 7 yrs pinmaker 5s

               Butter, Richard son of Thomas, basket maker, of Hartpury
               Wilkins, Richard [blank] wiredrawer [blank]

1/451   25 Dec Beale, Thomas son of Geoffrey, mercer, of Gloucester
                Beale, Geoffrey, his father, & Joan 8 yrs mercer 20s *fee given*

       25 May Whitfeild, Richard son of Richard, cordwainer, of Gloucester
               Broade, William & Elizabeth 8 yrs [baker] 5s

       25 Jul Jenkins, John son of Robert, miller, dec'd, of Gloucester
               Witcombe, John & Anne 8 yrs cordwainer 3s 4d

1/452   Lugg, Thomas son of Thomas, tanner, of Gloucester
               Lugg, Thomas, his father, & Anne 8 yrs tanner 5s *Mr Holliday*[1]

               Newman, John son of William, mercer, of Gloucester
               Newman, William, his father, & Alice 8 yrs mercer 5s *Mr Hollyday*

               Hughes, Timothy son of Richard, butcher, of Gloucester
               Hughes, Richard, his father, & Joan 8 yrs butcher 5s *Mr Hollyday*

---

[1] GBR B3/2 p 29 22 Jul 1634: To have £5 of Mr Holliday's money: William Maddocke son of [blank], Thomas Lugg son of Thomas, tanner, Timothy Hughes son of Richard, butcher, Henry Hayes son of Henry, clothworker, John Newman son of William, mercer, Richard Cowley son of Richard, blacksmith.

1/453	1634	25 Jul	Hayes, Henry son of Henry, clothworker, of Gloucester Wintle, Richard & Alice 7 yrs cordwainer 5s *Mr Hollyday*
			Smith, Brice son of John, yeoman, of Quedgeley Bubb, Toby & Mary 8 yrs cordwainer 2s 6d
			Cowley, Richard son of Richard, blacksmith, of Gloucester Cowley, Richard, his father, & Eleanor 8 yrs blacksmith 5s *Mr Hollyday*
1/454			Onyon, Thomas son of Humphrey, sievemaker, of Gloucester Hale, William 9 yrs silkweaver 12d
	1633	25 Dec	Iles, Henry son of Henry, weaver, of South Cerney Woodward, John & [*blank*] 7 yrs blacksmith 5s
	1634	24 Aug	Badger, Jeremiah son of Brian, cutler, of Gloucester Miles, Richard & Anne 8 yrs weaver 5s [*cf Appendix V*]
1/455		25 Jul	Hayward, John son of John, farmer, of Over Sturmy, Robert & Eleanor 7 yrs glover 3s 4d
	—	25 Mar	Angell, Robert son of Luke, yeoman, of St Davids, Pembs Haies, Christopher & Joan 7 yrs glazier 6s 8d
	1634	29 Sep	Suffeild, Henry son of Thomas, cook, of Gloucester Hoare, William & Margaret 7 yrs glover 6s 8d
1/456		25 Jul	Bond, Richard son of Richard, butcher, of Stroud Cooke, Thomas & Margaret 8 yrs chandler 2s 6d
		25 May	Collett, Anthony son of Anthony, farmer, of Slaughter Palmer, Edward & Hester 7 yrs baker 5s
			Knight, Robert son of Edward, yeoman, of Eastington Knight, Nathaniel & Joan 7 yrs chandler 5s
1/457		29 Sep	Gilbert, Lewis son of Henry, yeoman, of Whaddon Gilbert, Henry & [*blank*] 7 yrs cordwainer 3s 4d
	1635	25 Mar	Marsh, William son of Henry, tanner, of Thornbury Lycense, Daniel & [*blank*] 7 yrs woollen draper 3s 4d
	1634	25 May	Byford, John son of Nicholas, tanner, of Tibberton Warde, Philip & Mary 7 yrs cordwainer 3s 4d
1/458		6 Apr	Lugg, Peter son of Peter, haberdasher, of Gloucester Fowler, William & Abigail 9 yrs mercer 6s 8d
		29 Sep	Angell, Thomas son of Luke, yeoman, of St Davids, Herefs [*recte* Pembs] Abbot, Bernard & Elizabeth 7 yrs tailor 6s 8d [*Cancelled: see 1/466*]
		25 May	Atkyns, Abraham son of Thomas, gentleman, of Upton St Leonards Lugg, John & Jane 11 yrs haberdasher 10s
1/459			**John Browne, mayor [1634–5]** **Charles Hoare and Lawrence Singleton, sheriffs**
	1634	21 Dec	Colechester, Edward son of Richard, gentleman, of Gloucester Frannckombe, Henry & [*blank*] 7 yrs woollen draper 2s 6d

| | 1635 | 2 Feb | Parish, John son of Edward, skinner, dec'd, of Gloucester |
| | | | Fewterel, William & Margaret 7 yrs tailor 2s 6d *fee given* |

1/460

Heming, Thomas son of Henry
Eldridg, Thomas & Mary 7 yrs joiner 2s 6d

Whitorne, Walter son of Walter, yeoman, of Charleton
Jordan, John & Mary 7 yrs baker 12d

1634 25 Dec Cur, Robert son of Henry, yeoman, of Down Ampney
Curr, Henry & Sarah 7 yrs baker 2s 6d
[*Dated* All Saints [1 Nov], *deleted*]

1635 29 Sep Ricketts, Edward son of James, yeoman, of Hardwicke
Greene, Richard & Cristel 8 yrs baker 3s 4d

1/461   2 Feb Bridger, Samuel son of Arthur, yeoman, of Slimbridge
Saule, William 7 yrs cordwainer 2s 6d

29 Sep Symes, Robert son of John, yeoman, dec'd, of the Leigh
Payne, Robert & Elizabeth 10 yrs mercer 3s 4d

1634 25 Dec Chadd, William son of Alice, spinster, of Down Hatherley
Tilsley, Philip & Anne 16 yrs pinmaker 2s 6d

1635 25 Dec Massinger, William son of Witherston, draper, dec'd, of Brookthorpe
Cumalyn, James & Jane [*no term*] apothecary

1/462   25 Mar [*no name*]
Lugg, William & Eleanor 7 yrs tanner 6s 8d

29 Mar Parlor, William son of John, yeoman, of English Bicknor
Jordan, John & Eleanor 7 yrs baker 2s 6d

Chapman, James son of Thomas, smith, of Whaddon
Beard, William & Elizabeth 8 yrs tailor 2s 6d

1/463   25 Apr Willmore, William son of William, farmer, of Newent
Tither, Robert & Margaret [*no term*] tanner 3s 4d

—   —   Graffstocke, John son of [*blank*], of Hempsted
Strawford, Walter & Joan [*no term*] butcher

1635 17 May Dowle, Clement son of James, gentleman, of Bagendon
Wise, Denis & Hephzibah 9 yrs mercer 10s

24 Jun Baldwin, Roland son of William, yeoman, of Gloucester
Jordan, William & Jane 8 yrs silkweaver

1/464 17 May Woodward, John son of John, gentleman, of Gloucester
Payne, Robert & Elizabeth 8 yrs mercer 3s 4d

29 Sep Grevill, Edward son of Giles, gentleman, dec'd, of Charlton Kings
Grevill, Giles 8 yrs mercer [*blank*]

17 May Trippet, Thomas son of Charles, yeoman, of Awre
Taylor, Richard & Eleanor 8 yrs mercer 3s 4d

1634 29 Sep Merret, Thomas son of Richard, yeoman, of Whaddon
Harris, Walter & [*blank*] 8 yrs cordwainer 3s 4d
John Webb, mayor

1/465	1634	1 Nov	Haynes, James son of James, farmer, of Skenfrith, Mon Davis, William & Martha 8 yrs cooper 12d *John Browne mayor*
	1635	29 Mar	Cowles, Richard son of John, farmer, of Gloucester Cowles, Robert & Blanche 8 yrs butcher 5s
		29 Jun	Bubb, William son of Richard, farmer, of 'Elston' [Elkstone?] Eaton, Robert & Margery 7 yrs cordwainer 2s 6d
		29 Mar	Allanson, John son of Thomas, clerk, of Hasfield Taylor, John & Mary 8 yrs mercer 2s 6d
1/466	1634	1 Nov	Angell, Thomas son of Luke, yeoman, of St Davids, Pembs Abbotts, Bernard & Elizabeth 7 yrs tailor 6s 8d [*Replacing entry at 1/458*]
	1635	25 Jul	Marten, Miles son of John, clerk, of Brimpsfield Robins, James 10 yrs mercer 10s
		17 May	Hale, Miles son of Walter, farmer, of Gloucester Dunn, Thomas & Mary [*no term*] barber surgeon 2s 6d
1/467		24 Aug	Greene, John son of Richard, glover, of Gloucester Taylor, James & Margaret 7 yrs cordwainer 2s 6d *Holliday's money fee given*[1]
			Jones, Giles son of John, innholder, of Gloucester Townsend, Christopher & Elizabeth 8 yrs barber surgeon 3s 4d
			Russell, William son of William, tailor, of Gloucester Saule, William 7 yrs cordwainer [3s 4d *deleted*] 2s *Mr Hollidayes money*
1/468			Sprint, Zachariah son of John, clerk, dec'd, of Thornbury Nelme, John & Rachel 9 yrs mercer 2s 6d
			Jones, James son of William, tailor, of Gloucester Jones, William, his father, 7 yrs tailor 2s 6d *Mr Holliday*
		29 Sep	Allanson, Richard son of Thomas, clerk, of Hasfield Gresham, Thomas & Joan 9 yrs chandler [*blank*]
1/469			Bozley, Richard son of Richard, yeoman, of Churchdown Lane, William & Katharine 7 yrs feltmaker 12d [*Repeated, altered, at 1/509*]
			White, Anthony son of Anthony, farmer, of Huntley Taylor, Richard & Joan 8 yrs cordwainer 2s 6d
			Cleevly, Robert son of William, yeoman, of Charlton Kings Cooke, Richard & Eleanor 8 yrs chandler 2s 6d
1/470			Parker, Thomas son of John, yeoman, of Hampton Lovett, Worcs Pinke, John & Alice 8 yrs baker 12d

---

[1] GBR B3/2 p 40 21 Jul 1635: To have £5 of Mr Holliday's money: Henry Suffeild son of Thomas, cook, James Jones son of William, tailor, John Green son of Richard, William Russell son of William, tailor, Richard Lugg son of [*blank*], tanner, Gilbert Moore son of Thomas.

| | 1635 | 24 Jun | Webb, Edward son of John, yeoman, of Longford
Freeman, James & Alice 8 yrs feltmaker 12d |
| | | 25 Jul | Harris, Humphrey son of John, yeoman, of Whaddon
Harris, Walter & [blank] 7 yrs cordwainer 12d |

1/471 **William Hill, mayor [1635–6]**
Nicholas Webbe and John Nelme, sheriffs

    1635 1 Nov Barton, Michael son of Thomas, farmer, of Farmington
                      Bird, Andrew & Mary 8 yrs tailor 12d

    1636 6 Jan [blank], William son of William, farmer, of Stanton
                      Hooper, John & Anne 7 yrs vintner 5s

1/472 1635 25 Dec Payne, Thomas son of Robert, turner, of Gloucester
                            Kiddon, Charles & Mary 8 yrs milliner 2s 6d *pauper* [*fee*] *given*

    1636 25 Mar Allen, Thomas son of Thomas, yeoman, of Oddington
                      Collet, Edmund & Hester 7 yrs tanner 5s

          17 Apr Barret, Henry son of Thomas, cutler, of Gloucester
                  Barret, Thomas, his father, & Mary 7 yrs cutler 5s

1/473   Solas, Francis son of Richard, farmer, of Brimpsfield
                      Hill, John & Eleanor 7 yrs barber surgeon 2s 6d

                    Mudwell, Robert son of William, dec'd, of Gloucester
                    Bond, John & Frances 7 yrs cordwainer 2s 6d [*cf Appendix V*]

                    Symes, Thomas son of John, yeoman, of the Leigh
                    Eckley, Thomas & Elizabeth 8 yrs chandler 3s 4d

1/474   Massinger, Witherston son of Witherston, clerk, dec'd, of Gloucester
                    [blank] 7 yrs baker 2s 6d [*See complete entry at 1/494*]

          24 May Garner, Richard son of Isaac, clothier, of Godalming, Surrey
                  Dunne, Nathaniel 8 yrs tailor 2s 6d

          5 Jun Niblet, Richard son of John, yeoman, of Brookthorpe
                  Fewterel, William & Margaret 7 yrs tailor 2s 6d

1/475   22 Jun Bennet, Denis son of Anthony, clothier, of Gloucester
                  Carpenter, John & Bridget 8 yrs cordwainer 3s 4d

          24 Jul Williams, John son of Edward, farmer, of Newquay, Mon
                  Tither, Robert & Margaret 7 yrs tanner 5s

          29 Jun Alridge, Thomas son of Samuel, broadweaver, of Stroud
                  Beard, William & Elizabeth 8 yrs tailor 2s 6d

1/476   25 Jul Elliottes, Edward son of Henry, tailor, of Gloucester
                  Barnes, John & Joan 8 yrs cordwainer 10s *Mr Hollidaye's money*[1]

                    Higgins, John son of Thomas, carpenter, of Gloucester
                    Tayler, Richard & Joan 7 yrs [mercer] 2s 6d

---

[1] GBR B3/2 p 60 21 Jul 1636: To have £5 of Mr Holliday's money: John Bishop son of Robert, Edward Elliotts son of Edward, tailor, Nathaniel Teekell son of Samuel, ropier, Edward Charleton son of Edward, wiredrawer, Thomas Jones son of Thomas, victualler, Richard Mason son of Richard, silkweaver.

	1636	25 Jul	Jones, Thomas son of Thomas, victualler, of Gloucester
			Pitt, Samuel & Eleanor 7 yrs pinmaker 12d *Mr Holliday*
1/477		24 Jun	Tayloe, Thomas son of Thomas, clothier, of Gloucester
			Dewxell, John & Frances 8 yrs mercer 2s 6d
		25 Jul	Charleton, Edward son of Edward, wiredrawer, of Gloucester
			Charleton, Edward, his father, & Alice 7 yrs wiredrawer 2s 6d *Mr Holiday's money*
		24 Jul	Haynes, John son of Thomas, weaver, of Barton Street, Gloucester
			Cugley, John & Elizabeth 8 yrs cardmaker 2s 6d
1/478		25 Jul	Mason, John son of Richard, silkweaver, of Gloucester
			Wintle, Richard & Alice 7 yrs cordwainer 2s 6d *Mr Holliday*
		—	Teeckle, Nathaniel son of Samuel Teekle, ropemaker, of Gloucester
			Teeckle, Samuel, his father 7 yrs ropemaker [*Incomplete*]
		24 Aug	Mower, John son of John, yeoman, of Painswick
			Packer, William & Dorothy 8 yrs tanner 5s
		23 Sep	Scrivener, John son of Hugh, doctor of medicine, of Dorchester, Dorset
			Gresham, Thomas & Joan 8 yrs chandler 2s 6d
1/479		29 Sep	Edwards, Jeremiah son of Thomas, yeoman, of Westbury
			Reeve, William & Jane [*no term*] cordwainer 3s 4d
		29 Sep	Younge, Thomas son of John, yeoman, of Bulley
			Humfryes, Samuel & [*blank*] [*no term*] tailor 12d
		5 Jun	Lea, Henry son of Henry, yeoman, of Gloucester
			Lea, Francis & [*blank*] [*no term*] cordwainer 12d
		29 Sep	Mason, Thomas son of Edward, saddler, of Gloucester
			Mason, Edward, his father, & Alice 7 yrs saddler 10s

1/480			**William Lugg, mayor [1636–7]** **Edward Wagstaffe and James Wood, sheriffs**
	1636	18 Oct	Heming, Henry son of Henry, yeoman, of Over
			Hassington, Henry & Alice 7 yrs silkweaver 5s
		1 Nov	Smith, Thomas son of Thomas, farmer, of Birdlip
			Stephens, James & Anne [*no term*] tanner 2s 6d
		25 Dec	Aphowell, Thomas son of William, dec'd, of Sollers Hope, Herefs
			Symonds, Richard & Katharine [*no term*] [glover] 12d
1/481	1637	16 Jan	Seaborne, John son of Henry, cordwainer, of Hereford
			Smith, William & Margaret 7 yrs feltmaker 2s
		—	Taylor, William son of Anthony, tanner, of Turkdean
			Smith, William [*Incomplete*]

	1636 12 Nov	Bozley, John son of Richard, farmer, dec'd, of Churchdown Lane, William & Katharine 7 yrs feltmaker 12d
		Because the said Bozley was a married man and above 27 years of age when he was bound, it was agreed by the aldermen on 23 Mar 1637 that he should be discharged from his apprenticeship at the next sessions and lose the benefit of being a freeman
1/482	1637 2 Feb	Flucke, Thomas son of William, farmer, of Leckhampton [MS Leckington] Lugg, William, mayor of the city of Gloucester, & Eleanor [*no term*] tanner 3s 4d
	1636 25 Dec	Chambers, John son of John, dec'd, of Gloucester Taylor, John & Mary 8 yrs mercer 2s 6d
	1 Nov	Robins, Maurice son of Thomas, glover, of Evesham [Worcs] Lugg, Lawrence & Mary 9 yrs tanner 5s
	25 Dec	Ingley, William son of Thomas, milliner, of Gloucester Linckinholt, John & Sarah 7 yrs wiredrawer 2s 6d
1/483	1637 25 Mar	Bellamy, William son of Guy, dyer, of Ross, Herefs Gresham, Thomas & Joan 8 yrs chandler 2s 6d
	9 Apr	Elmes, Robert son of John, tailor, of Gloucester Hodges, Christopher & [*blank*] 8 yrs mercer 5s
		Warmington, Thomas son of John, yeoman, of Tirley Hall, Roger & Margery 7 yrs cooper 12d
1/484		Groving, John son of Richard, tailor, of Humber, Herefs Price, John & Anne [*no term*] vintner 20s
		Badger, Jeremiah son of Brian, cutler, of Gloucester Craker, John & Margaret [*no term*] weaver 2s 6d [*cf Appendix V*]
1/485	1 May	Webb, Robert son of Robert, yeoman, of Oxenton Gale, John & Alice 7 yrs cordwainer 2s 6d
	18 May	Caleowe, Arthur son of William, gentleman, of Mitcheldean Sturmy, Robert jr & Elizabeth 7 yrs glover 2s 6d
	28 May	Freeman, Samuel son of William, yeoman, formerly of Hardwicke Willis, James & Jane 7 yrs tanner 20s
		Webb, William son of Thomas, dyer, of Tytherington Hobbs, John & Cecily 8 yrs feltmaker 2s 6d
1/486	1636 1 Nov	Gelf, Thomas son of William, yeoman, of Hartpury Herd, Richard 7 yrs baker 2s 6d
	1637 6 Jan	Suckley, Geoffrey son of Roland, gentleman, of Hartpury Clarke, William & Joan 8 yrs mercer 2s 6d
	24 Jun	Pace, William son of John, yeoman, of Maisemore Springe, Lewis & Isabel 7 yrs joiner 5s
1/487	6 Jan	Cawson, Stephen son of Henry, weaver, of Gloucester Brewster, John, alderman, & Elizabeth 8 yrs maltster 3s 4d

	1637 24 Jun	Blicke, William son of John, yeoman, dec'd, of Somerford, Wilts Beale, Geoffrey [*no term*] mercer 10s
	29 Jun	Lawrence, Robert son of George, yeoman, of Cirencester Eldridge, Thomas & Mary [*no term*] joiner 2s 6d
1/488	1 May	Beard, Henry son of Richard, alderman, of Gloucester Wise, Denis & Hephzibah 9 yrs mercer 6s 8d
	29 Jun	Floucke, Edward son of John, yeoman, of Deerhurst Bishop, Thomas & Anne 9 yrs cordwainer 2s 6d
1/489	25 Jul	Lane, John son of John, baker, of Gloucester [*illegible*] John & Alice 7 yrs cutler 2s 6d *Mr Holiday's money*[1]
		Tyler, Thomas son of John, tailor, dec'd, of Gloucester Tyler, Alice, his mother, 7 yrs [tailor] 10s
		Vaughan, Thomas son of Richard sr, joiner, of Gloucester Vaughan, Richard, his father, & Isobel 7 yrs joiner 40s *Mr Hollidaye's money*
1/490		Wilkins, John son of Richard, wiredrawer, of Gloucester Wilkins, Richard, his father, & Elizabeth 7 yrs wiredrawer 40s *Mr Holiday's money*
		Little, Thomas son of John, cordwainer, of Gloucester Skinner, Robert & Anne [*no term*] glover, 3s 4d
	29 Jun	Pyckering, Luke son of William Pyckeringe, yeoman, of Bourton on the Hill Smyth, William & Margaret 8 yrs feltmaker 3s 4d
1/491	25 Jul	Mudwell, Robert son of William, feltmaker, of Gloucester S[myth] William & Margaret 7 yrs feltmaker 2s 6d [*cf Appendix V*]
	10 Aug	Davis, David son of James, broadweaver, of Gloucester Payne, John & Margaret 7 yrs feltmaker 20s
	24 Aug	Hall, John son of John, baker, of Kemble Lugg, Lawrence & Mary [*no term*] tanner 20s
1/492		Blisse, Nathaniel son of Thomas, weaver, of Gloucester Blisse, Thomas, his father, & Margaret 7 yrs weaver 5s
	25 Jul	Beard, John son of Thomas, mercer, of Stroud Powell, Joan 10 yrs silkweaver 12d *fee given by master*
	24 Aug	Smyth, William son of Thomas, yeoman, of Quedgeley Barnes, John & Joan 7 yrs cordwainer 2s 6d
1/493		Watts, Thomas son of Thomas, yeoman, of [*illegible; page torn*] Glos Little, Thomas & Anne 7 yrs ch[*illegible – chandler?*] 2s 6d

[1] GBR B3/2 p 80 21 Jul 1637: To have £5 of Mr Holliday's money: Thomas Vaughan son of Richard, joiner, John Wilkins son of Richard, wiredrawer, John Lane son of John, baker, Nathaniel Blisse son of Thomas, weaver, John Seyer son of John, tanner, Joseph Bayliss son of John, glover.

	1637	29 Sep	Syer, John son of John, tanner, of Gloucester Teakle, Samuel & Joan 7 yrs ropemaker 3s 4d *Mr Holliday*
		[blank]	Nash, Richard son of Anselm, yeoman, of Gloucester Window, Richard & Margaret 8 yrs chandler 2s 6d
1/494		29 Sep	Messinger, Witherstone son of Witherstone, clerk, of Brookthorpe Ellis, Godfrey & Margaret 7 yrs baker 2s 6d [*Replacing entry at 1/474*]
			Hancox, George son of Richard, innholder, of Pershore, Worcs Lea, Francis & Isabel 7 yrs cordwainer 2s 6d
			Vynor, Michael son of Thomas, yeoman, of Hucclecote Evans, Samuel & Elizabeth 8 yrs pinmaker 3s 4d
1/495	—	1 Nov	Collier, Henry son of [*blank*], farmer, of Lydiard Millicent [MS North Lydiard], Wilts Tither, Robert & Margaret tanner [*Incomplete & deleted: see 1/497*]
	1637	1 Nov	Jones, Thomas son of Hugh, labourer, of Gloucester Lugge, William & Eleanor 10 yrs tanner 3s 4d
		25 Jul	Bristoll, Henry son of Henry, farmer, of Great Witcombe Davis, William & Martha [*blank*] cooper 2s 6d
1/496		29 Sep	Colchester, Edward son of Richard, yeoman, of Forthampton Pearce, Thomas & Hester 9 yrs mercer 2s 6d

1/497			**William Singleton, mayor [1637–8]** **Anthony Edwardes and Richard Grymes, sheriffs**
	1637	1 Nov	Collier, Henry son of [*blank*], farmer, of Lydiard Millicent [MS North Lydiard], Wilts Tither, Robert & Margaret 7 yrs tanner 20s [*Replacing entry at 1/495*]
			Carpenter, Matthew son of Matthew, farmer, of Tirley Symondes, Nathaniel & Anne 7 yrs blacksmith 6s
	1638	6 Jan	Hergest, John son of Thomas, carpenter, of Lyonshall [MS Lynnolls], Herefs Nicholls, John & Joan 8 yrs tanner 5s
1/498	1637	1 Nov	Singleton, John son of William, butcher, of Longhope Lugg, William & Eleanor 7 yrs tanner 10s
	1638	2 Feb	Steedman, Richard son of William, gentleman, dec'd, of Gloucester Poole, Thomas & Sarah 7 yrs barber surgeon 2s 6d
		25 Mar	Low, Edward son of John Lowe, yeoman, dec'd, of Barnwood Chapman, Thomas & [*blank*] [*no term*] tailor 12d
1/499		2 Feb	Steedman, John son of William, gentleman, dec'd, of Gloucester Craker, John & Margaret 7 yrs weaver 2s 6d
		25 Mar	Blanchet, John son of John, yeoman, of Gloucester Cugley, Arthur & Elizabeth 7 yrs wiredrawer 3s 4d *fee given*

	1638	3 Apr	Kinne, Samuel son of Edward, vintner, of Stroud
			Eckly, Thomas & Elizabeth 7 yrs chandler 2s 6d
		25 Mar	Beale, John son of John, yeoman, of Chaceley, Worcs
			Lugg, Thomas & Mary 9 yrs haberdasher 10s
1/500		1 May	Roberts, John son of William, tailor, of city of Bristol
			Warwick, William & Anne [*no term*] vintner
		25 Mar	Driver, Anthony son of Matthew, sailor, dec'd, of Gloucester
			Mathewes, Henry & Joan [*no term*] tailor 12d
		24 Jun	Chadd, William son of Eleanor, spinster, of Down Hatherley
			Pitt, Robert & Anne [*no term*] pinmaker 12d *pauper*
1/501		25 Jul	Walker *alias* Weaver, Edward son of John
			Phelps, William & Margaret 8 yrs cordwainer 2s 6d
			Mr Holliday's money[1]
			Hassington, Henry son of Henry, silkweaver, of Gloucester
			Hassington, Henry, his father, & Alice 7 yrs silkweaver 2s 6d
			Mr Holliday's money
		24 Aug	Keene, John son of John, brewer, of Gloucester
			Keene, John, his father, & Susannah 7 yrs brewer 5s
1/502		25 Jul	Bishop, Alexander son of Thomas, cordwainer, of Gloucester
			Bishop, Thomas, his father, & Anne [*no term*] cordwainer 12d
			Mr Hollidaye's money
		24 Aug	Adams, John son of John, weaver, formerly of Gloucester
			Pearce, Giles of Kingsholm, & Eleanor 7 yrs miller 2s 6d
			Mr Hollydaye's money
		24 Jun	Bowher, William son of Thomas, smith, of Laugharne, Carms
			Massey, Richard & Joan 7 yrs feltmaker 3s 4d
1/503	—	1 Nov	Winston, John son of Henry, yeoman, of Witcombe
			Davis, William & Martha [*no term*] cooper
			[*Incomplete: see 1/505*]
	1638	25 Mar	Lugg, Jasper son of Jasper, tanner, of Gloucester
			Lugg, Jasper, his father, & Anne 7 yrs tanner 3s 4d
1/504			**William Caple, mayor [1638–9]**
			John Maddock and Henry Cugley, sheriffs and bailiffs
	1638	1 Nov	Wyneatt, John son of Henry, farmer, dec'd, of Kempley
			Brethers, Robert & Alice 7 yrs cardmaker 20s

---

[1] GBR B3/2 p 93 21 Jul 1638: To have £5 of Mr Holliday's money: Edward Walker *alias* Weaver son of John, chandler, dec'd, John Beard son of Thomas late of the city, mercer, Henry Hassington son of Henry, silkweaver, [Alexander] Bishop son of Thomas, cordwainer, [John] Addams, John Fleming son of John
  ibid p 107 7 Dec 1638: Simon Pryor to take John Fleminge apprentice from Michaelmas next and to have £5 of Mr Holliday's money if he seals a bond for the repayment of it to the mayor if John should die before Michaelmas.

1/505	1638	1 Nov	Winston, John son of Henry, yeoman, of Witcombe

1/505 1638 1 Nov Winston, John son of Henry, yeoman, of Witcombe
Davis, William & Martha 8 yrs cooper 2s 6d [*Replacing entry at 1/503*]

Sparks, Richard son of John, labourer, of Witcombe
Davis, William & Martha 8 yrs cooper 2s 6d *40s given by Richard Sparks his kinsman by the appointment of the justices*

25 Dec Tayler, Thomas son of Richard, yeoman, of Gloucester
Till, Richard & [*blank*] 7 yrs cutler 3s 4d

1/506 1639 6 Jan Stephens, James son of Henry, blacksmith, of Minster Lovell, Oxon
Wantner, Margaret, widow, 8 yrs [blacksmith] 3s 4d

2 Feb Organ, Henry son of Thomas, weaver, of Harescombe in parish of Haresfield
Lugg, Jasper & Anne 7 yrs tanner 12d

Danby, John son of John, yeoman, of Maisemore
Tither, Robert & Margaret 8 yrs tanner 2s 6d

1/507 French, John son of Walter, cordwainer, of Gloucester
Harris, Edward & Mary 7 yrs tailor 12d

Harward, Geoffrey son of Richard, woollen draper, of Gloucester
Harward, Richard, his father, & Margaret 7 yrs woollen draper 6s 8d

Cooper, Richard son of Francis, gentleman, of Charlton, Worcs
Pearce, Thomas & Hester [*no term*] mercer

25 Mar Boyfeilds, Thomas son of Richard Taylor, yeoman, of Minsterworth
Saule, Richard & Katharine 7 yrs tailor 1s

1/508 Poulton, Thomas son of Richard, yeoman, formerly of Hartpury
Webb, William & [*blank*] 7 yrs haberdasher 2s 6d

— — Witcombe, Joseph son of John, yeoman, formerly of Chaceley, Worcs
Greene, Thomas & Deborah [*no term*] mercer [*Incomplete entry*]

1639 25 Mar Hergest, Hugh son of Thomas, husbandman, of Lyonshall [MS Linnolls], Herefs
Collet, Edmund & Hester 9 yrs tanner 10s

14 Apr Harper, Philip son of Richard, husbandman, of Lyonshall [MS Linnolls], Herefs
Nicholls, John & Joan 7 yrs tanner 10s

1/509 Lewes, William son of Robert, glover, of Gloucester
Craker, John & Margaret 8 yrs weaver 6s 8d

1 May Clarke, Giles son of Thomas, farmer, of Castle Eaton [MS Churcheaton], Wilts
Lugge, Jasper & Anne 7 yrs tanner 2s 6d

1638 25 Dec Bosley, Richard son of Richard, farmer, of Churchdown
Lane, William & Katharine 7 yrs feltmaker 1s [*Repeating entry at 1/469 for 29 Sep 1635*]

1/510 1 Nov Pryor, Thomas son of Thomas, husbandman, of Alvescot, Oxon
Pryor, Simon & Margery 7 yrs feltmaker 3s 4d

	1639	2 Jun	Smith, William son of John, yeoman, of Badsey
			Cuffe, Thomas & [blank] 8 yrs mercer 20s
	—	2 Jun	Haward *alias* White[head], David son of William, yeoman, of Leonard Stanley
			Linckinholt, John & Sarah [*no term*] wiredrawer [*Deleted: see 1/511*]
1/511	1639		Haward *alias* Whitehead, David son of William, yeoman, of Leonard Stanley
			Linckinholt, John & Sarah [*no term*] wiredrawer
			[*Replacing entry at 1/510*]
			Thomas, Thomas son of Roland, labourer, of Gloucester
			Tither, Robert & Margaret 8 yrs tanner 12d
		29 Jun	Reynolds, James son of Oliver, chapman, of Welsh Newton, Herefs
			Eldridge, William & Hester 7 yrs silkweaver 2s 6d
1/512		24 Jun	Higgs, William son of Walter, yeoman, of Charlton Kings
			Webb, John 7 yrs mercer 2s 6d
			Knight, Richard son of Henry, innholder, of Gloucester
			Pincke, John & Alice 8 yrs baker 40s
		2 Jun	Pritchards, Henry son of Thomas, maltster, of Gloucester
			Beard, John & [*blank*] 8 yrs mercer 2s 6d
1/513			Long, John son of Richard Longe, cordwainer, of Gloucester
			Sturmey, Robert jr & Elizabeth 7 yrs glover 2s 6d
			Mr Holiday's money[1]
		25 Jul	Turner, John son of Thomas, cook, of Gloucester
			Turner, Thomas, his father, & Joan 7 yrs cook 10s
			Mr Holydaye's money
			Barrow, Robert son of Robert, butcher, of Gloucester
			Barrow, Robert, his father, & Joan 7 yrs butcher 20s
			Mr Hollidaye's money
1/514			Knipe, John son of Christopher, sealmaker, of Gloucester
			Knipe, Christopher, his father, & Joan 7 yrs sealmaker £5
			Mr Hollidaye's money
			Tayler, William son of Thomas, clothier, of Gloucester
			Tayler, Thomas, his father, & Magdalen 7 yrs clothier 20s
			Mr Hollidaye's money
		9 Nov	Morris, William son of Richard, husbandman, of Bourton on the Hill
			Smith, William & Margaret 7 yrs feltmaker 2s 6d
1/515		25 Jul	Bayley, Thomas son of John, glover, of Gloucester
			Doughton, Richard & Mary 8 yrs pinmaker 5s *Promised Mr Hollidaye's money next year. 1640, now he hath it*

---

[1] GBR B3/2 p 118 19 Jul 1639: To have £5 of Mr Holliday's money: Humphrey Beale son of Humphrey, mercer, dec'd, John Turner son of Humphrey, joiner, Robert Barrow son of Robert, butcher, William Tayler son of Thomas, clothier, John Long son of Richard, cordwainer, John Knipe son of Christopher, sealmaker.

| | 1639 | 24 Jun | Issard, Gabriel son of Richard, yeoman, of Brockworth |
| | | | Greene, Thomas & Deborah 9 yrs mercer 6s 8d |

            1 May Burrow, Thomas son of Nathaniel, cordwainer, of Gloucester
                   Edward, Anthony & Anne 8 yrs mercer 2s 6d

1/516   29 Sep Mitchell, George son of Richard, painter, of Gloucester
                   Craker, John & Margaret 7 yrs weaver [*cf Appendix V*]

                   Holman, James son of John, gentleman, formerly of Gloucester
                   Horsham, John & Ursula 8 yrs tailor 12d

           21 Apr Ingley *alias* Farmer, Robert son of John Ingly, miller, of Gloucester
                   Pitt, Samuel & Eleanor 7 yrs pinmaker 20s

1/517   **James Powell, mayor [1639–40]**
                   Richard Cugley and James Steephens, sheriffs

       1639 1 Nov Fones, Godfrey son of John, cleric, formerly of Kemerton
                   Atkins, John & [*blank*] 7 yrs cordwainer 3s 4d

                   James, William son of James Probert, yeoman, of Llanfihangel, Mon
                   Wood, John & Mary 8 yrs tanner 12d

                   Gearinge, Simon son of Simon Gearing, yeoman, of Lechlade
                   Haynes, William & Katrine 7 yrs baker 2s 6d

1/518   —   —   Cheltenham, William son of William, broadweaver, of Gloucester
                   Powell, Joan, widow of Thomas Powell, one of the burgesses of
                   Gloucester 8 yrs silkweaver [*Cancelled: see next entry*]

       1639 1 Nov Cheltenham, William son of William, broadweaver, of Gloucester
                   Powell, Joan, widow of Thomas Powell, one of the burgesses of
                   Gloucester 8 yrs silkweaver 5s [*Replacing last entry*]

       1640 6 Jan Francombe, Thomas son of Thomas, yeoman, formerly of Gloucester
                   Dowton, Richard & Mary 8 yrs pinmaker 5s

1/519   Clarke, Giles son of Giles, tanner, of Gloucester
                   Hoare, Alexander & Margery 8 yrs tanner 3s 4d [*cf Appendix V*]

                   Badcott, William son of John, husbandman, of Longhope
                   Tither, Robert & Eleanor 7 yrs tanner

           2 Feb Gilbert, Humphrey son of Henry, yeoman, of Whaddon
                   Lund, Walter & Hester 7 yrs baker 2s 6d

1/520   Whittington, William son of Robert, apothecary, dec'd, of Gloucester
                   Comalyne, James & Jane 8 yrs apothecary 5s

          26 Feb Armitage, John son of Richard, labourer, of Barton Street, Gloucester
                   Linckingholt, William & Elizabeth 7 yrs wiredrawer 5s
                   Five pounds of the gift of Mr Blackleech given with him

1/521   27 Feb Parish, Thomas son of John, skinner, dec'd, of Gloucester
                   Fewterell, William sr, dec'd, & Margaret 7 yrs tailor 5s
                   Five pounds of the gift of Mr Blackleech

	1640 24 Feb	Mathewes, John son of Richard, weaver, dec'd, of Gloucester
		Cugley, Arthur & Elizabeth 7 yrs wiredrawer 12d
	12 Mar	Hooper, Henry son of Henry, victualler, dec'd, of Gloucester
		Sturmy, Edward & Blanche 10 yrs glover 1s
		Five pounds of the gift of Mr Blackleech given with him
1/522	25 Mar	Hayes, Christopher son of Henry, shearman, of Gloucester
		Hayes, Christopher & Joan 7 yrs glazier 10s
	28 Feb	Welch, John son of John, ostler, of Gloucester
		Barrett, Thomas & Mary 9 yrs cutler 50s
		Five pounds of Mr Blackleech's gift
		Summers, Thomas son of Anthony, silkweaver, of Gloucester
		Eldridge, William & Hester [*no term*] silkweaver [*Entry incomplete*]
		Five pounds of Mr Blackleech's gift
1/523	5 Apr	Wolley, William son of Henry, barber surgeon, of Gloucester
		Bubb, Toby & Mary 7 yrs cordwainer 2s 6d
		Boyfield, William son of Thomas, yeoman, dec'd, of Minsterworth
		Tyler, James & Margaret 7 yrs cordwainer 2s 6d
	1639 25 Mar	Yate, Thomas son of Richard, esquire, of Arlingham
		Comelin, James & Jane 7 yrs apothecary 5s
	1640 1 May	Haynes, Peter son of William, baker, of Gloucester
		Hyron, Humphrey & Mary 7 yrs chandler 3s 4d
1/524	25 Apr	Bidle, William son of Thomas, farmer, of Brimpsfield
		Cowcher, William 8 yrs haberdasher 2s 6d
	1639 1 Nov	Adams, John son of William, yeoman, of Bourton on the Water
		Collet, Edmund & Hester 7 yrs tanner 2s 6d
	1640 14 May	Elmes, George son of John, yeoman, of Newent
		Collet, Edmund & Hester 7 yrs tanner 2s 6d
1/525	24 May	Joyner, Thomas son of Lawrence, trunkmaker, dec'd, of city of Bristol
		Evans, John & Alice 12 yrs sailor
		Saunders, Thomas son of William, farmer, of Great Witcombe
		Lugg, Jasper & Anne 8 yrs tanner 5s
	24 Jun	Shott, John son of William, husbandman, of Westbury
		Tither, Robert & Margaret 7 yrs tanner 20s
1/526	24 May	Hickes, Thomas son of William, yeoman, of Tirley
		Goode, Thomas & Katherine 7 yrs tailor 2s 6d
	24 Jun	Bickner, William son of [*blank*], dec'd, of Hartpury
		Beard, Richard & Armila 7 yrs tailor 1s
		Clarke, Giles son of Giles, tanner, of Gloucester
		Pace, Thomas & Margaret 8 yrs cooper 12d [*cf Appendix V*]
1/527		Springe, Henry son of Francis, yeoman, dec'd, of Haresfield
		Robins, James & [*blank*] 8 yrs mercer 3s 4d

	1640	25 Jul	Symons, Edward son of Lawrence, feltmaker, of Gloucester
			Doughton, Stephen & Elizabeth 8 yrs pinmaker 10s *Holliday*[1]
		5 Apr	Gwyn, Lewis son of Elias, farmer, of St Mary de Lode, Gloucester
			Stephens, Thomas & Alice 7 yrs pinmaker 2s 6d
1/528		25 Jul	Williams, Lewis son of John, farmer, of Cl[...]ke, Gloucester
			Gittoes, William & Joan 10 yrs glover 2s 6d
			Wilkinson *alias* Bevis, James son of John Bevis *alias* Wilkinson, innholder, of Gloucester
			Willets, George & Joan 7 yrs pinmaker 10s *Mr Hollyday*
		24 May	Mason, Edward son of Edward, saddler, of Gloucester
			Mason, Edward, his father, & Alice 7 yrs saddler 10s
1/529		24 Jun	Sturmy, George son of James, cordwainer, dec'd, of Painswick
			Brodgate, Richard & Alice 7 yrs barber 5s
		25 Jul	Taylor, Richard son of George, labourer, of Westbury
			Webly, Giles & Mary 7 yrs mercer 2s 6d
			Hitchins, Mathias son of Thomas, cordwainer, of Gloucester
			Lugg, William, late alderman of the city, & Eleanor 8 yrs tanner 10s
			£5 of Mr Hollidaye's money
1/530		24 Aug	Philpot, Samuel son of Samuel Philpet, glover, dec'd, of Gloucester
			Craker, Jonathan & Abigail 9 yrs silkweaver 5s
		24 Aug	Haynes, Thomas son of Thomas, linen weaver, of Barton Street
			Gresham, Thomas & Joan 8 yrs chandler 20s
			£5 of Mr Blackleeche's gift
		25 Jul	Perry, John son of Thomas, cordwainer, of Gloucester
			Willetts, George & Anne 8 yrs wiredrawer £10
			£5 of Mr Blackleeche's gift [deleted] *Hollidaye's money*
1/531		24 Aug	Woodward, Richard son of William, yeoman, of Gloucester
			Doughton, Richard & Mary 8 yrs pinmaker 5s
		25 Jul	Chandler, William son of Thomas, yeoman, of Gloucester
			Hayes, Anne, widow of John, 8 yrs baker 10s
		29 Sep	Pritchardes, Giles son of Giles, labourer, of Bisley
			Onyon, Humphrey & Eleanor 9 yrs sievemaker 2s 6d
1/532		6 Oct	Wilcoxe, Thomas son of John, clothier, dec'd, of Gloucester
			Williams, Isaac & Eleanor 8 yrs tailor 5s
			£5 of Mr Hollidaye's money in Alderman Hill's time
		29 Sep	Rider, Nicholas son of Nicholas, labourer, of Gloucester
			Steephens, James & Anne 7 yrs gentleman 2s 6d

---

[1] GBR B3/2 p 155 21 Jul 1640: To have £5 of Mr Holliday's money: Thomas Bayley son of John, glover, William Bird son of Thomas, yeoman, Mathias Hitchins son of Thomas, cordwainer, John Phillips son of [*blank*], dec'd, Edward Symonds son of Lawrence, feltmaker, James Bevis *alias* Wilkinson son of John, innholder, dec'd.

	1640 29 Sep	Williams, Henry son of Evan, carpenter, of Kinnersley [MS Kenersley], Herefs
		Messinger, Richard & Margaret 7 yrs maltster 4d
		Bingham, Walter son of Edward, salter, of Gloucester
		Horsam, John & Ursula 8 yrs tailor 2s 6d
1/533		Bullawaye, William son of William, farmer, of Crickley, Gloucester
		Wood, John & Margaret 8 yrs tanner [blank]
		Branch, John son of Walter, yeoman, dec'd, of Tibberton
		Taylor, Richard & Eleanor 8 yrs mercer 3s 4d
	24 May	Ward, Nathaniel son of William, tailor, of Tewkesbury
		Craker, Jonathan & Abigail 9 yrs silkweaver 12d

1/534 **Thomas Hill, mayor [1640–1]**
[Anthony Hathway and Edmund Palmer, sheriffs]

	1640 4 Nov	Hurlston, William son of Giles, yeoman, of Maisemore
		Jennings, Brian & Alice 7 yrs from Christmas baker 2s 6d The father to find him apparel all the term
	1 Nov	Poole, David son of Henry, feltmaker, of Cirencester
		Phelpes, Joseph & Barbara 7 yrs feltmaker 2s 6d
		Woodward, James son of William, brewer, of Gloucester
		Dowton, Stephen & Elizabeth 7 yrs pinmaker 10s
1/535		Woodward, John son of William, brewer, of Gloucester
		Dowton, Stephen & Elizabeth 7 yrs pinmaker 3s 4d
		Palmer, Edward son of Edward, baker, of Gloucester
		Palmer, Edward, his father, & Hester 7 yrs baker 20s
	30 Nov	Phillips, James son of [blank], haberdasher, dec'd, of Gloucester
		Dun, John & Margaret 9 yrs tailor 12d
1/536	1 Nov	Ward, Joseph son of William, tailor, of Tewkesbury
		Craker, Jonathan & Abigail 7 yrs silkweaver 5s
	1641 13 Jan	Rawlins, Thomas son of Thomas, yeoman, of Gloucester
		Phelpes, Joseph & Barbara 7 yrs feltmaker 2s 6d
	2 Feb	Dyer, Humphrey son of Humphrey, brewer, of Gloucester
		Lugg, William & Eleanor 9 yrs tanner 5s
		£5 of Mr Hollidaye's money, Mr Alderman Hill's time[1]
1/537		Moore, Henry son of Alexander, joiner, of Gloucester
		Powell, William & Alice 8 yrs pinner 15s
		Symonds, Nathaniel son of Richard, yeoman, dec'd, of Eldersfield, Worcs
		Cordell, James & Joan [no term] glover 2s 6d

---

[1] GBR B3/2 p 182 21 Jul 1641: To receive £5 of Mr Holliday's money: James son of William Farmer, glover, John son of Richard Lugge, tanner, Thomas Wilcox, Humphrey son of Humphrey Dyer, brewer, Richard son of Richard Bodenham, baker, Richard Garret.

	1641	24 Feb	Pricketts, Roland son of Howell, milliner, of Gloucester Willetts, George & Anne 7 yrs wiredrawer 6s 8d
1/538		12 Mar	Hawkins, Walter son of Eleanor, widow, of Barton Street, Gloucester Craker, Jonathan & Abigail 7 yrs silkweaver 3s 4d
		9 Mar	Jordan, Thomas son of Thomas, yeoman, of Stoke Orchard Cooke, William & [*blank*] 8 yrs mercer 3s 4d
		2 Feb	Brookes, Edward son of Thomas, cutler, of Monmouth Cowles, Robert & Blanche 10 yrs butcher 2s 6d
1/539		25 Mar	Pace, Samuel son of Walter, yeoman, of Ashleworth Harris, Humphrey & Anne 7 yrs baker 2s 6d
			Chandler, Richard son of Cuthbert, turner [MS ternell], dec'd, of Cheltenham Pedlingham, Thomas & Susannah 8 yrs saddler 2s 6d
			Baughe, William son of William, brewer, of Gloucester Pace, Thomas & Margaret 7 yrs cooper 2s 6d
1/540			Gregory *alias* Ridler, William son of Alice, spinster, of Witcombe Cox, Richard & Cecily 8 yrs distiller [MS. 'stiller of stronge water'] 2s 6d
		13 Jun	Hill, Edward son of Edward, gentleman, dec'd, of Gloucester Cooke, John & Katharine 8 yrs haberdasher 2s 6d
		25 Mar	Carpenter, John son of John, cordwainer, dec'd, of Gloucester Cugly, Arthur & Elizabeth 10 yrs wiredrawer 2s 6d *pauper*
1/541		1 May	Adeane, Thomas son of Richard, farmer, formerly of Temple Guiting Woodward, William & Anne 8 yrs blacksmith 2s 6d
			Browning, Thomas son of Thomas, tanner, of Gloucester Knight, James & Eleanor 8 yrs currier 10s
		25 Apr	Herne, John son of John, tailor, of Bulley Hayman, Thomas & Elizabeth 7 yrs tailor 2s 6d
1/542		2 May	Greene, William son of Richard, tailor, dec'd, of Westbury Harris, William & Susannah 7 yrs pinner *alias* pinmaker 2s 6d
		[*blank*]	Daunt, John son of William, gentleman, dec'd, of [Forest of] Dean Singleton, Lawrence & Joan [*blank*] woollen draper £10 *Cancelled*
		24 Jun	Wyman, Thomas son of John, farmer, of Huntley Nash, Richard & Rebecca 7 yrs feltmaker 12d
1/543		25 Jul	Hayes, William son of Richard, cutler, of Gloucester Barnes, John & Joan [*blank*] cordwainer 2s 6d
			Perry, John son of Thomas, yeoman, of Sollers Hope, Herefs Symons, Richard & Katharine [*blank*] glover 2s 6d
			Tanner, Roger son of Roger, husbandman, Kineton Taylor, George & [*blank*] 8 yrs barber surgeon 2s 6d

	1640	25 Jul	Garrett, Richard son of Nathaniel, broadweaver, of Gloucester Charleton, Edward & Alice 8 yrs wiredrawer 20s *£5 of Alderman Holliday's gift given him*
1/544			Lugge, John son of Richard, tanner, dec'd, of Gloucester Whitson, John & Joan 7 yrs pinmaker of Southgate Street 20s *£5 of Alderman Holliday's gift given him*
			Farmer, James son of Richard, glover, dec'd, of Gloucester Wilkins, Richard & Elizabeth 7 yrs wiredrawer 20s *£5 of Alderman Holliday's*
		6 Sep	Colley, Richard son of William, gentleman, dec'd, of Ross, Herefs Lycense, Daniel & Sarah 9 yrs woollen draper 2s 6d
1/545		24 Aug	Badger, Jeremiah son of Brian, cutler, of Gloucester Addames, Albert & Alice 7 yrs broadweaver 2s 6d [*cf Appendix V*]
			Suffeild, Thomas son of Thomas, cooper, of Gloucester Wintle, Richard & Alice 7 yrs cordwainer 2s 6d
		29 Sep	Smith, John son of Richard, haberdasher, of London Palmer, Edmund & Hester 8 yrs baker 2s 6d
			Kingscoate, Charles son of Mary Kingscoote, widow, of Blaisdon Heminge, William & Martha 7 yrs barber surgeon 3s 4d
1/546			Stock, Thomas son of Christopher, clerk, of Bromsberrow Ricketts, James & [*blank*] 8 yrs saddler 2s 6d
		24 Aug	Fewterer, Edward son of William, tailor, of Gloucester [Fewterer], William, his father, & Margaret 7 yrs tailor 5s
		25 Apr	Baker, Thomas son of Thomas, weaver, of Gloucester Williams, Michael & Elizabeth 8 yrs joiner 3s 4d
1/547		29 Sep	Gibbins, Richard son of William, farmer, dec'd, of Upton St Leonards Gibbins, Thomas & Frances 8 yrs wiredrawer 12d
			Bradford, John son of John, brewer, of Gloucester Hall, Roger & Margery 7 yrs cooper 2s 6d
			Sheppard, Thomas son of Thomas, tanner, dec'd, of Lyonshall, Herefs Nicholls, John & Joan 8 yrs tanner 10s

John Scriven, mayor [1641–2]
Edmund Collet and John Wood, sheriffs

	1641	23 Oct	Mills, John son of John, farmer, of Cowley Charleton, Edward & Alice 7 yrs wiredrawer 2s 6d
		1 Nov	Togwell, William son of William, yeoman, dec'd, of Brimpsfield Beard, Richard & Armyla 8 yrs tailor *The said William Togwell was discharged by me 26 Oct 1641 by the consent of me Sybil Togwell* [*marks of Sybil and William*] [*See next entry; the dates are puzzling*]
1/548		26 Oct	Togwell, William son of William, yeoman, dec'd, of Brimpsfield Atkins, John & Elizabeth 8 yrs cordwainer 2s *Enrolled for the former fee* [*See preceding entry*]

	1641	28 Oct	Mills, Richard son of William, husbandman, of Cowley Charleton, Edward & Alice 7 yrs wiredrawer 2s 6d
		1 Nov	Loggins, George son of Augustine, mason, of Gloucester Lucas, Elizabeth widow of Robert 7 yrs farrier 12d
			Bevan, Walter son of Edward, husbandman, of Lyonshall, Herefs Lugg, Jasper & Anne 7 yrs tanner £4
1/549		18 Oct	Powell, Edward son of Edward, farmer, of Mitcheldean Wintle, Richard & Alice 7 yrs cordwainer 5s 6d
		1 Nov	Merrett, Thomas son of Thomas, cordwainer, dec'd, of Gloucester Evans, Samuel & Elizabeth 10 yrs pinmaker 10s
		16 Nov	Sheppard, Samuel son of William, esquire, of Gloucester Beale, Thomas 9 yrs mercer 5s [cf Appendix V]
		1 Nov	Draper, John son of Thomas, upholsterer, dec'd, of Gloucester Plomer, Robert & Christian 8 yrs pewterer 20s
1/550			Apperly, William son of John, yeoman, dec'd, of Much Marcle, Herefs Hayes, Anne, widow of John 7 yrs baker 20s
			Theyer, Thomas son of Anne, widow, of Twigworth Horsam, John & Ursula 7 yrs tailor 2s 6d
			Jefferies, Thomas son of John, yeoman, of [blank], Glos Hiron, Humphrey jr & Margaret 9 yrs chandler 2s 6d
			Morse, Humphrey son of Thomas, gentleman, of Gloucester Tayler, John & Mary 8 yrs chandler 2s 6d
1/551		10 Oct	Holtham, William son of Oliver, yeoman, of Hardwicke Windowe, Richard & Margaret 9 yrs chandler 2s 6d
		1 Nov	Timbrell, Christopher son of Christopher, yeoman, of Ipsley, Warws Broad, William & Elizabeth 7 yrs baker 12d
	1642	29 Jan	Mills, Thomas son of John, yeoman, of Cowley Charleton, Edward & Alice 7 yrs wiredrawer 2s 6d
		25 Mar	Shott, Thomas son of Philip, farmer, of Westbury Atkins, John & Elizabeth 7 yrs cordwainer 12d
1/552		2 Feb	Williams, Thomas son of Robert, tanner, of Gloucester Lugg, William & Eleanor [blank] tanner [blank]
	1641	25 Dec	Hincksman, Joseph son of Edward, yeoman, of Prestbury Warwicke, William & Anne 8 yrs vintner 40s
	1642	15 Mar	Cooke, James son of James, yeoman, of Corse Fowler, William 9 yrs gentleman 3s 4d
1/553		25 Mar	Syms, William son of Thomas, yeoman, of Hempsted Tomes, John & Elizabeth 9 yrs mercer 2s 6d
		1 May	Payne, John son of John, labourer, of Broadway, Worcs Steephens, James, gentleman, & Anne 7 yrs maltster 40s

| | 1642 10 Apr | Cartwright, Edward son of Edward, yeoman, of Prestbury |
| | | Pincke, John & [blank] 7 yrs baker 2s 6d |

    1 May Hoare, Charles son of Thomas, saddler, of Gloucester
      Knight, Robert & [blank] 7 yrs chandler 5s

1/554 19 May Davis, Henry son of Thomas, cordwainer, of Gloucester
      Davis, Thomas, his father, & Margaret 7 yrs cordwainer 5s

    6 Jan Corbet, Arthur son of Arthur, cordwainer, of Gloucester
      Burrup, Thomas & Joan 7 yrs cordwainer 2s 6d

    29 May Robberts, Miles son of Giles, yeoman, of Barnwood
      Lye, Giles & Esther 8 yrs chandler 12d

    7 Jun Exton, John son of Barnabas, farmer, of Gloucester
      Wantner, Margaret widow of William 7 yrs farrier 12d

1/555 10 Apr Gardner, William son of William, tanner, formerly of Suckley, Worcs
      Greene, John & Katharine 7 yrs cooper 2s 6d

    1 Aug Wintle, William son of Thomas, yeoman, of Westbury
      Edwardes, John & Elizabeth 8 yrs haberdasher 2s 6d

      Willmotts, Robert son of Richard, of Newnham
      Stephens, Oliver 7 yrs saddler 2s 6d

    24 Jun Smith, John son of William, yeoman, of Boddington
      Hill, Eleanor, widow, 7 yrs barber surgeon 2s 6d

1/556 25 Jul Hart, Valentine son of James, cutler, of Gloucester
      Burrop, Thomas & Joan 7 yrs cordwainer 2s 6d

      [blank]
      Collet, John & Elizabeth 7 yrs tanner 2s 6d

      Cugley, James son of Arthur, wiredrawer, of Gloucester
      Cugley, John & Elizabeth [blank] cardmaker 20s
       Hollidayes money[1]

1/557   Tyler, John son of John, tailor, of Gloucester
      Gilbert, Henry & Mary 7 yrs cordwainer £5 *Hollidayes money*

      Ockford, Giles son of Giles Ockfords, yeoman, dec'd, of Gloucester
      Gilbert, Henry & Mary 7 yrs cordwainer £5 *Hollidayes money*

      Stephens, Thomas jr son of Thomas sr, farmer, of Prestbury
      Bishopp, Thomas & Anne 8 yrs cordwainer 2s

    24 Aug Burrows, Samuel son of Nathaniel Burrowes, cordwainer, of
       Gloucester
      Wise, Denis & Hephzibah 9 yrs mercer 2s 6d

1/558 25 Jul Phillips, John son of William, haberdasher, dec'd, of Gloucester
      Payne, John & Margaret 7 yrs feltmaker 20s *Hollidayes money*

---

[1] GBR B3/2 p 218 21 July 1642: To receive £5 of Alderman Holliday's money: Jacob son of Arthur Cugley, William son of Richard Hayes, John son of William Phillipps, William son of William Jeyne, John son of [blank] Tyler, Giles son of Giles Ockford.

	1642	29 Sep	Webb, John son of Sergent, yeoman, of Linton Price, Richard & Dinah, 7 yrs pewterer 20s

1/559

Dennis Wise, mayor [1642–3]
Edward Wagstaffe and James Wood, sheriffs

1643 29 Sep Gregory, Brice son of Henry, butcher, of Gloucester
  Humfreyes, Richard & Frances 7 yrs butcher 13s 4d
  Mr Hollidayes money[1]

  Cowley, John son of Richard, blacksmith, of Gloucester
  Tyler, James & Margaret 7 yrs cordwainer 20s
  Mr Hollidayes money

  Williams, Thomas son of John, dec'd, of Gloucester
  Williams, John, his brother, & Jane 7 yrs ropemaker 20s
  Mr Hollidayes money

1/560 9 Sep Bosley, John son of Richard, cordwainer, of Gloucester
  Harris, Humphrey & Elizabeth 7 yrs cordwainer 6s 8d
  Mr Hollidayes money

  25 Dec Pritchards, John son of Roger, mason, of Gloucester
  Pace, Thomas & Margaret 8 yrs cooper 2s 6d
  [*Inserted between existing entries in wrong mayoral year*]

  9 Sep Turner, Cuthbert son of John, cook, of Gloucester
  Barnes, John & Joan 7 yrs cordwainer 6s 8d
  Mr Hollidayes money

  25 Sep Hancocke, John son of John, yeoman, of Newington Bagpath
  Phelps, Joseph 7 yrs feltmaker

1/561 29 Sep Brothers *alias* Chapman, Toby son of John, tailor, of Gloucester
  [Brothers *alias* Chapman], John, his father, & Joan 7 yrs tailor
  6s 8d *Mr Hollidayes money*

Nicholas Webb, mayor [1643–4]
[James Stephens and Robert Tyther, sheriffs]

1644 1 May Dyer, Nathaniel son of Humphrey, brewer, of Gloucester
  Hadnot, Henry & Jane 8 yrs tailor 2s 6d

  25 Mar Webly, Richard son of Henry, yeoman, dec'd, of Rendcomb
  Fowler, William & Anne 7 yrs mercer 5s
  [*Inserted between existing entries*]

  24 Jun Garret, Thomas son of Nathaniel, broadweaver, of Gloucester
  Lugg, William, alderman, & Eleanor 8 yrs tanner 2s 6d

1/562 29 Jun Haynes, William son of Thomas, weaver, of Gloucester
  Atkins, John & Elizabeth 9 yrs cordwainer 2 suits of clothes

---

[1] GBR B3/2 p 270 21 July 1643: To receive £5 of Alderman Holliday's money: Thomas son of John Williams, dec'd, Cuthbert son of Thomas Turner, cook, Toby son of John Brothers *alias* Chapman, tailor, John son of Richard Cowley, blacksmith, Brice son of Henry Gregory, blacksmith, John son of Richard Bozley, cordwainer.

	1644 24 Jun	White, Samuel son of Richard, yeoman, of Dymock Nicholls, John & Elizabeth 7 yrs tanner 5s
	1 Aug	Denny, Daniel son of William, mercer, of Tetbury Lea, Francis & Joan 7 yrs cordwainer 2s 6d
1/563	21 Apr	Davis, William son of Roger, cordwainer, of Gloucester Lugg, Thomas & [blank] 9 yrs haberdasher 2s 6d
	25 Jul	Rix, Nathaniel son of Richard, clothier, dec'd, of Gloucester Burropp, Thomas & Joan 7 yrs cordwainer 2s 6d
	24 Jun	Pedlingham, Thomas son of Thomas, saddler, of Gloucester Pedlingham, Thomas, his father, & Susannah 8 yrs saddler 10s
1/564	25 Jul	Hall, John son of John, vintner, formerly of Gloucester Pedlingham, Thomas & Susannah 8 yrs saddler 5s [Mr Hollidayes money][1]
		Davis, William son of William, weaver, of Dursley Onyon, Humphrey & Eleanor 9 yrs sievemaker 2s 6d
		Greene, Thomas son of Edmund, cordwainer, of Gloucester Lea, Francis & [blank] 7 yrs cordwainer 3s 4d [Mr Hollidayes money]
1/565		Selwyn, Thomas son of Henry, cordwainer, of Gloucester Harris, Walter & Elizabeth 7 yrs cordwainer 10s [Mr Hollydayes money]
	25 Mar	Aram, Thomas son of John, yeoman, of Newent Browne, John & Elizabeth 7 yrs mercer 5s
	24 Aug	Griffeth, Jonathan son of David, farmer, of Eldersfield, Worcs Harris, Walter & Elizabeth 7 yrs cordwainer 5s
1/566	29 Sep	Edwards, Samuel son of Francis, farmer, of Colerne, Wilts Dunne, John 7 yrs tailor 2s 6d
		Stanby, Thomas, of Badgeworth Atkins, John & Elizabeth 7 yrs cordwainer 5s
		Hale, Young son of Walter, yeoman, of Burton Hayes, Anne, widow, 7 yrs baker 3s 4d
1/567	25 Jul	Tompson, William son of Francis, cook, of Gloucester Beard, Richard & Armela 8 yrs tailor 10s [Mr Hollidayes money]
	29 Sep	Boulter, John son of Richard Bowlter, farmer, of Eckington, Worcs Palmer, Edward & Hester 8 yrs baker 2s 6d
		Clutterbooke, Thomas son of John, yeoman, of Haresfield Edwardes, Anthony & Anne 8 yrs mercer 2s 6d

---

[1] GBR B3/2 p 305 22 July 1644: To receive £5 of Alderman Holliday's money: John son of John Hall, dec'd, Thomas son of Henry Selwyn, cordwainer, Thomas son of Edmund Greene, cordwainer, Francis son of Francis Tompson, cook dec'd, Samuel son of [blank] Pitt, Thomas son of [blank] Baker.

Luke Nurse, mayor [1644–5]
Toby Jordan and John Edwards, sheriffs

1644 1 Nov Surman, George son of John, yeoman, of Tirley
Goode, Thomas & Katharine 7 yrs tailor 2s 6d

Kayse, William son of John, farmer, of Huntley
Nash, Richard & Rebecca 8 yrs feltmaker 20s

1/568 25 Dec Coustons, Samuel son of John, yeoman, of Churcham
Chapman, Thomas & Elizabeth 7 yrs tailor 2s 6d

1645 6 Jan White, William son of Thomas, smith, of Banbury, Oxon
Phillips, John & Jane 7 yrs feltmaker 2s 6d

1644 25 Dec Oynion, Humphrey son of Humphrey, sievemaker, of Gloucester
Oynion, Thomas & [*blank*] 8 yrs silkweaver 5s [*cf Appendix V*]

1645 6 Jan Hayward, John son of Richard, yeoman, of Barnwood
Gittoes, William & Joan 7 yrs glover 12d

1/569 1644 1 Nov Blake, Edward son of Valentine, gentleman, of Winchcombe
Gilbert, Henry & Mary 7 yrs cordwainer 2s 6d

1645 6 Jan Smith, Matthew son of Thomas, yeoman, of Berkeley
Lugg, William, alderman, & Eleanor 7 yrs tanner 5s

Bell, John son of John, clerk, of Upper Slaughter
Onnyon, Thomas & [*blank*] 8 yrs silkweaver 2s 6d

1644 20 May Lews, John son of Abel, tiler, of Gloucester
Lews, Abel, his father, & Joan 7 yrs tiler 2s 6d
[*Wrong year. Added later*]

1/570 1645 2 Feb Cripps, Nathaniel son of Nathaniel, yeoman, of Upton in parish of Tetbury
Clayfeild, Edward & Alice 7 yrs turner 2s 6d

Marten, Thomas son of John, brewer, of Gloucester
Davis, Thomas & Jane 7 yrs wiredrawer 2s 6d

Gabb, Daniel son of Richard, blacksmith, dec'd, of Haresfield
Gwynn, Augustine & Alice 7 yrs cordwainer 5s

1/571 1644 29 Sep Denton, Edward son of John, yeoman, of Bagendon
Gilbert, Henry & Mary 7 yrs cordwainer 5s

1645 25 Mar Pigg, Richard son of David, farmer, of Hentland, Herefs
Payne, Richard & Margaret 7 yrs pinmaker 5s

— [*blank*] son of [*blank*]
Collet, Edmund & Hester tanner [*Incomplete*]

Purlewent, John son of John, baker, of Gloucester
Hobson, John & Joan 8 yrs mercer
21 Jan 1650: John Purlewent turned over to serve the residue of his term with William Fowler, mercer, with the consent of John Hobson & his own. Before Thomas Hill, alderman. The apprentice to find himself the clothes

1/572	1645	1 May	Neast, George son of George, feltmaker, of Gloucester Hobbs, John & Cecily 7 yrs feltmaker 5s
		6 Apr	Ellis, John son of John, yeoman, of Elmore Ellis, Godfrey & Margaret 7 yrs baker 5s
			Jones, William son of William, yeoman, of Gloucester Taylor, George & Eleanor 7 yrs cordwainer 3s 4d
		1 May	Edmonds, Charles son of Lewis, innholder, dec'd, of Lea Harris, Humphrey & Elizabeth 7 yrs cordwainer 5s
1/573		25 May	Frape, Joseph son of Robert, yeoman, of Westerleigh Donne, John & Margaret 7 yrs tailor 2s 6d
			Nash, Jesse son of Richard, tanner, dec'd, of Gloucester Bird, Daniel & Anne 7 yrs feltmaker 2s 6d
		25 Mar	Partridge, William son of John, farmer, dec'd, of Cowley Beale, Geoffrey & Edith 8 yrs mercer 5s
		25 May	Mayo, Edward son of Henry, clothier, of Tetbury Collett, John & Elizabeth 7 yrs tanner 5s
1/574			Miles, James son of William, baker, of Crudwell, Wilts Haynes, William & [blank] 7 yrs baker 2s 6d
		25 Mar	Webb, John son of Nicholas, alderman, of Gloucester Grevill, Giles & Anne 7 yrs mercer 10s
		24 Jun	Stephens alias White, Thomas son of John White, tanner, of Gloucester Wilkins, Richard & Maudlin 7 yrs wiredrawer 2s 6d
		25 Jul	Horsington, Thomas son of Henry, silkweaver, of Gloucester Shipton, John & Elizabeth 7 yrs bodicemaker 2s 6d *Mr Hollidaye's money*[1]
1/575		24 Jun	Tyler, James son of James, cordwainer, of Gloucester Tyler, James, his father, & Margaret 8 yrs cordwainer 10s
			Browne, Thomas son of George, turnmaker, dec'd, of Longhope Onnyon, Humphrey & Eleanor 9 yrs sievemaker 2s 6d
		6 April	Allen, George son of William, farmer, of Barnwood Pace, Thomas & Margaret 8 yrs cooper 2s 6d
1/576		24 Jun	Smyth, John son of Walter, farmer, of Coulston [MS Cowston], Wilts Clarke, William & Joan 8 yrs mercer 5s
			Griffin, David son of Hugh, farmer, of Minsterworth Beard, William & Elizabeth 7 yrs tailor 2s 6d
		29 Sep	Knipe, Simon son of William, horn maker, of Gloucester Taylor, George & Eleanor 8 yrs cordwainer 8s *Mr Hollidaye's money*

---

[1] GBR B3/2 p 333 21 Jul 1645: These boys to have £5 of Alderman Holliday's money, there being no more suitors for the same: Nathaniel Rickes, Thomas Horsington, William Witcombe, Simon Knipe, Samuel Teekle, Thomas Kircombe.

1/577	1645	25 Jul	Francombe, Luke son of Thomas, farmer, dec'd, of Gloucester Smyth, William & [*blank*] 7 yrs cordwainer 5s
		25 Dec	Price, Ralph son of Ralph, dec'd, of Gloucester Hill, Walter & Dorothy 7 yrs cordwainer 2s
		25 Jul	Shepheard, Samuel son of William, esquire, of Gloucester Dowle, Clement & Hannah 7 yrs mercer 2s 6d [*cf Appendix V*]
		29 Sep	Bower, Thomas son of Thomas, gentleman, dec'd, of Mitcheldean Pingry, Thomas & Anne 7 yrs weaver 5s
1/578		25 Jul	Clarke, John son of John, farmer, of Redmarley, Worcs Vaughan, Richard 7 yrs joiner 2s 6d
		29 Sep	Teekle, Samuel son of Samuel, ropemaker, of Gloucester Teekle, Richard & Katharine 7 yrs ropemaker 3s & 2 suits *Mr Hollidaye's money*
		24 Aug	Jordan, William son of William, silkweaver, of Gloucester Bubb, William & Judith 9 yrs apothecary 5s & 2 suits
1/579		29 Sep	Kircombe, Thomas son of John, blacksmith, of Gloucester Kircombe, John, his father, & Joyce 7 yrs blacksmith 10s *Mr Holliday's money*
		25 Jul	Witcombe, William son of William, weaver, of Gloucester Rutter, William & Alice 7 yrs weaver 5s *Mr Holliday's money*

Laurence Singleton, mayor [1645–6]
Anthony Edwards and Walter Lane, sheriffs

	1645	29 Sep	Fisher, William son of William, pinmaker, dec'd, of Gloucester Stephens, Thomas & Alice 8 yrs pinmaker 5s
1/580		1 Nov	Mans, Toby son of Richard, garter weaver, of Gloucester Craker, Margaret, widow, 8 yrs garter weaver 5s
			Hayward, Geoffrey son of Thomas, farmer, of Hartpury Beard, Richard & Armila 7 yrs tailor 2s 6d
1/581			Jordan, Thomas son of William, maltster, of Gloucester Beard, John & [*blank*] 8 yrs mercer
			Tipper, James son of Richard, labourer, of Churchdown Hill, Walter & Dorothy 7 yrs cordwainer 12d
			Wintle, Henry son of Henry, cooper, of Westbury Bingly, John & Elizabeth [*blank*] cooper 5s
1/582			Cole, William son of John, farmer, of Alveston Dean, John & Margaret 7 yrs tailor 3s 4d
	1646	2 Feb	Goldinge, Richard son of Richard, yeoman, of Oaksey, Wilts West, John & Mary [*blank*] tanner 2s 6d
	1645	25 Dec	Farley, Thomas son of George, cutler, of Gloucester Phillips, Thomas & Elizabeth 8 yrs cutler 2s 6d

1/583	1645	1 Nov	Bray, Henry son of Henry, gentleman Nelme, Richard & [blank] 9 yrs mercer 5s
	1646	2 Feb	Harmer, William son of John, gentleman, dec'd, of Gloucester Colchester, Thomas & Eleanor 8 yrs haberdasher 2s 6d
			Beard, John son of Richard, tailor, of Syde Neast, Alexander & Margaret 7 yrs silkweaver 2s 6d
1/584			Mason, Thomas son of Thomas, yeoman, of Hartpury Parker, Thomas & Margaret 8 yrs baker 5s
		25 Mar	Davis, Thomas son of Thomas, glover, of Gloucester Fones, John & Eleanor 7 yrs glover 12d
		29 Mar	Guy, Thomas son of Richard, yeoman, of Gloucester Knowles, Henry & Anne 7 yrs brazier 5s
1/585		1 May	Merryman, Charles son of John, husbandman, of Hardwicke Surman, John & Sybil 11 yrs glover 2s 6d
		29 Mar	Stephens, Richard son of James, gentleman, of Gloucester Taylor, Richard & [blank] 8 yrs mercer 10s
			Foorde, Thomas son of Humphrey, innholder, of Taynton Jennings, William & [blank] 8 yrs barber surgeon 5s
1/586		17 May	Woodcoke, William son of William, yeoman, of Whaddon Gwyn, Augustine & Alice 7 yrs cordwainer 5s
			Angell, William son of Richard, gentleman, of Bromsberrow Harris, Walter & Elizabeth 7 yrs cordwainer 2s 6d
		29 Mar	Payne, Robert son of Robert, mercer, of Gloucester Payne, Robert, his father, & Elizabeth 7 yrs mercer 10s
1/587		24 Jun	Mathews, Giles son of Thomas, yeoman, of Rissington Collett, Edward & Margery 7 yrs tanner 10s
		29 Mar	Hawker, Thomas son of Edward, yeoman, of Apperley Nicholls, John & Mary 7 yrs tanner 5s
		25 Mar	Overthrow, John son of John, carpenter, dec'd, of Bulley Greene, William & Margaret 7 yrs joiner 2s 6d
1/588		24 Jun	Badger, Thomas son of Richard, gentleman, of Prestbury Reynolds, Eleanor widow of Robert 7 yrs tanner 2s 6d

[On 1/591 is a memorandum relating to an apprenticeship in Tewkesbury, which is included below as Appendix III.]

1645–1668

GBR C10/2

2/1 **Laurence Singleton, mayor [1645–6]**
Anthony Edwards and Walter Lane, sheriffs

1646 24 Jun White, Richard son of Richard, yeoman, dec'd, of Dymock
White, Sergeant & Joan 7 yrs cordwainer 3s
[*Text of indenture given in full*]

2/2 7 Jul Stallard, Thomas son of Anselm, cooper, of Gloucester
Carter, William & Joyce 8 yrs cooper 11s 6d
[*Repeated, altered, at 2/14*]   *Mr Holliday's money*[1]

26 Jun Eldriedge, William son of William, silkweaver, dec'd, of Gloucester
Nest, Alexander & Margaret 7 yrs silkweaver 2s 6d

24 Jul Smith, Giles son of Walter, yeoman, of Corston [MS Chorson], parish of Malmesbury
Jennings, Alice, widow, 7 yrs baker 3s 4d

16 Jun Loxlie, William son of William, dec'd
Bird, Daniel & Anne 8 yrs feltmaker 2s 6d

2/3 24 Jun Smart, John son of Richard, farmer, of Over
Heminge, Thomas & Margery 8 yrs joiner 2s 6d

1645 25 Dec Robinson, Samuel son of Hester, widow, of Gloucester
Singleton, Laurence, esq, mayor, & [*blank*] 8 yrs woollen draper 10s

1646 24 Jun Hayes, William son of Josiah, cordwainer, of Gloucester
Tyler, James & Margaret 7 yrs cordwainer 5s

29 Jul Marten, Henry son of George, yeoman, of Gloucester
Maddocke, William and Sarah 7 yrs tailor 2s 6d

24 Jul Cugley, Thomas son of Thomas, cardmaker, of Gloucester
Cugley, Thomas, his father, & Joan 8 yrs cardmaker 2s 6d

2/4 24 Mar Bellamy, George son of George, dyer, of Ross, Herefs
Harris, Humphrey & Elizabeth 7 yrs cordwainer 2s 6d

10 Aug Townsend, John son of Thomas, blacksmith, of Barton Street, Gloucester
Davis, Thomas & Jane 7 yrs wiredrawer 12d

20 Aug Lea, Anthony son of Francis, cordwainer, of Gloucester
Greene, Edward & Eleanor 7 yrs cordwainer 5s
Mr Holliday's money

2/5 30 Aug Stephens William son of Matthew, cordwainer, of Gloucester
Smith, William & [*blank*] 7 yrs cordwainer 5s
Mr Holliday's money

---

[1] GBR B3/2 p 376 21 Jul 1646: To receive £5 of the gift of Alderman Holliday: John Thayer, William Jones, Anthony Leigh, Thomas Stallard, William Stephens, John Humphryes.

| | 1646 | 1 Sep | Humfreyes, John son of John, baker, of Gloucester |
| | | | Humfreyes, Richard & Frances 8 yrs butcher 20s |

3 Sep Thomas, John son of John, yeoman, of Eardisley, Herefs
   Lane, William & Susannah 7 yrs feltmaker 7s [?; MS 7 yrs]

2/6 14 Sep Reynolds, John son of Richard, farmer, of Forden, Mont
   Hayward, John & Sarah 7 yrs feltmaker 5s

28 Mar Woodward, Francis son of John, yeoman, of Newent
   Fowler, William & Anne 8 yrs mercer 2s 6d

2/7 29 Sep Lande, Robert son of Richard, husbandman, of Newent
   Hewes, John & Jane 8 yrs cordwainer 3s 4d

1 Sep Jones, Edward son of William, cordwainer, of Gloucester
   Bearde, Nathaniel & Jane 7 yrs tailor 2s 6d
   Mr Holidaye's money
   7 Jun 1650, turned over to Thomas Alridge, tailor, with the
   consent of his master & his own. Before James Stephens, mayor,
   Denis Wise & Jasper Clutterbuck. [Signed] *Edward Jones*

29 Sep Adeane, Richard son of Richard, yeoman, of Temple Guiting
   Butterton, Richard & Susannah 7 yrs currier 5s

2/8 Lloyde, Thomas son of Walter, of Cirencester
   Ricketts, James 8 yrs tanner 40s

7 Oct Farmer, Francis son of Edward, wiredrawer, of Gloucester
   Davis, David & Mary 7 yrs feltmaker 12d

24 Jun Ebbs, Philip son of Philip, husbandman, of Gloucester
   Bruckbancke, Margery, widow 7 yrs saddler

2/9 **Jasper Clutterbuck, mayor [1646–7]**
   [Thomas Pritchard and Henry Ellis, later Robert Paine, sheriffs]

1646 7 Oct Allen, Samuel son of William, yeoman, of Barnwood
   Pace, Thomas & Elizabeth 7 yrs cooper 2s 6d

31 Oct Hyron, Nicholas son of Nathaniel Hieron, dyer, of Wotton under Edge
   Coloricke, Daniel & Mary 8 yrs bodicemaker 12d

30 Oct Lugg, Lawrence son of Lawrence, tanner, of Gloucester
   Marten, John & [*blank*] 7 yrs baker 5s
   9 Sep 1650 turned over to Henry Edwards, baker. The
   apprentice to find himself clothes all the time. His master had 50s
   with him

2/10 2 Nov Rowles, John son of Benjamin, mason, of Hailes
   Chamley, Thomas & [*blank*] 8 yrs sealmaker 12d

25 Dec Wolston, Godfrey son of Henry, gentleman, of Maisemore
   Phillipes, James & Margery 8 yrs tailor 6s

1 Dec Pryor, John son of Thomas, yeoman, of Alvescot [MS Alscott], Oxon
   Hobbs, John & Cecily 7 yrs feltmaker 40s

2/11	1646	28 Nov	Jenkins, William son of William, mercer, dec'd, of Newent Cooke, Richard & Margaret 7 yrs chandler 1s 8d
		1 Dec	Cowcher, Robert son of Thomas, cordwainer, of Gloucester Jones, Thomas & Elizabeth 7 yrs pinmaker 2s 6d
		4 Dec	Browne, Joseph son of Thomas, yeoman, of Awre Trippet, Thomas & [blank] 8 yrs mercer 2s 6d
			Samson, Jonathon son of John, turner, of Gloucester Samson, William & [blank] 7 yrs turner [blank]
2/12		1 Dec	Ewins, John son of John, yeoman, of Marlcliff [MS Mart Cleeve], Warws Harward, Richard & [blank] 7 yrs draper 6s 8d
		5 Dec	Butter, Roger son of John, yeoman, of Hartpury Nash, Richard & [blank] 7 yrs chandler [blank]
		1 Dec	Townesend, William son of William, labourer, of Gloucester Pritchard, Thomas & Emit 7 yrs gentleman £6
		2 Nov	Smyth, Giles son of Richard, husbandman, of Painswick Gilbert, Giles & Margaret 7 yrs chandler 20s
2/13		25 Dec	Holborne, John son of John, mason, of Oddington Allen, Thomas & [blank] 7 yrs tanner 2s 6d
		1 Nov	Churches, Thomas son of Thomas, miller, of Cranham Wilkins, Richard & Matilda 7 yrs wiredrawer 3s 4d
	1647	2 Feb	Gurner, Richard son of George, weaver, dec'd, of Gloucester Stephens, Thomas & Alice 8 yrs pinmaker 2s 6d
2/14	1646	15 Oct	Wasfeild, John son of John, husbandman, dec'd, of Olveston Welsteedd, John & Elizabeth 7 yrs blacksmith 5s
	1647	1 Jan	Martin, Abraham son of Ewen, yeoman, dec'd, of Saintbury Lucas, Thomas & Elizabeth 7 yrs farrier 2s 6d
		18 Jan	Stallard, Thomas son of Anselm, cooper, dec'd, of Gloucester Carter, William & Joyce 7 yrs cooper 2s 6d [Replacing entry at 2/2]
2/15		11 Feb	Onyon, Humphrey son of Humphrey, sievemaker, of Gloucester Onyon, Humphrey, his father, & Eleanor 7 yrs sievemaker 5s [cf Appendix V]
		15 Feb	Wintle, John son of Richard, cordwainer, of Gloucester Wintle, Richard, his father, & Alice 7 yrs cordwainer 2s 6d
		2 Feb	Carew, Thomas son of Matthew, knight, of Middle Littleton, Worcs Comelyne, James & Jane 7 yrs apothecary 5s
2/16			Cooke, Richard son of John, thatcher, of Minsterworth Reeve, William & Elizabeth 7 yrs butcher 5s
		29 Sep	Wyniatt, Richard son of John, gentleman, of Dymock Singleton, William, alderman, & Frances 8 yrs draper 5s
			Nash, John son of John, of Mitcheldean Beard, John & Margaret 8 yrs mercer 2s 6d

2/17	1647	25 Mar	Caise, Robert son of John, yeoman, of Huntley Davis, Roger & Katharine 8 yrs glover 2s
		1 Mar	Vinar, Mathias son of Joan, widow, of Churchdown Browne, William & Elizabeth 8 yrs pewterer [2s 6d *deleted*] nil
		25 Mar	Bishop, Anthony son of Richard, yeoman, of Boddington Beale, Geoffrey & Edith 8 yrs mercer 10s
2/18			Heathfield, William son of Guy, farmer, of Slimbridge Singleton, John & Anne 7 yrs innholder 40s
		25 Apr	Whittingam, Jesse son of Thomas, baker, of Gloucester Whittingam, Thomas, his father, & Alice 7 yrs baker 5s *Mrs Browne's money*[1]
		21 Apr	Skillern, Richard son of Richard, tanner, of Gloucester Pullen, Thomas & Joan 8 yrs tailor 5s *Mrs Browne's money*
		29 Sep	Ackinson, George son of Anthony, of Elterwalter [Westmld] Knight, Nathaniel & Joan 7 yrs chandler 10s
2/19		21 Apr	Mills, Thomas son of William, yeoman, of Barnwood Broad, Richard & Mary 7 yrs baker 2s 6d
		22 Apr	Noven, Richard son of Richard, tailor, dec'd, of Gloucester Hookam, Nathaniel & Alice 7 yrs from 25 Mar last butcher 5s
		11 May	Mous, Richard son of Richard, garter weaver, of Gloucester Colericke, Daniel & Mary 7 yrs bodicemaker 2s 6d
	1648	1 Jan	Phelps, Joseph son of Edward, chandler, of Tewkesbury Knight, Nathaniel & Joan 7 yrs [from] the same day chandler 10s
2/20	1647	2 Jun	Cleeve William son of William, dec'd, of Arlingham Ley, Giles & Hester 8 yrs chandler 10s
		25 Mar	Powell, Henry son of Hugh, yeoman, dec'd, of Tibberton Fones, John & Eleanor, of Tibberton 8 yrs [from] 5 Jun glover 5s
		28 Jun	Wood, Thomas son of John, labourer, of Gloucester Symondes, John & Anne 8 yrs cordwainer 2s 6d *pauper* [*Entry deleted*]
2/21		1 Jun	Cooke, Benjamin son of William, dec'd, of Uckington Plott, Cornelius & [*blank*] 7 yrs [from] 2 Jun tailor 2s 6d
		8 Jun	Goodchep, Thomas son of Thomas, husbandman, of Hasfield Coxe, Winston & Anne 7 yrs cordwainer 2s 6d
		24 Jun	Bullocke, John son of William, dec'd, of Longney Barton, Richard & Anne 7 yrs glover 6d

---

[1] GBR B3/2 p 402 26 Mar 1647: To receive £4 of the legacy of Mrs Sarah Browne to place them apprentice with masters to be approved by the mayor and aldermen: Richard son of William Skillen, Jesse son of Thomas Whittingham, Thomas son of Thomas Perry.

2/22	1647	Bullocke, Joseph son of William, dec'd, of Longney Coxe, Richard & Susannah 7 yrs [from] the same day cordwainer 6d
	3 May	Drewry, John son of John, tailor, of Gloucester Plott, Cornelius & [blank] 7 yrs tailor 2s 6d
	24 Jun	Robins, Thomas son of Thomas, of Stow on the Wold Collett, John & Elizabeth 7 yrs tanner 2s 6d
2/23	20 Jul	Thayer, John son of Giles, baker, dec'd, of Gloucester Cuffe, Thomas & Frances 7 yrs [from] 20 Jul mercer [blank]
	29 Jul	Phillipps, William son of William, haberdasher, dec'd, of Gloucester Hayward, John & Sarah 7 yrs [from] 28 Jul feltmaker 1s
	25 Jul	Lugg, John son of Thomas, dec'd, of Gloucester Roberts, Elizabeth, widow, 7 yrs [from] 30 Jul pewterer 2s 6d
2/24		Putlie, Thomas son of George, labourer, of Berkeley Clayfield, Edward & Alice [from] 30 Jul 8 yrs tanner 2s 6d
		Packer, William son of William, gentleman, of Gloucester Hayes, Henry & [blank] 8 yrs [from] 31 Aug cordwainer 2s 6d
	10 Aug	Wright, Thomas son of Thomas, innholder, of Gloucester Wright, Thomas, his father, & Anne 7 yrs [from] 10 Aug innholder 5s
2/25	20 Aug	Butter, John son of John, of Hartpury Chapman, Thomas & [blank] 7 yrs [from] 2 Aug tailor 2s 6d

	25 Jul	Keene, John son of William, tailor, dec'd, of Gloucester
		   Harris, Edward & Mary 7 yrs [from] 30 Aug tailor 2s 6d
		   Mr Hollyday's money[1]

	29 Sep	Clarke, William son of John, dec'd, of Hartpury
		   Harris, Walter & Elizabeth 7 yrs cordwainer 6s 8d
		   [*Repeated & cancelled at 2/28*]

2/26	24 Aug	Greene, Philip son of Philip, of Great Malvern, Worcs Swayne, William & Joan 7 yrs [from] 24 Aug lantern maker 5s
	21 Jul	Greene, Richard son of Richard, cordwainer, of Gloucester Lea, Francis 8 yrs [from] 3 Aug cordwainer 3s 4d
	21 Sep	Bodman, Joan daughter of Richard, baker, of Gloucester Thomas, Henry & Joan 8 yrs [from] 2 Sep [*no trade*]
2/27	25 Sep	Nicholls, John son of Richard, labourer, of Harescombe Lugg, Anne, widow 8 yrs [from] 30 Sep tanner 4s
	29 Sep	Ellis, Jeremiah son of John, yeoman, late of Berkeley Bubb, Toby and Katharine 7 yrs [from] 28 Sep cordwainer 2s 6d

---

[1] GBR B3/2 p 420 21 Jul 1647: To receive £5 of Mr Hollidaye's money: John Lugge, Thomas Pettifer, Amity Clutterbooke, the widow Carver's son, William Phillips, John Keene, for whom the mayor gave his voice and not for Greene who was otherwise equal to him in the vote.

	1647	25 Jul	Petifor, Thomas son of Timothy, late of Gloucester
			Barrat, Thomas & Margaret 8 yrs cutler 2s 6d
			Mr Hollyday's money

2/28   **John Madocke, mayor [1647–8]**
        [Thomas Pearce and Thomas Lugg, sheriffs]

	1647	8 Oct	Scriven, Henry son of John, gentleman, of Gloucester
			Harward, Geoffrey & Mary 7 yrs draper
		29 Sep	Clarke, William son of John, dec'd, of Hartpury
			Harris, Walter & Elizabeth 7 yrs [from] 12 Oct cordwainer 6s 8d
			Cancelled, entered previously [See 2/25]

2/29   Thackwell, Joseph son of Thomas, tanner, dec'd, of Birtsmorton
                    [MS Birch Moreton], [Worcs]
                Collett, Edmund & Margery 8 yrs tanner 5s

        21 Oct Hiett, William son of Thomas, dec'd, of Minsterworth
                Phelpes, William & [*blank*] 7 yrs [from] 16 Oct cordwainer 2s 6d

2/30   23 Nov Iddin, John son of Richard, dec'd, of Gloucester
                Barker, Thomas & Margaret 7 yrs [from] 21 Oct pinmaker 2s 6d

        25 Dec Guyse, Henry son of George, gentleman, of Sherborne
                Whittington, William & [*blank*] 7 yrs [from] 28 Oct apothecary 5s

2/31   1 Nov   Wyse, Urian son of Denis, alderman, mercer, of Gloucester
                Wyse, Denis, his father, & Hephzibah 7 yrs [from] 13 Nov
                    mercer 7s

        15 Nov Barnewood, Richard son of Edmund, dec'd, of Gloucester
                Barnewood, John & Hester 7 yrs bellfounder 2s 6d

2/32   Harris, Henry son of Henry, of Upton St Leonards
                Brode, Elizabeth, widow 7 yrs baker [*blank*]

        17 Nov Wood, William son of John, gentleman, of Gloucester
                Grevill, Edward & Mary 8 yrs [from] 17 Nov mercer 2s 6d

        1 Dec   Ricotts, George son of William, of Newland
                Wood, John & Elizabeth 7 yrs tanner 1s

2/33   Symonds, William son of John, of Minsterworth
                Gray, Joan, widow 7 yrs butcher 2s 6d
                    9 Jul 1652: turned over by consent to complete his term with
                    Robert Jones, butcher. Before William Singleton, mayor, Thomas
                    Hill, Denis Wise, Luke Nurse, Lawrence Singleton

        25 Dec Fleminge, Thomas son of Thomas, butcher, of Gloucester
                Symes, Robert & Anne 7 yrs mercer 5s

                Bicke, Edward son of Edmund, innholder, dec'd, of Gloucester
                Warwicke, William & Anne 8 yrs innholder 10s 6d

2/34	1648	25 Mar	Clements, John son of John, dec'd, of Evesham, Worcs Jennings, Alice 7 yrs baker 3s 4d
		2 Feb	Pitt, Samuel son of Samuel, pinner, of Gloucester Ellis, Anthony & Joyce 7 yrs innholder 10s
2/35	1647	25 Dec	Marten, Alexander son of John, tailor, of Gloucester Grenninge, Richard & Alice 8 yrs tailor nil
		6 Oct	Wilse, John son of Thomas, yeoman, of Dymock Williams, Isaac & Eleanor 8 yrs tailor 2s 6d
	1648	25 Mar	Linkinholt, John son of John, dec'd, of Gloucester Linkinholt, William & Elizabeth 7 yrs wiredrawer 5s *Bound with the sum of £4 of Mrs Browne's gift*[1]

Enrolled 27 April

2/36	27 Apr	Lane, Nicholas son of Walter, gentleman, dec'd, of Gloucester Yates, Thomas & Elizabeth 8 yrs apothecary 5s
	25 Mar	Taylor, Robert son of Robert, late of Ross, Herefs Knipe, John & [*blank*] 7 yrs glover 5s 4 May
	5 May	Ducke, John son of Thomas, late of Upton St Leonards Stephens, Henry & Anne 7 yrs brewer 10s 7 May
2/37	10 May	Roberts, Thomas son of Edward, dec'd, of Ruardean Symons, Richard & Joan 7 yrs from 10 May glover 2s 6d *4 Jun 1651: turned over to James Cordell, glover, according to the covenants of this indenture by and with his own consent and the consent of Joan the wife of Richard Simons who hath absented himself from his dwelling and left the said apprentice with his said wife. Before Thomas Hill, one of the aldermen*
	3 May	Everett, Ambrose son of Ambrose, fuller, of Dursley Lysons, Daniel & Sarah 9 yrs from 3 May draper £5
2/38	20 Jun	Faulkner, Dennis son of Maurice, clothier, of Gloucester Hordell, John & Margaret 7 yrs tailor 5s
	25 Mar	Champnis, Arthur son of Arthur, yeoman, of Hull *alias* Hill Greene, John & Katharine 7 yrs cooper 10s
	22 Jun	Blye, Richard son of Richard, labourer, dec'd, of Gloucester Lews, Abel & Joan 7 yrs tiler 2s 6d *Mrs Browne's money*
2/39	14 Jul	Barrett, Thomas son of Arthur, yeoman, of Minsterworth Gwynn, Augustine jr & Margaret 8 yrs cordwainer 5s

---

[1] GBR B3/2 p 449 27 Mar 1648: To receive £4 of Mrs Browne's money: John Blye, John Linkinholt, John Barton.

	1648	24 Jun	Hall, John son of Thomas, tanner, of Gloucester

1648　24 Jun　Hall, John son of Thomas, tanner, of Gloucester
　　　　　　　Hayes, Anne, widow　7 yrs　baker　5s
　　　　　　　　12 Feb 1655: Alice Jennings otherwise Pincke, widow, came before Edmund Collett, mayor, William Caple and Laurence Singleton and confessed that John Hall, who is turned over to serve the residue of his term with her, has been absent from her service a whole year and as much as from Michaelmas last past to the day of the date hereof

2/40

　　　　　22 Jul　Bishopp, Giles son of Thomas, dec'd, of Painswick
　　　　　　　　Taylor, Richard jr & [*blank*]　7 yrs　mercer　2s 6d

　　　　　24 Jun　Morley, James son of John, clothier, of Ledbury, Herefs
　　　　　　　　Atkins, John & Elizabeth　7 yrs　cordwainer　5s

　　　　　7 Aug　Woodward, William son of William, blacksmith, of Gloucester
　　　　　　　　Woodward, William, his father, & Anne　7 yrs　blacksmith　5s
　　　　　　　　Mr Holliday's money[1]

2/41

　　　　　11 Aug　Jones, Richard son of Thomas, victualler, late of Gloucester
　　　　　　　　Tayler, George & Eleanor　7 yrs　cordwainer　[*Holliday*]
　　　　　　　　15 Aug 1651: turned over to John Tailor, cordwainer, to serve the residue of his term by his master's consent and his own. Before Anthony Edwardes, Thomas Hill, Jasper Clutterbuck

　　　　　　　　Bubb, Thomas son of Toby, cordwainer, of Gloucester
　　　　　　　　Bubb, Toby, his father, & Katharine　8 yrs　cordwainer　5s
　　　　　　　　Mr Hollyday's money

　　　　　　　　Savage, Henry son of Anthony, wiredrawer, of Gloucester
　　　　　　　　Wilkins, Richard & Matilda　7 yrs　wiredrawer　5s
　　　　　　　　Mr Holliday's money

2/42

　　　　　25 Jul　Lane, Thomas son of Walter, baker, dec'd, of Gloucester
　　　　　　　　Cooke, Thomas & Margaret　9 yrs　chandler　40s

　　　　　29 Aug　Fewtrell, Nicholas son of William, tailor, dec'd, of Gloucester
　　　　　　　　Fewtrell, Edward & Joan　7 yrs　tailor　2s 6d
　　　　　　　　Mr Holliday's money

　　　　　15 Sep　Younge, Robert son of John, currier, of Gloucester
　　　　　　　　Barker, Thomas & Margaret　8 yrs　pinmaker　2s 6d

2/43

Henry Cugley, mayor [1648–9]
[William Clark and Richard Taylor, sheriffs]

　　1648　18 Oct　Restall, Richard son of Richard, tanner, of Gloucester
　　　　　　　　Coxe, Richard & Susannah　7 yrs　cordwainer　1s　[*Holliday*]

---

[1] GBR B3/2 p 462　21 Jul 1648: To receive £5 of Mr Hollidaye's money: Toby Bubb, William Woodward, Richard Restall, Nicholas Fewtrell, Richard Jones, Henry Savage. 'The masters are to receive the said several £5 with their respective apprentices as has been formerly used.'

	1648	18 Dec	Crumlum, Giles son of Richard, clerk, dec'd, of Quedgeley
			Gwyn, Augustine sr & Alice 7 yrs cordwainer 5s
	1649	1 Jan	Greene, Richard son of Philip, husbandman, of Great Malvern, Worcs
			Powel, William & Joan 7 yrs haulier [MS hallier] 2s 6d
2/44		14 Jan	Lugg, William son of Jasper, tanner, dec'd, of Gloucester
			Sampson, William & Jane 7 yrs turner & combmaker 5s
		29 Jan	Beale, William son of Thomas, chandler, dec'd, of Ross, Herefs
			Lane, William & Katherine 7 yrs feltmaker 1s
2/45		2 Feb	Payne, Thomas son of Joseph, surgeon, of Cirencester
			Greene, Roland & Anne 7 yrs brewer 2s
		6 Feb	Johnsons, Thomas son of James, chapman, of Gloucester
			Stephens, Thomas & Alice 7 yrs pinmaker 2s 6d
		8 Feb	Cussens, Thomas son of William, farmer, of Hucclecote
			Greene, John & Katharine 7 yrs cooper 2s 6d
2/46		25 Mar	Band, Richard son of Richard, dec'd, of Harescombe
			Harris, Anne, widow 7 yrs baker 4s
	1646	1 May	Pinbury, Robert son of Charles, dec'd, of Cranham
			Knight, James & Katharine 7 yrs currier 12d
			This indenture was enrolled a great time after the making of it
	1648	29 Sep	Swett, Richard son of John, of Flaxley
			Hayes, Christopher & Joan 7 yrs glazier 2s
2/47	1649	5 Apr	Elridge, William son of William, silkweaver, late of Gloucester
			Onnyon, Thomas & Bridget 8 yrs silkweaver 3s
		25 Mar	Morse, John son of Thomas, gentleman, Tibberton
			Morse, Humphrey 7 yrs chandler 2s 6d
		26 Apr	Collett, Henry son of William, dec'd, of Cheltenham
			Sturmy, John 7 yrs glover 3s
2/48		1 May	Crumpe, Richard son of Richard, cordwainer, of Gloucester
			Grining, Richard & Alice 7 yrs tailor 10s
			Mrs Browne's money[1]
	1648	25 Dec	Mills, Bartholomew son of William, yeoman, of Barnwood
			James, Leigh & Christian 7 yrs baker 5s
	1649	1 May	Ockford, John son of John, yeoman, dec'd, of Gloucester
			Whitfield, Richard jr & Hannah 8 yrs baker 10s
2/49		5 May	Townsend, Lawrence son of Thomas, blacksmith, of Gloucester
			Townsend, Thomas, his father, & Joan 7 yrs blacksmith 10s
			[*Mrs Browne*]
		25 Mar	Younge, Robert son of John, late of St Mary's parish in Gloucester
			Loggins, Augustine & Anne 9 yrs mason 1s

---

[1] GBR B3/2 p 497 26 Mar 1649: To receive £4 of Mrs Browne's money: Richard son of Richard Crumpe, Lawrence son of Thomas Townsend, John son of Humphrey Dier.

| | 1649 | 22 May | Cowcher, William son of Thomas, cordwainer, of Gloucester |
| | | | Cowcher, John & Jane 8 yrs pinmaker 10s |

2/50   5 Jun   Haynes, Edward son of William, carpenter, dec'd, of Olveston
      Haines, Nicholas & Sarah 8 yrs milliner 2s 6d

25 Mar   Cooke, William son of William, baker, of Gloucester
      Cooke, William, his father, & [blank] 7 yrs baker 5s

24 Jun   Pedlingham, Richard son of Thomas, saddler, of Gloucester
      Pedlingham, Thomas, his father, & Susannah 7 yrs saddler 5s

2/51   14 Jul   Hickes, Christopher son of William, dec'd, of Tirley
      Hickes, Thomas 7 yrs tailor 2s

1 Mar   Suffield, Anthony son of Thomas, cook, of Gloucester
      Suffield, Thomas, his father, & Anne 7 yrs cook 10s
      [cf Appendix V]

24 Jul   Rixton, Ralph son of Ralph, clerk, of Kingsdon, Som
      Branch, John & [blank] 9 yrs mercer 5s

2/52   1647   25 Jul   Weaver, Thomas son of Thomas, butcher, dec'd, of Gloucester
      Charleton, Edward & Elizabeth 7 yrs wiredrawer 2s 6d
      Mr Hollyday's money

1649   25 Jul   Gregory, William son of Henry, dec'd, of Gloucester
      Humphries, Richard & Frances 7 yrs butcher 1s
      Mr Holliday's money

1 Aug   Tomkins, John son of John, blacksmith, of Gloucester
      Tomkins, John, his father, & Ursula 7 yrs blacksmith 6s 8d
      Mr Holiday's money

2/53   Pritchard, Thomas son of Henry, dec'd, of Gloucester
      Willmotts, Robert 8 yrs saddler 5s

18 Jul   Rainsford, Thomas son of William, innholder, dec'd, of Lechlade
      Massinger, Richard & Margaret 7 yrs brewer

13 Aug   Merrett, Richard son of Thomas of [blank]
      Phenix, Henry & Margaret 7 yrs pinmaker 2s 6d
      £4 of Mrs Browne's money

24 Jun   Parker, James son of John, farmer, of Hampton Lovett, Worcs
      Parker, Thomas & Margaret 7 yrs baker 5s

2/54   1 Aug   Addis, Edward son of Edward, cordwainer, of Gloucester
      Hill, Walter & Dorothy 9 yrs cordwainer 12d

24 Jun   Archer, George son of Edward, gentleman, late of Hanley, Worcs
      Fones, Godfrey & Anne 7 yrs cordwainer 5s
      11 Feb 1651: turned over to John Atkins, cordwainer, for the residue of his term with the consent of his master and his own. Before Thomas Hill

3 Aug   Keare, Henry son of Thomas, farmer, of Gloucester
      Stephens, Thomas & Alice 7 yrs pinmaker 2s 6d

2/55	1649	5 Sep	Berrow, Samuel son of George, tailor, of Gloucester Berrow, George, his father, & Alice 7 yrs tailor 1s *Mr Holidaie's money*[1]
		29 Sep	Williams, John son of John, farmer, of Gloucester Wheeler, William & Jane 7 yrs tailor 2s 6d
			Collet, Edmund son of Edmund, tanner, of Gloucester Cooke, John & Sarah 8 yrs haberdasher 2s 6d
2/56			Ryland, John son of Thomas, dec'd, of Quinton Collet, Edmund & Margery 7 yrs tanner 2s 6d
		24 Jun	Bennet, John son of William, surgeon, dec'd, of Longney Jennings, William & Bridget 7 yrs barber surgeon 2s 6d

James Stephens, mayor [1649–50]
[Robert Tyther and William Fowler, sheriffs]

	1649	10 Oct	Pritchard, Samuel son of Philip, yeoman, of North Cerney Stephens, James & Anne 7 yrs tanner 2s 6d
2/57		1 Nov	Badger, Albert son of Brian, cutler, of Gloucester Phenix, Henry & Margaret 7 yrs pinmaker 5s
			Jones, John son of John, feltmaker, of Salisbury [MS New Sarum], Wilts Phenix, Henry & Margaret 7 yrs pinmaker 5s
		26 Nov	Eliots, Robert son of Edward, dec'd, of Gloucester Haies, Christopher jr & Margaret 8 yrs glazier 40s *Mr Holidaie's money*
2/58	1650	18 Jan	George, William son of Robert, yeoman, dec'd, of Gloucester Phelpes, Thomas & Frances 7 yrs feltmaker 2s 6d *12 May 1651: turned over to Richard Bosley, feltmaker, for the residue of his term. Before Mr Hill and Mr Wise, aldermen*
		12 Jan	Francombe, Thomas son of Henry, woollen draper, dec'd, of Gloucester Phelpes, Thomas & Frances 10 yrs feltmaker 5s [*cf Appendix V*]
		19 Jan	Reade, John son of John, farmer, late of 'Batchfords Heath' [Besford Heath?], Worcs Deane, Thomas 7 yrs blacksmith 2s 6d
		28 Jan	Bayneham, John son of Thomas, wiredrawer, dec'd, of Gloucester Stapp, William & Sarah 7 yrs innholder 2s
2/59		8 Feb	Chandler, Nathaniel son of John, yeoman, of Eckington, Worcs Palmer, [Edmund] & Hester 7 yrs baker 2s

---

[1] GBR B3/2 p 510 21 Jul 1649: To receive £5 of Mr Hollidaye's money: Thomas Weaver, Samuel Berrow, Robert Elliotts, Samuel Roberts, Joan Gregory's son, John Tomkins's son. The £4 of Mrs Browne's money formerly granted to Humphrey Dier's son to be granted to one Merrett.

	1650	2 Feb	Bennett, Robert son of Robert, yeoman, of Berkeley Stephens, James, mayor, & Anne [*no term*] maltster 2s 6d

1 Mar Beale, Richard son of John, dec'd, of Tirley
Nicholls, John & Mary 7 yrs tanner 10s

2/60 29 Mar Alday, John son of John, dec'd, of Gloucester
Horsington, Thomas & Margery 7 yrs bodicemaker 2s 6d
£4 of Mrs Browne's money[1]
17 Feb 1654: turned over to serve the residue of his term with Daniel Colericke, bodicemaker
[*See 2/131*]

Wood, Thomas son of John, of Gloucester
Simons, John & Emma 7 yrs gardener 2s 6d
£4 of Mrs Browne's money

25 Mar Turner, Edward son of Edward, tailor, dec'd, of Gloucester
Clayfield, Edward & Alice 7 yrs tanner 2s 6d

Niblet, Jonathan son of John, tailor, dec'd, of Gloucester
Elliotts, John & Margaret 7 yrs wiredrawer 2s 6d

2/61 19 Apr Dunne, Thomas son of Nathaniel, tailor, of Gloucester
Dunne, Nathaniel, his father, & Jane 7 yrs tailor 5s [*Mrs Browne*]

2 Feb Boyes, John son of John, husbandman, of Cowley
Mills, John & Mary 8 yrs wiredrawer 40s

13 May *Ebbs, Philip, late apprentice of Margery Bruckbank, dec'd, turned over to serve the residue of his term with Robert Willmots, saddler. Before James Stephens, mayor, Thomas Hill & Luke Nourse*
[*See 2/8*]

16 May Litle, John son of John, yeoman, dec'd, of Hartpury
Jennings, Alice, widow 7 yrs baker 2s 6d

2/62 5 Mar Harmer, Francis son of John, gentleman, dec'd, of Gloucester Castle
Browne, John & Elizabeth 8 yrs mercer 2s 6d

21 Jun Reeve, Giles son of Giles, gunsmith, of Gloucester
Reeve, Giles, his father, & Mary 7 yrs gunsmith 5s

Reeve, Samuel son of Giles, gunsmith, of Gloucester
Reeve, Giles, his father, & Mary 8 yrs gunsmith 10s

20 July Shayle, Thomas son of Thomas, gentleman, of Dymock
Peirce, Thomas & Martha 8 yrs from 1 Aug mercer 3s 4d

23 May Sturmy, Daniel son of Daniel, yeoman, dec'd, of Cheltenham
Sturmy, John 7 yrs glover 2s 6d
This indenture was enrolled a great while after the making

---

[1] GBR B3/2 p 542 26 Mar 1650: To receive £4 of Mrs Browne's money: John Alday, Thomas Woods, Thomas Dunne.

2/63	1650	25 July	Bradgate, Richard son of Richard, barber surgeon, of Gloucester Bradgate, Richard, his father, & Alice 8 yrs barber surgeon 10s *£5 of Mr Hollidaie's gift*[1]
		[blank]	Jackson, Edward son of John, dec'd, of Gloucester Doughton, Richard & Elizabeth 7 yrs pinmaker 5s
		3 Aug	Turner, William son of Edward, yeoman, of Througham, Bisley Morse, Humphrey 7 yrs chandler 5s
		25 Jul	Bulbricke, Nicholas son of John, dec'd, of Gloucester Cowcher, John & Jane 7 yrs pinmaker 10s *£5 of Mr Hollidaie's gift*
2/64			Smith, John son of George, dec'd, of Gloucester Samson, Jonathan & Mary 7 yrs turner 5s *Mr Hollidaie's money*
		28 Aug	Silvester, Thomas son of Thomas, of Cirencester Samson, William & Jane 7 yrs turner 2s 6d
		29 Aug	Watkins, John son of Richard, of Gloucester Wise, Denis & Hephzibah 8 yrs mercer 5s

2/65   Anthony Edwards, mayor [1650–1]
[Henry Robins and Daniel Lysons, sheriffs]

	1650	2 Oct	Mearson, Nicholas son of Nicholas, dec'd, of Tewkesbury Longden, Robert & Joan 7 yrs ironmonger 2s 6d
			Whitfeild, Edmund son of Edmund, joiner, of Gloucester Davis, Henry & Elizabeth 7 yrs cordwainer 6d
		29 Sep	Harris, James son of Timothy, clerk, of Bockleton, Worcs Barton, Richard & Anne 7 yrs glover 5s
		23 Oct	Addys, John son of John, yeoman, of Frampton on Severn Nicolls, John & Mary 7 yrs tanner 5s
2/66		28 Oct	Smarte, Joseph son of Richard, husbandman, of Over Wellsteede, John & Elizabeth 7 yrs blacksmith 5s
		29 Oct	Cooke, William son of William, yeoman, of Uckington Morse, Humphrey & Blanche 7 yrs chandler 5s
		21 Nov	Bumford, William son of William, husbandman, of Upton St Leonards Shipton, John & Sarah 7 yrs bodicemaker 5s
2/67		3 Oct	Browne, Nathaniel son of Nathaniel, yeoman, of city of London Vaiers, Thomas & Margaret 7 yrs farrier 3s 4d

---

[1] GBR B3/2 p 559 22 Jul 1650: To receive £5 of Mr Hollidaye's money: John son of George Smith, Toby Keeble's son, Richard Bradgate's son, Richard son of Elizabeth Skillam, John Bulbricke's son, Edward Fewtrell's son.

	1650	29 Sep	Oker, John son of John, gentleman, late of Wells, Som Townsend, Elizabeth, widow, 7 yrs barber surgeon 5s
			Towey, Edward son of Lawrence, baker, dec'd, of Tewkesbury Cartwright, Edward 7 yrs baker 2s 6d
2/68		29 Oct	Singleton, William son of Francis, clerk, of Newent Singleton, William sr, alderman, & Frances [*blank*] woollen draper 3s 4d
	1651	15 Jan	Low, Robert son of Robert, dec'd, of Barnwood Linckinholt, William & Elizabeth 7 yrs wiredrawer 1s [*cf Appendix V*]
		18 Jan	Low, Richard son of Robert, dec'd, of Barnwood Davis, Thomas & Mary 7 yrs wiredrawer 5s
2/69	1644	10 Jun	Baker, John son of Griffin, butcher, of Gloucester Humfreys, Richard & Frances 7 yrs butcher 2s 6d *Time of Nicholas Webb, 1644*
	1651	4 Feb	Byrt, William son of Giles, yeoman, of Lydney Philips, James & Anne 7 yrs tailor 2s 6d
		17 Feb	Wooddinge, John son of John Wooding, husbandman, of Kingsholm Farley, George & Mary 8 yrs cutler 5s
2/70	1650	25 Dec	Haynes, Edward son of Francis, woollen draper, dec'd, of Worcester Singleton, Lawrence, alderman, & Mary 9 yrs woollen draper 10s
	1651	11 Feb	Hale, Richard son of Robert, husbandman, of Hartpury Tailor, John 7 yrs cordwainer 3s 4d
		14 Feb	Lye, Henry son of Francis, miller, of Barton Street, Gloucester Kercombe, John & Joyce 7 yrs blacksmith 6s 8d
2/71		10 Mar	Fewtrell, Thomas son of William, tailor, of Gloucester Horsington, Thomas & Margery 7 yrs bodicemaker £5 *city money*
	1642	18 Nov	Thomas, Jonathan son of William, shoemaker, of Gloucester Mathewes, Henry 7 yrs tailor
	1651	Mar	Haines, Thomas son of Thomas, dec'd, of Olveston Haines, Nicholas & Sarah 8 yrs milliner & hosier
2/72		24 Mar	Heath, Samuel son of Thomas, pewterer, dec'd, of Chipping Norton, Oxon Onion, Thomas & Bridget 8 yrs silkweaver
		25 Mar	Hignall, Thomas son of George, tailor, of Gloucester Hill, Walter & Dorothy 7 yrs cordwainer 2s
			Seaman, Robert son of William, maltster, of Gloucester Seaman, William, his father, & Edith 7 yrs maltster 5s
2/73		3 Apr	Neast, Joseph son of Alexander, silkweaver, dec'd Mitchell, George & Comfort 7 yrs garter weaver 2s 6d [*Repeated, altered, at 2/124*]
			Wright, John son of Richard, husbandman, of Gloucester Cowcher, John & Jane 7 yrs pinmaker 2s 6d

	1651	3 Apr	Laurence, Thomas son of Nicholas, husbandman, dec'd, of Gloucester
			Browne, John 7 yrs butcher 3s 4d
			£4 of Mrs Browne's money[1]
2/74			Abbat, Henry son of Henry, yeoman, of Gloucester
			Jennings, Alice, widow, 7 yrs baker 10s
		9 Apr	Baggatt, William son of John, cordwainer, late of Gloucester
			Hunt, John & Elizabeth 7 yrs garter weaver 2s 6d
			£4 of Mrs Browne's money
		12 Apr	Hall, William son of Thomas, yeoman, of Kilcot in parish of Newent
			Skinner, Anne, widow, 7 yrs glover
			9 Feb 1652 Thomas [sic] Hall delivered up his indenture of apprenticeship to the said Anne and both parts were cancelled
2/75		25 Mar	Davis, William son of Thomas, feltmaker, late of Gloucester
			Motley, Anthony & Joyce 7 yrs turner 2s 6d
	1650	25 Dec	Harry, John son of Robert, gentleman, late of Gloucester
			Chapman, Thomas & Eleanor 7 yrs tailor 2s 6d
	1651	25 Mar	Lugg Thomas son of Thomas, haberdasher, of Gloucester
			Beard, John & Margaret 8 yrs mercer 10s [cf Appendix V]
	1650	25 Dec	Wintle, Richard son of Richard, cordwainer, of Gloucester
			Wintle, Richard, his father, & Alice 7 yrs cordwainer 5s
2/76	1651	25 Mar	Goodwyn, Richard son of William, farmer, of Minsterworth
			Cox, Winston & Anne 7 yrs cordwainer 6d
		3 Apr	Randle, John son of James, yeoman, of Charlton Kings
			Smith, William & Katharine 7 yrs cordwainer 2s 6d
			[Entries from here on are in English]
		9 May	Terret, Thomas son of Samuel, husbandman, of Stroud
			Knight, Henry & Prudence 8 yrs innholder 1s
2/77		16 Jun	Raxhall, Richard son of Richard, dec'd, of city of London
			Atkins, John & Elizabeth 7 yrs cordwainer 12d
		24 Jun	Beale, James son of Richard, cordwainer, late of Gloucester
			Hughes, John & Jane 7 yrs cordwainer 12d
		6 Apr	Sandy, Mark son of Mark, husbandman, of Hasfield
			Burrup, Thomas & Joan 7 yrs cordwainer 12d
2/78		4 Jun	Hancksman, Thomas son of Thomas, victualler, dec'd, of Gloucester
			Eckly, Edward & Anne 8 yrs button maker 2s 6d
		4 Jul	Mercer, Robert son of Henry, yeoman, of Sandhurst
			Sare, John & Joan 7 yrs butcher 5s

---

[1] GBR B3/2 p 604 26 Mar 1651: To receive £4 of Mrs Browne's money: — Child, [William] Baggott, [Thomas] Laurence.

2/79	1651	24 Jun	Childs, John son of John, husbandman, late of Gloucester Greene, Thomas 8 yrs cordwainer 2s 6d *£4 of Mrs Browne's money*
		26 Mar	Fowler, John son of William, mercer, of Gloucester Fowler, William, his father, & Anne 8 yrs mercer 10s
		21 Jul	Phillips, John son of John, feltmaker, of Gloucester Phillips, John, his father, & Jane 8 yrs feltmaker 20s *£5 of Mr Hollidaie's gift*[1]
2/80		22 Jul	Morse, Thomas son of James, cordwainer, of Gloucester Cox, Winston & Anne 7 yrs cordwainer 6d *Mr Holliday's money*
		24 Jun	Marston, John son of John, clerk, dec'd, of Norton Arram, Thomas & [blank] 7 yrs mercer 2s 6d
		25 Jul	Danby, Thomas son of John, cordwainer, late of Gloucester Greene, Thomas & [blank] 7 yrs cordwainer 2s 6d *£5 of Mr Hollidaie's gift*
2/81		4 Aug	Hughes, Philip son of Thomas, pinmaker, late of Gloucester Gwin, Augustine jr & Margaret 7 yrs cordwainer 2s 6d *£5 of Mr Hollidaie's gift. 14 Oct 1651: turned over to Thomas Burrup, cordwainer, for the residue of his term by his own and his master's consent. Before Alderman Caple & Alderman Clutterbuck [cf Appendix V]*
		24 Jun	Townsend, Richard son of Christopher, barber surgeon, dec'd, of Gloucester Townsend, Elizabeth, widow, his mother 7 yrs barber surgeon 2s 6d
		25 Aug	Williams, Richard son of Anthony, nailer, of Westbury Stephens, James & Anne 7 yrs tanner £5
2/82		16 Jul	Clifford, James son of Thomas, of Gloucester Phenix, Henry & Margaret 8 yrs pinmaker 6d
		15 Aug	Townsend, Henry son of Christopher, barber surgeon, dec'd, of Gloucester Warwicke, William & Anne 8 yrs vintner 40s *[cf Appendix V]* *£5 of Mr Hollidaie's gift*
		16 Aug	Pinckutt, Jonathan son of Benjamin, broadweaver, late of Berkeley Gwyn, Augustine jr & Margaret 7 yrs cordwainer 2s 6d
2/83		1 Aug	Childe, Richard son of Richard, husbandman, of Upton St Leonards Martin, John & Jane 7 yrs baker 5s
		22 Sep	Best, Thomas son of Thomas, yeoman, of Kingsholm Fewtrell, Edward & Joan 7 yrs tailor 2s 6d
		29 Sep	Skillam, Isaac son of William, tanner, dec'd, of Barton Street Russell, William & Sarah 8 yrs skinner 5s *£5 of Mr Hollidaie's gift*

---

[1] GBR B3/2 p 620 21 Jul 1651: To receive £5 of Mr Hollidaye's money: John Phillips's son, Mary Danbye's son, James Morse's son, Mary Hughes's son, John Harris's son, widow Townsende's son.

2/84	1651	29 Sep	Wallington, Edward son of Stephen, cardmaker, of Wotton under Edge Elliotts, John & Margaret 8 yrs wiredrawer 2s 6d
			Petty, William son of John, dec'd, of Cirencester Gilbert, Giles & Mary 7 yrs chandler 5s
			Flemminge, John son of Thomas, tailor, of Gloucester Fleminge, Thomas, his father, & Rosamund 7 yrs tailor 5s
2/85		13 Aug	Hanksman, John son of Thomas, victualler, dec'd, of Gloucester Stap, William & Sarah 8 yrs innholder 12d
		29 Sep	Keene, William son of John, tailor, dec'd, of Barton Street Hiron, Humphrey & Margaret 7 yrs chandler 5s
			Savage, John son of John, husbandman, of Cowley Gwyn, Augustine sr & Alice 7 yrs shoemaker 3s 4d

2/86 **William Singleton, mayor [1651–2]**
[John Purlewent and Thomas Witcombe, sheriffs]

	1651	18 Nov	Low, Robert son of Robert, late of Barnwood Devis, Thomas & Mary 7 yrs wiredrawer 5s [*cf Appendix V*]
		1 Dec	Litle, Robert son of Thomas, yeoman, Uckington, parish of Elmstone [*sic*] Burroughs, Thomas & Comfort 7 yrs mercer 2s 6d
2/87		6 Dec	Guyse, Christopher son of John, gentleman, of Gloucester Yate, Thomas & Elizabeth 12 yrs apothecary 2s 6d
	1644	29 Sep	Cooke, Richard son of Richard, yeoman, of Poppinger [MS Popinge Joyes], Herefs Salcombe, John & Joan 7 yrs blacksmith 3s 4d *Enrolled 8 Dec 1651*
2/88	1651	25 Dec	Gracing, Aaron son of William, dec'd, of Over Church, Henry & Everin 7 yrs tailor 2s 6d
	1644	20 Aug	Wells, John son of Richard, tailor, of Kingsholm Hill, Walter 7 yrs cordwainer 5s *Enrolled 10 Dec 1651*
2/89	1651	25 Dec	Hayward, Samuel son of Richard, yeoman, of Barnwood Cleevely, Robert & Mary 8 yrs chandler 2s 6d
			Dowxell, William son of Thomas, husbandman, of Newent Messinger, Richard & Margaret 7 yrs brewer 5s
	1652	18 Jan	Chamley, Thomas son of Thomas Chamlyn, turner, dec'd, of Gloucester Greening, John & Frances 10 yrs turner 3s 4d
2/90	1651	7 Oct	Humphris, Richard son of Richard, butcher, of Gloucester Commelin, James & Jane 8 yrs apothecary
		25 Dec	Bicke, William son of Thomas, husbandman, dec'd, of Brockworth Gwyn, Augustine jr & Margaret 7 yrs cordwainer 2s 6d

	1652	2 Feb	Cox, Henry son of Henry, millwright, of Rudford Bicknell, William 7 yrs tailor 2s 6d
2/91		7 Feb	Sheppard, Joseph son of Edmund, dec'd, of St Andrew, [Pershore], Worcs Doughton, Stephen & Elizabeth 8 yrs from 25 Mar pinmaker 5s
			Goslinge, Thomas son of John, yeoman, dec'd, of Churcham Wintle, William & Elizabeth 8 yrs from 26 Mar haberdasher 5s
		10 Feb	Voare, Charles son of Charles, yeoman, of Weston under Penyard, Herefs Cawdle, William & Elizabeth 7 yrs woollen draper 5s
2/92	1651	18 Sep	Suffeild, Anthony son of Thomas, innholder, dec'd, of Gloucester Harris, Walter & Elizabeth 7 yrs shoemaker [cf Appendix V] *Enrolled 13 Feb 1652*
	1649	16 May	Keene, John son of Tacey, widow of John, of Little Witcombe Gilbert, Henry 7 yrs cordwainer *Enrolled 14 Feb 1652*
	1652	8 Mar	Hall, William son of Roger, wine cooper, dec'd, of Gloucester Merret, Thomas 7 yrs cordwainer 2s 6d [*Holliday*]
2/93		29 Mar	Webley, Robert son of Robert, husbandman, late of Brockworth Elliott, Edward & Margaret 7 yrs cordwainer 1s
		2 Apr	Lambert, Sylvester son of John, tobacco-pipe maker, of Gloucester Moore, Henry & Joan 7 yrs tobacco-pipe maker 10s *£4 of Mrs Browne's money*[1]
		5 Apr	Hussey, Anthony son of Arthur, husbandman, of Gloucester Meeke, Thomas & Margery 7 yrs currier 2s 6d *£4 of Mrs Browne's money*
2/94		2 Mar	Lugg, Thomas son of Thomas, haberdasher, of Gloucester Bleeke, William & Mary 7 yrs mercer 10s [*cf Appendix V*]
		10 Apr	Litle, John son of William, husbandman, dec'd, of Maisemore Wintle, Richard & Alice 7 yrs from 25 Mar last cordwainer 10s
		29 Apr	Dobbs, John son of John, glover, of Gloucester Paine, Margaret, widow 7 yrs [pinmaker] 2s 6d *21 Nov 1653: turned over to Richard Pigg, pinmaker.* *Before Jasper Clutterbooke*
2/95		3 May	Jones, Samuel son of William, dec'd, of Usk, Mon Hands, Richard 7 yrs bricklayer etc
		10 May	Mills, Giles son of Thomas, broadweaver, of Barton Street, Gloucester Greene, William & Mary 7 yrs pinmaker 1s
			Croker, Thomas son of Thomas, husbandman, of Elmore Williams, Nicholas & Joan 7 yrs joiner 2s 6d

---

[1] GBR B3/2 p 663 26 Mar 1652: To receive £4 of Mrs Browne's money: John Lambert, John Roberts, Anthony Hussey.

2/96	1652 25 Mar	Clark, Cyprian son of Godfrey, of Winchcombe Collett, John & Elizabeth 7 yrs tanner 5s
	24 May	Welsteede, John son of John, blacksmith, of Gloucester Welsteede, John, his father, & Elizabeth 7 yrs blacksmith 10s
	25 May	Thomas, John son of Richard, cook, of Gloucester Cox, Winston & Anne 7 yrs cordwainer 12d
2/97	26 May	Witcombe, Thomas son of Thomas, gentleman, of Gloucester Beard, John & Margaret 7 yrs mercer 2s 6d
	1 May	Nash, William son of Richard, tanner, dec'd, of Gloucester Nash, Richard & Joan 7 yrs feltmaker 2s 6d
		Carpenter, Henry son of Richard, husbandman, dec'd, of Maisemore Hayes, Henry & Joan 7 yrs cordwainer 2s 6d
2/98	15 Jun	Hartland, William son of William, wiredrawer, dec'd, of St Catherine's parish, Gloucester Coucher, John & Jane 7 yrs pinmaker 5s
	1 Jun	Parkes, William son of John, nailer, dec'd, of Gloucester Pitt, Samuel & Eleanor 7 yrs pinmaker 12d
	9 Jun	Lea, Henry son of Robert, of Gloucester Lea, Francis 7 yrs cordwainer 12d
2/99		Freeman, Joseph son of Thomas, clerk, of Naunton Till, Richard & Dorothy 7 yrs cutler 20s
	1 Jun	Vyner, Thomas son of Thomas, husbandman, of Gloucester Bradford, John & Anne 7 yrs button maker 20s
	29 Jun	Faulkner, Walter son of John, broadweaver, of Gloucester Pitt, Samuel & Eleanor 7 yrs pinmaker 12d
2/100	5 Jul	Yeeding, John son of Richard, husbandman, dec'd, of Gloucester Paine, Margaret, widow 7 yrs pinmaker 12d *21 Nov 1653 turned over to Richard Pigg, pinmaker, for the residue of his term. Jasper Clutterbook.* [*Cf John Dobbs, 2/94*]
		Whitle, Samuel son of John, husbandman, dec'd, of parish of St Mary de Lode, Gloucester Atkins, John & Elizabeth 7 yrs cordwainer 5s
	24 Jun	Merricke, George son of Humphrey, mercer, of Gloucester Allen, Lawrence & Anne 8 yrs chandler 5s *£5 of Mr Holliday's gift*[1]

---

[1] GBR B3/2 p 671 21 Jul 1652: To receive £5 of Mr Hollidaye's money: John Parker's son, Humphrey Merrick's son, John Jordan's son, Edward son of widow Dunne, Richard Doughton's son, William Hall. Robert Sturmy to have £4 now in the hands of Mr Alderman Wise of the gift of Mrs Browne to bind him apprentice.

2/101	1652	19 Jul	Guyse, William son of John, gentleman, of Gloucester Webbe, John 7 yrs mercer 2s 6d
		23 Jul	Hughes, Philip son of Thomas, pinmaker, dec'd, of Gloucester Beard, Nathaniel & Jane 7 yrs tailor 2s 6d [*cf Appendix V*]
		1 Jul	Sheppard, John son of Edward, feltmaker, of Gloucester Merrett, William 7 yrs cordwainer 2s 6d [*Holliday*]

2/102		26 Jul	Sturmy, Robert son of Robert, glover, dec'd, of Gloucester
			    Veysey, Walter & Margaret 8 yrs from 29 Sep next tailor 5s
			    £4 of Mrs Browne's money

		4 Aug	Perry, Henry son of John, husbandman, of Newent Graffstock, John & Elizabeth 7 yrs butcher 3s 4d

		6 Aug	Doughton, Richard son of Richard, pinmaker, dec'd, of Gloucester
			    Doughton, Stephen & Elizabeth 8 yrs pinmaker 10s
			    £5 of Mr Holliday's gift

2/103		14 Aug	Nelme, Richard son of Richard, tucker, of North Nibley
			    Clutterbooke, Daniel & Merriam 8 yrs from 24 Jun last
			    skinner 2s 6d

		20 Aug	Dunne, Lawrence son of Edward, chandler, dec'd, of Gloucester Merrett, Thomas & Esther 7 yrs cordwainer 2s 6d
		2 Aug	Addams, Thomas son of Thomas, yeoman, of Minsterworth Greene, John sr & Katharine 8 yrs cooper 3s 4d
2/104		31 Aug	Gwyn, David son of Allias, husbandman, dec'd, of Gloucester Stephens, Thomas & Alice 7 yrs pinmaker 2s 6d
		1 Sep	Wadman, Roger son of Roger, dec'd, of Cheriton [MS Cherington] Som Mitchell, George & Comfort 7 yrs garter weaver 2s 6d
		24 Aug	Wiltshire, Thomas son of John, broadweaver, of Tytherington Nash, Richard & Joan 7 yrs feltmaker 2s 6d
2/105		4 Sep	Hornedge, William son of William, husbandman, of Kingsholm Steevens, Thomas & Alice 7 yrs pinmaker 2s 6d
		3 Jul	Band, John son of John, cordwainer, dec'd, of Gloucester Pitt, Samuel & Eleanor 7 yrs pinmaker 12d
		24 Aug	Powell, Robert son of John, yeoman, of Tirley [MS Trinley *alias* Turley] Burrop, Thomas & Joan 7 yrs cordwainer 12d

		30 Aug	Dunne, Edward son of Edward, chandler, dec'd, of Gloucester
			    Sampson, Jonathon & Mary 7 yrs turner & combmaker 5s
			    £5 of Mr Holliday's gift. *No burgess*

2/106		27 Sep	Houlship, Edward son of John, husbandman, of Harthurstfield in parish of Cheltenham Mitchell, George & Comfort 7 yrs garter weaver 5s

William Caple, mayor [1652–3]
William Russell and John Singleton, sheriffs

1652 5 Oct Vyner, William son of Humphrey, of Churchdown
Bosly, Richard & Elizabeth 7 yrs feltmaker 2s 6d

14 Oct Barnad, James son of William, beer brewer, of Gloucester
Skillum, John 8 yrs skinner 10s
£4 of Mrs Browne's money [1]

4 Oct Ricketts, John son of James, husbandman, dec'd, of Hardwicke
Pedlingham, Thomas & Susannah 8 yrs saddler 5s

2/107 16 Oct Fletcher, Thomas son of Ralph, yeoman, of Maisemore
Fletcher, Thomas & Margaret 7 yrs tanner 2s 6d

22 Oct Hacker, Thomas son of Richard, yeoman, of Painswick
Jordan, John & Elizabeth 7 yrs baker 10s

28 Oct Coucher, Richard son of Thomas, cordwainer, dec'd, of Gloucester
Coucher, John & Jane 7 yrs pinmaker 15s

2/108 1 Nov Kearsey, Thomas son of Richard, fisher, dec'd, of Longford
Eckly, Henry & Anne 7 yrs milliner 2s 6d

Weaver, Edward son of Anthony, labourer, dec'd, of Westbury
Stephens, Thomas & Alice 7 yrs pinmaker 5s

1651 12 Mar Bower, Michael son of Anthony, gentleman, dec'd, of Mitcheldean
Plummer, Robert & Christian, of Mitcheldean and a burgess of
Gloucester 7 yrs pewterer *Enrolled 26 Nov 1652*

2/109 1652 10 Nov Mathews, William son of William, yeoman, of Minsterworth
Griffith, Jonathon & [*blank*] 7 yrs cordwainer 5s
*18 Nov 1653: turned over to John Tyler, cordwainer, for the
residue of his term. Before Anthony Edwards*

1 Nov Waye, William son of William, carpenter, dec'd, of Hankerton, Wilts
Vaughan, Richard & [*blank*] 7 yrs joiner 2s 6d

27 Nov King, Thomas son of Richard, clothier, dec'd, of Rodborough
Cooke, William & Anne 7 yrs baker 2s 6d

2/110 23 Dec Careless, Henry son of John, yeoman, of Tarrington [MS Taddington],
Herefs
Clutterbooke, Margaret, widow of Amity 7 yrs tailor 2s 6d

1650 9 Jul Chapman, Thomas son of Thomas, tailor, of Gloucester
King, Samuel & Mary 7 yrs tailor 5s *Enrolled 31 Jan 1653 and
turned over on that day to serve the residue of his term with
Thomas Hicke, with the consent of Samuel King & his own. Before
William Caple, mayor, & Denis Wise, alderman*

---

[1] GBR B3/2 p 700 24 Mar 1653: To receive £4 of Mrs Browne's money: son of Mary Canter, James Barnewood, Henry Tucker.

| | 1652 30 Nov | Churches, John son of Thomas, husbandman, of Cranham
Wilkins, Richard & Nanfun 7 yrs wiredrawer 4s *Enrolled 31 Jan 53*
*5 Oct 1658 John to complete his term with William Brymeyard,
wiredrawer, Richard Wilkins & his wife being dead* |
|-------|-------------|---|

2/111 1653 22 Feb Corr, Robert son of Robert, carrier, dec'd, of Gloucester
                  Downbell, Stephen & [blank] 7 yrs vintner 5s

       5 Mar Coale, John son of John, husbandman, of Churcham
              Pitt, Samuel & Eleanor 8 yrs pinmaker 1s

       9 Mar Underwood, Richard son of Richard, husbandman, of Taynton
              Baker, John & Anne 7 yrs butcher 5s

       15 Mar Smith, John son of John, baker, dec'd, of Gloucester
               Ellis, Godfrey & Margaret 7 yrs baker 2s 6d

2/112 26 Mar Staunton, Robert son of William, dec'd, husbandman, of Norton
               Barnwood, John & Hester 7 yrs bellfounder 12d

       1650 24 Jun Bullocke, Matthew son of Robert, yeoman, of Longney
                    Pace, Samuel 7 yrs baker *Enrolled 26 Mar 1653*

       1653 1 Apr Sare, James son of Ralph, pinmaker, dec'd, of Gloucester
                   Dunn, John & Margaret 7 yrs tailor 2s 6d

2/113 16 Apr Marden, Giles son of Thomas, yeoman, of Maisemore
               Franckis, Richard & Elizabeth 7 yrs cordwainer 2s 6d

       22 Apr Nicholls, George son of Otho, tailor, of Gloucester
               Beard, John & Sarah 8 yrs silkweaver 2s 6d

       18 Apr Linckinholt, John son of John, husbandman, dec'd, of Gloucester
               Fewtrell, William & Mary 7 yrs tailor 2s 6d

       23 Apr Williams, Richard son of John, husbandman, of Elkstone
               Pace, Thomas & Elizabeth 7 yrs cooper 2s 6d

2/114 10 May Davis, William son of John, gunsmith, of Ledbury, [Herefs]
               Goslinge, Thomas & [blank] 8 yrs sievemaker 5s

       16 May Tucker, Henry son of Thomas, tailor, dec'd, of Gloucester
               Plott, Cornelius & Margaret 8 yrs tailor 3s 4d
               £4 Mrs Browne's money

       18 May Franckis, Wiliam son of Henry, baker, dec'd, of Upton St Leonards
               Miles, James & Dorothy 7 yrs baker 5s

2/115 1 Mar Bower, Charles son of Anthony, yeoman, dec'd, of Mitcheldean
              Perkes, John & Alice 7 yrs baker 2s 6d

       30 May Bishop, Gregory son of William, yeoman, dec'd, of Donnington, Herefs
               Tailor, George & Joan 7 yrs cordwainer 3s 4d

       1 Jun Hopkins, John son of John, husbandman, of Cheltenham
              Mitchell, George & Comfort 7 yrs garter weaver 5s [*see 2/249*]

2/116 7 Jul Perkins, Richard son of Thomas, furrier, of city of Worcester
              Parish, John & Frances 7 yrs tailor 1s

| | 1653 24 Jun | Drury, William son of John, tailor, of Gloucester |
| | | Thomas, Jonathan & Joan 7 yrs tailor 10s |

    21 Jul Herbert, Edward son of Walter, gentleman, of Crickhowell, Brecon
              Nash, Richard & Joan 7 yrs grocer 1s

2/117   23 Jul Hill, Matthew son of Thomas, yeoman, of Ashleworth
              Fewtrell, Edward & Joan 7 yrs tailor 2s 6d

    25 Jul Holliday, Richard son of Maurice, husbandman, dec'd, of Upleadon
              Jennings, Alice, widow of Brian 7 yrs baker 2s 6d

    1 Aug Humphries, William son of John, baker, dec'd, of Gloucester
              Nicholls, John & Mary 8 yrs tanner 2s 6d
              £5 of Mr Holliday's gift [1] *No burgess*

2/118   25 Jul Dyer, James son of Humphrey, brewer, dec'd, of Gloucester
              Woogan, Thomas & Anne 7 yrs glover 5s
              £5 of Mr Holliday's gift   No burgess

           Eldridge, Richard son of William, tanner, late of Gloucester
              Phillips, John & Jane 8 yrs feltmaker 10s
              £5 of Mr Holliday's gift

    18 Aug Whitson, John son of John, pinmaker, dec'd, of Gloucester
              Tylor, Margaret, widow of James 7 yrs cordwainer 2s 6d but no clothes

2/119   Bishop, Robert son of John, yeoman, of Quedgeley
              Bishopp, Giles & [*blank*] 7 yrs mercer 2s 6d

    29 Aug Grainger, Thomas son of William, husbandman, late of Gloucester
              Phenix, Margaret, widow of Henry 7 yrs pinmaker 2s 6d
                22 Jul 1656: turned over to Thomas Baily, pinmaker, Margaret
                Phenix being dead. Before Anthony Edwards

    2 Sep Gee, George son of George, husbandman, of Morton in parish of
              Thornbury
              Lysons, Daniel & Sarah 10 yrs from 24 Jun woollen draper 5s

2/120   3 Sep Perkins, Walter son of Walter, husbandman, of Barnwood
              Doughton, Stephen & Elizabeth 7 yrs from 5 Sep pinmaker 20s

    1 Sep Clarke, Henry son of James, woollen draper, late of Gloucester
              Hayes, Christopher & Joan 7 yrs glazier 2s 6d [*Holliday*]
                20 Jun 1656: turned over to John Painter, glazier, by his own
                wish and that of Joan, widow of Christopher. Before Denis Wise,
                mayor, William Caple, Luke Nurse

    14 Sep Bowser, Thomas, son of George, gentleman, of Gloucester
              Greene, Roland & Anne 7 yrs from 29 Sep brewer 2s 6d
              [*cf Appendix V*]

---

[1] GBR B3/2 p 716 21 Jul 1653: To receive £5 of Mr Hollidaye's money: Henry son of James Clarke, James Dyer, Richard Elbridge, John Shepheard, William Humphries and also Philip Ward, placed apprentice by Mr Godfrey Ellis to Richard Harding, citizen and weaver of London by the appointment of this house.

2/121	1653	16 Sep	Clarke, Stephen, yeoman, dec'd, of Walford, Herefs Taylor, Richard & Dorothy 8 yrs from 2 Aug last mercer 5s
		17 Sep	Churches, John son of Robert, chandler, dec'd, of Mitcheldean Moore, George & Mary 7 yrs from 25 Jul last butcher 5s
		27 Sep	Stephenson otherwise Cowles, John son of Stephen, bodicemaker, of Gloucester Horsington, Thomas & Margery 7 yrs bodicemaker 2s 6d
2/122		1 Oct	Sulaway, William son of William, husbandman, of Cricklade, Wilts Wood, Thomas & Jane 8 yrs from 28 Aug last tanner 20s (Wm Caple, mayor)
		29 Sep	Jennings, William son of William, barber surgeon, of Gloucester Jennings, William, his father, & Bridget 7 yrs [barber surgeon] 5s

2/123 **Thomas Pury, mayor [1653–4]**
Robert Hill and William Bubb, sheriffs
The names of apprentices bound and enrolled in the year 1653

	1653	17 Oct	Keare, John son of Thomas, husbandman, of Gloucester Stephens, Thomas & Alice 7 yrs from 29 Sep last pinmaker 2s 6d
		18 Oct	Blunt, Charles son of Nicholas, leatherseller, dec'd, citizen of London Pedlingham, Thomas sr & Susannah 7 yrs from 20 Oct saddler 5s
2/124		25 Oct	Neast, Joseph son of Alexander, silkweaver, dec'd, of Gloucester Mitchell, George & Comfort 7 yrs from 29 Sep last garter weaver 5s [*Replacing entry at 2/73*]
			Merrett, John son of Thomas, cordwainer, dec'd, of Gloucester Lambe, William, vintner, & Joyce 7 yrs from 29 Sep last to be instructed in the art of cook and innholder 5s
		18 Nov	Marston, George son of John, clerk, of Charlton Kings Hill, Edward & [*blank*] 8 yrs haberdasher 2s 6d
2/125		10 Nov	Greene, Thomas son of Thomas, cordwainer, dec'd, of Gloucester Sampson, William & Jane 7 yrs turner 5s
		23 Nov	Danby, Thomas son of William, husbandman, dec'd, of Maisemore Carter, Lancelot & [*blank*] 7 yrs currier 2s 6d
		29 Nov	Elliotts, William son of Henry, tailor, dec'd, of Gloucester Lugg, John & Mary 9 yrs from 1 Nov pinmaker 5s
2/126			Monning, Samuel son of Samuel, cordwainer, dec'd, of Gloucester Lugg, John & Mary 9 yrs from 1 Nov pinmaker 5s
			Chamlyn, John son of Thomas, turner, dec'd, of Gloucester Tailor, George & Joan 9 yrs from 8 Nov cordwainer 5s
		5 Dec	Bowcer, Thomas son of George, gentleman, of Gloucester Whitington, William & Anne 7 yrs from 25 Dec apothecary 5s [*cf Appendix V*]

2/127	1653	6 Dec	Clutterbooke, Daniel son of Amity, tailor, dec'd, of Gloucester Hurlestone, William & Anne 7 yrs from 1 Dec baker 40s & 3 suits
		9 Dec	Monning, Isaac son of Samuel, cordwainer, dec'd, of Gloucester Powell, William & Alice 11 yrs from 25 Dec pinmaker 40s
		16 Dec	Ven, Henry son of John, feltmaker, of Gloucester Pigg, Richard & Eleanor 7 yrs from 1 Dec pinmaker 5s
2/128	1654	3 Jan	Bishop, John son of Richard, gentleman, dec'd, of Boddington Beale, Geoffrey & Edith 8 yrs from 1 Nov last mercer 13s 4d
		18 Jan	Freeman, Benjamin son of Thomas, clerk, of Naunton Collett, Edmund & Hester 8 yrs from 25 Dec last tanner 5s
		2 Feb	Branch, John son of Thomas, yeoman, of Highnam Broade, Richard & Mary 7 yrs baker 5s
2/129		30 Jan	Bridges, John son of John, wiredrawer, of Barton Street, Gloucester Hughes, Richard & Joan 7 yrs from 2 Feb butcher 5s
		2 Feb	Bishop, Richard son of Thomas, yeoman, dec'd, of Deerhurst Walton Greening, Richard & Alice 7 yrs tailor 10s
		8 Feb	Jones, John son of David, gentleman, dec'd, of 'Malechurch', Radnors Vaughan, Thomas & Ursula 7 yrs joiner 2s 6d
2/130			Beacon, Sampson son of Sampson, silkweaver, of Gloucester Hutchins, William & Anne 7 yrs silkweaver 2s 6d
		17 Feb	James, Leigh son of Leigh, baker, of Gloucester James, Leigh, his father, & Christian 7 yrs from 21 Sep last baker 10s
		2 Feb	Kent, Samuel son of John, husbandman, dec'd, of Aston Greene, William & Margaret 7 yrs joiner 2s 6d
2/131		17 Feb	*Alday, John: Whereas Thomas Horsington is lately gone away and hath forsaken this city and hath left his children and his apprentice John Alday upon the charge of Margery his wife which are likely to be chargeable to the parish of St Mary de Lode of this city, the said Thomas having not left any competent substance whereby they may be maintained, John Alday is turned over to serve the residue of his term with Daniel Colericke, bodicemaker, by the consent of the said John & Daniel. Before the justices Thomas Pury, mayor, Denis Wise & Jasper Clutterbuck [Signed] Daniel Colericke, John Alday his mark [See 2/60]*
		20 Feb	Wise, Denis son of Denis, alderman & mercer, of Gloucester Wise, Denis, his father, & Hephzibah 7 yrs from 25 Mar mercer 10s
2/132		2 Feb	Curr, Robert son of Robert, baker, dec'd, of Gloucester Crumwell, John & Anne, 7 yrs carrier 40s
		2 Mar	Young, Joseph son of Joseph, pinmaker, of Bristol Pitt, Samuel & Eleanor 7 yrs from 2 Feb pinmaker 2s 6d

	1654 10 Apr	Dowle, Samuel son of George, of Slimbridge
		Baily, Thomas & Elizabeth 8 yrs from 1 May pinmaker 5s
2/133	1 Apr	Powles, John son of William, husbandman, of Gloucester
		Bradford, John & Anne 8 yrs button [*deleted*] milliner 3s 4d
		Blisse, John son of Thomas, yeoman, of Painswick
		Clayfeild, Edward & Alice 7 yrs tanner 3s 4d
	13 Apr	Lewis, John son of James, feltmaker, of parish of St Mary de Lode
		Lugg, John & Mary 7 yrs from 25 Mar last pinmaker 4s
2/134	15 Apr	Sparrowhawk, Robert son of Robert, garter weaver, of Gloucester
		Bell, John & [*blank*] 7 yrs silkweaver 2s 6d
		Underhill, Jacob son of Jacob, narrow weaver, of Tewkesbury
		Bell, John & [*blank*] 7 yrs silkweaver 2s 6d
	24 Apr	Limbricke, John son of Richard, husbandman, of Frampton on Severn
		Crumwell, John & Anne 7 yrs victualler 2s 6d
		The apprentice is to have 3s a year for the first 5 years & 5s a year for the last 2 years
2/135	1 May	Mills, William jr son of William sr, husbandman, of Barton Street, Gloucester
		Saunders, Anthony & Sarah of Cheltenham 7 yrs tailor 2s 6d
		£4 of Mrs Browne's money[1] *No burgess*
	6 May	Lane, Samuel son of Brian, yeoman, dec'd, of Mitcheldean
		Cooke, Thomas & Margaret 7 yrs chandler 2s 6d
	3 Jun	Chappell, Thomas son of Robert, clothworker, of Wotton under Edge
		Welsteed, John & Elizabeth 7 yrs from 24 Jun blacksmith 2s 6d
2/136	8 Jun	Townsend, Henry son of Christopher, barber surgeon, dec'd, of Gloucester
		Bubb, Toby & Katharine 7 yrs from 24 Jun cordwainer 12d
		[*cf Appendix V*]
		Aldridge, Thomas son of John, clothier, of Stroud
		Lysons, Daniel & Sarah 10 yrs from 25 Mar last woollen draper 20s
	1 Apr	Burch, Thomas son of William, blacksmith, of Badgeworth
		Beard, John 9 yrs silkweaver 5s
2/137	10 Jun	Commelin, Daniel son of James, apothecary, of Gloucester
		Commelin, James, his father, & Jane 7 yrs from 25 Mar last apothecary 5s
		Causfeild, William son of Richard, narrow weaver, of Ashleworth
		Moore, Henry & Joan 7 yrs from 15 May tobacco-pipe maker 2s 6d
	14 Jun	Hulls, Richard son of Richard, yeoman, of Little Rissington
		Greene, John jr & [*blank*] 7 yrs from 1 May cooper 2s 6d

---

[1] GBR B3/2 p 761 27 Mar 1654: To receive £4 of Mrs Browne's money: John Clutterbooke, Walter Falkener, William Mills.

2/138	1654	17 Jun	Browne John, Henry son of Henry, gentleman, dec'd, of Zealhouse, parish of 'Eastwood', Southampton Paine, Robert jr & [blank] 8 yrs mercer 5s
		22 Jun	Etkins, Thomas son of John, yeoman, dec'd, of Hartpury Mason, Thomas & [blank] 7 yrs baker 2s 6d
		27 Jun	Hutchins, William son of William, innholder, of Gloucester Madocke, William & Sarah 7 yrs from 15 May tailor 10s
2/139			[The top part of the page has been torn out and there is probably one entry missing from 2/139 and from 2/140]
		3 Jul	Tray, Robert son of Edward, yeoman, of Bulley Smallwood, John & Jane 7 yrs from 24 Jun barber surgeon 2s 6d
		5 Jul	Churches, Caleb son of Robert, chandler, dec'd, of Mitcheldean Sturmy, Edmund & Blanche 8 yrs from 1 Jul glover 5s
2/140		1 Aug	Woollwright, John son of William, husbandman, of Slimbridge Heyward, John & Sarah 7 yrs feltmaker 1s
			Baugh, John son of John, tanner, dec'd, of Gloucester King, William & Phoebe 7 yrs pinmaker 5s
2/141		15 Aug	Holder, Richard son of Richard, pinmaker, of Gloucester Baily, Thomas & Elizabeth 7 yrs pinmaker 2s 6d
		19 Aug	Skinner, Samuel son of Robert, glover, late of Gloucester Cowdell, James & Anne 7 yrs from 1 Aug glover 2s 6d £5 Mr Hollidaie's gift [1]
			Clutterbooke, Joseph son of Amity, tailor, dec'd, of Gloucester Phillips, James jr & Anne 7 yrs from 1 Aug tailor 2s 6d £5 Mr Hollidaie's gift
2/142			Clutterbooke, John son of Amity, tailor, dec'd, of Gloucester Lugg, John & Mary 7 yrs from 1 Aug pinmaker 10s £4 Mrs Browne's gift
		30 Jul	Chapman, Selwyn son of Samuel, victualler, of Gloucester Bubb, William & Judith 8 yrs from 29 Sep apothecary 5s
		25 Aug	Symonds, Richard son of Richard, glover, of Gloucester Symonds, Richard, his father, & Joan 7 yrs from 1 Aug glover 5s £5 Mr Hollidaye's gift

---

[1] GBR B3/2 p 773 17 Jul 1654: The monies of the gift of Mr Holliday for the placing forth apprentices to be disposed of by the Common Council on Fri 28 Jul at one in the afternoon. It cannot be done sooner because the Assizes begin on 21 Jul.
  ibid p 774 28 Jul 1654: To receive £5 of Mr Hollidaye's money: Samuel Skinner, son of Elizabeth Cowdall, Joseph Clutterbooke, Thomas Eckly, son of Richard Symonds, Bromley son of Joan Wood. It passed for Skinner, Cowdall, Clutterbooke and Eckley by the majority of voices of the Common Council and for Symondes and Bromley having equal voices with Palmer by the mayor's casting vote.

2/143	1654 25 Aug	Bromly, Richard son of John, glover, dec'd, of Gloucester
		Bromley, Leonard & Jane 7 yrs from 1 Aug glover 2s 6d
		£5 Mr Hollidaie's gift
		14 May 1655: turned over to Thomas Woggan, glover. Before William Caple & Jasper Clutterbuck, aldermen
	8 Sep	Cowdale, John son of John, button maker, dec'd, of Gloucester
		Good, Thomas & Mary 7 yrs from 1 Aug tailor 5s
		£5 Mr Hollidaie's gift
	1 Aug	Winckworth, Jonas son of John, of Great Somerford [MS Broadsomerford], Wilts
		Bray, Henry 7 yrs mercer
2/145		**Edmund Collett, mayor [1654–5]**
		Thomas Cooke and James Comelin, sheriffs
		Names of apprentices bound and enrolled, 1654
	1654 7 Oct	Bishop, Daniel son of John, yeoman, dec'd, of Quedgeley
		Horrell, John & Mary 7 yrs from 24 Aug tailor 2s 6d
		Holliday, Giles son of Charles, carpenter, of Badgeworth
		Beard, John & [*blank*] 7 yrs from 29 Sep silkweaver 2s 6d
2/146	16 Oct	Wheelar, William son of Francis, husbandman, of Over
		Hunt, John & Elizabeth 8 yrs from 1 Nov garter weaver 5s
	14 Oct	Heyward, Zachariah son of Richard, yeoman, of Barnwood
		Perks, John & Alice 7 yrs from 29 Sep baker 2s 6d
	25 Oct	Rodway, Giles son of George, yeoman, of Badgeworth
		Atkins, John & [*blank*] 7 yrs cordwainer 3s 4d
2/147	16 Nov	White, William son of John, musician, of Gloucester
		White, John, his father, & Sybil 7 yrs from 29 Sep musician 5s
		Enrolled this 17th November 1654
	17 Nov	Arnold, Thomas son of John, hoop maker, dec'd, of Longhope
		Eldridge, Thomas & Mary 9 yrs joiner 50s
	11 Nov	Mills, Matthew son of William, mason, of Cowley
		Mills, Richard & [*blank*] 7 yrs from 1 Nov wiredrawer 5s
2/148	21 Nov	Fishpoole, Joseph son of Joseph, husbandman, of Badgeworth
		Ricketts, Jacob & Anne 7 yrs tanner 2s 6d
	1 Dec	Prosser, James son of John, husbandman, of Bulley
		Stephens, James & Anne 7 yrs [tanner *deleted*] maltster £4
	7 Dec	Pearce, Edmund son of John, weaver & clothier, of Tewkesbury
		Heyward, John & Sarah 7 yrs from 1 Nov feltmaker 2s 6d
2/149	12 Dec	Eckly, Thomas son of Thomas, chandler, of Gloucester
		Eckly, Thomas, his father, & Elizabeth 8 yrs from 25 Dec chandler 5s
		£5 Mr Hollidaye's gift
	15 Dec	Barnfull, Francis son of Francis, clothworker, dec'd, of Cirencester
		Onyon, Thomas & Bridget 8 yrs from 22 Dec silkweaver 2s 6d

GLOUCESTER APPRENTICESHIP REGISTERS, 1595–1700 135

	1654 21 Dec	Gillman, George son of Brian, yeoman, of Haresfield Price, Richard & Dinah 7 yrs from 25 Dec pewterer 5s & 3 suits
2/150		Pember, Thomas son of John, pinmaker, of Gloucester Coucher, John & Jane 7 yrs pinmaker 5s
	1655 16 Jan	Wastfeild, Nicholas son of John, husbandman, dec'd, of Olveston Wastfeild, John jr & [blank] 7 yrs from 16 Jan last blacksmith 5s
	2 Feb	Griffin, John son of John, yeoman, dec'd, of Llancloudy [MS Landcludocke], Herefs Partridge, Thomas & Elizabeth 7 yrs from 29 Sep last baker 2s 6d *The apprentice to have 50s yearly of his master to find him clothes*
2/151	1650 26 Dec	Cugly, Daniel son of Thomas, cardmaker, of Gloucester Cugly, Thomas, his father, 7 yrs cardmaker *Enrolled 11 Dec 1654, turned over the same day to serve the residue of his term with Thomas Cugly jr, cardmaker, with the consent of Daniel & Thomas the father. Before me, William Singleton*
	1655 22 Jan	Arnold, Thomas son of Thomas, husbandman, dec'd, of Barton Street, Gloucester Coucher, Robert & Margaret 7 yrs pinmaker 2s 6d
		Gibson, Thomas son of John, cook, dec'd, of Barton Street, Gloucester Coucher, Robert & Margaret 7 yrs pinmaker 2s 6d
2/152	2 Feb	Clifford, Thomas son of Thomas, tailor, dec'd, of Tuffley Sparrowhawke, Robert & Joan 7 yrs garter weaver 2s 6d
		Ludlo, Joseph son of Stephen, husbandman, of Shipton Moyne & Dovel Aram, Thomas & Margaret 8 yrs mercer 5s
2/153	19 Feb	Hannis, Thomas son of Thomas, husbandman, of Highnam Powell, William & Joan 8 yrs brewer 42s 6d
	24 Feb	Parlour, Edward son of William, yeoman, of English Bicknor Barrett, Thomas & Mary 9 yrs from 25 Mar cutler 20s
	1651 8 Oct	Thomas, George son of David, labourer, dec'd, of Cwmcarn [MS Combe Corran], Mon Mutlye, John & Joan 7 yrs fishhook maker 20s *Enrolled 21 Mar 1655*
2/154	1655 2 Apr	Waters, Andrew son of Thomas, labourer, of the Magdalens, Gloucester Coucher, John & Jane 7 yrs from 25 Mar pinmaker 2s 6d *£4 Mrs Browne's gift*[1]
		Jones, William son of William, pargeter, dec'd, of Gloucester Stephens, Thomas & Alice 7 yrs from 25 Mar pinmaker 2s 6d *£4 Mrs Browne's gift*

---

[1] GBR B3/2 p 810 26 Mar 1655: To receive £4 of Mrs Browne's money: Thomas Waters's son, William Jones *alias* Abbotts, George Dobbes.

2/155	1655	19 Apr	Lewis, Walter son of William, husbandman, dec'd, of Mitcheldean Jones, John & Margaret 7 yrs from 25 Mar butcher 2s 6d
		6 Apr	Dobbs, George son of John, glover, late of Gloucester Pigg, Richard & Eleanor 7 yrs from 25 Mar pinmaker 2s 6d *£4 Mrs Browne's gift*
		20 Apr	Goold, William son of Edward, feltmaker, dec'd, of Gloucester Powell, William & Alice 8 yrs pinmaker 2 suits *The apprentice is to have 4s weekly during the last year of the 8 yrs and the master and mistress to be excused from finding the apprentice meat, drink and apparel, the double apparel mentioned to be given in the end of the 8 yrs being only excepted*
2/156		11 May	Hilly, John son of John, mariner, dec'd, of Tewkesbury Phelpes, Joseph & [blank] 7 yrs from 1 May chandler & soap boiler 5s
		15 May	Stephens, John son of Thomas, pinmaker, of Gloucester Jennings, William & Bridget 8 yrs from 1 May barber surgeon 10s
		19 May	Shill, John son of Anthony, husbandman, of Withington Mills, Thomas & Hannah 8 yrs from 1 May wiredrawer 5s
2/157		28 May	Andros otherwise Andrewes, John son of Thomas, bricklayer, of Gloucester Barker, Thomas & Margaret 7 yrs from 1 Jun pinmaker 5s
			Lemster, William son of Richard, husbandman, dec'd, of Tewkesbury Pace, Thomas & Elizabeth 7 yrs cooper 12d
			Eckly, John son of Edward, milliner, of Gloucester Eckly, Edward, his father, & Anne 7 yrs from 1 May milliner 10s
2/158		1 Jun	Merricke, Walter son of Thomas, vintner, of Shrewsbury, Salop Tomes, John & Elizabeth 8 yrs from 25 Mar last mercer 2s 6d
		17 Jun	Hill, Thomas son of Christopher, blacksmith, dec'd, of Newnham Philips, George & Mary 7 yrs from 1 Jun feltmaker 20s
2/159	1649	1 Jul	Willis, Samuel son of Chris, mercer, dec'd, of Wotton under Edge Browne, William 9 yrs pewterer & brazier double apparel *Enrolled 4 Jul 1655*
	1655	29 Jun	Roberts, Giles son of Giles, yeoman, of Quedgeley Gwin, Augustine jr & Margaret 7 yrs from 24 Jun cordwainer [blank]
2/160		30 Jun	Brawne, Nathaniel son of William, yeoman, of Sandhurst Bicknell, William & Dorothy 7 yrs from 24 Jun tailor 2s 6d
			Morris, William son of William, husbandman, late of Hartpury Onyon, Humphrey jr & Elizabeth 9 yrs from 24 Jun sievemaker 5s
2/161		11 Jul	Lord, Henry son of Richard, blacksmith, of Hempsted Beard, John & Elizabeth 7¼ yrs from 24 Jun silkweaver 5s
		23 Jul	Glassenbury, John son of John, yeoman, of Newnham Nash, Jesse & [blank] 7 yrs from 25 Jul feltmaker 5s

| | 1655 | 23 Jul | Killmester, Alan son of Alan, gardener, dec'd, of Southgate Street, Gloucester |

                    Veysey, Walter & Margaret 7 yrs from 25 Jul tailor 2s 6d

2/162   25 Jul Savory, William son of William, farrier, of Gloucester
                    Savory, William, his father, & Mary 7 yrs farrier 5s
                    £5 Mr Hollidaye's gift[1]

              Davis, John son of John, cordwainer, dec'd, of Gloucester
                  Phenix, Margaret, widow of Henry 7 yrs pinmaker 1s
                  £5 Mr Hollidaye's gift

              Beard, Richard son of Richard, tailor, of Gloucester
                  Beard, Richard, his father, & Armilla 7 yrs tailor 20s
                  £5 Mr Hollidaye's gift

2/163   1 Aug Fry, Gabriel son of John, blacksmith, of Great Shurdington, parish of Badgeworth
                  Beard, John & Elizabeth 7 yrs silkweaver 2s 6d

              Stephens, Matthew son of Matthew, cordwainer, of Gloucester
                  Tyler, John & Anne 7 yrs cordwainer 2s 6d

              Parsons, Henry son of John, clerk, of Withington, Herefs
                  Perry, Robert & Elizabeth 7 yrs cordwainer 10s

2/164   28 Aug Price, James son of James, chapman, of Gloucester
                  Doughton, Stephen & Elizabeth 7 yrs pinmaker 5s

              Price, Francis son of Roland, labourer, dec'd, of All Hallows, city of Hereford
                  Bishop, Giles & Elizabeth 7 yrs from 1 Aug innkeeper 2s 6d
                  7 Oct 1656: Francis Price & Giles Bishop testified that Francis is discharged from his apprenticeship and the indentures of apprenticeship are burnt

2/165   1 Sep Mutley, Miles son of John, pinmaker, dec'd, of Gloucester
                  Hickes, Thomas & Joan 7 yrs tailor 2s 6d

      10 Sep Thompson, Richard son of Richard, clerk, of Ashleworth
                  Cox, Winston & Anne 7 yrs from 24 Aug cordwainer 1s

      20 Sep Perry, Samuel son of Nicholas, upholsterer, of Gloucester
                  Angell, William & [*blank*] 7 yrs from 1 May last merchant 5s

2/166   21 Sep Washborne, Samuel son of Thomas, clerk, of Dumbleton
                  Yate, Thomas & Elizabeth 8 yrs from 29 Sep apothecary 5s

      22 Sep Sparkes, William son of John, carpenter, of Gloucester
                  Williams, Isaac & Eleanor 7 yrs from 29 Sep tailor 2s 6d
                  £5 Mr Hollidaye's gift

---

[1] GBR B3/2 p 821 21 Jul 1655: To receive £5 of Mr Hollidaye's money: Widow Rickes's son, Hester Sparkes's son, Benjamin son of Richard Beard, William son of William Savory, Richard son of Richard Beard, tailor, John Davis.

	1655 26 Sep	Woodyatt, James son of Richard, husbandman, dec'd, of Barton Street, Gloucester
		Bradford, John & Alice 9 yrs button maker 3s 4d
2/167	28 Sep	Cudd, John son of John, husbandman, dec'd, of Longford
		Mills, Samuel & [blank] 7 yrs silkweaver 5s
	6 Oct	Cartwright, Thomas son of Edward, yeoman, of Prestbury
		Jelfe, Thomas & Elizabeth 7 yrs from 25 Jul baker 2s 6d
		Entered on the next leaf [*See 2/169*]
2/169		**Denis Wise, mayor [1655–6]**
		John Purlewent and Nicholas Webb bailiffs and sheriffs
		The names of apprentices enrolled in 1655
		John Dorney town clerk
	1655 6 Oct	Cartwright, Thomas son of Edward, yeoman, of Prestbury
		Jelfe, Thomas & Elizabeth 7 yrs from 25 Jul baker 2s 6d
		[*Repeating entry at 2/167*]
	20 Oct	Surman, Richard son of Thomas, husbandman, of Tirley
		Burrup, Thomas & Joan 7 yrs from 29 Sep cordwainer 2s 6d
2/170	24 Oct	Garner, Nathaniel son of John, husbandman, of Painswick
		Parker, Margaret, widow of Thomas 7 yrs from 1 Jan next baker 2s 6d
	1 Nov	Palmer, Stephen son of William, husbandman, of Cranham
		Mills, Richard & [blank] 7 yrs wiredrawer 5s
		Wilton, Joseph son of George, husbandman, dec'd, of Huntley
		Ricketts, Jacob & Anne 7 yrs tanner 1s
2/171	14 Nov	Williams, Thomas son of Thomas, merchant, dec'd, of Bristol
		Nash, Richard & Joan 7 yrs from 29 Sep grocer 12d
	15 Nov	Younge, John son of John, maltster, dec'd, of Gloucester
		Jordan, William jr & Katharine 7 yrs from 1 Nov apothecary 5s
	24 Nov	Cowper, Maurice son of Maurice, yeoman, of Chaceley, Worcs
		Robins, Thomas & [blank] 7 yrs from 1 Nov tanner £7
2/172	4 Dec	Adys, John son of Edward, cordwainer, dec'd, of Gloucester
		Hill, Walter & Dorothy 7½ yrs from 25 Dec cordwainer 2s 6d
	31 Dec	Cupitt, Andrew son of Arthur, trowman, late of Awre
		Stephens, James, alderman, & Anne 11 yrs from 1 Jan maltster 20s
		[*cf Appendix V*]
	1656 1 Jan	Chedworth, Giles son of John, mason, of the Magdalens, Gloucester
		Linkinholt, William & Elizabeth 7 yrs wiredrawer 2s 6d
2/173	19 Jan	Heaghe, Jacob son of Abraham, clerk, dec'd, of Ashleworth
		Holtham, William & Mary 7 yrs from 1 Feb chandler 2s 6d
		[*cf Appendix V*]
	19 Feb	Low, Nathaniel son of Henry, husbandman, of Barnwood
		Linkinholt, William & Elizabeth 7 yrs wiredrawer 2s 6d

	1656 14 Mar	Parlour, Henry son of William, cutler, dec'd, of Gloucester Pharley, George & Mary 7 yrs cutler 2s 6d *£5 Mr Hollidaye's gift*[1]
2/174	20 Mar	Hemming, John son of Richard sr, yeoman, of Barton Street, Gloucester Browne, John & Elizabeth 7 yrs from 1 Mar butcher 5s
	27 Mar	Manington, John son of John, husbandman, of Tirley Sparrowhawk, Robert & Joan 7 yrs from 25 Mar garter weaver 2s 6d
	7 Apr	Hartlen, Richard son of William, wiredrawer, dec'd, of Gloucester Doughton, Stephen & Elizabeth 7 yrs pinmaker 2s 6d
2/175	28 Apr	Cox, John son of Richard, cordwainer, of Gloucester Greene, Thomas & Margaret 7 yrs from 1 May cordwainer 2s 6d *£4 Mrs Browne's gift*[2]
		Vyner, Daniel son of Daniel, husbandman, of Churchdown Deane, Thomas & Katharine 7 yrs from 1 May blacksmith 2s 6d
	30 Apr	Vaughan, Richard son of James, cordwainer, dec'd, of Gloucester Mills, Samuel & Mary [*no term*] from 1 May silkweaver 2s 6d [*Mrs Browne*]
2/176	7 May	Rudge, George son of George, yeoman, of Huntley Lucas, Thomas & Elizabeth 7 yrs from 25 Mar farrier 10s
	26 May	Jelfe, George son of Richard, labourer, of Gloucester Brymeyard, William & Joan 7 yrs wiredrawer *18 Mar 1657 turned over to Roger Heath, wiredrawer, for the residue of his term. Before Alderman Collett*
2/177	31 May	Bowry, Samuel son of William, blacksmith, of Longney Ricketts, Jacob & Anne 7 yrs from 1 Jun tanner 12d
	2 Jun	Mill, Giles son of Thomas, broadweaver, of Barton Street, Gloucester White, Sergeant & Joan 7 yrs cordwainer 6d
	5 Jun	Cam, Arthur son of Thomas, gentleman, dec'd, of Newport Paine, Robert jr & Anne 8 yrs mercer 10s
2/178	7 Jun	Drue, John son of Richard, husbandman, dec'd, of Bulley Greene, John sr & Katharine 7 yrs from 20 May cooper 3s 4d
	9 Jun	Peachee, Thomas son of John, husbandman, dec'd, of Upton St Leonards Madocke, William & Sarah 7 yrs tailor 2s 6d
	12 Jan	Bishop, William son of Thomas, yeoman, dec'd, of Hempsted Beard, William & Elizabeth 7 yrs from 25 Dec last tailor 2s 6d
2/179	19 Jun	Witcombe, Thomas son of William, victualler, of Gloucester Beard, William & Elizabeth 7 yrs from 24 Jun tailor 2s 6d

---

[1] GBR B3/2 p 873 21 Jul 1656: To receive £5 of Mr Hollidaye's money: Henry Parlour, John Witcombe's son, John Palmer, Arthur Dudley, Thomas Goold, John Gwilliam.

[2] GBR B3/2 p 859 27 Mar 1656: To receive £4 of Mrs Browne's money: Richard Vaughan, widow Barneham's son, John Cox.

	1656	4 Jul	Sheppard, Thomas son of Edward, feltmaker, of Gloucester
			King, William & Phoebe 7 yrs from 24 Jun pinmaker 10s
			[cf Appendix V]
		9 Jul	Harris, Daniel son of Humphrey, baker, dec'd, of Gloucester
			Hurlestone, Anne widow of William 7 yrs from 24 Jun baker 5s

2/180 16 Jul Litle, Henry son of William, yeoman, of Cleeve
            Cooke, Thomas & Margaret 7 yrs from 25 Jul chandler 5s

       17 Jul Staniford, Charles son of Thomas, clerk, of Castle Eaton, Wilts
            Collins, Daniel & [blank] 7 yrs from 25 Jul mercer 5s

       26 Jul Sadler, John son of James, carpenter, of Brimpsfield
            Mills, Richard & [blank] 7 yrs from 24 Jun wiredrawer 5s

2/181 4 Aug Dudley, Arthur son of Arthur, butcher, of Gloucester
            Mathewes, John & Margaret 7 yrs from 25 Jul butcher 5s
            £5 Mr Hollidaye's gift

       6 Aug Powell, Charles son of William, brewer, of Gloucester
            Powell, William, his father, & Joan 7 yrs from 24 Jun brewer 10s
            [cf Appendix V]

              Foster, William son of William, tailor, of Winchcombe
            Hill, Walter & Dorothy 8 yrs from 25 Jul cordwainer 12d

2/182 1 Aug Good, William son of Thomas, tailor, late of Gloucester
            White, Sergeant & Joan 9 yrs cordwainer 2s 6d

       11 Aug Gun, Arthur son of Moses, yeoman, of Frampton on Severn
            Gwin, Augustine sr & Alice 7 yrs cordwainer 2s 6d

       14 Aug Palmer, John son of John, cooper, dec'd, of Gloucester
            Bubb, Toby & Katharine 7 yrs from 25 Jul cordwainer 2s 6d
            £5 Mr Hollidaye's gift

2/183 18 Aug Mill, Edward son of Toby, cordwainer, of Gloucester
            Beard, Walter & Alice 7 yrs tailor 6d
            £5 Mr Hollidaye's gift in 1657

       19 Aug Gwilliam, John son of John, tanner, of Gloucester
            Nash, Richard & Joan 7 yrs feltmaker 2s 6d £5 Mr Hollidaye's gift

       8 Aug Witcombe, John son of John, cordwainer, dec'd, of Gloucester
            Harris, Walter & Elizabeth 8 yrs from 29 Sep cordwainer 3s 4d
            £5 Mr Hollidaye's gift

2/184 25 Aug Jelfe, Richard son of Richard, labourer, of Gloucester
            Wood, John & Margaret [no term] button maker 2s 6d
            Placed by the chamber. The apprentice was bound presently after the said John Wood was sworn a burgess [See Freemen p 14]

       27 Aug Stocke, Walter son of William, yeoman, of Chaceley, Worcs
            Burrup, Thomas & Joan 7 yrs from 1 Aug cordwainer 2s 6d

       28 Aug Haines, Nicholas son of Nicholas, husbandman, dec'd, of Cheltenham
            Jones, John & Alice 7 yrs from 1 Sep pinmaker 2s 6d

2/185	1656 30 Aug		Pullum, John son of John, carpenter, of Matson Nicholls, William & Joan 7 yrs from 1 Sep tanner 2s 6d
		3 Sep	Webley, John son of William, gentleman, of Much Marcle, Herefs Grevile, Edward & Mary 7 yrs from 1 Aug mercer 10s
		12 Sep	Kettle, Thomas son of Thomas, wheelwright, the Margarets, Gloucester Lewis, Abel & Elizabeth 7 yrs from 24 Jun tiler & plasterer 2s 6d
2/186		15 Sep	Stone, John son of John, tailor, of Ledbury, Herefs Eckley, Edward & Anne 7 yrs from 29 Sep button maker 2s 6d
			Doughton, Stephen son of Stephen, pinmaker, of Gloucester Doughton, Stephen, his father, & Elizabeth 7 yrs from 29 Sep pinmaker 5s

			Doughton, William son of Richard, pinmaker, dec'd, of Gloucester
			   Doughton, Stephen & Elizabeth 8 yrs from 18 Sep pinmaker 5s
			   £5 Mr Hollidaye's gift

2/187		17 Sep	Hood, Richard son of Richard, wiredrawer, of Gloucester Jones, John & Alice 7 yrs pinmaker 2s 6d

		22 Jul	Williams, William son of Walter, gentleman, dec'd, of Brecon [MS Brecknock]
			   Williams, Isaac & Eleanor 7¼ yrs tailor 2s 6d
			   This was done in 1660 by the special appointment of the mayor & some of the aldermen

2/189			**Luke Nourse, mayor [1656–7]** **Geoffrey Beale and John Tomes, bailiffs of the city and sheriffs of the county of the city** **John Dorney, town clerk**
	1656	7 Oct	Bosly, John son of John, feltmaker, dec'd, of Gloucester Bosly, Richard & Elizabeth 7 yrs from 29 Sep feltmaker 5s
		8 Oct	Walker, Matthew son of Francis, husbandman, of Kidlington [MS Kettleton], Oxon Slicer, James & Elizabeth 7 yrs from 1 Oct tanner 5s
2/190	1654	2 Feb	Tomkins otherwise Brymeyeard, William Moore, Henry & Joan 7 yrs tobacco-pipe maker 2s 4d [*sic*]
	1656	18 Oct	Powell, John son of Thomas, tailor, of Southgate Street, Gloucester Bradford, John & Anne 7 yrs from 29 Sep milliner 2s 6d
		25 Oct	Braban, Francis son of William, husbandman, of Churcham Greene, John jr & Margaret 7 yrs from 18 Oct cooper £5

2/191		18 Oct	Carpenter, Thomas son of John, narrow weaver, late of Eldersfield, Worcs
			   Nicholls, John & Mary 7 yrs tanner 5s
			   12 Sep 1659: turned over to James Sliser, tanner, with the consent of himself and his master. Robert Tither, mayor, William Caple, Luke Nourse, James Stephens

	1656 31 Oct	Powell, George son of William, pinmaker, of Gloucester
		Powell, William, his father, & Alice 7 yrs from 1 Nov pinmaker 20s
	1 Nov	Cupitt, Andrew son of Arthur, trowman, of Awre
		Wood, Thomas & Jane 10 yrs from 29 Sep tanner £4 [*cf Appendix V*]
2/192	14 Nov	Rogers, Thomas son of Thomas, yeoman, of Bentham, parish of Badgeworth
		Mills, Thomas 7 yrs from 1 Nov baker 2s 6d
	1651 19 May	Gardner, John son of Philip, tanner, of Bengeworth, Worcs
		White, Sergeant & Joan 7 yrs cordwainer
		Enrolled 21 Nov 1656
	1656 22 Nov	Browne, Thomas son of Humphrey, husbandman, of Maisemore
		Carter, Lancelot [*no term*] currier 20s
2/193	1650 18 Jul	Jones, William, labourer, of Gloucester
		Hale, Anthony & Katharine 10 yrs from 24 June last carrier
		Enrolled 28 Nov 1656
	1656 28 Nov	Pine, Charles son of Charles, upholsterer, dec'd, of Cirencester
		Smallwood, John & Jane 7 yrs barber surgeon 5s
	1 Dec	Tarkinton, Joseph son of John, glover, dec'd of Gloucester
		Parish, John & Frances 7 yrs tailor 8s 6d
	1655 22 Sep	Nethaway, Edward son of Thomas Netheway, cordwainer, of Gloucester
		Donn, John & Margaret 8 yrs from 29 Sep tailor 2s 6d
		Enrolled 1 Dec 1656
2/194	1656 3 Dec	Sheppard, Thomas son of Edward, feltmaker, of Gloucester
		Willcox, Thomas & Mary 7 yrs from 1 Dec tailor 5s
		[*cf Appendix V*]
	1652 29 Sep	Cleevly, William son of William, ironmonger, late of Gloucester
		Haynes, Nicholas & Sarah 8 yrs ironmonger
		Enrolled 3 Dec 1656
	1656 13 Dec	Goodcheape, William son of Thomas, husbandman, dec'd, of Hasfield
		Goodcheape, Thomas & [*blank*] 7 yrs from 1 Dec cordwainer 5s
2/195		Winnard, Thomas son of Richard, cordwainer, of Mitcheldean
		Jones, John & Alice 7 yrs pinmaker 2s 6d
	27 Dec	Dole, John, gardener, of Cheltenham
		Meeke, Thomas & Margery 7 yrs from 1 Dec currier 5s
	1657 3 Jan	Coale, Christopher son of John, husbandman, dec'd, of Churcham
		Pitt, Samuel & Eleanor 9 yrs from 25 Dec last pinmaker 8s
2/196	17 Jan	Beale, Joseph son of William, yeoman, of Chaceley, Worcs
		Wintle, Richard & Alice 7 yrs from 25 Dec last cordwainer 2s 6d
	19 Jan	Bradshaw, Bartholomew son of Simon, narrow weaver, dec'd, of Marlborough, Wilts
		Wells, John & Sarah 9 yrs cordwainer 2s 6d

	1657 17 Jan	Perris, William son of Richard, butcher, of Cirencester
		Hughes, Richard & Joan 7 yrs from 25 Dec last butcher 10s
2/197	20 Jan	Paine, William son of Anthony, sawyer, dec'd, of Gloucester
		Jones, John & Alice 7 yrs from 25 Jan pinmaker 2s 6d
	23 Feb	Hill, John son of John, yeoman, dec'd, of Over
		Willmotts, Robert & Mary 7 yrs from 25 Mar saddler 2s 6d
	27 Feb	Winston, John son of Thomas, husbandman, dec'd, of Great Witcombe
		King, Samuel & Mary 7 yrs tailor 3s 6d
2/198	2 Mar	Penson, Stephen son of William, tailor, of Gloucester
		Elliott, Edward & Mary 7 yrs cordwainer 12d
	7 Mar	Hornedge, Thomas son of Christopher, yeoman, of Maisemore
		Colericke, Daniel & Mary 7 yrs bodicemaker 2s 6d
	10 Mar	Mount, William son of John, gentleman, of Maldon, Essex
		Perkes, John & Alice 7 yrs from 2 Mar baker 20s
2/199	11 Mar	Chamlin, John son of Chamlyn, Thomas, turner, dec'd, of Gloucester
		Robins, James & Mary 7 yrs from 2 Mar currier 20s
	16 Mar	Rogers, John son of John, broadweaver, dec'd, of Gloucester
		Lewis, John & Alice 9 yrs glover 2s 6d

2 Oct 1669 It appeared to the mayor and some of the aldermen that shortly after the binding of the aforesaid apprentice, John Lewis did leave of[f] his calling and that John Rogers did only serve him about a year of his apprenticeship.

Edward Mason and James King being called before the mayor and other aldermen did testify that Richard Loggins, son of Augustine, was bound to Thomas Weaver upon the day of the date of the indenture of apprenticeship. Whereupon it was ordered that the said indenture should be enrolled.

	1652 6 Nov	Loggins, Richard son of Augustine sr, mason, of Gloucester
		Weaver, Thomas 7 yrs from 1 Nov last past butcher
		Enrolled 16 Mar 1657
2/200	1657 20 Mar	Lye, Samuel son of Giles, chandler, of Gloucester
		Lye, Giles, his father, & Hester 9 yrs from 29 Sep last chandler 20s
	21 Mar	Carter, Samuel son of William, yeoman, of Cricklade St Sampsons, Wilts
		Lye, Giles & Hester 7 yrs from 25 Mar chandler 2s 6d
	26 Mar	Powell, Paul son of Edmund, husbandman, Naunton
		Jordan, John & Anne 7 yrs from 25 Mar baker 2s 6d

2/201	1657 30 Mar	Jones, Samuel son of Thomas, baker, dec'd, of Gloucester Baker, Richard & Joyce dwelling near the castle in the county of Glos 7 yrs from 25 Mar nailer 10s £4 of Mrs Browne's money.[1] *Richard Baker is not a freeman.*
	1 Apr	Pricket, John son of Prickett, Edward, button maker, late of Gloucester Gwin, Augustine jr & Margaret 9 yrs from 25 Mar cordwainer 5s £4 of Mrs Browne's money
	2 Apr	Haines, John son of John, yeoman, of Rollright, Oxon Barrett, Mary widow of Thomas 7 yrs from 25 Mar cutler 10s
	9 Apr	Hinton, William son of George, cordwainer, of Gloucester Sampson, William & Jane 8 yrs from 25 Mar turner 2s 6d
2/202	16 Apr	Hale, Thomas son of Thomas, feltmaker, of Gloucester Tyler, James & Mary 7 yrs from 25 Mar cordwainer 2s 6d £4 of Mrs Browne's money
		Smith, Henry son of Richard, gentleman, of Gloucester Flucke, Thomas & Elizabeth 7 yrs tanner 5s
	22 Apr	Jaquies, Aaron son of Richard, yeoman, of Broadwell Parker, Margaret widow of Thomas 7 yrs from 1 Apr baker
2/203	24 Apr	Smart, Richard son of Richard, yeoman, of Gloucester Merrett, Thomas & Hester 7 yrs cordwainer 2s 6d
	28 Apr	Ebbs, Thomas son of Philip, husbandman, dec'd, of Gloucester Ebbs, Philip & [blank] 7 yrs from 25 Mar saddler 2s 6d
	30 Apr	Evans, James son of John, clothdresser, dec'd, of Dulas, Herefs Peirson, William, one of the fraternity of cooks and innholders in the city, & Elizabeth 7 yrs from 25 Mar 20s
2/204	6 May	Hopkins, John son of Philip, husbandman, of Buckholt [MS the Buckall], parish of Monmouth Saunders, John & Isobel 7 yrs from 1 May victualler 5s
	9 May	Gwatkin, Walter son of Walter, gentleman, of Much Dewchurch, Herefs Collett, Edmund, alderman, & Hester 7 yrs from 1 May tanner 2s 6d
	13 May	Fowler, William son of William, mercer, dec'd, of Gloucester Tayler, George & Joan 7 yrs from 25 Jul barber surgeon 2s 6d £5 Mr Hollidaye's money[2]
2/205	16 May	Hale, William son of William, husbandman, of Upton St Leonards Huffe, Thomas & Joan 7 yrs from 1 May weaver 2s 6d
		Wilse, Joseph son of John, yeoman, of Dymock Harris, Walter & Elizabeth 7 yrs cordwainer 12d

---

[1] GBR B3/3 p 22 27 Mar 1657: To receive £4 of Mrs Browne's money: Thomas Hale, Samuel Jones, John Prickett.

[2] GBR B3/3 p 31 21 Jul 1657: To receive £5 of Mr Hollidaye's money: William Doughton, William Fowler, James Browne, Richard Cox, George Williams, Edward Mills.

	1657 25 May	Ridler, William son of Walter, clerk, dec'd, of Tibberton Philips, James jr & Anne 8 yrs from 1 May tailor 5s [*cf Appendix V*]
2/206	26 May	Etheridge, Joseph son of John, narrow weaver, of Apperley in parish of Deerhurst Nash, Richard & Joan 8 yrs from 1 Jun grocer 2s 6d
		Cardwell, John son of William, husbandman, of Winchcombe Charleton, Edward & Sarah 7 yrs wiredrawer 2s 6d
	3 Jun	Drue, Thomas son of John, yeoman, of Dymock Lane, Nicholas & [*blank*] 7 yrs from 1 Jun apothecary 5s
2/207	25 Jun	Goslinge, Henry son of John, gentleman, of Wotton [St Mary] Palmer, Edmund & Hester 7 yrs from 24 Jun baker 2s 6d
	30 Jun	Belcher, Richard son of Richard, yeoman, dec'd, of Linton Onyon, Thomas & Bridget 8 yrs from 24 Jun silkweaver 5s
	7 Jul	Randle, Daniel son of James, yeoman, of Charlton Kings Hemming, Thomas & Margery 7 yrs from 18 Jul joiner 2s 6d
2/208	17 Jul	Fowle, Joseph son of William, glover, of Westbury Davis, Thomas & Anne 7 yrs from 25 Jul glover 12d
	18 Jul	Smith, Nicholas son of William, husbandman, of Frocester Niccolls, John & Mary 7 yrs tanner 5s
	21 Jul	Belcher, Thomas son of Richard, yeoman, dec'd, of Linton Hurlestone, Anne widow of William 7 yrs baker 2s 6d
2/209	28 Jul	Cox, Richard son of Richard, cordwainer, of Gloucester Cox, Winston & Anne 7 yrs from 25 Jul cordwainer 2s 6d *£5 Mr Hollidaye's money*
	7 Aug	Griffes, Nathaniel son of Henry, narrow weaver, of Pontesbury, Salop Adams, John & Margaret 7 yrs from 1 Aug narrow weaver 2s 6d
	25 Aug	Williams, George son of John, wiredrawer, dec'd, of Gloucester Hannis, Thomas & Eleanor 7 yrs from 1 Aug pinmaker 10s [*Holliday*]
	29 Jul	Belcher, Daniel son of Richard, yeoman, dec'd, of Linton Hatton, William & Hester 7 yrs from 25 Jul button maker 2s 6d
2/210	31 Aug	Marten, Arthur son of William, cordwainer, of Gloucester Philips, James 7 yrs tailor 2s 6d
	4 Sep	Bradrist, Henry son of Henry, gardener, of Barton Street, Gloucester Greene, William & Mary 7 yrs from 16 Aug pinmaker 2s 6d
	8 Sep	Wood, Isaac son of John, gentleman, dec'd, of Gloucester White, Richard & [*blank*] 7 yrs from 24 Aug cordwainer 2s 6d
	15 Sep	Watkins, John son of John, husbandman, of Tirley Harris, Joseph & Tacy 9 yrs cordwainer 2s 6d
2/211	17 Sep	Berry, Thomas son of William, husbandman, dec'd, of Matson Lewis, Abel & Elizabeth 7 yrs tiler & plasterer 2s 6d

| | 1657 24 Sep | Bishop, Thomas son of Thomas, husbandman, of Churchdown
Greene, William & Mary 7 yrs pinmaker 2s 6d |

2/213
Laurence Singleton, mayor [1657–8]
Thomas Whitcombe and Thomas Russell, bailiffs of the city and sheriffs of the county of the city
John Dorney, town clerk

	1657 1 Oct	Plovy, William son of Thomas, husbandman, of Woodstock, Oxon Franckis, Richard & Elizabeth 7 yrs cordwainer 5s
	7 Oct	Bosly, Richard son of John, feltmaker, dec'd, of Churchdown Sturmy, John & Mary 7 yrs from 1 Oct glover 2s 6d
	13 Oct	Stephens, Thomas son of Matthew, cordwainer, of Gloucester Griffin, David & [blank] 7 yrs tailor 5s
2/214	15 Oct	Harris, Jeremiah son of Thomas, gunsmith, of Gloucester Smyth, Giles & Sybil 7 yrs from 29 Sep baker 3s 4d
	16 Oct	Cheesman, Robert son of John, cooper, dec'd, of Modbury, Devon Prytchetts, Simon & Sarah 7 yrs from 1 Nov cooper 2s 6d
	17 Oct	Alye, Joseph son of William, husbandman, dec'd, of Chaceley, Worcs Sparrowhawk, Robert & Joan 9 yrs from 29 Sep garter weaver 5s
2/215	31 Oct	Blisse, John son of Richard, broadweaver, of Arle Farmer, Francis & Elizabeth 7 yrs feltmaker 2s 6d
	4 Nov	Griffin, John son of Foulke, innkeeper, of Eckington, [Worcs] Sampson, Jonathan & Mary 7 yrs from 31 Oct turner & combmaker 2s 6d
	9 Nov	Wilse, John son of John, turner, of Much Marcle, Herefs Eliote, Henry & Jane 7 yrs joiner 2s 6d
	16 Nov	Prune, John son of Thomas, husbandman, of Haydon Swayn, William sr & Sarah 7 yrs brickmaker 40s [cf Appendix V]
2/216	25 Nov	Banaster, Willoughby son of Nathaniel, gentleman, of Staverton Cooke, John & Sarah 7 yrs from 1 Nov haberdasher 5s
	10 Dec	Price, Thomas son of Laurence, labourer, dec'd, of Malmesbury, Wilts Sampson, William & Jane 7 yrs turner 2s 6d
	1658 2 Jan	Clarke, William son of Thomas, merchant, dec'd, of Bristol Sampson, Jonathan & Mary 7 yrs from 1 Jan turner 1s
2/217	14 Jan	Browne, James son of John, butcher, dec'd, of Gloucester Smyth, Thomas & Joan 7 yrs from 1 Jan pewterer 2s 6d *£5 of Mr Hollidaye's money*
	1657 17 Dec	Hall, Francis son of John, gentleman, of Bullen, parish of Ledbury, Herefs Singleton, Lawrence & Mary 7 yrs woollen draper 10s *Enrolled 8 Feb 1658*

	1658 5 Feb	Warde, Anthony son of Anthony, husbandman, of Cheltenham
		Welsteed, John & Elizabeth 7 yrs from 2 Feb blacksmith 2s 6d
2/218	11 Feb	Heaghe, Jacob son of Abraham, clerk, dec'd, of Ashleworth
		Lane, Thomas & [*blank*] 7 yrs from 2 Feb chandler 5s [*cf Appendix V*]
	1 Mar	Jobbins, William son of William, broadweaver, dec'd, of Berkeley
		Farmer, Francis & Elizabeth 7 yrs feltmaker 3s 4d
	5 Mar	Gardner, John son of Thomas, husbandman, of Whitchurch, Herefs
		Farmer, Francis & Elizabeth 7 yrs from 1 Mar feltmaker 3s 4d
2/219	23 Mar	Evans, Thomas son of Owen, husbandman, of Gloucester
		Woodward, John & Elizabeth 7 yrs from 25 Dec last brewer 10s
	29 Mar	Kent, Giles son of Thomas, husbandman, of Sandhurst
		Smith, William & Katharine 7 yrs from 1 April cordwainer 2s
	2 Apr	Cantrell, John son of Henry, yeoman, dec'd, of Gloucester
		Symons, Richard & Joan 8 yrs from 1 Apr glover 2s 6d
2/220	7 Apr	Harbert, William son of Christopher, brewer, of Gloucester
		Borow, William & Eleanor 7 yrs tailor 2s 6d
		This indenture made void 17 May 1658 [*See 2/221*]
	9 Apr	Purlewent, Roger son of Daniel, broadweaver, dec'd, of Gloucester
		Adams, John & Margaret 7 yrs narrow weaver 2s 6d
		£4 Mrs Browne's money[1]
	10 Apr	Carell, John son of Kalo, husbandman, dec'd, of Little Dewchurch, Herefs
		Haines, Nicholas & Sarah 7 yrs from 25 Mar milliner & hosier 2s 6d
2/221	18 May	Harbert, William son of Christopher, brewer, of Gloucester
		Chapman, Thomas & Eleanor 8 yrs tailor 2s 6d [*See 2/220*]
	24 May	Lysons, Daniel son of Daniel, woollen draper, of Gloucester
		Lysons, Daniel, his father, & Sarah 7 yrs woollen draper 10s
	2 Jun	Gregory, Edmund son of Humphrey, yeoman, of Castle Eaton, Wilts
		Clutterbooke, Marian widow of Daniel 7 yrs from 24 Jun skinner 5s
2/222	5 Jun	Tompsin, Thomas son of Thomas, tailor, dec'd, of Much Birch, Herefs
		Moore, Henry & Joan 9 yrs from 25 Dec last tobacco-pipe maker 9s
	14 Jun	Bourne, Benjamin son of William, clerk, dec'd, of Brislington [MS Bristleton], Som
		Barrett, Mary widow of Thomas 7 yrs from 24 Jun cutler 5s
	17 Jun	Lord, James son of Richard, blacksmith, of Barton Street, Gloucester
		Coutcher, Robert & Margaret 8 yrs pinmaker 5s
2/223	14 Jun	Ridler, William son of Walter, clerk, dec'd, of Tibberton
		Greening, Richard & Alice 7 yrs tailor 2s 6d [*cf Appendix V*]

---

[1] GBR B3/3 p 65 26 Mar 1658: To receive £4 of Mrs Browne's money: William Hinton, Thomas Ebbes, Roger son of Daniel Purlewent.

	1658 26 Jun	Sparrowhawke, William son of Robert, garter weaver, of Gloucester
		Sparrowhawke, Robert, his father, & Joan 7 yrs from 24 Jun garter weaver 10s
		William [*Space for entry left blank*]
2/224	7 Jul	Welch, James son of William, miller, of Longhope
		Baylee, Thomas & Elizabeth 7 yrs pinmaker 10s
	23 Jul	Mill, Henry son of Tobias, cordwainer, of Gloucester
		Archard, George & Elizabeth, 7 yrs cordwainer 3s 4d
	28 Jul	Ferebee, John son of Thomas, yeoman, dec'd, of Frocester
		Veisey, Walter & Margaret 9 yrs from 25 Jul tailor 5s
2/225	31 Jul	Bingle, Daniel son of Daniel, yeoman, dec'd, of Upton St Leonards
		Jordan, William & Katharine 7 yrs from 25 Mar apothecary 5s
	2 Aug	Gittos, William son of William, glover, of Gloucester
		Willmott, Robert & Mary 8 yrs saddler 20s
	5 Aug	Boulton, Richard son of Richard, pinmaker, of Gloucester
		Barker, Thomas & Margaret 7 yrs pinmaker 2s 6d
	6 Aug	Broade, Edmund son of Edmund, yeoman, of Woodmancote, parish of North Cerney
		Broade, Richard & Mary 7 yrs from 1 Aug baker 5s
2/226	7 Aug	Tovey, Richard son of Thomas, yeoman, of Southwick, parish of Tewkesbury
		Cartwright, Edmund & Mary 7 yrs baker 3s 4d
		Aldridge, William son of William, mason, dec'd, of Hereford
		Shipton, John & Sarah 7 yrs bodicemaker 2s 6d
		Carter, William son of William, cooper, of Gloucester
		[Carter] [MS Cooper] William, his father, & Joyce 7 yrs from 25 Jul cooper 20s *£5 of Mr Hollidaye's money*[1]
	23 Aug	Mathews, Henry son of Henry, tailor, dec'd, of Gloucester
		Stephens, Thomas & Alice 8 yrs from 25 Jul pinmaker 2s 6d
		£5 of Mr Hollidaye's money
2/227	12 Aug	Dewxell, Richard son of Thomas, gentleman, of Barton Street, Gloucester
		Beard, Richard & Armilla 7 yrs tailor 2s
	17 Aug	Jones, James son of Arthur, gentleman, dec'd, of Gloucester
		Onion, Humphrey jr & Elizabeth 7 yrs silkweaver 3s 4d
		£5 of Mr Hollidaye's money
	1 Sep	Meeke, Richard son of Philip, yeoman, of Littledean
		Gardner, John & Margaret 8 yrs cordwainer 3s 4d
2/228	13 Sep	Hanks, Joseph son of Richard, dyer, of Tewkesbury
		Heyward, John & Sarah 7 yrs feltmaker 2s 6d

---

[1] GBR B3/3 p 71 21 Jul 1658: To receive £5 of Mr Hollidaye's money: James Jones, William Carter, James King's son, Henry Mathewes, John Lugg, son of Margery Nicholls.

	1658 16 Sep	Freeman, Roland son of Anthony, gentleman, of Badgeworth Beard, John & Margaret 8 yrs from 24 Jun mercer 2s 6d
	22 Sep	Curtis, Thomas son of [*blank*], narrow weaver, of Ganarew [MS Gannerrue], Herefs Massenger, William & Anne 7 yrs from 1 Sep victualler 3s 4d
2/229	25 Sep	Nicholls, Thomas son of Reece, brewer, dec'd, of Gloucester Goodcheape, Thomas & Sybil 7 yrs from 29 Sep cordwainer 2s 6d *£5 of Mr Hollidaye's money*
	2 Oct	Lugg, John son of John, haberdasher, of Gloucester Stapp, Sarah widow of William 8 yrs from 26 Jul innkeeper 5s *£5 of Mr Hollidaye's money*
	29 Aug	Lacy, William son of William, gardener, of King's Stanley Hieron, Humphrey & Margaret 7 yrs vintner & chandler 5s *Enrolled 1 Oct 1658*

2/231		**Robert Tither, mayor [1658–9]** **John Singleton and Richard Massinger sheriffs and bailiffs** **John Dorney, town clerk**
	1658 14 Oct	Okey, Daniel son of John, miller, dec'd, of Cheltenham Mitchell, George & Comfort 7 yrs from 29 Sep weaver 2s 6d
	20 Oct	Evans, Samuel son of Thomas, mercer, dec'd, of Westbury Cox, Winston & Anne 7 yrs cordwainer 6d
2/232	15 Oct	King, John son of James, scrivener, of Gloucester King, James, his father, & Isobel 7 yrs from 29 Sep scrivener 5s
	21 Oct	Francombe, Thomas son of Henry, woollen draper, dec'd, of Gloucester Atkins, John & Elizabeth 7 yrs cordwainer 15s [*cf Appendix V*]
	5 Nov	Tippinge, James son of William, husbandman, dec'd, of Great Malvern, Herefs [*recte* Worcs] Swayne, William jr & Joan 7 yrs lantern maker 2s 6d
2/233	20 Nov	Smith, William son of Thomas, husbandman, of Upton St Leonards Mills, Richard & Anne 7 yrs wiredrawer 2s 6d
	1659 10 Jan	Weaver, Francis son of Francis, butcher, dec'd, of Gloucester Farmer, John & Bridget 7 yrs silkweaver 2s 6d
	2 Feb	Pace, Thomas son of Thomas, cooper, dec'd, of Gloucester Pace, Elizabeth widow of said Thomas 7 yrs cooper 5s
2/234		Hadnett, John son of Henry, tailor, late of Gloucester Williams, Isaac & Eleanor 7 yrs tailor 10s
	[1658] 25 Dec	Commelin, Isaac son of James, apothecary, of Gloucester Commelin, James, his father, & Jane 7 yrs apothecary 10s
	1659 17 Feb	Aram, Arnold son of John, gentleman, of Newnham Hill, Edward & [*blank*] 7 yrs from 1 Jan haberdasher 2s 6d

	1659 16 Feb	Coale, William son of John, husbandman, dec'd, of Churcham
		Pitt, Samuel & Eleanor 7 yrs from 15 Feb pinmaker 12d
2/235	17 Feb	Hanx, John son of William, mercer, of Bampton [MS Bampton upon the Bush], Oxon
		Clayfeild, Edward & Anne 7 yrs from 15 Feb tanner 2s 6d
	3 Mar	Jeffes, William son of John, husbandman, of Ashleworth
		Syre, Daniel & [blank] 7 yrs from 1 Mar ropier 2s 6d
	6 Apr	Hall, William son of Francis, [blank], of Ledbury, Herefs
		Miles, James & [blank] 7 yrs baker 2s 6d
2/236	16 Apr	Hancocke, John son of John, broadweaver, of Barton Street, Gloucester
		Colericke, Daniel & Mary 7 yrs bodicemaker 2s 6d
		Lambert, Peter son of John, tobacco-pipe maker
		Freeman, Samuel & Jane 7 yrs jersey comber 2s 6d
		£4 Mrs Browne's money[1]
		Evans, William son of John, cordwainer, of Wotton under Edge
		Crumwell, John & Anne 7 yrs carrier 5s
2/237	7 May	Tayler, Jasper son of John, tanner, dec'd, of Weston under Penyard, Herefs
		Lugg, William & Eleanor 8 yrs from 2 Feb combmaker & turner 20s
	4 May	Feild, Edward son of Thomas Field, gentleman, dec'd, of Gloucester
		Hicks, Thomas & Joan 7 yrs from 25 Mar tailor 2s 6d
	6 May	Sinnox, John son of Thomas, blacksmith, dec'd, of Barton Street, Gloucester
		Sinnox, Thomas & Isabel 7 yrs from 25 Mar blacksmith
		2s 6d £4 Mrs Browne's money. The master is not a freeman
2/238	– May	Smith, William son of William, gentleman, of Deerhurst
		Hoare, Charles & Sarah 7 yrs from 1 May chandler 5s
	27 May	Gardner, Edward son of John, husbandman, of Painswick
		Bumford, William & [blank] 7 yrs from 1 May bodicemaker 2s 6d
2/239	– May	Browne, Richard son of Humphrey, husbandman, of Maisemore
		Horsington, Thomas & Margery 8 yrs bodicemaker 5s
	30 Jun	Belcher, John son of Richard, yeoman, dec'd, of Linton
		Berow, William & Eleanor 7 yrs tailor 2s
	—	Creese, George son of William, husbandman, dec'd, of Gloucester
		Bradford, John & Anne 8 yrs from 1 Jun milliner 10s
	1 Jun	Sisemore, Thomas son of Anthony, yeoman, dec'd, of Hartpury
		Beard, Richard & Armilla 7 yrs from 24 Jun tailor 2s 6d

---

[1] GBR B3/3 p 99 28 Mar 1659: To receive £4 of Mrs Browne's money: William son of Anne Ridler, widow, John son of Eleanor Senox, widow, Peter son of John Lambert, tobacco-pipe maker.

2/240	1659	8 Jun	Berry, Richard son of William, dec'd, of Matson

2/240 1659 8 Jun Berry, Richard son of William, dec'd, of Matson
Lewis, Abell & [blank] 7 yrs tiler & plasterer [blank]

18 May Parsons, Richard son of Richard, yeoman, of Much Birch, Herefs
Yates, Francis & Joan 7 yrs cordwainer 2s 6d

27 Jun Smith, William son of John, yeoman, dec'd, of Hill
Perry, Robert & Elizabeth 7 yrs from 24 Jun cordwainer 10s

2/241 28 Jun Byford, Joseph son of Joseph, cordwainer, of Gloucester
Sweate, Richard & Elizabeth 7 yrs glazier 20s

29 Jun Randle, Thomas son of John, yeoman, of Great Shurdington
Allen, Lawrence & Anne 7 yrs chandler 5s

2 Jul Colwell, Robert son of John, yeoman, of Newent
White, Anthony & Margaret 7 yrs from 24 Jun cordwainer 2s

2/242 6 Jul Morgan, Thomas son of John, husbandman, of Coleford
Colliar, Wm & Mary 7 yrs from 1 Jul blacksmith & gunsmith 2s 6d

12 Jul Monley, John son of Edward, tailor, of Shenington
Plott, Cornelius & Margaret 7 yrs tailor 2s 6d

11 Jul Parry, Daniel son of Daniel, mercer, dec'd, of Leonard Stanley
Selwyn, Thomas & Martha 7 yrs cordwainer 5s

2/243 30 Jul Jones, Richard son of Richard, smith, of Withington
Reeve, Giles & Mary 8 yrs gunsmith 2s 6d

4 Aug Pace, John son of Thomas, cooper, dec'd, of Gloucester
Newman, Augustine & Elizabeth 7 yrs from 25 Jul chandler 5s

9 Aug Bromley, James son of John, glover, dec'd, of Gloucester
Skillum, Richard & Sarah 7 yrs from 1 Aug tailor 2s 6d
£5 Mr Hollidaye's money[1]

2/244 9 Aug Bradgate, John son of Richard, barber surgeon, of Gloucester
Bradgate, Richard, his father, [no term] from 1 Aug barber surgeon 10s
£5 Mr Hollidaye's money

Atkins, Walter son of Thomas, cordwainer, of Gloucester
Atkins, John & Elizabeth 9 yrs from 20 Aug cordwainer 9s
£5 Mr Hollidaye's money

11 Aug Wiltshire, Lawrence son of Lawrence, gentleman, of Barton Street, Gloucester
Perks, John & Alice 7 yrs baker 5s
13 Jun 1660: John Perks came and certified that the indenture was cancelled by the consent of Lawrence Wiltshire father & son & the son was discharged from his apprenticeship

---

[1] GBR B3/3 p 105 31 Jul 1659: To receive £5 of Mr Hollidaye's money: William Reeve, John Brodgate, Walter Atkins, John Bromley, John Tilleson, Thomas Yarnold's son.

2/245	1659	3 Sep	Till, Richard son of Richard, cutler, of Gloucester Till, Richard, his father, & Dorothy 7 yrs cutler 20s £5 Mr Hollidaye's money
		30 Aug	Warde, John son of Robert, cordwainer, of Gloucester Moore, Henry & Joan [no term] from 24 Aug tobacco-pipe maker 5s
		24 Sep	Amos, Nathaniel son of Samuel, dyer, of Painswick Bumford, William & [blank] 7 yrs bodicemaker 2s 6d
		1 Oct	Scudamore, William son of William, woollen draper, of Gloucester Scudamore, William, his father, & [blank] 9 yrs from 29 Sep woollen draper 10s
2/246		1 Aug	Reeve, William son of William, butcher, of Gloucester Reeve, William, his father, 7 yrs butcher 10s £5 Mr Hollidaye's money

2/247 **Toby Jordan, mayor 1659[–60]**
William Scudamore and Nicholas Small, bailiffs and sheriffs
John Dorney, town clerk

	1659	4 Oct	Hill, Thomas son of Thomas, cordwainer, dec'd, of Gloucester Hill, Walter & Elizabeth 9 yrs cordwainer 2s
		5 Oct	Peter, John son of Giles, yeoman, of Oxenhall Niccolls, John & Mary 7 yrs from 29 Sep tanner 5s
		4 Oct	Skelton, Francis son of Richard, yeoman, of Great Malvern, Worcs Dunn, John & Margaret 7 yrs from 29 Sep maltster 10s
2/248		15 Oct	Filder, George son of Maurice, narrow weaver, of Sherston, Wilts Vayers, Thomas & Margaret 7 yrs from 29 Sep farrier & blacksmith 5s
		22 Oct	Randle, James son of John, [yeoman] of Great Shurdington Mercer, Robert & [blank] 7 yrs butcher 5s
			Randle, Giles son of John, yeoman, of Great Shurdington Beard, John & [blank] 7 yrs silkweaver 5s
2/249		1 Nov	Gardner, Thomas son of William, husbandman, of Gloucester Coutcher, John & Cecily 7 yrs pinmaker 5s
		28 Nov	Jones, Peter son of William, cordwainer, of Gloucester Atkins, Thomas & [blank] 7 yrs cordwainer 2s 6d
		10 Dec	Hopkins, John son of John, husbandman, dec'd, of Cheltenham Wadman, Roger & Elizabeth 7 yrs garter weaver 5s *2 Jun 1660: turned over to George Mitchell, garter weaver [see 2/115], to serve the residue of his term. Before Denis Wise.*
2/250		13 Dec	Winston, Walter son of Thos, husbandman, dec'd, of Great Witcombe Humphris, Richard & Frances 7 yrs from 25 Dec butcher 5s

1660 10 Jan Keene, Francis son of Joseph, dec'd, of Tewkesbury
Mills, Hannah widow of Richard 7 yrs silkweaver 6s 8d

6 Feb Heyward, Stephen son of Giles, gentleman, of Sandhurst
Broade, Richard & Mary 7 yrs from 2 Feb baker 2s 6d

2/251

Pockeridge, William son of Thomas, tailor, of Gloucester
Whitfeild, Richard & Hannah 8 yrs from 25 Mar last baker 5s
[*cf Appendix V*]
23 Feb 1662: indenture cancelled with the consent of his father Thomas Pockeridge. [Signed] Richard Whitfild

– Feb Nelme, Giles son of Giles, blacksmith, of Newnham
Tither, Robert, alderman, & Em [*no term*] from 29 Sep last tanner £4

19 Jan Hay, Alexander, son of Thomas, husbandman, dec'd, of Huntley
Philips, George & Mary 7 yrs feltmaker 2s 6d
George Philips is not a freeman

21 Jan Brooker, John son of [*blank*], butcher, dec'd, of Twyning
Viner, William & Constance 7 yrs feltmaker 2s 6d

2/252

2 Feb Baker, Jacob son of Abraham, scrivener, of Prestbury
Deane, Thomas & Katharine 7 yrs blacksmith 2s 6d

6 Jan Hodges, Nathaniel son of John, yeoman, of Longhope
Graftstocke, John & Elizabeth [*no term*] butcher 2s 6d

6 Mar Painter, John son of William, husbandman, of Wotton [St Mary]
Stephens, Richard & Margery 8 yrs tobacconist 40s

2/253

1 Mar Randle, Josiah son of James, yeoman, of Charlton Kings
Perkes, John & Alice 7 yrs baker 10s

26 Mar Cowdell, Robert son of Robert, silkweaver, of Gloucester
Unwin, Robert & [*blank*] 7 yrs feltmaker of Newnham 2s 6d
Alderman Clutterbuck, his gift[1]

Robinson, John son of Thomas, cordwainer, dec'd, of Gloucester
Pitt, Samuel & Eleanor 7 yrs pinmaker 2s
Alderman Clutterbuck, his gift

2 Apr Mayo, John son of William, miller, dec'd, of Saul
Sparrowhawke, William & Mary 8 yrs from 25 Mar garter weaver 5s

2/254

1 Apr Hancox, William son of John, button maker, of Gloucester
Bubb, Toby & [*blank*] 7 yrs cordwainer 12d
£4 Mrs Browne's gift[2]

3 May Rodway, John son of John, gentleman, of Upton St Leonards
Blicke, William & Mary 8 yrs from 1 May mercer 5s

---

[1] GBR B3/3 p 149 19 Sep 1660: Whereas the son of Henry Bradley had £5 of the gift of Mr Hollidaye granted to him but was not 14 years old at the time, the £5 is to be granted to Robert Cowdell who is already bound apprentice and was to have £5 of the gift of Alderman Clutterbuck but could not receive it.

[2] ibid p 129 26 Mar 1660: To receive £4 of Mrs Browne's gift: son of John Hancox of Barton Street, son of John Hancox of [St Mary de] Crypt parish, John son of William Taylor.

	1660 30 Apr	Madocke, James son of John, gentleman, of Barton Street, Gloucester Jennings, William & Bridget 7 yrs from 23 Apr barber surgeon 5s
	1 Apr	Jennings, John son of William, barber surgeon, of Gloucester Jennings, William, his father, & Bridget 10 yrs from 25 Mar barber surgeon 10s
2/255	28 May	Dring, William son of Simon, gentleman, of Great Shurdington Onyon, Thomas & Bridget 8 yrs silkweaver 2s 6d
	29 May	Varnum, Gregory son of Gregory, yeoman, of Kidderminster, Worcs Pritchards, Simon & Sarah 7 yrs cooper 2s 6d
	1 Jun	Reeve, George son of Giles sr, gunsmith, of Gloucester Reeve, Giles, his father, & Mary 7 yrs gunsmith 10s
	14 Jun	Chapman, John son of Thomas, tailor, dec'd, of Gloucester Bell, John & Joan 7 yrs from 29 Sep next silkweaver 2s 6d
2/256	25 Jun	Churches, Giles son of John, clothier, of Woodchester [MS Wichester] Cooke, Thomas & Margaret 7 yrs from 25 Mar last chandler 2s 6d *& 2 suits of apparel whereof one is to consist of 5 yards of broad cloth of the price of 10s at the least to make him a suit and cloak*
		Ives, Willliam son of John, joiner, of London Martley, Anthony jr & Anne 7 yrs from 24 Jun turner 2s 6d
	1 Jul	Wood, James son of Richard, yeoman, of Barton Street, Gloucester Lugg, Lawrence & Elizabeth 7 yrs baker 3s 4d
	24 Jun	Eckly, John son of John, yeoman, dec'd, of Wormsley, Herefs Lysons, Daniel & Sarah 9 yrs woollen draper 5s
2/257	1 Jul	Heaven, John son of John, clothier, of King's Stanley Payne, Robert jr & Anne 8 yrs from 24 Jun mercer 10s
		[*Entries from here on in Latin*]
	7 Jul	Bosly, Walter son of Thomas, yeoman, of Barnwood Bosly, Richard & Elizabeth 7 yrs feltmaker 5s
	1 Jul	Poole, John son of John, tucker, dec'd, of Malmesbury, [Wilts] Bell, John & Joan 8 yrs silkweaver 5s
	18 Jul	Ricketts, George son of George, yeoman, of Elmstone Hardwicke Freeman, Samuel & Jane 7 yrs jersey comber 2s 6d
2/258	23 Jul	Sparkes, Thomas son of Thomas, sievemaker, of Gloucester Beard, John & [*blank*] 8 yrs silkweaver 5s [*Entry in English*]
	21 Jul	Stephens, Thomas son of Thomas, pinmaker, of Gloucester Stephens, Thomas, his father, & Alice 7 yrs pinmaker 10s [*Holliday*]
	25 Jul	Tailor, William son of William, trowman, late of Gloucester Stephens, Thomas & Alice 8 yrs from 24 Jun pinmaker 5s
	1 Aug	Bosly, Thomas son of Thomas, yeoman, of Barnwood White, Sergeant & Joan [*no term*] cordwainer 2s 6d

2/259	1660	30 Jul	Huntley, Richard son of John, dec'd, of Newnham
			Nash, Jesse & Hester 7 yrs feltmaker 5s
		2 Aug	Woolley, James son of Thomas, gentleman, of Gloucester
			Plott, Cornelius & Margaret 7 yrs from 25 Jul tailor £3
		1 Aug	Ockold. Thomas son of Henry, gentleman, of Gloucester
			Tyler, John 7 yrs cordwainer 5s
		21 Jul	Endall, William son of William, butcher, late of Gloucester
			Elliotts, John & Margaret 7 yrs wiredrawer 5s
			£5 of Mr Hollidaye's gift in 1659[1]
		1 Sep	Longden, Thomas son of Robert, ironmonger, of Gloucester
			Longden, Robert, his father 7 yrs ironmonger 10s
2/260		25 Jul	Bingle, John son of John, cooper, of Gloucester
			Bingle, John, his father, & Elizabeth 7 yrs cooper 5s
			£5 of Mr Hollidaye's gift[2]
			Cooke, Richard son of Richard, blacksmith, of Gloucester
			Cooke, Richard, his father, & Eleanor 7 yrs blacksmith 5s
			£5 of Mr Hollidaye's gift
		4 Sep	Randle, William son of James, yeoman, late of Charlton Kings
			Bicknell, William & Dorothy 7 yrs tailor 2s 6d
		6 Sep	Hornedge, Henry son of William, farmer, of Kingsholm
			Cowcher, Robert & Margery [*no term*] pinmaker 2s 6d
2/261		14 Sep	Winiatt, Stephen son of William, farmer
			Webb, John & Ursula 7 yrs cooper 2s 6d
		17 Jul	Lovell, William son of William, carrier, of Malmesbury, Wilts
			Wood, John & Margaret 9 yrs button maker [*blank*]
		19 Sep	Madocke, Thomas son of Richard, farmer, of Cranham
			Thomas, Giles & Dorothy 7 yrs pinmaker 2s 6d
		26 Sep	Berry, Robert son of Robert, victualler, of Gloucester
			Philips, James jr & Anne 7 yrs from 29 Sep tailor 5s
2/262		2 Oct	Hornedge, John son of William, gardener, of Kingsholm
			Eckly, Henry 7 yrs button maker 2s 6d
		1 Sep	Parsons, Walter son of John, clerk, of Withington, Herefs
			Perry, Robert & Elizabeth 7 yrs currier 10s
		—	Jones, John son of Edmund, yeoman, of parish of Itton, Mon
			Powell, Robert & Alice 7 yrs barber surgeon 12d
			[*Repeated at 2/268*]

---

[1] GBR B3/3 p 140 21 Jul 1660: Whereas £5 was granted about a year ago to a son of Thomas Yearnold and he is beyond the sea and the moneys not accepted, it is agreed that this act be made void and the £5 granted to the son of Elizabeth Endall, widow, who is in a very low condition.

[2] ibid p 140 21 Jul 1660: To receive £5 of Mr Hollidaye's money: Thomas Morse's son, Thomas Stephens, Henry Bradley, John Bingle, Richard Cooke, John Simon's son.

1660 29 Sep Bubb, Henry son of John, carpenter, dec'd, of Wotton [St Mary]
              Russell, William, alderman, & Jane 7 yrs furrier 40s

2/263 **Robert Payne, mayor [1660–1]**
         Joseph Powell and Samuel Brewster, bailiffs and sheriffs

1660 3 Oct Powell, Charles son of William, brewer, of Gloucester
             Painter, John & Elizabeth 7 yrs from 29 Sep glazier 2s 6d
             [*cf Appendix V*]

      27 Oct Robins, John son of William, yeoman, dec'd, of Maugersbury
              Nash, William & Mary 7 yrs feltmaker 5s

      1 Nov Simons, William son of John, victualler, of Gloucester
             Wintle, Richard & [*blank*] 7 yrs currier 2s 6d
             £5 of Mr Hollidaye's gift

1661 2 Feb Price, James son of Richard, pewterer, of Gloucester
             Price, Richard, his father, & Dinah 7 yrs pewterer 10s

2/264 1660 15 Nov Hill, Thomas son of Thomas, yeoman, of Ashleworth
                      Tyler, John & Elizabeth 7 yrs from 18 Oct cordwainer 5s

              19 Nov Morse, John son of Thomas, currier, of Gloucester
                      Martley, Anthony jr & Anne 7 yrs feltmaker 5s [*Holliday*]

              20 Nov Pinnell, Henry son of Francis, yeoman, of Aust
                      Edmunds, John & Anne 7 yrs hosier 2s 6d

                —   Colway, Robert son of John, yeoman, of Newent
                      Holliday, Richard & [*blank*] 7 yrs baker 5s

2/265   1 Nov Chapman, George son of John, freemason, of Mitcheldean
                      Collier, William & Mary 8 yrs gunsmith & blacksmith 10s

               3 Dec Smarte, John son of John, mason, of Cheltenham
                      Weaver, Thomas & Blanche 7 yrs butcher 2s 6d

               8 Dec Hancox, Edward son of George, gentleman, dec'd, of Hide, Stanford
                      Bishop, Herefs
                      Bennett, John & Penelope 7 yrs barber surgeon 6s 8d

              10 Dec James, Richard son of Richard, yeoman, dec'd, of Gloucester
                      Stephens, Thomas & Alice 7 yrs pinmaker 2s 6d

2/266   17 Dec Price, Richard son of Richard, gardener, of Gloucester
                      Price, John & [*blank*] 7 yrs wiredrawer 2s 6d

              19 Dec Roberts, John son of Hugh, yeoman, of Hempsted
                      Wand, William & [*blank*] 7 yrs mercer 5s

        1661 1 Jan   Nash, Joseph son of William, yeoman, of Haresfield
                      Ricketts, James & Anne 7 yrs tanner 3s 4d

              9 Jan   Rogers, John son of Thomas, yeoman, dec'd, of Badgeworth
                      Pharley, George & Mary 7 yrs cutler 5s [*cf Appendix V*]

2/267	1661	21 Jan	Bannett, John son of John, miller, of Gloucester Onyon, Humphrey & Elizabeth 9 yrs silkweaver 5s
		1 Jan	Hickes, John son of William, yeoman, dec'd, of Tirley Partridge, Richard & Katharine 7 yrs baker 5s
		2 Feb	Bicke, Henry son of John, yeoman, of Up Hatherley Gwin, Augustine sr & Alice 7 yrs currier 5s
			Wilse, Giles son of Thomas, yeoman, of Barnwood Abbotts, Henry & Sarah 7 yrs baker 2s 6d
2/268		26 Feb	Barrett, Thomas son of Thomas, cutler, of Bristol Barrett, Thomas & [blank] 7 yrs cutler 40s
		1 Mar	Farmer, John son of John, silkweaver, of Gloucester Farmer, John, his father, & Bridget 7 yrs silkweaver 5s
		25 Mar	Bishop, Edmund son of Thomas, farmer, of Churchdown Cordell, James & Cecily 7 yrs glover 12d *Edmund Bishop is discharged from James Cordell and bound to William Greene, pinmaker, to be enrolled in this present year* [See 2/277]
		30 Mar	Tayler, Richard son of Richard, cutler, dec'd, of Gloucester Elliotts, John & Margaret 8 yrs from 25 Mar wiredrawer 2s 6d
		20 Feb	Jones, John son of Edmund, yeoman, of Itton, Mon Powell, Robert & Alice 7 yrs barber surgeon 12d [*Repeating entry at 2/262, with date added*]
2/269		1 Apr	Powell, John son of Richard, navigator, late of Bridgnorth [Salop] Samson, William & Jane 7 yrs turner 5s
		18 Apr	Pace, William son of John, late of Maisemore Merrett, Thomas & Hester 7 yrs currier 2s 6d
		8 Apr	Skinner, John son of John, glover, of Tewkesbury Sturmy, John & Mary 7 yrs glover 2s 6d
		1 May	Hancox, John son of John, currier, of Gloucester Roberts, Samuel & Elizabeth 7 yrs silkweaver 2s 6d [*Mrs Browne*][1]
2/270			Haines, William son of William, farmer, formerly of Barton Street, Gloucester Eliote, Edward & Mary 9 yrs victualler 5s
		15 May	Elliotts, Richard son of Richard, baker, of Leonard Stanley Jordan, John & [blank] [no term] from 25 Mar last baker 1s *23 Feb 1663: John Jordan testifies that Richard Elliotts fell sick and was never in his service.* [Signed] *John Jordan*
		17 May	Holloway, John son of Hugh, victualler, of Leonard Stanley Beard, Richard & Armilla 7 yrs from 25 Mar tailor 5s

---

[1] GBR B3/3 p 175 26 Mar 1661: To receive £4 of Mrs Browne's money: John son of John Hancox, cobbler, Henry Bubb, Widow Butt's son.

	1661 20 May	Thomas, Henry son of William, farmer, of Gloucester Roberts, Samuel & Elizabeth 7 yrs silkweaver 2s 6d
2/271	1 May	Butt, Robert son of James, pavior, dec'd, of Gloucester Waterson, Geoffrey & Joan 7 yrs pavior & gardener 3s 4d [Mrs Browne]
	21 May	Nethaway, Benjamin son of Thomas, currier, of Gloucester Onyon, Thomas & Bridget 8 yrs silkweaver 8s
	23 May	Gardner, Daniel son of William, labourer, of Gloucester Hartland, William & Martha [no term] pinmaker 5s
	29 May	Freame, John son of John, tailor, dec'd, of Barnwood Partridge, Richard & Katharine 7 yrs baker 5s
2/272	1 Jun	Harris, William son of William, brewer, of Gloucester Skillum Richard & Sarah 7 yrs tailor 2s 6d
		Freeman, George son of Anthony, gentleman, of Badgeworth Lugg, Thomas & Joan 8 yrs haberdasher 5s
	17 Jun	Tinsley, John son of Walter, farmer, of Benington, Lincs Nash, William & Mary 7 yrs feltmaker 2s 6d
	3 Jun	Heard, Humphrey son of Robert, yeoman, of Hempsted Cripps, Samuel & Mary 7 yrs butcher 5s
2/273	24 Jun	Marshall, George son of Thomas, farmer, of Berry Hill in the Forest [of Dean] Nash, Jesse & Hester 7 yrs feltmaker 5s
		Stephens, Samuel son of Thomas, pinmaker, of Gloucester Clark, John & [blank] 7 yrs joiner 2s 6d [cf Appendix V]
		Brocke, William son of William, farmer, late of Hasfield Swayne, Edward & Elizabeth [no term] collarmaker 2s 6d
		Curnocke, James son of James, currier, of Gloucester Merrett, Thomas & Hester 7 yrs currier 1s
2/274	10 Jul	Terrett, John son of Thomas, maltster, dec'd, of Gloucester Franckis, William & Elizabeth 7 yrs baker 5s [cf Appendix V]
		Stocke, Castle son of William, yeoman, of Chacely, Worcs Longden, Robert & [blank] 7 yrs ironmonger 5s
	24 Jun	Elridge, Thomas son of Eldridge, Henry, narrow weaver, of Hasfield Greene, John jr & Margaret 7 yrs cooper 5s
	1 Aug	Cowles, Richard son of Richard, butcher, of Gloucester Mitchell, George & Elizabeth 7 yrs garter weaver 3s 4d £5 of Mr Hollidaye's gift[1]

---

[1] GBR B3/3 p 193 22 Jul 1661: To receive £5 of Mr Hollidaye's money: John Bradley, Richard Cowles, Winston Cox, Edmund Turner *alias* Barnard, Robert Yearnold, Edmund Sturmy's son.

2/275	1661	25 Jul	Bradley, John son of Henry, feltmaker, of Gloucester Baker, John sr & [blank] 7 yrs butcher 5s *£5 of Mr Hollidaye's gift*

2/275   1661   25 Jul   Bradley, John son of Henry, feltmaker, of Gloucester
                Baker, John sr & [blank] 7 yrs butcher 5s
                £5 of Mr Hollidaye's gift

                Cox, Winston son of Winston, currier, of Gloucester
                Cox, Winston, his father, & Anne 7 yrs currier 5s
                £5 of Mr Hollidaye's gift

                Turner *alias* Barnard, Edmund son of John, joiner, dec'd, of Gloucester
                Wadman, Roger & Elizabeth 7 yrs garter weaver 5s
                £5 of Mr Hollidaye's gift

         1 Aug Yearnold, Robert son of Thomas, sailor, of Gloucester
                Withenbury, James & Joan 7 yrs carpenter 2s 6d
                £5 of Mr Hollidaye's gift

2/276   24 Jun White, William son of John, yeoman, of Dymock
                Hathaway, Elizeor & Mary 7 yrs carpet weaver 2s 6d

        25 Jul Simons, John son of John, victualler, of Gloucester
                Lea, Henry & [blank] 7 yrs currier 3s 4d

        23 Sep Springe, Francis son of Henry, yeoman, of Brookthorpe
                Gwin, Augustine jr & Margaret 7 yrs cordwainer 5s

2/277   25 Sep Bishop, Edmund son of Thomas, farmer, of Churchdown
                Greene, William & Mary 8 yrs pinmaker 2s 6d [*See 2/268*]

        28 Sep Hoskins, Thomas son of Gabriel, miller, of Stroud
                Beard, John & [blank] 7 yrs silkweaver 5s

                Winniat, George son of George, farmer, of Tewkesbury
                Heyward, John & Sarah 7 yrs feltmaker 3s 4d

2/279   **Thomas Peirce, mayor 1661[–2]**
                Thomas Yate and Thomas Price, sheriffs and bailiffs

        1661 9 Oct Clarke, Thomas son of Thomas, mat maker, of Newent
                     Harris, Joseph & Tacy 7 yrs currier 3s 4d

                     Woodward, John son of Thomas, mason, formerly of Tewkesbury
                     Sparrowhawke, William & Mary 8 yrs cotton weaver 5s

        11 Oct Sturmy, Edmund son of Edmund, glover, of Gloucester
                Hardinge, John & Elizabeth 7 yrs glover 2s 6d [*Holliday*]

        14 Oct Crumpe, Edward son of Henry, farmer, of Bulley
                Roberts, Samuel & Elizabeth 7 yrs silkweaver 2s 6d

2/280   21 Oct Weaver, William son of William, farmer, of Churchdown
                Hill, Walter & Elizabeth 8 yrs from 18 Oct currier 1s

                Davis, Anthony son of John, currier, dec'd, of Gloucester
                Badger, Albert & Elizabeth 7 yrs pinmaker 5s
                9 Mar 1664: turned over to Robert Coucher, pinmaker, to serve the residue of his term. Before Henry Ockold

        29 Oct Pearce, Thomas son of Henry, yeoman, of Wotton under Edge
                Sparrowhawke, Robert & Joan 7 yrs cotton weaver 2s 6d

	1661 29 Oct	Browne, Samuel son of William, yeoman, of Sandhurst Clarke, Henry & [blank] 7 yrs from 1 Nov glazier 2s 6d
2/281	31 Oct	Hulls, John son of Ralph, farmer, of Bourton on the Water Pharley, George & Mary 7 yrs from 1 Nov cutler 5s
	2 Nov	Newman, Edward son of Robert, butcher, of Harescombe Badger, Jeremiah & Margaret 9 yrs weaver 2s 6d
	14 Nov	Turner, William son of John, cook, of Gloucester Turner, John, his father, & Joan 7 yrs cook 5s
	5 Dec	Terrett, John son of Thomas, maltster, dec'd, of Gloucester Wadman, Roger & Elizabeth 7 yrs from 1 Oct cotton weaver 10s [cf Appendix V]
2/282	18 Dec	Soule, John son of William, farmer, of Woolstrop Warwicke, William & Anne 8 yrs from 25 Dec vintner 10s
	1662 3 Jan	Newman, Henry son of Christopher, carpenter, formerly of Gloucester Walker, James & Martha 10 yrs button maker 3s 4d
	1661 1 Aug	Watson, Humphrey son of Humphrey, victualler, of Bristol Hutchins, William & [blank] 7 yrs tailor 2s 6d
	— —	Cole, Charles son of Ralph, yeoman, of St Margarets, Gloucester Perkes, William & [blank] 7 yrs pinmaker [Incomplete entry; cf Appendix V]
2/283	1662 11 Mar	Marden, Giles son of Giles, yeoman, dec'd, of Maisemore Broade, Richard & Mary 7 yrs from 25 Mar baker 20s
	17 Mar	Sadler, William son of William, coachman, of London Crumwell, John & Anne 7 yrs carrier 20s
	26 Mar	Lumbard, James son of William, farmer, of Combe St Nicholas, Som Lumbard, Isaac & Jane 7 yrs serge weaver 5s
		Mathewes, Matthew son of John, brewer, of Gloucester Mathews, John, his father, & Joan 7 yrs brewer £5
2/284	2 Apr	Dubberly, William son of William, gardener, of Gloucester Coucher, John & Cecily 7 yrs from 1 May pinmaker 5s
	1656 7 Jul	Hutchins, Humphrey son of William, innholder, of Gloucester James, Humphrey 7 yrs of London draper *7 Mar 1662: turned over to Richard Cooke, blacksmith of Gloucester for the remainder of the 7 yrs*
	1662 7 Apr	Longe, John son of Gilbert, farmer, of Oxenhall Stephens, James, alderman, & Anne 7 yrs maltster 13s 4d
	19 Apr	Holliday, Richard son of Henry, basket maker, of Gloucester Morris, Richard & Katharine 7 yrs carpenter 5s[1]

---

[1] GBR B3/3 p 223 26 Mar 1662: To receive £4 of Mrs Browne's money: George Hintin's son, Henry Holliday's son, Anne Woodcock's son.

2/285	1662	Hinton, George son of George, currier, of Gloucester Woodward, John & Margaret 7 yrs combmaker 2s 6d [*Mrs Browne*]
	19 May	Denton, John son of Edward, farmer, of Brimpsfield Beedle, James & Avice 7 yrs haberdasher 5s
		Ryland, Richard son of William, yeoman, of Quinton Ryland, John & Hester 7 yrs tanner 5s
		Haines, William [*deleted*]
	24 Jun	Hancox, Thomas son of John, currier, of Gloucester Sumers, Thomas & Eleanor 7 yrs silkweaver 12d[1]
2/286	—	Hill, John son of Thomas, labourer, of Minsterworth Davis, Henry & Elizabeth 7 yrs currier 12d
	9 Jun	Woodcocke, William son of Giles, carpenter, dec'd, of Gloucester Onyon, Humphrey & Elizabeth 7 yrs silkweaver 2s 6d [*Mrs Browne*]
	15 Jul	Ferrett, Nathaniel son of John, glover, of Maisemore Cordell, James & Cecily 7 yrs glover 12d
	23 Jul	Gwyn, Samuel son of Lewis, pinmaker, of Gloucester Yates, Francis & [*blank*] 7 yrs from 1 Sep currier [*blank*]
	8 Aug	Davis, Thomas son of Thomas Davis *alias* Devis, wiredrawer, of Gloucester Davis, Thomas, his father, & Mary 7 yrs wiredrawer 5s [*Holliday*][2]
2/287	1656 7 Jan	Powell, William son of Roger, of Brockworth Smith, William & Katharine 8 yrs currier *25 Jun 1662: by the consent of Katharine Smith, turned over to Francis Yates, cordwainer, for the rest of his term. Before Lawrence Singleton*
	1662 19 Aug	Horrell, John son of John, tailor, of Gloucester Horell, John, his father, & [*blank*] 7 yrs from 24 Aug tailor 20s *£5 Mr Holliday's money*
	20 Aug	Williams, Elisha son of John, ropier, of Gloucester Williams, John, his father, & Jane 7 yrs from 25 Jul ropier 10s *£5 Mr Holliday's money*
	29 Aug	Kinge, William son of William, pinmaker, of Gloucester Kinge, William, his father, & Phoebe 7 yrs pinmaker 5s *£5 Mr Holliday's money*

---

[1] GBR B3/3 p 221 21 Feb 1662: Serjeant Seys wished the fee due to him as Recorder to be used to bind boys apprentice. The sons of John Hancox of St Aldate's and Richard Tayler, deceased, of St Mary de Crypt to have £3-6-8 each.

[2] ibid p 237 22 Jul 1662: To receive £5 of Mr Holliday's money: John Dewxell, Thomas Devis, William King, Elisha Williams, James Cooke, John Horell.

2/288	1662	8 Sep	Sparkes, Richard son of Thomas, sievemaker, of Gloucester White, Sergeant & Joan 8 yrs from 29 Sep currier 10s
		[blank]	Dewxell, Anthony son of John, gentleman, of Gloucester Barton, Richard & Anne 7 yrs glover 2s 6d £5 Mr Holliday's money
		29 Sep	Pearce, Henry son of Henry, farmer, of Wotton under Edge Sparrowhawke, Robert jr & Dorothy 7 yrs silkweaver 2s 6d
			Cawdle, Richard son of William, maltster, of Gloucester Smith, John & Margaret 7 yrs barber surgeon 5s
2/289			Farmer, William son of [blank], gunsmith, of Hardwicke Woolford, Thomas & Joan 11 yrs basket maker 5s

2/291 **William Russell, mayor [1662–3]**
Edward Tither and Toby Langford, sheriffs and bailiffs

	1662	7 Oct	Wintle, Samuel son of Henry, yeoman, of Westbury Wintle, Henry & Mary 7 yrs maltster 12d
		28 Oct	Prune, John son of Thomas, farmer, of Haydon Nash, Richard & Joan 7 yrs feltmaker 5s [cf Appendix V]
		1 Nov	Wilson, John son of John, butcher, of Gloucester Smith, William & Susannah 8 yrs glover 2s 6d
		17 Nov	Venton, Thomas son of John, farmer, formerly of Barton Street, Gloucester Coutcher, Robert & Margaret 8 yrs pinmaker 5s
2/292		20 Nov	Castle als Cooke, Nathaniel son of Walter, yeoman, dec'd of Painswick Perkes, John & Alice 7 yrs baker 2s 6d
		26 Nov	Knight, John son of George, farmer, of Miserden Axon, John & Elizabeth 7 yrs blacksmith & farrier 2s 6d
		24 Oct	Barrett, William son of Ralph, yeoman, of Minsterworth Gardner, John & Mary [no term] currier 2s 6d
		1 Dec	Williams alias Baker, William son of William, yeoman, of Newent Sare, James & Margaret 7 yrs tailor 5s
2/293		26 Dec	Dawe, William son of Richard, tanner, of Huntley Lewis, Abel & Elizabeth 7 yrs tiler & plasterer 6s
		30 Dec	Morris, John son of Robert, carpenter, of Gloucester Morris, Richard & Katharine 7 yrs carpenter 2s 6d
	1663	5 Jan	Osborne, Daniel son of Daniel, heelmaker, of Painswick Fowler, Henry & [blank] 7 yrs doctor in physic 5s
		14 Jan	Bryan, Thomas son of Thomas, clerk, of Painswick Kinge, Samuel & Mary 7 yrs from 5 Nov last tailor 2s 6d
2/293 [bis]		26 Feb	Smarte, Anthony son of Richard, yeoman, of Gloucester Merrett, Thomas & [blank] 7 yrs from 2 Feb currier 6s

	1663	29 Jan	Eckly, Samuel son of Thomas, chandler, of Gloucester Yate, Thomas, alderman, & Elizabeth 8 yrs from 2 Feb apothecary 5s
		14 Feb	Cowles, Thomas son of Thomas, glover, of Gloucester Chapman, Thomas & Elizabeth 7 yrs tailor 2s 6d [*cf Appendix V*]
		2 Feb	Maddinge, John son of John, brewer, dec'd, of Gloucester Perkes, William & [*blank*] 8 yrs pinmaker 8s
2/294		21 Feb	Baker, Thomas son of Thomas, yeoman, of Bromsgrove, Glos [*recte* Worcs] Clayfeild, Edward & Anne 8 yrs tanner 3s 4d
		24 Feb	Heyden, John son of Nathaniel, farmer, of Gloucester Bamford, William & Elizabeth 7 yrs bodicemaker 12d
		12 Mar	Cooke, Robert son of James, sawyer, of Gloucester Goodcheape, Thomas & Sybil 7 yrs currier 2s 6d [*Holliday*]
		18 Mar	Tainton, Walter son of Walter, grocer, dec'd, of Gloucester Tainton, Eleanor widow of Walter 7 yrs grocer 10s
2/295		25 Mar	Byford, Nathaniel son of Richard, narrow weaver, of Gloucester Parish, John & Frances 7 yrs tailor 2s 6d
		7 Apr	Bromly, William son of William, glover, formerly of Gloucester Hawkins, Giles & Eleanor 7 yrs comb maker 2s 6d *£4 Mrs Browne's money*[1]
		14 Apr	Nash, Richard son of Richard, feltmaker, of Gloucester Marston, John & Rebecca 7 yrs mercer 5s
		20 Apr	Churches, Jonathan son of John, yeoman, of Woodchester [MS Wichester] Partridge, Thomas & Elizabeth [*no term*] from 25 Mar baker 5s
2/296		1 May	Cowles, Thomas son of Thomas, glover, of Gloucester Hughes, John & Jane 7 yrs currier 3s 4d [*cf Appendix V*]
		4 May	Longe, Walter son of Thomas, farmer, of Ashleworth Singleton, John & Anne 7 yrs innholder 5s
		1 Jan	Garlicke, James son of James, tailor, dec'd, of Gloucester Onyons, Thomas & Bridget 8 yrs silkweaver 10s
		1 May	Copner, Richard son of Giles, currier, of Haresfield Barrett, Thomas & Joan 9 yrs cutler 30s
2/297	1662	5 Apr	Lange, James son of James, silk weaver, late of Gloucester Sparrowhawke, Robert jr & Dorothy 7 yrs silkweaver 2s 6d *Enrolled by the order of the mayor and justices*
	1663	28 May	George, Nathaniel son of John, yeoman, of Redmarley d'Abitot, Worcs Vaisie, Walter & Margaret 9 yrs from 25 Mar tailor [*blank*]

---

[1] GBR B3/33 p 255 26 Mar 1663: To receive £4 of Mrs Browne's money: William Bromley, George Wood, Sarah Harris's son.

	1663	1 Jun	Cooke, Henry son of Henry, yeoman, of Paganhill

1663　1 Jun　Cooke, Henry son of Henry, yeoman, of Paganhill
　　　　　　　Pharley, George & Mary 9 yrs cutler 50s

　　　　6 Jun　Roach. Abraham son of William, farmer, of Carew [MS Carey], Pembs
　　　　　　　George, William & Hester 7 yrs feltmaker 2s 6d

2/298　1 May　Drury, Jeremiah son of John, tailor, of Gloucester
　　　　　　　Cowdale, John & Patience 7 yrs tailor 2s 6d

　　　　18 Jun　Dowsinge, William son of Walter, farrier, of Gloucester
　　　　　　　Chapman, Thomas & Elizabeth 7 yrs tailor 2s 6d

　　　　17 Jun　Dimocke, Cressey son of Cressey Dymocke, gentleman, of London
　　　　　　　Webb, John & Jane 8 yrs mercer 5s

　　　　24 Jun　Jeffes, Richard son of John, yeoman, of Ashleworth
　　　　　　　Bosly, Richard & Elizabeth 7 yrs feltmaker 5s

　　　　　　　Knowles, Henry son of Henry, pewterer, of Gloucester
　　　　　　　Knowles, Henry, his father, & Mary 7 yrs pewterer 20s

2/299　4 Jul　Watts, William son of [*blank*], tailor, of Highnam
　　　　　　　Madocke, William & Sarah 7 yrs tailor 5s

　　　　6 Jul　Mathews, Thomas son of William, yeoman, of Minsterworth
　　　　　　　Greene, John sr & Katharine 7 yrs cooper 3s 4d

　　　　18 Jul　Kinge, Thomas son of Thomas, baker, dec'd, of Gloucester
　　　　　　　Yates, Francis & Joan 7 yrs from 29 Sep currier 12d

　　　　22 Jul　Ives, Samuel son of John, joiner, dec'd, of Deddington, Oxon
　　　　　　　Bumford, William & Elizabeth 7 yrs bodicemaker 2s 6d

2/300　7 Jul　Wootton *alias* White, William son of William, yeoman, dec'd, of Down Hatherley
　　　　　　　Cowdale, John & Patience 8 yrs tailor 5s

　　　　1 Aug　Price, Richard son of Richard, pewterer, dec'd, of Gloucester
　　　　　　　Price, Dinah widow of Richard 7 yrs pewterer 5s

　　　　　　　Longe, John son of Richard, currier, of Gloucester
　　　　　　　Bennett, John & Anne 7 yrs button maker 2s 6d

　　　　7 Aug　Haines, Peter son of Peter, chandler, of Gloucester
　　　　　　　Haines, Peter, his father, & Elizabeth 7 yrs chandler 10s

2/301　17 Aug　Griffin, Richard son of Richard, plasterer, of Gloucester
　　　　　　　Nash, Richard & Joan 7 yrs feltmaker 2s 6d

　　　　25 Jul　Savory, Edward son of William, farrier, of Gloucester
　　　　　　　Smith, Thomas & Joan 7 yrs pewterer 2s 6d [*Holliday*][1]

　　　　1 Sep　Ludlow, Christopher son of Stephen, yeoman, dec'd, of Shipton
　　　　　　　Ludlow, Joseph & [*blank*] 7 yrs mercer 5s

　　　　12 Sep　Milton, William son of John, farmer, of Upton St Leonards
　　　　　　　Pitt, Samuel & Eleanor 7 yrs pinmaker 2s 6d

---

[1] GBR B3/3 p 261 20 July 1663: To receive £5 of Mr Hollidaye's money: William Savory, John Hobson, Charles Tony, — Beard, April Dudley and — Dobbs.

2/302 1663 15 Sep Dudley, April son of Arthur, butcher, of Gloucester
Baker, John jr & Anne 7 yrs from 17 Sep butcher 5s [*Holliday*]

18 Sep Knowles, Edward son of John, cooper, of Worcester
Williams, Richard & [*blank*] 7 yrs cooper 3s 4d

2/304 **John Powell, mayor 1663[–4]**
Walter Harris and Clement Dowle, bailiffs and sheriffs

1663 10 Oct Turbett, Robert son of Robert, farmer, of Bredon, Worcs
Day, William & Joan 7 yrs from 29 Sep tanner 5s

15 Oct Longe, William son of Anthony, gentleman, formerly of Ashleworth
Lye, Hester widow of Giles 7 yrs from 25 Mar next chandler 2s 6d

1 Nov Dewxell, Thomas son of Thomas, gentleman, of Barton Street, Gloucester
Welsteed, John & Elizabeth 7 yrs blacksmith 5s

16 Oct Toney, Charles son of Thomas, currier, dec'd, of Gloucester
Ludnam, John & [*blank*] 7 yrs musician 20s [*Holliday*]

2/305 5 Oct Holman, Henry son of Henry, [*blank*], of Pershore, Worcs
Onyon, Humphrey & Elizabeth [*no term*] from 29 Sep silkweaver 2s 6d

7 Oct Meeke, Thomas son of Thomas, currier, of Gloucester
Meeke, Thomas, his father, & Margery 7 yrs from 29 Sep currier 7s

3 Nov Griffin, John son of Richard, plasterer, of Gloucester
Perkes, John & Katharine 7 yrs from 1 Nov pinmaker 2s 6d

5 Nov Jones *alias* Watts, John son of Richard, button-mould maker, of Gloucester
Whitfeild, Edward & Mary 7 yrs shoe mender 2s 6d

2/306 14 Nov Wily, James son of William, yeoman, of Frampton on Severn
Jordan, John & Anne 7 yrs from 1 Nov baker 2s 6d

6 Nov Man, John son of Robert, yeoman, of Eastcott, Wilts
Niccolls, William & Joan 7 yrs from 29 Sep tanner 5s

17 Nov Hobson, James son of John, mercer, dec'd, of Gloucester
Bennett, John & Anne [*no term*] button maker 2s 6d
£5 Alderman Hollidaye's money

30 Nov Dewe, John son of John, innkeeper, of Gloucester
Sare, James & Sarah 7 yrs tailor 4s [*cf Appendix V*]

2/307 4 Dec Pheasant, Thomas son of Thomas, farmer, of Gloucester
Baker, William & Elizabeth 8 yrs button maker 8s

1 Dec Freeman, Giles son of Robert, yeoman, of parish of Badgeworth
Smith, Giles & Sybil 7 yrs baker 12d

25 Dec Davis, Isaac son of William, tailor, of Sandhurst
Hicks, Thomas & Joan 7 yrs tailor 3s

	1663 21 Dec	Clarke, Francis son of Thomas, yeoman, of Cranborne, Dorset
		Mairis, Charles & [*blank*] 7 yrs brazier 5s
		1 Oct 1664: by the consent of himself and Charles Mairis, Francis Clarke is discharged from his apprenticeship and the indentures are cancelled
2/308		30 Dec Edmunds, Lewis son of Lewis, innkeeper, of the Leigh
		Hale, Richard & Alice 7 yrs currier
		7 Feb 1667: Richard Hale disenfranchised by act of Common Council for several misdemeanours. Lewis Edmunds was in fraudent manner bound only that he might be a freeman. He did not serve as an apprentice but openly exercised his trade as of himself. He should therefore not be admitted to be a burgess or freeman. [*Signed*] *Williams*
	1664 1 Jan	Cooke, John son of Thomas, innkeeper, dec'd, of Gloucester
		Lane, Thomas & Isobel 7 yrs chandler 30s
	12 Jan	Paule, Thomas son of Edward, farmer, of Naunton
		Sare, James & Margaret 7 yrs tailor 2s 6d
2/309	7 Mar	Whittorne, John son of Richard, vintner, dec'd, of Gloucester
		Tyler, John & Elizabeth 7 yrs currier 5s
	4 Mar	Perry, Robert son of Robert, currier, of Gloucester
		Nash, Richard & [*blank*] from 24 Jun next grocer & chandler
		[*Incomplete*]
		27 Jun 1664: Richard Nash signified to me that this apprentice was discharged by the consent of his father and the indentures cancelled.
		[*Signed*] *Thomas Williams, clerk to the council*
	10 Mar	Horne, George son of John, cooper, of Mitcheldean
		Williams, Richard & [*blank*] 8 yrs cooper 5s
	15 Mar	Workman, Richard son of John, butcher, of Dursley
		Hughes, Richard & [*blank*] 7 yrs butcher 5s
2/310	18 Mar	Gibbons, Richard son of William, farmer, of Awre
		Dowsinge, Walter & Dinah 7 yrs farrier 2s 6d
	14 Mar	Stephens, Samuel son of Thomas, pinmaker, of Gloucester
		Stephens, John & [*blank*] 7 yrs barber surgeon [*blank*]
		[*cf Appendix V*]
	25 Mar	Tanner, Thomas son of Humphrey, gentleman, of Sudeley
		Jordan, William jr & Alice 7 yrs apothecary 5s
	28 Mar	Moore, John son of John, dec'd, of Gloucester
		Sparrowhawke, Robert & Joan 7 yrs garter weaver 2s 6d
2/311	25 Mar	Hobbs, John son of John, feltmaker, dec'd, of Gloucester
		Cox, Winston & Anne 7 yrs currier 2s 6d

	1664 8 Apr	Williams, Thomas son of John, brewer, dec'd, of Gloucester George, William & Hester 9 yrs feltmaker 5s *£4 of the gift of the mayor and burgesses* [1]
	25 Mar	Gunn, Moses son of Moses, yeoman, of Frampton on Severn Plott, Cornelius & Joan 7 yrs tailor 2s 6d
	12 Apr	Cugly, John son of Thomas, miller, dec'd, of Gloucester Whitfeild, Richard & Anne 7 yrs baker 5s *£4 of the gift of the mayor and burgesses*
2/312	[1663] 29 Sep	White, Richard son of Giles, of Great Shurdington Hands, Richard 7 yrs bricklayer *Enrolled 19 May 1664*
	1664 16 May	Woadley, John son of John, yeoman, of Hasfield Parker, Margaret, widow, 7 yrs baker 2s 6d *26 Jun 1665: apprenticeship cancelled with the consent of John Woadley himself and Margaret Parker.* *Witnessed by Thomas Pearce*
	9 Apr	Bosly, Richard son of John, feltmaker, dec'd, of Gloucester Bosly, John & Mary 7 yrs feltmaker 5s
	10 Mar	Hall, John son of John, [*blank*] of Bridstow, Herefs Fowler, Henry, alderman, 7 yrs physician
2/313	20 Apr	Holsteed, Thomas son of Thomas, farmer, of Elmore Sparrowhawke, William & Mary 8 yrs silkweaver 5s
	21 Apr	Punter, Robert son of Joseph, yeoman, dec'd, of Westbury Lawrence, Robert & [*blank*] 7 yrs mercer 2s 6d
	18 Apr	Jennings, Richard son of Henry sr, yeoman, of Hempsted Griffin, David & Hester 7 yrs tailor 5s
	6 May	White, Thomas son of John, yeoman, of Dymock White, Richard & Joan 7 yrs from 25 Dec last currier 2s 6d
2/314	1 Apr	Heyter, Edward son of Edward, brazier, of Gloucester Nourse, John & Marian 7 yrs cooper 2s 6d [*cf Appendix V*] *£4 of the gift of the mayor and burgesses*
	16 May	Allen, John son of John, sawyer, of Gloucester Howlett, Thomas & Joan 7 yrs butcher 2s 6d
	25 May	Eldridge, Thomas son of Thomas, joiner, of Gloucester Eldridge, Thomas, his father, & Mary 7 yrs from 25 Mar joiner 20s
	30 May	Barker, William son of Thomas, pinmaker, of Gloucester Trowe, John & Margaret 7 yrs from 29 May pinmaker 10s
2/315	1 May	Freeman, John son of John, farmer, of Hasfield Hurlestone, Anne widow of William 7 yrs baker 2s 6d

---

[1] GBR B3/33 p 284 31 Mar 1664: To receive £4 of Mrs Browne's money: Thomas Williams, Edward Heyter and John Kugley.

	1664	Beedle, James son of James, victualler, of Gloucester
		Bubb, Toby & Joan 7 yrs cordwainer 2s 6d
		25 Sep 1667: turned over to John Cox for the residue of his term, Toby Bubb being dead. Before Henry Ockold
		Hornedge, Joseph son of John, farmer, of Barton Street, Gloucester
		Syre, Daniel & Anne 9 yrs ropier 5s
	2 Jul	Coopy, John son of Richard, farmer, of Tirley
		Carpenter, Thomas & [blank] 7 yrs tanner 10s
2/316	1 Jul	Woodward, Francis son of Allen, brewer, of Gloucester
		Baker, William & Elizabeth 7 yrs button maker 2s 6d
	25 Jul	Humfris, Joseph son of Toby, yeoman, dec'd, of Hempsted
		Nash, Richard & [blank] 7 yrs grocer 2s 6d
	22 Jul	Eliots, Walter son of John, wiredrawer, of Gloucester
		Eliots, John, his father, & Margaret 7 yrs wiredrawer 2s 6d
		Eliots, John son of John, wiredrawer, of Gloucester
		Cugley, James & Anne 7 yrs cardmaker 10s
		[*Holliday*]¹
2/317	23 Jul	Greene, William son of William, farmer, of Minsterworth
		Greene, Richard & Sarah 7 yrs clothier 2s 6d
	25 Jul	Browne, John son of John, mercer, of Gloucester
		Berrowe, Thomas & Mary 7 yrs tailor 2s 6d
		[*Holliday*]
	1 Aug	Church, William son of John, yeoman, of Sandhurst
		Williams, William & Hester 7 yrs butcher 5s
	12 Aug	Godsee, Thomas son of Thomas, farmer, of Aston
		Beard, John & Eleanor 10 yrs silkweaver 5s
2/318	24 Jun	Harris, John son of Thomas, gunsmith, of Gloucester
		Wasfeild, John & [blank] 7 yrs blacksmith 5s
	1 Sep	Brocke, John son of William, farmer, dec'd, of Hasfield
		Symons, Richard & Joan 7 yrs from 17 Sep glover 2s 6d
	12 Sep	Deane, Thomas son of Thomas, blacksmith, of Gloucester
		Deane, Thomas, his father, & Katharine 7 yrs blacksmith 20s
		[*Holliday*]
	15 Sep	Pearce, Nathaniel son of John, clothier, of Tewkesbury
		Pearce, Edward & [blank] 7 yrs feltmaker 2s 6d
2/319	25 Jul	Bubb, Toby son of Toby, currier, of Gloucester
		Bubb, Toby, his father, 7 yrs currier 5s
		£5 Alderman Hollidaye's money

---

[1] GBR B3/3 p 287 21 Jul 1664: To receive £5 of Mr Hollidaye's money: John Elliottes, Thomas Deane, Toby Bubb, John Niccolls, John Browne, John Perry.

2/320		**Robert Feilding, MD, mayor 1664[–5]** **William Hedges and Robert Longden, bailiffs and sheriffs**
	1664 18 Oct	Nicholls, John son of Richard, brewer, dec'd, of Gloucester Eckly, Edward & Anne 7 yrs from 29 Sep button maker 10s *£5 Alderman Hollidaye's money*
	20 Oct	Marowe, Benjamin son of Thomas, farmer, dec'd, of Mordiford [MS Mordivant], Herefs Mills, Thomas & Hester 7 yrs baker 5s
	22 Oct	Homes, Thomas son of John, yeoman, of Westington Park, Chipping Campden Mills, Thomas & Hester 7 yrs baker 10s
2/321	12 Nov	Wright, John son of John, victualler, of Newent Bell, John & Joan 7 yrs from 2 Feb next silkweaver 2s 6d
	14 Nov	Wilson, Charles son of John, butcher, of [Chipping] Campden Cor, Edward and [*blank*] 8 yrs from 25 Mar next button maker 2s 6d
	14 Dec	Reeve, Francis son of Joseph, joiner, of Tewkesbury Baldwin, Stephen & Mary 7 yrs stone carver 2s 6d
	1 Nov	Haies, John son of Henry, currier, of Gloucester Tufly, Charles & Katharine 8 yrs barber surgeon 10s
2/322	—	Fox, John son of William, mason, of Twigworth Baldwin, Stephen & Mary 7 yrs stone carver 2s 6d
	1665 26 Jan	Stowell, William son of William, pinmaker, of Gloucester Heath, Samuel & Mary 8 yrs from 1 May next silkweaver 5s *24 Sep 1667: turned over to John Jordan of the city of [Gloucester deleted] London, silkweaver, by order of the Sessions.* *Before Henry Ockold*
		Beale, William son of Thomas, yeoman, of Eldersfield, Worcs Goodcheape, Thomas & [*blank*] 7 yrs from 1 Nov last currier 5s
	1664 1 Dec	Andros, Richard son of George, baker, of Blakeney Woodward, Samuel & Susannah 7 yrs blacksmith 2s 6d
2/323	1665 7 Feb	Carter, Thomas son of William, cooper, dec'd, of Gloucester Sparrowhawke, William & Mary 8 yrs silkweaver 2s 6d
	17 Feb	Boyfeild, Thomas son of Thomas, tailor, of Huntley Stephens, James, alderman, [*no term*] from 25 Mar maltster 5s
	12 Apr	Baker, Thomas son of Thomas, joiner, late of Gloucester Hitchins, Daniel & [*blank*] 8 yrs from 27 Mar silkweaver 2s 6d *£8 from the mayor and burgesses*

	1665 25 Apr	Ravener, Thomas son of Thomas, tailor, of Gloucester
		Eldridge, William & Abigail 7 yrs silkweaver 5s
		£4 from the mayor and burgesses [1]
2/324	27 Apr	Wantner, William son of Abel, innkeeper, of Gloucester
		Taylor, George & Joan 7 yrs barber surgeon 5s
	13 May	Pace, John son of Thomas, farmer, of Maisemore
		Merrett, Thomas & Mary 7 yrs currier 2s 6d
	30 May	Symes, Francis son of Thomas, yeoman, dec'd, of Hempsted
		Bishop, Daniel & Eleanor 8 yrs from 25 Mar tailor 2s 6d
	9 Jun	Hill *alias* Hazleton, John son of [*blank*]
		Sampson, William & Joan 8 yrs from 1 May turner 30s
2/325	15 Jul	Huffe, Thomas son of Thomas, weaver, dec'd, of Gloucester
		Yates, Francis & Joan 7 yrs from 25 Jul currier 1s [*Holliday*][2]
	30 Jun	Higgs, John son of William, clerk, late of Little Birch [MS Litle Bury], Herefs
		Lye, Hester widow of Giles [*no term*] from 24 Jun chandler 2s 6d
	6 Jul	Shipton, John son of John, bodicemaker, of Gloucester
		Fowler, William & [*blank*] 7 yrs barber surgeon 2s 6d
	1 Jul	Haines, Nicholas son of Nicholas, ironmonger, of Gloucester
		Haines, Nicholas, his father, & Sarah 7 yrs from 24 Jun ironmonger 20s
2/326	25 Jul	Barnes, John son of John, joiner, dec'd, of Gloucester
		Springe, Lewis & [*blank*] 7 yrs joiner 5s
		£5 from the mayor and burgesses
	29 Aug	Turbervile, Francis son of John, dyer, dec'd, of Tewkesbury
		Heyward, John & Sarah 7 yrs from 30 Aug feltmaker 1s
	19 Jul	Cowles, William son of William, butcher, of Gloucester
		Cowles, William, his father, & Jane 7 yrs butcher 5s
	29 Jul	Barnes, William son of Thomas, yeoman, of Ruardean
		Wilmotts, Robert & Sarah 7 yrs from 29 Sep saddler 5s
2/327	1 Aug	Wadley, John son of John, yeoman, of Hasfield
		Slicer, James & Elizabeth 7 yrs tanner 2s 6d
	18 Aug	Hiett, John son of Jeremy, gentleman, dec'd, of Westbury
		Payne, Robert jr & Anne 7 yrs mercer 30s
	1 Aug	Williams, Richard son of Richard, innholder, of Littledean
		Stephens, John & Bridget 7 yrs barber surgeon 2s 6d
	4 Sep	Fewtrell, Thomas son of Edward, tailor, of Gloucester
		Nott, Thomas & Elizabeth 7 yrs silkweaver 2s 6d
		£5 Alderman Holliday's gift

---

[1] GBR B3/3 p 303 27 Mar 1665: To receive £4 of the gift of the mayor and burgesses: Thomas Ravener and Allen Woodward.

[2] ibid p 309 24 Jul 1665: To receive £5 of Mr Holliday's money: John Dewe, — Huffe, John Barnes, — Mathewes, Thomas Fewtrell, Thomas Gythins.

2/328	1665	8 Sep	Gythins, Thomas son of Robert, farmer, dec'd, of Gloucester
			Meeke, Thomas & Margery 8 yrs from 29 Sep currier 10s
			£5 Alderman Holliday's gift
		1 Sep	Mathewes, John son of John, butcher, dec'd, of Gloucester
			Mathewes, Margaret, [his mother], widow of John 7 yrs butcher 5s
			[*cf Appendix V*] £5 Alderman Holliday's gift
		15 Sep	Dewe, John son of John, innholder, dec'd, of Gloucester
			Hincksman, John & [*blank*] 7 yrs from 29 Sep vintner 5s
			[*cf Appendix V*] £5 Alderman Holliday's gift
		17 Sep	Wells, John son of John, currier, of Gloucester
			Wells, John, his father, & Sarah 7 yrs currier 5s [*cf Appendix V*]
2/329		28 Sep	Cartwright, Edward son of Edward, baker, of Gloucester
			Cartwright, Edward, his father, [*no term*] baker 5s

2/330
Thomas Yate, mayor 1665[–6]
Isaac Williams and John Gythens, bailiffs and sheriffs

	1665	3 Oct	Forty, John son of John, yeoman, dec'd, of Hartpury
			Byford, Joseph & Elizabeth 7 yrs from 29 Sep currier 5s
		10 Oct	Fluck, William son of William, yeoman, of Leckhampton
			Fluck, Thomas & Elizabeth 7 yrs from 29 Sep tanner 5s
			Heyter, Edward son of Edward, brazier, of Gloucester
			Cripps, Edward & Elizabeth 7 yrs from 29 Sep butcher 5s
			[*cf Appendix V*]
2/331		6 Nov	Clifford, Thomas son of William, haulier, of Gloucester
			Adys, John & Elizabeth 7 yrs currier 2s 6d
		8 Dec	Sheppard, Samuel son of John, worsted comber, of Tetbury
			Cox, Winston & Anne 7 yrs currier 2s 6d
		15 Dec	Cleevely, Robert son of Robert, chandler, of Gloucester
			Cleevely, Robert, [his father], & Mary 9 yrs chandler 20s
	1666	1 Jan	Jordan, William son of John, baker, of Gloucester
			Whitle, Samuel & Mary 7 yrs currier 2s 6d
2/332		10 Jan	Bonwell, Richard son of Richard, butcher, late of Gloucester
			Cowcher, William & Susannah 7 yrs pinmaker 5s
		19 Feb	Smith, Henry son of Thomas, farmer, of Moreton Valence
			Ricketts, James & Anne 8 yrs tanner 8s
		21 Feb	Pullen, Richard son of Richard, miller, of Cirencester
			Jordan, John & Anne 7 yrs from 24 Feb baker 5s
	1665	6 Oct	Knowles, John son of Henry, pewterer, of Gloucester
			Knowles, Henry, his father, & Mary 7 yrs from 29 Sep pewterer 10s
2/333	1666	24 Mar	Spillman, Thomas son of Thomas, carrier, of Great Shurdington
			Harrison, William & Sarah 7 yrs carrier 5s

	1666 26 Mar	Pearce, John son of William, wiredrawer, of Gloucester
		Cowcher, Rebecca widow of Richard 7 yrs pinmaker 2s 6d[1]
	1665 6 Oct	Smallwood, John son of John, barber surgeon, of Gloucester
		Smallwood, John, his father, & Jane 7 yrs from 24 June last barber surgeon 10s
	1666 16 Apr	Badger, Phoenix son of Brian, pinmaker, of Gloucester
		Baily, Thomas & Elizabeth 7 yrs from 25 Mar pinmaker 2s 6d
2/334	18 Apr	Hawkins, William son of Thomas, clothier, dec'd, of Gloucester
		Farmer, John & Bridget 7 yrs silkweaver 5s
	27 Apr	Humphris, John son of John farmer, of Whaddon
		Doughton, Stephen & Joan 9 yrs pinmaker 10s
	1 May	Herbert, Christopher son of Christopher, brewer, of Gloucester
		Hicks, Thomas & Joan 7 yrs tailor 2s 6d
	3 May	Layton, Jonathan son of Joseph, yeoman, of Elmore
		Gardiner, Nathaniel & Sarah 7 yrs baker 2s 6d
2/335	27 May	Beard, William son of William, tailor, of Gloucester
		Beard, Richard & Armilla 7 yrs from 18 Feb tailor 2s 6d
	8 May	Kinge, John son of Giles, yeoman, of Brockworth
		Heyward, John & Sarah 7 yrs feltmaker 2s 6d
		Gratian, John son of William, fisherman, dec'd, of Over
		Goodwin, Richard & Elizabeth 7 yrs currier 3s 4d
	12 May	Lane, John son of John, cutler, dec'd, of Gloucester
		Brimyeard, William & Elizabeth 7 yrs tobacco-pipe maker 7s
		£4 from the mayor and burgesses
2/336	14 May	Drury, John son of John, yeoman, dec'd, of Childswickham
		Allen, Lawrence & Anne 7 yrs chandler 2s 6d
	15 May	Woadley, William son of John, yeoman, of Hasfield
		Slicer, James & Elizabeth 7 yrs tanner 5s
	—	Lane, Robert son of John, cutler, dec'd, of Gloucester
		Brimeyeard, William & Elizabeth 8 yrs tobacco-pipe maker 8s
	22 May	Puxon, Richard son of Richard, carrier, of Gloucester
		Brimeyeard, William 7 yrs from 3 May tobacco-pipe maker 10s
		£4 from the mayor and burgesses
2/337	29 May	Sparrowhawke, Richard son of Robert, garter weaver, of Gloucester
		Sparrowhawke, Robert 7 yrs from 25 Dec last garter weaver 10s
	2 Jun	Dobbs, John son of John, labourer, dec'd, of Barton Street, Gloucester
		Hartland, William & Martha 8 yrs pinmaker 2s 6d

---

[1] GBR B3/3 p 318 27 Mar 1666: To receive £4 of the gift of the mayor & burgesses: William Pearce's son, Richard Puckson's son, John Lane.

	1666 25 Apr	Griffin, Thomas son of Richard, plasterer, of Gloucester Dunn, Edward & Mary 7 yrs combmaker 5s
	9 Jun	Ricketts, Charles son of John, farmer, of Longney Bell, John & Joan 7 yrs from 25 Jul silkweaver 2s 6d
2/338	1 Jun	Bicke, Thomas son of John, yeoman, of Up Hatherley Lugg, Lawrence & Elizabeth 7 yrs baker 5s
		Lucas, Robert son of Thomas, smith & farrier, dec'd, of Gloucester Lucas, Elizabeth, [his mother,] widow of Thomas 7 yrs smith & farrier 5s [*Holliday*]¹
	27 Jun	Webb, John son of John, yeoman, of Minsterworth Parker, Margaret widow of Thomas 7 yrs from 2 Jul baker 2s 6d
	2 Jul	Harward, Robert son of Geoffrey, gentleman, dec'd, of Gloucester Hoare, Charles & Sarah 7 yrs chandler 2s 6d
2/339		Lugg, John son of John, pinmaker, of Gloucester Lugg, John, his father, & Mary 7 yrs from 24 Jun pinmaker 20s
	4 Jul	Perry, William son of John, clothier, of Rudford Maddocke, William & Sarah 7 yrs from 1 Jul tailor 5s
	9 Jul	Coale, Charles son of Ralph, farmer, of Wotton [St Mary] Hartland, William & Martha 7 yrs pinmaker 2s 6d [*cf Appendix V*]
	16 Jul	Pate, Lynnett son of Lynnett, gentleman, of Charlton Kings Jordan, William & Alice 7 yrs apothecary 5s
2/340	28 Jul	Rogers, John son of Thomas, yeoman, dec'd, of Badgeworth Rogers, Thomas & Priscilla 7 yrs baker 2s 6d [*cf Appendix V*]
	1 Jul	Childe, Thomas son of Thomas, maltster, of Gloucester Jennings, Thomas & Mary of King's Barton [MS Barton Regis] 7 yrs from 24 Jun currier 1s *£5 of Alderman Holliday's money*
	25 Jul	Bickarton, John son of Edward, joiner, of Evesham, Worcs Reeve, Giles sr & Mary 7 yrs smith 5s
		Varnham, William son of John, yeoman, of Longford Beard, John & Eleanor 7 yrs silkweaver 5s
2/341	13 Aug	Browne, Elias son of John, blacksmith, of Longhope Onyon, Thomas & [*blank*] 9 yrs silkweaver 5s
	9 Jul	Atkins, John son of Robert, farmer, of Gloucester Hartland, William & Martha 7 yrs pinmaker 2s 6d *£5 of Alderman Holliday's money*
	3 Jun	Cooke, Moses son of John, gardener, of Gloucester Welsteed, John & Elizabeth 7 yrs blacksmith 5s

---

¹ GBR B3/3 p 322 31 Jul 1666: To receive £5 of Mr Holliday's money: Thomas son of Thomas Turner, William Cooke, Robert Lucas, John Atkins, Richard Beard, Thomas Childe.

	1666	30 Aug	Shipton, Thomas son of John, bodicemaker, of Gloucester Shipton, John, his father, & Sarah 7 yrs bodicemaker 5s
2/342		1 Sep	Turner, Thomas son of Thomas, yeoman, of Gloucester Tyler, James & Mary 7 yrs currier 2s 6d *£5 of Alderman Holliday's money*
		11 Sep	Turner, Thomas son of John, cook, [dec'd], of Gloucester Turner, Joan, [his mother,] widow of John 7 yrs cook 5s
		21 Sep	Langford, John son of Toby, stationer, of Gloucester Langford, Toby, his father, 7 yrs stationer 20s
		26 Sep	Clarke, William son of William, stationer, of Gloucester Clarke, William, his father, & Jane 7 yrs from 29 Sep stationer 5s
		25 Sep	Cooke, William son of Thomas, butcher, of Gloucester Cooke, Thomas, his father, & Margaret 7 yrs butcher [blank] [*Holliday*]
2/343		29 Jun	Medway, John son of Henry, clothier, of Gloucester Medway, Henry, his father, & Mary 7 yrs clothier 5s

2/344	**Thomas Price, mayor 1666[–7]** **Thomas Aram and Richard Stephens, bailiffs and sheriffs**

	1666	3 Oct	Dubberly, Jonathan son of William, gardener, of Gloucester Cowcher, Cecily [widow of John] 7 yrs pinmaker [*See 2/284*] 5s
		22 Oct	Jones, Henry son of Thomas, shoe mender, of Gloucester Jones, William & Margery 7 yrs shoe mender 2s 6d
			Jones, John son of Thomas, shoe mender, of Gloucester Jones, William & Margery 7 yrs shoe mender 2s 6d
		24 Oct	Herbert, Thomas son of Christopher, brewer, of Gloucester Gardner, John & Mary 7 yrs currier 5s
2/345		1 Nov	Cleevely, Henry son of Robert, chandler, of Gloucester Cleevely, Robert, his father, & Mary 7 yrs from 24 Aug chandler 20s
		6 Nov	Hale, Jesse son of Thomas, feltmaker, of Gloucester Swaine, John & [*blank*] 7 yrs from 25 Dec tailor 2s 6d
		29 Oct	Williams, William son of Toby, farmer, dec'd, of Quedgeley Sparrowhawke, Robert jr & Dorothy 8 yrs from 29 Sep silkweaver 5s
		30 Nov	Wall, Richard son of Richard, fisherman, dec'd, of parish of St John's [St John in Bedwardine], county of Worcester Berrowe, William & Eleanor 7 yrs tailor 6d
2/346		1 Dec	Nash, Nathaniel son of William, yeoman, of Haresfield Bell, John & Joan 7 yrs silkweaver 2s 6d
	1667	5 Jan	Baker, Benjamin son of Richard, feltmaker, dec'd, of Tewkesbury Nash, Richard & Anne 7 yrs feltmaker 2s 6d
		9 Jan	Bird, Daniel son of Daniel, feltmaker, of Gloucester Martley, Anthony jr & Anne 7 yrs feltmaker 2s 6d

	1667	1 Jan	Merrett, Peter son of Anthony, tailor, dec'd, of Upton St Leonards Merrett, Clement & Mary 7 yrs tailor 5s

2/347   1 Feb Pitt, Samuel son of Richard, yeoman, of Newent
                    Yates, Francis & Joan 8 yrs from 2 Feb currier 12d

                   Heyward, Edward son of Edward, yeoman, of Sandhurst
                    Beard, John & Eleanor 7 yrs silkweaver 5s

             2 Feb Gwyn, Lewis son of Lewis, pinmaker & chapman, of Gloucester
                    Gwyn, Lewis, his father, & Mary 7 yrs pinmaker & chapman 10s

        1666 25 Dec Price, Richard son of William, vintner, dec'd, of Longhope
                    Parker, William & Elizabeth 7 yrs currier 2s 6d

2/348   1667 14 Feb Restall, Peter son of Peter, coverlet [MS coverlid] weaver, of
                        Tewkesbury
                    Sparrowhawke, William & Mary 8 yrs silkweaver 5s

                   Smith, Peter son of William, feltmaker, of Gloucester
                    Wadman, Roger & Elizabeth 7 yrs weaver 5s

             11 Mar Ady, Thomas son of Thomas, yeoman, of Hardwicke
                    Perkes, John & Alice 7 yrs baker 2s 6d

             1 Mar Halsteed, Joseph son of Joseph, farmer, of Westbury
                    Randle, Daniel & [blank] 7 yrs joiner 2s 6d

2/349   11 Mar Ockey, William son of John, yeoman, of Norton
                    Brobon, Francis & Hester 7 yrs cooper 10s

             23 Mar Blackwell, Thomas son of Thomas, yeoman, of Rendcomb
                    Baldwin, Stephen & Mary 7 yrs stone carver
                    *19 Oct 1670: turned over for the residue of his term by Mary
                    Baldwin to Francis Reeve, stone carver, who is to find him food,
                    drink and clothing and give him at the end of the term 10s and
                    2 suits. Thomas's father is to give Francis 10s for clothing during
                    and at the end of the term*

        1666 2 Oct Rogers, John son of John, brewer, of Gloucester
                    Rogers, John, his father, & Mary 7 yrs brewer 20s

        1667 26 Mar Ragbourne, Giles son of Giles, yeoman, of Norton
                    Pace, Thomas & Bridget 7 yrs from 25 Mar cooper 2s 6d

2/350   17 Apr Sturmy, Henry son of Edward, glover, of Gloucester
                    Heath, Samuel & Mary 7 yrs from 1 May silkweaver 2s 6d

             4 Apr Barrett, Thomas son of Arthur, yeoman, late of Minsterworth
                    Cowdale, John & Patience 7 yrs tailor 2s 6d

             1 May Williams, Isaac son of Nicholas, joiner, of Gloucester
                    Williams, Isaac sr & Eleanor 7 yrs tailor 20s

             16 May Williams, Nicholas son of Nicholas, joiner, of Gloucester
                    Suffeild, Anthony & [blank] 7 yrs currier 2s 6d [*Holliday*]

2/351	1667 12 Jun	Hodges, Samuel son of John, yeoman, dec'd, of Longhope Nash, Jesse & [blank] 7 yrs from 29 Sep last feltmaker 5s
	18 Apr	Blissard, Stephen son of Thomas, yeoman, of Laverton Lumbard, Isaac & [blank] 7 yrs serge weaver & wool comber 5s
	26 Mar	Heaven, John son of Robert, clothier, of Stroud Beard, John & Eleanor 7 yrs silkweaver 6s 8d
	1 May	Willmotts, Thomas son of Robert, shipturner, of Littledean Lane, Thomas & Isobel 7 yrs chandler 2s 6d
2/352	24 Jun	Scanderight, Walter son of Walter, glover, dec'd, of Kington [MS Keynton], Herefs Pace *alias* Parris Francis & Phillida of Frampton on Severn 7 yrs baker 2s 6d
	26 Mar	Pitt, William son of Richard, gentleman, of Newent Stephens, Richard & Margery 7 yrs from 25 Mar tobacconist 5s
	1 May	Rountree, Leonard son of Christopher, brewer, dec'd, of Gloucester Woodiatte, James & [blank] 7 yrs button maker 5s *£4 of the gift of the mayor and burgesses*[1]
2/353	21 May	Terrett, John son of Thomas, maltster, dec'd, of Gloucester Bosly, Richard & Elizabeth 7 yrs feltmaker 20s [*cf Appendix V*]
	1 May	Ayleway, Richard son of Richard, gentleman, of Westbury Belcher, Thomas & Joan 7 yrs baker 2s 6d
	16 May	Wall, William son of William, baker, dec'd, of Gloucester Morris, Richard & Katharine 7 yrs carpenter 5s *£4 of the gift of the mayor and burgesses*
	7 Jun	Hammonds, Thomas son of Thomas, brewer, dec'd, of Gloucester Swett, Richard & Ursula 7 yrs glazier 12d *£4 of the gift of the mayor and burgesses*
2/354	11 Jun	Savory, William son of William, farrier, of Gloucester George, William & Hester 7 yrs feltmaker 2s 6d
	24 Jun	Adams, William son of Godwin, yeoman, of Mitcheldean Pitt, Samuel & Eleanor 8 yrs pinmaker 2s 6d
		Robins, Henry son of Henry, gentleman, dec'd, of Gloucester Newman, Augustine & Elizabeth 7 yrs chandler 5s
	6 Jul	Oldacre, James son of William, miller, dec'd, of Buckland Pitt, Godwin & Mary 7 yrs from 24 Jun currier 2s 6d
2/355	1 May	Wintle, Daniel son of Henry, farmer, dec'd, of Westbury Wintle, Henry & Mary 7 yrs maltster 2s 6d
	24 Jun	Walker, Benjamin son of Ralph, blacksmith, of Naunton Heath, Samuel & Mary 8 yrs silkweaver 5s

---

[1] GBR B3/3 p 334 4 Apr 1667: To receive £4: [Leonard] Rountree, William Wall.

	1667 24 Jun	Ashmeade, Henry son of Giles, victualler, of Prestbury
		Humphris, Richard & Frances 7 yrs butcher 2s 6d
	1 May	Greene, Richard son of William, pinmaker, of Gloucester
		Greene, William, his father, & Mary [no term] pinmaker 5s
2/356	5 Jul	Hanly, Joseph son of William, carpenter, dec'd, of Lancaster [Lancs]
		Bosly, John & Mary 7 yrs feltmaker 5s
	31 Aug	Gwin, John son of Joseph, farmer, of Dymock
		Gwin, Augustine sr & [blank] 7 yrs currier 2s 6d
	25 Jul	Worlocke, Guy son of Guy, tailor, late of Barton Street, Gloucester
		Onyon, Thomas & Bridget 7 yrs silkweaver 5s
	20 Sep	Sampson, Daniel son of William, turner, of Gloucester
		Sampson, Jonathan & Mary 7 yrs combmaker & turner 2s
		Sampson, Solomon son of William, turner, of Gloucester
		Sampson, Jonathan & Mary 7 yrs combmaker & turner 2s
2/357	23 Sep	Preist, John son of Peter, labourer, late of Barton Street, Gloucester
		Doughton, Stephen jr & Joan 8 yrs from 29 Sep pinmaker 8s
	26 Sep	Wells, John son of John, shoe mender, dec'd, of Gloucester
		Wintle, John & Sarah 7 yrs from 29 Sep currier 2s 6d
		[cf Appendix V]
2/358	28 Sep	Haines, Richard son of Richard, yeoman, of Ashchurch
		Edwards, Richard & [blank] 7 yrs jersey comber 7s

2/360		**John Woodward, mayor 1667[–8]**
		John Rogers and John Marston, bailiffs and sheriffs
	1667 5 Oct	Hawthorne, John son of Robert, yeoman, of Elmstone Hardwicke
		Charleton, Edward & Sarah 7 yrs wiredrawer 2s 6d
		Jaquies, Daniel son of John, currier, of Longborough
		Pickeringe, Luke & Sarah 7 yrs feltmaker 2s 6d
	24 Oct	Barnelme, Richard son of Richard, turner, of Gloucester
		Boreman, Joseph & Mary 7 yrs from 29 Sep combmaker 2s 6d
		£4 Mrs Sarah Browne's money [Holliday]
	29 Oct	Stayte, Robert son of John, yeoman, of Gretton in Winchcombe
		Miles, James & Dorothy 7 yrs baker 2s 6d
2/361	21 Oct	Yates, Walter son of Humphrey, farmer, dec'd, of Cheltenham
		Meeke, Thomas & Margery 7 yrs from 29 Sep currier 5s
	17 Nov	Clarvoe, Thomas son of William, yeoman, dec'd, of Kempley
		Lugg, William & Hannah 7 yrs haberdasher 2s 6d
	6 Nov	Phelpes, William son of Nicholas, brewer, of Gloucester
		Phelpes, Nicholas, his father, & Sarah [no term] from 29 Sep brewer 20s

2/362 **Anthony Arnold, mayor**[1]

1667 5 Nov Fewtrell, John son of William, tailor, of Gloucester
　　　　　　Selwyn, Thomas & Martha 7 yrs from 25 Jul last currier 2s 6d
　　　　　　£5 *Alderman Holliday's money*[2]

　　　15 Nov Tucker, Thomas son of Thomas, innkeeper, dec'd, of Gloucester
　　　　　　Hutchins, Nathaniel & Deborah 7 yrs silkweaver 2s 6d
　　　　　　£5 *Alderman Holliday's money*

　　　24 Dec Marten, Thomas son of Thomas, victualler, dec'd, of Gloucester
　　　　　　Bishop, William & Elizabeth 7 yrs tailor 5s
　　　　　　£5 *Alderman Holliday's money*

　　　23 Dec Clarvoe, John son of William, yeoman, [dec'd], of Kempley
　　　　　　Abbotts, Henry & Sarah 7 yrs from 25 Dec baker 5s

2/363 1668 27 Jan Bowler, Thomas son of George, tucker, dec'd, of Winchcombe
　　　　　　Swaine, Edward & Jane 7 yrs from 2 Feb collar maker 2s 6d

　　1667 1 Nov Humfries, William son of Edward, yeoman, of Naunton
　　　　　　Heath, Samuel & Mary 7 yrs silkweaver 2s 6d

　　1668 3 Feb Smith, Samuel son of Thomas, farmer, of Minsterworth
　　　　　　Thomas, John & Margaret 7 yrs currier 2s 6d

　　　24 Feb Hall, Edward son of Edward, surgeon, late of city of Bristol
　　　　　　Cowcher, Robert & Margaret 7 yrs pinmaker 2s 6d

2/364　1 Mar Joseph, Thomas son of Thomas, labourer, of Gloucester
　　　　　　Niccolls, John & Mary 7 yrs tanner 5s

　　　　　　Greening, Thomas son of John, turner, dec'd, of Gloucester
　　　　　　Sowdley, John & Eleanor 7 yrs wool comber 7s
　　　　　　£5 *Alderman Holliday's money*[3]

　　　10 Mar Brian, Daniel son of Thomas, farmer, dec'd, of Barnwood
　　　　　　Whitle, Samuel & Mary 7 yrs currier 5s

　　　25 Mar Minchin, John son of Anthony, yeoman, of Great Rissington
　　　　　　Broade, Richard & Mary 7 yrs baker 5s

2/365　31 Mar Broade, George son of Samuel, clerk, of Great Rissington
　　　　　　Lugg, Thomas jr & Sarah 7 yrs from 1 Feb mercer 10s

　　　24 Mar Hitchman, Daniel son of Edward, blacksmith, dec'd, of Upton St Leonards
　　　　　　Merrett, Clement & Mary [*no term*] tailor 5s

---

[1] GBR B3/3 p 243: In place of John Wodward, deceased.

[2] ibid p 338 9 Aug 1667: To receive £5 of Mr Hollidaye's money: Richard Barnelme, Nicholas Williams, Thomas Martyn, John Browne, William Smythe, William Fewtrell.

[3] ibid p 360 23 Jul 1668: To receive £5 of Mr Hollidaye's money: Thomas Greening, Thomas Tucker, George Marten's son, Robert Roberts, Samuel Lugg, John Adams.

1668 26 Mar Cheesman, John son of Nicholas, cooper, of Gloucester
   Cheesman, Robert & Sarah 7 yrs cooper 5s [*Mrs Browne*][1]

13 Apr Griffin, James son of James, farmer, dec'd, of Gloucester
   Bennett, John & Anne 7 yrs from 25 Mar button maker 3s

2/366

Havard, Daniel son of John, farmer, of Gloucester
   Colericke, Daniel & Mary 8 yrs bodicemaker 2s 6d

27 Mar Cooke, Anthony son of Richard, blacksmith, of Gloucester
   Cooke, Richard, his father, & Eleanor 7 yrs blacksmith 5s
   £4 Mrs Sarah Browne's money

1 May Hale, Giles son of Giles, of Barton Street, Gloucester
   Coucher, Robert & Margaret 7 yrs pinmaker 2s 6d

6 May Browne, Samuel son of John, mercer, of Gloucester
   Clarke, Henry & Amy 7 yrs from 25 Mar glazier 2s 6d
   £4 Mrs Sarah Browne's money

2/367

14 May Smarte, Thomas son of Richard, maltster, of Gloucester
   Smarte, Ric, his father, & Susannah 7 yrs from 1 May maltster 5s

5 May Smith, Michael son of Michael, farmer, of Coleford
   Nash, Jesse & Joan 7 yrs feltmaker 2s 6d

1 Apr Farmer, Edward son of John, silkweaver, of Gloucester
   Farmer, John, his father, & Bridget 7 yrs from 1 Mar silkweaver 5s

16 Apr May, Thomas son of Thomas, yeoman, dec'd, of Ashton Keynes, Wilts
   Bosly, John & Mary 7 yrs feltmaker 2s 6d

2/368

1 May Hathway, William son of Richard, farmer, of Prestbury
   Martly, John & Anne 7 yrs turner 5s

Simons, Charles son of John, labourer, of Norton
   Smallwood, John & Jane 8 yrs from 25 Mar innholder 40s

1667 1 Jan Roberts, Robert son of Anthony, spoonmaker, late of Gloucester
   Roberts, Samuel & Elizabeth 7 yrs silkweaver
   £5 Alderman Holliday's money

1668 13 Jun Dowdswell, Henry son of Henry, currier, of Shrewsbury, Salop
   Heath, Samuel & Mary 8 yrs from 24 Jun silkweaver 5s

2/369

16 Jun Foote, William son of Lawrence, turner, of St Erme [MS St Erram], Cornwall
   Till, Richard jr & [*blank*] 7 yrs cutler 5s

24 Jun Younge, James son of John, broadweaver, of Mitcheldean
   Cowcher, Rebecca & Jones, John 7 yrs pinmaker 5s

6 Jul Norman, John son of William, silkweaver, dec'd, of Gloucester
   Powell, Henry & Bridget 7 yrs glover 2s 6d

---

[1] GBR B3/3 p 354 27 Mar 1668: To receive £4 of Mrs Browne's money: John Cheesman, James Griffin, Richard Cooke's son.

1668 28 Jul Tench, Stephen son of Stephen, clothworker, of Tewkesbury
Underhill, James & [blank] 7 yrs silkweaver 2s 6d

2/370

16 Jul Merrett, Joseph son of Richard, yeoman, dec'd, of Whaddon
Yates, Francis & Joan 7 yrs from 25 Dec next currier 12d

15 Jul Spencer, William son of Edward, clothworker, of Mitcheldean
Lugg, John & Mary [*no term*] from 24 Jun pinmaker 5s

Adams, Joseph son of Joseph, yeoman, dec'd, of Taynton
Keare, John & Alice 7 yrs pinmaker 5s

1 Aug Price, William son of Thomas, narrow weaver, of Hasfield
Tyler, John & [blank] 7 yrs currier 2s 6d [*Repeated at 3/10*]

APPRENTICES FOR VIRGINIA AND BARBADOS
1659–1660

(GBR C10/2 *cont.*)

2/371   **For Virginia**

    1660 24 Aug Lye, John son of Francis, of Barton Street, Gloucester
        Bridger, James, merchant, of the city of Bristol 4 yrs an axe and a hoe and 50 acres of land according to the custom of the country

2/372   **For Barbados**

    1659 3 Dec Law, Thomas, husbandman, of Barnwood
        Woodward, John, merchant, 4 yrs the said John or his assigns are to give at the end of his term £10 according to the custom of the country

        Powell, William, husbandman, of Gloucester
        Woodward, John, merchant, 4 yrs £10

        Jones, Mary, spinster, of Llanidloes [MS Llanlidoll], Mont
        Woodward, John, merchant, 4 yrs £10

        Merricke, Katharine, spinster, of Abbey Dore, Herefs
        Woodward, John, merchant, 4 yrs £10

2/373   18 Nov Jones, Alice, spinster, of 'Dersum' [Dorstone?], Herefs
        Woodward, John, merchant, 4 yrs £10

        Smith, Hester, spinster, of Over
        Woodward, John, merchant, 4 yrs £10

        Lawrence, Thomas, husbandman, of Gloucester
        Woodward, John, merchant, 4 yrs £10

     7 Nov Butt, Sarah, spinster, of Norton
        Woodward, John, merchant, 4 yrs £10

2/374   Sparkes, Thomas, husbandman, of Eldersfield, Mon [*recte* Worcs]
        Woodward, John, merchant, 4 yrs £10

    18 Nov Cowcott, Sarah, spinster, of Saniger
        Woodward, John, merchant, 4 yrs £10

        Powell, Mary, spinster, of Llanvapley [MS Landwapley], Mon
        Woodward, John, merchant, 4 yrs £10

        Gawcam, Elizabeth, spinster, of Newland
        Woodward, John, merchant, 4 yrs £10

2/375   7 Nov Tasker, Dinah, spinster, of Gloucester
        Woodward, John, merchant, 4 yrs £10

        Hossum, Elizabeth, spinster, of Gloucester
        Woodward, John, merchant, 4 yrs £10

        Price, Jennett, spinster, of 'Wander' [Vaynor?], Brecon
        Woodward, John, merchant, 4 yrs £10

	1659 18 Nov	Jones, Joan, spinster, of Newent Woodward, John, merchant, 4 yrs £10
	7 Nov	Gardner, John, husbandman, of Eynsham Ferry, Oxon Woodward, John, merchant, 4 yrs £10
2/376		**For Virginia**
	6 Aug	Parker, George, labourer, of Gloucester Bridger, James, of city of Bristol, merchant, 5 yrs
		For Barbados
	7 Nov	Drinkwater, Elizabeth, of Haydon Woodward, John, merchant, 4 yrs £10
		Benfield, Mary, spinster, of Gloucester Woodward, John, merchant, 4 yrs £10
		Mathewes, Jane, spinster, of Gloucester Woodward, John, merchant, 4 yrs £10
		Vaughan, Judith, spinster, of Gloucester Woodward, John, merchant, 4 yrs £10
		Jones, Anne, spinster, of Gloucester Woodward, John, merchant, 4 yrs £10
2/377	26 Feb	Hall, Edward son of Edward, anchorsmith, of Stourbridge, Worcs Powell, John, merchant, 4 yrs £10
	27 Feb	Rogers, Mary, spinster, of Hereford Powell, John, merchant, 4 yrs £10
		For Virginia
	16 Jul	Price, William, labourer, of Churchdown Bridger, James, of Bristol, merchant, 5 yrs
	8 Aug	Baily, Jane, spinster, of Painswick Jennings, William, of Bristol, merchant, 4 yrs £10
		Wilks, Susannah, widow, of Ross, Herefs Jennings, William, of Bristol, merchant, 4 yrs £10
2/378	29 Aug	Browne, Elizabeth daughter of [*illegible*], maltster, dec'd, of Gloucester Viner, Thomas, gardener, & Eleanor, 5 yrs to be instructed in knitting 6s 8d [*This entry is on a loose page, without reference to Virginia, but continuing from the preceding entries and in the same hand*]

1668–1700

GBR C10/3

3/9	1668	27 Jul Wallen, Francis son of Thomas, farmer, of Gloucester Keare, John & Alice 7 yrs from 25 Jul farmer 5s
		25 Jul Adams, John son of John, narrow weaver, of Gloucester Adams, John, his father, & Margaret 7 yrs narrow weaver 5s [*Holliday*]
		Thomas, Anthony son of Anthony, narrow weaver, of the Margarets, [Gloucester] Hartland, William & Martha 7 yrs pinmaker 5s
		Powell, William son of William, haulier, of Gloucester Cox, John & [*blank*] 7 yrs currier 2s 6d [*Holliday*]
3/10		24 Jun Webly, Thomas son of George, mercer, of Gloucester Partridge, Thomas & Eleanor 8 yrs baker 2s 6d
		1 Aug Price, William son of Thomas, narrow weaver, of Hasfield Tyler, John & [*blank*] 7 yrs currier 2s 6d [*Repeating entry at 2/370*]
		25 Jul Marten, George son of George, turner, of Gloucester Marten, George, his father, & Mary 7 yrs turner 10s [*Holliday*]
		29 Sep Saunders, Benjamin son of John, mercer, dec'd, of Wotton under Edge Vaisie, Walter & Margaret 7 yrs tailor 5s
		1 Sep Owen *alias* Wood, Henry son of Henry, pinmaker, of Gloucester Keare, John & Alice 9 yrs pinmaker 5s
3/11		21 Sep Jones, Henry son of John, pinmaker, dec'd, of Gloucester Cowcher, Rebecca 8 yrs from 29 Sep pinmaker 5s
		26 Sep Tayler, Philip son of John, tanner, of Weston under Penyard, Herefs Taylor, Jasper & [*blank*] 7 yrs combmaker 20s
		29 Sep Aram, John son of Thomas, brewer, of Gloucester Aram, Thomas, his father, & Margaret 7 yrs [brewer] 20s
3/12		10 Sep Clarke, Thomas son of Nicholas, farmer, of Gloucester Kinge, William & Phoebe 7 yrs wiredrawer & pinmaker 5s

Henry Ockold, mayor [1668–9]
John Ewins and George Tayler, bailiffs and sheriffs

	1668	7 Oct Bergum, John son of Robert, yeoman, of Abenhall [MS Avenhill] Cowcher, Rebecca, widow, 7 yrs pinmaker 5s
		13 Oct Stephens, John son of John, farmer, dec'd, of Minsterworth Griffin, David & Hester 7 yrs tailor 2s 6d
3/13		Beakes, Benjamin son of Robert, currier, of Bristol Crumwell, John & Anne 7 yrs carrier 50s [*cf Appendix V*]
		15 Oct Bubb, William son of Thomas, blacksmith, of Barnwood Partridge, Richard & Anne 8 yrs baker 20s

	1668	16 Oct	Greene, John son of Roland, gentleman, dec'd, of Maisemore Cox, Winston & [blank] 7 yrs currier 1s
			Bourne, William son of Henry, baker, dec'd, of Paganhill Pace, Francis & Phillida 7 yrs baker 3s
3/14		21 Oct	Hieron, John son of Richard, yeoman, of Dymock Lea, Henry & Joan 7 yrs currier 2s 6d
			Lodge, Trustrum son of John, mason, late of Ruardean Greene, John sr & Katharine 7 yrs cooper 2s 6d
		[blank]	Hodges, William son of William, yeoman, of [blank] Ricketts, James & Anne 7 yrs from 29 Sep last tanner [blank]
		22 Oct	Titcombe, John son of John, labourer, dec'd, of Gloucester Hill, Walter & Elizabeth 7 yrs from 29 Sep currier 2s 6d
3/15		6 Oct	Rogers, Thomas son of Thomas, gentleman, of Oxenhall Jordan, William & Alice 8 yrs from 25 Mar last apothecary 20s
		26 Oct	Friar, Walter son of Walter, labourer, of Gloucester Cudd, John & Elizabeth 7 yrs silkweaver 2s
		3 Nov	Lovett, John son of John, yeoman, of Naunton Heath, Samuel & Mary 7 yrs from 29 Sep silkweaver 2s 6d
			Lovett, James son of John, yeoman, of Naunton Heath, Samuel & Mary 7 yrs from 29 Sep silkweaver 2s 6d
		1 Nov	Hands, William son of William, farmer, dec'd, of Highnam Williams, John & Jane 8 yrs ropier 10s
3/16			Stephenson *alias* Cowles, William son of Wm, tanner, of Winchcombe Bidle, Jonas & Bridget 7 yrs shoe mender 2s 6d
		17 Nov	Prince, John son of Thomas, yeoman, dec'd, of Hartpury Mayris, Charles & Elizabeth 7 yrs pewterer & brazier 5s
		19 Nov	Vaisie, Thomas son of Walter, gentleman, of Gloucester Burroughes, Samuel & Mary 7 yrs from 25 Mar next mercer 5s
		18 Nov	Baylis, Richard son of John, farmer, of Staunton, Worcs Gwilliam, John & Mary 7 yrs feltmaker 2s 6d
		28 Nov	Goodwyn, Joseph son of Joseph, yeoman, of Minsterworth Goodcheape, Thomas & Mary 7 yrs currier 2s 6d
3/17		1 Dec	Atkins, William son of William, farmer, of Upton St Leonards Heyward, John & Mary 7 yrs feltmaker 5s
		10 Dec	Turner, John son of William, farmer, of Gloucester Woodinge, William & [blank] 7 yrs button maker 5s
		26 Dec	Thomas, Thomas son of Thomas, labourer, of Gloucester Pitt, James & [blank] 8 yrs pinmaker 2s 6d
	1669	9 Jan	Rodway, Giles son of John, yeoman, of Upton St Leonards Rodway, John & Elizabeth 7 yrs from 29 Sep last mercer 5s

	1669	16 Jan	Adams, Daniel son of Joseph, farmer, dec'd, of Taynton
			Keare, John & Alice 7 yrs from 25 Jan pinmaker 10s
3/18		23 Jan	Sally, Thomas son of Thomas, gardener, of Gloucester
			Hill, Walter & Elizabeth 8 yrs currier 2s 6d
	1668	1 Nov	West, Stephen son of Robert, farmer, dec'd, of Painswick
			Heaghe, James & Hester 7 yrs chandler 2s 6d
	1669	2 Feb	Burford, Francis son of Francis, farmer, dec'd, of Newent
			Woodward, John & Margaret 7 yrs combmaker 2s 6d
			Palmer, Joseph son of George, baker, of Gloucester
			Chapman, Thomas & Elizabeth 7 yrs tailor 2s 6d [cf Appendix V]
3/19		8 Feb	Forreigne, Thomas son of Thomas, maltster, of Tewkesbury
			Jaquies, Aaron & Mary 7 yrs baker 6s 8d
		9 Feb	Norgrove, James son of James, pinmaker, of Bristol
			Coucher, Rebecca 7 yrs from 25 Dec last pinmaker 10s
		19 Feb	Smith, John son of Thomas, yeoman, of Upton Bishop, Herefs
			Nash, Richard & Anne 8 yrs feltmaker 2s 6d
		22 Feb	Knight, Thomas son of Thomas, broadweaver, of Kingswood, Wilts
			Onyon, Humphrey & Elizabeth 8 yrs silkweaver 2s 6d
		1 Mar	Cobb, Thomas son of Christopher, clothier, of Gloucester
			Merrett, Thomas & Mary 7 yrs currier 12d
3/20		2 Mar	Freeman, John son of Thomas, carpenter, of Eldersfield, Worcs
			Cordell, James & Anne 7 yrs glover 2s 6d
		[blank]	Mathewes, John son of John, butcher, late of Gloucester
			Perrys, William & Frances 7 yrs from 25 Dec last butcher 7s
			[cf Appendix V]
		8 Mar	Lewis, John son of Miles, pinmaker, of Gloucester
			Coucher, William & Susannah 8 yrs pinmaker 5s
		10 Mar	Man, Richard son of Richard, butcher, dec'd, of Cirencester
			Wasfield, John & [blank] 7 yrs locksmith 5s
		23 Feb	Wood, Thomas son of Thomas, tanner, of Gloucester
			Wood, Isaac & [blank] 7 yrs currier 2s 6d
3/21		24 Feb	Canon, Thomas son of Thomas, brewer, dec'd, of Barton Street, Gloucester
			Cripps, Edward & Elizabeth 7 yrs butcher 2 [sic]
		17 Mar	Mount, John son of William, merchant, of Dublin, kingdom of Ireland
			Perkes, John & Alice 7 yrs baker 5s
	1668	25 Dec	Procer, Hugh son of Henry, yeoman, of Holme Lacy, Herefs
			Plott, Cornelius & Joan 7 yrs tailor 3s 4d
	1669	23 Mar	Dimocke, Francis son of Giles, clothworker, of Randwick
			Randle, Josiah & Margery 7 yrs baker 2s 6d
		25 Mar	Hooper, Henry son of [blank], late of Gloucester
			Cowcher, Cecily 8 yrs pinmaker 2s 6d

3/22	1669	26 Mar	Jewett, Peter son of Peter, carpenter, dec'd, of Gloucester Farley, George & Mary 7 yrs cutler 12d
		2 Apr	Quench, Richard son of Richard, tailor, of Gloucester Chomlyn, Thomas & Mary 7 yrs turner 2s 6d
			Riggs, Stephen son of Francis, labourer, of Gloucester Perkes, William & Katharine 8 yrs pinmaker 2s 6d
		3 Apr	Turner, Richard son of Richard, carpenter, late of Tuffley Cox, Winston sr & [*blank*] 7 yrs currier 2s 6d
		1 Apr	Grevile, Henry son of Francis, gentleman, dec'd, of Charlton Kings Lysons, Daniel sr & Sarah 8 yrs from 2 Feb woollen draper 5s
3/23	1668	1 Nov	Dalton, James son of Andrew, saddler, late of Woodchester [MS Westchester] Harmer, William & Joan 7 yrs [*blank*] 40s
	1669	25 Mar	Abbotts, John son of Henry, baker, of Gloucester Abbotts, Henry, his father, & Sarah 7 yrs baker 10s [1]
		10 Apr	Beevan, Richard son of William, labourer, of Gloucester Walker, James & Martha 7 yrs button maker 2s 6d [*Mrs Browne*][2]
		1 Apr	Hazlewood, James son of Christopher, glover, dec'd, of Gloucester Berrowe, Samuel & Katharine 7 yrs from 25 Mar currier 5s *£4 of Mrs Browne's money*
		17 Apr	White, John son of William, butcher, of Newent Clayfeild, Edward sr & Anne 7 yrs tanner
3/24		15 Feb	Wood, George son of George, brewer, of Gloucester Bromley, Leonard & [*blank*] 7 yrs glover *26 Mar 1670: on a complaint to the common council that Bromley had taken Wood as his apprentice improperly, the indentures were cancelled*
		1 Apr	Wilmotts, John son of Robert, saddler, of Gloucester Wilmotts, Robert, his father, & Sarah 7 yrs from 25 Dec last saddler 20s
		22 Apr	Wilmotts, Robert son of Robert, saddler, of Gloucester Wilmotts, Robert, his father, & Sarah 7 yrs from 24 Jun next saddler 20s
		1 Apr	Fones, Thomas son of John, glover, of Gloucester Fones, John, his father, & Eleanor 7 yrs glover 10s
		28 Apr	Stone, Robert son of John, yeoman, of Bromsberrow Clayfield, Edward jr & Katharine 7 yrs from 27 Mar tanner 3s 4d
3/25		30 Apr	Parry, John son of Lancelot, joiner, of Wrexham, Denbigh Samson, William & Jane 7 yrs turner 10s

---

[1] GBR B3/3 p 639 27 Sep 1675: The son of Henry Abbottes to receive £10 of Sir Thomas Rich's money to bind him apprentice.

[2] ibid p 402 26 Mar 1669: To receive £4 of the gift of Mrs Sarah Browne lately deceased: James Hazlewood, John Houlton, Richard Beevan.

	1669	1 May	Stephens, William son of William, currier, of Gloucester
			Taylor, Jasper & [blank] 7 yrs combmaker 5s [*Holliday*]
			Reade, Robert son of John, yeoman, of Tuffley
			Singleton, Francis & Sarah 7 yrs ironmonger 5s
		25 Mar	Holton, John son of Richard, labourer, of Gloucester
			Doughton, Stephen & [blank] 8 yrs pinmaker 2s 6d
			£4 of the gift of Mrs Browne
3/26		31 May	White *alias* Wootton, Joseph son of William, yeoman, dec'd, of Down Hatherley
			Parker, Margaret 7 yrs from 22 May 1669 baker 2s 6d
			26 Mar 1670: Indentures cancelled by the common council because he did not live with Margaret Parker as an apprentice
		24 May	Lugg, Samuel son of John, haberdasher, of Gloucester
			Martley, Anthony and Anne 7 yrs horner 5s
			£5 of Mr Hollidaye's money
		20 May	Stocke, Thomas son of Edward, yeoman, dec'd, of Hasfield
			Cox, John & Alice 7 yrs currier 2s 6d
		31 May	Bucke, John son of Richard, mason, of Gloucester
			Williams, John & Jane 7 yrs ropier 10s
		1 May	Elmes, John son of Thomas, yeoman, of Wheatenhurst
			Selwyn, Thomas & Martha 7 yrs currier 2s 6d
3/27		5 Jun	Yates, Daniel son of Humphrey, farmer, of Cheltenham
			White, Sergeant & Joan 7 yrs from 16 Jun currier 2s 6d
		1 Jun	Mathewes, John son of John, farmer, of Ablington
			Ryland, John & Hester 8 yrs tanner 2s 6d
		12 Jun	Niccolls, Thomas son of John, miller, of Cheltenham
			Barnes, Thomas & Susannah 7 yrs from 1 Mar last plumber 2s 6d
		16 Jun	Nash, Richard son of William yeoman, of Haresfield
			Hancks, John & Elizabeth 7 yrs tanner 2s 6d
3/28		5 Jul	Phelpes, Matthew son of William, farmer, of the Leigh
			Gwillim, John & Mary 7 yrs feltmaker 5s
		9 Jul	Carter, William son of Thomas, farmer, dec'd, of Maisemore
			Sparrowhawke, William & Mary 8 yrs silkweaver 5s
		10 Jul	Knight, Richard son of Thomas, yeoman, of Ruardean
			Meeke, Thomas & Margery 7 yrs from 29 May currier 3s 6d
		13 Jul	Greene, Robert son of Richard, baker, of Gloucester
			Greene, Richard, his father, & [blank] 7 yrs baker 10s
		20 Jul	Price, Samuel son of William, yeoman, late of the Castle, Gloucester
			Prickett, John & Anne 7 yrs currier 2s 6d
3/29		21 Jul	Smith, Thomas son of William, glover, of Gloucester
			Smith, William, his father, & Susannah 7 yrs glover 20s

1669 22 Jul Merry, William son of William, yeoman, dec'd, of Sandhurst
              Phelpes, Joseph & Joan 7 yrs from 25 Jul chandler 2s 6d

      26 Jul Vaughan, Aaron son of Thomas, joiner, of Gloucester
              Vaughan, Thomas, his father, & Mary 7 yrs joiner 5s

      30 Jul Mills, John son of John, broadweaver, of Gloucester
              Wood, John & Margaret 7 yrs button maker 5s

      25 Jul Eliote, Thomas son of John, wiredrawer, of Gloucester
              Eliote, John, his father, & Margaret 7 yrs wiredrawer 5s
              £5 of Mr Hollidaye's money[1]

3/30 21 Jul Woolford, Richard son of Thomas, basket maker, of Gloucester
              Woolford, Thomas, his father, & Joan 7 yrs basket maker 5s
              £5 of Mr Hollidaye's money

       7 Aug Byard, Augustine son of Richard, yeoman, of Sandhurst
              Jeffes, William & Mary [blank] from 2 Aug ropemaker 5s

      25 Jul Merrett, Thomas son of Thomas, currier, of Gloucester
              Merrett, Thomas, his father, & Mary 7 yrs currier 20s [Holliday]

      10 Aug Tainton, Thomas son of Walter, grocer, late of Gloucester
              Tainton, Eleanor, widow of Walter 7 yrs from 1 Aug grocer 10s

      20 Jul Theyer, John son of William, farmer, of Alstone in Cheltenham
              Birt, William & Deborah 7 yrs tailor 5s

3/31   1 Aug Hill, John son of John, yeoman, of Highleadon
              Tyler, John & [blank] 7 yrs currier 2s 6d

      23 Aug Lugg, Thomas son of Jasper, combmaker, of Gloucester
              Martley, John & Anne 7 yrs from 24 Aug combmaker 5s [Holliday]
              18 Dec 1672: turned over to serve the residue of his term with
              Daniel Sampson, horner, with the consent of Anne Martley

      24 Aug Painter, John son of John, glazier, of Gloucester
              Painter, John, his father, & Elizabeth 7 yrs glazier 5s

       1 Aug Palmer, Joseph son of George, baker, of Gloucester
              Maddocke, William & Jane 7 yrs tailor 5s [cf Appendix V]

3/32 21 Aug Webly, Richard son of Richard, yeoman, dec'd, of Churchdown
              Bosly, Richard & Elizabeth 7 yrs feltmaker 5s

       1 Sep Rose, Benjamin son of Benjamin, gentleman, of Kilmore Church,
                County Monaghan in the kingdom of Ireland
              Rose, Samuel & Dorothy 7 yrs brewer 10s

       8 Sep Probert, Thomas son of Roger, yeoman, of Charlton Kings
              Phillips, James & Anne 7 yrs tailor 2s 6d

---

[1] GBR B3/3 p 416 21 Jul 1669: To receive £5 of Mr Holliday's money: Thomas Farmer, Thomas son of Jasper Lugg, William son of William Powell, the son of John Eliote, Thomas son of Thomas Merrett, the son of Thomas Woolford.

1669 30 Sep Lane, Richard son of William, gentleman, dec'd, of Norton
     Jordan, Toby & Anne 7 yrs from 29 Sep stationer

3/34   **John Wagstaff, mayor [1669–70]**
     Richard Broade and William Massinger, bailiffs and sheriffs

1669 11 Oct Harper, Nicholas son of John, tanner, of Gloucester
     Clifford, James & Mary 7 yrs pinmaker 2s 6d

   12 Oct Bishop, John son of Richard, farmer, of Churchdown
     Beard, John & Eleanor 7 yrs silkweaver 5s

     Bishop, John son of Giles, yeoman, of Churchdown
     Sparkes, Thomas & Sarah 7 yrs silkweaver 2s 6d

3/35   Gibbons, David son of Thomas, white wiredrawer, of Gloucester
     Stephens, Thomas jr & Frances 7 yrs pinmaker 2s 6d

   23 Oct Trotman, William son of William, clothworker, of Mitcheldean
     Pitt, James & [*blank*] 8 yrs pinmaker 2s 6d

   25 Oct Morgan, John son of Thomas, farmer, of Wotton [St Mary]
     Coucher, Cecily, widow, 9 yrs [pinmaker] 5s

   20 Oct Tomes, Daniel son of Matthew, farmer, of Hampnett
     Jeffes, William & Mary 7 yrs from 29 Sep ropier 2s 6d

   26 Oct Clifford, John son of Thomas, labourer, late of Gloucester
     Day, William & Joan 7 yrs from 29 Sep tanner 2s 6d

3/36   29 Oct Glaw, William son of William, cooper, of Ruardean
     Pritchards, Simon & Sarah 7 yrs from 1 Nov cooper 2s 6d

     Adams, John son of Joseph, yeoman, of Taynton
     Clifford, James & Mary 7 yrs pinmaker 2s 6d

   1 Nov Smith, John son of Giles, labourer, of Gloucester
     Samsons, William & Jane 8 yrs horner 5s

   8 Nov Ferrett, John son of John, glover, late of Maisemore
     Ferrett, Nathaniel & [*blank*] 7 yrs glover 2s 6d
      16 Jan 1671: discharged from his apprenticeship with the
      consent of himself and Nathaniel Ferrett and the indenture
      cancelled
      Witnessed: Benjamin Hyett

     Powell, Thomas son of Thomas, labourer, of Gloucester
     Pigge, Richard & Blanche 7 yrs pinmaker 2s 6d

3/37   8 Nov Berry, Samuel son of Zachariah, brushmaker, dec'd, of Gloucester
     Pigge, Richard & Blanche 7 yrs pinmaker 2s 6d

   1 Nov Arundell, William son of Samuel, clothier, late of Stroudwater
     Dowsinge, Walter & Dinah 7 yrs smith & farrier 5s

	1669		
		1 Nov	Smyth, Thomas son of Robert, glover, of city of London
			Smyth, Thomas & Joan 9 yrs from 29 Sep pewterer 40s
		6 Oct	Minchin, John son of Giles, yeoman, of Down Hatherley
			Cudd, John & Elizabeth 7 yrs from 29 Sep silkweaver 5s
		15 Nov	Puckeridge, William son of Thomas, tailor, of Gloucester
			Bishop, William & [blank] 7 yrs tailor 2s 6d [cf Appendix V]
3/38		7 Dec	Tacklyn, Thomas son of Thomas, labourer, of Gloucester

1669

1 Nov Smyth, Thomas son of Robert, glover, of city of London
          Smyth, Thomas & Joan 9 yrs from 29 Sep pewterer 40s

6 Oct Minchin, John son of Giles, yeoman, of Down Hatherley
          Cudd, John & Elizabeth 7 yrs from 29 Sep silkweaver 5s

15 Nov Puckeridge, William son of Thomas, tailor, of Gloucester
          Bishop, William & [blank] 7 yrs tailor 2s 6d [cf Appendix V]

3/38

7 Dec Tacklyn, Thomas son of Thomas, labourer, of Gloucester
          Roberts, Samuel & Elizabeth 7 yrs silkweaver 5s

Coale, John son of John, sawyer, of Gloucester
          Roberts, Samuel & Elizabeth 7 yrs silkweaver 5s

17 Nov Heminge, William son of Arnold, chandler, of Gloucester
          Gardner, Thomas & Anne 7 yrs pinmaker 10s

24 Nov Willis, Thomas son of William, yeoman, Hucclecote
          Shipton, John & Alice 7 yrs currier 12d

14 Dec Pegler, Joseph son of John, farmer, of Bledington
          Robins, Thomas & Hester 7 yrs tanner 2s 6d

3/39

13 Dec Browne, John son of Humphrey, farmer, of Maisemore
          Stephens, James & Anne 7 yrs from 25 Dec maltster 2s 6d

1670

4 Jan Okey, William son of William, farmer, of Dowdeswell
          Davis, John & Comfort 7 yrs from 25 Dec wool comber 10s

19 Jan Fisher, Robert son of Richard, tanner, of Upton Bishop, Herefs
          Hathway, Elizeus & Mary 7 yrs from 25 Mar clothier 2s 6d

13 Jan Bailee, Thomas son of Thomas, victualler, of Gloucester
          Taylor, George & Joan 7 yrs barber surgeon 5s[1]

3/40

2 Feb Clarke, John son of Nicholas, farmer, of Gloucester
          Byford, Joseph & Sarah 7 yrs glazier 2s 6d [cf Appendix V]
          [Mrs Browne][2]

Merry, John son of John, yeoman, late of Sandhurst
          Perkes, John & Alice 7 yrs baker 2s 6d

Heyter, Edward son of Edward, brazier, of Gloucester
          Price, James & Alice 9 yrs pewterer 5s [cf Appendix V]

18 Feb Clifford, Joshua son of Joshua, silkweaver, of Gloucester
          Underhill, James & Frances 7 yrs from 24 Feb silkweaver 2s 6d

2 Feb Dowle, Job son of Clement, mercer, of Gloucester
          Dowle, Clement, his father, & Hannah 7 yrs mercer 2s 6d

---

[1] GBR B3/3 p 423 16 Sep 1669: Thomas Knight, Thomas Wintle, Timothy Cartwright, Humphrey Merry, Edward Rogers to have £10 for clothing and placing them apprentice according to the will of our noble benefactor Sir Thomas Rich. Thomas son of Thomas Baily, one of the Bluecoat boys in the hospital of Sir Thomas Rich to be removed thence and given £10 for clothing and placing him apprentice, according to the will of Sir Thomas Rich.

[2] GBR B3/3 p 440 26 Mar 1670: To receive £4 of Mrs Browne's money: Nicholas son of John Clarke, William son of Jane Knott, John son of John Evans.

3/41	1670	11 Feb	Alford, Stephen son of Stephen, farmer, dec'd, of Tibberton Fownes, John & Eleanor 7 yrs glazier 5s
		25 Mar	Watts, Richard son of William, butcher, of Minsterworth Cowdale, John & Patience 7 yrs tailor 2s 6d
		2 Apr	Saunders, Thomas son of Thomas, farmer, dec'd, of Gloucester Reeve, Francis & Hannah 7 yrs from 29 Sep stone cutter 10s [*Holliday*]
			Mitchell, George son of George, garter weaver, dec'd, of Gloucester Wadman, Roger & Elizabeth 7 yrs from 25 Mar silkweaver 10s
3/42		1 Mar	Amos, Edward son of Samuel, dyer, of Painswick Amos, Nathaniel & [*blank*] 7 yrs bodicemaker 7s
		20 Mar	Dobles, Isaac son of Abraham, wool comber, late of Gloucester Greene, Edmund jr & [*blank*] 7 yrs from 8 Oct last cordwainer 2s 6d [*Repeated, altered, at 3/43*] £4 *of the gift of Mrs Sarah Browne deceased*
		6 Apr	Ferrett, Daniel son of John, dec'd, of Gloucester Ferrett, Nathaniel & [*blank*] 7 yrs glover 2s 6d
		8 Oct	Allen, William son of Lawrence, chandler, of Gloucester Allen, Lawrence, his father, & Anne 7 yrs chandler 5s
3/43		23 Mar	Allen, Thomas son of Lawrence, chandler, of Gloucester Allen, Lawrence, his father, & Anne 7 yrs chandler 5s
	1669	25 Dec	Aram, Edward son of John, gentleman, of Newnham Aram, Arnold & [*blank*] 7 yrs haberdasher 2s 6d
	1670	15 Apr	Knott, William son of Henry, bricklayer, dec'd, of Gloucester Sampson, William & Jane 8 yrs turner & combmaker 30s [*Mrs Browne*]
		20 Mar	Dobles, Isaac son of Abraham, wool comber, late of Gloucester Greene, Edmund jr & [*blank*] 7 yrs from 8 Oct last currier [*blank*] [*Repeating entry at 3/42*]
3/44		12 Apr	Berrowe, William son of William, yeoman, late of Down Hatherley Bosly, Richard & Elizabeth 7 yrs feltmaker 5s
		25 Apr	Charles, John son of John, farmer, of Upton St Leonards Hawkes, Richard & Anne 7 yrs sievemaker 7s
			Merry, Humphrey son of Humphrey, wiredrawer, of Gloucester Greene, Edmund jr & [*blank*] 7 yrs currier 5s
		27 Apr	Ovenell, John son of John, yeoman, dec'd, of Redmarley d'Abitot, Worcs Stephens, John & Bridget 7 yrs barber surgeon 2s 6d
3/45		2 May	Freeman, Thomas son of Thomas, carpenter, of Eldersfield, Worcs Hancocks, John & Philadelphia 7 yrs bodicemaker 2s 6d
		1 May	Hartland, John son of Richard, broadweaver, of Mitcheldean Dobbes, John & Jane [*no term*] barber surgeon 2s 6d

	1670		
		1 May	Hayward, Giles son of William, yeoman, of Minsterworth Griffin, David & Hester 7 yrs tailor 2s 6d
		28 May	Freame, William son of Daniel, yeoman, of Badgeworth George, William & Hester 7 yrs feltmaker 5s
3/46		1 May	Jordan, John son of William, apothecary, of Gloucester Jordan, William, his father, & Alice 7 yrs apothecary 20s
		8 Jun	Bishop, Richard son of William, yeoman, of Churchdown Sparrowhawke, William & Mary 7 yrs silkweaver 5s
		1 Jun	Rogers, James son of Thomas, gentleman, of Wrexham, Denbigh Samson, William & Jane 7 yrs from 17 Mar turner 2s 6d
		14 Jun	Wastfeild, Robert son of William, farmer, of Painswick Jaquies, Aaron & Mary 7 yrs baker 2s 6d
3/47		15 Jun	Hiett, Richard son of Robert, yeoman, dec'd, of Churcham Yates, Francis & Joan 7 yrs currier 1s
		16 Jun	Showell, Thomas son of John, yeoman, of Longford Rogers, Thomas & Priscilla 7 yrs baker 2s 6d
		17 Jun	Wadley, Richard son of John, haulier, of Gloucester Greene, John sr & Katharine 7 yrs from 24 Jun cooper 2s 6d
		24 Jun	Dring, John son of John, gentleman, dec'd, of Sherborne Lugg, Thomas sr & Joan 7 yrs haberdasher 20s
3/48		6 Jul	Blanch, Daniel son of Daniel, farmer, of Gloucester Greene, William & Mary 7 yrs pinmaker 5s
		24 Jun	Hooke, William son of Edward, yeoman, of Taynton Selwyn, Thomas & Martha 7 yrs currier 2s 6d
		9 Aug	Atkins, William son of Robert, gardener, of Gloucester Sparkes, Thomas & Sarah 8 yrs silkweaver 2s 6d [*Holliday*][1]
			Thomas, John son of Jonathan, tailor, dec'd, of Gloucester Norman, Edward & Joan 7 yrs butcher 5s
3/49		31 Aug	Hughes, John son of Thomas, weaver, of Gloucester Cudd, John & Elizabeth 7 yrs silkweaver 2s 6d
		5 Sep	Prickett, Samuel son of Howell, button maker, of Gloucester Hands, Richard & Sarah 7 yrs freemason 5s
		23 Sep	Hughes, Richard son of Thomas, silkweaver, of Gloucester Sparrowhawke, William & Mary 7 yrs silkweaver 2s 6d
		27 Mar	Cowles, Robert son of Richard, butcher, of Gloucester Gregory, William & Anne 7 yrs from 29 Sep butcher 5s

[1] GBR B3/3 p 444 22 Jul 1670: To receive £5 of Mr Hollidaye's money: Robert son of Richard Cowles, Thomas Saunders, John Thomas, William son of William Stephens cordwainer, John Warde, the son of Robert Atkins.

3/51		**Henry Fowler, mayor [1670–1]** **Edward Tither and Nicholas Phelpes, bailiffs and sheriffs**
	1670	11 Oct Pembridge, Thomas son of Thomas, cleric, of Corse Nash, Richard & [blank] 7 yrs grocer 2s 6d
		14 Oct Benfeild, Thomas son of Thomas, mercer, of Cheltenham Marston, John & Rebecca 8 yrs from 29 Sep merchant 5s
		Hamlin, James son of Robert, leather button maker, of Gloucester Hiron, Margaret 8 yrs vintner 8s
3/52		28 Oct Warde, John son of Philip, victualler, of Gloucester Whitle, Samuel & Mary 7 yrs from 17 Sep currier 5s
		4 Nov Dudley, John son of John, farmer, of Rodley Farmer, Bridget widow of John 7 yrs silkweaver 2s 6d
		Fry, Henry son of Henry, farmer, late of Gloucester Randle, Daniel & Anne 7 yrs tailor 2s 6d
		1 Nov Tayler, John son of John, blacksmith, dec'd, of Longford Cudd, John & Elizabeth 8 yrs silkweaver 5s
3/53		Badger, Jeremiah son of John, merchant, of Westbury Farmer, Bridget widow of John 7 yrs silkweaver 2s 6d
		21 Nov Bevan, Edward son of Edward, labourer, dec'd, of Gloucester Clifford, James & Mary 7 yrs pinmaker 2s 6d
		1 Dec Collett, Edmund son of Edmund, haberdasher, of Gloucester Collett, Edmund, his father, & Mary 7 yrs from 1 Nov haberdasher 10s
	1671	1 Jan Downbell, Edmund son of Stephen, vintner, dec'd, of Gloucester Bishopp, John & Hester 8 yrs merchant 5s [1]
3/54		11 Jan Short, John son of William, fisherman, of Southgate Street, Gloucester Martley, Anthony jr & Anne 7 yrs horner 5s
		12 Jan Knott, George son of Nicholas, yeoman, of Broadway, Worcs Knott, Lawrence & Elizabeth 7 yrs from 29 Sep last carpenter 5s
		31 Jan Puckeridge, Abraham son of Thomas, tailor, of Gloucester Suffeild, Anthony & Hester 7 yrs from 2 Feb currier 2s 6d
		2 Feb Clarke, John son of Nicholas, labourer, of Gloucester Fewtrell, William & Mary 7 yrs tailor 2s 6d [cf Appendix V]
3/55		Jelfe, Walter son of William, yeoman, of Hartpury Smith, Giles & Sybil 7 yrs baker 3s 4d
		13 Feb Hamlyn, Joseph son of Richard, yeoman, of Brimpsfield Hall, William & Elizabeth 7 yrs currier 3s 4d

---

[1] GBR B3/3 p 452 23 Dec 1670: To be removed from Sir Thomas Rich's hospital and receive £10 to bind them apprentice: Thomas Deane, William Howell, Thomas Probert, John Williams, Edmund Downbell.

	1670	26 Dec	Anstee, Charles son of Charles, butcher, of Gloucester
			Anstee, Charles, his father, & Mary 7 yrs butcher 10s
	1671	1 Mar	Collett, Samuel son of John, husbandman, of Cheltenham
			Lugg, Thomas & Joan 7 yrs haberdasher 20s
3/56		2 Mar	Keys, John son of John, farmer, of the parish of Newent
			Nash, Jesse & Elizabeth 7 yrs feltmaker 5s
		6 Mar	Bishop, William jr son of William sr, yeoman, of Hucclecote
			Davis, John & Comfort 7 yrs wool comber 5s
		27 Mar	Heminge, Robert son of Arnold, chandler, of Gloucester
			Sparrowhawke, Robert & Elizabeth 7 yrs silkweaver 3s
			Pace, William son of Thomas, yeoman, dec'd, of Maisemore
			Cooke, Benjamin & Sarah 7 yrs from 25 Mar tailor 5s
3/57		1 Apr	Jewett, Thomas son of Peter, carpenter, of Gloucester
			Till, Richard & [blank] 8 yrs cutler 10s [cf Appendix V]
		1 Apr	Till, Edward son of Richard, cutler, of Gloucester
			Till, Richard, his father, & [blank] 7 yrs cutler 20s
		3 Apr	Bradley, John son of Henry, yeoman, of Elmore
			Lye, Samuel & Sarah 8 yrs from 25 Mar chandler 2s 6d
			Gibbs, Thomas son of John, yeoman, of Minsterworth
			Welsteed, John & Elizabeth 7 yrs blacksmith 5s
3/58		11 Apr	Wyman, Ambrose son of Thomas, yeoman, of Quedgeley
			Cox, Winston sr & [blank] 7 yrs currier 2s 6d
		13 Apr	Weaver, Thomas son of Thomas, of city of Worcester
			Sparrowhawke, Robert & Elizabeth 7 yrs from 1 April silkweaver
			Harris, John son of William, brewer of Gloucester
			Lugg, Jasper & Alice 7 yrs combmaker 5s
		25 Apr	Hall, Henry son of William, yeoman, of the Leigh
			Reeve, Giles sr & [blank] 7 yrs gunsmith 2s 6d
3/59		17 Apr	Morris, John son of Justinian, carpenter, of Gloucester
			Aram, Thomas & Margaret 7 yrs from 25 Jul maltster 2s 6d
		19 Apr	Jelfe, James son of James, cook, of Barton Street, Gloucester
			Cowcher, William & Susannah 8 yrs pinmaker 5s
		8 Apr	Atkins, Joseph son of John, of [blank]
			White, Sergeant & Joan 7 yrs currier 2s 6d
		27 Apr	Jelfe, Oliver son of Thomas, baker, dec'd, of Gloucester
			Cooke, Richard & Margaret 7 yrs from 1 Apr chandler 2s 6d
3/60		28 Apr	Horrold, William son of John, of [blank]
			Browne, James & Elizabeth 7 yrs pewterer [blank]
		6 May	Weyman, John son of [blank], of Huntley, [blank]
			Hill, Walter & Elizabeth 8 yrs currier 2s 6d

| | 1671 | 8 May | Heminge, Richard son of Arnold, chandler, of Gloucester |
| | | | Killmister, Alan & Jane 7 yrs tailor 2s 6d |

        1 May Dobbs, Francis son of John, barber surgeon, of Gloucester
                 Dobbs, John, his father, & [blank] 7 yrs barber surgeon 5s
                 [cf Appendix V]

3/61   13 May Keele, James son of James, farmer, of Newent
                 Bell John & Joan 7 yrs from 1 May silk weaver 5s

       17 May Beakes, Benjamin son of Robert, currier, of the city of Bristol
                 Cox, Robert & Margaret 7 yrs surgeon 5s [cf Appendix V]

                 Barrett, Anthony son of Ralph, yeoman, of Minsterworth
                 Reeve, Samuel & Anne 7 yrs gunsmith 5s

        5 Jun Greene, Jonathan son of William, joiner, dec'd, of Gloucester
                 Greene, Margaret, his mother, widow of William 7 yrs [joiner] 10s

3/62   [blank] Gather, John son of Richard, yeoman, of Crudwell, Wilts
                 Williams, Richard & [blank] 8 yrs cooper 2s 6d

       20 Jun Yate, Josiah son of Humphrey, [blank], late of Cheltenham
                 Randle, William & Hester 8 yrs tailor [blank] [cf Appendix V]

       19 Jun Mosely, Charles son of John, gentleman, dec'd, of Redmarley d'Abitot, Worcs
                 Smarte, Richard & Margaret 7 yrs currier 5s

        3 May Mills, Thomas son of Edward, miller, of Flaxley
                 Hartland, William & Martha 8 yrs pinmaker 5s

3/63   24 Jun Price, Thomas son of Richard sr, gardener, of Gloucester
                 Lea, Anthony & [blank] 7 yrs currier 2s 6d

        5 Jul Ford, James son of John, tailor, of Gloucester
                 Vaisey, Walter & Margaret 7 yrs from 24 Jun tailor 2s 6d

       20 Jul Biles, Ephraim son of Thomas, gentleman, of Manston, Dorset
                 Onion, Thomas & Bridget 7 yrs silkweaver 5s

                 Osborne, Joseph son of Thomas, mason, of Painswick
                 Cooke, Henry & [blank] 7 yrs cutler 2s 6d

3/64   10 Aug Pontin, William son of William, [blank], dec'd, of Wotton under Edge
                 Gibbons, Richard & [blank] 7 yrs farrier 2s 6d

       24 Aug Warneford, Walter son of William, gentleman, of Miserden
                 Whitson, John & [blank] 7 yrs currier 5s

       12 Sep Davis, Joseph son of Randle, yeoman, of Newent
                 Byford, Joseph & Elizabeth 7 yrs [no trade] 5s

       13 Sep Fewtrell, Edward son of Edward, tailor, dec'd, of Gloucester
                 Hawkins, Eleanor, widow, 7 yrs combmaker 5s [Holliday][1]

---

[1] GBR B3/3 p 479 7 Aug 1671 To receive £5 of Mr Hollidaye's money: [blank] Bird, Moses Pickeringe, Edward Fewtrell, [blank] Badger, [blank] Turner, William Lugg.

3/65	1671	18 Sep	Onyon, John son of Thomas, silkweaver, of Gloucester Onyon, Thomas, his father, & Bridget 7 yrs silkweaver 20s
		25 Sep	Card, John son of Henry, weaver, dec'd, of Gloucester Russell, William, alderman, & [blank] 7 yrs skinner 2s 6d
		27 Sep	Cowles, Thomas son of Thomas, [blank], dec'd, of Gloucester Suffeild, Anthony & Hester 8 yrs currier 6d
		28 Sep	Lugge, William son of Edward, butcher, dec'd, of Gloucester Cowles, William & Jane 7 yrs butcher 5s [Holliday]

3/66   **Henry Fowler, mayor [1671–2]**
Willliam Lamb and Samuel Rose, sheriffs and bailiffs

	1671	4 Oct	Turner, John son of Thomas, victualler, dec'd, of Gloucester Whittorne, John & his wife 7 yrs cordwainer 5s [Holliday]
		13 Oct	Riman, James son of Thomas, farmer, of Ashton Keynes, Wilts Bosley, Richard & Elizabeth 7 yrs feltmaker 2s 6d
		15 Oct	Holtham, William son of William, chandler, of Gloucester Holtham, William, his father, & [blank] 7 yrs chandler 10s
		1 Nov	Mans, Richard son of Richard, yeoman, of Barnwood Shipton, John & [blank] 7 yrs currier 2s 6d
3/67		14 Nov	Broad, Samuel son of Samuel, yeoman, dec'd, of North Cerney Mardin, Richard & his wife 7 yrs baker 2s 6d
			Keyse, Joseph son of John, gentleman, of Hope Mansell, Herefs Payne, Robert & [blank] 7 yrs merchant 2s 6d
			Downbell, Stephen son of Stephen, vintner, dec'd, of Gloucester White, Richard & Joan 8 yrs from 25 Jul last currier 5s
			England, Joshua son of Richard, currier, of Gloucester Matley, Anthony & [blank] 7 yrs turner & combmaker [blank]
3/68		15 Nov	Man, James son of James, farmer, dec'd, of Lydney Marten, Thomas & Katharine 7 yrs glover 2s 6d
			Knowles, John son of Richard Cowles, coalminer, of Coleford Cudd, John & Elizabeth 8 yrs silkweaver 10s
	1672	16 Jan	Baker, Edmund son of Edward, gardener, of Barton Street [Gloucester] Wilkins, John & Mary 7 yrs wiredrawer 3s 4d
		14 Feb	Jenkins, William son of William, labourer, of Gloucester Price, John & Hester 7 yrs brewer £5 14s
3/69		1 Apr	Cowcher, William son of John, pinmaker, dec'd, of Gloucester Goodcheape, Thomas & Mary 7 yrs currier 5s
		27 Apr	Browne, John son of Thomas, husbandman, of Wotton [St Mary] Thomas, Morgan & Dorothy 7 yrs wiredrawer 5s

	1672 14 May	Walkley, Thomas son of Thomas, clothier, late of Wraxall, Som Hayward, Samuel & Deborah 7 yrs from 25 Dec next chandler 2s 6d

1672 14 May Walkley, Thomas son of Thomas, clothier, late of Wraxall, Som
 Hayward, Samuel & Deborah 7 yrs from 25 Dec next chandler 2s 6d

20 May Jones, Robert son of Richard, butcher, dec'd, of Gloucester
 Hughes, Daniel & Elizabeth 7 yrs cordwainer 5s[1]

3/70 21 May Tayler, William son of Richard, cutler, dec'd, of Gloucester
 Winston, John & Elizabeth 7 yrs tailor 5s

24 May Haynes, Edward son of William, joiner, dec'd, of Frampton on Severn
 Dobbs, Thomas & Jane 7 yrs barber & periwig maker 2s 6d

25 May Jewett, Thomas son of Peter, carpenter, dec'd, of Gloucester
 Selwyn, Thomas & Martha 7 yrs currier 2s 6d [*cf Appendix V*]

 Yelfe, Ezra son of Richard, yeoman, dec'd, of Longney
 Mills, Thomas & [*blank*] 7 yrs baker 2s 6d

3/71 3 Jun Withenbury, James son of James, carpenter, of Gloucester
 Reeve, Francis & Hannah 7 yrs stone carver 10s

1 Jun Meadway, Edward son of Henry, clothier & hosier, of Gloucester
 Meadway, Henry, his father, & Mary 7 yrs clothier & hosier 10s

1 Nov Moore, James son of George, butcher, of Gloucester
 Jelfe, Elizabeth, widow, 7 yrs baker 5s

24 Jun Harding, Edward son of Edward, bodicemaker, of Gloucester
 Hornedge, John & Sarah 7 yrs button maker 5s

3/72 Staple, William son of Thomas, rugmaker, of Woodchester
 Sheppard, John & Susannah 7 yrs cordwainer 2s 6d

28 Jun Greene, Thomas son of Thomas, currier, of Gloucester
 Greene, Edmund jr & [*blank*] 7 yrs from 25 Mar last currier 5s

29 Jun Hobson, Joseph son of John, merchant, dec'd, of Gloucester
 Cowles *alias* Stephenson, John & Anne 7 yrs from 25 Mar last
  bodicemaker 5s

28 Jun Lawrence, Simon son of William, yeoman, of Bromsberrow
 Selwyn, Thomas & Martha 7 yrs currier 5s

3/73 1 May Ready, Thomas son of John, gentleman, of Bulley
 Cox, John & Alice 7 yrs currier 2s 6d

25 Jul Humfris, Samuel son of Richard, butcher, dec'd, of Gloucester
 Humfris, Frances widow of Richard, his mother, 7 yrs butcher 10s

18 Jul Garners *alias* Mashfield, John son of John, victualler, of Gloucester
 Williams, Nicholas & Jane 7 yrs joiner 2s 6d

27 May Chestro, George son of Nathaniel, maltster, dec'd, of Cheltenham
 James, Leigh sr & [*blank*] 7 yrs baker 5s

---

[1] GBR B3/3 p 482 22 Sep 1671: To be removed from the hospital of Sir Thomas Rich and given £10 to place them apprentice: Richard Lugg, John Hobson, William Tayler, James Devis, Thomas Greene, Robert Jones.

3/74	1672	28 Sep	Campion, John son of John, painter stainer, of Gloucester Campion, John, his father, 7 yrs [painter stainer] 20s
		24 Jun	Merry, Thomas son of John, yeoman, of Sandhurst Yates, Francis & [blank] 8 yrs currier 2s 6d
		1 Sep	Potter, Anthony son of Anthony, yeoman, of Bishop's Cleeve Winston, Walter & Alice 7 yrs butcher 2s 6d
		3 Sep	Childe, John son of Thomas, currier, of Gloucester Childe, Thomas, his father, 7 yrs currier 5s [*Holliday*][1]

3/80 Henry Norwood, mayor [1672–3]
William Jordan and John Price, sheriffs and bailiffs

	1672	8 Oct	Eger, John son of Thomas, yeoman, of Frampton on Severn Cox, Winston & [blank] 7 yrs currier 1s 6d
		1 Oct	Warde, John son of George, yeoman, of Longford Washfield, John & [blank] 7 yrs blacksmith 5s
		15 Oct	Hinton, Daniel son of George, currier, of Gloucester Samsons, William & Jane 7 yrs horner 2s 6d [*Mrs Browne*][2]
		1 Oct	Aldington, Isaac son of Anthony, victualler of Childswickham Pace, Thomas & Mary 7 yrs cooper 5s
3/81			Barradell, John son of John, blacksmith, of Bishop's Cleeve Green, John sr & [blank] 7 yrs cooper 2s 6d
		26 Oct	White, William son of Samuel, tanner, of Gloucester White, Samuel, his father, & [blank] 7 yrs tanner 20s
		13 Nov	Merrett, Samuel son of Richard, of Leonard Stanley Parry, Daniel & [blank] 7 yrs currier 2s 6d
		1 Oct	Prior, Thomas son of Thomas, feltmaker, dec'd, of Gloucester Barnelme, Richard & [blank] 7 yrs horner & combmaker 5s [*Holliday*]
3/82			Wood, John son of John, button maker, of Gloucester Wood, John, his father, & Margaret 7 yrs button maker 10s [*Holliday*]
		2 Dec	Higgins, Nicholas son of Thomas, yeoman, dec'd, of Gloucester Ricketts, John & [blank] 7 yrs saddler 2s 6d
			Webb, Nicholas son of John, merchant, of Gloucester Webb, John, his father, & Jane 7 yrs merchant 2s 6d
	1673	1 Jan	Chandler, Thomas son of Richard, saddler, of Gloucester Chandler, Richard, his father, & Susannah 7 yrs saddler 5s

---

[1] GBR B3/3 p 510 9 Aug 1672: To receive £5 of Mr Holliday's money: William Smith, John Wood, William Skillum, Thomas Prior, James Stephens, John Childe.

[2] ibid p 511 9 Aug 1672: To receive £4 of Mrs Browne's money: Daniel Hinton, James Baker, William Thomas & [*name deleted*].

3/83	1673	6 Jan	Browne, Thomas son of Thomas, sievemaker, of Gloucester
			Browne, Thomas, his father, & Sarah 7 yrs sievemaker 5s
		1 Jan	Trinder, William son of William, farmer, of Ashton Keynes, Wilts
			Bosly, John & Mary 7 yrs feltmaker 2s 6d
		18 Jan	Jeynes, Thomas son of John, yeoman, of Ashchurch
			Pearce, Edmund & Sarah 7 yrs feltmaker 5s
		1 Feb	Fords, Richard son of William, farmer, of Cowley
			Greene, John jr & Margaret 8 yrs from 25 Mar next cooper 40s
3/84		8 Feb	Lawrence, Thomas son of William, yeoman, of Bromsberrow
			Randle, Josiah & Margery 7 yrs baker 2s 6d
			Richmond, Thomas son of John, farmer, of Kingsholm
			Best, John & Anne 7 yrs gardener 2s 6d
		10 Feb	Crasse, William son of William, yeoman, dec'd, of Gloucester
			Hancocks, John & Philippa 7 yrs bodicemaker 1s
		18 Feb	Thomas, John son of John, feltmaker, of Gloucester
			Samson, Daniel &[blank] 7 yrs horner 2s 6d
3/85		1 Mar	Curtis, Edward son of Christopher, maltster, dec'd, of Tewkesbury
			Perkes, William & Jane 10 yrs pinmaker 2s 6d
		20 Mar	Rogers, Thomas son of John, alderman, of Gloucester
			Webb, John & Jane 7 yrs from 25 Mar merchant 5s
		1 Jan	Harvey, Abraham son of Walter, innholder, of Gloucester
			Harvey, Walter, his father, & Anne 7 yrs innholder [blank]
		25 Mar	Beale, Geoffrey son of Geoffrey, merchant, of Gloucester
			Beale, Geoffrey, his father, & Edith 7 yrs merchant 5s
3/86		10 Apr	Brookes, Joseph son of Joseph, linen draper, dec'd, of Gloucester
			Sampsons, William & Jane 7 yrs horner 5s
		22 Apr	Humfries, Nathaniel son of Toby, butcher, of Gloucester
			Humfras, Joseph & [blank] 7 yrs chandler 5s
		24 Apr	Hammons, William son of Thomas, yeoman, late of Gloucester
			Barnelme, Richard & [blank] horner & combmaker [blank]
	1672	4 Oct	Skillum, William son of Richard, tailor, of Gloucester
			Skillum, Richard, his father, & [blank] 7 yrs tailor 5s [Holliday]
3/87	1673	1 May	Elliote, Henry son of John, wiredrawer, of Gloucester
			Aram, Thomas & Margaret 7 yrs glassmaker 5s
			Townsend, William son of Lawrence, blacksmith, dec'd, of Barton Street, Gloucester
			Greene, William & Mary 10 yrs pinmaker 2s 6d
			Browne, John son of John, butcher, dec'd, of Gloucester
			Browne, James & Elizabeth 7 yrs pewterer 5s [1]

[1] GBR B3/3 p 515 13 Sep 1672: To be removed from Sir Thomas Rich's hospital and given £10 to be placed apprentice to 'such masters as shall be approved by this house': Edmund Browne, John Brown, Thomas Phillipps, Lazarus Willmott, John Thomas, John Hickman.

	1672	21 Dec	Hickman, John son of John, scrivener, of Gloucester
			Dowsinge, William & Katharine 7 yrs tailor 5s[1]
3/88	1673	6 Jun	Forty, Daniel son of Thomas, tiler, of Cheltenham
			Knowles, Henry & [blank] 8 yrs brazier 20s
		9 Jun	Parker, George son of George, petty chapman, dec'd, of Gloucester
			Cowcher, William & Susannah 8 yrs pinmaker 2s 6d
		6 Jun	Brookes, Jonathan son of Jonathan, currier, dec'd, of Maisemore
			Cox, John & Alice 7 yrs currier 2s 6d
		1 May	Davis, Samuel son of James, gentleman, dec'd, of Standish
			Randle, Daniel & Anne 7 yrs joiner £3
3/89		19 Jun	Browne, Edmund son of John, merchant, dec'd, of Gloucester
			Hanbury, Caple & Anne 7 yrs [no trade] 5s
		24 Jun	Mills, Jeremiah son of Jeremiah, clothier, of King's Stanley
			Randle, William & Hester 7 yrs tailor 2s 6d
		26 Jun	Greene, Stephen son of Roland, yeoman, dec'd, of Maisemore
			Cox, Winston sr & [blank] 7 yrs currier 6d
		30 Jun	Mayzee, Benjamin son of John Maysee, clothier, of Bisley
			Panter, John & Mary 7 yrs [no trade] 2s 6d
3/90		2 Jul	Birton, William son of William, tailor, dec'd, of Newent
			Hill, Walter & Elizabeth 8 yrs shoe mender 2s 6d
		9 Jul	Norris, John son of Richard, husbandman, of Ashleworth
			Walker, James & Martha 7 yrs [button maker] 2s 6d
		25 Jul	Tanner, William son of Isaac, labourer, of Newnham
			Aram, Thomas & Margaret 9 yrs glassmaker 2s 6d
		25 Mar	Phillipps, Thomas son of George, feltmaker, of Gloucester
			Phillipps, James & Anne 7 yrs tailor 2s 6d
3/91		23 Jul	Baker, James son of James, yeoman, of Gloucester
			Woodward, John & Margaret 7 yrs combmaker 10s
			[Mrs Browne]
		24 Jul	Clarke, Nicholas son of Nicholas, farmer, of Gloucester
			Higgins, John and Nanfan 7 yrs currier 2s 6d
		30 Jul	Heyford, Thomas son of Henry, farmer, of Southgate Street, Gloucester
			Whitfeild, Edward & Mary 8 yrs from 1 Aug shoe mender 5s
		31 Jul	Ditton, George son of [blank], cleric, of Longhope
			Wilmott, Robert & Sarah 7 yrs from 29 Sep next saddler 5s

---

[1] GBR B3/3 p 549 29 Nov 1672: This house doth upon the petition of — Hickman of the said city, widow, consent that her son, one of the boys in the hospital of Sir Thomas Rich, may be placed apprentice to William Dowsinge of the said city, tailor, he giving good security as usually.

3/92	1673	1 Jun	Bridger, Desborowe son of Samuel, gentleman, dec'd, of Slimbridge Heard, Humphrey & Dorothy 7 yrs butcher 5s
		25 Jul	Greene, Nicholas son of John, blackware man, of Gloucester Wolford, Thomas & Joan 7 yrs basket maker 5s [*Mrs Browne*]¹
		1 Aug	Young, Abraham son of Walter, currier, of Gloucester Young, Walter, his father, & Joan 7 yrs currier 5s [*Holliday*]²
		25 Jul	Crafte, Samuel son of William, silkweaver, of Arlingham Sparrowhawk, Richard & [*blank*] 7 yrs silkweaver 2s 6d
3/93		1 Aug	Smart, John son of John, joiner, of Gloucester Brabban, Francis & Hester 7 yrs cooper 5s
		25 Mar	Cooke, Henry son of Richard, blacksmith, of Gloucester Cooke, Richard, his father, & Eleanor 7 yrs blacksmith 5s
			Birch, Thomas son of Thomas, yeoman, dec'd, of Ashton Keynes, Wilts Bosly, John & Mary 7 yrs feltmaker 2s 6d
		27 Aug	Rives, Henry son of Thomas, yeoman, of Newland Gwillim, John & Anne 7 yrs feltmaker 5s
3/94		12 Sep	Hale, John son of Thomas, feltmaker, of Gloucester Beard, John & Eleanor 7 yrs silkweaver 2s 6d [*Holliday*]
		29 Sep	Bennett, Robert son of Edward, feltmaker, of Gloucester Stephens, Thomas & Frances 7 yrs pinmaker 2s 6d
			Stephens, John son of William, currier, of Gloucester Stephens, Thomas & Garnet 7 yrs tailor 5s
			Jenkins, Richard son of Richard, carpenter, of Ross, Herefs Woodward, William 8 yrs physician & surgeon 10s
3/95			Featherston, George son of Richard, farmer, of Welsh Newton, Herefs Nash, Jesse & Elizabeth 7 yrs feltmaker 3s 6d
			Hall, John son of John, wiredrawer, of Gloucester Hughes, Daniel & Elizabeth 7 yrs currier 2s 6d
		25 Jul	Browne, Joseph son of Joseph, merchant, of Gloucester Fowler, William & Mary 7 yrs barber surgeon 2s 6d [*Holliday*]
		24 Jun	Pembrug, Samuel son of Thomas, clerk, of Corse Parker, Margaret, widow, 7 yrs baker 2s 6d
3/96		29 Sep	Edwards, Thomas son of John, gentleman, of Badgeworth Haines, Peter jr & Elizabeth 7 yrs grocer 5s

---

¹ GBR B3/3 p 562 18 Jul 1673: To have £4 of Mrs Browne's money: Nicholas Green, [*blank*] Cook, [*blank*] Hall, [*name deleted*].

² ibid p 564 22 Jul 1673: To have £5 of Mr Holliday's money: William Barett's son, Joseph Browne's son, Thomas Hale's son, Thomas Summer's son, John Wintle, Abraham Yonge.

3/99			**William Cooke, mayor [1673–4]** **Richard Stephens and Nicholas Phelpes, bailiffs and sheriffs**

3/99   **William Cooke, mayor [1673–4]**
            Richard Stephens and Nicholas Phelpes, bailiffs and sheriffs

          1673   25 Dec   Travis, John son of Matthew, farmer, of Gloucester
                         Sere, James & Margaret   7 yrs   tailor   [*blank*]

3/100   7 Oct   Burridge, Thomas son of John, hosier, of Pershore, Worcs
                        Lumbert, Isaac & [*blank*]   7 yrs   serge weaver   2s 6d

                  1 Nov   Rathbone, Richard son of Richard, gunsmith, of Worcester
                        Brimiard, William & Elizabeth   7 yrs   tobacco-pipe maker   2s 6d

                10 Jun   Salcombe, Samuel son of Samuel, yeoman, of Churcham
                        Jeffes, William & Mary   7 yrs   ropemaker   2s 6d

                  1 Nov   Blanch, William son of Thomas, farmer, of Frampton on Severn
                        Horrell, John jr & Anne   7 yrs   tailor   5s

3/101   3 Dec   Hall, Thomas son of John, wiredrawer, of Gloucester
                        Hughes, Daniel & Elizabeth   7 yrs   currier   2s 6d

                31 Dec   Moore, John son of John, currier, of Cheltenham
                        Sparrowhawk, Richard & Eleanor   7 yrs from 1 Jan   silkweaver   2s 6d

          1674   1 Jan   Wintle, John son of John, currier, of Gloucester
                        Bell, Joan, widow,   7 yrs   silkweaver   2s 6d   [*Holliday*]

                15 Jan   Cor, Richard son of Richard, surgeon, of Down Ampney
                        Cor, Robert & Margaret   7 yrs   surgeon   10s

3/102   Freeman, Ferebe son of Anthony, gentleman, of Badgeworth
                        Hyett, John & [*blank*]   7 yrs   merchant   5s

                  2 Feb   Price, John son of John, gentleman, of Gloucester
                        Woodward, Elizabeth widow of John   7 yrs   brewer   20s

          1673   26 Dec   Mathewes, James son of John, innholder, of Gloucester
                        Selwyn, Thomas & [*blank*]   7 yrs   currier   6s

                22 Dec   Parker, John son of James, baker, of Gloucester
                        Sare, James & Margaret   7 yrs   tailor   2s 6d [1]

3/103   1674   25 Mar   Workeman, Charles son of Morgan, butcher, of Mitcheldean
                        Pace, Francis & Phyllida   7 yrs   baker   2s 6d

                17 Mar   Saunders, John son of William, farmer, dec'd, of Rodley, Westbury
                        Hornedge, John & Sarah   7 yrs from 25 Mar   button maker   2s 6d

                23 Mar   Garner, John son of John, yeoman, of Painswick
                        Freame, John & Elizabeth   7 yrs   baker   5s

          1673   25 Dec   Farley, George son of Thomas, cutler, of Gloucester
                        Farley, Thomas, his father,   7 yrs   cutler   10s

---

[1] GBR B3/3 p 574 5 Sep 1673: To be removed from Sir Thomas Rich's Hospital and given £10 to bind them apprentice: Samuel Hircombe, Litle Wintle, William Wood, John Parker, Thomas Kemplea, John Simonds.
    ibid p 587 3 Nov 1673: Little Wintle, son of John, to be apprenticed to John Swift of Worcester.

3/104	1674 23 Apr	Barrett, John son of William, cutler, late of Gloucester Brooke, John & Mary 7 yrs glover & fellmonger 2s 6d [*Holliday*]
	25 Mar	Mayo, John son of John, yeoman, of Pendock, Worcs Goodcheape, Thomas & M[ary] 7 yrs currier 2s 6d
	2 Feb	Simons, John son of William, butcher, of Gloucester Meeke, Thomas [sr] & Margery 7 yrs currier 7s [1]
	1 May	Tayler, John son of [*blank*], carpenter, of Badgeworth Rogers, John & Margaret 7 yrs baker 2s 6d
3/105		Roberts, Joseph son of Joseph, wool comber, of Gloucester Cugley, James & Anne 7 yrs cardmaker 2s 6d
	6 May	Baker, Charles son of Edmund, gardener, of Barton Street [Gloucester] Beard, John & Eleanor 7 yrs silkweaver 2s 6d
	1 May	Hathway, Henry son of Richard, [*blank*], of Prestbury Deane, Thomas & Katharine 7 yrs blacksmith 2s
	12 May	Bishop, Daniel son of Daniel, [*blank*], of Gloucester Madocke, William & Sarah 7 yrs tailor 2s 6d [*Mrs Browne*][2]
3/106	23 May	Hill, Thomas son of Richard, yeoman, of Taynton Nash, Richard & Anne 7 yrs feltmaker 2s 6d
	1 Jun	Bradstocke, Thomas son of Ric, yeoman, dec'd, of Pendock, Worcs Smart, Richard & Margaret 7 yrs currier 2s 6d
	24 Jun	Tayler, Thomas son of Thomas, gentleman, of Gloucester Hickes, Edward & Grace 7 yrs tobacco-pipe maker 2s 6d
	29 Jun	Wooles, John son of Thomas, currier, of Westbury Horrell, John & Anne 7 yrs tailor 2s 6d
3/107	24 Jun	Morse, John son of Walter, rugmaker, of Rodborough Ady, Thomas & [*blank*] 7 yrs baker 2s
	14 Jul	Harris, Joseph son of Thomas, yeoman, of Whaddon Broade, Mary, widow, 7 yrs baker 10s
	16 Jul	Beard, John son of Thomas, clothworker, of Stroud Beard, John & Eleanor 7 yrs silkweaver 2s 6d
	1 Jul	Kersey, Thomas son of Richard, husbandman, of Kingsholm Gardner, Thomas & Anne 7 yrs pinmaker 5s
3/108	14 Aug	Rigges, Nathaniel son of Francis, labourer, of Gloucester Cudd, John & Elizabeth 7 yrs silkweaver 5s
		Berry, Zachariah son of Zachariah, brushmaker, of Gloucester Turbett, Thomas & [*blank*] 8 yrs tanner 5s

[1] GBR B3/3 p 603 8 Mar 1674: John Simons given £10 of Sir Thomas Rich's bequest.
[2] ibid p 605 16 Apr 1674: To receive £4 of Mrs Browne's money: John Neast, Daniel Bishop, John Harris.

        1674 1 Sep Shipton, Daniel son of John sr, bodicemaker, of Gloucester
                          Shipton, John & [blank] 7 yrs barber surgeon 2s 6d

              7 Sep Thomas, Abraham son of John, feltmaker, of Gloucester
                          Wood, John & Margaret 7 yrs button maker 2s 6d

3/109   12 Sep Lovell, Edward son of John, silkweaver, of Gloucester
                          Randle, Giles & Joan 7 yrs silkweaver 5s

            18 Sep Foords, James son of Richard, miller, of Leonard Stanley
                        Gwin, Augustine sr & [blank] 7 yrs currier 2s 6d

              8 Sep Mathewes, Richard son of William, apothecary, of Gloucester
                        Mathews, William, his father, & Mary 7 yrs apothecary 5s

            17 Sep Norman, Edward son of Edward, butcher, of Gloucester
                        Norman, Edward, his father, & Joan 8 yrs butcher 10s [*Holliday*][1]

3/110   Neast, John son of John, carpenter, of Gloucester
                        Holliday, Henry & Elizabeth 7 yrs carpenter 5s [*Mrs Browne*]

            29 Sep Jobbins, James son of Thomas, tiler, of Gloucester
                        Hayward, John & Mary 7 yrs feltmaker 1s [*cf Appendix V*]

            10 Apr Cornish, John son of Thomas, [blank], dec'd, of Gloucester
                        Aram, Thomas & [blank] 7 yrs glassmaker [blank]

            25 Jul Vaughan, Joshua son of Thomas, joiner, of Gloucester
                        Vaughan, Thomas, his father, & Margaret 7 yrs joiner £5 [*Holliday*]

3/115   **Duncombe Colchester, mayor [1674–5]**
             John Campion & Walter Vaisey, bailiffs and sheriffs

        1674 5 Oct Poole, John son of John, brewer, dec'd, of Gloucester
                        Dawe, William & [blank] 7 yrs tiler & plasterer 2s 6d

              8 Oct Oliffe, Richard son of Richard, farmer, of Gloucester
                        Wooding, William & Susannah 7 yrs button maker 2s 6d

                    Hall, Henry son of John, farmer, of Standish and Oxlinch
                        Ricketts, James & Anne 7 yrs tanner 2s 6d

            16 Oct Harris, James son of William, yeoman, of Newland
                        Powell, William & Alice 9 yrs pinmaker 2s 6d

3/116   27 Oct Woodward, Richard son of Richard, pinmaker, of Gloucester
                        Woodward, Richard, his father, & Mary 7 yrs from 1 Nov pinmaker 5s
                        [*Holliday*]

            17 Nov Allen, John son of John, yeoman, dec'd, of Flaxley
                        Willmott, Robert & Sarah 9 yrs from 25 Dec glassmaker 5s

            23 Nov Randle, Thomas son of Simon, yeoman, dec'd, of Cowley
                        Wadman, Roger & Elizabeth 7 yrs weaver 2s 6d

---

[1] GBR B3/3 p 613 29 Jul 1674: To receive £5 of Mr Hollidaye's money: Thomas Vaughan, Jonah Bidle, William Stephens, Edward Norman, Richard Woodward, Ben Croker.

	1674 24 Nov	Sowdley, John son of John, jersey comber, of Gloucester Soudley, John, his father, & Eleanor 7 yrs jersey comber 20s
	25 Dec	Smith, William son of Giles, yeoman, of Gloucester Flucke, Thomas & Elizabeth 8 yrs tanner 5s
3/117	1 Dec	Sowle, William son of William Soule, farmer, of Woolstrop Jennings, John & Jane 7 yrs barber surgeon 2s 6d
	14 Dec	Soule, Thomas son of William, farmer, of Woolstrop Soule, John 7 yrs vintner 10s
		Croker, Benjamin son of Thomas, joiner, of Gloucester Croker, Thomas, his father, & Eleanor 7 yrs joiner £5 [*Holliday*]
	28 Dec	Butt, John son of Edmund, yeoman, of Norton Price, Brian & Anne 7 yrs pinmaker 5s
3/118	26 Dec	Ingley, Thomas son of Thomas, wool comber, of Gloucester Wilmott, Robert & Sarah 9 yrs glassmaker [*blank*]
	1675 2 Jan	Heaven, Henry son of Robert, clothier, dec'd, of Stroud Heaven, John & [*blank*] 7 yrs from 29 Sep last silkweaver 2s 6d
	1 Jan	George, John son of William, feltmaker, dec'd, of Gloucester George, Hester widow of William 7 yrs feltmaker 5s [*Holliday*]
	13 Jan	Tomkins, William son of [*blank*], labourer, of Newent Davis, John & Christian 7 yrs pinmaker 2s 6d
3/119		Morse, Thomas son of Thomas, cordwainer, of Gloucester Davis, John & Christian 7 yrs pinmaker 2s 6d
	1674 24 Dec	Hannis, Samuel son of Samuel, gentleman, of city of London Sparkes, Thomas & Sarah 7 yrs silkweaver 2s 6d
	1675 2 Feb	Bidawell, John son of John, glover, of Gloucester Stowell, William & [*blank*] 7 yrs silkweaver 2s 6d
		Reeve, Francis son of Francis, stone carver, of Gloucester Reeve, Francis, his father, & Hannah 7 yrs stone carver 10s
3/120		Reakes, George son of George, farmer, of Redmarley, Worcs Wilse, Giles & Anne 7 yrs baker 2s 6d
	27 Feb	Ricketts, John son of William, labourer, of Newent Cowcher, Thomas & Mary 7 yrs pinmaker 5s
	2 Feb	Charleton, Edward son of Edward, wiredrawer, of Gloucester Charleton, Edward, his father, & Sarah 7 yrs wiredrawer 10s
	25 Jul	Stephens, Thomas son of William, cordwainer, of Gloucester Springe, Francis & Elizabeth 7 yrs cordwainer 5s [*Holliday*]
3/121	2 Feb	Tandy, John son of Michael, victualler, of Gloucester Gardner, John & Mary 7 yrs cordwainer 5s

	1675		
		16 Feb	Elliotts, John son of John, victualler, of Gloucester Greene, John jr & Honour 7 yrs cooper 5s[1]
		1 Mar	Watts, John son of William, [*blank*], of Gloucester Watts, William, his father, & Sarah 7 yrs [*blank*] 10s
		26 Mar	Walker, Anthony son of Anthony, gardener, of Gloucester Cooke, Richard & Margaret 7 yrs blacksmith 2s 6d [*Holliday*]
3/122		6 Apr	Tayler, William son of William, yeoman, dec'd, of Hempsted Perkes, William & Joan 7 yrs pinmaker 2s 6d
		12 Apr	Arnell, William son of William, narrow weaver, of Tirley Wadman, Roger & Elizabeth 7 yrs silkweaver 5s
		14 Apr	Waite, William son of William, carpenter, of Charlton Kings Cheeseman, Robert & Sarah 9 yrs from 3 May cooper 5s
		27 Apr	Wellavise, William son of Thomas, farmer, of Leigh [MS Lye], Ashton Keynes, Wilts Nash, Richard & Anne 7 yrs feltmaker 5s
3/128		10 May	Colericke, Adam son of Daniel, bodicemaker, of Gloucester Caudle, Richard & Barbara 7 yrs barber & periwig maker [*blank*] [*Cancelled: see 3/142 for similar entry, also cancelled*]
3/129		25 Mar	Nourse, John son of John, cooper, of Hempsted Nourse, John sr & [*blank*] 7 yrs cooper 10s
		28 Apr	Bidle, George son of Jonah, shoe mender, of Gloucester Simons, Richard sr & Joan 7 yrs glover 2s 6d [*Holliday*]
		26 Mar	Hide, Joseph son of Joseph, cutler, of Sheffield, [Yorks] Till, Richard & Mary 9 yrs cutler 10s
		13 May	Clarke, Richard son of Nicholas, ostler, of Gloucester King, William & Elizabeth 7 yrs pinmaker 5s
3/130			Bradford, William son of Robert, husbandman, of Maisemore Winniett, Thomas & Elizabeth 9 yrs pinmaker 10s [*cf Appendix V*]
		1 Jun	Blizard, John son of Thomas, yeoman, of Guiting Power Perkes, John & Alice 7 yrs baker 5s
		26 Mar	Ebsworth, John son of Richard, yeoman, of Shipton Solers Parker, Thomas & Margaret 7 yrs [baker] 5s
		26 May	Williams, John son of Griffith, glover, of Wrexham, Denbigh Simons, Richard sr & Joan 7 yrs glover 2s 6d
3/131			Elton, Samuel son of Richard, tailor, of Newent Cowcher, Thomas & Mary 8 yrs pinmaker 5s
			Coale, Henry son of Thomas, tanner, of Newent Cowcher, Thomas & Mary 9 yrs pinmaker 5s

---

[1] GBR B3/3 p 615 16 Sep 1674: To receive £10 of Sir Thomas Rich's money: John Wintle, John Elliotts, Richard Pigg, Thomas Goodcheape, Richard Wintle, John Martin.

	1675 29 May	Mathewes, Thomas son of William, apothecary, of Gloucester Mathewes, William, his father, & Mary 7 yrs apothecary 20s
	8 Jun	Turner, Ralph son of Samuel, farmer, of Badgeworth Heath, Samuel & Mary 8 yrs silkweaver 5s
3/132	14 Jun	Dewe, Robert son of John, gentleman, dec'd, of Walford, Herefs Harward, Robert & Anne 7 yrs from 1 Jun chandler 2s 6d
	10 May	Edwards, William son of John, gentleman, of Badgeworth Aram, Arnold & Elizabeth 7 yrs haberdasher of hats 5s
	26 Mar	Howell, Joseph son of William, blacksmith, of Coleford Wasfield, John & Elizabeth 7 yrs blacksmith 5s
	24 Jun	Bradford, William son of Robert, farmer, of Maisemore Brimyard, William & Elizabeth 10 yrs tobacco-pipe maker 5s [cf Appendix V]
3/133		Plumer, Daniel son of John, clothier, of Pitchcombe Heaven, John & [blank] 7 yrs silkweaver 2s 6d
		Weale, Thomas son of Thomas, gentleman, of Longhope Tainton, Toby 7 yrs grocer 5s
	17 Jul	Jones, George son of Thomas, yeoman, dec'd, of Painswick Abbotts, Henry & Sarah 7 yrs baker 5s
	28 Jul	Beard, Thomas son of Thomas, clothmaker, of Stroud Beard, John & Eleanor 8 yrs silkweaver 2s 6d
3/134	25 Jul	Blanch, Seth son of Daniel, carpenter, dec'd, of Gloucester Croker, Thomas & Eleanor 7 yrs joiner 2s 6d [Mrs Browne][1] *Thomas Croker is disfranchised by act of common council*
	31 Jul	Davis, Robert son of Robert, yeoman, dec'd, of Painswick Mairis, Charles & Elizabeth 7 yrs from 1 Aug brazier 5s
		Evans, Charles son of James, yeoman, of Gloucester Greene, John jr & Honour 7 yrs from 1 Aug cooper 5s
	24 Jun	Goddard, Anthony son of Anthony, vintner, of Dursley Price, James & Alice 7 yrs pewterer 5s
3/135	13 Aug	Bleeke, Edward son of Richard, yeoman, of Cheltenham Allen, Lawrence & Anne 7 yrs chandler 5s
	16 Aug	Webb, John son of Richard, wool comber, of Gloucester Horrell, John & Anne 7 yrs tailor 5s
	29 Sep	Williams, Charles son of Nicholas, joiner, dec'd, of Gloucester Willey, Roger & Isabelle 7 yrs tailor 5s

---

[1] GBR B3/3 p 631 4 May 1675: To receive £4 of Mrs Browne's money: Thomas son of Nicholas Clarke, Seth son of Daniel Blanch, Abraham son of John Thomas.

	1675	1 Oct	Clifford, James son of James, pinmaker, of Gloucester Clifford, James, his father, & [blank] 7 yrs pinmaker 10s [Holliday][1]
3/140			**William Selwyn, mayor [1675–6]** **William Corsley and Nicholas Lane, bailiffs & sheriffs**
	1675	6 Oct	Cooke, Charles son of Thomas, butcher, of Gloucester Cooke, Thomas, his father, & [blank] 7 yrs butcher 5s
		1 Nov	Eliote, Samuel son of John, wiredrawer, of Gloucester Eliote, John, his father, & [blank] 7 yrs wiredrawer 5s [Holliday]
		14 Oct	Jennings, Michael son of Henry jr, yeoman, of Hempsted Cooke, Thomas jr & Anne 7 yrs from 29 Sep butcher 5s
			Bennett, Charles son of Thomas, farmer, of Alston Wilkins, John & Mary 7 yrs from 29 Sep wiredrawer 5s
3/141		30 Nov	Eliote, Robert son of Edward, innkeeper, of Gloucester Hayward, Samuel & Deborah 7 yrs from 1 May next grocer 5s
		1 Nov	Hopcutt, William son of John, farmer, of Forthampton Heath, Samuel & Mary 8 yrs silkweaver 5s
			Sweate, Thomas son of Richard, glazier, late of Gloucester Clark, Henry & Mary 8 yrs glazier 2s 6d [Mrs Browne]
		21 Dec	Smyth, Thomas son of Thomas, clerk, of Huntley Childe, Thomas & Elizabeth 7 yrs currier 5s
3/142			Griffin, Lawrence son of David, tailor, of Gloucester Griffin, David, his father, & Hester 7 yrs tailor 10s
	1676	8 Feb	Merrett, Daniel son of Richard, farmer, of Standish Perry, Daniel & [blank] 7 yrs cordwainer 2s 6d
		1 Feb	Baker, James son of John, butcher, dec'd, of Gloucester Moore, George & Mary 7 yrs butcher 5s *£10 of Sir Thomas Rich's gift given to him*[2]
		1 May	Dobbs, Francis son of John, barber surgeon, of Gloucester Dobbs, John, his father, & [blank] 7 yrs barber surgeon 5s [cf Appendix V]
		10 May	Colericke, Adam son of Daniel, bodicemaker, of Gloucester Caudle, Richard & Barbara 7 yrs periwig maker & barber surgeon [blank] [Cancelled: see 3/128 for similar entry]

[1] GBR B3/3 p 638 16 Sep 1675: To receive £5 of Mr Hollidaye's money: James son of James Clifford, Edmund son of Thomas Greene, serjeant, Anthony son of Anthony Walker, Richard son of Giles Collins, John George's son, Samuel son of John Eliote, wiredrawer.

[2] ibid p 636 16 Sep 1675: To receive £10 of Sir Thomas Rich's money: James Baker, Thomas Barrett, Benjamin Cooke, John Lewis, John Yates; ibid p 651 9 Mar 1676 James Baker proposed to be placed apprentice to George Moore, butcher, and is approved of.

3/143	1676	14 Feb	Church, Richard son of Thomas, yeoman, of Sandhurst
			Smyth, Giles & Sybil 7 yrs baker 3s 4d
		10 Apr	Powell, Robert son of Francis, husbandman, of the Margarets, [Gloucester]
			George, Hester, widow, 7 yrs feltmaker 2s 6d
			Ready, Alexander son of John, gentleman, dec'd, of Bulley
			Bicknell, William & [blank] 7 yrs tailor 2s 6d
			Lewis, John son of John, tiler, of Gloucester
			Barnelme, Richard & [blank] 7 yrs horner 5s [1]
		10 Mar	Godwyn, Richard son of Henry, farmer, of Gloucester
			Harris, Jeremiah & Mary 7 yrs tobacco man 5s [Mrs Browne] [2]
3/144		1 May	Skinner, William son of John, coalman, of Newent
			Dewxel, Thomas 8 yrs locksmith 5s
		10 May	Younge, Thomas son of [blank], yeoman, of Sandhurst
			Badger, Albert & Elizabeth 8 yrs pinmaker 5s
		1 Jun	Sparkes, Solomon son of Richard, cooper, of Gloucester
			Colericke, Daniel & [blank] 7 yrs bodicemaker 2s 6d
		5 Jun	Onyon, Joseph son of Thomas, silkweaver, of Gloucester
			Onyon, Thomas, his father, & Bridget 7 yrs silkweaver 5s
			Pitt, Joseph son of Joseph, cordwainer, of Newent
			Phelpes, Joseph & Sarah 7 yrs [blank] 2s 6d
3/145		25 Mar	Knott, Lawrence son of Lawrence, carpenter, of Gloucester
			Knott, Lawrence, his father, & Elizabeth 7 yrs carpenter 5s
		7 Jun	Checketts, Richard son of Richard, yeoman, of Stow on the Wold
			Ebbs, Philip & Hester 7 yrs saddler 5s
		1 May	Nash, Richard son of Seabright, gentleman, of Bridgnorth, Salop
			Singleton, Francis & Sarah 7 yrs ironmonger 10s
		24 Jun	Randalph, Reignold son of Reignold, ironmonger, of Ledbury, Herefs
			Wastfeild, John & Elizabeth 7 yrs blacksmith 5s
3/146		10 Jul	Griffith, Simeon son of Henry, miner, of Coleford
			Gwillim, John & Anne 8 yrs feltmaker 5s
		8 Aug	Horsington, Henry son of Thomas, bodicemaker, of Gloucester
			[blank] & his wife 7 yrs [blank] 5s [Holliday] [3]
			[One line of the entry has been left blank]
		[blank]	Tyler, John jr son of John sr, currier, of Gloucester
			Palmer, Hester, widow, 7 yrs baker [blank]

---

[1] GBR B3/3 p 652 5 Apr 1676: John son of John Lewis, Bluecoat boy, to be placed apprentice to Richard Barnelme, horner, he giving security as usually.

[2] ibid p 652 5 Apr 1676: To receive £4 of Mrs Browne's money: Samuel Wood, Thomas Swett, Henry Goodwin.

[3] ibid p 657 21 Jul 1676: To receive £5 of Mr Hollidaye's money: Jesse Painter, John Elliottes, Thomas Horsington, James Childe, Arthur Woolforde, John Hardinge.

	1676 29 Aug	Gibbs, John son of John, yeoman, of Minsterworth Vaughan, Thomas & Margaret 7 yrs joiner, carver & turner 5s
3/147	4 Sep	Pyrton, Philip son of John, yeoman, of Minsterworth Cox, Winston sr & [*blank*] 7 yrs cordwainer 1s
	10 Jul	Parry, Francis son of Francis, miner, of Coleford Nash, Jesse & Elizabeth 8 yrs feltmaker 5s
	24 Jun	Wooles, Richard son of Richard, carpenter, of Standish Reeve, William & Katharine 7 yrs butcher 2s 6d
	16 Sep	Dowe, James son of James, farmer, of Barnwood Cheeseman, Robert & Sarah 8 yrs cooper 2s 6d
3/148	29 Sep	Nott, Nathan son of Lawrence, carpenter, of Gloucester Underhill, James & Frances 7 yrs silkweaver 5s
	1 Sep	Rowles, Robert son of Robert, tailor, of Minsterworth Cripps, Edward & Elizabeth 7 yrs butcher 2s 6d
	24 Jun	Childe, James son of Thomas, maltster, of Gloucester Heyward, Edward & Mary 7 yrs silkweaver 5s [*Holliday*]
	25 Jul	Wolford, Arthur son of Thomas, basket maker, of Gloucester Wolford, Thomas, his father, & Joan 7 yrs basket maker 10s [*Holliday*]
3/149	29 Sep	Greene, Edmund son of Thomas, cordwainer, of Gloucester Greene, John jr & Margaret 7 yrs cooper 5s [*Holliday*]
	1 Jan	Cowles, Josiah son of Thomas, glover, of Gloucester Cowles, Thomas, his father, & Susannah 7 yrs glover 2s 6d
3/158		**William Russell, mayor [1676–7]** **John Bishop and Richard Bosley, bailiffs and sheriffs**
	1676 16 Oct	Merry, Richard son of Richard, yeoman, of Sandhurst Sowdley, John & Eleanor 7 yrs wool comber 20s
	1 Nov	Harding, John son of John, glover, of Gloucester Gardner, Thomas & Anne 7 yrs pinmaker 5s [*Holliday*]
	29 Nov	Brooke, Joseph son of John, yeoman, of Aston Ingham, Herefs Heyward, Edward & Mary 7 yrs silkweaver 3s
		Turner, William son of John, yeoman, of Longhope Heyward, Edward & Mary 7 yrs silkweaver 2s 6d
	6 Oct	Wilkins, Thomas son of Nicholas, yeoman, of Hurst Farm, Slimbridge Gregory, William & Anne 7 yrs from 29 Sep butcher [*blank*]
3/159	16 Dec	Workeman, Anthony son of Anthony, victualler, of Coleford Williams, William & Hester 7 yrs butcher 2s 6d
	1677 1 Jan	Eliote, Edward son of John, victualler, of Gloucester Smarte, Anthony & Anne 7 yrs cordwainer 2s 6d

	1676	8 Oct	Clifford, John son of James, pinmaker, of Gloucester
			Clifford, James, his father, & Mary 7 yrs from 29 Sep pinmaker 5s
	1677	20 Jan	Ellis, Guy son of Guy, gentleman, of Cheltenham
			Longden, Thomas & Anne 7 yrs ironmonger 5s
3/160		31 Jan	Collins, Charles son of Giles, yeoman, dec'd, of Hartpury
			Swaine, Edward & Jane 8 yrs collar maker [blank]
		10 Feb	Bruckbancke, Robert son of Robert, hoopmaker, dec'd, of Huntley
			Winniatt, Thomas & Elizabeth 8 yrs pinmaker 2s 6d
		1 Nov	Young, Joseph son of Richard, gentleman, of Westbury
			Hyett, John & Elizabeth 7 yrs mercer 5s
		28 Mar	Stone, William son of William, tailor, Bromsberrow, Herefs [recte Glos]
			Randle, William & Hester 7 yrs tailor 2s 6d
3/161		4 Apr	Phillips, John son of Roger, turner, of Gloucester
			Gravestocke, John & Elizabeth 7 yrs from 25 Mar butcher 2s 6d
		5 Apr	Freame, Jasper son of Daniel, yeoman, of Staverton
			Partridge, Richard & Anne 7 yrs from 25 Mar baker 5s
		7 May	Davis, Richard son of Richard, yeoman, of Charlton Kings
			Beard, John & Eleanor 7 yrs silkweaver 2s 6d
			23 Jul 83: turned over to Elizabeth Beard, silkweaver
		1 May	Selwyn, Thomas son of Thomas, cordwainer, of Gloucester
			Selwyn, Thomas, his father, & [blank] 7 yrs cordwainer 10s [1]
3/162		10 May	Gravestocke, John son of George, yeoman, of Hempsted
			Wilse, Giles & Anne 7 yrs baker 5s
		1 Jun	Meeke, Edward son of William, cordwainer, of Mitcheldean
			Gardiner, Daniel & Rebecca 7 yrs pinmaker 5s
		10 Jan	Bishop, John son of John, mercer, of Gloucester
			Bishop, John, his father, & Hester 7 yrs mercer 20s
		18 Jun	Puckson, Thomas son of Richard, carrier, of Gloucester
			Sumers, Thomas & Eleanor 7 yrs silkweaver 2s 6d
3/163		10 Aug	Nourse, George son of John jr, yeoman, of Hempsted
			Nourse, John & [blank] 7 yrs from 24 Jun cooper 10s
		17 Aug	Cordell, Alexander son of James, glover, of Gloucester
			Cordell, James, his father, & Anne 7 yrs glover 2s 6d [Holliday][2]
		21 Aug	Yates, John son of John, cordwainer, of Gloucester
			Browne, James & Elizabeth 7 yrs pewterer [blank][3]

---

[1] GBR B3/3 p 660 11 Aug 1676: To receive £10 of Sir Thomas Rich's money: Cornelius Barrett, Richard Holliday, Emmanuel Powell, Richard Mason, Thomas Selwyn, James Sare.

[2] ibid p 681 14 Aug 1677: To receive £5 of Mr Hollidaye's money: John Wells, James Cordell's son, Curtis Powell, William Symmons's son, John Hayward's son, Abel Lewis.

[3] ibid p 680 14 Aug 1677: John Yates, Bluecoat boy, to be apprenticed to James Browne, pewterer.

	1677	29 Sep	Church, Thomas son of John, wiredrawer, of Gloucester Pitt, James & [blank] 7 yrs pinmaker 2s 6d
3/164		24 Jun	Thorpe, Richard son of John, doctor of medicine, of Berkeley Burroughs, Samuel & Mary 7 yrs mercer 2s 6d
	1676	18 Nov	Turner, Henry son of John, labourer, of Longhope Heyward, Edward 7 yrs silkweaver *23 Jul [1683]: turned over to Elizabeth Beard [cf 3/161]*

3/172
Thomas Price, mayor [1677–8]
John Marston and Samuel Rose, bailiffs and sheriffs

	1677	6 Oct	Smarte, William son of John, joiner, of Gloucester Smarte, John, his father, & Mary 7 yrs from 29 Sep joiner 10s
		20 Oct	Wood, William son of William, yeoman, of Barnwood Wood, James & Hannah 7 yrs baker 5s
		15 Oct	Parker, Timothy son of Anthony, farmer, of Bishop's Cleeve Dudley, April & Elizabeth 7 yrs butcher [blank]
		24 Oct	Miles, James son of James, baker, of Gloucester Niccolls, William & Joan 7 yrs tanner 5s
3/173		27 Oct	Smarte, Richard son of Thomas, clothier, of Tibberton George, Hester, widow of William 7 yrs feltmaker 5s
		1 Nov	Grenden, John son of Thomas, gentleman, of Upleadon Bosly, John & Mary 7 yrs feltmaker 10s
			Rowles, Timothy son of Timothy sr, silkweaver, of Gloucester Wolford, Thomas & Joan 7 yrs basket maker 5s
	1678	1 Jan	Hill, Richard son of Thomas, shoe mender, of Gloucester Badger, Albert & Elizabeth 7 yrs pinmaker 3s 4d
3/174		7 Jan	Badcocke, Henry son of Henry, farmer, of Longhope Smith, William & Susannah 8 yrs glover 3s 4d
			Badcocke, James son of Henry, [farmer, of Longhope] Hill, Walter & Elizabeth 8 yrs shoe mender 2s 6d
	1677	21 Dec	Cooke, Anthony son of Benjamin, tailor, dec'd, of Gloucester Cooke, Sarah widow of Benjamin 7 yrs [tailor] 5s
			Sere, James son of James, tailor, of Gloucester Sere, James, his father, & Margaret 7 yrs tailor 10s[1]
3/175	1678	31 Jan	Neast, Daniel son of John, carpenter, of Gloucester Collier, William & Mary 7 yrs gunsmith 5s
		4 Apr	Butterton, John son of John, pinmaker, of Gloucester Pitt, James 7 yrs pinmaker 2s 6d

---

[1] GBR B3/3 p 697 21 Jun 1678: James Seyer to be bound to James his father, tailor, Samuel Cuffe to Thomas Goodcheape, cordwainer, Clement Heyward to David Griffin, tailor, with £10 of Sir Thomas Rich's money.

	1678 24 Jun	Roper, Thomas son of Thomas, yeoman, of Cleeve
		Heard, Humphrey & Dorothy 7 yrs butcher 2s 6d
	1 Mar¹	Clarke, William son of William, yeoman, dec'd, of Upleadon
		Lugg, Lawrence & Elizabeth 7 yrs baker 5s
3/176	1 May	Bayton, John son of Samuel, plasterer, of Gloucester
		Stephenson *alias* Cowles, John & Anne 7 yrs bodicemaker 5s
	29 May	Potter, John son of John, yeoman, of Gloucester
		Heyward, John & Mary 7 yrs feltmaker 2s 6d
	3 Jun	Watson, John son of John, gentleman, of Evesham, Worcs
		Medway, Henry & Sarah 7 yrs silkweaver 2s 6d
	24 Jun	Overthrowe, William son of William, carpenter, of Minsterworth
		Badger, Albert & Elizabeth 7 yrs pinmaker 2s 6d
3/177		Ham, William son of William, butcher [dec'd], of Gloucester
		Ham, Martha widow of William 7 yrs [butcher] 10s
		Sumers, Nathaniel son of Thomas, of Gloucester
		Sumers, Thomas, his father, & Eleanor 7 yrs silkweaver 2s 6d
	20 May	Preene, William son of John, gardener, of Stroud
		Vaisey, Walter & Margaret 7 yrs tailor 5s
	2 Oct	Webley, William son of Giles, feltmaker, of Gloucester
		Gardner, Daniel & Rebecca 7 yrs from 29 Sep pinmaker 2s 6d
3/178	24 Aug	Jacksons, Robert son of Robert, jersey spinner, of Gloucester
		Pitt, James & [blank] 7 yrs pinmaker 2s 6d
	1 Oct	Fox, Thomas son of William, stone cutter, of Gloucester
		Brymyard, William & Elizabeth 9 yrs tobacco-pipe maker 5s
	3 Oct	Davis, Thomas son of Richard, farmer, of Charlton Kings
		Beard, Eleanor, widow, 7 yrs from 29 Sep silkweaver 2s 6d
		[*Repeated at 3/184 in correct mayoral year*]
	1 Jan	Yeedinge, Thomas son of John, pinmaker, of Gloucester
		Yeedinge, John, his father, & Mary 7 yrs pinmaker 10s [*Holliday*]²
3/179	20 Dec	Porter, John son of Robert, mercer, of Gloucester
		Porter, Robert, his father, 9 yrs mercer 20s
	20 May	Cuffe, Samuel son of Thomas, merchant, dec'd, of Gloucester
		Goodcheape, Thomas & Mary 7 yrs cordwainer 2s 6d³
	26 Mar	Bevan, John son of Richard, gentleman, formerly of Frocester
		Humphris, Joseph & Mary, 7 yrs grocer
		10 Sep 1683: turned over to Samuel Hayward

¹ GBR B3/3 p 694 26 Mar 1678: To receive £4 of Mrs Browne's money: James Wintle, — Holtam, John Thomas.

² ibid p 701 1 Aug 1678: To receive £5 of Mr Hollidaye's money: Walter Miles, William Phelpes, — Borrow, — Saunders, — Beard, John Yeeding.

³ ibid p 682 24 Sep 1677: To receive £10 of Sir Thomas Rich's money: Clement Hayward, Samuel Cuffe, Charles Jones, Thomas Ryland, Richard Deane.

3/184			**John Wagstaffe, mayor [1678–9]** **Benjamin Hyett and Thomas Mills, bailiffs and sheriffs**
	1678	3 Oct	Davis, Thomas son of Richard, farmer, of Charlton Kings Beard, Eleanor, widow, 7 yrs silkweaver 2s 6d [*Repeating entry at 3/178*] *23 Jul 1683: turned over to Elizabeth Beard, widow*
3/187	1679	13 Mar	Wheeler, Samuel son of Thomas, carpenter, of Gloucester Smith, Peter & Margaret 8 yrs carpenter 2s 6d
3/188	1678	10 Oct	Lewis, Walter son of Adam, currier, of Monmouth Vosse, Matthew & Elizabeth 7 yrs victualler 10s
		10 Nov	Heyward, Clement son of John, feltmaker, of Gloucester Griffith, David & Hester 7 yrs tailor 5s [*Holliday*]
		29 Nov	Massinger, William son of William, gentleman, dec'd, of Gloucester Rodway, John & his wife 7 yrs mercer 5s
		2 Dec	Jobbins, James son of Thomas, tiler, of Gloucester Nash, Jesse & Elizabeth 7 yrs feltmaker 5s [*cf Appendix V*]
3/189		27 Dec	Braban, Francis son of Francis, cooper, of Gloucester Braban, Francis, his father, & Hester 8 yrs cooper 5s
	1679	12 Feb	Tailer, George son of George, gentleman, dec'd, of Gloucester Goslinge, Thomas & Elizabeth 7 yrs haberdasher of hats 2s 6d
		14 Feb	Andrewes, William son of Anthony, cleric, of Haresfield Barnes, William & Joan 7 yrs saddler 2s 6d
		2 Apr	Morgan, James jr son of James sr, yeoman, of Much Marcle, Herefs Nash, Jesse & Elizabeth 8 yrs feltmaker 5s
3/190		31 May	Eckly, Lawrence son of John, button maker, dec'd, of Gloucester Trowe, John & Margaret 7 yrs pinmaker 2s 6d
		11 Jun	Watts, Richard son of Thomas, yeoman, of Minsterworth Brian, Daniel & Anne 7 yrs cordwainer 7s 6d
		29 Jun	Hooper, Thomas son of Thomas, feltmaker, of Tewkesbury George, Hester, widow, 7 yrs feltmaker 2s 6d
		5 Jun	Harris, John son of John, butcher, of Newnham Whittingham, Edward, of Westbury, & Elizabeth 7 yrs [*no trade*] 1s
3/191		24 Jun	Ireland, William son of Richard, victualler, of Gloucester Parker, Margaret 7 yrs baker 5s
		21 Sep	Wiggett, Samuel son of William, maltster, of Tewkesbury Martin, Thomas & Catherine 7 yr glover 2s 6d
		31 Aug	Baker, William son of James, gardener, of Gloucester Probert, Thomas 7 yrs tailor 2s 6d

3/192	1679	29 Sep	Pritchard, Joseph son of Thomas, maltster, dec'd, of Gloucester Lea, Robert 7 yrs tobacco-pipe maker 1s
			Hall, John son of John, dec'd, of Gloucester King, William 7 yrs pinmaker 2s 6d
		24 Aug	Carpenter, Richard son of Robert, gentleman, dec'd, of Maisemore James, Leigh sr 7 yrs baker 5s
3/193		29 Sep	Mitchell, Jeremiah son of George, garter weaver, dec'd, of Gloucester Badger, Jeremiah & Margaret 7 yrs silkweaver 5s [Holliday][1]
		22 Dec	Price, Richard son of Richard, yeoman, dec'd, of Cheltenham Dawes, William & Elizabeth 7 yrs tiler & plasterer 2s 6d
		29 Sep	Andrews, Charles son of Anthony, S.T.P.,[2] dec'd, of Haresfield Cowdall, John & Mary 8 yrs tailor 2s 6d
3/194		5 Sep	Bretherton, Jeremiah son of Jeremiah, cordwainer, of Gloucester Atkins, Walter & Mary 7 yrs [no trade] 5s
		17 Nov	Dancocks, William son of Thomas Clifford, James & Mary 7 yrs pinmaker 1s
		26 Dec	Higgins, John son of John Higgins, John, his father, & Nanfan 7 yrs [currier] 5s
3/195	1680	7 Jan	Bosley, John son of John, of Sandhurst Bennett, John & Penelope [no term] barber surgeon 5s
		1 Mar	Butter, Edward son of Charles, of Churcham Horrall, John & Anne 7 yrs tailor 5s
	1679	25 Mar	Bedwell, Charles son of John Stowell, William & Mary 7 yrs pinmaker 2s 6d *Turned over to John Core*
3/196	1680	8 Apr	Bishop, Daniel son of Daniel, tailor, of Gloucester Shipton, John & Elizabeth [no term] barber surgeon 2s 6d[3]
		1 May	Baker, Thomas son of Thomas, baker Wilkes, John 7 yrs cordwainer 2s 6d
			Stephens, Philip son of Thomas, of Lower Southgate Street, Gloucester Swaine, John 7 yrs tailor 2s 6d
	1678	10 Oct	Rogers, Herbert son of John, brewer, of Gloucester Rogers, John, his father, & Mary 7 yrs brewer *[Entry added at foot of page]*

---

[1] GBR B3/3 p 737: 30 Sep 1679: To receive £5 of Mr Hollidaye's money: Jeremiah son of George Mitchell, James son of Walter Young, William Bubb, John Hale, John Swaine, John Thomas.

[2] *Sacrae Theologiae Professor* (i.e. professor of sacred theology).

[3] GBR B3/3 p 737 30 Sep 1679: To receive £10 of Sir Thomas Rich's money: Samuel Taylor, Henry Gregory, Thomas Packer, William Merrett, Richard Wells, Daniel Bishop.

3/197	1679	25 —	Whitfeild, Jeremiah son of Anthony, of Ashton Keynes [MS Ashen Caine], Wilts
			Nash, Jesse & Elizabeth 7 yrs feltmaker 2s 6d
		same day	Wells, Richard son of John, cordwainer, of Gloucester
			Wells, John 7 yrs cordwainer 5s

3/198 **Henry Fowler, mayor [1679–80]** [1]
John Smallwood and John Rodway, bailiffs and sheriffs

1679	25 Dec	Beale, James son of Geoffrey, merchant, dec'd, of Gloucester
		Beale, Edith widow of Geoffrey 7 yrs merchant 20s
1680	12 Apr	Gwinnet, Richard son of George, gentleman, of Badgeworth
		Randle, Josiah & Margery 7 yrs baker 2s 6d
	1 May	Wilkins, William son of William, clothier, of Nailsworth in Horsley
		Selwyn, Thomas & Martha 7 yrs cordwainer 2s 6d

3/199 25 Apr Yate, Matthew son of Matthew, apothecary, dec'd, of Gloucester
Yate, Elizabeth widow of Thomas 7 yrs [apothecary] 20s

24 Jun Yate, Richard son of Richard, gentleman, dec'd, of Arlingham
Stephens, James 7 yrs tanner 10s [*entry deleted*]

19 Jul Goodin, John son of Richard, cordwainer, of Woodford
Bishop, Daniel & Eleanor 7 yrs tailor 2s 6d

24 Jun Griffiths, Edward son of John, yeoman, of Ross, Herefs
Langford, Toby 7 yrs bookseller

3/200 26 Jul Beard, Andrew son of Andrew, [*blank*] dec'd, of Gloucester
Cox, Winston sr 7 yrs cordwainer

29 Jul Birt, William son of William, tailor, of Gloucester
Browne, James & Elizabeth 7 yrs pewterer

2 Aug Bevan, William son of William, yeoman, of Gloucester
Martin, Thomas 7 yrs tailor [*Mrs Browne*][2]

3/201 29 Jun Mandbee, John son of John, haulier, of Gloucester
Whitfeild, Edward & Mary 7 yrs cordwainer

24 Jun White, Anthony son of Anthony, cordwainer, of Gloucester
White, Anthony, his father, 7 yrs cordwainer 2s 6d

29 Sep Sweat, Richard son of Richard, glazier, of Gloucester
Gwin, John & Martha 7 yrs silkweaver 5s [*Holliday*][3]

---

[1] Pages 194–7 are incorrectly headed 'John Wagstaffe, mayor': see *Freemen* p 35 n 4.

[2] GBR B3/3 p 752 6 May 1680: To receive £4 of Mrs Browne's money: William Baker, William Beaven, — Harrison.

[3] ibid p 755 16 Aug 1680: To receive £5 of Mr Hollidaye's money: [*blank*] Bishop, [*blank*] Prickett, [*blank*] Sweate, [*blank*] Lugg, [*blank*] Swaine, William Axon.

3/202	1680	21 Jun	Hinton, Nathan son of George, shoe mender, of Gloucester
			Whitfeild, Edward & Mary 7 yrs shoe mender 2s 6d [*Mrs Browne*][1]
		24 Jun	Barrow, James son of John, of Bridstow, Herefs
			Vaughan, Moses & Elizabeth of Much Marcle, Herefs 7 yrs joiner 2s 6d
			Puxon, William son of Richard, currier, of Gloucester
			Lovett, John & Mary 7 yrs silkweaver 2s 6d
3/203			Bliss, William son of Thomas, of Painswick
			Lugg, Lawrence & Elizabeth 7 yrs baker 5s
		20 Sep	Jones, Thomas son of Thomas, farmer, of Longhope
			Smith, Thomas & Jane 8 yrs glover 2s 6d
		30 Aug	Greenway, Charles son of Charles, of Gloucester
			Atkins, Walter & Mary 7 yrs cordwainer 2s 6d
3/204		17 Aug	Clutterbucke, William son of William, of Quedgeley
			Lovett, John & Mary 8 yrs silkweaver 2s 6d
		1 Aug	Randle, Ralph son of Ralph, yeoman, of Leckhampton
			Smith, Giles & Elizabeth 7 yrs baker 2s 6d

3/206 **John Gythens, mayor [1680–1]**
Isaac Williams and William Phelps, sheriffs and bailiffs

	1680	29 Sep	Birt, John son of William, tailor, of Gloucester
			Russell, William 7 yrs furrier 2s 6d
		1 Nov	Lugg, Peter son of John, vintner, of Gloucester
			Doughton, Stephen & Elizabeth 7 yrs pinmaker 2s 6d
		25 Oct	Bishop, William son of William, tailor, of Gloucester
			Jennings, Richard & Margaret 7 yrs tailor 2s 6d [*Holliday*]
3/207		28 Oct	Underhill, George son of James, silkweaver, of Gloucester
			Bell, Joan, widow, 7 yrs silkweaver 6d
		1 Nov	Monning, Thomas son of Thomas, mason, dec'd, of Gloucester
			Brymyard, William & Elizabeth 7 yrs pipe maker 2s 6d
		27 Dec	Neale, Joseph son of John, yeoman, dec'd, of Northleach
			Gwillim, John & Anne 7 yrs feltmaker 50s
			[*Cancelled*] *by agreement*
3/208		29 Nov	Plott, Henry son of Cornelius, tailor, of Gloucester
			Haynes, Peter jr 7 yrs grocer 20s
		1 Nov	Swaine, Richard son of Edward collar maker
			Swaine, Edward, his father, 7 yrs collar maker 2s 6d [*Holliday*]
		29 Sep	Ellmes, Richard son of Thomas, dec'd, of Wheatenhurst
			Bell, Joan, widow, 7 yrs silkweaver 6d

---

[1] GBR B3/3 p 723 20 Mar 1679: To receive £4 of Mrs Browne's money: William Beard, Samuel Hynton, John Williams.

	1681	12 Jan	Broben, William son of John, cordwainer, of Churcham Seyer, James 7 yrs tailor
3/209	1680	18 Oct	Cake, Samuel son of Oliver, soap boiler, of Gloucester Jones, James 7 yrs silkweaver 2s 6d
		29 Sep	Bishop, William son of Thomas, farmer, of Hempsted Goodcheape, Thomas & Mary 7 yrs cordwainer 2s 6d
	1681	19 Jan	Wilton, James son of Morgan, carpenter, of Coleford Gwiliam, John & Anne 7 yrs feltmaker 5s
3/210		1 Jun	Howard, Thomas son of Richard, gentleman, dec'd, of Gloucester Reade, Robert 7 yrs ironmonger 5s
		25 Jan	Drue, William *alias* Farmer son of John, farmer, of Upleadon Underwood, Richard & Mary 7 yrs butcher 2s 6d [*entry deleted*]
		8 Feb	Foster, William son of Robert, miller, of Bloxham, Oxon Horne, George & Anne 7 yrs cooper £5
3/211		9 Feb	Vaughan, John son of David, of Longhope Sparkes, Thomas & Sarah 7 yrs weaver 2s 6d
		20 Feb	Bidle, Jonas son of Jonas, shoe mender, formerly of Gloucester Dowsing, William & Katharine 7 yrs tailor 5s[1]
		26 Feb	Young, James son of Walter, currier, of Gloucester Young, Walter, his father, & Joan 7 yrs currier 5s
3/212			Prickett, John son of John, cordwainer, of Gloucester Prickett, John, his father, 7 yrs cordwainer 5s [*Holliday*]
		26 Mar	Bodnam, Emmanuel son of Samuel, wiredrawer, of Huntley Sparrowhawk, Richard & Eleanor 8 yrs garter weaver 2s 6d
		24 Mar	Cambray, William son of Richard, yeoman, of Haslington [Ches?] Cooke *alias* Castle, Nathaniel 7 yrs baker 2s 6d
		25 Apr	Long, Moses son of Giles, salter, of Gloucester Long, Giles, his father, & his mother 7 yrs salter 5s
3/213	1680	4 Dec	Yate, Samuel son of Francis, cordwainer, of Gloucester Allen, Anne 7 yrs grocer 5s
	1681	24 Mar	Neale, Thomas son of Arthur, innholder, of Berkeley Lugg, Samuel & Sarah 7 yrs horn breaker 2s 6d
		18 Apr	Lovett, Henry son of John, farmer, of Naunton Lovett, James, his brother, & Elizabeth 7 yrs [*silkweaver*] 5s *Not yet agreed upon by the mayor*

---

[1] GBR B3/3 p 763 27 Sep 1680: To receive £10 of Sir Thomas Rich's money: John Palmer, Thomas Ham, Amity Clutterbuck, Jeremiah Norman, Jonas Biddle, John Browne.

ibid p 764: Townsend's son to have the £5 voted for William Ackson's son and Widow Cowle's son to have the £5 voted for William Woolley's son.

	1681 25 Mar[1]	Rogers, Thomas son of William, farmer, of Badgeworth

1681 25 Mar[1] Rogers, Thomas son of William, farmer, of Badgeworth
Rogers, John & Margaret 7 yrs baker

3/214   1 Aug Rawlings, William son of William, yeoman, of Badgeworth
Greene, Margaret 7 yrs joiner 2s 6d

15 Aug Vaughan, William son of William, gentleman, of Bronllys [MS. Brunlesse], Brecon
Bennett, John & Penelope 7 yrs barber surgeon [blank]

1 Aug Roberts, Nicholas son of Thomas, clerk, of Stanway
Knowles, Henry 7 yrs brazier

3/215   20 Aug Allord, Nathaniel son of Walter, yeoman, of Gloucester
Evans, Samuel & Elizabeth 7 yrs cordwainer 2s 6d

29 Aug Harrison, Thomas son of Henry, feltmaker, of Gloucester
Nash, Richard & Anne 7 yrs feltmaker 2s 6d

Burroughs, Samuel son of Samuel, mercer, of Gloucester
Burroughs, Samuel, his father, 8 yrs mercer 2s 6d

3/216   29 Jun Cherrington, Thomas son of Thomas, farmer, of Stroud
Jones, James 7 yrs silkweaver 5s

5 Sep Idding, John son of John, pinmaker, of Gloucester
Yate, Daniel 7 yrs cordwainer 5s [Holliday][2]

25 Mar Lysons, Silvanus son of Thomas, gentleman, of Hempsted
Beard, Thomas 7 yrs mercer

3/217   **John Rogers, mayor [1681–2]**
John Hill and John Wilcocks, bailiffs and sheriffs

1681 29 Sep Green, Richard son of Thomas, yeoman, of Churcham
Cooke, Charles & Mary 7 yrs butcher

1 Nov Oakes, Francis son of Francis, trowman, of Broseley, Salop
Hayes, Henry & Joan 7 yrs cordwainer 5s

Thomas, Richard son of John, cordwainer, of Gloucester
Thomas, John, his father, & his mother 7 yrs cordwainer 2s 6d
[Holliday]

3/218   Young, Samuel son of Joseph, pinmaker, of Gloucester
Young, Joseph, his father, & his mother 7 yrs pinmaker
[Holliday]

---

[1] GBR B3/3 p 785 9 Apr 1681: To receive £4 of Mrs Browne's money: Joseph Webly, Thomas Wheeler, Richard Wilkins.

[2] ibid p 796 1 Aug 1681: To receive £5 of Mr Hollidaye's money: John son of John Idding, Abraham son of John Wood, Samuel son of Joseph Young, Richard son of John Thomas, Edward son of Thomas Owting, John son of John Lugg.

	1681	1 Oct	Owting, Edward son of Thomas, yeoman, of Gloucester Horne, George & Anne 7 yrs cooper [*Holliday*]
			Browne, Daniel son of Thomas, sievemaker, of Gloucester Browne, Thomas, his father, & Martha 7 yrs sievemaker 2s 6d
			Browne, Jonathan son of Mary, single woman, of Longhope Sparks, Thomas & Sarah 7 yrs weaver 2s 6d
3/219		31 Oct	Mason, Richard son of Edward, mason, of Oxenhall Gwilliam, John & Anne 7 yrs feltmaker 5s
		21 Nov	Yate, Josiah son of Humphrey, yeoman, of Cheltenham Yate, Daniel 7 yrs cordwainer 2s 6d [*cf Appendix V*]
			Wilcocks, William son of John, merchant, of Gloucester Wilcocks, John & Mary 7 yrs merchant 5s
3/220		4 Dec	Wood, Abraham son of John, button maker, of Gloucester Wood, John, his father 7 yrs button maker 2s 6d [*Holliday*]
		25 Oct	Newman, Samuel son of Robert, yeoman, of Forthampton Parker, Thomas & Margaret 7 yrs baker 2s 6d
		25 Dec	Turbett, John son of John, carpenter, of Gloucester Vaughan, Thomas & Joyce 7 yrs joiner
3/221			Beale, William son of Thomas, yeoman, of Stanton Jelfe, Thomas & Elizabeth 7 yrs baker 2s 6d
	1682	2 Feb	Niblett, Daniel son of Samuel, yeoman, of Haresfield Palmer, Edward & Elizabeth 7 yrs baker 2s 6d
		22 Feb	Lugg, John son of John, pewterer, of Gloucester Price, James & Alice 7 yrs pewterer [*Holliday*]
3/222		27 Feb	Prosser, William son of James, tailor, of Coleford Gwilliam, John & Anne 7 yrs feltmaker
			Davis, John son of John, pinmaker, of Gloucester Davis, John, his father, & his mother 7 yrs pinmaker
	1681	25 Dec	Weaver, Richard son of Richard, yeoman, of Gloucester Welsteed, John & Elizabeth 7 yrs blacksmith[1]
3/223	1682	2 Feb	Beard, Henry son of Henry, farmer, of Painswick Longdon, John & Susannah 7 yrs ironmonger
		20 Mar	Ackson, William son of William, cordwainer, of Gloucester Cox, Winston sr 7 yrs cordwainer[2]

---

[1] GBR B3/3 p 802 21 Dec 1681: To receive £10 of Sir Thomas Rich's money: John Barnelme, Richard Weaver, John Gregory, William Ackson, Anthony George, Henry King.

ibid p 812 11 Jan 1682: Richard Weaver, Bluecoat boy, to be apprenticed to John Welsteed, blacksmith, and to receive £10

[2] ibid p 814 20 Feb 1682: William Axton's son to have £6 of the gift of Baron Gregory to bind him apprentice.

	1682	8 Apr	Clarke, Walter son of Nicholas, labourer, of Gloucester
			Clarke, Thomas 7 yrs pinmaker [Mrs Browne][1]
3/224		5 May	Way, John son of John, labourer, of Gloucester
			Porter, Anthony 7 yrs butcher [Mrs Browne]
		1 Apr	Skinner, William son of William, clothier, of Newent
			Selwyn, Thomas & Martha 7 yrs cordwainer
		25 Mar	Bradshaw, Henry son of William, labourer, of Gloucester
			Onion, Thomas 7 yrs silkweaver
3/225			Knott, Nathan son of Lawrence, carpenter, of Gloucester
			Clarke, Henry & Amicia 7 yrs glazier
		6 Jul	Davis, Thomas son of Thomas, innholder of Gloucester
			Blanch, William 7 yrs tailor
		31 Jul	Barnelme, John son of Edward, labourer, of Gloucester
			Harris, John 7 yrs blacksmith
3/226		25 Jun	Fletcher, Thomas son of John, blacksmith, of Tewkesbury
			Lodge, Trustram & Mary 7 yrs cooper
			Brooke, Jonathan son of Jonathan [*entry deleted*]
		14 Aug	Motloe, James son of James, blacksmith, formerly of Gloucester
			Smith, Thomas & Jane 7 yrs glover
		24 Jun	Symons, Edward son of Joan, widow, of Gloucester
			Veysee, Walter & Margaret 7 yrs tailor [*Mrs Browne*]
3/227		21 Aug	Cugley, John son of Daniel, cardmaker, of Gloucester
			Cugley, Thomas 7 yrs cardmaker [*Holliday*][2]
		1 Jul	Witt, Richard son of John, gentleman, dec'd, of Newland
			Paine, Robert 7 yrs mercer
		22 Jan	George, Anthony son of [William], feltmaker, dec'd, of Gloucester
			George, Hester, widow 7 yrs [feltmaker]
3/228		25 Dec	George, William son of William, feltmaker, dec'd, of Gloucester
			Coucher, William & Margaret 7 yrs cordwainer [*Holliday*]
		1 Sep	Randle, William son of Giles, silkweaver, of Gloucester
			Randle, Giles, his father, 7 yrs silkweaver [*Holliday*]
		[*blank*]	Ball, Thomas son of John, collar maker, of Gloucester
			Beard, John [*no term*] silkweaver [*Holliday*]

[1] GBR B3/6 f 9 7 Apr 1682: To receive £4 of Mrs Browne's money: Walter son of Nicholas Clarke, John son of John Way, Edward Symons.

[2] GBR B3/3 p 819 7 Aug 1682: To receive £5 of Mr Hollidaye's money: Thomas Ball, Giles Randle, John Cugley, John Bishopp, William Miles, Thomas Vaughan.

James son of James Tyler to receive £5 of the gift of Alderman Powell.

ibid p 823 22 Sep 1682: To receive £10 of Sir Thomas Rich's money: Sturmey, Bradgate, Badger, Cugley, Warwicke, Clayfeild.

	1682	1 Sep	Vaughan, Samuel son of Thomas, joiner, of Gloucester

1682 1 Sep Vaughan, Samuel son of Thomas, joiner, of Gloucester
Vaughan, Thomas, his father, 7 yrs joiner [*Holliday*]

3/229 2 Sep James, Thomas son of Thomas, yeoman, of Longhope
Williams, John & Margaret 7 yrs glover

1 Sep Bishoppe, John son of Daniel, tailor, of Gloucester
Bishoppe, Daniel, his father, 7 yrs tailor [*Holliday*]

3/230 **John Webb, mayor [1682–3]**
George Broad & Richard Chandler, bailiffs and sheriffs

1682 12 Nov Maddockes, Thomas son of Walter, cordwainer, of Ross, Herefs
Gyttos, William & Alice 7 yrs saddler

29 Sep Bubb, Giles son of Thomas, blacksmith, of Barnwood
White, John 7 yrs cordwainer

20 Nov Cox, Thomas son of William, yeoman, of Barton Street, Gloucester
Powell, William & Alice 7 yrs of Barton Street cordwainer
Thomas Cox discharged from his master by order of His Majesty's Justices of the Peace for that William Powell is not capable of keeping an apprentice to follow the trade and not living in the city [Indenture cancelled]

3/231 1 Dec Cooke, Giles son of William, husbandman, of Maisemore
Tyler, John & Anne 7 yrs cordwainer

1683 2 Feb Furney, William son of John, husbandman, of Brockworth
Gibbs, Philip & Mary 7 yrs hemp dresser

25 Mar Elliotts, Edward son of Edward, glassmaker, of Gloucester
Willcockes, John & Mary 7 yrs glassmaker

3/232 1682 13 Jun Furney, James son of Alice, widow, of Ross, Herefs
Longden, Thomas & Anne 7 yrs ironmonger

1683 16 Apr Puckeridge, Thomas son of Thomas, tailor, of Gloucester
Parker, John & Martha 7 yrs tailor

Fisher, John, [son of —] Fisher, yeoman, of Ross, Herefs
Barnes, William & Joan 7 yrs saddler

13 Apr Coucher, Philip son of Edmund, gentleman, of Ledbury, Herefs
Gosling, Thomas & Elizabeth 7 yrs haberdasher 2s 6d

3/233 16 Apr Perkins, Thomas son of John, yeoman, of Cheltenham
Meeke, Thomas & Mary 7 yrs currier

30 Apr Davis, John son of Thomas, wool comber, of Gloucester
Coucher, William 7 yrs cordwainer

25 Mar Sturmey, Samuel son of Samuel, of Gloucester
Tyler, Edward 7 yrs cordwainer

	1683	21 May	Armitage, Giles son of Richard, shoe mender, of Gloucester Savory, Robert 7 yrs blacksmith [*Mrs Browne*]¹
3/234		3 Jun	Bradshaw, Thomas son of William, carpenter, of Gloucester Sparks, Richard & Anne 7 yrs cordwainer [*Mrs Browne*]
		16 Jul	Skinner, Stephen son of William, clothier, of Newent Shipton, John & Elizabeth 7 yrs barber surgeon
		20 Jun	Collings, James son of Thomas, yeoman, of Brampton Abbotts, Herefs Lye, Samuel 7 yrs grocer
3/235		24 Jun	Palmer, Francis son of Richard, tailor, of Bredon, Worcs Turbett, Thomas & Margery 7 yrs tanner
		22 Jul	Carpenter, Richard son of Richard, miller, of Leonard Stanley Grene, John & Joan 7 yrs cordwainer
		24 Jun	Turbett, John son of William, yeoman, of Bredon, Worcs Turbett, Thomas & Margery 7 yrs tanner
3/236		25 Jul	Hosey, Edward son of Edward, feltmaker, of Gloucester Hayward, John 7 yrs feltmaker [*cf Appendix V*] [*Mrs Browne*]
		29 May	Badger, Jeremiah son of Albert, pinmaker, of Gloucester Hartland, John 7 yrs barber surgeon
		15 Jun	Spencer, Thomas son of Giles, wool comber, of Upton St Leonards Brobent, Francis & Hester 7 yrs [cooper]
3/237		1 May	Filders, George son of George, blacksmith, of Gloucester Filders, George, his father, 7 yrs blacksmith
		27 Aug	Bower, Samuel son of Samuel, tanner, of Gloucester Hicks, Edward & Grace 7 yrs tobacco-pipe maker 2s 6d [*Holliday*]
		17 Sep	Skelton, Richard son of Francis, clothier, of Gloucester Jordan, William 7 yrs apothecary
3/238			Hughes, Philip son of Philip, tailor, of Gloucester Bishopp, Daniel 7 yrs tailor 2s 6d [*Holliday*]
		22 Jul	Robbins, Benjamin son of James, currier, of Gloucester Swaine, John 7 yrs tailor

3/239			**John Price, mayor [1683–4]** **[Giles Rodway and Josiah Randle, bailiffs and sheriffs]**
	1683	15 Oct	Sparrowhawk, Robert son of Robert, silkweaver, of Gloucester Palmer, Joseph 7 yrs tailor [*Holliday*]²
			Matthews, William son of John, yeoman, of Gloucester Robbins, James 7 yrs currier

---

¹ GBR B3/3 p 838 19 Apr 1683: To receive £4 of Mrs Browne's money: William Bradshaw, Giles Armitage, William Hosey.

² ibid p 844 2 Aug 1683: To receive £5 of Mr Hollidaye's money: Denis Beard, Joseph Phelps, William George, Samuel Bower, Philip Hughes, Robert Sparrowhawke.

	1683	29 Sep	Jackson, John son of Robert, labourer, of Gloucester Clifford, James 7 yrs pinmaker
3/240		10 Nov	Hancocks, Vincent [MS Vinient] son of Paul, clothier, of Worcester Bennett, John 7 yrs barber surgeon
		5 Nov	Cugley, John son of John, labourer, of Gloucester Weyman, Ambrose 7 yrs cordwainer
		29 Sep	Jones, John son of John, weaver, of Worcester Barnelme, Richard & Elizabeth 7 yrs horner
3/241		19 Nov	Beard, Dennis son of William, tailor, of Gloucester George, Nathaniel & Mary 7 yrs tailor [*Holliday*]
		1 Oct	Corsley, Richard son of William, goldsmith, of Gloucester Corsley, William, his father 7 yrs goldsmith
		7 Dec	Phelps, Joseph son of Joseph, feltmaker, of Gloucester Nash, Jesse & Elizabeth 7 yrs feltmaker [*Holliday*]
3/242		1 Dec	Felton, Joseph son of Joseph, cutler, of Gloucester Seysmore, John & Joan 7 yrs barber surgeon
	1684	21 Jan	Trolley, Joseph son of John, cordwainer, of Gloucester Evans, Samuel & Elizabeth 7 yrs cordwainer
	1683	1 Nov	Poole, Joseph son of Joseph, blacksmith, of Maisemore Bicknell, William & Dorothy 7 yrs tailor
		25 Dec	Floyd, John son of John, of Llangadog [MS Llangattock], Carms Tyler, John 7 yrs baker
3/243		22 Dec	Bevan, John son of Edward, labourer, formerly of Gloucester Clifford, James & Mary 7 yrs pinmaker
	1684	28 Jan	Stephens, John son of John, pargeter, of Gloucester Stephens, Thomas & Frances 7 yrs pinmaker
			Williams, John son of Phyllis, single woman, of Gloucester Stephens, Thomas & Frances 7 yrs pinmaker
3/244		14 Feb	Davis, Arnold son of Thomas, yeoman, of Churcham Mills, Thomas & Margaret 7 yrs baker
		3 Mar	Mathews, Richard son of John, brazier, of Mitcheldean Howell, Joseph & Elizabeth 7 yrs blacksmith
		10 Mar	Holliday, Henry son of Henry, carpenter, of Gloucester Cheesman, Robert & Sarah 7 yrs cooper[1]
3/245		16 Apr	Steight, John son of John, yeoman, of Aston Somerville Mayris, Charles & Elizabeth 7 yrs pewterer
		25 Mar	Gregory, John son of Abraham, S.T.P.,[2] of Gloucester Webb, John & Jane 7 yrs merchant

[1] GBR B3/3 p 849 27 Sep 1683: To receive £10 of Sir Thomas Rich's money: Griffin, Browne, Wolley, Pritchard, Holliday, Lugg.

[2] *Sacrae Theologiae Professor* (i.e. professor of sacred theology).

| | 1684 | 4 Apr | Mathews, John son of William, yeoman, of Awre
Bubb, William & Elizabeth 7 yrs baker |
| 3/246 | | 28 Apr | Nickolson, Thomas son of John, yeoman, formerly of Frocester
Smith, William & Susannah 7 yrs glover |
| | | 7 May | Humphris, Thomas son of Richard, apothecary, dec'd, of Gloucester
Dobbs, Thomas & Jane 7 yrs barber & periwig maker |
| | | 5 May | Vyner, William son of William, feltmaker, formerly of Gloucester
Trow, John 7 yrs pinmaker |
| | | 8 May | Beard, Henry son of Katharine, widow, of Gloucester
Dobbs, Thomas & Jane 7 yrs barber & periwig maker [*Holliday*] |
| 3/247 | | 12 May | Hayford, John son of Mary, of Littleworth
Powell, George 7 yrs pinmaker |
| | | 29 May | Perkins, William son of Samuel, cordwainer, of Gloucester
Tyler, John & Anne 7 yrs cordwainer [*Mrs Browne*]¹ |
| | | 26 May | Cooke, Florice son of Florice, yeoman, of Eldersfield, [Worcs]
Castle, Nathaniel [*no term*] baker |
| 3/248 | | 23 Jul | Wright, John son of Edward, labourer, of Charlton Kings
Randle, William & Hester 8 yrs tailor |
| | | 10 May | Daw, George son of John, yeoman, of Longhope
Tyler, Edward 7 yrs cordwainer |
| | | 24 Jun | Williams, John son of William, labourer, of Gloucester
Crass, William & Sarah 7 yrs bodicemaker [*cf Appendix V*] |
| | | | Keylock, John son of Thomas, dec'd, of Minsterworth
Cowles, Robert & Joan 7 yrs butcher [*Repeated at 3/249*] |
| 3/249 | | 7 Jul | Underwood, Christopher
Knott, George & Jane 7 yrs carpenter |
| | | 24 Jun | Keylock, John son of Thomas, dec'd, of Minsterworth
Cowles, Robert & Joan 7 yrs butcher [*Repeating entry at 3/248*] |
| | | 18 Jul | Greene, Adam son of Adam, yeoman, of Ashton Keynes, Wilts
Brocke, John & Mary 7 yrs glover |
| 3/250 | | 1 Aug | Bacon, Thomas son of Nollard, silkweaver, of Gloucester
Hathaway, Anne 7 yrs [*no trade*] [*Mrs Browne*] |
| | | 8 Sep | Wood, Isaac son of John
Cowdall, John & Mary 7 yrs tailor [*Holliday*]² |

[1] GBR B3/3 p 858 27 Mar 1684: To receive £4 of Mrs Browne's money: William son of Samuel Perkins, Roger son of Eleanor Church, [Thomas] son of Nollard Bacon.

[2] ibid p 862 22 Aug 1684: To receive £5 of Mr Hollidaye's money: Isaac son of John Wood, Richard son of Thomas Sparkes, John son of Anne Biddle, John son of Katharine Beard, John son of George Ward, Henry son of Henry Cor.

ibid p 863 4 Sep 1684: To receive £10 of Sir Thomas Rich's money: Henry Lugg, Robert Abbott, Thomas Cooke, George Phillipps, Thomas Hale, Samuel Ryland.

	1684	1 Oct	Randle, James son of Daniel, joiner, of Gloucester
			Randle, Daniel, his father, 6 yrs joiner 5s
3/251		8 Sep	Sparkes, Richard son of Thomas, weaver, of Gloucester
			Beard, Elizabeth 7 yrs weaver 2s 6d [*Holliday*]
		17 Sep	Young, Henry son of John, yeoman, of Mitcheldean
			Hartland, William & Martha 7 yrs pinmaker
			Dyer, John son of John, pinmaker, of Gloucester
			Dowten, Stephen & Elizabeth 7 yrs pinmaker 2s 6d
3/252			**William Lamb, mayor [1684–5]**
			Thomas Wilcox and James Price, bailiffs and sheriffs
	1684	29 Sep	Biddle, John son of John, cordwainer, formerly of Gloucester
			Bowler, Thomas 7 yrs collar maker [*Holliday*]
		20 Oct	Davis, William son of William, yeoman, dec'd, of Abenhall
			Vaughan, Edward & Margaret 7 yrs vintner
		7 Nov	Ready, Edward son of John, yeoman, of Bulley
			Phillips, James & Elizabeth 7 yrs saddler
3/253		13 Dec	Hopkins, John son of John, cleric, of Hankerton, Wilts
			Williams, Richard & Anne 7 yrs cooper
		26 Dec	Beach, John son of Robert, farmer, of Ledbury, Herefs
			Mason, Mary 7 yrs baker 5s
	1685	2 Feb	Reeve, Joseph son of Francis, stone cutter, of Gloucester
			Reeve, Francis, his father, 7 yrs stone cutter
3/254		25 Mar	Beard, William son of Henry, gentleman, of Painswick
			Hyett, John & Elizabeth 7 yrs merchant
		26 Mar	Hayward, Thomas son of William, yeoman, of Gloucester
			Goodcheap, Thomas & Mary 7 yrs cordwainer 2s 6d
3/259			**William Jordan, mayor [1685–6]**
			John Chapman and Nathaniel Castle [*alias* Cooke], bailiffs and sheriffs
	1685	3 Oct	Wilse, Thomas son of Giles, baker, of Gloucester
			Wilse, Giles, his father, & Anne 7 yrs baker 20s
			Carsey, John son of John, labourer, of Gloucester
			Heard, Humphrey & Dorothy 7 yrs from date of indenture butcher 5s
3/260		19 Oct	Jelfe, Henry son of Richard, yeoman, of Ruardean
			Palmer, Edmund & Elizabeth 7 yrs baker
		9 Nov	Skynner, Samuel son of Samuel Skinner, glover, of Gloucester
			Skinner, Samuel, his father, & Mary 7 yrs from 25 Mar last glover 20s

| | 1685 | 9 Nov | Marshall, Thomas son of Thomas, of English Bicknor
Gwillim, John & Anne 7 yrs feltmaker 2s 6d |

Heale, Thomas son of Thomas, cordwainer, dec'd, of Gloucester
Veysey, Walter & Margaret 7 yrs from 25 Jul last tailor 2s 6d

3/261 16 Nov Dyer, Philip son of James, glover, of Gloucester
Dowsing, William & [*blank*] 8 yrs from 14 Nov tailor 5s

Weaver, Henry son of Richard, labourer, of Gloucester
Gibbons, Richard & Dina 7 yrs from 11 Jun farrier & blacksmith 2s 6d [*Holliday*][1]

Fluck, William son of William, yeoman, dec'd, of Eldersfield, Worcs
Marden, Giles & Margaret 7 yrs from 25 Aug baker 10s

Manning, John son of Thomas, stone cutter, dec'd, of Gloucester
Jones, James & Anne 8 yrs from 14 Nov silkweaver 2s 6d

3/262 Brotherton, Joshua son of Jeremiah, labourer, of Gloucester
Quench, Richard & Mary 7 yrs from 14 Nov horn turner 1s

9 Nov Harding, Charles son of John, glover, of Gloucester
Cowcher, Richard & Margaret 7 yrs from 24 Jun last pinmaker 2s 6d [*Holliday*]

7 Dec Chaundler, John son of John, dec'd, of Gloucester
Anstee, Charles 7 yrs from 20 Nov butcher 2s 6d [*Holliday*]

14 Dec Corr, Edward son of Edmund Cor, button maker, of Gloucester
Reeve, Giles & Sarah 7 yrs from 20 Nov gunsmith 10s
[*Holliday*]

3/263 14 Dec Warnor, Charles son of Edward Warner, yeoman, of Haresfield
Humfris, Samuel 7 yrs from 26 Mar last butcher 2s 6d

Rone, John son of Joseph, narrow weaver, dec'd, of Tibberton
Sly, William & Mary 7 yrs from 29 Sep tailor 2s 6d

Fletcher, Thomas son of John, yeoman, of Corse
Wilse, Giles & Anne 7 yrs from 5 Nov baker 2s 6d

31 Dec Pritchard, John son of John, butcher, of Longtown, Herefs
Wall, William 7 yrs from date of indenture carpenter 10s

3/264 1686 25 Jan Gammon, John son of William, gardener, of Rendcomb
Lugg, Lawrence & Elizabeth 7 yrs from 21 Dec baker 5s

Rodway, Thomas son of Thomas, yeoman, of Great Witcombe
Moore, George & Elizabeth 7 yrs from 25 Dec butcher 5s

15 Feb Crosse, Henry son of John, labourer, of Gloucester
Farley, Thomas & Eleanor 7 yrs from 2 Feb cutler 10s

---

[1] GBR B3/3 p 891 25 Aug 1685: To receive £5 of Mr Hollidaye's money: Richard Weaver's son, Edward Corr, [*blank*] Harding, [*blank*] Partridge, John Chandler, Albert Badger

3/265	1686	25 Feb	Pritchard, Charles son of William, husbandman, of 'Langdila', Mon Evans, Samuel & Eliz 7 yrs from date of indenture cordwainer 2s 6d
			Badger, Albert son of Albert, pinmaker, dec'd, of Gloucester Winniett, Thomas & Eliz 7 yrs from date of indenture pinmaker 5s [*Holliday*]
		15 Mar	Panter, William son of John, wool comber, dec'd, of Gloucester Greene, John & Joan 7 yrs from date of indenture cordwainer 1s [1]
		19 Mar	Stepherson, Stephen son of John, bodicemaker, dec'd, of Gloucester Harrold, William & Jane 7 yrs from date of indenture pewterer 5s
3/266			Watkins, John son of Peter, husbandman, dec'd, of Painswick Reade, Thomas & Elizabeth 7 yrs from 2 Feb cordwainer 5s
			Woodward, Samuel son of Samuel, blacksmith, dec'd, of Gloucester Washborne, Daniel & Mary 7 yrs from date of indenture tinplate worker 2s 6d [2]
		26 Apr	Griffis, Owen son of Michael, cordwainer, of Gloucester Smith, Humphrey & Joan 7 yrs from date of indenture skinner & glover 2s 6d [*Mrs Browne*] [3]
		19 Apr	Hannis, Charles son of William, labourer, of Longhope Rudge, George & Milberrow 7 yrs from 25 Mar farrier 2s 6d
3/267			Leigh, Thomas son of Henry, cordwainer, of Gloucester Freame, Jasper 7 yrs from 25 Mar baker 5s
		26 Apr	Howell, James, of Gloucester Cowcher, Richard & Margaret 8 yrs from date of indenture pinmaker 2s 6d
		19 Apr	Carter, Henry son of Henry, chandler, of Arlingham Cooke, Charles & Mary 7 yrs from 25 Mar butcher 4s
		26 Apr	Rowbrey, Timothy son of Wm, husbandman, of Hanley Child, Worcs Clarke, Anne, widow of John, 7 yrs from 24 Dec joiner 2s 6d
3/268		10 May	Wilcocks, Daniel son of Thomas, tailor, dec'd, of Gloucester Coldricke, Adam & Anne 7 yrs from date of indenture barber 2s 6d
			Beale, Benjamin son of Thomas, husbandman, of Staunton, Worcs Walker, Anthony & Mary 7 yrs from date of indenture smith 2s 6d
			Fletcher, William son of Richard, miller, of Barnwood Allen, John & Margaret 7 yrs from 25 Mar butcher 2s 6d
		21 May	Diston, Isaac son of Isaac, mercer, dec'd, of Evesham, Worcs Ebbs, Philip & Hester 7 yrs from date of indenture saddler 5s

[1] GBR B3/3 p 892 16 Sep 1685: To receive £10 of Sir Thomas Rich's money: Stephen Cowles, Samuel Woodward, Lawrence Wilshire, William Panter, William Nash, Thomas Dudley. Masters to be approved of by the mayor and aldermen according to the will.

[2] ibid p 905 15 Mar 1686: John son of Samuel Woodward to have £5 of the gift of Mr Powell.

[3] ibid p 879 14 Apr 1685: To receive £4 of Mrs Browne's money: Owen Griffen, Joseph Trolly, John Nest.

3/269	1686	14 Jun	Nest, William son of John, carpenter, of Gloucester Nest, John jr & [blank] 7 yrs from 25 Mar carpenter 10s [*Mrs Browne*]
			Hemsley, Ric, son of [blank], victualler, dec'd, of St Owen's, Gloucs Wynniatt, Thomas 7 yrs from date of indenture pinmaker 5s
			Jeffreys, John son of William husbandman, dec'd, of Duntisbourne Hayward, John & [blank] 7 yrs from date of indenture feltmaker 2s 6d
3/270			Feild, Thomas son of Thomas, woollen draper, of Stratford [on Avon], Warws Hyett, John & Elizabeth 7 yrs from 7 Jun mercer 10s
		16 Jun	Stiles, William son of William, labourer, of Cheltenham Medway, Abraham & Mary 7 yrs from 1 May bricklayer 2s 6d
		21 Jun	Williams, Anthony son of James, husbandman, dec'd, of Dumbleton Baker, Thomas 7 yrs from date of indenture barber 2s 6d
		5 July	Boddenham, Samuel son of Samuel, wiredrawer, of Huntley Keare, John & Anne 8 yrs from date of indenture pinmaker 2s 6d
3/271			Gwinnell, Richard son of Richard, butcher, dec'd, of Minsterworth Allen, William 7 yrs from 19 Mar chandler 2s 6d
		2 Aug	Halford, John son of Edmund, yeoman, dec'd, of Maisemore Wells, John 7 yrs from 26 Jul cordwainer 2s 6d
			Woodward, John son of John, broadweaver, of Dursley Daws, William & Elizabeth 7 yrs from 24 Jun plasterer 5s
		10 May	Lane, Richard son of Nicholas, apothecary, of Gloucester Lane, Nicholas, his father, & Mary 7 yrs from date of indenture apothecary 20s
3/272		16 Aug	Lord, Samuel son of Richard, yeoman, dec'd, of Barnwood Bryan, Daniel & Anne 7 yrs from 24 Jun cordwainer 10s
		18 Aug	Lawrence, Anthony son of Thomas, butcher, dec'd, of Gloucester Cannon, Thomas & Katherine 7 yrs from date of indenture butcher 2s 6d [*Holliday*][1]
		13 Aug	Sisemore, Samuel son of Charles, tailor, of Gloucester Weyman, Ambrose & Mary 7 yrs from date of indenture cordwainer 1s [*Holliday*]
		30 Aug	Longden, Robert son of Thomas, ironmonger, of Gloucester Longden, Thomas, his father, & Anne 7 yrs from date of indenture ironmonger 20s
3/273		1 Sep	Bathorne, Jeremiah son of Robert, yeoman, dec'd, of Minsterworth Mason, Mary, widow, 7 yrs from date of indenture baker 2s 6d
		6 Sep	Davis, William son of Thomas, wool comber, of Gloucester Hayward, Clement 7 yrs from date of indenture tailor 5s

---

[1] GBR B3/3 p 907 6 Aug 1686: To receive £5 of Mr Hollidaye's money: Samuel Sisemore, Isaac Manning, John Bower, Anthony Lawrence, Joseph Wynniatt, Philip Philips.

John Hill, mayor [1686–7]
Joseph Phelpes and Robert Punter, bailiffs and sheriffs

3/274

1686 11 Oct Wood, William son of William, mercer, of Gloucester
  Wood, William, his father, & Eleanor 7 yrs from date of indenture mercer 10s

8 Nov Crumpe, Richard son of Thomas, yeoman, of Westbury
  Davis, Robert & Rebecca 7 yrs from 5 Oct brazier 2s 6d

Wynniatt, Joseph son of Thomas, pinmaker, of Gloucester
  Badger, John & Joan 7 yrs from date of indenture pinmaker 5s
  [*Holliday*]

3/275 Reynolds, William son of William, husbandman, of Newent
  Gwillim, John & Anne 8 yrs from 25 Mar next feltmaker 2s 6d

15 Nov Turner, John son of John, cordwainer, of Gloucester
  Savory, Thos & Joan 7 yrs from date of indenture farrier & smith 2s 6d

29 Nov Manning, Samuel son of Isaac, pinmaker, of Gloucester
  Wynniatt, Thomas & Eliz 7 yrs from date of indenture pinmaker 2s 6d
  [*Holliday*]

3/276 6 Dec Mathews, Edward son of John, brazier, of Mitcheldean
  Cooke, Richard & Margaret 7 yrs from 15 Feb next blacksmith 2s 6d
  12 Jul 1689: turned over to Anthony Walker by order of Sessions

20 Dec Turbett, Thomas son of John, carpenter, of Gloucester
  Poole, John & Sarah 7 yrs from date of indenture tiler 2s 6d
  [*Mrs Browne*][1]

1687 17 Jan Conklin, Thomas son of James, glassmaker, of Gloucester
  Garway, Jonathan & Edith 7 yrs from date of indenture grocer 10s

24 Jan Bower, John son of Samuel, tanner, of Gloucester
  Cowles, Josiah & Mary 7 yrs from 20 Dec glover 2s 6d [*Holliday*]

3/277 Punter, Robert jr son of Robert sr, mercer, of Gloucester
  Punter, Robert, his father, & Mary 7 yrs from date of indenture mercer 20s

Niblett, Henry son of John, weaver, of Haresfield
  Mathews, John & Anne 7 yrs from 24 Jun butcher 2s 6d

14 Feb Webb, Samuel son of William, salter, of London
  Mower, Thomas & Eliz 7 yrs from date of indenture barber surgeon 2s 6d

Webb, Thomas son of Thomas, husbandman, of Ruardean
  Annetts, John 7 yrs from 25 Jan blacksmith 2s 6d

3/278 1 Mar Watkins, Samuel son of Peter, husbandman, dec'd, of Painswick
  Tyler, Edward & Mary 7 yrs from 10 Jan cordwainer 1s

---

[1] GBR B3/3 p 905 15 Mar 1686: To receive £4 of Mrs Browne's money: John son of Thomas Hooper, Thomas son of John Turbett, [*blank*] son of Jeremiah Brotherton.

	1686 18 Mar	Mountague, Henry son of William, innholder, dec'd, of Over
		Ready, Thomas & Eliz 7 yrs from 24 Mar [next] cordwainer 2s 6d
		Okey, James son of William, husbandman, of Down Hatherley
		Ball, Giles & Sarah 7 yrs from 2 Feb cooper 2s 6d
		Watts, James son of John, yeoman, of Linton, Churcham
		Sheppard, John 7 yrs from date of indenture barber surgeon 2s 6d
3/279		Cooke, Richard son of Richard, innholder, of Paganhill, Stroud
		Grafstock, John & Margaret 7 yrs from 5 Oct baker 2s 6d
	1 Apr	Stephenson *alias* Cowles, William son of John, bodicemaker, dec'd, of Gloucester
		Fords, James & Mary 7 yrs from 25 Mar tailor 2s 6d
	8 Apr	Sparrowhawke, William son of William, silkweaver, of Gloucester
		Yate, Francis & Mary 7 yrs from 28 Mar cordwainer 1s
		Rowles, John son of William, broadweaver, dec'd, of Arlingham
		Anstee, Charles 7 yrs from date of indenture butcher 2s 6d
3/280	12 Apr	Freeman, Giles son of Giles, baker, of Gloucester
		Fletcher William & Katherine 7 yrs from date of indenture blacksmith 2s 6d[1]
	28 Apr	Williams, John son of William, labourer, dec'd, of Gloucester
		White, John & Hannah 7 yrs from 25 Mar cordwainer 1s
		[cf Appendix V]
		Window, William son of Richard, gardener, of Gloucester
		Parker, John & Martha 7 yrs from 25 Apr tailor 2s 6d
		Meeke, Thomas son of Thomas, currier, of Gloucester
		Meeke, Thomas, his father, & Frances 7 yrs from 25 Mar currier 5s
3/281	18 May	Davis, Anthony son of John, pinmaker, of Gloucester
		Davis, John, his father, & Christian 7 yrs from 25 Mar pinmaker 2s 6d
		Davis, James son of John, pinmaker, of Gloucester
		Davis, John, his father, & Christian 7 yrs from 25 Mar pinmaker 2s 6d
	20 May	Wheeler, Thomas son of Thomas, carpenter, of Gloucester
		Birt, William & Deborah 7 yrs from 1 May tailor 2s 6d [*Mrs Browne*][2]
	25 May	Hunt, William son of Samuel, dyer, of Newland
		Randle, Daniel & Anne 7 yrs from date of indenture joiner 10s
3/282		Butcher, William son of William, maltster, of Winterbourne
		Elliott, John & Jane 7 yrs from 24 Jun next upholsterer 5s
	27 May	Hemsley, Thomas son of Richard, vintner, dec'd, of Littleworth
		Sparkes, Richard & Anne 7 yrs from date of indenture cordwainer 2s 6d
		[*Mrs Browne*]

[1] GBR B3/3 p 921 27 Sep 1686: To receive £10 of Sir Thomas Rich's money: Joseph Holder, Giles Freeman, Thomas Meeke, Lawrence Whitterne, Henry Worrall, Samuel Ackson.

[2] ibid f 151 5 Apr 1687: To receive £4 of Mrs Browne's money: Thomas Wheeler, John Jennings, Thomas Hemsley, Samuel Streete.

	1687	1 Jun	Evenis, John son of James, wheelwright, dec'd, of Upton St Leonards Castle, Nathaniel 7 yrs from date of indenture baker 2s 6d
		25 May	Poole, Samuel son of William, blacksmith, of Maisemore Hayes, William jr & Judith 7 yrs cordwainer
3/283		1 Aug	Marden, John son of William, farmer, of Maisemore Tyler, John & Anne 7 yrs cordwainer
		15 Aug	Endall, Thomas son of Stephen, of Ross, Herefs Seysmore, William & Eleanor 7 yrs barber surgeon
		25 Aug	Seyer, John son of Daniel, ropemaker, of Gloucester Seyer, Daniel, his father, & Anne 7 yrs ropemaker
		29 Aug	Dudley, Thomas son of April, butcher, of Gloucester Dudley, April, his father, 7 yrs butcher
3/284		1 Aug	Madocke, William son of Walter, cordwainer, of Ross, Herefs Bishop, Daniel & Anne 7 yrs barber surgeon
		25 Jun	Bretherton, Daniel son of Jonathan, labourer, of Gloucester Beard, Elizabeth 7 yrs silkweaver [*Mrs Browne*]
3/285		19 Sep	Underwood, Anthony son of [*blank*], of Walford, Herefs Andrews, William 7 yrs saddler
			Lewis, John & Richard sons of Abel, pargeter, of Gloucester Lewis, John [*no term*] combmaker [*Holliday*][1]
		25 Sep	Driver, Richard son of Matthew, yeoman, of Awre Gosling, Thomas 7 yrs haberdasher
3/286		29 Sep	Harding, William son of John, glover, of Gloucester Gardner, Daniel & Rebecca 7 yrs pinmaker [*Holliday*]
		16 Nov	Blissard, William son of William, farmer, of Up Hatherley Randle, Josiah & Margery 7 yrs baker *Indenture to be delivered up and cancelled and William to have no privilege of the freedom of Gloucester having served only 3 years 4 months. William Blisard, Josiah Randle Witness: D Weyman*
		5 Nov	Taylor, Matthew son of Richard, farmer, of Newnham Martin, Thomas & Katharine 7 yrs glover
3/287		6 Oct	Wadley, William son of John, farmer, of Ashleworth Sowdley, John & Eleanor 7 yrs wool comber

---

[1] GBR B3/6 f 160v 9 Aug 1687: Nominated for Mr Hollidaye's money: Richard son of Edward Cor, George Bowler's son, Henry Symons, William son of John Harding, Zachary son of Thomas Barrow, Richard son of Abel Lewis.
Richard son of William Hemming to have £5 of Alderman Powell's money.

	1687	24 Oct	Cook, Samuel son of William, victualler, of Gloucester
			Andrews, William 7 yrs saddler
		25 Oct	Cor, Richard son of Edward, button maker, of Gloucester
			Cor, Edward, his father, 7 yrs button maker
			[*Holliday*]
3/288		6 Oct	Rudge, Charles son of John, farmer, of Aston Ingham, Herefs
			Pembrudge, Samuel 7 yrs baker
		29 Sep	Spencer, William son of Giles, wool comber, of Gloucester
			Sowdley, John & Eleanor 7 yrs wool comber
	1688	6 Jan	Hampton, Philip son of Thomas, yeoman, of Westbury
			Pegler, Joseph & Jane 7 yrs tanner
3/289		14 Feb	Mericke, John son of Merricke, Richard, yeoman, of Taynton
			Berrow, Stephen 7 yrs tailor
		26 Mar	Austin, Hugh son of Richard Augustin, of Bromsberrow
			Perkins, George & Sarah 7 yrs pinmaker
		12 Mar	Lewis, John son of John, labourer, of Gloucester
			Slye, William & Mary 7 yrs tailor
		9 Apr	Mayo, William son of William, yeoman, of Minsterworth
			Bubb, William 7 yrs barber
3/290	1687	24 Jun	Buckle, Richard son of Richard, yeoman, of Harescombe [MS Hascombe]
			Bycke, Thomas & Eleanor 7 yrs baker
	1688	28 Feb	Drew, Thomas son of Thomas, yeoman, of Churcham
			White, John & Hannah 7 yrs cordwainer
		26 Mar	Meeke, Edward son of Thomas, currier, of Gloucester
			Brian, Daniel & Anne 7 yrs cordwainer [*Holliday*]
3/291		25 Mar	Brian, Richard son of Richard, yeoman, of Ashleworth
			Knowles, Henry 7 yrs pewterer
		20 Apr	Mutley, Miles son of Miles, tailor, of Gloucester
			Pace, John & Anne 7 yrs cordwainer
		23 Apr	Evenis, William son of James, yeoman, of Upton St Leonards
			Goodcheape, Thomas & Mary 7 yrs cordwainer
3/292		7 Aug	Munday, Toby son of Toby, yeoman, of Framilode
			Slye, William & Mary 7 yrs tailor
		29 Sep	Nelme, Jasper son of Robert, yeoman, of Upton St Leonards
			Sellwyn, Martha 7 yrs cordwainer
		22 Jun	Robinson, Edward son of Philip, nailer, of Littledean
			Read, Robert & Anne 7 yrs ironmonger

3/293 **Anselm Fowler, mayor [Oct–Nov 1688]**
[William Reeves and Thomas Longden, bailiffs and sheriffs]

1688 12 Oct Baker, Richard son of Benjamin, feltmaker, of Gloucester
Norman, Edward & Joan 7 yrs [butcher] [*Holliday*][1]

William Cooke, mayor

1689 1 Jan Greenway, Walter son of Charles, of Longford
Hill, Richard & Jane 7 yrs pinmaker

15 Mar Willy, John son of Roger, tailor, formerly of Gloucester
Pembrudge, Thomas & Elizabeth 7 yrs chandler[2]

3/294 13 Mar Grace, George son of John, innkeeper, of Dursley
Fowler, William & Mary 7 yrs barber surgeon

25 Mar Randle, Giles son of Giles, silkweaver, of Gloucester
Sparkes, Thomas & Sarah 7 yrs silkweaver [*Holliday*]

18 Feb Hornidge, Matthew son of Thomas, bodicemaker, of Gloucester
Jennings, Richard & Margaret 7 yrs tailor

3/295 20 May King, John son of John, scrivener, of Gloucester
Nott, George & Jane 7 yrs carpenter [*Holliday*]

24 Jun Grove, William son of John, glassmaker, of Gloucester
Meek, Thomas & Frances 7 yrs currier

1 May Vernon, Henry son of George, clerk, of Gloucester
Eckly, Samuel 7 yrs apothecary

7 Jun Walker, Daniel son of Richard, yeoman, of Gloucester
Coldricke, Daniel 7 yrs bodicemaker [*Mrs Browne*][3]

3/296 24 Jul Butler, John son of Thomas, formerly of London
Phillipps, Thomas & Elizabeth 7 yrs tailor [*Mrs Browne*]

26 Mar Washborne, John son of John, maltster, of Bengeworth, Worcs
Wastfield, Nicholas & Jane 7 yrs blacksmith

1 Aug Carpenter, James son of Robert, gentleman, formerly of Gloucester
Longden, Thomas & Anne 7 yrs ironmonger

---

[1] GBR B3/6 f 209v 10 Oct 1688: To receive £5 of Mr Hollidaye's money: James Bidle, Giles Randle, Richard Baker, Thomas Sturmey, John Woodward, John King.

[2] ibid f 210 10 Oct 1688: To receive £5 of Alderman Powell's money: John Willy.

[3] ibid f 192 30 Apr 1688: Nominated for Mrs Browne's money: John Buttler son in law to John Bradley, William Beard son in law to Richard Jennings, John son of Henry Jennings, William son of John Beard, Robert son of Thomas Millard, Daniel Walker, Joseph Raylee son in law to Nathaniel Veysee, Samuel son of John Evans. No votes were recorded and the money was presumably not awarded since the following year 6 boys instead of 3 received £4.

ibid f 227 1 Mar 1689: To receive £4 of Mrs Browne's money: John Buttler, John Jennings, William Beard son in law to Richard Jennings (all nominated in 1688), Joan Walker's son, Daniel Bishop's son, James Lugg.

3/297	1689	26 Mar	Beard, John son of John, clerk, formerly of Gloucester Longden, Thomas & Anne 8 yrs ironmonger
		21 Oct	Davis, Thomas son of John, pinmaker, of Gloucester Davis, John, his father 7 yrs pinmaker [*Holliday*]
		23 Apr	Hamlin, Edward son of Arthur, farmer, formerly of Brimpsfield Wells, John & Anne 7 yrs cordwainer
		28 Oct	Webb, John son of Arthur, dec'd, of Uley Vaughan, Thomas & Margaret 7 yrs joiner & carver for turner

3/298   **William Hodges, mayor [1689–90]**
                   [Samuel Palmer and Benjamin Rose, bailiffs and sheriffs]

	1689	28 Oct	Beard, William son of John, tailor, formerly of Haresfield Bubb, Giles 7 yrs shoemaker [*Mrs Browne*]
			Munns, Charles son of Robert, turner, of Gloucester Vaughan, Thomas & Margaret 7 yrs joiner & carver for joiner
		1 Nov	Nicholls, Edward son of William, alderman, of Gloucester Colley, Richard & Eleanor 7 yrs woollen draper
		2 Feb	Steell, Samuel son of Stephen, smith, of Littledean Hornidge, James & Mary 7 yrs smith *This boy was upon trial ¾ of a year before he was bound*
3/299		29 Sep	Lewis, James son of James, yeoman, of Gloucester Evans, Samuel & Elizabeth [*no term*] cordwainer
		4 Dec	Hampton, James son of William, narrow weaver, of Huntley Cowles, Josiah & Mary 7 yrs glover
	1690	25 Mar	Filders, Joseph son of George Filders, George, his father, 7 yrs [blacksmith]
		31 Mar	Bidle, James son of John, of Gloucester Weyman, Ambrose 7 yrs cordwainer [*Holliday*] *12 Jul 1693: turned over to Daniel Bryan*
3/300		2 Jun	Terrett, Richard son of John, formerly of English Bicknor, Glos Yates, Francis & Mary 7 yrs cordwainer
		9 Jun	Chapman, John son of George, blacksmith, of Hereford Chapman, George, his father, 7 yrs blacksmith
			Chapman, George son of George, blacksmith, of Hereford Chapman, George, his father, 7 yrs blacksmith
		11 Jul	Barrett, John son of Thomas, dec'd Atkyns, Walter & Mary 7 yrs cordwainer

3/301	1690	21 Jul	King, James son of John, of Gloucester Maverly, William & Barbara, 7 yrs button maker [*Holliday*]¹
		1 Mar	Cooke, Bernard son of George, grocer, of Gloucester Cooke, George, his father 7 yrs grocer
		21 Aug	Merritt, Thomas son of Thomas, clerk, of Gloucester Wyly, Thomas & Martha 7 yrs baker 10s
3/302		25 Jul	Cooke, Richard son of Thomas, chandler, of Gloucester Turner, Thomas & Anne 7 yrs cordwainer 5s [*sum deleted*] [*Holliday*]²
		17 Sep	Browne, John son of John, yeoman, of Whaddon Harris, Joseph & Elizabeth 7 yrs baker
		26 Mar	Morse, John son of John, horn turner, of Gloucester Weaver, Richard & Anne 7 yrs butcher 20s
		1 Aug	Ollive, Henry son of Richard, labourer, of Gloucester Bradley, John & Mary 7 yrs butcher 5s [*Mrs Browne*]³
3/303		13 Oct	Hosey, Edward son of Edward, feltmaker, of Gloucester Nash, Jesse & Elizabeth 2½ yrs feltmaker [*cf Appendix V*]
		29 Sep	Savory, Robert son of Robert, blacksmith, of Gloucester Savory, Robert, his father, 7 yrs blacksmith [*Holliday*]
		29 Oct	Davis, Samuel son of Comfort, widow Baker, James & Anne [*no term*] butcher [*Holliday*]
		29 Sep	Dowsen, William son of William, tailor, of Gloucester Broben, Francis jr [*no term*] cooper⁴
3/304		12 Oct	Weaver, Richard son of Richard, yeoman, of Longford Ward, John & Elizabeth 7 yrs smith
		29 Sep	Medway, Henry son of Henry, silkweaver, of Gloucester Medway, Henry, his father 7 yrs silkweaver [*Holliday*]
			Wooding, William son of William, yeoman, of Minsterworth Miles, Walter & Elizabeth 7 yrs baker
		1 Nov	Gwinnett, Francis son of Lawrence, gentleman, of Great Shurdington Newman, Samuel 7 yrs baker

---

[1] GBR B3/6 f 236v 5 Aug 1689: To receive £5 of Mr Hollidaye's money: Thomas son of John Davis, John son of April Dudley, John son of James Miles, Thomas son of Henry Lea, John King's son, Edward son of Thomas Meek.
  ibid f 239 14 Aug 1689 To receive £5 of Alderman Powell's money: Giles Freeman.

[2] ibid f 276 6 Aug 1690: To receive £5 of Mr Hollidaye's money: Richard son of Thomas Cooke, Thomas Gardner's son, Samuel son of Comfort Davies, Robert son of Robert Savory, Henry son of Henry Medway, William son of William Dewxell.
  To receive £5 of Alderman Powell's money: Francis Hutchings.

[3] ibid f 269 16 Apr 1690: To receive £4 of Mrs Browne's money: James Hermitage, Richard Olive, Solomon Bretherton.

[4] GBR B3/7 f 6v 3 Oct 1690: William Dowson's son, lately come out of the Bluecoat Hospital, to be apprenticed to Francis Braban, cooper.

3/305	1690	29 Sep	Gardner, William son of Thomas, pinmaker, of Gloucester
			Gardner, Thomas, his father, 7 yrs pinmaker [*Holliday*]
			[*Entered twice, duplicate entry deleted*]
			Sparkes, Thomas son of Richard, cordwainer, of Gloucester
			Sparkes, Richard, his father, 7 yrs cordwainer
		18 Oct	Carter, John son of John, of Elmore
			Bryan, Daniel 7 yrs cordwainer

3/306 **Sir John Guise, mayor [1690–1]**
[Peter Haines and Thomas Webb, bailiffs and sheriffs]

	1690	1 Nov	Lugg, James son of John, vintner, dec'd, of Gloucester
			Reeve, Giles & Sarah 7 yrs gunsmith [*Mrs Browne*]
		28 Oct	Hermitage, James son of Richard, dec'd, of Gloucester
			Turner, John & Margaret 7 yrs cordwainer [*Mrs Browne*]
		1 Nov	Shaw, John son of Joan, widow, of Awre
			Gibbons, Richard & Mary 7 yrs blacksmith & farrier
		8 Nov	Gundy, Tobias son of Walter, cordwainer, of Ross on Wye, Herefs
			Jennings, Richard & Margaret 7 yrs tailor
3/307		24 Nov	Parry, James son of John, collier, of Coleford
			Nash, Jesse & Elizabeth 7 yrs feltmaker
		16 Dec	Barker, John son of William, pinmaker, of Gloucester
			Skinner, Stephen 7 yrs barber
	1691	21 Jan	Hutchings, Francis son of Sarah, of Gloucester
			Robbins, Benjamin 8 yrs tailor
			9 Feb 1693: turned over to William George, tailor, for the residue of his term, Benjamin Robbins being gone off
		13 Jan	Higgs, William son of Eleanor, widow, of Cheltenham
			Broben, Francis & Hester 7 yrs cooper
3/308		1 Jan	Kingman, John son of John, of Frome Selwood, Som
			Wilkins, Mary 7 yrs wiredrawer
		7 Feb	Cartrell, John son of John, of Newent
			Baldwyne, William & Mary 7 yrs from 23 Apr tobacconist
		16 Feb	Wantner, Thomas son of Abel, clerk, of Gloucester
			Tyler, John & Anne 7 yrs cordwainer[1]
			Styles, James son of James, labourer, of Gloucester
			Williams, Richard & Anne 7 yrs cooper
3/309		2 Feb	Wintle, Robert son of Robert, of Blaisdon
			Mills, Thomas & Margaret 7 yrs baker

---

[1] GBR B3/7 f 23v 13 Feb 1691: Abel Wantner's son, lately come out of Bluecoat Hospital, to be apprenticed to John Tyler, cordwainer.

	1690	1 Nov	Mayoe, John son of Richard, of Gloucester Fisher, William & Anne 7 yrs pinmaker
	1691	7 Mar	Hopkins, Theophilus son of John, of Hankerton, Wilts Kent, Samuel 7 yrs joiner
		24 Mar	Daw, Eleazor son of Elizabeth, widow, of Gloucester Nest, John & Barbara 7 yrs carpenter
3/310		11 Apr	Merrett, Samuel son of John, of Haresfield Wiggett, Samuel 7 yrs glover
		9 Feb	Baldwyn, Thomas son of John Balldwyn, yeoman, of Newent Skinner, William & Mary 7 yrs cordwainer
		2 Feb	Griffin, Hugh son of Griffen, Daniel, yeoman, of Minsterworth Cowles, Robert & Sarah 7 yrs butcher *5 Feb 1693: turned over to Thomas Bright of Tibberton, butcher, a freeman of this city, by Robert Cowles*
		23 Apr	Randle, Daniel son of William, tailor, of Gloucester Jennings, Jeremiah & Anne 7 yrs tailor
3/311		1 Apr	Poulton, Richard son of Richard, gentleman, of Newent Webb, Thomas [*no term*] mercer
		28 Apr	Charles, John son of John, wool comber, of Gloucester Weyman, John 7 yrs cordwainer
	1690	10 Oct	Hathaway, Richard son of Richard, horner, of Gloucester Wooding, William & Margaret 7 yrs button maker [*Mrs Browne*][1]
	1691	6 May	Maverly, Thomas son of William, button maker, of Gloucester Watts, Robert 8 yrs tailor [*Mrs Browne*]
3/312		28 Mar	Niblett, James son of Samuel, yeoman, of Standish Gregory, William & Anne 7 yrs butcher
		1 Apr	Fowler, William son of Daniel, yeoman, of Hempsted Gwinnet, Sarah, widow, 7 yrs baker
		16 Jul	Butter, Charles son of Charles, yeoman, of Highnam Butter, Edward & Elizabeth 7 yrs tailor *Easter 1693: turned over to William Perry tailor, by order of Sessions*
		2 Feb	Stephens, Francis son of Paul, apothecary, of Cirencester Gwilliam, John & Anne 7 yrs feltmaker
3/313		22 Jun	Merryman, Newman son of Edward, yeoman, of Alstone Hayward, Clement 7 yrs tailor
		29 Jun	Higgs, Robert son of Eleanor, widow, of Cheltenham Wells, Richard 6 yrs cordwainer

---

[1] GBR B3/7 f 28v 13 Feb 1691: To receive £4 of Mrs Browne's money: Thomas Maverly, William Baker, Richard Hathaway (on the mayor's casting vote).

| | 1691 | 3 Aug | Luther, John son of John, glass founder, of Gloucester |
| | | | Matthews, John 7 yrs from 29 Sep 1688 butcher |

He was 3 years with his master before he was bound

| | | 25 Jul | Smith, Thomas son of Thomas, saddler, of Winchcombe |
| | | | Willmott, Robert & Sarah 7 yrs saddler |

14 Apr 1693: At the Tolsey, before Robert Payne, mayor, and some of the aldermen, Robert Willmott said Thomas Smith had delivered up his indenture to him and they were discharged each from other

3/314

Lander, Thomas son of James, wool comber, of Gloucester
  Humphris, Samuel 7 yrs butcher

Russell, Hugh son of John, baker, formerly of 'Lay'
  Castle, Nathaniel 7 yrs baker

1 Aug Man, Joseph son of George, glover, of Ross on Wye, Herefs
  Jones, Joseph 7 yrs barber surgeon

24 Jun Beard, Richard son of John, clerk, dec'd, of Gloucester
  Beard, Henry & Grace 7 yrs [*no trade*]

3/315

Davis, Henry son of John, pinmaker, of Gloucester
  Davis, John, his father, 7 yrs [pinmaker]

Thomas Brown, mayor [1691–2]
[Samuel Lye and John Bell, bailiffs and sheriffs]

1691 29 Sep Iles, Thomas son of Thomas, victualler, of Gloucester
  Brown, Samuel 7 yrs glazier

Churches, John son of Thomas, wiredrawer, of Gloucester
  Kare, John & Anne 7 yrs pinmaker

12 Oct Hawling, William son of Robert, farmer, of Churchdown
  Palmer, Edmund & Elizabeth 7 yrs baker

3/316

29 Sep Bacon, Walter son of Oliver, silkweaver, formerly of Gloucester
  Perry, William 8 yrs from 1 Aug tailor

Rush, John son of James, victualler, of Gloucester
  Humphris, Thomas & Anne 7 yrs barber

Coopey, John son of John, tanner, of Gloucester
  Green, John & Margaret 7 yrs cooper [*Holliday*][1]

1 Nov Cove, William son of William, yeoman, of Pucklechurch
  Bowler, Thomas & Anne 7 yrs collar maker

3/317 21 Dec Smith, John son of John, feltmaker, of Gloucester
  Bosley, Walter 7 yrs feltmaker [*Holliday*]

15 Jun 1696: turned over to Anne Nash, widow, by Walter Bosley

---

[1] GBR B3/7 f 36 10 Apr 1691: To receive £5 of Mr Hollidaye's money: John Smith, John Coopey, Joseph Hanks, Henry Hornidge, William Taylor, Thomas Hossington.

	1691	17 Nov	Cor, Henry son of Edmund, button maker, of Gloucester Prinn, William 7 yrs tailor[1]
		3 May	Sparrow, William son of William, yeoman, of Sandhurst [MS Sainthurst] Graffstocke, John 7 yrs butcher *10 Jun 1693: turned over to John Allen, butcher*
		29 Sep	Bradley, Thomas son of Henry, feltmaker, of Gloucester White, John 7 yrs cordwainer [*Repeated at 3/326*]
		24 Jul	Higgings, Ephraim son of Higgins, Ephraim, feltmaker, of the Margarets, [Gloucester] Meadway, Abraham 7 yrs bricklayer
3/318	1692	15 Jan	Green, William son of Philip, dec'd, of Gloucester Greening, John & Ursula 7 yrs butcher
		7 Apr	Townsend, Giles son of Giles, dec'd, of Minsterworth Elliotts, Henry jr & Jane 7 yrs joiner
		9 May	Drinkwater, Thomas son of William, of Cheltenham Hornidge, Joseph & Mary 7 yrs ropemaker
3/319		14 Jun	Fletcher, Robert son of Robert, gentleman, of Winchcombe Jaques, Aaron & Mary 7 yrs baker
		27 Jun	Lodge, William son of Trustram, cooper, of Gloucester Lodge, Trustram, his father, 7 yrs cooper
		4 Jul	Hooper, John son of John, tailor, dec'd, of Hartpury Pace, John 7 yrs from 25 Mar cordwainer
		11 Jul	Evans, Hardwicke son of Eleanor, widow, of Gloucester Davis, Robert & Rebecca 7 yrs brazier
3/320		—	Fordes, William son of William, placed by the parish of St Catherine's, Gloucester Care, John, of the same parish, 8 yrs from 24 May pinmaker
		18 Jul	Felton, Thomas son of Joseph, cutler, dec'd, of Gloucester Felton, Joseph, his brother, 7 yrs from 24 Jun barber surgeon
		23 Jul	Portus, William son of Thomas, yeoman, of Upton, Tetbury Humphris, Edward & Elizabeth 7 yrs from 6 Jul currier
		26 Jul	Swayne, Edward son of Edward, collar maker, dec'd, of Gloucester Jeffryes, Henry & Mary 7 yrs from 24 Jun joiner[2]
3/321		24 Jun	Budding, Richard son of Henry, yeoman, of Slimbridge Lewis, Thomas 7 yrs goldsmith & watchmaker
		29 Jun	Painter, George son of Richard, barber surgeon, of Ross, Herefs Madocke, Thomas 7 yrs saddler

---

[1] GBR B3/7 f 36v 10 Apr 1691: To receive £5 of Mr Powell's money: Henry son of Edmund Cor.
[2] ibid f 59 5 Jul 1692: Edward Swayne from Bluecoat Hospital to be apprenticed to Henry Jeffryes.

	1692	29 Sep	Farley, James son of Thomas, cutler, of Gloucester
			Farley, Thomas, his father, 7 yrs [cutler]
3/322		1 Jun	Mountague, George son of William, yeoman, of Over
			Browne, John 7 yrs tailor
		1 May	Gabb, Thomas son of Thomas, yeoman, of Hardwicke
			Hornidge, William 7 yrs cordwainer
		7 Sep	Heyford, John son of John, pavior, of Gloucester
			Heyford, John, his father, 7 yrs pavior [*Mrs Browne*]¹
			Pritchard, Edward son of Thomas, labourer, of Lower Southgate Street
			Byford, Joseph 7 yrs glazier
3/323		9 Sep	Price, William son of Alice, widow, of Gloucester
			Price, Alice, his mother, 7 yrs [pewterer]
		25 Sep	Swaine, Thomas son of Frances, widow, of Gloucester
			Price, Richard 7 yrs plasterer [*Holliday*]²
		29 Sep	Powell, Samuel son of Anne, widow
			Smyth, Giles & Sybil 7 yrs baker
		21 Sep	Makepeace, Samuel son of John, clerk, of Quedgeley
			Partridge, Richard & Anne 7 yrs baker
		24 Sep	King, John jr son of John sr, brewer, of Gloucester
			Prynn, William & Margaret 7 yrs from 29 Sep tailor [*Holliday*]
3/324		28 Sep	Hill, Samuel son of William, yeoman, dec'd, of Minsterworth
			Cooke, Charles & Mary 7 yrs from 25 Dec last butcher
		5 Oct	Smith, Maurice son of William, yeoman, dec'd, of Slimbridge
			Chandler, Richard 7 yrs from 21 Jul saddler
	1691	10 Oct	Wood, James son of William, mercer, dec'd, of Gloucester
			Wood, Eleanor 7 yrs mercer
	1692	1 May	Lewis, Edward son of Abel, tiler, of Gloucester
			Bicknell, William 7 yrs tailor³
		1 Jun	Branch, William son of Thomas, yeoman, of Highnam
			Yate, Samuel 7 yrs grocer
		1 Aug	Nest, Thomas son of Thomas, carpenter, of Gloucester
			Paynter, John & Elizabeth 7 yrs glazier
3/325		13 Aug	Elsmore, Joseph son of John, of Longhope
			Smith, Thomas & Jane 7 yrs glover
		17 Sep	Cockerell, Thomas son of Thomas, clothier, of Feering [MS Fearrell], Essex
			Bicknell, William & Abigail 7 yrs tailor

¹ GBR B3/7 f 57v 6 Apr 1692: To receive £4 of Mrs Browne's money: the sons of Francis Beale, John Hayford, Michael Griffiths.

² ibid f 66v 1 Sep 1692: To receive £5 of Mr Hollidaye's money: Thomas Swaine, John King, Walter Young, William Glover, John Thomas, Thomas Horsington.

³ ibid f 59 5 Jul 1692: Edward Lewis from Bluecoat Hospital to be apprenticed to William Bicknell.

	1692	1 Mar	Rodway, Thomas son of Giles, mercer, of Gloucester Rodway, Giles, his father, 7 yrs mercer
		29 Sep	Waldin, Thomas son of Henry, blacksmith, of Ruardean Reeve, John & Sarah 8 yrs gunsmith
		1 Mar	Rodway, John son of John, mercer, dec'd, of Gloucester Rodway, Elizabeth, his mother, 7 yrs mercer
3/326	1691	29 Sep	Bradley, Thomas son of Henry, feltmaker, of Gloucester White, John & Hannah 7 yrs cordwainer [*Repeating entry at 3/317*] *13 Nov 1696: turned over by consent to William Hornage, cordwainer. Before John Hyett, mayor*

3/330			**Robert Payne, mayor [1692–3]** **Caple Payne and William Nicholls, bailiffs and sheriffs**
	1692	11 Oct	Estcott, Samuel son of Christopher, pinmaker, of Gloucester Hartland, Thomas & Margaret 7 yrs pinmaker
		6 Oct	Partridge, Robert son of Thomas, baker, dec'd, of Gloucester Hayes, William & Judith 7 yrs cordwainer[1]
		14 Oct	Holder, Joseph son of Joseph, pinmaker, of Gloucester Sysemore, Alice 7 yrs widow *2 Jul 1696: turned over to Mary Bayly, widow*
		15 Oct	Young, Walter son of Walter, currier, dec'd, of Gloucester Atkins, Walter & Mary 7 yrs cordwainer [*Holliday*]
		18 Oct	Cooke, Richard son of Richard, blacksmith, dec'd, of Gloucester Wintle, John & Anne 7 yrs cordwainer
3/331		22 Oct	Hall, Giles son of Robert, tailor, of Slimbridge Gibbs, Thomas & Sarah 7 yrs blacksmith formerly of Gloucester, now of Dursley
		25 Oct	Collett, Samuel son of Samuel, haberdasher of hats, of Gloucester Bosley, Walter & Joyce 7 yrs feltmaker
		29 Oct	Barker, Thomas son of Nicholas, innholder, of Tirley Lugg, Lawrence & Elizabeth 7 yrs from 1 Nov baker
		8 Nov	Swayne, Samuel son of William, victualler, of St Mary de Lode, Wotton, Gloucester Weaver, Henry & Sarah 7 yrs from 2 Nov farrier
	1693	2 Jan	Bland, Josiah son of Bridget, widow, of Bristol Payne, Robert, esquire, 8 yrs from 29 Sep [merchant]
3/332		9 Jan	Cowles, John son of Thomas, cordwainer, of Gloucester Church, Roger & Sarah 7 yrs tailor [*cf Appendix V*]
		23 Jan	Barrett, Thomas son of William, wool comber Martin, Thomas 7 yrs tailor

---

[1] GBR B3/7 f 67v 1 Sep 1692: To receive £5 of Mr Powell's money: Robert Partridge.

| | 1693 24 Jan | Lewis, Richard son of Abel, pargeter, of Gloucester
Howell, Joseph & Elizabeth 7 yrs blacksmith [*cf Appendix V*]
23 Nov 1695: turned over to Jasper Nelme, cordwainer. Before Thomas Longden, mayor |

| | 11 Feb | Partridge, Henry son of Henry sr, gentleman, of Wishanger, Ruardean
Webb, Thomas & Anne 7 yrs from 1 Dec mercer |

3/333 27 Mar Dawby, Giles son of John, victualler, formerly of Hardwicke
Green, John & Joan 7 yrs from 25 Mar cordwainer

10 Apr Stephens, John son of Thomas, yeoman, dec'd, of Cheltenham
Spencer, Thomas & Beata 7 yrs cooper

13 Apr Dicks, William son of Thomas, labourer, dec'd, of Gloucester
Meadway, Abraham & Mary 7 yrs bricklayer [*Mrs Browne*][1]

3 May Lewis, Richard son of Abel, tiler & pargeter, of Gloucester
Cowcher, William & Elizabeth 7 yrs cordwainer [*cf Appendix V*]

3/334 12 May Pritchard, John jr son of John, tiler & plasterer, of Gloucester
Pritchard, John, his father, 7 yrs tiler & plasterer [*Mrs Browne*]

Hale, William son of William, innholder, dec'd, of Gloucester
Kent, Samuel & Jane 7 yrs joiner

23 May White, William son of Giles, mason, of Littleworth
Barker, William & Lucy 7 yrs tiler & plasterer

2 Jun Jeffs, Edward son of Thomas, yeoman, of Charlton Kings
Nash, Anne, widow 7 yrs [feltmaker] [*cf Appendix V*]

3/335 5 Jun Hyett, William son of John, alderman, of Gloucester
Hyett, John, his father, & Elizabeth 7 yrs [merchant]

23 Jun Elliott, Richard son of Edward, glassmaker, dec'd, of Gloucester
Oatley, Francis & Sarah 7 yrs feltmaker

27 Jun Best, Francis son of Francis, malt maker, of Gloucester
Parker, John & Martha 7 yrs from 29 Sep past tailor

7 Jul Ashmead, John son of John, coverlet weaver, of Cheltenham
Hyett, John, alderman, & Elizabeth 7 yrs [merchant]

3/336 8 Jul Lander, James son of James, wool comber, of Gloucester
Pendris, Humphrey & Margaret of Droitwich, Worcs 7 yrs from 1 May baker

11 Jul Bradshaw, William son of William, sawyer, of Gloucester
Randle, Daniel & Anne 7 yrs joiner

13 Jul Ady, Edward son of Thomas, baker, of Gloucester
Ady, Thomas, his father, & Margery 7 yrs baker

17 Jul Drew, John son of Thomas, yeoman, dec'd, of Churcham
Sysemore, William 7 yrs barber surgeon

---

[1] GBR B3/7 f 93v 10 Apr 1693: To receive £4 of Mrs Browne's money: William Dicks, John Pritchard, Edward Sollers.

3/337	1693	22 Jul	Clarke, Thomas son of Diana, widow, of Malswick, Newent Jaques, Aaron & Mary 7 yrs baker
		28 Jul	Adams, John son of John, weaver, of Gloucester Cowcher, Richard & Margaret 10 yrs pinmaker
		21 Jul	Griffith, Philip son of Bridget, widow, of Coleford Fowler, William & Mary 7 yrs barber surgeon
		14 Aug	Harris, Richard son of John, yeoman, dec'd, of Harescombe Bubb, William 7 yrs from 24 Jun barber surgeon
3/338		4 Sep	Williams, Richard son of Richard, cooper, of Gloucester Williams, Richard, his father, & Anne 7 yrs cooper
		5 Sep	Berry, William son of Thomas, tiler & plasterer, dec'd, of Gloucester Browne, John & Hester 7 yrs from 29 Jun tailor [*Holliday*][1]
			Randle, John son of Giles, silkweaver, of Gloucester Attwood, John & Susannah 7 yrs tiler & plasterer [*Holliday*]
		25 Sep	Dubberley, Thomas son of John, pinmaker, dec'd, of Gloucester Gardner, Thomas & Joan 7 yrs pinmaker [*Holliday*]
3/339		29 Sep	Gittos, William son of William, saddler, of Gloucester Furney, James & Sarah 7 yrs ironmonger
			Dowson, Joseph son of William, tailor, of Gloucester Dowson, William, his father, & Katharine 7 yrs tailor[2]
3/340			**John Ewins, mayor [1693–4]** **Samuel Hayward and Samuel Burroughs, bailiffs and sheriffs**
	1693	12 Oct	Sandford, Thomas son of Thomas, yeoman, dec'd, of Taynton Edwards, Thomas 7 yrs from 29 Sep grocer
		2 Nov	Motley, John son of William, glover, dec'd, of Gloucester Corsnett, Richard & Martha 7 yrs vintner
		3 Nov	Ellis, John son of Thomas, collier, dec'd, of Coleford Rudge, Milberrow, widow 7 yrs [farrier]
3/341		25 Nov	Cole, Thomas son of John, yeoman, dec'd, of Shurdington Collins, James & Sarah 7 yrs grocer
		1 Dec	Sollars, Edward son of James, yeoman, dec'd, of Cranham Heard, Humphrey & Jane 7 yrs butcher [*Mrs Browne*]
		6 Dec	Flower, John son of Samuel, barber surgeon, dec'd, of London Crowdy, James & Mary 7 yrs tailor

[1] GBR B3/7 f 98 4 Aug 1693: To receive £5 of Mr Hollidaye's money: Thomas Berry, Richard Beard, Giles Randle, Isaac Puckeridge, Richard Sleight, Thomas Dubberly.

[2] ibid f 98v 4 Aug 1693: To receive £5 of Alderman Powell's charity money: Joseph son of William Dowson.

3/342	1694	15 Jan	Cowlsey, William son of Thomas, yeoman, dec'd, of Hartpury
			Allen, William & Mary 7 yrs from 1 Nov grocer
		19 Jan	Hamonds, Thomas son of Thomas, glazier, dec'd, of Gloucester
			Rogers, Thomas & Mary 7 yrs from 25 Mar next baker
		24 Jan	Puckeridge, Isaac, of Gloucester
			Puckeridge, Thomas 7 yrs from 29 Sep past tailor [*Holliday*]
		22 Jan	Gardner, Anthony son of Thomas, clothworker, of Painswick
			Gammond, John 7 yrs from 1 Dec baker
3/343		25 Jan	Savory, William son of Robert, farrier, of Gloucester
			Savory, Robert, his father, & Mary 7 yrs farrier
		2 Feb	Hawtherne, Charles son of John, wiredrawer, dec'd, of Gloucester
			Wythenbury, Thomas & Sarah 7 yrs carpenter
		16 Feb	Tyler, Edward son of Edward, trowman, dec'd, of Tewkesbury
			Wilmott, Robert & Sarah 7 yrs from 2 Feb saddler
		19 Feb	Pitt, John son of Roger, carpenter, of Gloucester
			Pitt, Joseph & Mary 7 yrs feltmaker
3/344		21 Feb	Gardner, John son of Richard, yeoman, of St Mary de Lode, Tuffley
			Jennings, Michael & Abigail 7 yrs from 2 Feb butcher
		3 Mar	Vyner, William son of John, yeoman, dec'd, of Hartpury
			Whittingham, Edward & Abigail 7 yrs from 5 Feb baker
		26 Mar	Nurse, John son of Giles sr, yeoman, of Upton St Leonards
			Walker, Anthony & Mary 7 yrs blacksmith
			Mason, William son of William, wool comber, of Gloucester
			Price, John & Anne 7 yrs gardener
3/345		5 May	Deane, Thomas son of George, yeoman, of Hyde Farm, Pinnock
			Lawrence, William 7 yrs from 25 Mar baker
		17 May	Turbett, Thomas son of Thomas, tanner, of Gloucester
			Sexstone, Clement & Anne of Wantage, Berks 7 yrs currier [*Mrs Browne*][1]
			Joy, John son of David, yeoman, dec'd, of Gloucester
			Davis, John & Margaret 7 yrs pinmaker [*Mrs Browne*]
		28 May	Lightfoot, Mark son of William, yeoman, of Newent
			Skynner, William & Mary 7 yrs cordwainer
3/346		18 Jun	Hatton, John son of John, butcher, dec'd, of Gloucester
			Way, John & Susannah 7 yrs butcher [*Mrs Browne*]
		27 Jun	Man, John son of Edward, yeoman, of Westbury
			Man, James & Mary 8 yrs from 9 Apr glover

---

[1] GBR B3/7 f 98 19 Apr 1694: To receive £4 of Mrs Browne's money: John Joy, Thomas Turbett, John Hatton.

| | 1694 | 17 Jul | Barrett, William son of William, wool comber, of Gloucester |
| | | | Webb, Richard & Elizabeth 7 yrs wool comber |

 1 Aug Rudhall, Abraham son of Abraham, bellfounder, of Gloucester
         Rudhall, Abraham, his father, & Elizabeth 7 yrs bellfounder

3/347 10 Aug Sparks, Thomas son of Thomas, silkweaver, of Gloucester
         Pegler, Joseph & Jane 7 yrs from 25 Jul tanner

 27 Aug Clarke, Samuel son of John, tanner, of Gloucester
         Clarke, Philip & Joan 7 yrs butcher
         26 May 1699: turned over by consent to Thomas Lander, butcher. Before Alderman Rodway

William Tayler, mayor [1694–5]
[Thomas Edwards and William Edwards, bailiffs and sheriffs]

 1694 2 Oct Nash, Richard son of William, feltmaker, of Gloucester
         Workman, Anthony & Anne 7 yrs butcher [*cf Appendix V*] [*Holliday*]¹
         12 Nov 1695: turned over by consent to John Graffstocke, butcher

 6 Oct Aylburton, William son of John, gentleman, dec'd, of Westbury
         Veysey, Thomas & Mary 7 yrs from 29 Sep mercer

3/348 12 Oct Colles, Thomas son of Thomas, cordwainer, of Gloucester
         Benson, John & Elizabeth 7 yrs from 24 Aug pargeter

 16 Oct Hobson, James son of James, button maker, of Gloucester
         Atkins, Walter & Mary 7 yrs cordwainer [*Holliday*]

 22 Oct Powell, John son of Thomas silkweaver, of Gloucester
         Hicks, Edward & Grace 7 yrs pipe maker

 16 Nov Bossom, Thomas son of Thomas, innholder, of Mitcheldean
         Heaven, John & Deborah 7 yrs from 23 Sep barber surgeon

3/349 24 Nov Merrett, Giles son of Thomas, clerk, of Gloucester
         Walter, John & Margery 7 yrs ship's carpenter

 18 Dec Bird, John son of Daniel, horn breaker, of Gloucester
         Bird, Daniel, his father, & Anne 7 yrs horn breaker [*Holliday*]

 1695 16 Jan Barnfield, Richard son of Richard, yeoman, of Cranham
         Hornage, James & Mary 7 yrs from 1 Nov blacksmith

 17 Jan Johnson, Samuel son of Michael, yeoman, of Wormington
         Bell, John, gentleman, & Mary 7 yrs from 20 Dec [mercer]

3/350 24 Jan Horrold, Edward son of Edward, yeoman, dec'd, of Hankerton, Wilts
         Williams, Richard & Anne 7 yrs cooper

---

¹ GBR B3/7 f 98 7 Aug 1694: To receive £5 of Mr Hollidaye's money: Thomas Cowles, George Nott, Arthur Barrett, Richard Nash, John Bird, James Hobson.

| | 1695 | 19 Mar | Collett, John son of Samuel, haberdasher, dec'd, of Gloucester |
| | | | Kent, Hannah 7 yrs widow |

                   26 Mar Emes, Richard son of Jonathan, pewterer, formerly of Pershore, Worcs
                            Ward, John & Elizabeth 7 yrs from 25 Nov blacksmith

                   29 Mar Sexty, John son of John sr, cheesemonger, of Gloucester
                            Sexty, John, his father, & Susannah 7 yrs cheesemonger

3/351   10 Apr Barrett, Arthur son of Thomas, tailor, dec'd, of Gloucester
                            Watts, Thomas & Elizabeth of Over 7 yrs from 25 Mar tailor
                                [*Holliday*]

                   15 Apr Fownes, Godfrey son of Godfrey, maltster, dec'd, of Gloucester
                            Cowdall, John jr & Sarah 7 yrs grocer

                   18 Apr Randle, Josiah, son of William, gentleman, of Gloucester
                            Randle, Josiah & Margery 7 yrs baker

                              Hone, John son of Henry, yeoman, of Brockworth
                            Jennings, Jeremiah & Anne 7 yrs tailor

3/352   19 Apr Nott, George son of George, carpenter, dec'd, of Gloucester
                            Jones, Charles & Anne 7 yrs cooper [*Holliday*]

                   29 Apr Gregory, William son of William, wheelwright, of Hucclecote
                            Davis, Jonathan & Elizabeth 7 yrs tailor 5s

          1694 1 Nov Englee, Richard son of Richard, bricklayer, of Gloucester
                            Englee, Richard, his father, & Alice 7 yrs bricklayer

          1695 17 May Harris, John son of Richard, yeoman, of Hawling
                            Punter, Robert & Mary 7 yrs from 27 Mar merchant

3/353   21 May Sexty, William son of John, cheesemonger, of Gloucester
                            Sexty, John, his father, & Susannah 7 yrs cheesemonger

                    1 Jun White, Nathaniel son of Nathaniel, butcher, of Newent
                            Pace, Francis & Susannah of Newent 7 yrs from 19 Apr cordwainer

                   22 Jun Cooke, James son of John, yeoman, dec'd, of Charlton Kings
                            Randle, James & Jane 7 yrs from 10 Jun joiner

                              Barnwood, Thomas son of Thomas, yeoman, of Hardwicke
                            Tyler, John & Anne 7 yrs from 29 May cordwainer

                   24 Jun Barton, John son of Thomas, labourer, dec'd, of Gloucester
                            Ingly, Richard & Alice 7 yrs bricklayer [*Mrs Browne*][1]

3/354   3 Jul Armitage, John son of John, wool comber, of Barton Street, Gloucester
                            Till, Richard & Mary 7 yrs cutler [*Mrs Browne*]

                   30 Jul Merchant, John son of Henry, yeoman, of Haydon, Boddington
                            Brocke, John & Mary 7 yrs from 29 May skinner

---

[1] GBR B3/7 f 118 10 May 1695: To receive £4 of Mrs Browne's money: John Barton, John Dudson, John Armitage.

| | 1695 | 5 Aug | Gill, William son of William, of Barton Street, St Mary de Lode |
| | | | Seyer, Daniel 7 yrs from 2 Oct last ropemaker |

        1695 5 Aug Gill, William son of William, of Barton Street, St Mary de Lode
                       Seyer, Daniel 7 yrs from 2 Oct last ropemaker

                   Hawkins, John son of Jonathan, serge weaver, dec'd, of Tewkesbury
                       Seyer, Daniel 7 yrs from 2 Oct last ropemaker

            13 Aug Perrys, John son of William, butcher, of Gloucester
                   Perrys, William, his father, & Frances 7 yrs butcher [*Holliday*][1]

3/355   8 Aug Veysey, Nathaniel son of Nathaniel, tailor, of Gloucester
                   Veysey, Nathaniel, his father, & Dorothy 7 yrs from 21 Dec tailor

            15 Aug Field, John son of Thomas, mason, of Tewkesbury
                   Cartwright, Edward 7 yrs from 24 Jun baker
                       10 Jan 1699: turned over to Robert Wintle, baker, by consent

            5 Sep Hope, John son of William, gentleman, of Llanthony
                   Matthews, Thomas 8 yrs from 1 Aug apothecary

            2 Sep Fordes, Henry son of Fords, James, tailor, of Gloucester
                   Fordes, James, his father, & Mary 7 yrs tailor [*Holliday*]

            9 Sep Sysemore, John son of Dennis, barber surgeon, dec'd, of Gloucester
                   Sysemore, John sr & Joan 7 yrs barber surgeon [*Holliday*]

3/356   Ingly, Thomas son of John, bricklayer, of Gloucester
                   Perrys, Richard & Mary 7 yrs butcher [*Holliday*]

            11 Sep Baldwyn, John son of Thomas, gardener, dec'd, of Tewkesbury
                   Brabant, Francis & Margaret 7 yrs cooper
                       These indentures are in English, so not in the usual form, 'for that we wanted others stamped which could not be got for the present occasion'

            20 Sep Keene, John son of William, glazier, of Dorchester, Oxon
                   Sheppard, John & Adoliza 7 yrs barber surgeon

            23 Sep Shaw, William son of John, farmer, of Bledisloe, Awre
                   Lucas, Samuel & Elizabeth 7 yrs joiner

            30 Sep Scudamore, William jr son of William, former alderman, of Gloucester
                   Scudamore, William sr 7 yrs woollen draper

3/357   **Thomas Longden, mayor [1695–6]**
                   [Thomas Veisey and Richard Corsnett, bailiffs and sheriffs]

        1695 4 Oct Sermon, Richard son of Richard, cordwainer, of Tirley
                   Oateley, Francis & Sarah 7 yrs feltmaker
                       18 Aug 1701: turned over by Francis Oatley to John Pearce of Tewkesbury, feltmaker

            9 Oct Holder, John son of Joseph, pinmaker, of Gloucester
                   Gardner, William & Hannah 7 yrs pinmaker

---

[1] GBR B3/7 f 126 2 Aug 1695: To receive £5 of Mr Hollidaye's money: John Perrys, Henry Fords, John Sysemore, Thomas Ingly, John Hornage, Isaac Monning.

	1695 19 Oct	Swayne, Edward son of William, yeoman, dec'd, of Kingsholm
		Aldridge, Henry & Sarah 7 yrs tailor
	24 Oct	Lovell, Samuel son of John, silkweaver, of Gloucester
		Davis, John & Margaret 7 yrs pinmaker

3/358   25 Oct   Jones, William son of William, metalman, of Lower Southgate Street, Gloucester
Stephens, James & Mary 7 yrs pinmaker

Cowles, Edmund son of William, butcher, of Gloucester
Cowles, William, his father, & Anne 7 yrs butcher

5 Nov   Gyles, Isaac son of Adam, tailor, of Gloucester
Winston, Thomas & Margaret 7 yrs from 5 Nov 1693 tailor

Griffiths, Alexander son of John, gentleman, of Llanfyllin [MS Lanvilling], Mont
Hyett, John, alderman, & Elizabeth 7 yrs [merchant]

6 Nov   Darke, Richard son of William, wheelwright, dec'd, of Twyning
Reeve, Giles & Sarah 7 yrs from 1 Nov gunsmith

3/359   8 Nov   Elliott, Thomas son of Thomas, wiredrawer, of Gloucester
Selwyn, Thomas & Mary 7 yrs from 25 Mar next cordwainer

Monning, William son of Isaac, pinmaker, of Gloucester
Wynniatt, Thomas 7 yrs from 1 Nov pinmaker [*Holliday*]

Hornage, John son of Joseph, ropemaker, of Gloucester
Hornage, Joseph, his father, & Mary 7 yrs ropemaker [*Holliday*]

11 Nov   Haynes, Edward son of Edward, tailor, dec'd, of Gloucester
Gardner, William & Hannah 7 yrs pinmaker

12 Nov   Lugg, Edward son of John, tanner, of Gloucester
Oatley, Francis 7 yrs from 29 Sep feltmaker

3/360   21 Nov   May, John son of Thomas, dec'd, of Little Badminton
Ady, Thomas & Margery 7 yrs baker

22 Nov   Dudson, John son of John, labourer, of Gloucester
Atkyns, Walter & Mary 7 yrs from 25 Dec next cordwainer [*Mrs Browne*]

25 Nov   Longden, Caple son of Thomas, now mayor, ironmonger, of Gloucester
Longden, Thomas, his father, & Anne 7 yrs ironmonger

2 Dec   Mince, John son of John, clothier, dec'd, of Bledington
Palmer, Edward & Elizabeth 7 yrs from 1 Nov baker

3/361   6 Dec   Hill, Thomas son of Richard, pinmaker, of Gloucester
Hill, Richard, his father, & Jane 7 yrs pinmaker

16 Dec   Barnes, Edward son of Thomas, gentleman, of Longdon, Worcs
Crumpe, Richard & Christian 7 yrs from 30 Oct brazier

	1696 31 Jan	Bullocke, Richard son of Richard, farmer, of Minsterworth Marshfield, James & Mary 7 yrs fisherman
		Taylor, William son of William, schoolmaster, of Gloucester Wyly, Thomas & Martha 7 yrs from 4 Dec baker
3/362	2 Apr	Fryer, Walter son of Mary, dec'd, of Hartpury Pytt, James & Joyce 12 yrs from 1 May last pinmaker
	16 Apr	Williams, Richard son of John, glover, of Gloucester Williams, John, his father, & Margaret 7 yrs from 1 May last glover
	17 Apr	Arnold, Anthony son of Joyce Church, of Gloucester Gardner, Daniel & Rebecca 7 yrs from 1 Jan pinmaker *22 Sep 1698: turned over to Richard Hill, pinmaker, & Jane*
		Hopley, Thomas son of Thomas, labourer, of Gloucester Hill, Richard & Jane 7 yrs from 25 Mar pinmaker
3/363	30 Apr	Dowle, James Clement son of James, clerk, dec'd, of Wellington, Som Dowle, Job 7 yrs from 29 Sep merchant
	20 Apr	Sparks, Richard son of Richard, victualler, of Barton Street, Gloucester Seyer, John 7 yrs from 21 Dec ropemaker
	29 Apr	Price, John son of David, labourer, of Gloucester Burridge, Thomas & Frances 7 yrs from 1 May next weaver
	11 May	Keys, John son of Patrick, tailor, formerly of Londonderry, Ireland Sayer, James sr & Margaret 7 yrs from 25 Mar tailor
	12 May	Washborne, Samuel son of John, clockmaker, of Barton Street, Gloucester Horrold, William & Jane 7 yrs from 4 May pewterer & brazier
	4 May	Castle, Nathaniel son of Nathaniel, baker, of Gloucester Castle, Nathaniel, his father, & Anne 7 yrs from 25 Mar baker
3/364	12 May	Cripps, Edward son of Edward, butcher, dec'd, of Gloucester Moore, John & Jane 7 yrs butcher[1]
	18 May	Cheesman, John son of John, cooper, dec'd, of Gloucester Jones, Charles & Anne 7 yrs cooper [*Holliday*][2]
	27 May	Webb, Richard son of Stephen, yeoman, dec'd, of Berrow, Worcs Wilmott, Robert & Sarah 7 yrs saddler
	9 Jun	Hayward, Samuel son of Samuel, gentleman, of Gloucester Bishopp, Daniel & Anne 7 yrs barber surgeon
	12 Jun	Smith, James son of James, yeoman, of Tockenham Wick, Wilts Brabant, Francis jr & Margaret 7 yrs from 21 May cooper

[1] GBR B3/7 f 130v 18 Sep 1695: To receive £10 of Sir Thomas Rich's money: Edward Cripps, Richard Bishopp, Anthony Motley, Stephen Wiltshire, James Jonsy, James Lovett.

[2] ibid f 151v 31 Jul 1696: To receive £5 of Mr Hollidaye's money: Joseph Young, John Cheesman, Henry Bradley, Henry Brimyard, Thomas Hughes, John Motley.

3/365	1696	15 Jun	Gyles, James son of Adam, tailor, of Gloucester
			Skillerne, William 7 yrs from 29 Sep next tailor [*Mrs Browne*]¹
			Symon, David son of David, innholder, dec'd, of Gloucester
			Beedle, John 7 yrs from 12 Apr collar maker
		16 Jun	Grove, Samuel son of John, glassmaker, of Gloucester
			Hornage, William & Anne 7 yrs from 1 Jun cordwainer
		22 Jun	Tayler, Edward son of Thomas, dec'd, of Gloucester
			Benson, William & Mary 7 yrs plasterer
		2 Jul	Bryan, Daniel son of Daniel, cordwainer, of Gloucester
			Farmer, Samuel & Anne 7 yrs apothecary
3/366		6 Jul	Tayler, Philip son of John, farrier, dec'd, of Brampton Abbotts, Herefs
			Randle, William 7 yrs barber surgeon
		17 Jul	Worrall, James son of Joshua, silkweaver, of Gloucester
			Wood, John & Elizabeth 7 yrs haberdasher
		25 Jul	Woolvin, Thomas son of Thomas, wool comber, of Winchcombe
			Smith, John & Frances 7 yrs currier
		6 Aug	Hodges, Samuel son of Thomas, yeoman, of Churchdown
			Aylway, Richard & Mary 7 yrs from 25 Jun baker
		7 Aug	Durham, James son of John, gentleman, of Willersey [MS Willersley]
			Webb, Thomas, alderman, & Anne 7 yrs from 24 Jun [mercer]
3/367		10 Aug	Hannis, Thomas son of Thomas, pinmaker, of Gloucester
			Brymyard, William & Alice 7 yrs pinmaker
		13 Aug	Goodman, Edward son of Charles, yeoman, of Linton, Churcham
			Perry, William & Anne 7 yrs from 6 May tailor
		2 Oct	Jenings, Henry son of Henry, tailor, of Gloucester
			Veysey, Nathaniel & Dorothy 7 yrs from 25 Mar tailor
			[*Mrs Browne*]
			Hughes, Thomas son of John, silkweaver, of Gloucester
			Trow, John 7 yrs from 29 Sep pinmaker [*Holliday*]
			Mutlow, John son of Miles, fishhook maker, of Gloucester
			Mutlow, Miles jr 7 yrs from 29 Sep cordwainer [*Holliday*]
			3 May 1699: turned over to William Browne, cordwainer

3/368 **John Hyett, mayor [1696–7]**
[John Gwillim and Edmund Gregory, bailiffs and sheriffs]

	1696	12 Oct	Brymyard, Henry son of William, pinmaker, dec'd, of Gloucester
			Wells, Richard & Mary 7 yrs cordwainer [*Holliday*]
		13 Oct	Cheeseman, Paul son of John, cooper, dec'd, of Gloucester
			Kent, Samuel & Jane 7 yrs from 29 Sep joiner

---

¹ GBR B3/7 f 148v 22 May 1696: To receive £4 of Mrs Browne's money: James Gyles, Isaac Jennings, Thomas Morse.

	1696	7 Nov	Barrow, William son of William, yeoman, of Longford, St Catherine's

1696 7 Nov Barrow, William son of William, yeoman, of Longford, St Catherine's
Kearsy, Thomas & Anne 7 yrs button maker

13 Nov Nash, George son of Jesse jr, feltmaker, dec'd, of Gloucester
Jones, Thomas & Jane 8 yrs glover

23 Nov Bradley, Henry son of John, butcher, of Gloucester
Bradley, John, his father, & Mary 7 yrs butcher [*Holliday*]

3/369 28 Nov Finch, Richard son of William, bodicemaker, of Westminster
Collericke, Daniel & Elizabeth 7 yrs from 6 Oct bodicemaker

25 Nov Bacon, Robert son of Nollard, silkweaver, dec'd, of Gloucester
Church, Roger & Sarah 7 yrs from 24 Jun next tailor[1]

30 Dec Hardwicke, Nathaniel son of William, yeoman, dec'd, of Lassington
Jaques, Aaron & Mary 7 yrs from 25 Dec baker

1697 7 Jan Hopkins, Benjamin son of Anthony, clothier, of Ledbury, Herefs
Field, Thomas & Edith 7 yrs from 24 Jun past mercer

25 Jan Stephens, Thomas son of Thomas, tailor, dec'd, of Barton Street, Gloucester
Bowler, George jr & Mary 7 yrs from 21 Dec tailor[2]

3/370 2 Feb Hagborne, Thomas son of William, farmer, of Quedgeley
Palmer, Edmund & Elizabeth 7 yrs baker

26 Mar Toney, James son of Charles, labourer, dec'd, of Gloucester
Kingman, John & Anne 7 yrs from 25 Mar wiredrawer

7 Apr Bradshaw, John son of William, carpenter, of Gloucester
Jones, Thomas & Martha 7 yrs feltmaker

17 Apr Collett, William son of Samuel, haberdasher, dec'd, of Gloucester
Pembruge, Thomas & Elbeata 7 yrs grocer

16 Apr Hawkins, Samuel son of Thomas, yeoman, of Hardwicke
Hawkins, Thomas & Elizabeth 7 yrs grocer

3/371 1 May Organ, John son of Samuel, yeoman, dec'd, of Painswick
Drew, Thomas & Hannah 7 yrs cordwainer

7 Apr Hooper, Charles son of James, weaver, of Much Marcle, Herefs
Graffstocke, John & Sarah 7 yrs from 2 Feb butcher

17 May Williams, Thomas son of Thomas, gardener, of Gloucester
Guy, John & Sarah 7 yrs from 25 Mar maltster

29 May Worme, William son of Henry, wool comber, of South Cerney
Humphris, Edward & Elizabeth 7 yrs from 1 Nov past currier

---

[1] GBR B3/7 f 151v 31 Jul 1696: To receive Alderman Powell's £5: Robert Bacon.
[2] ibid f 155 3 Sep 1696: To receive £4 of Sir Thomas Rich's money: James Phelps, John Cowcher, John Hale, Thomas Stephens, Thomas Canon, Samuel Kendricke.

3/372	1697	11 Jun	Tanner, David son of David, gentleman, dec'd, of Gloucester Beale, Benjamin & Anne 7 yrs blacksmith [*Mrs Browne*][1]
		24 Jun	Williams, Thomas son of Thomas, dec'd, of Barton Street, Gloucester Weaver, Richard & Anne 7 yrs from 1 May butcher
		16 Jul	Price, Charles son of Thomas, cordwainer, dec'd, of Gloucester Jakeman, William & Elizabeth 7 yrs baker
		31 Jul	Stocke, John son of John, yeoman, of Chaceley, Worcs Gwinnell, Richard & Mary 7 yrs from 29 Jun grocer
3/373		2 Aug	Window, William son of William, silkweaver, of Gloucester Greenway, Charles & Rebecca 7 yrs cordwainer [*Mrs Browne*]
		27 Aug	Lye, Thomas son of Thomas, miller, dec'd, of Barton Street, Gloucester Berwicke, Thomas & Barbara 7 yrs from 2 Aug button maker
		7 Sep	Lee, William son of John, yeoman, dec'd, of Hampton, Salop Lee, John & Elizabeth 7 yrs tailor
		20 Sep	Maddocks, Thomas son of William, gentleman, of Gloucester Palmer, Edmund & Elizabeth 7 yrs from 4 Sep baker
3/374		30 Sep	Perry, Robert son of Robert, innkeeper, dec'd, of Gloucester Beach, John & Margaret 7 yrs from 3 Sep baker [*Holliday*][2]
			Wadley, John son of John, waggoner, of Gloucester Cope, Thomas & Mary 7 yrs from 29 Sep baker

Giles Rodway, mayor [1697–8]
[William Randle and Thomas Farley, bailiffs and sheriffs]

	1697	6 Oct	Haynes, William son of William, yeoman, of Ashchurch Burroughs, Samuel jr & Elizabeth 7 yrs innkeeper
		11 Oct	Hooke, Jonathan son of Edward, yeoman, of Taynton Freeman, Robert & Frances 7 yrs from 29 Sep joiner
3/375		23 Oct	Careles, Ebenezer son of John, gentleman, dec'd, of Gloucester Lane, Nicholas jr & Hester 7 yrs apothecary
			Mason, William son of William, tanner, of Gloucester Window, William & Elizabeth 7 yrs tailor
		1 Nov	Panther, Samuel son of Samuel, labourer, of St Catherine's Gloucester Webb, John & Anne 7 yrs from 29 Sep tailor
		5 Nov	Launder, James son of James, maltster, of Gloucester Lane, John & Sarah 7 yrs from 9 Oct grocer & tallow chandler

[1] GBR B3/7 f 169 15 Apr 1697: To receive £4 of Mrs Browne's money: William Window, Daniel Meeke, David Tanner, John Benson.

[2] ibid f 175 5 Aug 1697: To receive £5 of Mr Hollidaye's money: Robert Perry, John Gwynn, Robert Burridge, Thomas Philipps, Charles Young, John Turner.

ibid f 175v 5 Aug 1697: To receive £5 of Alderman Powell's money: John Wiltshire.

3/376	1697	30 Nov	Philips, John son of Thomas, tailor, of Gloucester Philips, Thomas, his father, & Elizabeth 7 yrs from 24 Jun tailor [*Holliday*]
		3 Dec	Young, Charles son of James, pinmaker, of Gloucester Gardner, William & Hannah 7 yrs from 22 Nov pinmaker [*Holliday*]
		6 Dec	Lovegrove, John son of John, yeoman, dec'd, of Barton Street, Gloucester Lovegrove, Giles 7 yrs plasterer & tiler
		8 Dec	Benson, John son of John, tiler & plasterer, of Gloucester Benson, John, his father, & Eliz 7 yrs from 1 Jun tiler & plasterer [*Mrs Browne*]
3/377		18 Dec	Gardner, Thomas son of Edward, mercer, of Corse Tyler, John jr & Mary 7 yrs from 5 Nov baker
		20 Dec	Burridge, Robert son of Thomas, weaver, of Gloucester Burridge, Thomas, his father, & Frances 7 yrs weaver [*Holliday*]
	1698	11 Jan	Cannon, Thomas son of Thomas, butcher, dec'd, of Gloucester Perrys, William & Elizabeth 7 yrs 5 Nov butcher
		13 Jan	Skynner, Thomas son of William, gentleman, of Preston Mason, Mary, widow 7 yrs from 29 Sep [baker] *1 Jun 1698: turned over by Mary Mason to William Godwin, baker*
3/378		24 Jan	Niccolls, Thomas son of Thomas, cordwainer, of Gloucester Philipps, James & Mary 7 yrs saddler
	1697	13 Dec	Pawldin, Daniel son of John, baker, of Painswick Gamond, John 7 yrs baker
	1698	4 Mar	Turner, William son of John, button maker, dec'd, of Gloucester Randle, William & Susannah 8 yrs serge weaver [*Holliday*]
		1 Apr	Nash, Richard son of William, feltmaker, dec'd, of Gloucester Nash, William 7 yrs carpenter [*cf Appendix V*]
3/379		11 Apr	Meadway, Joseph son of Henry, silkweaver, dec'd, of Gloucester Bubb, William 7 yrs from 25 Mar barber surgeon [1]
		4 Apr	Woodrooffe, William son of Francis, stone cutter, dec'd, of London Weaver, Richard & Mary 7 yrs from 25 Mar blacksmith
		11 Apr	Wantner, Charles son of Abel, clerk, of Gloucester Fowler, William & Mary 7 yrs barber surgeon
			Butt, Thomas son of Thomas, yeoman, dec'd, of Bishop's Norton Greene, John & Joan 7 yrs from 25 Mar cordwainer
3/380			Turner, Samuel son of Samuel, maltster, of Bisley Pedlingham, Richard & Jane 7 yrs saddler
		4 May	Gardner, Richard son of Richard, yeoman, of Tuffley Humphris, Anne, widow, 7 yrs from 25 Nov [barber]

---

[1] GBR B3/7 f 179 8 Sep 1697: To receive £10 of Sir Thomas Rich's money: Robert Hoskins, Joseph Meadway, William Bradgate, Henry Grevile, John Badger, Thomas Bullocke.

	1698 10 May	Hendy, Samuel son of Thomas, clothier, dec'd, of Periton [MS Pyrton], Som

1698 10 May Hendy, Samuel son of Thomas, clothier, dec'd, of Periton [MS Pyrton], Som
                Thorpe, Anne, widow, 7 yrs from 25 Dec past [*no trade*]

30 May Vice, Jonathan son of Jonathan, glover, of Gloucester
        Wiggett, Samuel & Alice 7 yrs glover

3/381 Rogers, Thomas son of John, baker, dec'd, of Gloucester
        Jeenes, Thomas & Martha 7 yrs feltmaker

8 Jun Andrews, Robert, with consent of George Cooke & Thomas Somers, overseers of the poor of St Aldate's parish, Gloucester
        Ricketts, John until age of 24 years pinmaker

20 Jun Gwynn, John son of John, silkweaver, of Gloucester
        Roan, Charles, of Down Hatherley 7 yrs from 25 Mar collar maker [*Holliday*]

22 Jun Freeman, William son of Vereby, mercer, dec'd, of Gloucester
        Archer, Abraham & Mary 7 yrs from 1 Jun bricklayer [*Mrs Browne*][1]

3/382 16 Jul Wynniatt, John, pauper, placed by James Engly & Thomas Monnington, overseers of the poor of St Catherine's parish, Gloucester
        Ricketts, John until age of 21 years pinmaker

8 Aug Belcher, Richard son of Edward, yeoman, of Saintbridge, Upton St Leonards [*sic*]
        Browne, William & Joan 7 yrs cordwainer

13 Aug Bower, Thomas son of Thomas, tanner, dec'd, of Newent
        Niccolls, William & Elizabeth 7 yrs tanner

        Long, William son of Thomas, yeoman, of Ashleworth
        Pace, Francis & Susannah 7 yrs from 1 Aug cordwainer

3/383 17 Aug White, William son of John, tanner, of Newent
        White, John, his father, & Mary 7 yrs from 25 Mar tanner

26 Aug Kingman, James son of John, yeoman, dec'd, of Frome, Som
        Wilkins, Mary, widow 7 yrs [wiredrawer]

1 Sep Jeffs, Edward son of Thomas, yeoman, of Charlton Kings
        Phelps, Matthew & Joyce 7 yrs feltmaker [*cf Appendix V*]

5 Sep Fordes, John son of John Fords, pinmaker, of Gloucester
        Fords, John, his father, & Isobel 7 yrs from 25 Mar pinmaker

9 Sep Toms, William son of John, gentleman, of Stanley Pontlarge
        Gregory, John & Hester 7 yrs from 1 Sep mercer

3/384 20 Sep Bradshaw, Robert son of William, sawyer, of Gloucester
        Meadway, Abraham & Mary 7 yrs from 29 Aug bricklayer [*Mrs Browne*]

23 Sep Bullocke, Thomas son of Thomas, scrivener, dec'd, of Gloucester
        Heming, Richard & Mary 7 yrs from 25 Mar tailor

---

[1] GBR B3/7 f 193 5 May 1698: To receive £4 of Mrs Browne's money: William Marden, Thomas Shatford, William Bradshaw, William Freeman.

Thomas Wilcox, mayor [1698–9]
[James Furney and Thomas Field, bailiffs and sheriffs]

1698   4 Oct   Brocke, Joseph son of Joseph, yeoman, dec'd, of Westbury
       Hyett, John & Elizabeth   7 yrs   mercer

25 Oct   Ward, John son of John, blacksmith, of Gloucester
       Ward, John, his father, & Elizabeth   7 yrs from 5 Nov next   blacksmith
       [*Holliday*][1]

12 Nov   Ravener, George son of Thomas, gardener, of Gloucester
       Matthews, Giles & Susannah of Upton St Leonards   7 yrs from 29 Sep
       butcher   [*Holliday*]

3/385   28 Nov   Lugg, John son of John, pinmaker, of Gloucester
       Browne, Samuel & Hester   7 yrs   glazier   2s 6d

29 Nov   Fryer, William son of Walter, yeoman, of Gloucester
       Price, Richard & Isobel   7 yrs   plasterer & tiler   [*Holliday*]
       These indentures were lost and new ones made for the remaining
       6 years of his service
       2 Jun 1701: turned over to Thomas Swayne, tiler & plasterer, his
       former master being dead. Before Nicholas Webb, mayor

5 Dec   Land, Thomas son of Thomas, yeoman, dec'd, of Lower Sheephouse
       Humphris, Samuel   7 yrs from 29 Sep   butcher

1699   28 Jan   Crockett, James son of Thomas, yeoman, of Taynton
       Skynner, William & Mary   7 yrs from 1 Nov   cordwainer

3/386   31 Jan   Mills, Thomas son of Thomas, plasterer, of Gloucester
       Pool, John & Sarah   7 yrs from 2 Feb next   plasterer

4 Feb   Turner, Thomas son of Thomas, cordwainer, of Gloucester
       Turner, Thomas, his father, & Anne   7 yrs   cordwainer

6 Feb   Parker, Thomas son of Thomas, baker, of Gloucester
       Nash, Anne, widow   7 yrs   [feltmaker]

Farmer, Francis son of Francis, labourer, of Gloucester
Prynn, William & Margaret   7 yrs from 2 Feb   tailor[2]
       17 Sep 1700: turned over by William Prynn to James Crody,
       tailor. Before Thomas Longden, alderman

Garrett, Thomas son of Thomas, yeoman, of Hanley, Worcs
Parker, John & Martha   7 yrs from 25 Mar   tailor
       24 Mar 1706: crossed out by order of John Bell, mayor

Cowdall, Aaron son of Robert, feltmaker, of Gloucester
Howell, Joseph & Elizabeth   7 yrs from 29 Sep   blacksmith

---

[1] GBR B3/7 f 198v 16 Aug 1698: To receive £5 of Mr Hollidaye's money: John Elliott, John Ward, William Fryer, Joseph Nurse, William Matthews, George Ravener.

[2] ibid f 200v 14 Sep 1698: To receive £10 of Sir Thomas Rich's money: Francis Farmer, George Bishopp, Thomas Turner, Henry Hayes, John Parker, Thomas Veysey.

3/387	1699	7 Feb	Bishopp, George son of Daniel, tailor, dec'd, of Gloucester Heaven, John & Deborah 7 yrs from 25 Jan barber surgeon
		13 Feb	Nourse, Joseph son of Joseph, currier, of Gloucester Mutlow, Anthony & Eleanor 7 yrs tailor [*Holliday*]
		3 Apr	Veysey, Thomas son of Nathaniel, tailor, of Gloucester Veysey, Nathaniel, his father, & Dorothy 7 yrs from 21 Dec tailor
		24 Apr	Braddis, Richard son of Richard, bricklayer, of Gloucester Jones, Nathaniel 7 yrs from 1 Mar tailor[1]
			Organ, John son of Nathaniel, dec'd, of Tuffley, parish of St Mary de Lode Webb, John & Anne 7 yrs from 1 Mar tailor *11 Sep 1700: turned over by John Webb by consent to Thomas Cooper alias Allen, tailor. Before John Hyett, alderman*
3/388		27 Apr	Walker, Richard son of Richard, carpenter, dec'd, of Gloucester Nest, William & Mary 7 yrs from 1 Jan carpenter
		11 May	Tayler, Thomas son of Robert, yeoman, dec'd, of Bushley, Worcs Cooke, Thomas & Susannah 7 yrs from 25 Mar tailor
		12 May	Smith, Thomas son of Thomas, flax dresser, of Gloucester Bicknell, William & Abigail 7 yrs from 25 Mar tailor [*Mrs Browne*][2]
		24 Apr	Sermon, Samuel son of Samuel, yeoman, of Cheltenham Blizzard, John & Mary 7 yrs from 22 Apr baker
3/389		22 Jun	Hyett, Henry son of Zachariah, gentleman, dec'd, of Painswick Platt, Henry & Anne 7 yrs from 2 Feb grocer
		15 Jul	Pates, Leonard son of Leonard, dec'd, of Charlton Kings Fletcher, Thomas & Sarah 7 yrs from 11 Jun baker
		17 Jul	Layton, William son of Richard, yeoman, dec'd, of Elmore Barker, John & Anne 7 yrs barber surgeon
		16 Aug	Butt, Richard son of John, dyer, of Over Willis, Samuel & Elizabeth 7 yrs from 24 Jun haberdasher
		21 Aug	Archer, Thomas son of Sampson, silkweaver, of Gloucester Farley, Thomas & Eleanor 7 yrs cutler
3/390		1 Sep	Bound, Thomas son of Thomas, maltster, of Lower Southgate Street, Gloucester Lane, Richard & Anne 7 yrs from 3 Aug grocer
		21 Sep	Marden, William son of William, silkweaver, of Gloucester Gwillim, John 7 yrs from 15 May feltmaker [*Mrs Browne*]
		22 Sep	Ravener, Thomas son of Joseph, serge weaver, of Gloucester Ravener, Joseph, his father, & Margery 7 yrs from 17 Sep serge weaver [*Holliday*]

---

[1] GBR B3/7 f 198v 16 Aug 1698: To receive £5 of Alderman Powell's money: Richard Braddis.
[2] ibid f 215v 27 Apr 1699: To receive £4 of Mrs Browne's money: Adam Mason, Thomas Archer, Thomas Smith, John Field.

	1699	25 Sep	Rogers, John son of William, yeoman, of Bentham, Badgeworth Rogers, Thomas & Mary 7 yrs from 25 Mar baker
			Brymyard, John son of William, pipe maker, dec'd, of Gloucester Wells, Richard & Mary 7 yrs from 17 Sep cordwainer[1]
			Lane, John son of John, pipe maker, dec'd, of Gloucester Browne, William & Joan 7 yrs from 17 Sep cordwainer [Holliday]
3/391		22 Sep	Cole, John son of Thomas, gentleman, of Tirley Lane, Nicholas jr & Hester 7 yrs from 2 Apr apothecary

Thomas Snell, mayor [1699–1700]
[Henry Plat and Samuel Beale, bailiffs and sheriffs]

	1699	7 Oct	Roffe, John son of Jasper, carpenter, of Gloucester Bicknell, James 7 yrs from 24 Jun tailor
		26 Oct	Ravenhall, James son of John, cooper, of Coleford Workman, Anthony & Anne 7 yrs butcher
		2 Nov	Wells, Joseph son of Michael, yeoman, of Quedgeley Partridge, Richard & Anne 7 yrs from 20 Aug baker & maltster
3/392		10 Nov	Vaughan, Charles son of William, cordwainer, dec'd, of Gloucester Hopkins, Theophilus & Susannah 7 yrs joiner
		14 Nov	Archer, Anthony son of Anthony, bricklayer, dec'd, of Gloucester Davis, Thomas & Joan 7 yrs serge weaver
		18 Nov	Pegler, Andrew son of John, yeoman, of Bledington Wilmott, Robert 7 yrs from 29 Sep saddler & upholsterer
		20 Dec	Buckle, John son of Walter, gentleman, of Cheltenham Burroughes, Samuel jr, gentleman, & Elizabeth 7 yrs [innkeeper]
3/393	1700	2 Jan	Witcombe, Richard son of Samuel, serge weaver & comber, of Gloucester Witcombe, Samuel, his father, & Elizabeth 7 yrs from 1 Nov serge weaver & comber
		3 Jan	Gardner, James son of John, joiner, dec'd, of Gloucester Luter, John & Elizabeth 7 yrs from 29 Sep butcher
			Hayes, Josiah son of William, cordwainer, of Gloucester Hornage, William & Anne 7 yrs from 25 Dec cordwainer [Holliday][2]
		17 Jan	Mann, Thomas son of Thomas, yeoman, of Hucclecote, Churchdown Smith, Sybil, widow 7 yrs from 1 Jul [baker]

---

[1] GBR B3/7 f 217v 11 Aug 1699: To receive £5 of Alderman Powell's money: Brymyard's son.

[2] ibid f 217 11 Aug 1699: To receive £5 of Mr Hollidaye's money: Thomas Ravener, John Lane, John Merry, Henry Cleavly, Thomas son of widow Webly, Josiah Hayes (on the mayor's casting vote).

3/394	1700	29 Jan	Collett, John son of John, toyman, dec'd, of London Punter, Robert & Mary 7 yrs from 1 Jan mercer
		25 Jan	Hayes, William son of William, cordwainer, of Gloucester Hayes, William, his father, & Judith 7 yrs cordwainer[1]
		29 Jan	Cleavley, Henry son of Henry, grocer, dec'd, of Gloucester Jennings, Margaret, widow 7 yrs from 1 Jan [tailor] [*Holliday*]
		2 Feb	Cowles, John son of Thomas, cordwainer, dec'd, of Gloucester Evenis, William & Katharine 7 yrs from 3 Jan cordwainer [*cf Appendix V*]
		26 Feb	Dymocke, Jonathan son of John, broadweaver, of Randwick, Stroud Way, John & Susannah 7 yrs from 24 Feb butcher
3/395		27 Feb	Perkins, Samuel son of George, clerk, dec'd, of Fretherne Perkins, George 7 yrs from 29 Sep baker
		2 Mar	Mason, Walter son of Walter, gentleman, dec'd, of Cheltenham Matthews, John & Dorcas 7 yrs from 1 Nov tanner
		30 Mar	Hunt, Robert son of Robert, broadweaver, of Painswick White, Richard & Rebecca 7 yrs from 25 Mar mason & bricklayer
		18 Apr	Aycrigg, William son of Elizabeth Hancocke, of Twyning Jordan, William 7 yrs apothecary
3/396		18 May	Stephens, Henry son of William, combmaker, dec'd, of Gloucester Summers, Thomas & Elizabeth 7 yrs from 2 Feb silkweaver
		30 May	Brocke, John son of John, glover, of Gloucester Brocke, John, his father, & Mary 7 yrs from 1 May glover [*Mrs Browne*][2]
		3 Jun	Morse, Thomas son of John, dec'd, of Berkeley Bicknell, William & Abigail 7 yrs from 3 May tailor
		11 Jun	Davis, Thomas son of John, wool comber, of Gloucester Winston, Thomas & Margaret 7 yrs tailor [*Mrs Browne*]
3/397			Ashmead, Giles son of Giles, glover, of Cheltenham Beard, William 7 yrs from 29 Sep last mercer
			Fordes, John son of James, tailor, of Gloucester Parker, John & Martha 7 yrs from 1 Jun tailor
		13 Jun	Jennings, Jeremiah son of Jeremiah, tailor, of Gloucester Jenings, Jeremiah, his father, & Anne 7 yrs from 29 May tailor
		14 Jun	Silly, Thomas son of Richard, yeoman, of Tuffley, St Mary de Lode Bright, Thomas & Joyce 7 yrs from 8 Mar butcher

---

[1] GBR B3/7 f 219 29 Aug 1699: To receive £10 of Sir Thomas Rich's money: John Cowles, William Hayes, William Wellavise, John Lodge, James Read, Edmund Ready.

[2] ibid f 234v April 1700: To receive £4 of Mrs Browne's money: William Grove, Thomas Davis, John Brocke.

3/398	1700	22 Jun	Browne, Philip son of Philip, yeoman, of Market Lavington, Wilts Weaver, Henry & Sarah 7 yrs from 25 Mar farrier
		5 Jul	Wellavise, William son of William, feltmaker, dec'd, of Gloucester Browne, John & Hester 7 yrs from 24 Jun tailor
		6 Jul	King, Stephen son of Stephen, carpenter, of Bisley Bliss, William & Hester 7 yrs from 25 Mar baker
		8 Jul	Davenall, William son of William, weaver, of Wellington, Salop Meadway, Abraham & Mary 7 yrs from 24 Jun bricklayer
3/399		19 Jul	Webley, Thomas son of Thomas, baker, dec'd, of Gloucester Davis, Robert & Rebecca 8 yrs from 24 Jun brazier [*Holliday*]
		24 Jul	Pace, William son of William, gentleman, of Longney Yate, Samuel 7 yrs from 5 Mar grocer
		21 Aug	King, Thomas son of John, scrivener, of Gloucester Humphris, Samuel 7 yrs from 24 Dec past butcher
		17 Sep	Foords, James son of James, tailor, of Gloucester Ravener, Joseph & Margery 7 yrs from 17 Oct next weaver[1]
3/400		26 Sep	Lawrence, Eleazor son of William, yeoman, of Bromsberrow Lawrence, Thomas & Margaret 7 yrs baker

---

[1] GBR B3/7 f 242v 28 Jun 1700 To receive £5 of Mr Hollidaye's money: John Mamby, Joseph Coopy, James Foords, Joseph Cowles, William Hathway, John Heaven.
John Lea to have the £5 of Mr Powell's gift.

APPENDIX I
SPECIMEN APPRENTICESHIP INDENTURES

1. The indenture of apprenticeship, in Latin, which was the basis for the first of the entries in the registers calendared above.

Hec indentura facta in festo Sancti Johannis Baptiste anno regni domine nostre Elizabete, dei gratia Anglie, Francie et Hibernie regine, fidei defensoris etc., tricesimo septimo. Testatur quod Jasper Greninge filius Johannis Greninge de Moreton Valence, husbandman, posuit seipsum apprenticium Johanni Gwilliam de civitate Gloucestrie silkweaver et Johanne uxori eius in arte qua predictus Johannes modo utitur erudiendum, et cum ipsis more apprenticii sui commoraturum et deserviturum a festo supradicto usque ad finem termini octo annorum extunc proxime sequentium et plenarie complendorum, durante quo termino predictus Jasper Greninge prefatis Johanni Gwilliam et Johanne tamquam magistro et magistre suis bene, benigne et fideliter deserviet. Secreta eorum celabit; precepta eorum licita et honesta libenter ubique faciet. Damnum eis non faciet nec fieri procurabit quovismodo quin pro posse suo impediet aut statum dictos magistrum vel magistram suos premonebit; bona vel catalla dictorum magistri et magistre suorum non devastabit nec alicui accommodabit sine licencia dictorum magistri vel magistre suorum; fornicationem in domibus dictorum magistri et magistre suorum neque extra non committet; matrimonium sive contractum cum aliqua infra terminum predictum non contrahet; ad talos seu aliqua alia ioca vel luda illicita non ludet; tabernas consuetas non frequentabit; cum bonis suis propriis aut alienis (durante dicto termino) non marchandizabit. A servitio suo predicto (termino non finito) non recedet, nec se elongabit sed seipsum in omnibus tamquam bonum et fidelem apprenticium geret et habebit per totum terminum predictum; et predicti Johannes et Johanna apprenticium suum predictum in arte de silkweavers craffte optimo modo quo sciverint aut poterint docebunt, tractabunt et informabunt aut doceri et informari facient; debito modo castigando, inveniendoque ei omnia necessaria ut victualia, vestitum lineum [et] laneum, calciamentum et lectum sufficientia pro tali serviente talis artis vel scientie per totum terminum predictum; necnon dabunt ac solvent prefato servienti eorum in fine termini predicti 3*s* 4*d* legalis monete Anglie nomine stipendii sui cum duplici vestitu, viz. pro diebus ferialibus et operariis prout talem servientem decet. In cuius rei testimonium huic presenti indenture partes predicti sigilla suas alternativim apposuerunt. Tempore Henrici Hazard maioris civitatis predicte, Christopheri Caple et Johannis Brewster vicecomitatum eiusdem civitatis. Datum festo et anno supradictis.

Ref. Glos RO, GBR C10/1, p. 1.

2. An indenture of apprenticeship, in English. Although not related to any of the entries calendared above, it comes from the same period and gives a literal translation of most of the conditions. The spelling has been modernised.

This indenture witnesseth that Thomas Lowe son of Sir Thomas Lowe, knight and alderman of London, hath put himself apprentice to Robert Offley, citizen and haberdasher of London and one of the merchant adventurers of England and merchant of the staple of England and merchant of the Levant, in the art in which he useth to be instructed, and with him after the manner of his apprentice to abide and serve from the feast day of the nativity of St. John Baptist last past before the date hereof unto the end and term of nine years from thence next ensuing and fully to be complete and ended. During which term the said apprentice shall serve his said master well and faithfully; his secrets he shall keep; his commandments lawful and honest willingly he shall everywhere do; damage to his master he shall not do, nor know to be done by any other, but the same to his power shall hinder, or his said master thereof forthwith forewarn; the goods of his master he shall not waste, nor them to any person unlawfully lend; fornication he shall not commit; matrimony he shall not contract; at dice or cards or any other unlawful games he shall not play; taverns he shall not frequent; with his own goods or any others during the said term without licence of his master he shall not buy or sell; from his service aforesaid day or night he shall not unlawfully depart or prolong himself, but in all things as a good and faithful apprentice towards his master and all his shall gently bear and behave himself during the said term. And the said Robert, the said Thomas his apprentice, in the art which he useth in the best manner that he knoweth or can, shall teach, instruct and inform or cause to be informed with due manner of chastisement. And shall find unto him meat, drink, apparel both linen and woollen, shoes and bedding and all other things necessary for him as it becometh such an apprentice of the said art to be found according to the custom of the city of London during the said term. And to these covenants all and singular on the said apprentice's part well and faithfully to be holden and performed in manner aforesaid, the said apprentice firmly bindeth himself to his said master and his executors by these presents. In witness whereof the parties aforesaid to these indentures interchangeably have set their seals. Given the five and twentieth day of September in the year of the reign of our sovereign lord James, by the grace of God king of England, Scotland, France and Ireland, defender of the faith etc., that is to say of England, France and Ireland the second and of Scotland the 38th. 1604.

Ref. Glos RO, D1448/Z 1

APPENDIX II
APPRENTICING CHARITIES

Several charities for apprenticeship were administered by the corporation. They are discussed above, pages xx–xxiii, as also in *VCH Glos* iv. 356–7. Their recipients are recorded in the apprenticeship registers, and the calendar includes footnotes referring to decisions about the application of the charities that have been found in the corporation's minutes. It is to be noted that by no means all the intended recipients named in the minutes are recorded in the registers.

Abraham Blackleech (d. 1639) gave a sum of money which was evidently not treated as an endowed charity. The capital sum was a notional £50, of which £30 was spent in 1640 on apprenticing six boys at £5 each, as recorded at **1**/520–2, 530. If there was any remaining money it is not recorded in the registers.

Mrs Sarah Browne: the application of her charity is recorded in the calendar from 1647 at **2**/18, 35, 38, 48–9, 53, 60–1, 73–4, 79, 93, 102, 106, 114, 135, 142, 154–5, 175, 201–2, 220, 236–7, 254, 271, 285–6, 295, 360, 365–6; **3**/23, 25, 40, 42–3, 80, 91–2, 105, 110, 134, 141, 143, 175*n*, 200, 202, 213*n*, 223–4, 226, 233–4, 236, 247, 250, 266, 269, 276, 281–2, 284, 295–6, 298, 302, 306, 311, 322, 333–4, 341, 345–6, 353–4, 360, 365, 367, 372–3, 376, 381, 384, 388, 390, 396.

Jasper Clutterbuck (d. 1659), by his will dated 1648 gave leasehold land from which £10 was to be used for apprenticing two boys each year. The application of the money is recorded in the calendar at **2**/253. The charity probably lapsed on the expiry of the lease.

William Holliday (or Halliday): see above, pages xx–xxii. The registers often indicate the recipients of the charity; where they do not but the relevant entries can confidently be matched with the decisions recorded in the minutes, the calendar adds '[*Holliday*]' to those entries. From 1625 the calendar records the application of the charity so frequently that it would be pointless to list all the references.

John Powell (d. 1666): the relevant register does not mention his charity, but from 1682 the calendar notes decisions in the minutes about the application of the charity, at **3**/227*n*, 266*n*, 285*n*, 293*n*, 301*n*, 302*n*, 317*n*, 330*n*, 339*n*, 369*n*, 374*n*, 387*n*, 390*n*, 399*n*. The earliest entry in the register that matches the record of a decision is of 1686 (**3**/266).

Sir Thomas Rich in founding, by will dated 1666, his Bluecoat school or Bluecoat Hospital directed that part of the income should be used to apprentice the boys from the school. The registers do not refer to the charity, but from 1669 some of the entries are for boys whose apprenticing was the subject of decisions recorded in the corporation's minutes, as noted at **3**/23*n*, 39*n*, 53*n*, 69*n*, 87*n*, 102*n*, 104*n*, 121*n*, 142*n*, 143*n*, 161*n*, 163*n*, 174*n*, 179*n*, 196*n*, 211*n*, 222*n*, 228*n*, 244*n*, 250*n*, 265*n*, 280*n*, 303*n*, 308*n*, 320*n*, 324*n*, 364*n*, 369*n*, 379*n*, 386*n*, 394*n*.

APPENDIX III
AGREEMENT TO DISCHARGE A TEWKESBURY APPRENTICE

[The memorandum is written in the Gloucester apprenticeship register, GBR C10/1, at p. 588. The reasons for its inclusion are obscure, but the names of Denis Wise and, apparently, John Dorney, town clerk of Gloucester, suggest that the city was directly concerned with the agreement. The agreement may have arisen from the preparations early in 1642 for the city's defence: cf. *VCH Glos* iv. 92–3.]

18 March 1642

Memorandum: that it was concluded and agreed between us, Theophilus Alye of Tewkesbury in the county of Gloucestershire, mercer, and Samuel Baxter, apprentice of the said Theophilus, in form following: That Whereas the said Samuel did heretofore bind himself by indenture to serve the said Theophilus as an apprentice for the term of certain years whereof some part are yet to come and is desirous with my consent to serve the residue of his time with Lieutenant Fleminge (or some other), I the said Theophilus do hereby voluntarily discharge the said Samuel of any further service to be performed to me and do agree that he shall serve the residue of his time with the said Lieutenant Fleminge (or some other) as aforesaid. And I the said Samuel do willingly accept the said discharge and promise to place myself with the said Lieutenant Fleminge (or some other) to serve as aforesaid. Any covenant in the said indenture contained to the contrary of this agreement in any wise notwithstanding. In witness whereof we hereunto set our hands the day and year above written
Theo Alye
Samuel Baxter

I Stephen Baxter brother to the said Samuel do freely consent to the said agreement [*deleted*]. This agreement made in the presence of
De[nis] Wise
Dorney
Steph Baxter
E Wheeler

APPENDIX IV
ADMISSIONS OF FREEMEN, 1595–1641

Freemen admitted by fine

The names listed below have been taken from the minutes of Gloucester city common council. From 1641 the names of freemen are recorded in registers which have been published as *A Calendar of the Registers of the Freemen of the City of Gloucester 1641–1838* (Glos. Record Series vol. 4).

GBR B3/1

157v	1595	19 Dec	Tickell, Walter, of Over coming to be innkeeper of the Bear. Fine: £6-13-4
			Wise, Thomas. Fine: £6-13-4
159v	1596	29 Jan	Browne, Francis. Fine: £6-13-4
162v		27 Sep	Window, John, servant to the mayor. Fine: £3-6-8
170v	1597	29 Sep	Wade, John, late servant to Alderman Taylor. Fine: £3-6-8
178v	1598	15 Sep	Haydon, Henry, gentleman, having married the widow of Robert Ingram of the Boothall. Fine: £10[1]
182	1599	20 Aug	Haydon, Henry. Fine: £7
183v		8 Nov	Greene, Richard. Fine: £4
185	1600	5 Jun	Paunt, John, brazier. Fine: 53s 4d
189	1601	4 Sep	Carpenter, John. Fine: £4
			Elton, Edward. Fine: £6-13-4
190v	1601	2 Oct	Thornbury, Giles. Fine: £6-13-4
192	1602	7 May	Powell, James. Fine: £3-6-8
			Barston, James, gentleman. Fine: £6-13-4
			Norton, Philip. Fine: £5
208	1603	13 Oct	Webb, John; Heath, Richard; and Prior, Henry; who had been disfranchised for 'contempt against the ordinances for preserving the city from plague' were readmitted.
211	1605	9 Sep	Oliver, Thomas. Fine: 20 nobles
			Tomes, Robert. Fine: £20 nobles
215	1606	20 Mar	Wheeler, Henry, if he installs three 'plumps' to drain water
			One Hauxwell if he makes 'a good and sufficient receipt for water'
217v		9 Sep	Howell, John, who brought a certificate to testify that he served 7 years in London as apprentice to a feltmaker. Fine: £5
220v	1607	4 Jun	Drinkwater, Samuel, restored to the freedom despite having his sign torn down for keeping an inn while disfranchised. Fine: 5 marks

---

[1] He had not paid the fine by 28 Jan 1599 and was barred from keeping an inn: GBR B3/1 f 180v.

222	1607	1 Oct	Awberye, George. Fine: nil
227v	1609	20 Jul	Traye, Robert. Fine: £10
230v	1610	23 Jan	Synger, Thomas, dyer, by the consent of the rest of the dyers. Fine: £10
231v		29 Mar	John Smith and Henry Wheeler if they supply oak boards for building the Boothall
			Field, Thomas, brewer, to be readmitted if he provides a good dinner for the mayor
232		5 Jun	Vaughan, Richard, joiner. Fine: £3
233		10 Jul	Robinson, Anthony, gentleman. Fine: £5
234		20 Sep	Gilbert, William. Fine: £10
236v	1611	30 Apr	Mayo, John. Fine: £8
237v		21 Aug	Bennett, Abel, at the request of the mayor. Fine: 40s
239v	1612	2 Jan	Ellis, John. Fine: 20 marks
240		17 Jan	Waggestaffe, Edward. Fine: 20 marks
243v		3 Sep	Wevere, Edward. Fine: 40s
247	1613	28 May	Gilbert, William. Fine: £10
252		2 Dec	Phillippes, John, late servant, who is to marry the widow Price. Fine: £5
256v	1614	7 Sep	Shewringe, Edmund, servant to Luke Garnons. Fine: £10
260v		5 Dec	Bradley, Thomas, who is to marry a freeman's daughter. Fine: £4
261	1615	9 Mar	West, David, who is to marry the widow Price. Fine: £5
			Lloyd, John, servant to the Bishop of Gloucester. Fine: £5
268		26 Aug	Holland, John. Fine: nil
270		22 Dec	Pell, Pauncefoote. Fine: nil
440v	1616	17 Dec	Symonds, Edward, feltmaker. Fine: £5
444	1617	19 Jun	Kym, John. Fine: £10
446		21 Jul	Freeman, James, feltmaker. Fine 20 nobles
			Beard, Andrew, tailor, if he agrees with the company of tailors. Fine: £10
448		8 Aug	James, Jasper. Fine: nil
449		16 Sep	Townesend, Humphrey, wheeler, having married a freeman's widow. Fine: £5
453v	1618	30 Mar	Clarke, John keeper of the Northgate. Fine: nil
			Hore, William. Fine: 40s
455		8 Jun	Kym, John, clothier. Fine: £10
			Beaton, Moses. Fine: £10
459v	1619	15 Jan	Grace, William. Fine: 20 nobles
461		16 Jul	Mitchell, Edward. Fine: nil
461v		6 Aug	Powell, James, of the Bell. Fine: £10

APPENDIX IV: ADMISSIONS OF FREEMEN, 1595–1641

462v	1619	1 Sep	Stewart, Andrew, merchant, at request of Henry Gibb, esq, one of the gentlemen of His Majesty's bedchamber. Fine: nil
			Wright, Robert. Fine: £5
463v		14 Sep	Rogers, Morris, servant of the Lord Bishop, at the request of the Lord Bishop and having married a freeman's widow
465v		25 Nov	Loggins, John, mason. Fine: nil
481	1621	21 Aug	Hopkins, John. Fine: 5 marks
482			Tomson, Francis, Sir William Guise's man – to dress the mayor's dinner yearly
			Blinkhorne, George, pargeter, on condition he repairs the gallery of St Nicholas's church
484	1622	18 Jan	Little, John, having married Richard Portman's daughter and being very poor. To pay a fine of £5 to this chamber if he sets up shop without the consent of the company of shoemakers
487v		13 Sep	Kinge, William who has been living in the Low Countries as a sergeant in the army but was born in Gloucester and is prepared to live there and teach his skills to the trained band. Fine: nil
			Partridge, John, at the request of Dr Seaman, Chancellor. Fine: 5 marks
491v	1623	14 Jul	Archard, Edward, having married Alderman Thorne's grandchild, if he makes a stone wall level with the causeway from Mr Deighton's pump to his own pump house. Fine: 20 nobles
496	1624	8 Jan	Holland, John, having served the town clerk for many years. Fine: nil
499		27 May	Machin, William, grandchild of Thomas Machin. Fine: 40s. Mr Machin did not accept. Act repealed 15 Jun
499v		15 Jun	Morris, John. Fine: £5
500v		9 Aug	Jones, John, victualler at the quay. Fine: £5
503v		12 Nov	Smyth, Gervase, eldest son of the late Lord Bishop of Gloucester
504v	1625	28 Jan	Suffeild, Thomas, sometime servant to the late Lord Bishop and having married a freeman's daughter
505v		9 Apr	Baughe, Thomas, on condition he marries the widow Endall before being sworn. Fine: 40s
507		19 Jul	Pope, Richard, of Westgate Street. Fine: £20
508v		13 Sep	Pryor, Simon, feltmaker, having married a burgess's daughter
513v	1626	25 Sep	Bull, Anthony, having married Mr Holman's daughter. Fine: £5
515		2 Nov	Mauncell, William, for his good carriage and his readiness to perform any service to this city. Fine: nil
			Tyler, John, tailor, servant to the widow Farmer, having agreed with the company of tailors for his admission into their company. Fine: £5
515v	1627	19 Jan	Bird, Thomas, upon request of Mr Recorder. Fine: 5 marks
516		20 Mar	Bingham, Edward. Fine: £10

518v	1627	17 Aug	Hanbury, John, having married Ald Caple's daughter. Fine at his own discretion
522	1628	21 Jan	Hooper, Henry, having served 7 years as an apprentice at the Boothall and lost his indenture. Fine: £5
522v		15 Jul	Wolley, Richard, having married Richard Cugley's daughter. Fine: £6 13s 4d
523		30 Sep	Hall, John, servant to the Lord Bishop, having married Thomas Weblie's daughter. Fine: £5
528v	1629	14 Jan	Bennett, John, having married a freeman's widow. Fine: 20 nobles
532		17 Mar	Brett, Henry esq, having married Ald Seaman's daughter
			Messinger, William, freeman's son to be an attorney in the court of this city being first sworn a burgess
535		23 Sep	Webly, William. Fine: £5
538v	1630	14 Jan	Hill, John, to marry the widow of John Dunne, barber, having got the goodwill of the company of barbers. Fine: 4 marks
541		9 Apr	Chandler, Thomas, having married the daughter of John Hayes. Fine: £5
541v			Sarson, Humphrey, sievemaker, for his 'honest carriage'. Fine: 5 marks
543v		21 Jul	Barnard, James, mariner who has married a freeman's daughter and transports merchandise to this city from foreign parts and is likely to serve as a good master pilot for this city. Fine: nil
544v		12 Aug	Swayne, Thomas. Fine: £5
546v		20 Sep	Clent, James. Fine left to his own generous disposition
557v	1632	16 Jan	Pryce, John, carpenter if he repairs 3 decayed posts in the Boothall
559		22 Sep	Barret, Thomas, cutler, having agreed with the company of smiths and hammermen. Fine: £10
			Webly, Thomas, grandchild to Thomas Webly, clothier. Fine: 20s

GBR B3/2

2	1632	4 Dec	Addys, William, yeoman. Fine: £19
8	1633	9 May	Evans, John, trowman, if he brings to the quay 300 tunn of pebble stones before Michaelmas
38		8 Apr	Onyon, Humphrey, for taking a poor boy of this city apprentice
43		11 Sep	Comelyn, James, having married a freeman's daughter and agreed with the company. Fine: £5
			Atwood, Thomas, watchmaker. Fine: 20 nobles
45		30 Sep	Rich, Thomas, cook, at the request of the Lord Bishop. Fine: nil
47		2 Oct	Maddock, John, having served Mr Powell above 7 years as an apprentice though he was not bound by indenture
59	1636	21 Jul	Gibbs, Matthew, having married the daughter of Mr Reade. Fine: 20 nobles
64		22 Sep	Hinxman, Thomas, servant to Charles Hoare for 8 years. Fine: £10

APPENDIX IV: ADMISSIONS OF FREEMEN, 1595–1641

65	1636	26 Sep	Hinxman, Thomas to have 5 marks abated from his fine and pay only 20 nobles if he marries the widow of George Martin, freeman
			Parrat, Thomas, servant to the Lord Bishop, paying nothing at his Lordship's request
71	1637	3 Feb	Hobbes, John, feltmaker, having married a freeman's widow. Fine: £5
			Blanch, John, who intends to use clothing and set many poor people on work. Fine: £10
79		18 Jul	Dewxell, Anthony, born in this city and brought up at sea as a mariner, on undertaking to be serviceable to the city by navigation. Fine: 5 marks
86		15 Dec	Keene, John, yeoman. Fine: £20
87	1638	13 Jan	Jones, Robert, servant to the Lord Bishop who is to marry the widow of Mr Hall, late burgess. Fine: 5 marks
94		7 Dec	Butterton, Ralph served — Knight, currier, for 8 years but because Knight was not a freeman until 2 years after he was bound, by the custom of the city he cannot be made free. Because he is a poor man he shall be admitted to his freedom without fine or fees
107	1639	8 Aug	Brotherton, John. Fine: £10
			Webley, Samuel. Fine: 20 nobles
			Sampson, William. Fine: 20 nobles
123		14 Aug	Horsham, John, tailor, paying to the company of tailors 20 nobles & the chamber £10
			Shepheard, Edward, feltmaker. Fine: £5
138		4 Nov	Fox, Thomas, late servant to Ald John Browne, dec'd, and now servant to his widow. Fine: 5 marks
140		10 Dec	Phillips, John, labourer of St Catherine's parish, for marrying the widow Syer who has 7 children chargeable on the parish. Fine: 40s or sufficient security to discharge the parish
144	1640	3 Feb	Wright, Thomas, feltmaker, having married a freeman's daughter and served 7 years at the trade and having a house of his wife's inheritance in Southgate Street. Fine: 5 marks
145		15 Mar	Lenthall, William, esq, recorder of the city, by the whole vote of this house desired to take the oath of common burgess
147			Chapman, Samuel, having married a freeman's daughter by whom he has 2 children if he puts in such security as the mayor and alderman think fit to save harmless the parish where he shall come to inhabit from any charge by his wife or children and pay for a fine to the Chamber £5
166		29 Oct	Shewell, Thomas, having married the daughter of Richard Cater, dec'd. Fine: 20 nobles
168		13 Dec	Cawston, William, having married a freeman's daughter. Fine: £5
			Cowper, Thomas, having married Taylor's widow. Fine: 20 marks
196	1641	30 Sep	Bicke, Edward, if he accepts within 1 month. Fine: £10

Freemen by patrimony and apprenticeship

The names listed below are taken from the chamberlains' accounts, which record the payments made on enrolment but are not available for all years during the period. New freemen were required to contribute to the provision of buckets for fire-fighting, the 'bucket money' for new freemen admitted by patrimony or apprenticeship being 2s 8d, the price of one bucket, and for those admitted by fine 5s 4d, the price of two.

GBR F4/4

Freemen for mayoralty of Henry Browne (**1628–9**)

Freemen's sons and apprentices

Barnwod, John	Woodward, John	Greene, Richard
Sellwine, Henry	Haynes, Francis	Capenor, Giles
Lugg, Thomas	Lea, Francis	Vayers, Thomas
Angle, William	Lysance, Daniel	Bosley, Richard
Payntor, Thomas	Rodway, Thomas	Clutterbuck, Amity
Ellis, Anthony	Reve, William	Tylor, James
Meachen, James	Smart, Joseph	Williams, Richard
Lugg, Lawrence		
Parker, Daniel		

All pay 2s 8d bucket money
John Bennett and William Webly pay 2 buckets, 5s 4d

GBR F4/5

f 29 **1635–6**

For every freeman's son and those who served 7 yrs apprenticeship – 2s 8d for one bucket; for those made free by fine – 5s 4d for two buckets.

Freemen's sons	*Apprentices*
Phillips, William	Donne, Nathaniel
Fleming, John	Symonds, Nathaniel
Mr Lugg's son	Mathews, Henry
Fletcher, Edward	Stephens, Oliver
	Penson *alias* Jonas, William
	Symonds, Richard
	Lord, Richard
	Lea, James
	Thomas Coke's man
	Humfris, Samuel
	Gibbs, Robert

f 56 1636–7

Freemen's sons

Warwicke, William
Bartone, Richard
Huttson, Thomas
Morgan, John
Knight, Robert
Hughes, Miles
Cugley, John
Wagestaff, John
Price, Thomas
Bubb, William
Russell, William

Apprentices

Lugge, Richard
Smith, John
Hodges, Christopher
Heath's prentice
Hobbs, John
Price, James
Cleevely, William
Webb, Thomas
Hathway, George
Dewxell, Anthony
Holshipp, William
Payne, John
Blanch, John

f 64v 1637–8

Howlett, Thomas
Till, Richard
Phillipps, Thomas
Allen, Lawrence
Dowsen, Walter
Lugge, Jasper
Bishopp, John
Russell, Francis
Tarne, Leonard
Plummer, Thomas
Jones, Richard
Horwarde, Anthony
Scudamore, William

Webb, John
Broade, Richard
Lye, Giles
Chapman, Thomas
Baker, William
Beard, Richard
Dowton, Richard
Webb, William
Edmondes, John
Seizemore, John
Browne, James
Dudley, Arthur
Williams, John

f 94v **1638–9**

Freemen's sons
Singleton, Richard
Hughes, Giles
Grimes, Richard
Palmer, John
Cuffe, Thomas
Atkins, John
Seare, John
Pincke, Samuel
Horner, John
Langford, Toby
Beale, Thomas
Rix, Peter
Broadway, Richard
Ellis, John
Pury, Thomas
Hill, Robert
Whitfield, Edward
Harris, Francis
Hallinge, William
Hillary, Simon
Browne, John

Apprentices
Webly, Giles
Cooke, William
Gibbons, Thomas
Merrett, George
Cassell *alias* Cooke, Thomas
Winton, Humphrey
Price, John
Powell, John
Hawkes, Richard
Gwilliam, John
Williams, John
Beard, John
Day, William
Githis, William
Rudd, William
Jones, John, fee forgiven by the mayor
Hill, John, fee forgiven by the mayor

f 125 **1639–40**

Pritchard, Francis
Wiliams, Nicholas
Cowcher Edmund
Wood, John, gentleman
Grey, John
Freeman, John
Scriven, John
Hayes, Thomas
Lucas, Thomas
Teinton, Thomas
Cowcher, Lewis
Donne, John
Nash, Richard
Craker, Jonathan
Davys, John
Woolley, Thomas, gentleman
Roberts, Henry
Wadley, John
Cox, Winston

Greene, William
Pace, Thomas
Taylor, George
Kinge, Thomas
Clayfield, Edward
Dowton, Stephen
Pingrey, Thomas
Chedworth, Thomas
Steephens, Thomas
Linkenholt, William
Tully, Thomas
Mills, Toby
Kinge, Henry
Perry, Robert
Ricketts James
Baker, Thomas
Mills, John
Longe, Thomas
Travell, William
Bidwell, James

1640–41

Freemen's sons

Kible, John
Cawdle, John
Hatton, William
Martyn, John
Robbertes, John
Hatton, John
Rixe, John
Messinger, William
Phelpes, Nicholas
Charleton, John
Tuckye, John
Harberte, Charles
Williams, John
Palmer, William
Plummer, Samuel (fees forgiven)
Knowles, Henry
Hughes, Timothy
Whyte, Sergeant
Carpenter, William
Bromleye, Leonard
Pittman, John
Hillarye, John
Phelpes, John
Knighte, Henry
Major, Thomas
Harris, Thomas
Davis, John

Apprentices

Sparkes, Thomas
Hughes, John
Corbett, Roger
Tombes, John
Powell, William
Barker, Thomas
Collett, John
Tayler, John
Martynn, William
Randford, John
Barnes, John
Swayne, William
Shipton, John
Hall, Walter
Collett, Anthony
Barnes, Thomas
Linkinholte, Thomas
Davis, Thomas
Browne, Robert
Wyman, John
Goslinge, William
Marshe, William
Byrd, Nathaniel
Batt, John
Payne, Richard
Barnelme, William
Walters, Giles
Harris, William

APPENDIX V
APPRENTICES POSSIBLY BOUND MORE THAN ONCE

More than seventy of the entries in the registers calendared above record the assignment of the apprentice to a new master. A comparable number of apprentices apparently figure in a second or even a third entry in the registers without any indication that the apprentice had been reassigned or bound anew. Some instances are noted in the calendar; others of the more obvious instances are listed below.

apprentice	father	craft	master	year	entry
Addames, Robert	Thomas, of Minsterworth, husbandman	baker baker	John Haies William Johns	1615 1617	1/237 1/259
Archard, John	William, of Down Ampney, yeoman	baker cordwainer	John Heyford John Coxe	1617 1618	1/267 1/276
Badger, Jeremiah	Brian, of Gloucester, cutler	weaver weaver broadweaver	Richard Miles John Craker Albert Addames	1634 1637 1641	1/454 1/484 1/545
Barrett, Robert	Robert, of Gloucester, tailor	tailor tailor	John Moore William Higginson	1598 1599	1/32 1/46
Beakes, Benjamin	Robert, of Bristol, currier	carrier surgeon	John Crumwell Robert Cox	1668 1671	3/13 3/61
Bowser (Bowcer), William	George, of Gloucester, gentleman	brewer apothecary	Rowland Greene William Whitington	1653 1653	2/120 2/126
Bradford, William	Robert, of Maisemore, husbandman/farmer	pinmaker tobacco-pipe maker	Thomas Wynniatt William Brymyard	1675 1675	3/130 3/132
Bullock, Edward	Thomas, of Highleadon, dec'd/yeoman, dec'd	mercer clothier	Thomas Witcombe James Bullock	1620 1624	1/295 1/334
Clarke, Giles	Giles, of Gloucester, tanner	tanner cooper	Alexander Hoare Thomas Pace	1640 1640	1/519 1/526
Clarke, John	Nicholas, of Gloucester, farmer/labourer	glazier tailor	Joseph Byford William Fewtrell	1670 1671	3/40 3/54
Cole (Coale), Charles	Ralph, of St Margaret's/ Wotton, yeoman/farmer	pinmaker pinmaker	William Perkes William Hartland	1661 1666	2/282 2/339
Cowles, John	Thomas, of Gloucester, cordwainer/cordwainer, dec'd	tailor cordwainer	Roger Church William Evenis	1693 1700	3/332 3/394
Cowles, Thomas	Thomas, of Gloucester, glover	tailor currier	Thomas Chapman John Hughes	1663 1663	2/293 [bis] 2/296
Cugley, Henry	Thomas, of Gloucester, woollen draper/draper	woollen draper mercer	Henry Browne John Baugh	1597 1600	1/23 1/68
Cupitt, Andrew	Arthur, of Awre, trowman	maltster tanner	James Stephens Thomas Wood	1655 1656	2/172 2/191
Dewe, John	John, of Gloucester, innkeeper/innholder	tailor vintner	James Sare John Hincksman	1663 1665	2/306 2/328

APPENDIX V: APPRENTICES POSSIBLY BOUND MORE THAN ONCE

apprentice	father	craft	master	year	entry
Dobbes, Francis	John, of Gloucester, barber surgeon	barber surgeon barber surgeon	John Dobbes John Dobbes	1671 1676	3/60 3/142
Dobbes, Lawrence	John, of Gloucester, baker	glover cordwainer	Robert Sturmey Richard Dobbes	1605 1606	1/129 1/138
Francombe, Thomas	Henry, of Gloucester, woollen draper, dec'd	feltmaker cordwainer	Thomas Phelpes John Atkins	1650 1658	2/58 2/232
Gale, John	William, dec'd	cordwainer shoemaker	William Crompe Francis Baughe	1611 1612	1/189 1/201
Gretton, William	William, of Gloucester, feltmaker/feltmaker, dec'd	lantern maker tanner	Thomas Cosby William Lugg	1617 1625	1/260 1/344
Harris, Humphrey	Thomas, of Gloucester, gunsmith	baker baker	John Lane Thomas Whittingham	1627 1628	1/361 1/364
Heaghe, Jacob	Abraham, of Ashleworth, clerk, dec'd	chandler chandler	William Holtham Thomas Lane	1656 1658	2/173 2/218
Heyter, Edward	Edward, of Gloucester, brazier	cooper butcher pewterer	John Nourse Edward Cripps James Price	1664 1665 1670	2/314 2/330 3/40
Hodghson (Hodgshon), Jeremiah	Marmaduke, of Gloucester, dec'd	cordwainer tanner	William Clarke John Niccolls	1620 1628	1/292 1/375, 388
Hosey, Edward	Edward, of Gloucester, feltmaker	feltmaker feltmaker	John Hayward Jesse Nash	1683 1690	3/236 3/303
Hughes, Philip	Thomas, of Gloucester, pinmaker, dec'd	cordwainer tailor	Augustine Gwin Nathaniel Beard	1651 1652	2/81 2/101
Jeffs, Edward	Thomas, of Charlton Kings, yeoman	feltmaker feltmaker	Anne Nash Matthew Phelps	1693 1698	3/334 3/383
Jewett, Thomas	Peter, of Gloucester, carpenter/carpenter, dec'd	cutler currier	Richard Till Thomas Selwyn	1671 1672	3/57 3/70
Jobbins, James	Thomas, of Gloucester, tiler	feltmaker feltmaker	John Hayward Jesse Nash	1674 1678	3/110 3/188
Lewis, Richard	Abel, of Gloucester, pargeter, tiler/pargeter	blacksmith cordwainer	Joseph Howell William Cowcher	1693 1693	3/332 3/333
Low, Robert	Robert, of Barnwood, dec'd	wiredrawer wiredrawer	Wm Linckinholt Thomas Devis	1651 1651	2/68 2/86
Lugg, Thomas	Thomas, of Gloucester, haberdasher	mercer mercer	John Beard William Bleeke	1651 1652	2/75 2/94
Mathewes, John	John, of Gloucester, butcher, dec'd	butcher butcher	Margaret Mathewes William Perrys	1665 1669	2/328 3/20
Maysey (Meysey), Theophilus	Ralph (of Randwick), clerk	apothecary stationer	Robert Whittington Toby Langeford	1608 1610	1/160 1/179
Mitchell (Michell), George	Richard, of Gloucester, painter	garter weaver weaver	Rob Sparrowhawke John Craker	1634 1639	1/447 1/516
Mudwell, Robert	William, of Gloucester, dec'd/feltmaker	cordwainer feltmaker	John Bond William S[myth]	1636 1637	1/473 1/491
Nash, Richard	William, of Gloucester, feltmaker/feltmaker, dec'd	butcher carpenter	Anthony Workman William Nash	1694 1698	3/347 3/378
Onyon (Oynion), Humphrey	Humphrey, of Gloucester, sievemaker	silkweaver sievemaker	Thomas Oynion Humphrey Onyon	1644 1647	1/568 2/15

apprentice	father	craft	master	year	entry
Palmer, Joseph	George, of Gloucester, baker	tailor	Thomas Chapman	1669	3/18
		tailor	William Maddocke	1669	3/31
Pingery (Pingrey), Thomas	John, of Lea (Herefs), yeoman/clothier	innholder	John Woodward	1623	1/326
		clothier	John Craker	1629	1/395
Powell, Charles	William, of Gloucester, brewer	brewer	William Powell	1656	2/181
		glazier	John Painter	1660	2/263
Prune, John	Thomas, of Haydon, husbandman/farmer	brickmaker	William Swaine sr	1657	2/215
		feltmaker	Richard Nash	1662	2/291
Puckeridge (Pockeridge), William	Thomas, of Gloucester, tailor	baker	Richard Whitfeild	1660	2/251
		tailor	William Bishop	1669	3/37
Ridler, William	Walter, of Tibberton, clerk, dec'd	tailor	Richard Greening	1657	2/205
		tailor	James Philips jr	1658	2/223
Robertes, Giles	Thomas, of Harescombe, yeoman	—	John Cooke	1615	1/246
		draper	Nathaniel Byshop	1617	1/269
Robertes, William	William, of Harescombe, yeoman	cordwainer	Augustine Gwinne	1631/2	1/407
		baker	John Purlewent	1632	1/428
Rogers, John	Thomas, of Badgeworth, yeoman, dec'd	cutler	George Pharley	1661	2/266
		baker	Thomas Rogers	1666	2/340
Sheppard (Shepheard), Samuel	William, of Gloucester, esquire	mercer	Thomas Beale	1641	1/549
		mercer	Clement Dowle	1645	1/577
Sheppard, Thomas	Edward, of Gloucester, feltmaker	pinmaker	William King	1656	2/179
		tailor	Thomas Willcox	1656	2/194
Stephens, Samuel	Thomas, of Gloucester, pinmaker	joiner	John Clark	1661	2/273
		barber surgeon	John Stephens	1664	2/310
Suffeild, Anthony	Thomas, of Gloucester, cook/innholder, dec'd	cook	Thomas Suffield	1649	2/51
		shoemaker	Walter Harris	1651	2/92
Terrett, John	Thomas, of Gloucester, maltster, dec'd	baker	William Franckis	1661	2/274
		cotton weaver	Roger Wadman	1661	2/281
		feltmaker	Richard Bosly	1667	2/353
Townsend, Henry	Christopher, of Gloucester, barber surgeon, dec'd	vintner	William Warwicke	1651	2/82
		cordwainer	Toby Bubb	1654	2/136
Weaver, Francis	Francis, of Gloucester, butcher, dec'd	cordwainer	Robert Hedges	1617	1/271
		vintner	John Whoppere	1624	1/331
Wells, John	John, of Gloucester, currier/shoe mender, dec'd	currier	John Wells	1665	2/328
		currier	John Wintle	1667	2/357
Williams, John	William of Gloucester, labourer/labourer, dec'd	bodicemaker	William Crass	1684	3/248
		cordwainer	John White	1687	3/280
Witcombe, John	John, of Hempsted, husbandman/yeoman, dec'd	shoemaker	Augustine Gwynn	1624	1/337
		cordwainer	John Carpenter	1626	1/358
Yate, Josiah	Humphrey, of Cheltenham, dec'd/yeoman	tailor	William Randle	1671	3/62
		cordwainer	Daniel Yate	1681	3/219

INDEX OF PERSONS

References to the calendar are to the volumes and pages of the MSS., which are given in the left-hand column of the calendar; references preceded by 'p.' or 'pp.' are to the pages of the introduction or the appendixes. An asterisk * indicates that the reference is to more than one occurrence of the name concerned. The index does not attempt to distinguish different people with the same forename and surname. References to men acting as justice, mayor, alderman or sheriff, however, are distinguished from those to apprentices, fathers, or masters. A widow or a daughter recorded without a forename is indexed under (respectively) her first husband's or her father's surname, as 'widow' or (for a daughter) with an em dash, but a widow remarrying is not indexed under her new husband's surname. The entries in Appendix V are not indexed, since they repeat the substance of entries in the body of the calendar.

The occurrence of a name in a footnote is not separately indexed where a person is named on the page of the MS. to which the footnote is appended. Where a forename or a civic title is not given in the calendar but can be confidently inferred, the reference is indexed under the forename or the civic title.

Where a space for a forename has been left in the MS. (given in the calendar as [*blank*]), the name has been indexed with an em dash.

Abbot (Abbat, Abbots, Abbottes, Abbotts), Anne, 1/180, 256, 290; Bernard, 1/458, 466; Edw, 1/257; Eliz, 1/94, 458, 466; Henry, 2/74*, 267, 362; 3/23*, 133; John, 3/23; Ralph, 1/257; Ric, 1/94*, 180, 256, 290, 404*n*, 405; Rob, 3/250*n*; Sarah, 2/267, 362; 3/23, 133; Wm, 1/94, 405; Wm (*alias* Jones), 2/154*n*

Abrahall (Abrahell), Hugh, 1/343; Jas, 1/343; Simon, 1/180; Thos, 1/180

Ackinson, Ant, 2/18; Geo, 2/18; *and see* Atkinson

Ackley, John, 1/330; Ric, 1/330

Ackson (Axon, Axton), Eliz, 2/292; John, 2/292; Sam, 3/280*n*; Wm, 3/201*n*, 211*n**, 222*n*, 223*; *and see* Exton

Adams (Adammes, Addames, Addams), Albert, 1/33, 134, 136, 161, 545; Alice, 1/545; Anne, 1/33, 134, 136, 161; Dan, 3/17; Eliz, 1/147; Francis, 1/147, 260; Godwin, 2/354; Jane, 1/25, 105, 122, 173; John, 1/14, 211, 260, 273, 501*n*, 502*, 524; 2/209, 220, 364*n*; 3/9*, 36, 337*; Joseph, 2/370*; 3/17, 36; Marg, 2/209, 220; 3/9; Margery, 1/211; Ric, 1/14; Rob, 1/237, 259; Thos, 1/25, 105, 122, 173*, 237, 259; 2/103*; Thos, justice, 1/162, mayor, 1/200*, 207, sheriff, 1/103, 157; Wm, 1/524; 2/354; —, 1/273, 396*

Addis (Addys, Adys), Edw, 2/54*, 172; Eliz, 2/331; John, 1/177; 2/65*, 172, 331; Wm, 1/177; p. 268

Adeane, Ric, 1/541; 2/7*; Thos, 1/541; *and see* Dean

Ady, Edw, 3/336; Margery, 3/336, 360; Thos, 2/348*; 3/107, 336*, 360; —, 3/107

Adys *see* Addis

Alday, John, 2/60*, 131*; p. xix

Aldington, Ant, 3/80; Isaac, 3/80

Aldridge (Alridge), Henry, 3/357; John, 2/136; Sam, 1/475; Sarah, 3/357; Thos, 1/475; 2/7, 136; Wm, 2/226*

Alford, Stephen, 3/41*

Allanson, John, 1/465; Ric, 1/468; Thos, 1/465, 468

Allen, Anne, 2/100, 241, 336; 3/42–3, 135, 213; Arnold, 1/307*; Edm, 1/282; Edw, 1/119, 148, 282; Geo, 1/575; John, 2/314*; 3/116*, 268, 317; Lawr, 1/148; 2/100, 241, 336; 3/42*–3*, 135; p. 271; Marg, 3/268; Mary, 3/342; Ric, 1/119, 158; Rob, 1/158; Sam, 2/9; Thos, 1/472*; 2/13; 3/43; Thos (*alias* Cooper) 3/387; Wm, 1/575; 2/9; 3/42, 271, 342; —, 2/13

Allord, Nat, 3/215; Wal, 3/215

Alridge *see* Aldridge

Alye, Giles, 1/381; Joseph, 2/214; Theophilus, p. 264; Wm, 2/214

Amos, Edw, 3/42; Nat, 2/245; 3/42; Sam, 2/245; 3/42; —, 3/42

Amphlett, Joan, 1/357; Ric, 1/357

Andrews (Andrewes, Andros), Ant, 3/189, 193; Chas, 3/193; Chris, 1/10; Geo, 2/322; John, 2/157; Ric, 2/322; Rob, 3/381; Thos, 1/10; 2/157; Wm, 3/189, 285, 287

Angell (Angle), Abel, 1/109, 169, 263*, 380; Abel, sheriff, 1/372; Anne, 1/110; Edw, 1/148; Luke, 1/455, 458, 466; Mary, 1/109, 169, 263; Ric, 1/148, 586; Rob, 1/110, 455; Thos, 1/458, 466; Wm, 1/263, 586; 2/165; p. 270; —, 2/165

Annetts, John, 3/277

277

Anstee (Anstick), Chas, **3**/55*, 262, 279; Henry, **1**/386*n*, 387; Joan, **1**/313, 387; Mary, **3**/55; Ralph (Randall), **1**/313, 386*n*, 387*

Ap Gwilliam, Ric, **1**/23; *and see* Gwilliam; Williams

Ap Rice, Powell, **1**/63; Ric, **1**/63; *and see* Price; Rice

Aphowell, Thos, **1**/480; Wm, **1**/480; *and see* Howell; Powell

Apperly, John, **1**/550; Wm, **1**/550

Aram (Arram), Arnold, **2**/234; **3**/43, 132; Edw, **3**/43; Eliz, **3**/132; John, **1**/565; **2**/234; **3**/11, 43; Marg, **2**/152; **3**/11, 59, 87, 90; Thos, **1**/565; **2**/80, 152; **3**/11*, 59, 87, 90, 110; Thos, sheriff, **2**/344; —, **2**/80; **3**/43, 110

Archard, Edw, p. 267; Eliz, **2**/224; Geo, **2**/224; John, **1**/267, 276; Wm, **1**/267, 276

Archer, Abraham, **3**/381; Ant, **3**/392*; Edw, **2**/54; Geo, **2**/54; Mary, **3**/381; Sampson, **3**/389; Thos, **3**/388*n*, 389

Ardwaie (Ardwaye), Cath, **1**/36; John, **1**/36, 93; Wm, **1**/93

Arkell, Edw, **1**/5; Nic, **1**/5

Armitage, Giles, **3**/233; Henry, **1**/343, John, **1**/520; **3**/353*n*, 354*; Ric, **1**/343, 520; **3**/233

Arnold (Arnell), Ant, **3**/362; John, **2**/147; Thos, **2**/147, 151*; Wm, **3**/122*; *and see* Yarnold

Arram *see* Aram

Arthur, Abraham, **3**/333*n*; Giles, **1**/268; Rob, **1**/268

Arundell, Jas, **1**/261; Sam, **3**/37; Thos, **1**/261; Wm, **3**/37

Ashbie, John, **1**/117; Sam, **1**/117

Ashmead (Ashmeade), Giles, **2**/355; **3**/397*; Henry, **2**/355; John, **1**/279, 283; **3**/335*; Wm, **1**/279, 283

Aspden, Guy, **1**/100; John, **1**/100

Aspin, Wm, **1**/268*–9*

Asteman, Thos, **1**/22*

Atkins (Atkings, Atkyns, Etkins), Abraham, **1**/458; Eliz, **1**/548, 551, 562, 566; **2**/40, 77, 100, 232, 244; Francis, **1**/15; Henry, **1**/354; Jane, **1**/113; John, **1**/24, 134, 172, 436*n*, 438, 517, 548, 551, 562, 566; **2**/40, 54, 77, 100, 138, 146, 232, 244, 338*n*, 341; **3**/59; p. 272; Joseph, **3**/59; Martha, **1**/172; Mary, **3**/194, 203, 300, 330, 348, 360; Mathea, **1**/134; Ric, **1**/15; Rob, **1**/436*n*, 438; **2**/40, 77, 100, 232, 244; **3**/48; Sybil, **1**/24; Thos, **1**/197*, 354, 458; **2**/138, 244, 249; Thos, town clerk, **1**/39; Wal, **2**/243*n*, 244; **3**/194, 203, 300, 330, 348, 360; Wm, **3**/17*, 48; —, **1**/517; **2**/146, 249

Atkinson, Edw, **1**/8; Wm, **1**/8; *and see* Ackinson

Atkyns *see* Atkins

Atwood (Attwood), John, **3**/338; Maurice, **1**/114; Susannah, **3**/338; Thos, p. 268; Wm, **1**/114

Austin (Augustin), Hugh, **3**/289; Ric, **3**/289

Awberye, Geo, p. 266

Axon (Axton) *see* Ackson

Aycrigg, Wm, **3**/395

Aylburton, John, **3**/347; Wm, **3**/347

Ayleway (Aylway), Mary, **3**/366; Ric, **2**/353*; **3**/366

Bacon, Oliver (Nollard), **3**/247*n*, 250, 316, 369; Rob, **3**/369; Thos, **3**/247*n*, 250; Wal, **3**/316

Badcocke, Henry, **3**/174*; James, **3**/174

Badcott, John, **1**/519; Wm, **1**/519

Badger, Albert, **2**/57, 280; **3**/144, 173, 176, 236, 261*n*, 265*; Brian, **1**/129, 401, 454, 484, 545; **2**/57, 333; Eliz, **2**/280; **3**/144, 173, 176; Giles, **1**/129, 401; Jeremiah, **1**/454, 484, 545; **2**/281; **3**/53, 193, 228*n*, 236; Joan, **3**/274; John, **3**/53, 274, 379*n*; Marg, **2**/281; **3**/193; Phoenix, **2**/333; p. xvi; Ric, **1**/314, 588; Thos, **1**/588; —, **3**/64*n*

Baggot (Baggatt, Baggott, Bagott), John, **1**/81, 377, 436*n*, 437; **2**/74; Thos, **1**/81; Wm, **1**/436*n*, 437; **2**/73*n*, 74

Baily (Bailee, Bayley, Baylee, Baylie, Bayly), Abigail, **1**/228*, 335, 352; Eliz, **2**/132, 141, 224, 333; Jane, **2**/377; John, **1**/121, 228*, 255, 335, 352, 527*n*, 515; Mary, **3**/330; Thos, **1**/527*n*, 515; **2**/119, 132, 141, 224, 333; **3**/39*; p. xvi; Wm, **1**/121; *and see* Baylis

Baker, Abraham, **2**/252; Anne, **2**/111, 302; **3**/303; Benj, **2**/346; **3**/293; Chas, **3**/105; Edm, **3**/68*, 105; Eliz, **2**/307, 316; Griffin, **2**/69; Henry, **1**/293; Jacob, **2**/252; Jas, **1**/360; **3**/80*n*, 91*, 142, 191, 303; Joan, **1**/360; John, **1**/99; **2**/69, 111, 275, 302; **3**/142; Joyce, **2**/201; Luke, **1**/52; Ric, **1**/420; **2**/201*, 346; **3**/293; Ric, town clerk, **1**/1; Thos, **1**/287*, 381, 417, 546*, 564*n*; **2**/294*, 323*; **3**/196*, 270; p. 272; Wm, **1**/52, 99, 293, 381, 417, 420; **2**/307, 316; **3**/191, 200*n*, 311*n*; p. 271; Wm (*alias* Williams) **2**/292*; —, **1**/564*n*; **2**/275

Baldwin (Baldwyn, Baldwyne, Balldwyn), John, **3**/310, 356; Mary, **2**/321–2, 349*; **3**/308; Roland, **1**/463; Stephen, **2**/321–2, 349; Thos, **3**/310, 356; Wm, **1**/463; **3**/308

Ball, Giles, **3**/278; John, **3**/228; Nat, **1**/112; Rob, **1**/112; Sarah, **3**/278; Thos, **3**/227*n*, 228

Balldwyn *see* Baldwin

Ballenger *see* Bellinger

Bamford (Bumford), Eliz, **2**/294, 299; Wm, **2**/66*, 238, 245, 294, 299; —, **2**/238, 245

Banaster *see* Banister

Banckes *see* Banks

Band (Bande), Henry, **1**/8; John, **2**/105*; Ric, **2**/46*; Thos, **1**/8; *and see* Bond; Bound

INDEX OF PERSONS

Banister (Banaster), Giles, **1**/249; Nat, **2**/216; Wm, **1**/249; Willoughby, **2**/216

Banks (Banckes, Bankes), Henry, **1**/248, 334; John, **1**/334; Philip, **1**/248

Bannett, John, **2**/267*; *and see* Bennett

Barber (Barbour), Jas, **1**/202; Joan, **1**/202; John, **1**/307; Thos, **1**/307

Bardle, Wm, **1**/86*, 104*

Barker, Anne, **3**/389; John, **1**/370, 445*; **3**/307, 389; Lucy, **3**/334; Nic, **3**/331; Marg, **2**/30, 42, 157, 225; Thos, **1**/370; **2**/30, 42, 157, 225, 314; **3**/331; p. 273; Wm, **2**/314; **3**/307, 334

Barkesdale, Giles, **1**/143, 259; John, **1**/143, 208; Nic, **1**/208; —, **1**/259

Barnad *see* Barnwood

Barnard (Barnarde), Edm (*alias* Turner), **2**/275; Jas, p. 268; John (*alias* Turner), **2**/275; Wm, **1**/69*

Barneham *see* Barnham

Barnelme, Edw, **3**/225; Eliz, **3**/240; John, **3**/222*n*, 225; Ric, **2**/360*, 362*n*; **3**/81, 86, 143, 240; Wm, **1**/66, 255; p. 273; —, **3**/81, 86, 143

Barnes, Anne, **1**/8, Edw, **3**/361; Eliz, **1**/45; Joan, **1**/476, 492, 543, 560; **3**/189, 232; John, **1**/8, 476, 492, 543, 560; **2**/325*n*, 326*; p. 273; Susannah, **3**/27; Thos, **1**/45; **2**/326; **3**/27, 361; p. 273; Thos, sheriff, **1**/61; Wm, **1**/439*; **2**/326; **3**/189, 232

Barnewood *see* Barnwood

Barnfield, Ric, **3**/349*

Barnfull, Francis, **2**/149*

Barnham (Barneham), widow, **2**/175*n*; —, **2**/175*n*

Barnwood (Barnad, Barnwod, Barnewood) Edm, **2**/31; Eliz, **1**/107; Henry, **1**/12; Hester, **2**/31, 112; Jas, **2**/106; John, **2**/31, 112; p. 270; Ric, **2**/31; Thos, **1**/107; **3**/353*; Wm, **1**/12; **2**/106

Barradell, John, **3**/81*

Barrett (Barrat, Barret), Alice, **1**/41, 142; Ant, **3**/61; Arthur, **2**/39, 350; **3**/347*n*, 351; Chris, **1**/41, 142; Cornelius, **3**/161*n*; Henry, **1**/472; Joan, **2**/296; John, **3**/92*n*, 104, 300; Marg, **2**/27; Mary, **1**/472, 522; **2**/153, 201, 222; Ralph, **2**/292; **3**/61; Rob, **1**/32*, 46*; Roger, **1**/5; Thos, **1**/5, 123*, 472*, 522; **2**/27, 39, 153, 201, 222, 268*, 296, 350; **3**/142*n*, 300, 332, 351; p. 268; Wm, **1**/340*; **2**/292; **3**/92*n*, 104, 332, 346*; —, **2**/268

Barrow (Barrowe), Anne, **1**/414; Henry, **1**/413–14; Jas, **3**/202; Joan, **1**/513; John, **3**/202; Rob, **1**/513*; Thos, **3**/285*n*; Wm, **3**/368*; Zachary, **3**/285*n*; *and see* Berrow; Borrow; Burroughs

Barston, Jas, p. 265

Barton (Bartone), Anne, **2**/21, 65, 288; Eleanor, **1**/245; John, **2**/35*n*; **3**/353; Michael, **1**/471; Ric, **2**/21, 65, 288; p. 271; Thos, **1**/471; **3**/353; Wm, **1**/245

Bathorne, Jeremiah, **3**/273; Rob, **3**/273

Batt, Anne, **1**/5; Dan, **1**/137; Edm, **1**/5; John, p. 273; Wm, **1**/137

Batten, Bridget, **1**/324; Eliz, **1**/159, 171, 187; John, **1**/159, 171, 187; Ric, **1**/324

Battie (Batty, Battye), Eliz, **1**/98; John, **1**/53, 98; Ric, **1**/53, 157

Baugh (Baughe), Eleanor, **1**/30, 86, 110, 125, 201–2; Francis, **1**/30, 86, 110, 125, 201–2; John, **1**/3, 68, 81, 280, 353*, 411; **2**/140*; John, mayor, **1**/157, 297, 302, sheriff, **1**/19; Marg, **1**/3, 81, 280; Thos, p. 267; Wm, **1**/411, 539*

Baxter, Sam, p. 264; Stephen, p. 264

Bayley (Baylee, Baylie, Bayly) *see* Baily

Baylis (Bayliss), John, **1**/489*n*; **3**/16; Joseph, **1**/489*n*; Ric, **3**/16; *and see* Baily

Bayneham, John, **2**/58; Thos, **2**/58

Bayton, John, **3**/176; Sam, **3**/176

Beach, John, **3**/253, 374; Marg, **3**/374; Rob, **3**/253

Beacon, Sampson, **2**/130*

Beakes, Benj, **3**/13, 61; Rob, **3**/13, 61; *and see* Beck; Beeke

Beale, Anne, **3**/372; Benj, **3**/268, 372; Edith, **1**/573; **2**/17, 128; **3**/85, 198; Frances, **1**/84; Francis, **3**/322*n*; Geof, **1**/10, 42, 84, 144, 404, 451*, 487, 573; **2**/17, 128; **3**/85*, 198*; Geof, justice, **1**/227, 261, 269, mayor, **1**/246, 267, sheriff, **1**/141; **2**/189; Humph, **1**/112, 238, 501*n**; Jas, **2**/77; **3**/198; Joan, **1**/10, 42, 84, 144, 161, 238, 451; John, **1**/284*, 499*; **2**/59; Joseph, **2**/196; Matt, **1**/277; Ric, **2**/59, 77; Sam, sheriff, **3**/391; Thos, **1**/161, 451, 549; **2**/44, 322; **3**/221, 268; p. 272; Wm, **1**/277; **2**/44, 196, 322; **3**/221; —, **1**/112; **3**/322*n*

Beard (Bearde), Alice, **2**/183; Andrew, **1**/297, 313, 388, 400*, 446; **3**/200; p. 266; Anne, **1**/109, 327, 342, 389; Armilla (Armela, Armyla), **1**/526, 547, 567, 580; **2**/162, 227, 239, 270, 334; Benj, **2**/162*n*; Denis, **3**/239*n*, 241; Eleanor, **2**/317, 340, 347, 351; **3**/34, 94, 105, 107, 133, 161, 178, 184; Eliz, **1**/329, 462, 475, 576; **2**/161, 163, 178–9; **3**/161, 164, 184, 251, 284; Geo, **1**/106; Grace, **3**/314; Henry, **1**/488; **3**/223*, 246, 254, 314; Isobel, **1**/303, 329; Jane, **2**/7, 101; John, **1**/109, 389, 492, 501*n*, 512, 581, 583; **2**/16, 75, 97, 113, 136, 145, 161, 163, 228, 248, 258, 277, 317, 340, 347, 351; **3**/34, 94, 105, 107*, 133, 161, 228, 250*n*, 295*n*, 297*, 298, 314; pp. xxv, 272; Kath, **3**/246, 250*n*; Marg, **2**/16, 75, 97, 228; Mary, **1**/297, 313, 388, 400, 446; Nat, **2**/7, 101; Ric, **1**/109, 131, 248, 292, 303, 327, 329, 342, 389, 400, 488, 526, 547, 567, 580, 583; **2**/162*, 227, 239, 270, 334, 338*n*; **3**/314, 338*n*; p. 271;

INDEX OF PERSONS

Beard (*cont.*)
  Ric, mayor, **1**/360, 382, sheriff, **1**/227; Sarah, **2**/113; Thos, **1**/106, 109, 188, 389, 492, 501*n*; **3**/107, 133*, 216; Wal, **2**/183; Wm, **1**/462, 475, 576; **2**/178–9, 334*; **3**/202*n*, 241, 254, 295*n**, 298, 397; —, **1**/131, 512, 581; **2**/145, 248, 258, 277, 301*n*; **3**/178*n*; *and see* Byard
Beaton, Moses, p. 266
Beaven *see* Bevan
Beck (Becke), Ant, **1**/142*; Chris, **1**/20; Ric, **1**/20; *and see* Beakes; Beeke
Bedwell, Chas, **3**/195; John, **3**/195
Beedle (Beedell) *see* Biddle
Beeke, John, **1**/445, Thos, **1**/445; *and see* Beakes; Beck
Beevan *see* Bevan
Belcher, Dan, **2**/209; Edw, **3**/382; Joan, **2**/353; John, **2**/239; Ric, **2**/207*, 208–9, 239; **3**/382; Thos, **2**/208, 353
Bell, Joan, **2**/255, 257, 321, 337, 346; **3**/61, 101, 207–8; John, **1**/569*; **2**/134*, 255, 257, 321, 337, 346; **3**/61, 349, 386; John, sheriff, **3**/315; Mary, **3**/349; —, **2**/134*
Bellamy (Billamy), Geo, **2**/4*; Guy, **1**/483; Thos, **1**/198; p. xv; Wm, **1**/198, 483
Bellinger (Ballenger), Chris **1**/37, 209; John, **1**/37*; Thos, **1**/37
Benfield (Benfeild), Mary, **2**/376; Thos, **3**/51*
Bennett (Bennet), Abel, p. 266; Anne, **1**/72, 97–8; **2**/300, 306, 365; Ant, **1**/138, 281, 302, 334, 344, 348, 442, 475; Arthur, **1**/138, 179; Chas, **1**/288; **3**/140; Denis, **1**/475; Edw, **3**/94; Eliz, **1**/281, 302, 334, 344, 348; Henry, **1**/82; Jas, **1**/101; Jesse, **1**/442; John, **1**/75*, 101, 144*; **2**/56, 265, 300, 306, 365; **3**/195, 214, 240; pp. 268, 270; Mary, **1**/137, 179, 180–1, 246; Penelope, **3**/195, 214; **2**/265; Rob, **1**/159*; **2**/59*; **3**/94; Thos, **1**/72, 82, 97–8, 137, 179*, 180–1, 246; **3**/140; Wm, **1**/288, 325*; **2**/56; *and see* Bannett
Benson, Eliz, **3**/348, 376; John, **3**/348, 372*n*, 376*; Mary, **3**/365; Wm, **3**/365
Bergum, John, **3**/12; Rob, **3**/12
Berrow (Berow, Berrowe), Alice, **2**/55; Eleanor, **2**/239, 345; Geo, **1**/104; **2**/55*; Kath, **1**/104; **3**/23; Mary, **2**/317; Sam, **2**/55; **3**/23; Stephen, **3**/289; Thos, **2**/317; Wm, **2**/239, 345; **3**/44*; *and see* Barrow; Borrow; Burroughs
Berry, John, **1**/173; Ric, **1**/173; **2**/240; Rob, **2**/261*; Sam, **3**/37; Thos, **2**/211; **3**/338; Wm, **2**/211, 240; **3**/338; Zachariah, **3**/37, 108*
Berwicke, Barbara, **3**/373; Thos, **3**/373
Besall (Bezell, Bussell) *alias* Tackley (Tacly), Eliz, **1**/261, 275, 439; Thos, **1**/261, 275, 439

Best, Anne, **3**/84; Francis, **3**/335*; John, **1**/293*, 315; **3**/84; Thos, **1**/315; **2**/83*
Bevan (Beaven, Beevan), Edw, **1**/548; **3**/53*, 243; John, **3**/179, 243; Lewis, **1**/172*; Ric, **3**/23, 179; Wal, **1**/548; Wm, **3**/23, 200*; *and see* Evans; Heaven
Bevis, Jas (*alias* Wilkinson), **1**/527*n*, 528; John (*alias* Wilkinson), **1**/527*n*, 528; Lawr, **1**/8; Ric, **1**/8
Bezell *see* Tackley
Bickarton, Edw, **2**/340; John, **2**/340
Bicke (Bycke), Edm, **2**/33; Edw, **2**/33; p. 269; Eleanor, **3**/290; Henry, **2**/267; John, **2**/267, 338; Thos, **2**/90, 338; **3**/290; Wm, **2**/90
Bicknell (Bikenell), Abigail, **3**/325, 388, 396; Dorothy, **2**/160, 260; **3**/242; Jas, **3**/391; John, **1**/1; Theophilus, **1**/1; Wm, **2**/90, 160, 260; **3**/143, 242, 324–5, 388, 396; —, **3**/143
Bickner, Wm, **1**/526; —, **1**/526
Bidawell, John, **3**/119*; *and see* Bidwell
Biddle (Beedle, Beedell, Bidle), Anne, **3**/250*n*; Avice, **2**/285; Bridget, **3**/16; Geo, **3**/129; Jas, **1**/42; **2**/285, 315*; **3**/293*n*, 299; John, **3**/250*n*, 252*, 299, 365; Jonas (Jonah), **3**/16, 109*n*, 129, 211*; Thos, **1**/524; Wm, **1**/42, 524
Bidwell, Jas, p. 272; *and see* Bidawell
Biglin, Edw, **1**/141; Sybil, **1**/141
Bikenell *see* Bicknell
Biles, Ephraim, **3**/63; Thos, **3**/63
Billamy *see* Bellamy
Bingham, Edw, **1**/532; p. 267; Wal, **1**/532
Bingle (Bingly), Dan, **2**/225*; Eliz, **1**/581, **2**/260; John, **1**/581; **2**/260*
Birch (Birche, Burch), John, **1**/338*; Thos, **2**/136; **3**/93*; Wm, **2**/136
Birchley, John, **1**/30; Thos, **1**/30,
Bird (Birde, Burd, Byrd, Byrde), Andrew, **1**/341*, 349, 375, 471; Anne, **1**/573; **2**/2; **3**/349; Dan, **1**/573; **2**/2, 346*; **3**/349*; Ferdinand, **1**/167, 210; Joan, **1**/210; John, **1**/170; **3**/349; Mary, **1**/341, 349, 375, 471; Nat, p. 273; Ric, **1**/167; Thos, **1**/527*n*; p. 267; Wm, **1**/170, 341, 527*n*; —, **3**/64*n*
Birt (Burt, Burte, Byrt), Deborah, **3**/30,281; Giles, **2**/69; Joan, **1**/285; John, **3**/206; Ric, **1**/281; Rob, **1**/146*, 285; Thos, **1**/281; Wm, **2**/69; **3**/30, 200*, 206, 281
Birton, Wm, **3**/90*
Bishop (Bishopp, Bishoppe, Bisshop, Bushop, Bushoppe, Busshope, Byshop, Byshopp), Alan, **1**/360; Alex, **1**/187, 197, 212*, 333, 377, 394, 403, 501*n*, 502; Anne, **1**/208–9, 257, 292, 321, 397, 423, 488, 502, 557; **3**/284, 364; Ant, **1**/247, 355; **2**/17; Bridget, **1**/187, 197, 212, 377; Dan,

INDEX OF PERSONS

2/145, 324; 3/105*, 196*, 199, 229*, 238, 284, 295n, 364, 387; Edm, 2/268*, 277; Eleanor, 2/324; 3/199; Eliz, 2/164, 362; Geo, 3/386n, 387; Giles, 2/40, 119, 164*; 3/34; Gregory, 2/115; Hester, 3/53, 162; Isobel, 1/42, 49, 227, 269*; John, 1/92, 247, 355, 360, 396n, 397, 476n; 2/119, 128, 145; 3/34*, 53, 162*, 227n, 229; p. 271; John, sheriff, 3/158; Mary, 1/121, 160, 438; Maurice, 1/307; Nat, 1/42, 49, 227, 269*, 321; Nat, sheriff, 1/129; Peter, 1/17*; Ric, 1/11; 2/17, 128–9; 3/34, 46, 364n; Rob, 1/121, 160, 438, 476n; 2/119; Rob, sheriff, 1/279; Thos, 1/92, 208–9, 257, 292, 396n, 397*, 423, 488, 501n, 502*, 557; 2/40, 129, 178, 211*, 268, 277; 3/209; Wm, 1/11, 307, 355; 2/115, 178, 362; 3/37, 46, 56*, 206*, 209; —, 2/119; 3/37, 201n, 295n

Blackborne, Henry, 1/403; Ric, 1/403
Blackleech, Abraham (Mr), 1/520, 521*–2*, 530*; p. xxiii and see p. 263
Blackwell, Thos, 2/349*
Blake, Edw, 1/569; Valentine, 1/569
Blanche (Blanch), Dan, 3/48*, 134; John, 1/40; pp. 269, 271; Miles, 1/40; Seth, 3/134; Thos, /100; Wm, 3/100, 225
Blanchet, John, 1/499*
Blanchflower, Edm, 1/207; Edw, 1/207
Bland, Bridget, 3/331; Josiah, 3/331
Blicke (Bleeke), Arthur, 1/144; Edw, 3/135; John, 1/487; Mary, 2/94, 254; Ric, 1/144; 3/135; Wm, 1/487; 2/94, 254
Blinkhorne, Geo, p. 267
Blisard see Blizzard
Bliss (Blisse), Anne, 1/6, 100, 124; Hester, 3/398; John, 1/34, 428; 2/133, 215 Marg, 1/492; Nat, 1/489n, 492; Ric, 1/200; 2/215; Thos, 1/6, 100, 124, 182, 489n, 492*; 2/133; 3/203; Wm, 1/34, 182, 200, 428; 3/203, 398; —, 1/407n
Blissard see Blizzard
Blisse see Bliss
Blizzard (Blisard, Blissard, Blizard), John, 3/130, 388, Mary, 3/388; Stephen, 2/351; Thos, 2/351; 3/130; Wm, 3/286*
Blomer (Blowmer), Giles, 1/342; Mary, 1/342; Thos, 1/13, 207; Wm, 1/207
Blunt, Chas, 2/123; Nic, 2/123
Blye, John, 2/35n; Ric, 2/38*
Boddenham (Bodenham) see Bodnam
Bodman, Joan, 2/26; p. xxiv; Ric, 2/26
Bodnam (Boddenham, Bodenham), Emmanuel, 3/212; John, 1/167; Marg, 1/326, 363; Ric, 1/167, 326, 363*, 536n*; Sam, 3/212, 270*
Boilson, Thos, 1/16*
Bond (Bonde), Frances, 1/473; John, 1/283*, 473; Ric, 1/456*; and see Band; Bound
Bonwell, Ric, 2/332*
Booth (Bothe), Ant, 1/211; Thos, 1/211
Boreman, Joseph, 2/360; Mary, 2/360
Borrow (Borow), Eleanor, 2/220; Wm, 2/220; —, 178n; and see Barrow; Berrow; Burroughs
Bosley (Bosly, Bozley), Eliz, 2/106, 189, 257, 298, 353; 3/32, 44, 66; John, 1/481, 559n, 560; 2/189*, 213, 312*, 356, 367; 3/83, 93, 173, 195*; p. xiv; Joyce, 3/331; Mary, 2/312, 356, 367; 3/83, 93, 173; Ric, 1/208, 469*, 481, 509*, 559n, 560; 2/58, 106, 189, 213*, 257, 298, 312, 353; 3/32, 44, 66; p. 270; Ric, sheriff, 3/158; Thos, 1/172*; 2/257, 258*; Wal, 2/257; 3/317*, 331; Wm, 1/208
Bossom, Thos, 3/348*
Bothe see Booth
Boulter (Bowlter), John, 1/567; Ric, 1/567
Boulton, Ric, 2/225*; Thos, 1/431; Wm, 1/431
Bound, Thos, 3/390*; and see Band; Bond
Bourne, Benj, 2/222; Henry, 3/13; Wm, 2/222; 3/13
Bowar see Bower
Bowcer (Bowser), Geo, 2/120, 126; Thos, 2/120, 126
Bowen, Edw, 1/332; Jas, 1/332
Bower (Bowar, Bowher), Anne, 1/80, 145; Ant, 2/108, 115; Chas, 2/115; John, 1/80, 145; 3/272n, 276; Michael, 2/108; Sam, 3/237*, 239n, 276; Thos, 1/502, 577*; 3/382*; Wm, 1/502
Bowland, Jane, 1/33; Thos, 1/33
Bowle, Henry, 1/133; Tacy, 1/133
Bowler, Anne, 3/316; Geo, 2/363; 3/285n, 369; Mary, 3/369; Thos, 2/363; 3/252, 316; —, 3/285n
Bowlter see Boulter
Bowry, Sam, 2/177; Wm, 2/177
Bowser see Bowcer
Boyes, John, 2/61*
Boyfield (Boyfeild, Boyfeilds), Thos, 1/507, 523; 2/323*; Wm, 1/523
Bozley see Bosley
Brabant (Braban, Brabban, Broben, Brobent, Brobon), Francis, 2/190, 349; 3/93, 189*, 236, 303, 307, 356, 364; Hester, 2/349; 3/93, 189, 236, 307; John, 3/208; Marg, 3/356, 364; Wm, 2/190; 3/208
Braddis, Ric, 3/387*
Bradford, Alice, 2/166; Anne, 2/99, 133, 190, 239; Arnold, 1/127; John, 1/547*; 2/99, 133, 166, 190, 239; Rob, 3/130, 132; Thos, 1/127, 210; Wm, 3/130, 132
Bradgate (Broadgate, Brodgate), Alice, 1/529; 2/63; John, 2/243n, 244; Ric, 1/357n*, 358*, 529; 2/63*, 244*; p. xxi; Wm, 3/379n; —, 3/228n

Bradley, Henry, 2/253*n*, 260*n*, 275; 3/57, 317, 326, 364*n*, 368; p. xxii; John, 2/253*n*, 274*n*, 275; 3/57, 275, 295*n*, 302, 368*; Mary, 3/302, 368; Thos, 3/317, 326; p. 266

Bradrist, Henry, 2/210*

Bradshaw, Bart, 2/196; Henry, 3/224; John, 3/370; Rob, 3/384; Simon, 2/196; Thos, 3/234; Wm, 3/224, 238*n*, 234, 336*, 370, 381*n*, 384

Bradstocke, Ric, 3/106; Thos, 3/106

Bradwell, Ric, 1/80; Thos, 1/80

Bramley *see* Bromley

Branch, John, 1/533; 2/51, 128; Thos, 2/128; 3/324; Wal, 1/533; Wm, 3/324; —, 2/51

Brawne, Nat, 2/160; Wm, 2/160

Bray, Henry, 1/583*; 2/143

Brethers (Breethers), Alice, 1/504; Blanche, 1/382; Rob, 1/504; Thos, 1/382

Bretherton (Brotherton), Dan, 3/284; Jeremiah, 3/194*, 262, 276*n*; John, p. 269; Jonathan, 3/284; Joshua, 3/262; Solomon, 3/302*n*; —, 3/276*n*

Brett, Henry, p. 268

Brewer, Thos (*alias* Liddiat), 1/16*

Brewster (Bruster), Eliz, 1/327, 487; John, 1/88, 100, 327, 487; John, alderman, 1/327, 342, 389, mayor, 1/167, 408, sheriff, 1/1, 39, 207, 267; p. 261; Kath, 1/88, 100; Sam, sheriff, 2/263

Brian *see* Bryan

Bridger, Arthur, 1/461; Desborowe, 3/92; Jas, 2/371, 376–7; p. xxiii; Sam, 1/461; Thos, 3/92

Bridges (Bridgges), Isobel, 1/10; John, 1/120, 147; 2/129*; Thos, 1/120, 147; Wm, 1/10, 51

Bright, Joyce, 3/397; Thos, 3/310, 397

Brimyard (Brimeyeard, Brimiard, Brymyard, Brymyrd), Alice, 3/367; Eliz, 2/335–6; 3/100, 132, 178, 207; Henry, 3/364*n*, 368; Joan, 2/176; John, 3/390; Wm, 2/110, 176, 335, 336*; 3/100, 132, 178, 207, 367–8, 390; Wm (*alias* Tompkins), 2/190

Brinkwell, Geo, 1/318; —, 1/318

Bristol, Henry, 1/495*

Broad (Broade, Brode), Edm, 1/230; 2/225*; Eliz, 1/451, 551; 2/32; Geo, 2/365; Geo, sheriff, 3/230; Mary, 2/19, 128, 225, 250, 283, 364; 3/107; Ric, 2/19, 128, 225, 250, 283, 364; p. 271; Ric, sheriff, 3/34; Sam, 1/375; 2/365; 3/67*; Thos, 1/375; Wm, 1/230, 451, 551

Broadgate *see* Bradgate

Broadway, Ric, p. 272

Broben (Brobent, Brobon) *see* Brabant

Brocke, John, 2/318; 3/249, 354, 396*; Joseph, 3/384*; Mary, 3/249, 354, 396; Wm, 2/273*, 318

Brode *see* Broad

Brodgate *see* Bradgate

Bromley (Bramley, Bromleye, Bromly), Anne, 1/32, 66; Jas, 2/243; Jane, 2/143; John, 1/32, 66, 130*, 436*; 2/143, 243; Leonard, 1/436; 2/143; 3/24; p. 273; Ric, 2/143; Sarah, 1/436; Wm, 2/295*; —, 3/24

Brooke (Brookes), Alice, 1/305; Edw, 1/538; Giles, 1/187, 189; John, 1/33, 96; 3/104, 158; Jonathan, 3/88*, 226*; Joseph, 3/86*, 158; Martin, 1/344; Mary, 3/104; Ric, 1/344; Roger, 1/33; Thos, 1/538; Wm, 1/96, 187, 189, 305

Brookebank *see* Bruckbanke

Brookehowse, Joan, 1/108, 144*; John, 1/108, 144*; Thos, 1/144

Brooker, John, 2/251; —, 2/251

Brookes *see* Brooke

Brothers *alias* Chapman, Joan, 1/561; John, 1/559*n*, 561*; Toby, 1/559*n*, 561

Brotherton *see* Bretherton

Brown (Browne), Dan, 3/218; Edm, 3/87*n*, 89; Edw, 1/257; Eleanor, 1/16, 51, 55; Elias, 2/341; Eliz, 1/16, 565; 2/17, 62, 174, 378; 3/60, 87, 163, 200; Francis, 1/16, 98; p. 265; Geo, 1/575; Henry, 1/23, 99, 391; Henry, mayor, 1/372, 419; p. 270, sheriff, 1/187; Hester, 3/338, 385, 398; Humph, 2/192, 239; 3/39; Isobel, 1/99; Jas, 1/333; 2/204*n*, 217; 3/60, 87, 163, 200; p. 271; Jane, 1/109, 147, 211, 229, 262; Joan, 3/382, 390; John, 1/15–16, 51, 55, 98, 159, 162, 200, 348*n*, 351*, 391, 565; 2/62, 73, 174, 217, 316*n*, 317*, 341, 362*n*, 366; 3/39, 69, 87*, 89, 211*n*, 302*, 322, 338, 398; pp. 269, 272; John, mayor, 1/187, 191, 311, 459, 465, sheriff, 1/111; Jonathan, 3/218; Joseph, 2/11; 3/92*n*, 95*; Margery, 1/22, 91; Martha, 3/218; Mary, 3/218; Nat, 2/67*; Nic, 1/22, 91, 117; Philip, 3/398*; Ric, 1/109, 147, 211, 229, 257, 262; 2/239; Rob, p. 273; Sam, 2/280, 366; 3/315, 385; Sarah, 3/83*; pp. xix, xxii *and see* p. 263; Thos, 1/575; 2/11, 192; 3/69, 83*, 218*; Thos, mayor, 3/315; Wm, 1/200, 321*, 333; 2/17, 159, 280; 3/367, 382, 390; widow, p. 269; —, 1/159; 3/244*n*

Browne John *see* Brownjohn

Browning (Browninge, Browneinge), Edw, 1/433; John, 1/121, 125, 129, 143; Kath, 1/121, 125, 129, 143; Ric, 1/300, 433; Thos, 1/300, 541*

Brownjohn (Browne John), Henry, 2/138*

Bruckbanke (Brookebanke, Bruckebancke), Eliz, 1/351; Giles, 1/351; Margery, 2/8, 61; Rob, 3/160*

Brushe, Thos, 1/85; Wm, 1/85

Bruster *see* Brewster

Bryan (Brian), Anne, 3/190, 272, 290; Dan, 2/364; 3/190, 272, 290, 299, 305, 365*; p. xvi; Ric,

INDEX OF PERSONS

3/291*; Rob, 1/411*; Thos, 2/293*, 364
Brymeyard (Brymyard) *see* Brimyard
Bubb (Bub, Bubbe), Beatrice, 1/271; Bridget, 1/72; Cecily, 1/34; Eleanor, 1/126, 145, 259, 350, 412*; Eliz, 3/245; Giles, 3/230, 298; Henry, 2/262, 269n; Joan, 1/203, 330; 2/315; John, 1/126, 145, 259, 350; 2/262; Judith, 1/578; 2/142; Kath, 2/27, 41, 136, 182; Mary, 1/453, 523; Ric, 1/465; Thos, 1/34, 72, 271, 422*; 2/41; 3/13, 230; Toby, 1/412, 453, 523; 2/27, 40n, 41*, 136, 182, 254, 315*, 316n, 319*; Wal, 1/95; Wm, 1/95*, 203, 330, 401*, 465, 578; 2/142; 3/13, 193n, 245, 289, 337, 379; p. 271; Wm, sheriff, 1/287; 2/123; —, 2/254
Bucke, John, 3/26; Ric, 3/26
Buckle, John, 3/392; Ric, 3/290*; Wal, 3/392
Budding, Henry, 3/321; Ric, 3/321
Bulbrick (Bulbricke), Anne, 1/305, 408; John, 1/305, 408; 2/63; p. xxiv; Nic, 2/63
Bull, Ant, p. 267
Bullawaye, Wm, 1/533*
Bullock (Bullocke, Bullucke), Ant, 1/198; Edw, 1/295, 334; Jas, 1/248, 334; John, 2/21; John, sheriff, 1/255; Joseph, 2/22; Matt, 2/112; Ric, 3/361*; Rob, 1/198; 2/112; Thos, 1/248, 295, 334, 358; 3/379n, 384*; Toby, alderman, 1/377, mayor, 1/407, sheriff, 1/177; Wm, 2/21-2
Bumford *see* Bamford
Burch *see* Birch
Burd *see* Bird
Burford, Francis, 3/18*
Burridge, Frances, 3/363, 377; John, 3/100; Rob, 3/374n, 377; Thos, 3/100, 363, 377*
Burropp (Burrop) *see* Burrup
Burroughs (Burroughes, Burrow, Burrowes, Burrows), Comfort, 2/86; Dorothy, 1/350, 393; Eliz, 3/374, 392; Mary, 3/16, 164; Nat, 1/288, 305, 350, 393, 449, 515, 557; Sam, 1/557; 3/16, 164, 215*, 374, 392; Sam, sheriff, 3/340; Thos, 1/515; 2/86; —, 1/288, 305; *and see* Barrow; Berrow; Borrow
Burrup (Burrop, Burropp), Joan, 1/554, 556, 563; 2/77, 105, 169, 184; Thos, 1/554, 556, 563; 2/77, 81, 105, 169, 184
Burt (Burte) *see* Birt
Bushop (Busshop, Busshoppe) *see* Bishop
Bussell *see* Tackley
Butcher, Wm, 3/282*
Butler (Buttler), John, 1/201; 3/295n*, 296; Rob, 1/168; Thos, 1/2*, 168, 201; 3/296
Butt, Alice, 1/85; Edm, 3/117; Jas, 2/271; John, 1/97; 3/117, 389; Ric, 1/197; 3/389; Rob, 2/269n, 271; Sarah, 2/373; Thos, 1/85; 3/379*; Wal, 1/97, 197; widow, 2/269n

Butter, Chas, 3/195, 312*; Edw, 3/312, 195; Eliz, 3/312; John, 2/12, 25*; Ric, 1/294, 450; Roger, 2/12; Thos, 1/450; Wm, 1/294, 259*
Butterton, John, 3/175*; Ralph, p. 269; Ric, 2/7; Susannah, 2/7
Buttler *see* Butler
Button, Bridget, 1/248; Ric, 1/248
Byard, Augustine, 3/30; Ric, 3/30; *and see* Beard
Bycke *see* Bicke
Byford (Byforde), Eliz, 2/330; 3/64; Geo, 1/15; Hugh, 1/15; John, 1/457; Joseph, 2/241*, 330; 3/40, 64, 322; Nat, 2/295; Nic, 1/457; Ric, 2/295; Sarah, 3/40
Byrd (Byrde) *see* Bird
Byrt *see* Birt
Byshop (Byshopp) *see* Bishop

Cadell, Wm, 1/250*
Caise, Rob, 2/17; John, 2/17; *and see* Keyse
Cake, Oliver, 3/209; Sam, 3/209
Caleowe, Arthur, 1/485; Wm, 1/485
Cam (Camme), Arthur, 2/177; Francis, 1/37; John, 1/37; Thos, 2/177
Cambray, Ric, 3/212; Wm, 3/212
Camme *see* Cam
Campion, John, 3/74*; John, sheriff, 3/115
Cannon (Canon), Kath, 3/272; Thos, 3/21*, 272, 369n, 377*
Canter, Mary, 2/106n; —, 2/106n
Cantrell, Henry, 2/219; John, 2/219
Capell *see* Caple
Capener (Capenor), Giles, 1/299; p. 270; John, 1/51, 299; Wm, 1/51; *and see* Copner
Caple (Capell), Chris, 1/10, 38*, 39-40, 118, 133, 238, 261, 284; Chris, mayor, 1/31, 139, 287, 299-300, sheriff, 1/1; p. 261; Grace, 1/10, 38-40, 118, 133, 238, 261, 284; Mary, 1/337, 356; Wm, 1/38, 337, 356; p. 268; Wm, alderman, 2/39, 81, 120, 143, 191, mayor, 1/504; 2/106, 110, sheriff, 1/287; —, p. 268
Card, Henry, 3/65; John, 3/65
Cardwell, John, 2/206; Wm, 2/206
Care, John, 3/320
Careles (Careless), Ebenezer, 3/375; Henry, 2/110; John, 2/110; 3/375
Carell, John, 2/220; Kalo, 2/220
Carew, Matt, 2/15; Thos, 2/15
Carne, Henry, 1/173; Hugh, 1/173
Carpenter (Carpinter), Bridget, 1/348, 358, 411, 475; Dorothy, 1/16, 94, 135, 202; Guy, 1/113; Henry, 1/16, 94, 290; 2/97; Jas, 1/379; 3/296; Joan, 1/113; John, 1/21, 51, 62*, 135, 202, 348, 358, 411, 475, 540*; 2/191; p. 265; Lawr, 1/113,

Carpenter (*cont.*)
246; Matt, **1**/497*; Ric, **1**/21, 290, 344, 447; **2**/97; **3**/192, 235*; Rob, **3**/192, 296; Thos, **1**/103, 113; **2**/191, 315; Toby, **1**/344; Wm, **1**/103, 379, 447; p. 273; —, **2**/315

Carsey, John, **3**/259*; *and see* Casye

Carter, Giles, **1**/53; Henry, **3**/267*; John, **3**/305*; Joyce, **2**/2, 14, 226; Lancelot, **2**/125, 192; Mary, **1**/53; Sam, **2**/200; Thos, **2**/323; **3**/28; Wm, **1**/369*; **2**/2, 14, 200, 226*, 323; **3**/28; —, **2**/125

Cartrell, John, **3**/308*

Cartwright, Edm, **1**/38*; **2**/226; Edw, **1**/553*; **2**/67, 167, 169, 329*; **3**/355; Mary, **2**/226; Thos, **2**/167, 169; Tim, **3**/39*n*

Carver, widow, **2**/25*n*; —, **2**/25*n*

Castle (Cassell), Anne, **3**/363; Nat, **3**/247, 282, 314, 363*; Nat (*alias* Cooke), **2**/292; **3**/212; Nat (*alias* Cooke), sheriff, **3**/259; Thos (*alias* Cooke), p. 272; Wal (*alias* Cooke), **2**/292

Casye, Ric, **1**/132*; *and see* Carsey

Cater, Giles, **1**/341; Ric, **1**/341; p. 269; —, p. 269

Caudle *see* Cawdle

Causfeild, Ric, **2**/137; Wm, **2**/137

Cawdle (Caudle), Barbara, **3**/128, 142; Eliz, **2**/91; John, p. 273; Ric, **2**/288; **3**/128, 142; Wm, **2**/91, 288

Cawson, Henry, **1**/487; Stephen, **1**/487

Cawston, Wm, p. 269

Ceely, Joan, **1**/76, 101, 135; Thos, **1**/31, 76, 101, 135

Chadd, Alice, **1**/461; Eleanor, **1**/500; Wm, **1**/461, 500

Chambers, John, **1**/482*

Chamlin (Chamley, Chamlyn, Chomlyn), John, **2**/126, 199; Mary, **3**/22; Thos, **1**/347*; **2**/10, 89*, 126, 199; **3**/22; —, **2**/10; *and see* Commelin

Champnis, Arthur, **2**/38*

Chandler (Chaundler), Cuthbert, **1**/539; John, **2**/59; **3**/261*n*, 262*; Nat, **2**/59; Ric, **1**/539; **3**/82*, 324; Ric, sheriff, **3**/230; Susannah, **3**/82; Thos, **1**/531; **3**/82; p. 268; Wm, **1**/531

Chapman, Arthur (*alias* Willmetts), **1**/331; Eleanor, **2**/75, 221; Eliz, **1**/568; **2**/293, 298; **3**/18; Geo, **2**/265; **3**/300*; Jas, **1**/462; Joan (*alias* Brothers), **1**/561; John, **2**/255, 265; **3**/300; John (*alias* Brothers) **1**/559*n*, 561*; John, sheriff, **3**/259; Sam, **2**/142; p. 269; Selwyn, **2**/142; Thos, **1**/388*, 462, 498, 568; **2**/25, 75, 110*, 221, 255, 293*b*, 298; **3**/18; p. 271; Toby (*alias* Brothers), **1**/559*n, 561*; —, **1**/498; **2**/25

Chappell, Rob, **2**/135; Thos, **2**/135

Charles, John, **3**/44*, 311*

Charlton (Charleton), Alice, **1**/209, 299, 477, 543, 547–8, 551; Edw, **1**/125, 209, 299, 317, 476*n*, 477*, 543, 547–8, 551; **2**/52, 206, 360; **3**/120*; Eliz, **2**/52; John, p. 273; Michael, **1**/73; Ric, **1**/125; Roger, **1**/73; Sarah, **2**/206, 360; **3**/120

Chatterton, Edw, **1**/101; Howell, **1**/101

Chaundler *see* Chandler

Checketts, Ric, **3**/145*

Chedworth, Giles, **2**/172; John, **2**/172; Thos, **1**/364*; p. 272

Cheesman (Cheeseman), John, **2**/214, 365; **3**/364*, 368; Nic, **2**/365; Paul, **3**/368; Rob, **2**/214, 365; **3**/122, 147, 244; Sarah, **2**/365; **3**/122, 147, 244

Cheltenham, Wm, **1**/518*

Cherrington, Thos, **3**/216*; *and see* Sherington

Chestro, Geo, **1**/412*; **3**/73; Nat, **3**/73

Chewe, Michael, **1**/187; Thos, **1**/187

Childe (Childs), Eliz, **3**/141; Jas, **3**/146*n*, 148; John, **2**/79*; **3**/74; Ric, **2**/83*; Thos, **2**/338*n*, 340*; **3**/74*, 141, 148; —, **2**/73*n*

Chomlyn *see* Chamlin

Church (Churche), Eleanor, **3**/247*n*; Everin, **2**/88; John, **2**/317; **3**/163; Henry, **2**/88; Joyce, **3**/362; Ric, **1**/138; **3**/143; Roger, **3**/247*n*, 332, 369; Sarah, **3**/332, 369; Thos, **1**/138; **3**/143, 163; Wm, **2**/317

Churches, Caleb, **2**/139; Giles, **2**/256; p. xix; John, **2**/110, 121, 256, 295; **3**/315; Jonathan, **2**/295; Rob, **2**/121, 139; Thos, **2**/13*, 110; **3**/315

Cissell (Cicill), David, **1**/20, 92, 103, 111; Eleanor, **1**/20, 92, 103, 111; Jas, **1**/83; Philip, **1**/83

Clark (Clarck, Clarke), Amy (Amicia), **2**/366; **3**/225; Anne, **3**/267; Ant, **1**/326; Cyprian, **2**/96; Dan, **1**/129; Diana, **3**/337; Edw, **1**/210, 312; Eleanor, **1**/292, 312*; Francis, **2**/307*; Giles, **1**/509, 519*, 526*; Godfrey, **2**/96; Henry, **1**/64, 133; **2**/117*n*, 120, 280, 366; **3**/141, 225; Jas, **1**/321; **2**/117*n*, 120; Jane, **2**/342; Joan, **1**/486, 576; **3**/347; John, **1**/67, 125*, 133, 135, 187, 229, 256, 272, 578*; **2**/25, 28, 273; **3**/40, 54, 267, 347; p. 266; Josiah, **1**/210; Margery, **1**/67, 125, 133, 135, 187, 229; Martin, **1**/136; Mary, **3**/141; Nic, **3**/12, 40, 54, 91*, 129, 134*n*, 223; Philip, **3**/347; Ric, **1**/136; **3**/129; Rob, **1**/129; Roger, **1**/64; Sam, **3**/347; Stephen, **2**/121; Thos, **1**/54, 125, 202–3, 321, 509; **2**/216, 279*, 307; **3**/12, 134*n*, 223, 337; Wal, **3**/223; Wm, **1**/133, 202–3, 256, 292, 312, 326, 486, 576; **2**/25, 28, 216, 342*; **3**/175*; Wm, sheriff, **2**/43; —, **1**/272; **2**/273, 280

Clarver, Matt, **1**/446; Ric, **1**/446

Clarvo (Clarvoe), Geo, **1**/133, 249; John, **1**/133; **2**/362; Thos, **1**/130*–1*; **2**/361; Wm, **2**/361–2

Clayfield (Clayfeild), Alice, **1**/570; **2**/24, 60, 133; Anne, **2**/235, 294; **3**/23; Edw, **1**/407, 570; **2**/24,

INDEX OF PERSONS

60, 133, 235, 294; **3**/23–4; p. 272; Kath, **3**/24; Sam, **1**/407; —, **3**/228*n*
Cleadly (Cleavley) *see* Cleevely
Clebery (Clibery), Alice, **1**/1, 111–12; Anne, **1**/61; John, **1**/1, 61, 111–12
Cleeve, Wm, **2**/20*
Cleevely (Cleadly, Cleavley, Cleavly, Cleevly, Clevely), Adam, **1**/160; Henry, **2**/345; **3**/393*n*, 394*; Joan, **1**/188; John, **1**/70, 188; Mary, **2**/89, 331, 345; Rob, **1**/469; **2**/89, 331*, 345*; Thos, **1**/70; Wm, **1**/160, 269, 379*, 469; **2**/194*; p. 271; —, **1**/269
Clements (Clemence), Anne, **1**/103, 124, 167; Edm, alderman, **1**/249, justice, **1**/212, 249, 280*, 328, master of Mercers, **1**/31, mayor, **1**/237, 327, 334, 337*, sheriff, **1**/111, 167; Edw, **1**/103, 124*, 167*, 212; John, **2**/34*; Thos, **1**/25*, 124, ; Toby, **1**/167
Clent, Jas, p. 268
Clevely *see* Cleevely
Clibery *see* Clebery
Clifford, Jas, **2**/82; **3**/34, 36, 53, 135*, 159*, 194, 239, 243; John, **3**/35, 159; Joshua, **3**/40*; Mary, **3**/34, 36, 53, 135, 159, 194, 243; Ric, **1**/443*; Thos, **2**/82, 152*, 331; **3**/35; Wm, **2**/331; —, **3**/135
Clinch, Ric, **1**/132; Thos, **1**/132
Clissolde, Giles, **1**/41; John, **1**/41
Clotterbooke *see* Clutterbuck
Cluffe, Henry, **1**/383; John, **1**/383
Clutterbuck (Clotterbooke, Clutterbok, Clutterbook, Clutterbooke, Clutterbucke), Amity, **1**/289, 405; **2**/25*n*, 110, 127, 141–2; **3**/211*n*; p. 270; Arthur, **1**/270; Dan, **1**/179, 189, 368; **2**/103, 127, 221; Fabian, **1**/273; Jasper, p. xxiii *and see* p. 263; Jasper, alderman, **2**/7, 41, 81, 94, 100, 131, 143, 253*; p. xxii, mayor, **2**/9, sheriff, **1**/407; John, **1**/130, 567; **2**/135*n*, 142; Joseph, **2**/141; Marg, **1**/405; **2**/110; Marian (Merriam, Miriam), **1**/368; **2**/103, 221; Ric, **1**/270; Rob, **1**/33; Sam, **1**/179; Sapience, **1**/33; Stephen, **1**/273; Thos, **1**/130, 567; Wal, **1**/189, 289; Wm, **3**/204*
Coale *see* Cole
Cobb, Chris, **3**/19; Thos, **3**/19
Cockerell, Thos, **3**/325*
Coke *see* Cooke
Colchester (Colechester), Duncombe, mayor, **3**/115; Edw, **1**/459, 496; Eleanor, **1**/583; Ric, **1**/410, 459, 496; Thos, **1**/410, 583
Coldricke (Colericke, Collericke, Coloricke), Adam, **3**/128, 142, 268; Anne, **3**/268; Dan, **2**/9, 19, 60, 131, 198, 236, 366; **3**/128, 142, 144, 295, 369; Eliz, **3**/369; John, **1**/123; Mary, **2**/9, 19, 198, 236, 366; Thos, **1**/123; —, **3**/144
Cole (Coale), Chas, **2**/282, 339; Chris, **2**/195; Henry, **3**/131; Humph, **1**/303; Jasper, **1**/432; John, **1**/303, 582; **2**/111*, 195, 234; **3**/38*, 341, 391; Ralph, **2**/282, 339; Thos, **1**/432; **3**/131, 341, 391; Wm, **1**/582; **2**/234
Colechester *see* Colchester
Colericke (Collericke) *see* Coldricke
Colles *see* Cowles
Collett (Collet), Ant, **1**/402, 456*; p. 273; Edm, **1**/315, 332, 402*, 472, 508, 524*, 571; **2**/29, 55*, 56, 128, 204; **3**/53*; Edm, alderman, **2**/176, mayor, **2**/39, 145, sheriff, **1**/547; Edw, **1**/200, 212, 587; Eliz, **1**/556, 573; **2**/22, 96; Henry, **2**/47; Hester, **1**/315, 332, 402*, 472, 508, 524*, 571; **2**/128, 204; John, **1**/200, 212, 402, 556, 573; **2**/22, 96; **3**/55, 350, 394*; p. 273; Margery, **1**/587; **2**/29, 56; Mary, **3**/53; Sam, **3**/55, 331*, 350, 370; Wm, **2**/47; **3**/370
Colley, Eleanor, **3**/298; Ric, **1**/544; **3**/298; Wm, **1**/544
Collier (Colliar) *see* Collyer
Collings, Jas, **3**/234; Thos, **3**/234
Collins, Chas, **3**/160; Dan, **2**/180; Giles, **3**/135*n*, 160; Jas, **3**/341; Ric, **3**/135*n*; Roland, **1**/357; Sarah, **3**/341; Wm, **1**/357*; —, **1**/357; **2**/180
Collyer (Colliar, Collier), Henry, **1**/495, 497; John, **1**/160; Mary, **2**/242, 265; **3**/175; Wm, **1**/160; **2**/242, 265; **3**/175; —, **1**/495, 497
Coloricke *see* Coldricke
Colstance (Colstons) *see* Coulstons
Colway, John, **2**/264; Rob, **2**/264
Colwell, John, **2**/241; Rob, **2**/241
Commelin (Comalyne, Comelin, Comelyn, Comelyne, Cumalyn), Dan, **1**/337; **2**/137; Isaac, **2**/234; Jas, **1**/337, 461, 520, 523; **2**/15, 90, 137*, 234*, 294; p. 268; Jas, sheriff, **2**/145; Jane, **1**/461, 520, 523; **2**/15, 90, 137, 234; *and see* Chamlin
Comminge, Thos, **1**/73*
Conklin, Jas, **3**/276; Thos, **3**/276
Cooke (Coke), Anne, **1**/260, 370; **2**/109; **3**/140; Ant, **2**/365*n*, 366; **3**/174; Benj, **2**/21; **3**/57, 142*n*, 174*; Bernard, **3**/301; Chas, **3**/140, 217, 267, 324; Dina, **1**/246; Eleanor, **1**/469; **2**/260, 366; **3**/93; Florice, **3**/247*; Geo, **3**/301*, 381; Giles, **3**/231; Henry, **2**/297*; **3**/63, 93; Jas, **1**/350, 552*; **2**/286*n*, 294; **3**/353; Jeremiah, **1**/22; Joan, **1**/66, 138, 208; John, **1**/66, 83, 158, 246, 322, 540; **2**/16, 55, 216, 308, 341; **3**/353; Juliana, **1**/99; Kath, **1**/65, 424, 540; Marg, **1**/249, 324, 334, 385, 456; **2**/11, 42, 135, 180, 256, 342; **3**/59, 121, 276; Mary, **3**/217, 267, 324; Moses, **2**/341; Nat (*alias* Castle), **2**/292; **3**/212; Nat (*alias* Castle), sheriff,

Cooke (*cont.*)

3/259; Peter, **1**/65, 99, 138; Ric, **1**/45, 280, 358, 362, 392, 469; **2**/11, 16, 87*, 260*, 284, 365*n*, 366*; **3**/59, 93*, 121, 276, 279*, 302, 330*; Rob, **2**/294; Sam, **3**/287; Sarah, **2**/55, 216; **3**/57, 174; Stephen, **1**/66, 138, 208, 322; Susannah, **3**/388; Thos, **1**/22, 44–5, 66, 83, 107, 143, 249, 260, 324, 334, 370, 385, 401, 424, 456; **2**/42, 135, 180, 256, 308, 342*; **3**/140*, 250*n*, 302, 388; pp. xix, 270; Thos, sheriff, **2**/145; Thos (*alias* Cassell), p. 272; Wal, **1**/358, 362; Wal (*alias* Castle), **2**/292; Wm, **1**/44, 107, 280, 350, 392, 400, 538; **2**/21, 50*, 66*, 109, 338*n*, 342; **3**/231, 287; p. 272; Wm, mayor, **3**/99, 293; —, **1**/143, 538; **2**/50; **3**/63, 92*n*, 140

Cooper (Cowper), Francis, **1**/507; John, **1**/167; Maurice, **2**/171*; Ric, **1**/507; Thos, p. 269; Thos (*alias* Allen), **3**/387; Wal, **1**/167

Coopey (Coopie, Coopy), Edw, **1**/353; John, **1**/429*, 430; **2**/315; **3**/316*; Joseph, **3**/399*n*; Ric, **1**/430; **2**/315; Thos, **1**/353

Cope, Mary, **3**/374; Ric, **1**/310; Thos, **3**/374; —, **1**/310

Copland (Coplande), John, **1**/177; Ric, **1**/177

Copner, Anne, **1**/340; Giles, **2**/296; Ric, **1**/120; **2**/296; Rob, **1**/120, 340; *and see* Capener

Cor *see* Corr

Corbet (Corbett), Arthur, **1**/554*; Roger, p. 273

Cordell, Alex, **3**/163; Anne, **3**/20, 163; Cecily, **2**/268, 286, 344; Jas, **1**/537; **2**/37, 268*, 286; **3**/20, 163*; Jane, **1**/36; Joan, **1**/537; Margery, **1**/341; Ric, **1**/341*; Wm, **1**/341

Core *see* Corr

Cornewall, John, **1**/295; Ric, **1**/295

Cornish, John, **3**/110; Thos, **3**/110

Corr (Cor, Core, Cur, Curr), Edm, **3**/262, 317; Edw, **2**/321; **3**/261*n*, 262, 285*n*, 287*; Henry, **1**/460*; **3**/250*n**, 317; John, **3**/195; Marg, **3**/101; Ric, **3**/101*, 285*n*, 287; Rob, **1**/460; **2**/111*, 132*; **3**/101; Sarah, **1**/460; —, **2**/321

Corsley, Ric, **3**/241, Wm, **3**/241*; Wm, sheriff, **3**/140

Corsnett, Martha, **3**/340; Ric, **3**/340; Ric, sheriff, **3**/357

Cosby (Cosbie), Alice, **1**/260; Eliz, **1**/118, 146; Jasper, **1**/159; John, **1**/30, 118, 146, 210, 255*, 326; Ric, **1**/30, 43, 159; Thos, **1**/43, 210, 260, 326; Toby, **1**/255

Cosens, Thos, **1**/8; *and see* Cussens

Cotterell, Henry, **1**/179*

Cotton, Sam, **1**/5; Thos, **1**/5

Coucher *see* Cowcher

Coulstons (Colstance, Colstons, Coustons, Cowlstons), Geo, **1**/84*, 99, 210; John, **1**/84, 568; Sam, **1**/568

Coutcher *see* Cowcher

Cove, Wm, **3**/316*

Cowarne, Jas, **1**/76, 101; Wal, **1**/76, 101

Cowcher (Coucher, Coutcher), Cecily, **2**/249, 284, 344; **3**/21, 35; Edm, **3**/232; p. 272; Eliz, **3**/333; Jane, **2**/49, 63, 73, 98, 107, 150, 154; Joan, **1**/200, 298; John, **1**/49, 65, 200; **2**/63, 73, 98, 107, 150, 154, 249, 284, 344; **3**/69, 369*n*; Kathleen, **1**/65; Lewis, p. 272; Marg, **2**/151*, 222, 291, 363, 366; **3**/228, 262, 267, 337; Margery, **2**/260; Mary, **3**/120, 131*; Philip, **3**/232; Rebecca, **2**/233, 369; **3**/11–12, 19; Ric, **2**/107, 333; **3**/262, 267, 337; Rob, **2**/11, 151*, 222, 260, 280, 291, 363, 366; Susannah, **3**/20, 59, 88; **2**/332; Thos, **2**/11, 49, 107; **3**/120, 131*; Wm, **1**/298, 524; **2**/49, 332; **3**/20, 59, 69, 88, 228, 233, 333

Cowcott, Sarah, **2**/374

Cowdall (Cowdale, Cowdell), Aaron, **3**/386; Anne, **2**/141; Eliz, **2**/141*n*; Jas, **2**/141; John, **1**/31; **2**/143*, 298, 300, 350; **3**/41, 193, 250, 351; Mary, **3**/193, 250; Patience, **2**/298, 300, 350; **3**/41; Rob, **2**/253*; **3**/386; p. xxii; Sarah, **3**/351; Thos, **1**/31; —, **2**/141*n*

Cowell, John, **1**/65; Wm, **1**/65

Cowles (Colles), Anne, **3**/358; Anne (*alias* Stephenson, **3**/72, 176; Blanche, **1**/465, 538; Edm, **3**/358; Jane, **2**/326; **3**/65; Joan, **3**/248–9; John, **1**/319, 366, 465; **3**/332, 394; John (*alias* Stephenson), **2**/121, **3**/72, 176, 279; Joseph, **3**/399*n*; Josiah, **3**/149, 276, 299; Mary, **3**/276, 299; Ric, **1**/465; **2**/274*; **3**/48*n*, 49 *and see* Knowles; Rob, **1**/319, 465, 538; **3**/48*n*, 49, 248–9, 310*; Sarah, **3**/310; Stephen, **3**/265*n;* Stephen (*alias* Stephenson), **2**/121; Susannah, **3**/149; Thos, **2**/293*b**, 296*; **3**/65*, 149*, 332, 347*n*, 348*, 394; Wal, **1**/142; Wm, **1**/366; **2**/326*; **3**/65, 358*; Wm (*alias* Stephenson), **3**/16*, 279; widow, **3**/211*n*; —, **3**/211*n*

Cowley (Cowly), Eleanor, **1**/277, 323, 453; John, **1**/559; Ric, **1**/122, 277, 323, 452*n**, 453*, 559; Thos, **1**/122

Cowlsey, Thos, **3**/342; Wm, **3**/342

Cowlstons *see* Coulstons

Cowly *see* Cowley

Cowper *see* Cooper

Cox (Coxe), Alice, **3**/26, 73, 88; Anne, **2**/21, 76, 80, 96, 165, 209, 231, 275, 311, 331; Cecily, **1**/540; Eleanor, **1**/30; Eliz, **1**/49, 69, 93, 112, 148, 177, 276; Henry, **2**/90*; Isobel, **1**/75; John, **1**/12*, 49, 69, 93, 112, 148, 177, 275–6; **2**/175, 315; **3**/9, 26, 73, 88; Marg, **3**/61; Ric, **1**/75, 540; **2**/22, 43, 175,

204*n*, 209*; Ric, mayor, **1**/103; Rob, **3**/61; Roger, **1**/275; Susannah, **2**/22, 43; Thos, **1**/30, 357*n*, 359; **3**/230*; Toby, **1**/359; Wm, **3**/230; Winston, **2**/21, 76, 80, 96, 165, 209, 231, 274*n*, 275*, 311, 331; **3**/13, 22, 58, 80, 89, 147, 200, 223; p. 272; —, **3**/9, 13, 22, 58, 80, 89, 147

Craddocke, Mary, **1**/159, 202; Ric, **1**/159, 202

Crafte, Sam, **3**/92; Wm, **3**/92

Craker, Abigail, **1**/530, 533, 536, 538; Giles, **1**/36, 45; John, **1**/36, 45, 170, 289, 304*, 351, 379, 395, 397, 412, 484, 499, 509, 516; Jonathan, **1**/530, 533, 536, 538; p. 272; Marg, **1**/170, 289, 304, 379, 395, 396*n*, 397, 412, 484, 499, 509, 516, 580; *and see* Croker

Crass (Crasse), Sarah, **3**/248; Wm, **3**/84*, 248

Crease (Creese), Geo, **2**/239; John, **1**/427; Wm, **1**/427; **2**/239

Cripps, Edw, **2**/330; **3**/21, 148, 364*; Eliz, **2**/330; **3**/21, 148; Mary, **2**/272; Nat, **1**/570*; Sam, **2**/272

Crockett, Jas, **3**/385; Thos, **3**/385

Crody *see* Crowdy

Croes *see* Crowes

Croker, Benj (Ben), **3**/109*n*, 117; Eleanor, **3**/117, 134; Thos, **2**/95*; **3**/117*, 134; p. xiv; *and see* Craker

Crompe *see* Crumpe

Cromwall *see* Crumwell

Crosse, Henry, **3**/264; John, **3**/264; *and see* Crowes

Crowdy (Crody, Crowday, Crowdey, Crowdyer), Edw, **1**/122; Jas, **3**/341, 386; John, **1**/323*, 404*n*, 407*n*, 419*; Mary, **3**/341; Nic, **1**/55; Ric, **1**/122; Thos, **1**/55; widow, **1**/404*n*

Crowes (Croes), Jasper, **1**/48; John, **1**/352*; Wm, **1**/48; *and see* Crosse

Crumlum, Giles, **2**/43; Ric, **2**/43

Crumpe (Crompe), Anne, **1**/136, 199, 281, 310*, 331, 352, 356; Christian, **3**/361; Edw, **1**/368*n*, 369; **2**/279; Giles, **1**/136, 188, 199, 237, 281, 310*, 331, 352, 356, 368*n*, 369, 400; Henry, **1**/188; **2**/279; Joan, **1**/124, 160, 189; John, **1**/188, 191; Ric, **2**/48*; **3**/274, 361; Rob, **1**/191; Thos, **3**/274; Wm, **1**/24, 126, 160

Crumwell (Cromwall), Anne, **2**/132, 134, 236, 283; **3**/13; Henry, **1**/99; John, **2**/132, 134, 236, 283; **3**/13; Thos, **1**/99

Cudd, Eliz, **3**/15, 37, 49, 52, 68, 108; John, **2**/167*; **3**/15, 37, 49, 52, 68, 108

Cue, John, **1**/376*

Cuffe, Frances, **2**/23; John, **1**/404; Sam, **3**/174*n*, 179; Thos, **1**/404, 510; **2**/23; **3**/179; p. 272; —, **1**/510

Cugley (Cuglie, Cugly, Kugley), Anne, **1**/157, 239, 270*, 323; **2**/316; **3**/105; Arthur, **1**/347, 403, 499, 521, 540, 556; Dan, **2**/151*; **3**/227; Eliz, **1**/2, 347, 394, 403, 477, 499, 521, 540, 556; Henry, **1**/23, 68; Henry, mayor, **2**/43, sheriff, **1**/504; Jas, **1**/556; **2**/316; **3**/105; Joan, **1**/73, 86, 125; **2**/3; John, **1**/357, 393–4, 477, 556; **2**/311; **3**/227, 240*; pp. xxi, 271; Ric, **1**/2, 157, 239, 270*, 323; p. 268; Ric, sheriff, **1**/517; Rob, **1**/73, 86, 125, 357; Thos, **1**/23, 68; **2**/3*, 151*, 311; **3**/227; Wal, **1**/394*; —, **3**/228*n*; p. 268

Cumalyn *see* Commelin

Cupitt, Andrew, **2**/172, 191; Arthur, **2**/172, 191

Curnocke, Jas, **2**/273*

Curr (Cur) *see* Corr

Currye, Arthur, **1**/75; Thos, **1**/75

Curtis, Chris, **3**/85; Edw, **3**/85; Thos, **2**/228; —, **2**/228

Cussens, Thos, **2**/45; Wm, **2**/45; *and see* Cosens

Daliner, John, **1**/280

Dallome, Rob, **1**/338*

Dalton, Andrew, **3**/23; Jas, **3**/23

Danby, John, **1**/506*; **2**/80; Mary, **2**/79*n*; Thos, **2**/79*n*, 80, 125; Wm, **2**/125

Dance (Daunce), Joan, **1**/132, 148; Ric, **1**/132, 148

Dancocks, Thos, **3**/194; Wm, **3**/194

Dappin, John, **1**/119*

Darby (Darbie), Henry, **1**/110; Henry, justice, **1**/80, mayor, **1**/129, sheriff, **1**/29, 91; Marg, **1**/110

Darke, Ric, **3**/358; Wm, **3**/358

Daunce *see* Dance

Daunt, John, **1**/542; Wm, **1**/542

Davenall, Wm, **3**/398*

Daves *see* Davies

David, David, **1**/13; Wm, **1**/13

Davies (Daves, Davis, Davys, Davyes, Devis) Anne, **2**/208; Ant, **2**/280; **3**/281; Arnold, **1**/91, **3**/244; Christian, **3**/118–19, 281*; Chris, **1**/144; Comfort, **3**/39, 56, 302*n*, 303; David, **1**/491; **2**/8; Edw, **1**/86; Eliz, **1**/210, 259, 316, 373, 432–3; **2**/65, 286; **3**/352; Giles, **1**/238*; Henry, **1**/554; **2**/65, 286; **3**/315; Hugh, **1**/47; Humph, **1**/95; Isaac, **2**/307; Jas, **1**/144, 491; **3**/69*n*, 88, 281; Jane, **1**/570; **2**/4; Joan, **3**/392; John, **1**/31*, 91, 227, 317, 389, 399; **2**/114, 162*, 280; **3**/39, 56, 118–19, 222*, 233, 281*, 297*, 301*n*, 315*, 345, 357, 396; pp. 272–3; Jonathan, **3**/352; Joseph, **3**/64; Kath, **1**/437; **2**/17; Marg, **1**/271, 554; **3**/345, 357; Martha, **1**/315, 350, 407, 465, 495, 503, 505*; Mary, **2**/8, 68, 86, 286; Randle, **3**/64; Rebecca, **3**/274, 319, 399; Ric, **1**/169, 227, 317, 423, 437; **3**/161*, 178, 184; Rob, **1**/169, 207, 345*; **3**/134*, 274, 319, 399; Roger, **1**/97, 210, 259, 316, 373, 399, 432–3, 563; **2**/17; Sam, **1**/158,

Davies (*cont.*)
  160; **3**/88, 302*n*, 303; Thos, **1**/47, 97, 158, 160, 271, 317, 423, 554*, 570, 584*; **2**/4, 68, 75, 86, 208, 286; **3**/178, 184, 225*, 233, 244, 273, 297, 301*n*, 392, 396; p. 273; Wal, **1**/389; Wm, **1**/86, 207, 315, 350, 407, 465, 495, 503, 505*, 563, 564*; **2**/75, 114, 307; **3**/252*, 273; —, **1**/317, 495
Daw *see* Dawes
Dawby, Giles, **3**/333; John, **3**/333
Dawes (Daw, Dawe, Daws), Geo, **3**/248; Eleazor, **3**/309; Eliz, **3**/193, 271, 309; John, **3**/248; Kath, **1**/359; Ric, **1**/359; **2**/293; Wm, **2**/293; **3**/115, 193, 271; —, **3**/115
Day (Daye), Joan, **2**/304; **3**/35; Ric, **1**/367; Wm, **1**/367; **2**/304; **3**/35; p. 272
Dean (Deane), Geo, **3**/345; John, **1**/311, 582; Kath, **2**/175, 252, 318; **3**/105; Marg, **1**/582; Ric, **3**/179*n*; Thos, **1**/311; **2**/58, 175, 252, 316*n*, 318*; **3**/53*n*, 105, 345; *and see* Adeane
Deighton, Anne, **1**/87; Jane, **1**/138; John, **1**/87, 138, 411; John, sheriff, **1**/297, 337; Ric, **1**/138; Sam, **1**/87; Thos, **1**/87; Wm, **1**/138; Mr, p. 267
Denny, Dan, **1**/562; Wm, **1**/562
Denton, Edw, **1**/571; **2**/285; John, **1**/571; **2**/285
Deveris, John, **1**/104, 142; Margery, **1**/104, 142
Devis *see* Davies
Dewe, John, **2**/306*, 325*n*, 328*; **3**/132; Rob, **3**/132
Dewxell (Dewxel, Dowxell), Ant, **2**/288; pp. 269, 271; Frances, **1**/477; John, **1**/344, 477; **2**/286*n*, 288; Ric, **2**/227; Thos, **1**/344; **2**/89, 227, 304*; **3**/144; Wm, **2**/89; **3**/302*n**
Deymonte, Roger, **1**/70; Wm, **1**/70
Dickinson, Edw, **1**/74; Marg, **1**/74
Dicks, Thos, **3**/333; Wm, **3**/333
Dier *see* Dyer
Dimocke *see* Dymocke
Diston, Isaac, **3**/268*
Ditton, Geo, **3**/91; —, **3**/91
Dobbes (Dobbs), Anne, **1**/36; Francis, **3**/60, 142; Geo, **2**/154*n*, 155; Jane, **3**/45, 70, 246*; Joan, **1**/294; John, **1**/20, 36*, 129, 138, 294, 422; **2**/94*, 155, 337*; **3**/45, 60*, 142*; Lawr, **1**/129, 138, 328, 422; Ric, **1**/138, 146, 201, 237, 302, 341*; Thos, **1**/20; **3**/70, 246*; Welthian(e) (Wealthinque), **1**/138, 146, 201, 237, 302; —, **2**/301*n*; **3**/60, 142
Dobles, Abraham, **3**/42–3; Isaac, **3**/42–3
Dole, John, **2**/195
Donn (Done, Donne) *see* Dunn
Doppinge, Giles, **1**/267; Sam, **1**/267
Dorney, John, town clerk, **2**/169, 189, 213, 231; p. 264
Doughton (Dowton Dowten, Dowtonne), Arnold, **1**/4*; Eleanor, **1**/4; Eliz, **1**/527, 534–5; **2**/63, 91, 102, 120, 164, 174, 186*; **3**/206, 251; p. xxviii; Joan, **2**/334, 357; Mary, **1**/515, 518, 531; Ric, **1**/4, 515, 518, 531; **2**/63, 100*n*, 102*, 186; p. 271; Stephen, **1**/527, 534–5; **2**/91, 102, 120, 164, 174, 186*, 334, 357; **3**/25, 206, 251; p. xxviii, 272; Wm, **2**/186, 204*n*; —, **3**/25
Dowdswell, Henry, **2**/368*; Henry (*alias* Whiller), **1**/419*
Dowe, Jas, **3**/147
Dower, Rob, **1**/51
Dowers, Ric, **1**/391*
Dowle, Clement, **1**/463, 577; **3**/40*; Clement, sheriff, **2**/304; Geo, **2**/132; Hannah, **1**/577; **3**/40; Jas, **1**/463; **3**/363; Jas Clement, **3**/363; Job, **3**/40, 363; John, **1**/228; Sam, **2**/132; Wm, **1**/50*, 228
Downbell, Edm, **3**/53; Stephen, **2**/111; **3**/53, 67*; —, **2**/111
Dowsing (Dowsen, Dowseinge, Dowsinge, Dowson), Dinah, **2**/310; **3**/37; Eliz, **1**/364; John, **1**/12, 103, 119, 182, 359, 447; Joseph, **3**/339; Kath, **3**/87, 211, 339; Marg, **1**/14, 52, 142, 198; Sybil, **1**/12, 103, 119, 182, 447; Wal, **2**/298, 310; **3**/37; p. 271; Wm, **1**/14, 52, 142, 198, 364; **2**/298; **3**/87, 211, 261, 303*, 339*; —, **1**/359; **3**/261
Dowton (Dowten, Dowtonne) *see* Doughton
Dowxell *see* Dewxell
Drackett, Giles, **1**/306; John, **1**/306
Draper, John, **1**/549; Thos, **1**/549
Drew (Drue), Hannah, **3**/371; John, **2**/178, 298; **3**/336; John (*alias* Farmer), **3**/210; Ric, **2**/178; Thos, **2**/206; **3**/290*, 336, 371; Wm (*alias* Farmer), **3**/210
Drewry *see* Drury
Dring, John, **3**/47*; Simon, **2**/255; Wm, **2**/255
Drinkwater (Drinkewater), Alice, **1**/248; p. xxiv; Edm, **1**/4, 173; Edw, **1**/182, 248; Eliz, **2**/376; p. xxiii; Ric, **1**/173, 182; Sam, p. 265; Thos, **1**/272; **3**/318; Wm, **1**/4, 272; **3**/318
Driver, Ant, **1**/500; Matt, **1**/500; **3**/285; Ric, **3**/285
Drue *see* Drew
Drury (Drewry), Jeremiah, **2**/298; John, **2**/22*, 116, 298, 336*; Wm, **2**/116
Dubberly, John, **3**/338; Jonathan, **2**/344; Thos, **3**/338; Wm, **2**/284*, 344
Ducke, John, **2**/36; Thos, **2**/36
Dudley, April, **2**/301*n*, 302; **3**/172, 283*, 301*n*; Arthur, **2**/173*n*, 181*, 302; p. 271; Eliz, **3**/172; John, **3**/52*, 301*n*; Thos, **3**/265*n*, 283
Dudson, John, **3**/353*n*, 360*
Duglas, Wm, **1**/434*
Dunn (Done, Donn, Donne, Dun, Dunne), Arthur, **1**/126; Edw, **1**/345*, 444; **2**/100*n*, 103, 105*, 337;

INDEX OF PERSONS

Gabriel, **1**/349; Jane, **2**/61; John, **1**/535, 566, 573; **2**/112, 193, 247; pp. 268, 272; Lawr, **2**/103; Marg, **1**/535, 573; **2**/112, 193, 247; Mary, **1**/466; **2**/337; Nat, **1**/349, 474; **2**/61*; p. 270; Ric, **1**/444; Rob, **1**/126; Thos, **1**/466; **2**/60*n*, 61; widow, **2**/100*n*; p. 268

Durham, Jas, **3**/366; John, **3**/366

Durin (Duringe, Duryn), Darius (Derias), **1**/6, 210; Eliz, **1**/210; Paul, **1**/6

Dutton, Henry, **1**/81; Marg, **1**/318; Ric, **1**/145, 318; Thos, **1**/81, 145

Dyer (Dier), Humph, **1**/262, 536*, 561; **2**/48*n*, 55*n*, 118; Jas, **2**/117*n*, 118; **3**/261; John, **2**/48*n*, 55*n*; **3**/251*; Nat, **1**/561; Philip, **3**/261; Thos, **1**/262

Dymocke (Dimocke), Cressey, **2**/298*; Francis, **3**/21; Giles, **3**/21; Jane, **1**/129, 141; John, **3**/394; Jonathan, **3**/394; Thos, **1**/129, 141; Wm, **1**/261*

Eaton, Margery, **1**/465; Peter, **1**/119; Rob, **1**/119, 465

Ebbs (Ebbes), Hester, **3**/145, 268; Philip, **2**/8*, 61, 203*; **3**/145, 268; Thos, **2**/203, 220*n*; —, **2**/203

Ebsworth, John, **3**/130; Ric, **3**/130

Eckley (Eckly), Anne, **2**/78, 108, 157, 186, 320; Edw, **2**/78, 157*, 186, 320; Eliz, **1**/473, 499; **2**/149; Henry, **2**/108, 262; John, **2**/157, 256*; **3**/190; Lawr, **3**/190; Ric, **1**/333; Rob, **1**/333, 384*; Sam, **2**/293*b*; **3**/295; Thos, **1**/384, 473, 499; **2**/141*n*, 149*, 293*b*; Wal, **1**/384; Wm, **1**/384

Ecoat, Thos, **1**/291; Wm, **1**/291

Edge, Barbara, **1**/260, 298; John, **1**/29; Thos, **1**/29, 157, 177, 260, 298; —, **1**/177

Edmonds (Edmondes, Edmunds), Anne, **2**/264; Chas, **1**/572; John, **2**/264; p. 271; Lewis, **1**/572; **2**/308*

Edwards (Edward, Edwardes), Alice, **1**/247; Anne, **1**/346, 392, 515, 567; Ant, **1**/346, 392, 515, 567; Ant, alderman, **2**/41, 109, 119, mayor, **2**/65, sheriff, **1**/497, 579; **2**/1; David, **1**/64; Eliz, **1**/410, 555; Francis, **1**/566; Henry, **1**/315; **2**/9; Humph, **1**/342; Jeremiah, **1**/479; John, **1**/178, 306, 315, 410, 555; **3**/96, 132; John, sheriff, **1**/567; Mary, **1**/420; Ric, **1**/2; **2**/358; Rob, **1**/43; Sam, **1**/566; Thos, **1**/43, 197, 479; **3**/96, 340; Thos, sheriff, **3**/347; Urian, **1**/420; Wm, **1**/64, 178, 182, 197, 342, 429*; **3**/132; Wm, sheriff, **3**/347; —, **1**/2, 182, 306; **2**/358

Egby, Rob, **1**/135; Wm, **1**/135

Eger, John, **3**/80; Thos, **3**/80

Elbridge (Elbridg), Alice, **1**/23; Jas, **1**/272, 280; Joan, **1**/4, 9, 17, 97*, 105, 133, 181, 187, 208, 238, 245, 347; John, **1**/4, 9, 17, 97*, 105, 133, 181, 187, 208, 238, 245, 347; Ric, **1**/280; **2**/117*n*; Wm, **1**/23, 272

Eldridge (Eldridg, Eldriedge, Elridge), Abigail, **2**/323; Henry, **2**/274; Hester, **1**/411, 511, 522; Mary, **1**/460, 487; **2**/147, 314; Ric, **2**/118; Thos, **1**/346*, 401, 460, 487; **2**/147, 274, 314*; p. xix; Wm, **1**/292*, 411, 511, 522; **2**/2*, 47*, 118, 323

Eliote (Eliots, Eliotts) *see* Elliott

Elles *see* Ellis

Elliott (Eliote, Eliots, Eliotts, Ellietts, Elliottes, Elliotts), Edw, **1**/27*, 146, 188, 289, 405*, 476 *and n**; **2**/57, 93, 198, 270; **3**/141, 159, 231*, 335; Eliz, **1**/146, 188, 405; Henry, **1**/119, 436*, 476; **2**/125, 215; **3**/87, 318; Jane, **2**/215; **3**/282, 318; Jasper, **1**/446; John, **1**/404*n*, 405; **2**/60, 84, 259, 268, 316*; **3**/29*, 87, 121*, 135*n*, 140*, 146*n*, 159, 282, 384*n*; Marg, **2**/60, 84, 93, 259, 268, 316*; **3**/29; Mary, **2**/198, 270; Ric, **1**/446; **2**/270*; **3**/335; Rob, **2**/55*n*, 57; **3**/141; Russell, **1**/289; Sam, **3**/135*n*, 140; Thos, **1**/76*, 119; **3**/29, 359*; Wal, **1**/394*; **2**/316; Wm, **2**/125; —, **3**/140

Ellis (Elles), Ant, **2**/34; p. 270; Godfrey, **1**/332, 403, 494, 572; **2**/111, 117*n*; Guy, **3**/159*; Henry, **1**/373; Henry, sheriff, **2**/9; Jeremiah, **2**/27; John, **1**/332, 396*n*, 397*, 572*; **2**/27; **3**/340; pp. 266, 272; Joyce, **2**/34; Marg, **1**/373, 403, 494, 572; **2**/111; Thos, **3**/340

Elmes (Ellmes), Geo, **1**/524; John, **1**/483, 524; **3**/26; Ric, **3**/208; Rob, **1**/483; Thos, **3**/26, 208

Elridge *see* Eldridge

Elsmore, Joseph, **1**/449; **3**/325; John, **3**/325; Rob, **1**/449

Elton, Edw, p. 265; Ric, **3**/131; Sam, **3**/131

Emes, Jonathan, **3**/350; Ric, **3**/350

Emmett (Emott, Emmotte), Bennet, **1**/73; John, **1**/73, 160; Wm, **1**/160

Endall, Alice, **1**/158; Anne, **1**/65, 91, 148, 246, 333; Eliz, **2**/259*n*; John, **1**/158; Stephen, **3**/283; Thos, **3**/283; Wm, **1**/65, 91, 148, 246; **2**/259*; widow, p. 267

England, Joshua, **3**/67; Ric, **3**/67

Englea (Englee), Alice, **3**/352; Jas, **3**/382; John, **1**/142; Ric, **3**/352*; Wm, **1**/142

Erro, John, **1**/325; Thos, **1**/325

Estcott, Chris, **3**/330; Sam, **3**/330

Etheridge, Geo, **1**/32; John, **1**/32, 376; **2**/206; Joseph, **2**/206; Margery, **1**/376; Wal, **1**/272

Etkins *see* Atkins

Evan, Anne, **1**/96; Ric, **1**/96

Evans (Evens), Alice, **1**/525; Anne, **1**/41; Augustine, **1**/438; Chas, **3**/134; David, **1**/112; Edw, **1**/112; Eleanor, **3**/319; Eliz, **1**/329, 494, 549; **3**/215, 242, 265, 299; Hardwicke, **3**/319;

INDEX OF PERSONS

Evans (*cont.*)
  Hugh, **1**/335; Jas, **2**/203; **3**/134; Joan, **1**/46, 120; John, **1**/40*n**, 46, 120, 146, 168, 180*, 525; **2**/203, 236; **3**/295*n*; p. 268; Matt, **1**/94, 145; Morgan, **1**/146; Nat, **1**/168; Owen, **2**/219; Ric, **1**/145, 199; Rob, **1**/137*, 199; Sam, **1**/329, 494, 549; **2**/231; **3**/215, 242, 265, 295*n*, 299; Thos, **1**/41, 94, 438; **2**/219, 231; Wm, **1**/335, 409; **2**/236; *and see* Bevan; Heaven

Evenis, Jas, **3**/282, 291; John, **3**/282; Kath, **3**/394; Wm, **3**/291, 394

Evens *see* Evans

Everett, Ambrose, **2**/37*

Ewins, John, **2**/12*; John, mayor, **3**/340, sheriff, **3**/12

Exton, Barnabas, **1**/554; John, **1**/554; *and see* Ackson

Faireley, Wm, **1**/401*

Falkner (Falkener) *see* Faulkner

Farley (Pharley), Eleanor, **3**/264, 389; Geo, **1**/582; **2**/69, 173, 266, 281, 297; **3**/22, 103; Jas, **3**/321; John, **1**/271*; Mary, **2**/69, 173, 266, 281, 297; **3**/22; Thos, **1**/582; **3**/103*, 264, 321*, 389; Thos, sheriff, **3**/374

Farmer (Farmar), Anne, **3**/365; Bridget, **2**/233, 268, 334, 367; **3**/52–3; Edw, **1**/209; **2**/8, 367; Eliz, **2**/215, 218*; Francis, **2**/8, 215, 218*; **3**/386*; Jas, **1**/536*n*, 544; John, **1**/147; **2**/233, 268*, 334, 367*; **3**/52–3; John (*alias* Drew) **3**/210; Marg, **1**/33; Ric, **1**/33, 47, 83, 209, 544; Rob, **1**/83; Rob (*alias* Ingley), **1**/516; Sam, **3**/365; Thos, **3**/29; Wm, **1**/47, 147, 536*n*; **2**/289; Wm (*alias* Drew) **3**/210; widow, p. 267; —, **2**/289

Farr (Farre), Agnes, **1**/43; Anne, **1**/70, 118; John, **1**/43, 70, 118

Farrington, Edm, **1**/53; Thos, **1**/53

Faulkner (Falkener, Falkner, Fawkener), Denis, **2**/38; John, **1**/35, 414; **2**/99; Maurice, **2**/38; Rob, **1**/35, 414; Wal, **2**/99, 135*n*

Featherstone, Geo, **3**/95; Ric, **3**/95

Feild *see* Field

Feilding, Rob, mayor, **2**/320

Felton, Joseph, **3**/242*, 320*; Thos, **3**/320

Ferebee, John, **2**/224; Thos, **2**/224

Ferrett, Dan, **3**/42; John, **2**/286; **3**/36*, 42; Nat, **2**/286; **3**/36*, 42; —, **3**/36, 42

Ferris, Geo, **1**/434*

Fewtrell (Fewterel, Fewterell, Fewterer), Edw, **1**/546; **2**/42, 63*n*, 83, 117, 327; **3**/64*; Joan, **2**/42, 83, 117; John, **2**/362; Marg, **1**/443, 459, 474, 521, 546; Mary, **2**/113; **3**/54; Nic, **2**/40*n*, 42; Thos, **2**/71, 325*n*, 327; Wm, **1**/443*, 459, 474, 521, 546*; **2**/42, 71, 113, 362; **3**/54; —, **2**/63*n*

Field (Feild, Fielde, Fild, Fyld), Edith, **3**/369; Edw, **2**/237; Isobel, **1**/262; John, **3**/355, 388*n*; Nat, **1**/181; Thos, **1**/101, 181, 262, 368*; **2**/237; **3**/270*, 355, 369; p. 266; Thos, sheriff, **1**/197, 245; **3**/384

Filder (Filders), Geo, **2**/248; **3**/237*, 299*; Joseph, **3**/299; Maurice, **2**/248

Finch, Ric, **3**/369; Wm, **3**/369

Fisher, Anne, **3**/309; John, **3**/232; Ric, **3**/39; Rob, **3**/39; Wm, **1**/579*; **3**/309

Fishpoole, Joseph, **2**/148*

Fitche, Francis, **1**/188; Thos, **1**/188

Fleming (Fleminge, Flemminge, Flemynge), John, **1**/182*, 191*, 501*n*; **2**/84; p. 270; Lieutenant, p. 264; Ric, **1**/3, 25, 327, 358; Rosamund, **2**/84; Tabitha, **1**/3, 25, 327; Thos, **2**/33*, 84*

Fleshall, Agnes, **1**/4; Rob, **1**/4

Fletcher, Edw, **1**/20, 110; p. 270; Francis, **1**/110; Henry, **1**/327, 421–2; John, **1**/281; **3**/226, 263; Kath, **3**/280; Marg, **2**/107; Margery, **1**/20, 110, 421–2; Ralph, **2**/107; Ric, **3**/268; Rob, **3**/319*; Sarah, **3**/389; Thos, **1**/281, 327; **2**/107*; **3**/226, 263, 389; Wm, **3**/268, 280

Flouke (Floucke) *see* Fluck

Flower, John, **3**/341; Sam, **3**/341

Flowke *see* Fluck

Floyd, John, **3**/242*; *and see* Lloyde

Fluck (Floucke, Flouke, Flowke, Flucke), Edw, **1**/62*, 488; Eliz, **2**/202, 330; **3**/116; John, **1**/488; Thos, **1**/482; **2**/202, 330; **3**/116; Wm, **1**/482; **2**/330*; **3**/261*

Fones (Foanes, Fownes), Alice, **1**/409; Anne, **2**/54; Eleanor, **1**/584; **2**/20; **3**/24, 41; Godfrey, **1**/517; **2**/54; **3**/351*; John, **1**/409, 434*, 517, 584; **2**/20; **3**/24*, 41; Thos, **3**/24

Foorde (Foords) *see* Ford

Foote, Lawr, **2**/369; Wm, **2**/369

Ford (Foorde, Foords, Fordes, Fords), Henry, **3**/354*n*, 355; Humph, **1**/585; Isobel, **3**/383; Jas, **3**/63, 109, 279, 355*, 397, 399*; John, **3**/63, 383*, 397; Mary, **3**/279, 355; Ric, **3**/83, 109; Thos, **1**/585; Wm, **3**/83, 320*

Forreigne, Thos, **3**/19*

Forty, Dan, **3**/88; John, **2**/330*; Thos, **3**/88

Foster, Rob, **3**/210; Wm, **2**/181*; **3**/210

Fowle, Joseph, **2**/208; Ric, **1**/123; Thos, **1**/170; Wm, **1**/123, 170; **2**/208

Fowler, Abigail, **1**/431, 458; Anne, **1**/561; **2**/6, 79; Anselm, **1**/302; Anselm, mayor, **3**/293; Dan, **1**/238; **3**/312; Ferdinand, **1**/157; Henry, **2**/293, 312; Henry, mayor, **3**/51, 66, 198; John, **2**/79; Mary, **3**/95, 294, 337, 379; Sam, **1**/238, 339; Wm,

INDEX OF PERSONS

1/302, 431, 458, 552, 561, 571; 2/6, 79*, 204*, 325; 3/95, 294, 312, 337, 379, 431, 458; Wm, sheriff, 2/56 ; —, 1/157; 2/293, 325

Fownes *see* Fones

Fox, John, 2/322; Thos, 3/178; p. 269; Wm, 2/322; 3/178

Franckis *see* Frankis

Francombe (Frannckombe), Henry, 1/352, 459; 2/58, 232; Luke, 1/577; Thos, 1/518*, 577; 2/58, 232; Wm, 1/352; —, 1/459

Frankis (Franckis, Frankys), Eliz, 2/113, 213, 274; Henry, 1/363; 2/114; Ric, 1/402; 2/113, 213; Wm, 1/363, 402; 2/114, 274

Frannckombe *see* Francombe

Frape, Joseph, 1/573; Rob, 1/573

Freame (Freeme), Dan, 3/45, 161; Dorothy, 1/288, 313, 340, 405; Eliz, 1/396; 3/103; Jasper, 3/161, 267; John, 1/177, 288, 313, 340, 396, 405; 2/271*; 3/103; Mary, 1/22, 24; Ric, 1/22, 24; Thos, 1/177; Wm, 3/45

Freeman, Alice, 1/326, 351, 470; Ant, 2/228, 272; 3/102; Benj, 2/128; Ferebe (Vereby), 3/102, 381; Frances, 3/374; Geo, 2/272; Giles, 2/307; 3/280*, 301*n*; Jas, 1/295, 326, 351, 400, 470; p. 266; Jane, 2/236, 257; John, 1/400; 2/315*; 3/20; p. 272; Joseph, 2/99; Rob, 2/307; 3/374; Roland, 2/228; Sam, 1/485; 2/236, 257; Thos, 2/99, 128; 3/20, 45*; Wm, 1/485; 3/381

Freeme *see* Freame

French, Eliz, 1/256; John, 1/507; Wal, 1/256, 507

Frewen, John, 1/2; Ric, 1/168; Thos, 1/159*,168; —, 1/2

Friar *see* Fryer

Fry, Gabriel, 2/163; Henry, 3/52*; John, 2/163

Fryer (Friar), Maurice, 3/362; Wal, 3/15*, 362, 385; Wm, 3/384*n*, 385

Furney, Alice, 3/232; Jas, 3/232, 339; Jas, sheriff, 3/384; John, 3/231; Sarah, 3/339; Wm, 3/231

Fyld *see* Field

Gabb, Dan, 1/570; Ric, 1/570; Thos, 3/322*

Gale (Galle), Alice, 1/323, 372, 402, 444, 485; John, 1/189, 201, 323, 372, 402, 444, 485; Wm, 1/189, 201

Gammond (Gammon, Gamnon, Gamon, Gamond), Edw, 1/137; John, 1/67; 3/264, 342, 378; Thos, 1/137; Wm, 3/264

Garbrande, Edw, 1/77, 200; Marg, 1/200; Ric (*alias* Harkes), 1/77

Gardiner (Gardner), Anne, 3/38, 107, 158; Ant, 3/342; Dan, 2/271; 3/162, 177, 286, 362; Edw, 2/238; 3/377; Eliz, 1/51, 79; Hannah, 3/357, 359, 376; Jas, 3/393; Joan, 3/338; John, 1/301; 2/192, 218, 227, 238, 292, 344, 375; 3/121, 344, 393; Marg, 2/227; Mary, 2/292, 344; 3/121; Nat, 2/334; Philip, 2/192; Rebecca, 3/162, 177, 286, 362; Ric, 3/344, 380*; Sarah, 2/334; Thos, 1/301; 2/218, 249; 3/38, 107, 158, 302*n*, 305*, 338, 342, 377; Wm, 1/51, 79, 178*, 555*; 2/249, 271; 3/302*n*, 305, 357, 359, 376

Garlick (Garlicke), Jas, 1/327; 2/296*; Thos, 1/282*, 327

Garne, Henry, 1/331; Wm, 1/331

Garner (Garners), Isaac, 1/474; John, 1/136; 2/170; 3/103*; John (*alias* Mashfield), 3/73*; Nat, 2/170; Ric, 1/474; Wm, 1/136

Garnons, Luke, p. 266; Luke, mayor, 1/79

Garnsum *see* Gransum

Garrett, Nat, 1/543, 561; Ric, 1/536*n*, 543; Thos, 1/561; 3/386*; Wal, 1/172; Wm, 1/172

Garway, Edith, 3/276; Jonathan, 3/276

Gather, John, 3/62; Ric, 3/62

Gatherne, Ric, 1/343*

Gawcam, Eliz, 2/374

Gearing (Gearinge), Simon, 1/517*

Gee, Geo, 2/119*

Geffreys *see* Jefferis

Gelf *see* Jelfe

George, Ant, 3/222*n*, 227; Hester, 2/297, 311, 354; 3/45, 118, 143, 173, 190, 227; John, 2/297; 3/118, 135*n*; Mary, 3/241; Nat, 2/297; 3/241; Rob, 2/58; Wm, 2/58, 297, 311, 354; 3/45, 118*, 173, 227, 228*, 239*n*, 307; —, 3/135*n*

Geste, Alan, 1/14; Wm, 1/14

Gibb, Henry, p. 267; *and see* Gibbs

Gibbons (Gibbins), David, 3/35; Dina, 3/261; Frances, 1/547; Mary, 3/306; Ric, 1/547; 2/310; 3/64, 261, 306; Thos, 1/423, 547; 3/35; p. 272; Wm, 1/423, 547; 2/310; —, 3/64

Gibbs (Gybbes), Jas, 1/274; John, 3/57, 146*, 383; Mary, 3/231; Matt, p. 268; Philip, 3/231; Ric, 1/99*; Rob, 1/274; p. 270; Sarah, 3/331; Thos, 3/57, 331; *and see* Gibb

Gibson (Gybson), Edw (*alias* Rawlings), 1/48; Eliz (*alias* Rawlings), 1/48; John, 1/383; 2/151; Paul, 1/383; Thos, 2/151

Gide, Ric, 1/349; Rob, 1/349

Gilbert (Gilberte), Giles, 2/12, 84; Henry, 1/352*, 457*, 519, 557*, 569, 571; 2/92; Humph, 1/519; John, 1/298*; Lewis, 1/457; Marg, 2/12; Mary, 1/557*, 569, 571; 2/84; Nic, 1/141; Roger, 1/400; Simon, 1/141; Wm, p. 266; —, 1/457

Gill (Gyll), Thos, 1/238*; Wm, 3/354*; *and see* Gyles

Gillman, Brian, 2/149; Geo, 2/149

Gittoes (Githis, Gitto, Gittos, Gyttos), Alice, **3**/230; Joan, **1**/528, 568; John, **1**/417; Wm, **1**/528, 568; **2**/225*; **3**/230, 339*; p. 272; Wm (*alias* Jones), **1**/417

Glassenbury, John, **2**/161*

Glaw, Wm, **3**/36*

Gloucester, bishop of, pp. 266, 267*–9*; chancellor of *see* Seaman, Dr

Glover, Wm, **3**/323*n*

Goade, John, **1**/63; Thos, **1**/63; *and see* Good

Goddard, Ant, **3**/134*

Godfree, Ric, **1**/228; Thos, **1**/228

Godsee, Thos, **2**/317*

Godwin (Godwyn), Henry, **3**/143; Ric, **3**/143; Wm, **3**/377 *and see* Goodwin

Goldinge, Ric, **1**/582*

Good (Goode), Isobel, **1**/135; Kath, **1**/526, 567; Mary, **2**/143; Ric, **1**/362; Thos, **1**/135, 362, 526, 567; **2**/143, 182; Wm, **2**/182; *and see* Goade

Goodcheap (Goodcheape, Goodchep), Mary, **3**/16, 69, 104, 179, 209, 254, 291; Sybil, **2**/229, 294; Thos, **2**/21*, 194*, 229, 294, 322; **3**/16, 69, 104, 121*n*, 174*n*, 179, 209, 254, 291; Wm, **2**/194; —, **2**/194, 322

Goodinge (Goodin), John, **3**/199; Ric, **3**/199; Thos, **1**/382*

Goodman, Chas, **3**/367; Edw, **3**/367

Goodwin (Goodwyn), Eliz, **2**/335; Joseph, **3**/16*; Ric, **2**/76, 335; Wm, **2**/76; *and see* Godwin

Goold, Edw, **2**/155; Thos, **2**/173*n*; Wm, **2**/155

Gorway, Anne, **1**/14, 52; Humph, **1**/14*; John, **1**/14, 52

Gosling (Goslin, Goslinge), Arthur, **1**/302; Eliz, **3**/189, 232; Henry, **2**/207; John, **1**/367, 433; **2**/91, 207; Thos, **1**/302, 367, 433; **2**/91, 114; **3**/189, 232, 285; Wm, p. 273; —, **2**/114

Gotheridge, Wm, **1**/2

Grace, Geo, **3**/294; John, **1**/421–2; **3**/294; Wm, **1**/421–2; p. 266

Gracing, Aaron, **2**/88; Wm, **2**/88

Graffstocke (Grafstock, Grafstocke) *see* Gravestock

Grainger (Granger), John, **1**/272; Joseph, **1**/272; Thos, **2**/119; Wm, **2**/119

Gransum (Garnsum), John, **1**/423, 425; Nic, **1**/423, 425

Gratian, John, **2**/335; Wm, **2**/335

Gravestock (Graffstock, Graffstocke, Grafstock, Grafstocke), Eliz, **2**/102, 252; **3**/161; Geo, **1**/402; **3**/162; John, **1**/402, 463; **2**/102, 252; **3**/161–2, 279, 317, 347, 371; Marg, **3**/279; Sarah, **3**/371; —, **1**/463

Gray (Grey, Graye), Alice, **1**/93 Brice, **1**/268, 299, 369; Joan, **1**/268, 299, 369; **2**/33; John, p. 272; Wm, **1**/210

Green (Greene, Grene), Adam, **3**/249*; Alice, **1**/436; Anne, **2**/45, 120; Augustine, **1**/276, 405, 436; Cristel, **1**/460; Deborah, **1**/508, 515; Edm, **1**/564; **3**/42–4, 72, 135*n*, 149; Edw, **1**/384, 432; **2**/4; Eleanor, **1**/384, 432; **2**/4; Eliz, **1**/247, 294, 418; Hercules, **1**/246; Honour, **3**/121, 134; Isobel, **1**/103, 108; Joan, **3**/235, 265, 333, 379; John, **1**/5, 42, 103, 108, 178, 276, 405, 438, 467, 555; **2**/38, 45, 103, 137, 178, 190, 274, 299; **3**/13–14, 47, 81, 83, 92, 121, 134, 149, 235, 265, 316, 333, 379; Jonathan, **3**/61; Kath, **1**/555; **2**/38, 45, 103, 178, 299; **3**/14, 47; Marg, **1**/48, 167, 587; **2**/130, 175, 190, 274; **3**/61, 83, 149, 214, 316; Margery, **1**/5, 42; Mary, **2**/95, 210–11, 277, 355; **3**/48, 87; Nic, **3**/92; Philip, **2**/26*, 43; **3**/318; Ric, **1**/48, 189, 246*, 298, 303, 361*, 438, 460, 467, 542; **2**/26*, 43, 317, 355; **3**/28*, 217; pp. 265, 270; Ric, sheriff, **1**/391; Rob, **1**/9, 298; **3**/28; Roland, **2**/45, 120; **3**/13, 89; Sam, **1**/178; Sarah, **2**/317; Simon, **1**/111, 247, 261, 294, 353, 418*; Stephen, **3**/89; Thos, **1**/9, 303, 327, 389, 402, 508, 515, 564; **2**/79, 80, 125*, 175; **3**/69*n*, 72*, 135*n*, 149, 217; Wm, **1**/111, 405, 407*n*, 418, 542, 587; **2**/95, 130, 210–11, 268, 277, 317*, 355*; **3**/48, 61*, 87, 318; p. 272; —, **1**/189; **2**/80; **3**/28, 42–4, 72, 81

Greeneberry, John, **1**/181; —, **1**/181

Greening (Greeninge, Greninge, Grenninge, Grining), Alice, **2**/35, 48, 129, 223; Frances, **2**/89; Jasper, **1**/1, 131, 137; p. 261; John, **1**/1; **2**/89, 364; **3**/318; p. 261; Ric, **2**/35, 48, 129, 223; Tacy, **1**/137; Thos, **2**/364; Ursula, **3**/318; —, **1**/131

Greenway, Chas, **3**/203*, 293, 373; Rebecca, **3**/373; Wal, **3**/293

Gregory, Abraham, **3**/245; Alice (*alias* Ridler), **1**/540; Anne, **3**/49, 158, 312, 352; Baron, **3**/223*n*; p. xxiii; Brice, **1**/559; Edm, **2**/221; Edm, sheriff, **3**/368; Henry, **1**/370, 559; **2**/52; **3**/196*n*; ; Hester, **3**/383; Humph, **2**/221; Joan, **1**/370; **2**/55*n*; John, **3**/222*n*, 245, 383; Wm, **2**/52; **3**/49, 158, 312, 352*; Wm (*alias* Ridler), **1**/540; —, **2**/55*n*

Grenden, John, **3**/173; Thos, **3**/173

Grene *see* Green

Greninge (Grenninge) *see* Greening

Gresham (Grosham), Henry, **1**/327; Joan, **1**/468, 478, 483, 530; Thos, **1**/327, 434, 468, 478, 483, 530; —, **1**/434

Gretton, Wm, **1**/260*, 344*

Grevile (Grevill, Grivell), Anne, **1**/574; Edw, **1**/464; **2**/32, 185; Francis, **3**/22; Giles, **1**/329*, 413, 464*, 574; Henry, **3**/22, 379*n*; Mary, **2**/32, 185

Grey *see* Gray

Griffen *see* Griffin; Griffith

Griffeth (Griffes) *see* Griffith

Griffin (Griffen), Dan, **3**/310; David, **1**/285, 576; **2**/213, 313; **3**/12, 45, 142*, 174*n*; Foulke, **2**/215; Hester, **2**/313; **3**/12, 45, 142; Hugh, **1**/576; **3**/310; Jas, **2**/365*, John, **2**/150*, 215, 305; Lawr, **3**/142; Ric, **1**/285; **2**/301*, 305, 337; Thos, **2**/337; —, **2**/213; **3**/244*n*

Griffith (Griffes, Griffeth, Griffis, Griffiths), Alex, **3**/358; Bridget, **3**/337; David, **1**/565; **3**/188; Edw, **3**/199; Francis, **1**/162, Henry, **1**/306*; **2**/209; **3**/146; Hester, **3**/188; John, **3**/199, 358; Jonathan, **1**/565; **2**/109; Michael, **3**/266; **3**/322*n*; Nat, **2**/209; Owen, **3**/266; Philip, **3**/337; Rob, **1**/162; Simeon, **3**/146; —, **2**/109; **3**/322*n*

Grigg, Wm, **1**/147*

Grimes (Grime, Gryme, Grymes), Joan, **1**/207, 328, 347; Ric, **1**/12*, 207, 328, 347*; p. 272; Ric, sheriff, **1**/497; Thos, **1**/169*, 444*

Grining *see* Greening

Grivell *see* Grevill

Grosham *see* Gresham

Grove, John, **3**/295, 365; Sam, **3**/365; Wm, **3**/295, 396*n*

Groving, John, **1**/484; Ric, **1**/484

Grymes *see* Grimes

Guise (Guyse), Chris, **2**/87; Geo, **2**/30; Henry, **2**/30; John, **2**/87, 101; Sir John, mayor, **3**/306; Wm, **2**/101; p. xiv; Sir Wm, p. 267

Gun (Gunn), Arthur, **2**/182; Moses, **2**/182, 311*

Gundy, Tobias, **3**/306; Wal, **3**/306

Gunn *see* Gun

Gurner, Geo, **2**/13; Ric, **2**/13

Guy (Guye), Eleanor, **1**/92; Eliz, **1**/6, 31, 64, 126, 160; Hugh, **1**/92; John, **3**/371; Ric, **1**/584; Sarah, **3**/371; Thos, **1**/6, 31, 64, 126, 160, 584

Guylden, Geo, **1**/260; Ric, **1**/260

Guylliam *see* Gwilliam

Guyse *see* Guise

Gwatkin, Wal, **2**/204*; *and see* Watkins

Gwilliam (Guylliam, Gwiliam, Gwillim), Anne, **3**/93, 146, 207, 209, 219, 222, 260, 275, 312; Cecily, **1**/120, 130, 144, 161, 173, 238–9, 291; Geo, **1**/245; Joan, **1**/1, 11, 48; p. 261; John, **1**/1, 11, 48, 120, 130, 144, 161, 173, 238–9, 291; **2**/173*n*, 183*; **3**/16, 28, 93, 146, 207, 209, 219, 222, 260, 275, 312, 390; pp. 261, 272; John, sheriff, **1**/297, 345; **3**/368; Mary, **3**/16, 28; Wm, **1**/245; *and see* Ap Gwillim; Williams

Gwin (Gwinne) *see* Gwynne

Gwinnell, Mary, **3**/372; Ric, **3**/271*, 372

Gwinnett (Gwinnet), Francis, **3**/304; Geo, **3**/198; Lawr, **3**/304; Ric, **3**/198; Sarah, **3**/312

Gwynne (Gwin, Gwinne, Gwyn, Gwynn), Alice, **1**/337, 348, 407, 427, 570, 586; **2**/43, 85, 182, 267; Allias *see* Elias; Augustine, **1**/160, 337, 348, 366, 369, 407, 427, 570, 586; **2**/39, 43, 81–2, 85, 90, 159, 182, 201, 267, 276, 356; **3**/109; p. xix; David, **2**/104; Elias (Allias), **1**/527; **2**/104; John, **2**/356; **3**/201, 374*n*, 381*; Joseph, **2**/356; Lewis, **1**/527; **2**/286, 347*; Marg, **2**/39, 81–2, 90, 159, 201, 276; Martha, **3**/201; Mary, **2**/347; Sam, **2**/286; Thos, **1**/160; —, **1**/366; **2**/356; **3**/109

Gybbes *see* Gibbs

Gybson *see* Gibson

Gyles, Adam, **3**/358, 365; Isaac, **3**/358; Jas, **3**/365

Gyll *see* Gill

Gythens (Gythins), John, sheriff, **2**/330, mayor, **3**/206; Rob, **2**/328; Thos, **2**/325*n*, 328

Gyttos *see* Gittoes

Hacker, Ric, **2**/107; Thos, **2**/107

Hadnett (Hadnot), Henry, **1**/561; **2**/234; Jane, **1**/561; John, **2**/234

Hagborne (Hagburne) Abraham, **1**/288; Ric, **1**/71, 347*; Thos, **1**/190; **3**/370; Wm, **1**/71, 190, 288; **3**/370

Haies *see* Hayes

Haines (Haynes, Heynes), Anne, **1**/386; Edw, **1**/198; **2**/50, 70; **3**/70, 359*; Eliz, **2**/300; **3**/96; Francis, **2**/70; p. 270; Jas, **1**/465*; John, **1**/106*, 160, 477; **2**/201*; Kath (Katrine), **1**/268, 338, 517; Nic, **2**/50, 71, 184*, 194, 220, 325*; Peter, **1**/523; **2**/300*; **3**/96, 208; Peter, sheriff, **3**/306; Ric, **1**/340; **2**/358*; Rob, **1**/208*, 340; Sarah, **2**/50, 71, 194, 220, 325; Thos, **1**/198, 477, 530*, 562; **2**/71*; Wm, **1**/112, 160, 268, 338, 386, 454, 517, 523, 562, 574; **2**/50, 270*, 285; **3**/70, 374*; —, **1**/574

Hale, Alice, **2**/308; Ant, **2**/193; Giles, **2**/366*; Jesse, **2**/345; John, **1**/112; **3**/92*n*, 94, 193*n*, 369*n*; Kath, **2**/193; Miles, **1**/466; Ric, **2**/70, 308*; Rob, **2**/70; Thos, **1**/351*; **2**/201*n*, 202*, 345; **3**/92*n*, 94, 250*n*; Wal, **1**/466, 566; Wm, **1**/112, 454; **2**/205*; **3**/334*; Young, **1**/566; *and see* Hall; Haule

Halford, Edm, **3**/271; John, **3**/271; Rob, **1**/10; Stephen, **1**/10

Hall (Halle), Edw, **1**/210, 256*; **2**/363*, 377*; Eleanor, **1**/306, 321, 397; Elias, **1**/134; Eliz, **3**/55; Francis, **2**/217, 235; Giles, **3**/331; Henry, **1**/357, 435; **3**/58, 115; Jas, **1**/74; John, **1**/134, 256*, 491*, 564*; **2**/39, 217, 312*; **3**/95*, 101, 115, 192*; p. 268; Margery, **1**/411, 483, 547; Ric, **1**/74, 100; Rob, **1**/357; **3**/331; Roger, **1**/74, 411, 483, 547; **2**/92; Thos, **1**/210, 306, 321, 396*n*, 397; **2**/39, 74*; **3**/101; Wal, **1**/435; p. 273; Wm, **2**/74, 92, 100*n*, 235; **3**/55, 58; Mr, p. 269; widow, p. 269; —, **3**/92*n*; *and see* Hale; Haule

Hallinge, Cath, **1**/168; Joan, **1**/111; John, **1**/168; Wm, **1**/111; p. 272; *and see* Hawling

Halsey, Thos, **1**/385; Wm, **1**/385

Halsteed (Hawsteed, Holsteed), John, **1**/200; Joseph, **2**/348*; Thos, **2**/313*; Wm, **1**/200

Ham, Martha, **3**/177; Thos, **3**/211*n*; Wm, **3**/177*

Hamlyn (Hamlin), Arthur, **3**/297; Edw, **3**/297; Jas, **3**/51; Joseph, **3**/55; Ric, **3**/55; Rob, **3**/51

Hammonds (Hammons, Hamonds, Hamons), Anne, **1**/187; John, **1**/8, 70, 127, 171, 187; Martha, **1**/8, 70, 127; Thos, **2**/353*; **3**/86, 342*; Wm, **3**/86; —, **1**/127, 171

Hampton, Jas, **3**/299; Philip, **3**/288; Ric, **1**/189; Thos, **3**/288; Wm, **1**/189; **3**/299

Hanbury, Anne, **3**/89; Caple, **3**/89; John, p. 268

Hancks *see* Hanks

Hancksman *see* Hanksman

Hancocks (Hancock, Hancocke, Hancox), Anne, **1**/343; Edw, **2**/265; Eliz, **3**/395; Geo, **1**/494; **2**/265; Henry, **1**/343; John, **1**/560*; **2**/236*, 254 *and n**, 269*, 285; **3**/45, 84; Paul, **3**/240; Philippa (Philadelphia), **3**/45, 84; Ric, **1**/494; Thos, **2**/285; Vincent, **3**/240; Wm, **2**/254; —, **2**/254*n*

Hands (Handes), Alex, **1**/170; Isaac, **1**/368*n*; John, **1**/170; Ric, **2**/95, 312; **3**/49; Sarah, **3**/49; Wm, **3**/15*; —, **1**/368*n*

Hanks (Hancks, Hankes, Hanx), Eliz, **3**/27; John, **1**/382; **2**/235; **3**/27; Joseph, **2**/228; **3**/316*n*; Ric, **1**/382; **2**/228; Wm, **2**/235

Hanksman (Hancksman), John, **2**/85, Thos, **2**/78*, 85

Hanly, Joseph, **2**/356; Wm, **2**/356

Hanman, John, **1**/24; Thos, **1**/24

Hannis (Hannys), Chas, **3**/266; Eleanor, **2**/209; Ric, **1**/258; Sam, **3**/119*; Thos, **1**/258; **2**/153*, 209; **3**/367*; Wm, **3**/266

Hanx *see* Hanks

Harbert (Harberte), Chas, p. 273; Chris, **2**/220–1; John, **1**/44, 75, 83; Peter, **1**/402*; Ric, **1**/75, 83; Wm, **1**/44; **2**/220, 221; *and see* Herbert

Harding (Hardinge), Chas, **3**/261*n*, 262; Edw, **3**/71*; Eliz, **2**/279; John, **1**/68; **3**/146*n*, 158*, 261*n*, 262, 279, 285*n*, 286; Marg, **1**/198; Ric, **2**/117*n*; Thos, **1**/68, 198; Wm, **3**/285*n*, 286

Hardwicke, John, **1**/158, 317; Nat, **3**/369; Wal, **1**/158; Wm, **1**/317; **3**/369

Harkes, Ric *(alias* Garbrande), **1**/77

Harmer, Francis, **2**/62; Joan, **3**/23; John, **1**/583; **2**/62; Wm, **1**/583; **3**/23

Harper, John, **3**/34; Nic, **3**/34; Philip, **1**/508; Ric, **1**/508

Harriettes (Harriates), Ant, **1**/173; Giles, **1**/260; John, **1**/173, 260

Harris (Harrys), Anne, **1**/539; **2**/46; Dan, **2**/179; Edw, **1**/357, 436*, 507; **2**/25; Eliz, **1**/560, 565*, 572, 586; **2**/4, 25, 28, 92, 183, 205; **3**/302; Francis, **1**/342; p. 272; Henry, **2**/32*; Humph, **1**/20, 361, 364, 470, 539, 560, 572; **2**/4, 179; Jas, **1**/449; **2**/65; **3**/115; Jeremiah, **2**/214; **3**/143; John, **1**/259, 326, 330, 332, 355*, 470; **2**/79*n*, 318; **3**/58, 105*n*, 190*, 225, 337, 352; Joseph, **2**/210, 279; **3**/107, 302; Mary, **1**/342, 357, 436, 507; **2**/25; **3**/143; Ric, **3**/337, 352; Rob, **1**/197; Sarah, **2**/295*n*; Susannah, **1**/542; Tacy, **2**/210, 279; Thos, **1**/20, 275, 326, 342*, 361, 364; **2**/214, 318; **3**/107; p. 273; Tim, **2**/65; Wal, **1**/332, 464, 470, 565*, 586; **2**/25, 28, 92, 183, 205; Wal, sheriff, **2**/304; Wm, **1**/197, 259, 330, 449, 542; **2**/272*; **3**/58, 115; p. 273; —, **1**/463, 470; **2**/79*n*, 295*n*; *and see* Harry

Harrison, Henry, **3**/215; Sarah, **2**/333; Thos, **3**/215; Wm, **2**/333; —, **3**/200*n*

Harrold, Jane, **3**/265; Wm, **3**/265

Harry, John, **1**/125; **2**/75; Rob, **2**/75; *and see* Harris

Harrys *see* Harris

Hart, Jas, **1**/556; Valentine, **1**/556

Hartland (Hartlen), Edw, **1**/437; John, **3**/45, 236; Marg, **3**/330; Martha, **2**/271, 337, 339, 341; **3**/9, 62, 251; Ric, **2**/174; **3**/45; Thos, **1**/437; **3**/330; Wm, **2**/98*, 174, 271, 337, 339, 341; **3**/9, 62, 251

Harvey, Abraham, **3**/85; Anne, **3**/85; Wal, **3**/85*

Harward (Harwood), Alice, **1**/395; Anne, **3**/132; Ant, **1**/395; Geof, **1**/507; **2**/28, 338; Marg, **1**/507; Mary, **2**/28; Ric, **1**/395*, 507*; **2**/12; Ric, sheriff, **1**/441; Rob, **2**/338; **3**/132; —, **2**/12

Hassard *see* Hazard

Hassington (Horsington, Hossington), Alice, **1**/480, 501; Henry, **1**/480, 501*, 574; **3**/146; Margery, **2**/60, 71, 121, 131, 239; p. xix; Thos, **1**/574; **2**/60, 71, 121, 131, 239; **3**/146, 316*n*, 323*n*; p. xix

Hathaway (Hathwaie, Hathway, Hathwaye), Anne, **3**/250; Ant, **1**/237, 379; Ant, sheriff, **1**/534; Elizeor (Elizeus), **2**/276; **3**/39; Geo, **1**/395; p. 271; Henry, **3**/105; Mary, **2**/276; **3**/39; Ric, **1**/395; **2**/368; **3**/105, 311*; Wm, **2**/368; **3**/399*n*

Hatton, Anne, **1**/211; Hester, **2**/209; John, **1**/211; **3**/345*n*, 346*; p. 273; Wm, **1**/211*; **2**/209; p. 273

Haule (Hawle), Anne, **1**/121; Ric, **1**/121; Roger, **1**/160, 170, 260; —, **1**/160, 170; *and see* Hale; Hall

Hauxwell, —, p. 265

Havard (Haward), Dan, **2**/366; David (*alias* Whitehead), **1**/510–11; John, **1**/131; **2**/366; Peter, **1**/131; Wm (*alias* Whitehead), **1**/510–11; *and see* Hayward; Horward; Howard

INDEX OF PERSONS

Hawcome, Henry, **1**/169; John, **1**/169
Hawker, Edw, **1**/587; Thos, **1**/587
Hawkes, Anne, **3**/44; John, **1**/51, 247*, 267*, 269*; Ric, **3**/44; p. 272; Wm, **1**/51
Hawkins, Eleanor, **1**/538; **2**/295; **3**/64; Eliz, **3**/370; Giles, **1**/9; **2**/295; Joan, **1**/45*, 65; John, **1**/45*, 65; **3**/354; Jonathan, **3**/354; Sam, **3**/370; Thos, **2**/334; **3**/370*; Wal, **1**/538; Wm, **1**/9; **2**/334
Hawle *see* Haule
Hawling (Hawlinge, Hawlins), Francis, **1**/42; Giles, **1**/145; Henry, **1**/145; John, **1**/61, 80; Kath, **1**/80; Ric, **1**/314; Rob, **1**/314; **3**/315; Wal, **1**/61; Wm, **1**/42; **3**/315; *and see* Halling
Hawsteed *see* Halsteed
Hawthorne (Hawtherne), Chas, **3**/343; John, **2**/360; **3**/343; Rob, **2**/360
Hay, Alex, **2**/251; Thos, **2**/251
Haydon, Henry, p. 265*; *and see* Heyden
Hayers, John, **1**/311; Thos, **1**/311
Hayes (Haies, Hayse), Anne, **1**/82, 146, 229, 237, 279, 281, 332, 350, 354, 421–2, 531, 550, 566; **2**/39; p. xxvii; Chris, **1**/181, 348, 455, 522*; **2**/46, 57, 120*; Eleanor, **1**/401; Henry, **1**/452*n**, 453*, 522; **2**/24, 97, 321; **3**/217, 386*n*; Joan, **1**/348, 455, 522; **2**/46, 97, 120*; **3**/217; John, **1**/82, 146, 229, 237, 279, 281, 354, 421–2, 531, 550; **2**/321; pp. xxvii, 268; Josiah, **2**/3; **3**/393; Judith, **3**/282, 330, 394; Marg, **2**/57; Margery, **1**/159; Ric, **1**/159, 401, 543, 556*n*; Thos, **1**/137*, 181, 354; p. 272; Wm, **1**/543, 556*n*; **2**/3; **3**/282, 330, 393, 394*; —, **2**/24; p. 268
Hayford (Heyford), Anne, **1**/199; Henry, **3**/91; Joan, **1**/267, 322; John, **1**/199, 258, 267, 322; **3**/247, 322*; Mary, **3**/247; Thos, **3**/91; —, **1**/258
Hayman, Eliz, **1**/541; Thos, **1**/541
Haynes *see* Haines
Hayse *see* Hayes
Hayward (Heyward), Clement, **3**/174*n*, 179*n*, 188, 273, 313; Deborah, **3**/69, 141; Edm, **1**/10; Edw, **1**/114, 210*, 239, 258, 322, 325, 404*; **2**/347*; **3**/148, 158*, 164; Geof, **1**/580; Giles, **2**/250; **3**/45; Henry, alderman, **1**/30*n*; Jas, **1**/96; Joan, **1**/133, 239, 258, 322, 325, 404; John, **1**/32, 114, 133, 181, 187, 228, 273, 299–300, 404, 427, 455*, 568; **2**/6, 23, 140, 148, 228, 277, 326, 335; **3**/17, 110, 163*n*, 176, 188, 236, 269; John, sheriff, **1**/311; Mary, **1**/228, 273, 299–300; **3**/17, 110, 148, 158*, 176; Ric, **1**/10, 124, 328, 568; **2**/89, 146; Sam, **2**/89; **3**/69, 141, 179, 364*; Sam, sheriff, **3**/340; Sarah, **2**/6, 23, 140, 148, 228, 277, 326, 335; Stephen, **2**/250; Thos, **1**/124, 181, 187, 328, 427, 580; **3**/254; Wal, **1**/32, 35; Wm, **1**/35, 96; **3**/45, 254; Zachariah, **2**/146; —, **3**/163*n*, 269; *and see* Havard; Horward; Howard
Hazard (Hassard, Hazarde), Alice, **1**/257; Arthur, **1**/124*, 137, 257; Henry, **1**/256; Henry, alderman, **1**/30, mayor, **1**/1, 111; p. 261; John, **1**/137; Thos, **1**/199*, 256
Hazlewood, Chris, **3**/23; Jas, **3**/23
Hazleton, John (*alias* Hill), **2**/324
Heaghe, Abraham, **2**/173, 218; Hester, **3**/18; Jacob (James), **2**/173, 218; **3**/18; *and see* Heath
Heale, Thos, **3**/260*
Heane, Roland, **1**/122; Wal, **1**/122
Heard (Herd), Charles, **1**/387; Dorothy, **3**/92, 175, 259; Humph, **2**/272; **3**/92, 175, 259, 341; Jane, **3**/341; Ric, **1**/486; Rob, **2**/272
Heare, Ric, **1**/104; Wm, **1**/104
Hearynge, Ric, **1**/99; Thos, **1**/99
Heath (Heathe), Anne, **1**/443; John, **1**/319; Mary, **2**/322, 350, 355, 363, 368; **3**/15*, 131, 141; Matilda, **1**/107, 131, 207; Ric, **1**/107, 131, 207, 319; p. 265; Roger, **2**/176; Sam, **2**/72, 322, 350, 355, 363, 368; **3**/15*, 131, 141; Thos, **1**/319, 368, 443; **2**/72; —, p. 271; *and see* Heaghe
Heathfield, Guy, **2**/18; Wm, **2**/18
Heaven, Deborah, **3**/348, 387; Henry, **3**/118; John, **2**/257*, 351; **3**/118, 133, 348, 387, 399*n*; Rob, **2**/351; **3**/118;—, **3**/118, 133; *and see* Bevan; Evans
Hedges, Marg, **1**/352; Nat, **1**/352; Nat, sheriff, **1**/441; Rob, **1**/271; Sybil, **1**/271; Thos, **1**/298; Wm, **1**/283, 298; Wm, sheriff, **2**/320
Helpe, John, **1**/409; Thos, **1**/409
Heming (Heminge, Hemming, Hemminge), Arnold, **1**/300; **3**/38, 56, 60; Henry, **1**/300, 460, 480*; **2**/174; Margery, **2**/3, 207; Martha, **1**/545; Mary, **3**/384; Ric, **2**/174; **3**/60, 285*n*, 384; Rob, **3**/56; Thos, **1**/460; **2**/3, 207; Wm, **1**/545; **3**/38, 285*n*
Hemsley, Ric, **3**/269, 282; Thos, **3**/281*n*, 282; —, **3**/269
Hendy, Sam, **3**/380; Thos, **3**/380
Henlock, Godfrey, **1**/187; Roger, **1**/187
Herbert, Chris, **2**/334*, 344; Edw, **2**/116; Thos, **2**/344; Wal, **2**/116; *and see* Harbert
Herd *see* Heard
Hergest, Hugh, **1**/508; John, **1**/497; Thos, **1**/497, 508
Hermitage, Jas, **3**/302*n*, 306; Ric, **3**/306
Herne, John, **1**/541*
Hewes (Heues) *see* Hughes
Hewson, Thos, **1**/142; Yewen, **1**/142
Heyden, John, **2**/294; Nat, **2**/294; *and see* Haydon
Heyford *see* Hayford
Heynes *see* Haines
Heyter, Edw, **2**/311*n*, 314*, 330*; **3**/40*

Heyward *see* Hayward
Hicke (Hickes) *see* Hicks
Hickman, John, **1**/382, 417; **3**/87*; Mary, **1**/382, 417; —, **3**/87*n*
Hicks (Hicke, Hickes), Chris, **2**/51; Edw, **3**/106, 237, 348; Grace, **3**/106, 237, 348; Joan, **2**/165, 237, 307, 334; John, **2**/267; Miles, **1**/111; Thos, **1**/281, 526; **2**/51, 110, 165, 237, 307, 334; Wm, **1**/111, 281, 526; **2**/51, 267; *and see* Higgs
Hide *see* Hyde
Hieron *see* Hiron
Hiett *see* Hyett
Higges *see* Higgs
Higgins (Higgings, Higgyns), Edw, **1**/352; Ephraim, **3**/317*; John, **1**/476; **3**/91, 194*; Nanfan, **3**/91, 194; Nic, **3**/82; Ric, **1**/352; Thos, **1**/476; **3**/82
Higginson, Eleanor, **1**/46; Wm, **1**/46
Higgs (Higges), Eleanor, **3**/307, 313; John, **2**/325; Ric, **1**/387*; Rob, **3**/313; Wal, **1**/512; Wm, **1**/512; **2**/325; **3**/307; *and see* Hicks
Higgyns *see* Higgins
Hignall, Geo, **2**/72; Thos, **2**/72
Hill, Anne, **1**/2, 5; Chas, **1**/299; Chris, **2**/158; **2**/124, 234; Dorothy, **1**/577, 581; **2**/54, 72, 172, 181; Edw, **1**/540*; **2**/124, 234; Eleanor, **1**/430, 473, 555; Eliz, **2**/247, 280; **3**/14, 18, 60, 90, 174; Geof, **1**/2, 5; Henry, **1**/16; Jas, **1**/45; Jane, **3**/293, 361, 362*; Joan, **1**/299; p. xxvii; John, **1**/16, 45, 393, 408, 430, 473; **2**/197*, 286; **3**/31*; pp. 268, 272; John (*alias* Hazleton), **2**/324; John, mayor, **3**/274, sheriff, **3**/217; Marg, **1**/75; Matt, **2**/117; Ric, **1**/291; **3**/106, 173, 293, 361*–2*; Rob, **1**/291, 403; p. 272; Rob, sheriff, **2**/123; Sam, **3**/324; Thos, **1**/299*, 393, 403*, 408; **2**/117, 158, 247*, 264*, 286; **3**/106, 173, 361; Thos, alderman, **1**/571; **2**/33, 37, 41, 54, 58, 61, mayor, **1**/534, sheriff, **1**/351; Wal, **1**/577, 581; **2**/54, 72, 88, 172, 181, 247, 280; **3**/14, 18, 60, 90, 174; Wm, **1**/9, 75; **3**/324; Wm, alderman, **1**/327, 342, 377, 389, 412, mayor, **1**/190, 197, 321, 471, sheriff, **1**/79; —, **2**/124, 234, 324
Hillaker, John, **1**/328; Rob, **1**/328
Hillary (Hillarie, Hillarye), John, **1**/48, 436*n*; p. 273; Simon, **1**/48, 436*n*; p. 272
Hilli *see* Hilly
Hilliard, John, **1**/437; Simon, **1**/437*; Sybil, **1**/437
Hilly (Hilli, Hillie), John, **1**/354; **2**/156*; Philip, **1**/426; Thos, **1**/354, 426
Hilman, John, **1**/181*
Hincksman (Hinxman), Edw, **1**/552; John, **2**/328; Joseph, **1**/552; Thos, pp. 268–9; —, **2**/328
Hinton (Hintin, Hynton), Dan, **3**/80; Geo, **2**/201, 284*n*, 285*; **3**/80, 202; Nathan, **3**/202; Sam, **3**/202*n*; Wm, **2**/201, 220*n*
Hinxman *see* Hincksman
Hircombe, Sam, **3**/102*n*
Hiron (Hieron, Hyron), Audrey, **1**/178; Blanche, **1**/257, 260, 277, 339, 359; Humphrey, **1**/178, 257, 260, 277, 339*, 359, 444, 523, 550; **2**/85, 229; John, **3**/14; Marg, **1**/444, 550; **2**/85, 229; **3**/51; Mary, **1**/523; Nat, **2**/9; Nic, **2**/9; Ric, **3**/14
Hitche, John, **1**/120; Thos, **1**/120
Hitchins, Dan, **2**/323; Eleanor, **1**/21; Grimbald, **1**/21; Grimbald, mayor, **1**/19; Margery, **1**/291–2; Mathias, **1**/527*n*, 529; Thos, **1**/132*, 527*n*, 529; Wm, **1**/291–2; —, **2**/323; *and see* Hutchings
Hitchman, Ant, **1**/11, 72, 268; Dan, **2**/365; Edw, **1**/349; **2**/365; John, **1**/72, 268; Rob, **1**/349; Thos, **1**/11
Hoare (Hore), Alex, **1**/339, 519; Anne, **1**/143, 190*; Chas, **1**/41*, 47, 53, 136, 148*, 188, 256, 346*, 553; **2**/238, 338; p. 268; Chas, sheriff, **1**/459; Joan, **1**/188, Marg, **1**/455; Margery, **1**/41, 47, 53, 136, 148, 256, 346, 519; Ric, **1**/143, 190*, 339; Ric, sheriff, **1**/237; Sarah, **2**/238, 338; Thos, **1**/148, 346, 553; Wm, **1**/455; p. 266
Hobbs (Hobbes), Cecily, **1**/486, 572; **2**/10; John, **1**/486, 572; **2**/10, 311*; pp. 269, 271
Hobson, Jas, **2**/306; **3**/347*n*, 348*; Joan, **1**/571; John, **1**/431, 571*; **2**/301*n*, 306; **3**/69*n*, 72; Joseph, **3**/72; Sam, **1**/431
Hockham *see* Hookam
Hodges, Chris, **1**/368, 483; p. 271; John, **2**/252, 351; Nat, **2**/252; Rob, **1**/171, 201; Sam, **2**/351; **3**/366; Thos, **1**/201, 368; **3**/366; Wm, **1**/171; **3**/14*; Wm, mayor, **3**/298 ; —, **1**/483
Hodgskins, Wm, **1**/400
Hodshon (Hodghson, Hodgshon, Hodgson), Jeremiah, **1**/292, 375, 386*n*, 388; p. xx; Marmaduke, **1**/120, 292, 375, 386*n*, 388; Ric, **1**/120, 407; Thos, **1**/407
Hogg, Peter, **1**/170*
Holborne, John, **2**/13*
Holder (Houlder), Anne, **1**/130; Cath, **1**/4, 50; Henry, **1**/209; John, **3**/357; Joseph, **3**/280*n*, 330*, 357; Ric, **2**/141*; Thos, **1**/4, 50, 130; Wal, **1**/209
Holforde, Stephen, **1**/67
Holland, John, pp. 266–7; —, **1**/382
Holliday (Holiday), Chas, **2**/145; Eliz, **3**/110; Giles, **2**/145; Henry, **2**/284; **3**/110, 244*; Lawr, **1**/3; Maurice, **2**/117; Ric, **2**/117, 264, 284; **3**/161*n*; Sam, **1**/3; Susan *see* Rich; Wm, pp. xvii, xx–xxiii *and see* p. 263; —, **2**/264
Holloway, John, **2**/270; Hugh, **2**/270
Holman, Henry, **1**/134; **2**/305*; Humph, **1**/11, 54,

INDEX OF PERSONS

134; Humph, sheriff, **1**/177; Jas, **1**/516; John, **1**/516; Mary, **1**/11, 54; Mr, p. 267; —, p. 267
Holshipp, Wm, p. 271
Holsteed *see* Halsteed
Holtham (Holtam), Mary, **2**/173; Oliver, **1**/551; Wm, **1**/551; **2**/173; **3**/66*; —, **3**/66, 175*n*
Holton (Houlton), Geo, **1**/260; John, **1**/260; **3**/23*n*, 25; Ric, **3**/25
Homes, John, **2**/320; Thos, **2**/320
Hone, Henry, **3**/351; John, **3**/351
Hoockham *see* Hookam
Hood, Ric, **2**/187*
Hookam (Hockham, Hoockam, Hookham), Alice, **2**/19; Anne, **1**/279, 322, 342; Eliz, **1**/402; Henry, **1**/279, 322, 342; John, **1**/279; Nat, **1**/279, 366, 402; **2**/19
Hooke, Edw, **1**/338; **3**/48, 374; Jas, **1**/408; John, **1**/338; Jonathan, **3**/374; Ric, **1**/408; Wm, **3**/48
Hookham *see* Hookam
Hooper, Anne, **1**/441, 471; Chas, **3**/371; Henry, **1**/521*; **3**/21; p. 268; Jas, **3**/371; Jesse, **1**/332, 392; John, **1**/199, 441, 471; **3**/276*n*, 319*; Nat, **1**/273; Sarah, **1**/332, 392; Thos, **3**/190*, 276*n*; Wm, **1**/199; —, **1**/273; **3**/21; *and see* Whooper
Hopcutt, John, **3**/141; Wm, **3**/141
Hope, John, **3**/355; Wm, **3**/355
Hopkins, Ant, **3**/369; Benedick, **1**/179; Benj, **3**/369; Jane, **1**/362, 421; John, **1**/202, 356, 362, 396*n*, 401, 420–1; **2**/115*, 204, 249*; **3**/253*, 309; pp. xix, 267; Philip, **2**/204; Ralph, **1**/179; Susannah, **3**/392; Theophilus, **3**/309, 392; Wm, **1**/202
Hopley, Thos, **3**/362*
Hopton, Ferdinand, **1**/199; Wm, **1**/199
Hordell, John, **2**/38; Marg, **2**/38
Hore *see* Hoare
Horell *see* Horrell
Hornage *see* Hornidge
Horne, Anne, **3**/210, 218; Eliz, **1**/86; Geo, **2**/309; **3**/210, 218; Henry, **1**/6; John, **2**/309; Nic, **1**/6; Thos, **1**/86,
Hornedge *see* Hornidge
Horner, Brian, **1**/126; John, p. 272
Hornidge (Hornage, Hornedge), Anne, **3**/365, 393; Chris, **2**/198; Henry, **1**/297; **2**/260; **3**/316*n*; Jas, **3**/298, 349; John, **2**/262, 315; **3**/71, 103, 354*n*, 359; Joseph, **2**/315; **3**/318, 359*; Mary, **3**/298, 318, 349, 359; Matt, **3**/294; Sarah, **3**/71, 103; Thos, **1**/146; **2**/198; **3**/294; Wm, **1**/146, 297; **2**/105*, 260, 262; **3**/322, 326, 365, 393
Horrell (Horell, Horrall), Anne, **3**/100, 106, 135, 195; John, **2**/145, 286*n*, 287*; **3**/100, 106, 135, 195; Mary, **2**/145

Horrold, Edw, **3**/350*; Jane, **3**/363; John, **3**/60; Wm, **3**/60, 363
Horsham (Horsam, Hossum), Eliz, **2**/375; John, **1**/516, 532, 550; p. 269; Ursula, **1**/516, 532, 550
Horsington *see* Hassington
Horsley, Francis, **1**/53; Wm, **1**/53
Horward (Horwarde), Ant, p. 271; Edw, **1**/313; Henry, **1**/313; *and see* Howard
Horwood, Ric, **1**/317
Hosey, Edw, **3**/236*, 303*; Wm, **3**/233*n*
Hoskins, Gabriel, **2**/277; Rob, **3**/379*n*; Thos, **2**/277
Hossington *see* Hassington
Hossum *see* Horsham
Houlder *see* Holder
Houlship, Edw, **2**/106; John, **2**/106
Houlton *see* Holton
House, Chas, **1**/416*; Joan, **1**/416; John, **1**/416
Howard, Ric, **3**/210; Thos, **3**/210; *and see* Havard; Hayward; Horward
Howe, Chas, **1**/11; Jas, **1**/147; Mary, **1**/11; Stephen, **1**/147
Howell, Eliz, **3**/244, 332, 386; James, **3**/267; John, p. 265; Joseph, **3**/132, 244, 332, 386; Meredith, **1**/14*; Wm, **3**/53*n*, 132; *and see* Aphowell
Howford, Anne, **1**/391; Ant, **1**/391
Howlett (Howlet), Anne, **1**/169; Ant, **1**/169, 300*, 322; Joan, **2**/314; John, **1**/258, 322; Margery, **1**/387; Ric, **1**/125; Thos, **1**/125; **2**/314; p. 271; Wm, **1**/258, 387
Hues *see* Hughes
Huffe, Joan, **2**/205; Thos, **2**/205, 325*
Hughes (Heues, Hewes, Hues), Dan, **3**/69, 95, 101; Edw, **1**/159; Eliz, **3**/69, 95, 101; Giles, **1**/348; p. 272; Henry, **1**/70; Jane, **2**/7, 77, 296; Joan, **1**/268, 452; **2**/129, 196; John, **2**/7, 77, 296; **3**/49, 367; p. 273; Mary, **2**/79*n*; Miles, p. 271; Philip, **2**/79*n*, 81, 101; **3**/238*, 239*n*; Ric, **1**/170*, 268, 452*; **2**/129, 196, 309; **3**/49; Thos, **1**/159, 348; **2**/81, 101; **3**/49*, 364*n*, 367; Tim, **1**/452; p. 273; Wm, **1**/70; —, **2**/309
Hulls, John, **2**/281; Ralph, **2**/281; Ric, **2**/137*;—, **2**/137
Humphreys (Humfras, Humfreyes, Humfries, Humfris, Humfryes, Humphries, Humphris), Anne, **3**/316, 380; Edw, **2**/363; **3**/320, 371; Eliz, **3**/320, 371; Frances, **1**/559; **2**/5, 52, 69, 250, 355; **3**/73; John, **1**/291; **2**/2*n*, 5*, 117, 334*; Joseph, **2**/316; **3**/86, 179; Mary, **3**/179; Nat, **3**/86; Ric, **1**/360, 559; **2**/5, 52, 69, 90*, 250, 355; **3**/73, 246; Sam, **1**/375, 479; **3**/73, 263, 314, 385, 399; p. 270; Thos, **1**/291, 360, 375; **3**/246, 316; Toby, **2**/316; **3**/86; Wm, **2**/117, 363; —, **1**/479; **3**/86

Hunt (Hunte), Eliz, **2**/74, 146; John, **1**/15*, 126, 389, 412; **2**/74, 146; Ric, **1**/126; Rob, **3**/395*; Sam, **3**/281; Thos, **1**/389, 412; Wm, **3**/281

Huntley, John, **2**/259; Ric, **2**/259

Hurlestone (Hurlston), Anne, **2**/127, 179, 208, 315; Giles, **1**/534; Wm, **1**/534; **2**/127, 179, 208, 315

Hurte, Eliz, **1**/144, 200; John, **1**/144, 200

Hussey, Ant, **2**/93; Arthur, **2**/93

Hutchings (Hutchins), Anne, **2**/130; Deborah, **2**/362; Francis, **3**/302*n*, 307; Humph, **2**/284; Nat, **2**/362; Sarah, **3**/307; Wm, **2**/130, 138*, 282, 284; —, **2**/282; *and see* Hitchins

Huttson, Thos, p. 271

Hyam, Barnabas, **1**/334; John, **1**/377*; Nic, **1**/334

Hyde (Hide), Francis, **1**/79; John, **1**/79; Joseph, **3**/129*

Hye, Ric, **1**/411

Hyett (Hiett), Benj, alderman, **3**/36, sheriff, **3**/184; Eliz, **3**/160, 254, 270, 335*, 358, 384; Henry, **3**/389; Jeremiah, **2**/327; John, **2**/327; **3**/102*, 160, 254, 270, 335*, 358, 384; John, alderman, **3**/387, mayor, **3**/326, 368; Ric, **3**/47; Rob, **3**/47; Thos, **2**/29; Wm, **3**/335; **2**/29; Zachariah, **3**/389; —, **3**/102; *and see* Wiett

Hynton *see* Hinton

Hyron *see* Hiron

Idding (Iddin), John, **2**/30; **3**/216*; Ric, **2**/30

Iles, Henry, **1**/454*; Thos, **3**/315*

Ingley (Ingly) Alice, **3**/353; John, **1**/516; **3**/356; Ric, **3**/353; Rob (*alias* Farmer), **1**/516; Thos, **1**/482; **3**/118*, 354*n*, 356; Wm, **1**/482

Ingram, Rob, p. 265; widow, p. 265

Ireland, Ric, **3**/191; Wm, **3**/191

Irish, Roger, **1**/406

Issard, Gabriel, **1**/515; Ric, **1**/515

Itheridge (Itheridg), John, **1**/136; Rob, **1**/136; Wal, **1**/188*

Ives, John, **2**/256, 299; Sam, **2**/299; Wm, **2**/256; **3**/45, 118*, 173

Jackson (Jacksons), Edw, **2**/63; John, **2**/63; **3**/239; Rob, **3**/178*, 239

Jakeman, Eliz, **3**/372; Wm, **3**/372

James, Christian, **2**/48, 130; Humph, **2**/284; Jasper, p. 266; Jasper, justice, **1**/271; Joan, **1**/352; John, **1**/121; Leigh, **1**/352; **2**/48, 130*; **3**/73, 192; Lewis, **1**/121; Ric, **2**/265*; Thos, **3**/229*; Wm, **1**/147, 517; —, **3**/73

Jans, Janes *see* Jeynes

Jaquies (Jaques), Aaron, **2**/202; **3**/19, 46, 319, 337, 369; Dan, **2**/360; John, **2**/360; Mary, **3**/19, 46, 319, 337, 369; Ric, **2**/202

Jayne (Jeanes, Jeenes) *see* Jeynes

Jefferies (Geffreys, Jefferis, Jefferyes, Jeffreys, Jeffryes), Henry, **3**/320; John, **1**/247, 359*, 550; **3**/269; Mary, **3**/320; Ric, **1**/9*, 229, 311; Rob, **1**/247; Thos, **1**/229, 550; Wm, **3**/269; —, **1**/311

Jeffs (Jeffes), Edw, **3**/334, 383; John, **2**/235, 298; Mary, **3**/30, 35, 100; Ric, **2**/298; Thos, **3**/334, 383; Wm, **2**/235; **3**/30, 35, 100

Jelfe (Gelf), Eliz, **2**/167, 169; **3**/71, 221; Geo, **2**/176; Henry, **3**/260; Jas, **3**/59*; John, **1**/122; Oliver, **3**/59; Ric, **2**/176, 184*; **3**/260; Thos, **1**/122, 486; **2**/167, 169; **3**/59, 221; Wal, **3**/55; Wm, **1**/486; **3**/55

Jeninge (Jeninges, Jenings) *see* Jennings

Jenkins, John, **1**/451; Ric, **3**/94*; Rob, **1**/451; Wm, **2**/11*; **3**/68*

Jennings (Jeninge, Jeninges, Jenings), Abigail, **3**/344; Alice, **1**/159, 291, 333, 352, 534; **2**/2, 34, 61, 74, 117; p. xxvii; Alice (*alias* Pincke), **2**/39; Anne, **1**/43; **3**/310, 351, 397; Brian, **1**/159, 291, 333, 352, 534; **2**/117; Bridget, **2**/56, 122, 156, 254*; Chris, **1**/43; Henry, **1**/277; **2**/313; **3**/140, 295*n*, 367*; Isaac, **3**/365*n*; Jane, **3**/117; Jeremiah, **3**/310, 351, 397*; John, **1**/105, 178*; **2**/254; **3**/117, 281*n*, 295*n**; Marg, **3**/206, 294, 306, 394; Martha, **1**/433; Mary, **2**/340; Michael, **3**/140, 344; Ric, **2**/313; **3**/206, 294, 295*n**, 306; Roland, **1**/105; Thos, **1**/277; **2**/340; Wm, **1**/433, 585; **2**/56, 122*, 156, 254*, 377*; p. xxiii; —, **1**/585

Jewett, Peter, **3**/22*, 57, 70; Thos, **3**/57, 70

Jeynes (Janes, Jans, Jayne, Jeanes, Jeenes, Jeyne), Eliz, **1**/262, 301; Joan, **1**/161; John, **3**/83; Martha, **3**/381; Matt, **1**/262; Ric, **1**/262; Thos, **1**/262; **3**/83, 381; Wm, **1**/117*–18*, 161, 301, 556*n**

Jobbins Jas, **3**/110, 188; Thos, **3**/110, 188; Wm, **2**/218*

Johns (Johnes) *see* Jones

Johnson (Johnsons, Jonson), Harman, **1**/304; Jas, **2**/45; John, **1**/273; Michael, **3**/349; Sam, **3**/349; Thos, **2**/45; Tim, **1**/304; Wm, **1**/2*, 54*, 273

Jonas (*alias* Penson), Wm, p. 270

Jones (Johnes, Johns, Joones), Alice, **2**/184, 187, 195, 197, 373; Anne, **2**/376; **3**/261, 352, 364; Arthur, **2**/227; Chas, **3**/179*n*, 352, 364; David, **1**/13, 54, 100, 180, 342, 377; **2**/129; Edm, **2**/262, 268; Edw, **2**/7*; Eliz, **1**/258; **2**/11; Emmanuel, **1**/113, 258; Evan, **1**/210; Francis, **1**/326; Geo, **3**/133; Giles, **1**/210, 467; Henry, **1**/326; **2**/344; **3**/11; Hugh, **1**/495; Iorwerth, **1**/432; Jas, **1**/467*n*, 468; **2**/226*n*, 227; **3**/209, 216, 261; Jane, **1**/259, 342; **3**/368; Joan, **1**/64, 178, 228; **2**/375; John, **1**/24, 54, 100–1, 108*, 181, 197, 211, 342, 376*, 377, 467; **2**/57*, 129, 155, 184, 187, 195, 197,

INDEX OF PERSONS

262, 268, 344, 369; **3**/11, 240*; pp. 267, 272; John (*alias* Watts), **2**/305; John, alderman, **1**/377, justice, **1**/328, mayor, **1**/129, 279, 345–6, 358; Joseph, **3**/314; Lewis, **1**/125, 147, 432; Marg, **1**/7; **2**/155; Margery, **2**/344*; Martha, **3**/370; Mary, **2**/372; Moses, **1**/180; Nat, **1**/177; **3**/387; Nic, **1**/36; Peter, **2**/249; Rebecca, **1**/376; Ric, **1**/16, 36; **2**/40*n*, 41, 243*; **3**/69; p. 271; Ric (*alias* Watts), **2**/305; Rob, **1**/16; **2**/33; **3**/69; p. 269; Sam, **1**/113, 177; **2**/95, 201; Thos, **1**/7, 181, 211, 247*, 374, 476*, 495; **2**/11, 41, 201, 344*; **3**/133, 203*, 368, 370; Wm, **1**/64, 71, 159, 162, 178, 228, 259, 330, 341*n*, 342, 374, 376, 467*n*, 468*, 572*; **2**/2*n*, 7, 95, 154*, 193, 249, 344*; **3**/358*; p. xxiv; Wm (*alias* Abbotts), **2**/154*n;* Wm (*alias* Gitto), **1**/417

Jonson *see* Johnson

Jonsy, Jas, **3**/364*n*

Joones *see* Jones

Jordan (Jorden), Alice, **2**/310, 339; **3**/15, 46; Anne, **1**/76; **2**/200, 306, 332; **3**/32; Edw, **1**/334; Eleanor, **1**/462; Eliz, **2**/107; Jane, **1**/463; John, **1**/334, 460, 462; **2**/100*n*, 107, 200, 270*, 306, 322, 331–2; **3**/46; Kath, **2**/171, 225; Mary, **1**/460; Thos, **1**/76, 96*, 239, 538*, 581; **3**/32; Toby, mayor, **2**/247, sheriff, **1**/567; Wm, **1**/239, 463, 578*, 581; **2**/171, 225, 310, 331, 339; **3**/15, 46*, 237, 395; Wm, sheriff, **3**/80, mayor, **3**/259; —, **2**/100*n*, 270

Joseph, Thos, **2**/364*

Joy, David, **3**/345; John, **3**/345

Joyner, Giles, **1**/282, 393; Lawr, **1**/525; Thos, **1**/282, 525; —, **1**/393

Kare *see* Kear
Kay *see* Key
Kayse *see* Keyse

Keare (Kare), Alice, **2**/370; **3**/9–10, 17; Anne, **3**/270, 315; Eliz, **1**/21; Henry, **2**/54; John, **1**/21; **2**/123, 370; **3**/9–10, 17, 270, 315; Thos, **2**/54, 123

Kearsey (Kearsy, Kersey), Anne, **3**/368; Ric, **2**/108; **3**/107; Thos, **2**/108; **3**/107, 368

Keeble (Keble, Kible), Agnes, **1**/87; Bernard, **1**/345; John, p. 273; Mary, **1**/428; Thos, **1**/87; Toby, **1**/407, 428; **2**/63*n*; Wm, **1**/345; —, **2**/63*n*

Keele, Jas, **3**/61*; Nic, **1**/199; Rob, **1**/199

Keene (Kene), Ant, **1**/94; Francis, **2**/250; Joan, **1**/94, 250; John, **1**/94, 148, 501*; **2**/25, 85, 92*; **3**/356; p. 269; Joseph, **2**/250; Miles, **1**/94, 250; Susannah, **1**/501; Tacey, **2**/92; Wm, **1**/148; **2**/25, 85; **3**/356; *and see* Kinne

Kemble, John, **1**/435; Wm, **1**/435

Kemp (Kempe), Jane, **1**/119; John, **1**/382*, 404*n*, 405; Thos, **1**/119

Kemplea, Thos, **3**/102*n*

Kendricke, Sam, **3**/369*n*

Kene *see* Keene

Kent, Alice, **1**/315; Giles, **2**/219; Hannah, **3**/350; Jane, **3**/334, 368; John, **2**/130; Sam, **2**/130; **3**/309, 334, 368; Thos, **2**/219; Wm, **1**/315

Kerby *see* Kirby

Kercombe *see* Kircombe

Kerke *see* Kirke

Kerry, John, **1**/135; Wm, **1**/135

Kersey *see* Kearsey

Kettle, Thos, **2**/185*

Key (Kay), Edw, **1**/9, 120, 198; p. xv; Grace, **1**/9; Grisegan (Grisgard), **1**/120, 198; Joan, **1**/21, 80*; Thos, **1**/21

Keylock (Keylocke), Jas, **1**/169; John, **3**/248–9; Ric, sheriff, **1**/360; Thos, **3**/248–9; Wm, **1**/169

Keyse (Kayse, Keys), John, **1**/135*, 567; **3**/56*, 67, 363; Joseph, **3**/67; Patrick, **3**/363; Wm, **1**/567; *and see* Caise

Kible *see* Keeble

Kiddon (Kydden, Kydon), Chas, **1**/367, 472; Eleanor, **1**/137, 406, 435; Mary, **1**/367, 472; Rob, **1**/137, 351, 406, 435

Kifte *see* Kiste

Killmister (Killmester), Alan, **2**/161*; **3**/60; Jane, **3**/60

King (Kinge, Kinges), Anne, **1**/446; Chris, **1**/347, 431; Eliz, **3**/129; Giles, **2**/335; Henry, **1**/200; **3**/222*n*; p. 272; Isobel, **2**/232; Jas, **2**/148, 199, 226*n**, 232*; **3**/301; Joan, **1**/431; John, **1**/446; **2**/232, 335; **3**/293*n*, 295*, 301, 323*, 399; Mary, **2**/110, 197, 293; Phoebe, **2**/140, 179, 287; **3**/12; Ric, **2**/109; Sam, **2**/110*, 197, 293; Simon, **1**/200; Stephen, **3**/398*; Thos, **1**/148; **2**/109, 299*; **3**/399; p. 272; Wm, **2**/140, 179, 286*n*, 287*; **3**/12, 129, 192; p. 267

Kingman, Anne, **3**/370; Jas, **3**/383; John, **3**/308*, 370, 383

Kingscoate (Kingscoote), Chas, **1**/545; Mary, **1**/545

Kinne, Edw, **1**/499; Sam, **1**/499; *and see* Keene; Kynner

Kirby (Kerby, Kirbie), Edw, **1**/228; John, **1**/11*; Marg, **1**/105, 319; Rob, **1**/228; Thos, **1**/105; Thos, sheriff, **1**/111

Kircombe (Kercombe), John, **1**/178, 579*; **2**/70; Joyce, **1**/579; **2**/70; Thos, **1**/178, 574*n*, 579

Kirke (Kerke), Joan, **1**/306; Ric, **1**/207, 300, 306; Thos, **1**/207

Kiste (Kifte, Kyste), Edw, **1**/24, 30, 97, 123, 142, 295, 351; Eliz, **1**/123; Juliana, **1**/24, 30, 97, 142, 295

INDEX OF PERSONS

Knight (Knighte), Edw, **1**/146, 324, 456; Eleanor, **1**/541; Geo, **2**/292; Henry, **1**/442*, 512; **2**/76; pp. xxx, 273; Jas, **1**/541; **2**/46; Joan, **1**/400, 456; **2**/18–19; John, **2**/292; Kath, **2**/46; Nat, **1**/324, 400, 456; **2**/18–19; Prudence, **2**/76; p. xxx; Ric, **1**/512; **3**/28; Rob, **1**/456, 553; p. 271; Thos, **3**/19*, 28, 39*n*; Wm, **1**/146; —, **1**/553; p. 269

Knipe, Chris, **1**/513*n*, 514*; Edw, **1**/107; Joan, **1**/514; John, **1**/107, 513*n*, 514; **2**/36; Simon, **1**/574*n*, 576; Wm, **1**/576 ; —, **2**/36

Knott, Eliz, **3**/54, 145; Geo, **3**/54, 249; Henry, **3**/43; Jane, **3**/40*n*, 249; Lawr, **3**/54, 145*, 225; Nathan, **3**/225; Nic, **3**/54; Wm, **3**/40*n*, 43

Knowles, Anne, **1**/584; Edw, **2**/302; Henry, **1**/584; **2**/298*, 332*; **3**/88, 214, 291; p. 273; John, **1**/35, 441; **2**/302, 332; Mary, **1**/35; **2**/298, 332; Ric, **1**/106*, 441; Ric (Cowles), **3**/68; —, **3**/88

Kugley *see* Cugley

Kydden (Kydon) *see* Kiddon

Kym, John, p. 266*

Kynner, Joan, **1**/145; Wm, **1**/145; *and see* Kinne

Kyste *see* Kiste

Lacy (Lacye), John, **1**/279, 281; Wm, **1**/279; **2**/229*

Ladde, John, **1**/13; Wm, **1**/13

Lamb (Lambe), Joyce, **2**/124; Wm, **2**/124; Wm, mayor, **3**/252, sheriff, **3**/66

Lambert, John, **1**/67*; **2**/93, 236; Peter, **2**/236; Sylvester, **2**/93; *and see* Lumbert

Lanckford *see* Langford

Land (Lande), Ric, **2**/7; Rob, **2**/7; Thos, **3**/385*

Lander (Launder), Jas, **3**/314, 336*, 375*; Thos, **3**/314, 347; Wm, **1**/34*

Lane, Anne, **1**/124; **3**/390; Brian, **2**/135; Cecily, **1**/35; Edw, **1**/157; Eliz, **1**/307–8, 345, 361, 363; Henry, **1**/308; Hester, **3**/375, 391; Isobel, **1**/334; **2**/308, 351; Joan, **1**/4, 25; John, **1**/98*, 129, 262, 307, 308*, 335*, 345, 361, 363, 489*; **2**/333*n*, 335–6; **3**/375, 390*, 393*n*; Kath, **1**/399, 408, 469, 481, 509; **2**/44; Mary, **3**/271; Mic, **1**/157; Nic, **2**/36, 206; **3**/271*, 375, 391; Nic, sheriff, **3**/140; Ric, **1**/4, 25, 116; **3**/32, 271, 390; Rob, **2**/336; Sam, **1**/4; **2**/135; Sarah, **3**/375; Susannah, **2**/5; Thos, **1**/4; **2**/42, 51, 218, 308, 351; Wal, **1**/258*, 334; **2**/36, 42; Wal, sheriff, **1**/579; **2**/1; Wm, **1**/35, 124, 129, 199, 262, 399, 408, 469, 481, 509; **2**/5, 44; **3**/32; —, **2**/206, 218

Lange, Jas, **2**/297*

Langford (Lanckford, Langeford, Langforde), Anne, **1**/73; Edw, **1**/212; Eleanor, **1**/179; Henry, **1**/49; John, **1**/92, 105; **2**/342; Nic, **1**/3*, 49, 73, 105, 136, 212; Nic, sheriff, **1**/19, 103; Ralph, **1**/24, 92; Rob, **1**/24; Toby, **1**/122; 179; **2**/342*; **3**/199; p. 272; Toby, sheriff, **2**/291; —, **1**/122, 136

Latton, Francis, **1**/317; John, **1**/317

Launder *see* Lander

Laurence *see* Lawrence

Law, Thos, **2**/372

Lawrence (Laurence, Lawrrance) Ant, **3**/272; Eleazor, **3**/400; Geo, **1**/311*, 487; Henry, **1**/182; Marg, **3**/400; Nic, **2**/73; Rob, **1**/487; **2**/313; Simon, **3**/72; Thos, **1**/180*–1*, 182; **2**/73, 373; **3**/84, 272, 400; p. xxiii; Wm, **3**/72, 84, 345, 400; —, **2**/313

Layton, Jonathan, **2**/334; Joseph, **2**/334; Ric, **3**/389; Wm, **3**/389,

Lea (Lee, Leigh), Ant, **2**/2*n*, 4; **3**/63; Eliz, **3**/373; Francis, **1**/259, 405, 438, 479, 494, 562, 564; **2**/4, 26, 98; p. 270; Henry, **1**/259, 479*; **2**/98, 276; **3**/14, 267, 301*n*; Isobel, **1**/405, 438, 494; Jas, **3**/192; p. 270; Joan, **1**/562; **3**/14; John, **3**/373*, 399*n*; Rob, **2**/98; **3**/192; Thos, **3**/267, 301*n*; Wm, **3**/373; —, **1**/479, 564; **2**/276; **3**/63; *and see* Lye

Leader, Henry, **1**/301*

Leavens (Leavon, Levens), Ant, **1**/295, 330; John, **1**/295; Thos, **1**/330*

Lee (Leigh) *see* Lea

Lemster, Ric, **2**/157; Wm, **2**/157

Lenthall, Wm, p. 269

Levens *see* Leavens

Lewis (Lewes, Lews), Abel, **1**/569*; **2**/38, 185, 211, 240, 293; **3**/163*n*, 285, 324, 332–3; Adam, **3**/188; Alice, **2**/199; Edw, **3**/324; Eliz, **2**/185, 211, 293; Humph, **1**/108; Jas, **2**/133; **3**/299*; Joan, **1**/569; **2**/38; John, **1**/54*, 569; **2**/133, 199*; **3**/20, 142*n*, 143*, 285*, 289*; Miles, **3**/20; Nat, **1**/365; Ric, **1**/147; **3**/285, 332–3; Rob, **1**/509; Thos, **1**/108, 356; **3**/321; Wal, **2**/155; **3**/188; Wm, **1**/257*, 509; **2**/155; —, **2**/240

Ley *see* Lye

License *see* Lysons

Liddiat, Thos (*alias* Brewer), **1**/16*

Lightfoot (Lightfoote), Joan, **1**/7; Mark, **3**/345; Wm, **1**/7; **3**/345

Limbricke, John, **2**/134; Ric, **2**/134

Lincecombe *see* Lindsecom

Linckinholt (Linckingholt) *see* Linkenholt

Lindsecom (Lincecombe), John, **1**/22; Sam, **1**/35; Wm, **1**/22, 35

Linkenholt (Linckinholt, Linckingholt, Linkinholte), Eliz, **1**/520; **2**/35, 68, 172–3; John, **1**/317, 482, 510–11; **2**/35*, 113*; Sarah, **1**/482, 510–11; Thos, **1**/317; p. 273; Wm, **1**/520; **2**/35, 68, 172–3; p. 272

Linnet, John, **1**/120; Ric, **1**/120

Lisney, Ric, **1**/363*

INDEX OF PERSONS

Little (Litle), Anne, **1**/493; Henry, **2**/180; John, **1**/385, 490; **2**/61*, 94; p. 267; John, sheriff, **1**/39; Rob, **1**/328*; **2**/86; Thos, **1**/385, 490, 493; **2**/86; Wm, **1**/63*; **2**/94, 180

Llewellyn (Llewellin), Alice, **1**/392; John, **1**/392, 393*

Lloyde (Lloyd), Cecily, **1**/238; John, **1**/111*, 238; p. 266; Thos, **2**/8; Wal, **2**/8; *and see* Floyd

Loader, Henry, **1**/329; John, **1**/329

Locksmith, Wm, sheriff, **1**/157

Lodge, John, **3**/14, 394*n*; Mary, **3**/226; Trustram, **3**/14, 226, 319*; Wm, **3**/319

Loggins, Anne, **1**/378*; **2**/49; Augustine, **1**/548; **2**/49, 199*; Geo, **1**/548; John, **1**/378*; p. 267; Lawr, **1**/378; Ric, **2**/199*

Long (Longe), Ant, **2**/304; Edm, **1**/46; Gilbert, **2**/284; Giles, **1**/135, 316*; **3**/212*; Henry, **1**/46; Humph, **1**/304*, 379; p. xx; Jas, **1**/403, 406; John, **1**/406, 513; **2**/284, 300; Moses, **3**/212; Ric, **1**/135, 513; **2**/300; Rob, **1**/304, 379; Thos, **1**/403; **2**/296; **3**/382; p. 272; Wal, **2**/296; Wm, **2**/304; **3**/382

Longden (Longdon), Anne, **3**/159, 232, 272, 296–7, 360; Caple, **3**/360; Joan, **2**/65; John, **3**/223; Rob, **1**/404; **2**/65, 259*, 274; **3**/272; Rob, sheriff, **2**/320; Susannah, **3**/223; Thos, **1**/404; **2**/259; **3**/159, 232, 272*, 296–7, 360*; Thos, alderman, **3**/386, mayor, **3**/332, 357, sheriff, **3**/293; —, **2**/274

Longe *see* Long

Lord, Henry, **1**/373*; **2**/161; Jas, **2**/222; Ric, **2**/161, 222; **3**/272; p. 270; Sam, **3**/272

Lothingham, Joan, **1**/15, 20; John, **1**/15, 20

Lovegrove, Giles, **3**/376; John, **3**/376*

Lovell, Edw, **3**/109; John, **3**/109, 357; Sam, **3**/357; Wm, **2**/261*

Lovelock, Wm, **1**/179; Zacheus, **1**/179

Lovett, Eliz, **3**/213; Henry, **3**/213; Jas, **3**/15, 213, 364*n*; John, **3**/15*, 202, 204, 213; Mary, **3**/202, 204

Low (Lowe), Edw, **1**/498; Henry, **2**/173; John, **1**/498; Nat, **2**/173; Ric, **2**/68; Rob, **2**/68*, 86*; Thos, pp. 261–2; Sir Thos, p. 261

Loxlie, Wm, **2**/2*

Lucas (Lukas), Eliz, **1**/381, 548; **2**/14, 176, 338; **3**/356; Kath, **1**/47, 141; Rob, **1**/47, 141, 381, 548; **2**/338; Sam, **3**/356; Thos, **2**/14, 176, 338*; p. 272

Ludlow (Ludlo), Chris, **2**/301; Joseph, **2**/152, 301; Stephen, **2**/152, 301; — **2**/301

Ludnam, John, **2**/304; —, **2**/304

Lugg (Lug, Lugge), Alice, **3**/58; Anne, **1**/321, 325, 389, 399, 423, 425, 452, 503, 506, 509, 525, 548; **2**/27; Edw, **3**/65, 359; Eleanor, **1**/263, 284–5, 316, 319, 339, 344, 363–4, 407–8, 482, 495, 498, 529, 536, 552, 561, 569; **2**/237; Eliz, **2**/256, 338; **3**/175, 203, 264, 331; Hannah, **2**/361; Henry, **3**/250*n*; Jas, **3**/295*n*, 306; Jane, **1**/406, 458; Jasper, **1**/503*, 506, 509, 525, 548; **2**/44; **3**/29*n*, 31, 58; p. 271; Joan, **1**/95, 383; **2**/272; **3**/47, 55; John, **1**/134, 322, 362, 406, 458, 536*n*, 544; **2**/23, 25*n*, 125–6, 133, 142, 226*n*, 229*, 339*, 370; **3**/26, 206, 218*n**, 221*, 306, 359, 385*; Juliana, **1**/227; Lawr, **1**/389, 425, 482, 491; **2**/9*, 256, 338; **3**/175, 203, 264, 331; p. 270; Marg, **1**/19, 136, 162, 159, 178, 293; Mary, **1**/425, 482, 491, 499; **2**/125–6, 133, 142, 339, 370; Peter, **1**/85, 134, 178, 293, 362*, 458*; **3**/206; Peter, sheriff, **1**/327, 337*; Ric, **1**/95, 311, 383, 467*n*, 536*n*, 544; **3**/69*n*; p. 271; Sam, **2**/364*n*; **3**/26, 213; Sarah, **2**/365; **3**/213; Toby, **1**/87; Thos, **1**/87, 134, 227, 293, 321, 325, 383, 399, 423, 425, 452*, 499, 563; **2**/23, 75*, 94*, 272, 365; **3**/29*n*, 31, 47, 55; p. 270; Thos, sheriff, **2**/28; Wm, **1**/19, 136, 159, 162, 255, 263, 284–5, 293, 316, 319, 339, 344, 363–4, 400, 407–8, 482, 495, 498, 529, 536, 552, 561, 569; **2**/44, 237, 361; **3**/64*n*, 65; Wm, mayor, **1**/480, sheriff, **1**/267; Mr, p. 270; —, **1**/134, 311, 322, 467*n*, 563; **3**/201*n*, 244*n*; p. 270

Lukas *see* Lucas

Lumbard (Lumbert), Isaac, **2**/283, 351; **3**/100; Jas, **2**/283; Jane, **2**/283; Wm, **2**/283; —, **2**/351; **3**/100; *and see* Lambert

Lund, Hester, **1**/519; Wal, **1**/519

Lustie, Jas, **1**/69; Ric, **1**/69

Luther (Luter), Eliz, **3**/393; John, **3**/313*, 393

Lycense *see* Lysons

Lye (Ley), Francis, **2**/70, 371; Giles, **1**/554; **2**/20, 200*, 304, 325; p. 271; Henry, **2**/70; Hester (Esther), **1**/554; **2**/20, 200*, 304, 325; John, **2**/371; Sam, **2**/200; **3**/57, 234; Sam, sheriff, **3**/315; Sarah, **3**/57; Thos, **1**/331; **3**/373*; Wm, **1**/131, 331; *and see* Lea

Lysons (License, Lysance, Lycense, Lysence), Chris, **1**/101, 105; Dan, **1**/457, 544; **2**/37, 119, 136, 221*, 256; **3**/22; p. 270; Dan, sheriff, **2**/65; Edm, 101; Edw, **1**/105, 143*; Henry, **1**/343; Miles, **1**/343; Sarah, **1**/544; **2**/37, 119, 136, 221, 256; **3**/22; Silvanus, **3**/216; Thos, **3**/216 ; —, **1**/457; family, p. xxxi

Mace, Ferdinand, **1**/172; John, **1**/172

Machen (Machien, Machin, Meachen), Henry, **1**/297; Jas, **1**/297, 342; p. 270; John, **1**/188–9; Kath, **1**/342; Thos, **1**/188–9; p. 267; Thos, mayor, **1**/91; Wm, p. 267

Maddinge, John, **2**/293*b**

Maddock (Maddocke, Maddockes, Maddocks, Madock, Madocke), Jas, **2**/254; Jane, **3**/31; John, **1**/25, 33, 35, 70, 124, 247; **2**/254; p. 268; John, sheriff, **1**/61, 504, mayor, **2**/28; Juliana, **1**/70; Lewis, **1**/35; Marg, **1**/25, 124; Ric, **1**/370; **2**/261; Sarah, **2**/3, 138, 178, 299, 339; **3**/105; Thos, **1**/247, 280; **2**/261; **3**/230, 321, 373; Wal, **3**/230, 284; Wm, **1**/33, 280, 370, 452*n*; **2**/3, 138, 178, 299, 339; **3**/31, 105, 284, 373; —, **1**/452*n*

Mager *see* Mayer

Maio *see* Mayo

Mairis *see* Mayris

Major *see* Mayer

Makepeace, John, **3**/323; Sam, **3**/323

Maltby (bookbinders) of Oxford, p. xxx

Mamby (Mandbee), John, **3**/201*, 399*n*

Man *see* Mann

Mandbee *see* Mamby

Manington, John, **2**/174*

Mann (Man, Manns, Mans), Edw, **3**/346; Francis, **1**/289, 171; Geo, **3**/314; Jas, **3**/68*, 346; John, **2**/306; **3**/346; Joseph, **3**/314; Mary, **3**/68, 346; Ric, **1**/580; **3**/20*, 66*; Rob, **1**/289; **2**/306; Thos, **1**/171; **3**/393*; Toby, **1**/580

Manning (Manninge, Monning), Isaac, **2**/127; **3**/272*n*, 275, 359; John, **3**/261, 354*n*; Sam, **1**/348, 418; **3**/275; **2**/126*, 127; p. xix; Thos, **3**/207*, 261; Toby, **1**/348; Wm, **3**/359

Manns (Mans) *see* Mann

Marckle, John, **1**/66; Marg, **1**/66

Marden (Mardin), Giles, **2**/113, 283*; **3**/261; John, **3**/283; Marg, **3**/261; Ric, **3**/67; Thos, **2**/113; Wm, **3**/283, 381*n*, 390*

Mardey, John, **1**/249; Wm, **1**/249

Mardin *see* Marden

Marowe, Benj, **2**/320; Thos, **2**/320; *and see* Mero; Merry

Marsh (Marshe), Henry, **1**/457; Wm, **1**/457; p. 273

Marshall, Cath, **1**/200; Geo, **2**/273; Henry, **1**/200; Joan, **1**/16; John, **1**/16; Sybil, **1**/63, 104; Thos, **1**/63, 104; **2**/273; **3**/260*

Marshe *see* Marsh

Marshfield, Jas, **3**/361; Mary, **3**/361; *and see* Masfield

Marson Edw, **1**/181; Ralph, **1**/181; *and see* Mason

Marston, Edw, **1**/289; Geo, **2**/124; John, **2**/80*, 124, 295; **3**/51; John, sheriff, **2**/360; **3**/172; Rebecca, **2**/295; **3**/51

Marten *see* Martin

Martimer, Giles, **1**/92; Thos, **1**/92

Martin (Marten, Martyn), Abraham, **2**/14; Alex, **2**/35; Arthur, **2**/210; Ewen, **2**/14; Geo, **1**/159, 278; **2**/3, 364*n*; **3**/10*; p. 269; Henry, **1**/12; **2**/3; Jane, **2**/83; John, **1**/159, 466, 570; **2**/9, 35, 83; **3**/121*n*; p. 273; Kath, **3**/68, 191, 286; Marg, **1**/278; Mary, **3**/10; Miles, **1**/466; Ric, **1**/12; Thos, **1**/278, 570; **2**/362*; **3**/68, 191, 200, 286, 332; Wm, **1**/278; **2**/210; p. 273; widow, p. 269; —, **2**/9, 364*n*

Martley, Anne, **2**/256, 264, 346, 368; **3**/26, 31*, 54; Ant, **2**/256, 264, 346; **3**/26, 54; John, **2**/368; **3**/31 *and see* Motley

Martyn *see* Martin

Masfield (Mashfield), Giles, **1**/293; John (*alias* Garner), **1**/293; Thos, **1**/335*; *and see* Marshfield

Mason, Adam, **3**/388*n*; Alice, **1**/35, 382, 430, 479, 528; Deenes, **1**/178; Edw, **1**/109, 306, 382, 405, 430, 479, 528*; **2**/199; **3**/219; John, **1**/35, 478; Marg, **1**/52, 169; Mary, **1**/5; **3**/253, 273, 377*; Ric, **1**/476*n**, 478; **3**/161*n*, 219; Rob, **1**/52, 178; Thos, **1**/5, 479*, 584*; **2**/138; Wal, **3**/395*; Wm, **1**/52*, 109, 169; **3**/344*, 375*; —, **1**/306; **2**/138; *and see* Marson

Massey, Joan, **1**/502; Ric, **1**/502

Massinger (Messinger), Anne, **2**/228; Arthur, **1**/227; Chris, **1**/3; Eleanor, **1**/227; John, **1**/3; Marg, **1**/532; **2**/53, 89; Ric, **1**/532; **2**/53, 89; Ric, sheriff, **2**/231; Rob, **1**/397; Wm, **1**/461; **2**/228; **3**/188*; pp. 268, 273; Wm, sheriff, **3**/34; Witherston, **1**/396*n*, 397, 461, 474, 494*

Massock (Massocke), John, **1**/66*

Masters, Wm, **1**/280*

Mathews (Mathewes, Matthews), Anne, **3**/277; Dorcas, **3**/395; Edw, **3**/276; Eliz, **1**/329; Giles, **1**/587; **3**/384; Henry, **1**/374, 500; **2**/71, 226*; p. 270; Jas, **3**/102; Jane, **2**/376; Joan, **1**/500; **2**/283; John, **1**/329*, 521; **2**/181, 283*, 325*n*, 328*; **3**/20*, 27*, 102, 239, 244–5, 276–7, 313, 395; Marg, **2**/181, 328; Mary, **3**/109, 131; Matt, **2**/283; Nic, **1**/450; Ric, **1**/374, 450, 521; **3**/109, 244; Susannah, **3**/384; Thos, **1**/329, 346*, 442, 587; **2**/299; **3**/131, 355; Wm, **2**/109*, 299; **3**/109*, 131*, 239, 245, 384*n*

Matley *see* Motley

Matthews *see* Mathews

Mauncell, Wm, p. 267

Maverly, Barbara, **3**/301; Thos, **3**/311; Wm, **3**/301, 311

May, John, **3**/360; Thos, **2**/367*; **3**/360

Mayden, Humph, **1**/315; John, **1**/315

Mayer (Mager, Major, Mayor), Giles, **1**/396, 427; Mary, **1**/396, 427; Thos, p. 273; Wm, **1**/84*, 92

Mayo (Maio, Mayoe), Abraham, **1**/119, 146, 212; Alice, **1**/119, 146, 212; Edw, **1**/573; Gregory, **1**/201; Guy, **1**/201; Henry, **1**/573; John, **2**/253; **3**/104*, 309; p. 266; Lawr, **1**/212; Ric, **3**/309; Rob, **1**/212; Wm, **1**/277; **2**/253; **3**/289*

INDEX OF PERSONS 303

Mayor *see* Mayer
Mayris (Mairis), Chas, **2**/307*; **3**/16, 134, 245; Eliz, **3**/16, 134, 245; —, **2**/307
Maysey (Maysee, Mayzee, Meysey), Benj, **3**/89; John, **3**/89; Ralph, **1**/160, 179; Theophilus, **1**/160, 179; p. xx
Meachen *see* Machen
Meadway *see* Medway
Mearson, Nic, **2**/65*
Medhopp, John, **1**/302; Roger, **1**/302
Medway (Meadway), Abraham, **3**/270, 317, 333, 384, 398; Edw, **3**/71; Henry, **2**/343*; **3**/71*, 176, 302*n**, 304*, 379; John, **2**/343; Joseph, **3**/379; Mary, **2**/343; **3**/71, 270, 333, 384, 398; Sarah, **3**/176
Meek (Meeke), Dan, **3**/372*n*; Edw, **3**/162, 290, 301*n*; Frances, **3**/280, 295; Margery, **2**/93, 195, 305, 328, 361; **3**/28, 104; Mary, **3**/233; Philip, **2**/227; Ric, **2**/227; Thos, **2**/93, 195, 305*, 328, 361; **3**/28, 104, 233, 280*, 290, 295, 301*n*; Wm, **3**/162
Mercer (Merser), Henry, **2**/78; Mary, **1**/106; Rob, **1**/106, 212, 272*; **2**/78, 248; Wm, **1**/212*, 396*; —, **2**/248
Merchant, Henry, **3**/354; John, **3**/354
Meredith *alias* Younge, Marg, **1**/141; Wm, **1**/141
Merewether, Ric, **1**/124; Sam, **1**/124
Mericke *see* Merrick
Meringe, Joan, **1**/72, 170, 173; Ric, **1**/72, 170, 173
Mero (Meroe, Merro, Murrowe), Alice, **1**/312*, 335, 349; Joan, **1**/422; John, **1**/312; Ric, **1**/312*, 330*, 335, 349, 422; *and see* Marowe; Merry
Merrett (Merret, Merritt), Ant, **2**/346; Chris, **1**/341; Clement, **2**/346, 365; Dan, **3**/142; Edm, **1**/285; Geo, **1**/341; p. 272; Giles, **3**/349; Hester (Esther), **2**/103, 203, 269, 273; John, **1**/208, 310; **2**/124; **3**/310; Joseph, **2**/370; Kath, **2**/372; Mary, **2**/324, 346, 365; **3**/19, 30; Peter, **2**/346; Ric, **1**/44, 285, 310, 464; **2**/53, 370; **3**/81, 142; Sam, **3**/81, 310; Thos, **1**/44, 208, 310*, 464, 549*; **2**/53, 92, 103, 124, 203, 269, 273, 293*b*, 324; **3**/19, 29*n**, 30*, 301*, 349; Wm, **2**/101; **3**/196*n*; —, **2**/55*n*, 293
Merrick (Mericke, Merricke), Geo, **2**/100; Henry, **1**/73; Humph, **1**/52*, 261; **2**/100; John, **3**/289; Kath, **2**/372; Lewis, **1**/52; Ric, **3**/289; Thos, **1**/261; **2**/158; Wal, **2**/158
Merrie *see* Merry
Merritt *see* Merrett
Merro *see* Mero
Merry (Merrie, Mirrie), Humph, **3**/39*n*, 44*; John, **3**/40*, 74, 393*n*; Ric, **1**/145; **3**/158*; Thos, **1**/145; **3**/74; Wm, **3**/29*; *and see* Marowe; Mero
Merryman, Chas, **1**/585; Edw, **3**/313; John, **1**/585;

Newman, **3**/313
Merser *see* Mercer
Messinger *see* Massinger
Meysey *see* Maysey
Michell *see* Mitchell
Micklewright, Joan, **1**/38, 79; Wal, **1**/38, 79
Middlewright (Midlewrighte), Humph, **1**/367; Joan, **1**/172*; John, **1**/359; Leonard, **1**/359; Thos, **1**/367; Wal, **1**/172*
Miles (Mill) *see* Mills
Millard (Millards), John, **1**/277; Ric, **1**/277; Rob, **3**/295*n*; Thos, **3**/295*n*
Millechep, Ric, **1**/359; Thos, **1**/359
Mills (Miles, Mill), Anne, **1**/454; **2**/233; Bart, **2**/48; Dorothy, **2**/114, 360; Edw, **1**/345; **2**/183, 204*n*; **3**/62; Eliz, **3**/304; Giles, **2**/95, 177; Hannah, **1**/366, 389, 435; **2**/156, 250; Henry, **2**/224; Hester, **2**/320*; Humph, **1**/345; Jas, **1**/574; **2**/114, 235, 360; **3**/172*, 301*n*; Jeremiah, **3**/89*; John, **1**/425, 547*, 551; **2**/61; **3**/29*, 301*n*; p. 272; Marg, **3**/244, 309; Mary, **2**/61, 175; Matt, **2**/147; Ric, **1**/366, 389, 435, 454, 548; **2**/147, 170, 180, 233, 250; Sam, **2**/167, 175; Thos, **1**/404, 551; **2**/19, 95, 156, 177, 192, 320*; **3**/62, 70, 244, 309, 386*; Thos, sheriff, **3**/184; Toby, **2**/183, 224; p. 272; Wal, **3**/178*n*, 304; Wm, **1**/404, 425, 548, 574; **2**/19, 48, 135*, 147; **3**/227*n*; —, **2**/147, 167, 170, 180, 235; **3**/70
Milton, John, **1**/246; **2**/301; Reginald, **1**/65; Rob, **1**/65; Wm, **1**/246; **2**/301
Mince, John, **3**/360*
Minchin (Minchyn, Mynchin), Ant, **2**/364; Giles, **3**/37; John, **2**/364; **3**/37; Michael, **1**/161; Ric, **1**/161
Mirrie *see* Merry
Mitchell (Michell), Comfort, **2**/73, 104, 106, 115, 124, 231; Edm, sheriff, **1**/337; Edw, p. 266; Eliz, **2**/274; Geo, **1**/447, 516; **2**/73, 104, 106, 115, 124, 231, 249, 274; **3**/41*, 193; Jeremiah, **3**/193; Ric, **1**/447, 516; Rob, **1**/122; Roger, **1**/122
Molgrave, John, **1**/62; Wal, **1**/62
Monley, Edw, **2**/242; John, **2**/242
Monning *see* Manning
Monnington, Thos, **3**/382
Monnsloe, Thos, **1**/67*
Moore (More), Alex, **1**/135, 386*, 426, 537; Eliz, **3**/264; Evan, **1**/313; Ferdinand, **1**/239; Geo, **2**/121; **3**/71, 142, 264; Gilbert, **1**/313, 467*n*; Henry, **1**/537; **2**/93, 137, 190, 222, 245; Jas, **3**/71; Jane, **3**/364; Joan, **1**/386; **2**/93, 137, 190, 222, 245; John, **1**/6*, 23, 32, 51, 386; **2**/310*; **3**/101*, 364; Jonathan, **1**/426; Marg, **1**/23, 32, 51; Mary, **1**/354; **2**/121; **3**/142; Thos, **1**/69, 135, 172*, 239, 354, 467*n*; Wm, **1**/9*

Moreton, Edw, **1**/322; John, **1**/322

Morgan, Eliz, **1**/167; Jas, **3**/189*; John, **2**/242; **3**/35; p. 271; Thos, **1**/3*; **2**/242; **3**/35; Wm, **1**/167

Moris *see* Morris

Morley, Jas, **2**/40; John, **2**/40

Morrall, John, **1**/268; Wm, **1**/268

Morris (Moris), David, **1**/210; Henry, **1**/210; John, **1**/430*; **2**/293; **3**/59; p. 267; Justinian, **3**/59; Kath, **2**/284, 293, 353; Ric, **1**/514; **2**/284, 293, 353; Rob, **2**/293; Wm, **1**/514; **2**/160*

Morse, Blanche, **2**/66; Eliz, **1**/126*, 161, 168; Humph, **1**/550; **2**/47, 63, 66; Lewis, **1**/314; Jas, **2**/79*n*, 80; John, **1**/314, 423; **2**/47, 260*n*, 264; **3**/107, 302*, 396; Marg, **1**/270, 293*, 300; Thos, **1**/44, 83, 126*, 161, 168, 181, 199, 270, 293*, 300, 407*n*, 423, 550; **2**/47, 79*n*, 80, 260*n*, 264; **3**/119*, 365*n*, 396; Thos, sheriff, **1**/321; Wal, **3**/107

Mosely, Chas, **3**/62; John, **3**/62

Motley (Matley, Motloe, Mutley, Mutlow, Mutlye), Ant, **2**/75; **3**/67, 364*n*, 387; Eleanor, **3**/387; Jas, **3**/226*; Joan, **2**/153; John, **1**/396*n*; **2**/153, 165; **3**/340, 364*n*, 367; Joyce, **2**/75; Miles, **2**/165; **3**/291*, 367*; Wm, **3**/340; —, **3**/67

Mount, John, **2**/198; **3**/21; Wm, **2**/198; **3**/21

Mountague, Geo, **3**/322; Henry, **3**/278; Wm, **3**/278, 322

Mous, Ric, **2**/19*

Mower, Eliz, **3**/277; John, **1**/478*; Ric, **1**/386; Thos, **1**/386; **3**/277

Mudwell, Rob, **1**/473, 491; Wm, **1**/473, 491

Munday, Toby, **3**/292*

Munns, Chas, **3**/298; Rob, **3**/298

Murrey, Ric, **1**/295

Murrowe *see* Mero

Mutlow (Mutley, Mutlye) *see* Motley

Mynchin *see* Minchin

Nash (Nashe), Anne, **2**/346; **3**/19, 106, 122, 215, 317, 334, 386; Anselm, **1**/493; Blanche, **1**/272, 281, 318; Eliz, **3**/56, 95, 147, 188–9, 197, 241, 303, 307; Geo, **3**/368; Hester, **2**/259, 273; Jesse, **1**/573; **2**/161, 259, 273, 351, 367; **3**/56, 95, 147, 188–9, 197, 241, 303, 307, 368; Joan, **2**/97, 104, 116, 171, 183, 206, 291, 301, 367; John, **2**/16*; Joseph, **2**/266; Mary, **2**/263, 272; Nat, **2**/346; Rebecca, **1**/542, 567; Ric, **1**/21*, 272, 281, 318, 493, 542, 567, 573; **2**/12, 97*, 104, 116, 171, 183, 206, 291, 295*, 301, 309*, 316, 346; **3**/19, 27, 51, 106, 122, 145, 215, 347, 378; p. 272; Seabright, **3**/145; Wm, **2**/97, 263, 266, 272, 346; **3**/27, 265*n*, 347, 378*; —, **2**/12, 161, 309, 316, 351; **3**/51

Neale, Arthur, **3**/213; Jas, **1**/372; John, **1**/372; **3**/207; Joseph, **3**/207; Thos, **3**/213

Neast (Nest), Alex, **1**/583; **2**/2, 73, 124; Barbara, **3**/309; Dan, **3**/175; Geo, **1**/572*; John, **3**/105*n*, 110*, 175, 266*n*, 269*, 309; Joseph, **2**/73, 124; Marg, **1**/583; **2**/2; Mary, **3**/388; Thos, **3**/324*; Wm, **3**/269, 388; —, **3**/269

Nelme (Nelmes), Ant, **1**/136; Giles, **2**/251*; Jasper, **3**/292, 332; Jeremiah, **1**/136; John, **1**/131*, 132, 158, 267, 276, 327, 360, 399, 468; John sheriff, **1**/471; Nic, **1**/276; Rachel, **1**/327, 360, 399, 468; Ric, **1**/365*, 420*, 583; **2**/103*; Rob, **3**/292; Thos, **1**/132; Wm, **1**/158, 288; —, **1**/158, 583

Nest *see* Neast

Nethaway (Netheway), Benj, **2**/271; Edw, **2**/193; Thos, **2**/193, 271

Newman, Alice, **1**/335, 338, 345, 452; Augustine, **2**/243, 354; Chris, **2**/282; Edw, **2**/281; Eliz, **2**/243, 354; Henry, **2**/282; John, **1**/337, 452; Ric, **1**/337; Rob, **2**/281; **3**/220; Sam, **3**/220, 304; Wm, **1**/143*, 335, 338, 345, 351, 452*

Niblet (Niblett), Dan, **3**/221; Henry, **3**/277; Jas, **3**/312; John, **1**/209, 474; **2**/60; **3**/277; Jonathan, **2**/60; Ric, **1**/237, 474; Sam, **3**/221, 312; Thos, **1**/209; Wm, **1**/237

Niccolls (Niccols) *see* Nicholls

Niccolson *see* Nicholson

Nicholls (Niccolls, Niccols, Nichols, Nickolls, Nicolls), Chas, **1**/104; Edw, **3**/298; Eliz, **1**/562; **3**/382; Geo, **2**/113; Joan, **1**/375, 388, 420, 445, 497, 508, 547; **2**/185, 306; **3**/172; John, **1**/105, 188*, 353, 375, 388, 420, 445, 497, 508, 547, 562, 587; **2**/27, 59, 65, 117, 191, 208, 247, 316*n*, 320, 364; **3**/27; Margery, **2**/226*n*; Mary, **1**/587; **2**/59, 65, 117, 191, 208, 247, 364; Otho, **2**/113; Reece, **2**/229; Ric, **2**/27, 320; Thos, **2**/226*n*, 229; **3**/27, 378*; Wal, **1**/104; Wm, **1**/105; **2**/185, 306; **3**/172, 298, 382; Wm, sheriff, **3**/330

Nicholson (Niccolson, Nickolson, Nicollson), Ant, **1**/119, 138; Chris, **1**/356; John, **1**/119; **3**/246; Knowles *alias* Knolles, **1**/356; Thos, **3**/246; Wm, **1**/138

Nickolls *see* Nicholls

Nickolson (Nicollson) *see* Nicholson

Nicolls *see* Nicholls

Nicollson *see* Nicholson

Norgrove, Jas, **3**/19*

Norman, Edw, **3**/48, 109*, 293; Jeremiah, **3**/211*n*; Joan, **3**/48, 109, 293; John, **2**/369; Wm, **2**/369

Norris, John, **3**/90; Ric, **3**/90

Norton, Philip, p. 265

Norwood, Henry, mayor, **3**/80

Note, Henry, **1**/189; Ric, **1**/189

Nott, Geo, **3**/295, 347*n*, 352*; Eliz, **2**/327; Jane,

INDEX OF PERSONS

3/295; Lawr, 3/148; Nathan, 3/148; Thos, 2/327; *and see* Nutt
Nourse (Nurse, Nursse), Anne, 1/294, 301, 314, 364; Eliz, 1/147; Geo, 3/163; Giles, 3/344; John, 1/117*, 121*, 294, 301, 314, 364; 3/129*, 163*, 213, 344; Joseph, 3/384*n*, 387*; Luke, 1/55, 297, 372, 391; Luke, alderman, 2/33, 61, 120, 191, justice, 1/85, 98, mayor, 1/567; 2/189, sheriff, 1/399; Marg, 1/55, 297; Marian, 2/314; Mary, 1/391; Wal, 1/55*, 147; —, 3/129, 163
Noven, Ric, 2/19*
Nurse (Nursse) *see* Nourse
Nurth, Wm, 1/181
Nutt (Nutte), Margery, 1/30, 119, 199, 274, 290; Wm, 1/30, 119, 199, 274, 290; *and see* Nott

Oakes, Francis, 3/217*
Oatley (Oateley), Francis, 3/335, 357*, 359; Sarah, 3/335, 357
Ocford *see* Ockford
Ockey (Okaye, Okey), Aaron, 1/406; Anne, 1/439; Dan, 2/231; Jas, 3/278; John, 1/406; 2/231, 349; Marg, 1/12, 81; Mary, 1/157, 230; Wm, 1/12, 81, 157, 230; 2/349; 3/39*, 278
Ockford (Ocford, Ockfords, Oxford), Giles, 1/110, 268–9, 556*n**, 557*; Joan, 1/268–9; John, 1/110; 2/48*
Ockold, Arnold, 1/303, 332, 349, 375; Henry, 2/259; Henry, alderman, 2/280, 315, 322, mayor, 3/12; Sybil, 1/332, 349, 375; Thos, 2/259; —, 1/303
Ockwell (Okewell), Arnold, 1/108; John, 1/108
Odie (Odye), Thos, 1/64; Wm, 1/64,
Offley, Rob, pp. 261–2
Okaye *see* Ockey
Oker, John, 2/67*
Okewell *see* Ockwell
Okey *see* Ockey
Oldacre, Jas, 2/354; Wm, 2/354
Oliffe (Ollive), Henry, 3/302; Ric, 3/115*, 302
Oliver, Thos, p. 265
Onion (Onnyon, Onyon, Onyons, Oynion), Bridget, 2/47, 72, 149, 207, 255, 271, 296, 356; 3/63, 65, 144; p. xxviii; Eleanor, 1/531, 564, 575; 2/15; Eliz, 2/160, 227, 267, 286, 305; 3/19; Humph, 1/454, 531, 564, 568*, 575; 2/15*, 160, 227, 267, 286, 305; 3/19; p. 268; John, 3/65; Joseph, 3/144; Thos, 1/454, 568–9; 2/47, 72, 149, 207, 255, 271, 296, 341, 356; 3/63, 65*, 144*, 224; p. xxviii; —, 1/568–9; 2/341
Oram (Owram), Ric, 1/9, 12
Organ, Henry, 1/506; John, 3/371, 387; Nat, 3/387; Sam, 3/371; Thos, 1/506

Osborne, Dan, 2/293*; Joseph, 3/63; Thos, 1/409*; 3/63
Osgood, Gabriel, 1/417; Wm, 1/417
Ovenell, John, 3/44*
Overthrow (Overthrowe), John, 1/587*; Wm, 3/176*
Overton, Humph, 1/132; Ric, 1/132
Owbery, John, 1/238; Thos, 1/238
Owen, Edw (*alias* Robins), 1/131; Eliz, 1/110; Gabriel, 1/442; Henry (*alias* Wood), 3/10*; John, 1/97*, 110, 442
Owram *see* Oram
Owting, Edw, 3/216*n*, 218; Thos, 3/216*n*, 218
Oxford *see* Ockford
Oynion *see* Onion

Pace, Anne, 3/291; Bridget, 2/349; Eliz, 2/9, 113, 157, 233; Francis, 3/13, 103, 353, 382; Francis (*alias* Parris), 2/352; John, 1/202, 403, 486; 2/243, 269, 324; 3/291, 319; Marg, 1/526, 539, 560, 575; Mary, 3/80; Phillida, 3/13, 103; Phyllida (*alias* Parris), 2/352; Sam, 1/539; 2/112; Susannah, 3/353, 382; Thos, 1/202, 415*–16*, 526, 539, 560, 575; 2/9, 113, 157, 233*, 243, 324, 349; 3/57, 80; p. 272; Wal, 1/403, 539; Wm, 1/486; 2/269; 3/57, 399*
Packer, Dan, 1/421; Dorothy, 1/478; Ric, 1/328, 421; Thos, 3/196*n*; Wm, 1/328, 478; 2/24*
Packington (Pakington), Joan, 1/171; Thos, 1/108, 171; —, 1/108
Paine (Payne), Anne, 2/177, 257, 327; Ant, 2/197; Caple, sheriff, 3/330; Eliz, 1/398, 461, 464, 586; Giles, 1/50, 63*, 81, 326; Joan, 1/50, 63*, 81; John, 1/270, 304, 359, 388, 491, 553*, 558; p. 271; John, sheriff, 1/3; Joseph, 2/45; Marg, 1/359, 491, 558, 571; 2/94, 100; Mark, 1/79; Ric, 1/107, 329*, 361, 571; p. 273; Rob, 1/248*, 270, 304, 345, 347, 361, 398, 461, 464, 472, 586*; 2/138, 177, 257, 327; 3/67, 227, 331; Rob, mayor, 2/263; 3/313, 330, sheriff, 2/9; Roger, 1/107; Thos, 1/338*, 472; 2/45; Wm, 1/79; 2/197; —, 2/138; 3/67; —, alderman, 1/341*n*
Painter (Paynter, Payntor), Eliz, 2/263; 3/31, 324; Geo, 3/321; Giles, 1/318, 323; Jane, 1/438; Jesse, 3/146*n*; John, 2/120, 252, 263; 3/31*, 324; Ric, 3/321; Thos, 1/318, 323, 438; p. 270; Wm, 2/252; *and see* Panter
Paite *see* Pate
Pakington *see* Packington
Palmer, Edm, 1/274, 410, 413, 545; 2/59, 207; 3/260, 315, 370, 373; Edm, sheriff, 1/534; Edw, 1/109, 456, 535*, 567; Edw [Edm?], 3/221, 360; Eliz, 3/221, 260, 315, 360, 370, 373; Francis,

Palmer (*cont.*)
  3/235; Geo, 3/18, 31; Hester, 1/410, 413, 456, 535, 545, 567; 2/59, 207; 3/146; John, 1/173, 197, 386*; 2/173*n*, 182*; 3/211*n;* p. 272; Joseph, 3/18, 31, 239; Marg, 1/197, 386; Ric, 3/235; Sam, sheriff, 3/298; Stephen, 2/170; Thos, 1/109; Wm, 2/170; p. 273; —, 1/173, 274; 2/141*n*
Panter, John, 3/89, 265; Mary, 3/89; Wm, 3/265; *and see* Painter; Punter
Panther, Sam, 3/375*
Parish, Edw, 1/459; Frances, 2/116, 193, 295; John, 1/459, 521; 2/116, 193, 295; Thos, 1/521
Parker, Ant, 3/172; Dan, p. 270; Edw, 1/42; Eliz, 2/347; Geo, 2/376; 3/88*; Jas, 2/53; 3/102; John, 1/470; 2/53, 100*n*; 3/102, 232, 280, 335, 386 *and n*, 397; Marg, 1/584; 2/53, 170, 202, 312*, 338; 3/26*, 95, 130, 191, 220; p. xxvii; Martha, 3/232, 280, 335, 386, 397; Nat, 1/273, Rob, 1/42; Thos, 1/26*, 273, 470, 584; 2/53, 170, 202, 338; 3/130, 220, 386*; Tim, 3/172; Wm, 2/347; —, 2/100*n*
Parkes, John, 2/98; Wm, 2/98
Parlour (Parler, Parlor), Edw, 2/153; Henry, 2/173; John, 1/462; Wm, 1/76*, 462; 2/153, 173
Parrat, Thos, p. 269
Parris, Francis (alias Pace), 2/352; Phillida, (alias Pace), 2/352
Parry, Dan, 2/242*, 3/81; Francis, 3/147*; Jas, 3/307; John, 3/25, 307; Lancelot, 3/25; —, 3/81; *and see* Perry; Pirry; Pury
Parsons Henry, 2/163; John, 2/163, 262; Ric, 2/240*; Wal, 2/262
Partridge (Partredge), Anne, 1/109; 3/13, 161, 323, 391; Arthur, 1/333; Eleanor, 3/10; Eliz, 2/150, 295; Henry, 3/332*; John, 1/573; p. 267; Kath, 2/267, 271; Ric, 2/267, 271; 3/13, 161, 323, 391; Rob, 1/109, 340*; 3/330; Thos, 1/333; 2/150, 295; 3/10, 330; Wm, 1/573; —, 3/261*n*
Pate (Paite, Pates, Payte), John, 1/71, 239, 326, 386*n*, 388*; Leonard, 3/389*; Lynnett, 2/339*; Nat, 1/326; Thos, 1/71; Wal, 1/386*n*, 388; Wm, 1/239
Paule, Edw, 2/308; Thos, 2/308
Paunt, John, p. 265
Pawldin, Dan, 3/378; John, 3/378
Payle, John, 1/270; Wm, 1/270
Payne *see* Paine
Paynter (Payntor) *see* Painter
Payte *see* Pate
Peachee, John, 2/178; Thos, 2/178
Peacocke, Henry, 1/104; John, 1/104
Pearce (Pearse, Peirce), Edm, 2/148; 3/83; Edw, 1/133; 2/318; Eleanor, 1/502; Giles, 1/161, 502; Henry, 2/280, 288*; Hester, 1/496, 507; John, 1/306; 2/148, 318, 333; 3/357; Martha, 2/62; Nat, 2/318; Ric, 1/306; Rob, 1/209; Sarah, 3/83; Thos, 1/7*, 133, 209, 391, 496, 507; 2/62, 280; Thos, alderman, 2/312, mayor, 2/279, sheriff, 2/28; Wm, 1/161, 284*; 2/333; —, 2/318; *and see* Perris; Purse
Pedlingham, Jane, 3/380; Ric, 1/324; 2/50; 3/380; Susannah, 1/401, 539, 563–4; 2/50, 106, 123; Thos, 1/324, 401, 539, 563*, 564; 2/50*, 106, 123
Pegler (Peglar), Andrew, 3/392; Jane, 3/288, 347; John, 3/38, 392; Joseph, 3/38, 288, 347
Peirce *see* Pearce
Peirson, Eliz, 2/203; Wm, 2/203
Pell, Pauncefoote, p. 266
Pember, John, 2/150; Thos, 2/150
Pembridge (Pembrudge, Pembrug, Pembruge), Eliz (Elbeata), 3/293, 370; Sam, 3/95, 288; Thos, 3/51*, 95, 293, 370
Pendris, Humph, 3/336; Marg, 3/336
Penson, Stephen, 2/198; Wm, 2/198; Wm (*alias* Jonas), p. 270
Perkes (Perckes, Perks), Alice, 2/115, 146, 244, 198, 253, 292, 348; 3/21, 40, 130; Dan, 1/355; Geo, 1/98; Jane, 3/85; Joan, 3/122; John, 1/355; 2/115, 146, 198, 244*, 253, 292, 305, 348; 3/21, 40, 130; Kath, 2/305; 3/22; Ric, 1/98; Wm, 2/282, 293*b*; 3/22, 85, 122; —, 2/282, 297
Perkins, Geo, 3/289, 395*; John, 3/233; Ric, 2/116; Sam, 3/247, 395; Sarah, 3/289; Thos, 2/116; 3/233; Wal, 2/120*; Wm, 3/247, 250*n*
Perks *see* Perkes
Perris (Perrys), Eliz, 3/377; Frances, 3/20, 354; John, 3/354; Mary, 3/356; Ric, 2/196; 3/356; Wm, 2/196; 3/20, 354*, 377; *and see* Pearce; Purse
Perry, Anne, 3/367; Dan, 3/142; Eliz, 2/163, 240, 262, 309; Henry, 2/102; John, 1/530, 543; 2/102, 316*n*, 339; Nic, 2/165; Rob, 2/163, 240, 262, 309; 3/374*; p. 272; Sam, 2/165; Thos, 1/530, 543; 2/18*n**; Wm, 2/339; 3/312, 316, 367; —, 3/142; *and see* Parry; Pirry; Pury
Perrys *see* Perris
Persivall, John, 1/119; Wm, 1/119
Pester, Alex, 1/373; Chris, 1/373
Peter, Giles, 2/247; John, 2/247
Pettifer (Petifer, Petifor, Pettefer, Pettipher), Anne, 1/444; Joseph, 1/245, 339, 360; Juliana, 1/360; Marg, 1/12, 109; Rob, 1/12, 109; Rob, sheriff, 1/111, 167; Tim, 1/245, 444; 2/27; Thos, 1/245, 339*; 2/25*n*, 27
Petty, John, 2/84; Wm, 2/84
Pharley *see* Farley
Pheasant, Thos, 2/307*
Phelpes (Phelepes, Phellpe, Phelps), Barbara, 1/534,

INDEX OF PERSONS

536; Edw, **2**/19; Eleanor, **1**/80; Frances, **2**/58*; Henry, **1**/126; Jas, **1**/350, 369*n*; Joan, **3**/29; John, p. 273; Joseph, **1**/534, 536, 560; **2**/19, 156; **3**/29, 144, 239*n*, 241*; Joseph, sheriff, **3**/274; Joyce, **3**/383; Marg, **1**/308, 501; Matt, **3**/28, 383; Nic, **1**/88; **2**/361*; p. 273; Nic, sheriff, **3**/51, 99; Ric, **1**/80; Sarah, **2**/361; **3**/144; Thos, **2**/58*; Wm, **1**/88, 126, 255, 308, 350, 501; **2**/29, 361; **3**/28, 178*n*; Wm, sheriff, **3**/206;—, **2**/29, 156

Phenix, Henry, **2**/53, 57*, 82, 119, 162; Marg, **2**/53, 57*, 82, 119*, 162

Phillips (Philipps, Philips, Phillippe, Phillippes, Phillipps), Anne, **2**/69, 141, 205, 261; **3**/32, 90; Eliz, **1**/582; **3**/252, 296, 376; Geo, **1**/85, 94; **2**/158, 251*; **3**/90, 250*n*; Jas, **1**/535; **2**/10, 69, 141, 205, 210, 261; **3**/32, 90, 252, 378; Jane, **1**/429, 568; **2**/79*, 118; John, **1**/21, 312, 429, 527*n*, 556*n*, 558, 568, 582; **2**/79, 118; **3**/161, 376; pp. 266, 269; Margery, **2**/10; Mary, **2**/158, 251; **3**/378; Philip, **3**/272*n*; Ric, **1**/21; Roger, **3**/161; Thos, **1**/85, 94, 312, 582; **3**/87*n*, 90, 296, 374*n*, 376*; p. 271; Wm, **1**/556*n*, 558; **2**/23*, 25*n*; p. 270; —, **1**/527*n*, 535

Philpot (Philpet), Sam, **1**/530*

Pickeringe (Pyckeryng, Pyckerynge), Luke, **1**/490; **2**/360; Moses, **3**/64*n*; Sarah, **2**/360; Wm, **1**/490

Piddinge, Thos, **1**/392; Wm, **1**/392

Pigg (Pigge), Blanche, **3**/36–7; David, **1**/571; Eleanor, **2**/127, 155; Ric, **1**/571; **2**/94, 100, 127, 155; **3**/36–7, 121*n*

Pinbury, Chas, **2**/46; Rob, **2**/46

Pincke *see* Pinke

Pinckutt, Benj, **2**/82; Jonathan, **2**/82

Pine, Chas, **2**/193*

Pingery (Pingrey, Pingry), Anne, **1**/577; John, **1**/326, 395; Thos, **1**/326, 395, 577; p. 272

Pinke (Pincke, Pynke), Alice, **1**/379, 434, 470, 512; Alice (*alias* Jennings), **2**/39; Eleanor, **1**/410; Joan, **1**/104, 138, 180; John, **1**/138, 180, 355, 379, 410, 434, 470, 512, 553; Margery, **1**/167, 177, 381; Wal, **1**/167, 177, 381; Sam, p. 272; Wm, **1**/104, 138*, 180*; —, **1**/553

Pinnell, Francis, **2**/264; Henry, **2**/264

Piperd, Thos, **1**/177*

Pirry, Henry, **1**/133; Kath, **1**/133; Rob, **1**/133; Thos, **1**/133–4; Wal, **1**/134; *and see* Parry; Perry; Pury

Pitt (Pytt), Anne, **1**/500; Edw, **1**/93; Eleanor, **1**/328–9, 476, 516; **2**/98–9, 105, 111, 132, 195, 234, 253, 301, 354; p. xxviii; Eliz, **1**/365, 373; Godwin, **2**/354; Henry, **1**/40*; Jas, **3**/17, 35, 163, 175, 178, 362; Joan, **1**/160; John, **1**/76, 87, 114, 159, 207, 261*; **3**/343; Joseph, **3**/144*, 343; Joyce, **3**/362; Marg, **1**/76, 87, 114, 159, 207, 261; Mary, **2**/354; **3**/343; Nic, **1**/289; Ric, **1**/93; **2**/347, 352; Rob, **1**/365, 373, 500; Roger, **3**/343; Sam, **1**/328–9, 476, 516, 564*n*; **2**/34*, 98–9, 105, 111, 132, 195, 234, 253, 301, 347, 354; p. xxviii; Thos, **1**/67, 160, 229, 289, 344; Wm, **1**/229; **2**/352; —, **1**/564*n*; **3**/17, 35, 163, 178

Pittman, John, p. 273

Plaister, John, **1**/36; Thos, **1**/36

Platt *see* Plott

Plomer *see* Plummer

Plott (Platt), Anne, **3**/389; Cornelius, **2**/21–2, 114, 242, 259, 311; **3**/21, 208; Henry, **3**/208, 389; Henry, sheriff, **3**/391; Joan, **2**/311; **3**/21; Marg, **2**/114, 242, 259; —, **2**/21–2

Plovy, Thos, **2**/213; Wm, **2**/213

Plummer (Plomer, Plumer), Christiane, **1**/435, 549; **2**/108; Dan, **3**/133; Giles, **1**/131; John, **1**/131; **3**/133; Rob, **1**/435, 549; **2**/108; Sam, p. 273; Thos, p. 271

Pockeridge *see* Puckeridge

Pomec, John, **1**/76; Thos, **1**/76

Pontin, Wm, **3**/64*

Poole (Pool), Chas, **1**/346; David, **1**/534; Henry, **1**/327, 534; John, **2**/257*; **3**/115*, 276, 386; Joseph, **3**/242*; Sam, **3**/282; Sarah, **1**/431, 498; **3**/276, 386; Thos, **1**/327, 346, 431, 498; Wm, **3**/282

Pope, John, **1**/402; Ric, **1**/402; p. 267

Porter, Ant, **3**/224; Eliz, **1**/179, 201–2, 276, 346; Joan, **1**/62; John, **1**/188; **3**/179; Mary, **1**/446; Rob, **1**/62, 68, 179, 201–2, 276, 346, 401, 446; **3**/179*; p. xix; Wal, **1**/188

Portman, Ric, **1**/308; p. 267; Rob, **1**/308; —, p. 267

Portus, Thos, **3**/320; Wm, **3**/320

Potter, Ant, **3**/74*; John, **3**/176*

Poulton, Ric, **1**/508; **3**/311*; Thos, **1**/508

Powell, Alice, **1**/537; **2**/127, 155, 191, 262, 268; **3**/115, 230; Anne, **3**/323; Bridget, **2**/369; Chas, **1**/356; **2**/181, 263; Curtis, **3**/163*n*; Edm, **2**/200; Edw, **1**/549*; Emmanuel, **3**/161*n*; Francis, **3**/143; Geo, **2**/191; **3**/247; Henry, **2**/20, 369; Hugh, **2**/20; Jas, **1**/187; pp. 265–6; Jas, mayor, **1**/517, sheriff, **1**/311; Jeremiah, **1**/187; Joan, **1**/492, 518*; **2**/43, 153, 181; John, **1**/162, 335, 372; **2**/105, 190, 269, 377*; **3**/348; pp. xxii, 272 *and see* p. 263; John, mayor, **2**/304; Joseph, sheriff, **2**/263; Mary, **2**/374; Paul, **2**/200; Ralph, **1**/372; Ric, **2**/269; Rob, **2**/105, 262, 268; **3**/143; Roger, **2**/287; Sam, **3**/323; Thos, **1**/335, 356, 518*; **2**/190; **3**/36*, 348; Wm, **1**/537; **2**/43, 127, 153, 155, 181*, 191*, 263, 287, 372; **3**/9*, 29*n**, 115, 230*; pp. xviii, xxiii, 273; Mr, p. 268; *and see* Aphowell

Powles, John, **2**/133; Wm, **2**/133

Poyner, Edw, **1**/145; John, **1**/145
Precdy (Preedie), Wm, **1**/274, 348; p. xix; —, **1**/274
Preene, John, **3**/177; Wm, **3**/177
Preist, John, **2**/357; Peter, **2**/357
Prentice, John, **1**/103
Price (Pryce), Albert, **1**/23; Alice, **1**/304, 354, 361; **3**/40, 134, 221, 323*; Anne, **1**/32, 294, 484; **3**/117, 344; Brian, **3**/117; Chas, **3**/372; David, **3**/363; Dinah, **1**/558; **2**/149, 263, 300; Eliz, **1**/161, 302, 349; Francis, **2**/164*; Henry, **1**/135, 304, 354, 361; Henry, sheriff, **1**/408; Hester, **3**/68; Isobel, **3**/385; Jas, **1**/349, 368, 380*; **2**/164*, 263; **3**/40, 134, 221; p. 271; Jas, sheriff, **3**/252; Jennet, **2**/375; Joan, **1**/21, 71, 96, 112–13, 147, 171, 180, 188, 197; John, **1**/294, 319, 328*, 349, 484; **2**/266; **3**/68, 102*, 344, 363; pp. 268, 272; John, mayor, **3**/239, sheriff, **1**/372; **3**/80; Lawr, **2**/216; Matt, **1**/21, 71, 96, 113, 135, 147, 171, 180, 188, 197, 245; Matt, justice, **1**/212, mayor, **1**/255, 328, 351, sheriff, **1**/129; Ralph, **1**/170, 577*; Ric, **1**/32, 368, 558; **2**/149, 263*, 266*, 300*, 347; **3**/63, 193*, 323, 385; Roland, **2**/164; Sam, **3**/28; Sybil, **1**/23; Thos, **1**/238; **2**/216, 370; **3**/10, 63, 372; p. 271; Thos, mayor, **2**/344; **3**/172, sheriff, **2**/279; Wal, **1**/23; Wm, **1**/32, 112, 161, 170, 302, 349; **2**/347, 370, 377; **3**/10, 28, 323; Wm, mayor, **1**/399, sheriff, **1**/197; widow, p. 266*; —, **1**/319; **2**/266; *and see* Ap Rice; Rice
Pricharde, Pricharde, Prichardes, Prichards) *see* Pritchard
Pricket (Prickett, Pricketts), Anne, **3**/28; Edw, **2**/201; Howell, **1**/537; **3**/49; John, **2**/201; **3**/28, 212*; Roland, **1**/537; Sam, **3**/49; —, **3**/201*n*; *and see* Ricketts
Pridaye (Prydye), Wm, **1**/245*, 313
Prince, John, **3**/16; Thos, **3**/16
Prinn *see* Prynn
Prior (Pryor), Anne, **1**/75, 168; Henry, **1**/75, 168; p. 265; John, **2**/10; Margery, **1**/510; Simon, **1**/501*n*, 510; p. 267; Thos, **1**/510*; **2**/10; **3**/74*n*, 81*
Pritchard (Prichard, Prichardes, Prichards, Pritchards, Prytchette, Prytchetts), Ant, **1**/24; Chas, **3**/265; Edw, **3**/322; Emit, **2**/12; Francis, p. 272; Gabriel, **1**/350; Geo, **1**/396; Giles, **1**/531*; Henry, **1**/512; **2**/53; John, **1**/118, 560; **3**/263*, 333*n*, 334*; Joseph, **3**/192; Kath, **1**/315; Philip, **1**/118; **2**/56; Rob, **1**/350; Roger, **1**/560; Sam, **2**/56; Sarah, **2**/214, 255; **3**/36; Simon, **1**/350; **2**/214, 255; **3**/36; Thos, **1**/7, 24, 315, 512; **2**/12, 53; **3**/192, 322; Thos, sheriff, **2**/9; Wal, **1**/261; Wm, **1**/261, 350, 396; **3**/265; —, **3**/244*n; and see* Richards

Probert, Jas, **1**/517; Roger, **3**/32; Thos, **3**/32, 53*n*, 191; *and see* Roberts
Prosser (Procer), Henry, **3**/21; Hugh, **3**/21; Jas, **2**/148; **3**/222; John, **2**/148; Wm, **3**/222
Prune, John, **2**/215, 291; Thos, **2**/215, 291
Pryce *see* Price
Prydye *see* Pridaye
Prynn (Prinn), Wm, **3**/317, 323, 386*; Marg, **3**/323, 386
Pryor *see* Prior
Prytchette (Prytchetts) *see* Pritchard
Puckeridge (Pockeridge), Abraham, **3**/54; Isaac, **3**/338*n*, 342; Thos, **2**/251*; **3**/37, 54, 232*, 342; Wm, **2**/251; **3**/37
Puckson *see* Puxon
Pullen (Pullin), Francis, **1**/137; Joan, **2**/18; Ric, **2**/332*; Rob, **1**/137; Thos, **2**/18
Pullum, John, **2**/185*
Punter, Joseph, **2**/313; Mary, **3**/277, 352, 394; Rob, **2**/313; **3**/277*, 352, 394; Rob, sheriff, **2**/274; *and see* Painter; Panter
Purlewent (Purlwent), Bridget, **1**/428; Dan, **2**/220; Eliz, **1**/248; p. xxiv; John, **1**/268, 340, 428, 571*; John, sheriff, **2**/86, 169; Michael, **1**/325, 343; Roger, **1**/33, 268; **2**/220; Sybil, **1**/343; Wm, **1**/33
Purrocke, Jane, **1**/279, 283; Thos, **1**/279, 283
Purse, Edw, **1**/71; Rob, **1**/71; *and see* Pearce; Perris
Pury, Eliz, **1**/280; Thos, **1**/280; p. 272; Thos, sheriff, **1**/351, mayor **2**/123, 131; *and see* Parry; Perry; Pirry
Putlie, Geo, **2**/24; Thos, **2**/24
Puxon (Puckson), Ric, **2**/333*n*, 336*; **3**/162, 202; Thos, **3**/162; Wm, **3**/202;
Pyckering (Pyckerynge) *see* Pickeringe
Pynke *see* Pinke
Pyrton, John, **3**/147; Philip, **3**/147
Pytt *see* Pitt

Quench, Mary, **3**/262; Ric, **3**/22*, 262

Ragbourne, Giles, **2**/349*
Rainsford, Thos, **2**/53; Wm, **2**/53
Randalph, Reignold, **3**/145*
Randell (Randle), Abel, **1**/290; Anne, **3**/52, 88, 281, 336; Dan, **2**/207, 348; **3**/52, 88, 250*, 281, 310, 336; Edm, **1**/239; Geo, **1**/378; Giles, **1**/271; **2**/248; **3**/109, 227*n*, 228*, 293*n*, 294*, 338; Hester, **3**/62, 89, 160, 248; Jas, **2**/76, 207, 248, 253, 260; **3**/250, 353; Jane, **3**/353; Joan, **3**/109; John, **2**/76, 241, 248*; **3**/338; Josiah, **2**/253; **3**/21, 84, 198, 286*, 351*; Josiah, sheriff, **3**/239; Margery, **3**/21, 84, 198, 286, 351; Ralph, **3**/204*; Ric, **1**/208; Simon, **3**/116; Susannah, **3**/378; Thos, **1**/378; **2**/241; **3**/116; Wm, **1**/208, 239, 271, 290;

2/260; 3/62, 89, 160, 228, 248, 310, 351, 366, 378; Wm, sheriff, 3/374; —, 2/348
Randford, John, p. 273
Rathbone, Ric, 3/100*
Ravener, Geo, 3/384; Joseph, 3/390*, 399; Margery, 3/390, 399; Thos, 2/323*; 3/384, 390, 393*n*
Ravenhall, Jas, 3/391; John, 3/391
Rawlings (Rawlins, Rawlynge), Edw (*alias* Gybson), 1/48; Eliz (*alias* Gybson), 1/48 Hugh, 1/144; Thos, 1/536*; Wm, 1/144; 3/214*
Raxhall, Ric, 2/77*
Raylee, Jospeh, 3/295*n*
Raynoldes *see* Reynolds
Rea, John, 1/46; Nic, 1/157; Ric, 1/46; Thos, 1/157
Read (Reade), Anne, 3/292; David, 1/117, 123; Eliz, 1/117; 3/266; Jas, 3/394*n*; John, 1/117*, 123*; 2/58*; 3/25; John, sheriff, 1/345; Rob, 3/25, 210, 292; Thos, 3/266; Mr, p. 268; —, p. 268
Ready, Alex, 3/143; Edm, 3/394*n*; Edw, 3/252; Eliz, 3/278; John, 3/73, 143, 252; Thos, 3/73, 278
Reakes, Geo, 3/120*
Redfin (Redven, Redvin), Henry, 1/74, 83, 277; Henry, sheriff, 1/327, 337*; Isobel, 1/277; Sam, 1/312; Thos, 1/74, 83, 312
Reeve (Reeves, Reve, Rives), Anne, 3/61; Eliz, 2/16; Francis, 2/321, 349; 3/41, 71, 119*, 253*; Geo, 2/255; Giles, 2/62*, 243, 255*, 340; 3/58, 262, 306, 358; Hannah, 3/41, 71, 119; Henry, 3/93; Jane, 1/479; John, 3/325; Joseph, 2/321; 3/253; Kath, 3/147; Mary, 2/62*, 243, 255, 340; Sam, 2/62; 3/61; Sarah, 3/262, 306, 325, 358; Thos, 1/299; 3/93; Wm, 1/299, 479; 2/16, 243*n*, 246*; 3/147; p. 270; Wm, sheriff, 3/293; —, 3/58
Restall (Restell), John, 1/104; Peter, 2/348*; Ric, 1/104; 2/40*n*, 43*
Reve *see* Reeve
Reynolds (Raynoldes), Alice, 1/46; Eleanor, 1/588; Eliz, 1/272, 283; Henry, 1/133, 392; Jas, 1/511; John, 1/46, 135, 230, 247, 392; 2/6; John, sheriff, 1/245; Mary, 1/135, 230, 247; Oliver, 1/511; Ric, 2/6; Rob, 1/133, 272, 283, 588; Wm, 3/275*
Rice (Ryce), Eliz, 1/145, 158, 314, 348; Geo, 1/145; Henry, 1/158; John, 1/44, 88, 158, 314, 348, 396*n*; Wm, 1/158; *and see* Ap Rice; Price
Rich (Riche), Anne, 1/25, 47, 71, 114; Susan, countess of Warwick, widow of Wm Holliday, 1/386*n*; p. xxi; Thos, 1/25, 47, 71, 114; p. 268; Thos, mayor, 1/111, sheriff, 1/3; Sir Thos, p. xxii *and see* p. 263
Richards, Ferdinand, 1/141; Henry, 1/141; *and see* Pritchard
Riche *see* Rich

Richmond, John, 3/84; Thos, 3/84
Rickes *see* Rix
Ricketts (Rickettes, Ricotts), Anne, 2/148, 170, 177, 266, 332; 3/14, 115; Chas, 2/337; Edw, 1/460; Geo, 2/32, 257*; Jacob, 2/148, 170, 177; Jas, 1/383, 401*, 460, 546; 2/8, 106, 266, 332; 3/14, 115; p. 272; John, 1/383; 2/106, 337; 3/82, 120, 381–2; Wm, 3/32, 120; —, 1/546; 3/82 *and see* Pricket
Rider, Nic, 1/532*
Ridler, Alice (*alias* Gregory), 1/540; Anne, 2/236*n*; Wal, 2/205, 223; Wm, 2/205, 223, 236*n*; Wm (*alias* Gregory), 1/540
Riggs (Rigges), Francis, 3/22, 108; Nat, 3/108; Stephen, 3/22
Riman *see* Ryman
River, John, 1/316; Rob, 1/316
Rives *see* Reeve
Rix (Rickes, Rixe), Ant, 1/173; Eleanor, 1/287; Humph, 1/106; John, 1/348, 440; p. 273; Nat, 1/563, 574*n*; Peter, p. 272; Ric, 1/173, 287, 348, 440, 563; Sam, 1/106; widow, 2/162*n*; —, 2/162*n*
Rixton, Ralph, 2/51*
Roach (Roache), Abraham, 2/297; Chas, 1/72, 80; Ric, 1/80; Thos, 1/72; Wm, 2/297
Roadway *see* Rodway
Roan (Rone), Chas, 3/381; John, 3/263; Joseph, 3/263
Robartes (Robberts) *see* Roberts
Robbins *see* Robins
Roberts (Robartes, Robbertes, Robberts, Robertes), Ant, 2/368; Arthur, 1/274; Dan, 1/249; Edw, 2/37; Eliz, 2/23, 269–70, 279, 368; 3/38*; Geo, 1/262; Giles, 1/246, 269, 554; 2/159*; Henry, 1/86, 449*; p. 272; Hugh, 2/91, 266; John, 1/400, 500; 2/93*n*, 266; p. 273; Joseph, 3/105*; Miles, 1/554; Nic, 3/214; Percy, 1/91; Rob, 1/86; 2/364*n*, 368; Sam, 2/59*n*, 269–70, 279, 368; 3/38*; Thos, 1/97*, 246, 262, 269, 274; 2/37; 3/214; Wm, 1/249, 407*, 428*, 500; *and see* Probert
Robins (Robbins, Robyns), Alice, 1/31; Benj, 3/307*, 238; Edw (*alias* Owen), 1/31; Geo, 1/263; Henry, 2/354*; Henry, sheriff, 2/65; Hester, 3/38; Jas, 1/466, 327, 527; 2/199; 3/238–9; John, 1/327; 2/263; Mary, 2/199; Maurice, 1/482; Nat, 1/263; Ric, 1/337*; Thos, 1/482; 2/22*, 171; 3/38; Wm, 2/263; —, 1/527; 2/171
Robinson, Ant, 1/201, 239; p. 266; Ant, mayor, 1/330, 391, sheriff, 1/255; Edw, 3/292; Hester, 1/201, 239; 2/3; John, 2/253; Philip, 3/292; Sam, 2/3; Thos, 1/313; 2/253
Robyns *see* Robins
Rodman, Francis, 1/111*

Rodway (Roadway), Eliz, **3**/17, 325; George, **2**/146; Giles, **2**/146; **3**/17, 325*; Giles, mayor, **3**/374, sheriff, **3**/239; John, **2**/254*; **3**/17*, 188, 325*; John, sheriff, **3**/198; Thos, **1**/292; **3**/264*, 325; p. 270; Wm, **1**/292

Roffe, Jasper, **3**/391; John, **3**/391

Rogers, Edw, **3**/39*n*; Francis, **1**/274, 275*, 283, 305; Herbert, **3**/196; Jas, **3**/46; John, **1**/87; **2**/199*, 266, 340, 349*; **3**/85, 104, 196*, 213, 381, 390; John, mayor, **3**/217, sheriff, **2**/360; Marg, **3**/104, 213; Mary, **1**/305; **3**/342; **2**/349, 377; **3**/196, 390; p. xxiv; Morris, p. 267; Nic, **1**/283; Priscilla, **2**/340; **3**/47; Ric, **1**/87, 396; Thos, **1**/396; **2**/192*, 266, 340*; **3**/15*, 46–7, 85, 213, 342, 381, 390; Wm, **1**/274; **3**/213, 390

Rone *see* Roan

Roper, Thos, **3**/175*

Rose, Benj, **3**/32*; Benj, sheriff, **3**/298; Dorothy, **3**/32; Sam, **3**/32; Sam, sheriff, **3**/66, 172

Rountree, Chris, **2**/352; Leonard, **2**/352

Rowbrey, Tim, **3**/267; Wm, **3**/267

Rowles, Benj, **2**/10; John, **1**/366*; **2**/10; **3**/279; Philip, **1**/8; Rob, **1**/8, 401; **3**/148*; Tim, **3**/173*; Wm, **3**/279

Rudd, Wm, p. 272

Rudge, Chas, **3**/288; Geo, **2**/176*; **3**/266; John, **3**/288; Milberrow, **3**/266, 340

Rudhall, Abraham, **3**/346*; p. xxxi; Eliz, **3**/346

Rush, Jas, **3**/316; John, **3**/316

Russell, Alice, **1**/87, 189; Eliz, **1**/442; Francis, p. 271; Henry, **1**/32; Hugh, **3**/314; Jane, **2**/262; John, **1**/32, 319, 399; **3**/314; Sarah, **2**/83; Thos, **1**/87, 189, 319; Thos sheriff, **1**/237; **2**/213; Wm, **1**/147*, 399, 442, 467*; **2**/83, 262; **3**/65, 206; p. 271; Wm, mayor, **2**/291; **3**/158, sheriff, **2**/106; —, **3**/65

Rutter, Alice, **1**/579; Joan, **1**/113; Luke, **1**/113; Wm, **1**/579

Ryce *see* Rice

Ryland, Hester, **2**/285; **3**/27; John, **2**/56, 285; **3**/27; Ric, **2**/285; Sam, **3**/250*n*; Thos, **2**/56; **3**/179*n*; Wm, **2**/285

Ryman (Riman), Edw, **1**/116; Jas, **3**/66; John, **1**/116; Thos, **3**/66

Sadler, Jas, **2**/180; John, **2**/180; Wm, **2**/283*

Salcombe, Joan, **2**/87; John, **2**/87; Sam, **3**/100*

Sally, Thos, **3**/18*; *and see* Solly

Sampson (Sampsons, Samson, Samsons), Dan, **2**/356; **3**/31, 84; Jane, **2**/44, 64, 125, 201, 216, 269; **3**/25, 36, 43, 46, 80, 86; Joan, **2**/324; John, **2**/11; Jonathan, **2**/11, 64, 105, 215–16, 356*; Mary, **2**/64, 105, 215–16, 356*; Solomon, **2**/356; Wm, **2**/11, 44, 64, 125, 201, 216, 269, 324, 356*; **3**/25, 36, 43, 46, 80, 86; p. 269; —, **2**/11; **3**/82

Sandes *see* Sands

Sandford (Sandforde, Sanford), Ancell, **1**/15; Edw, **1**/67, 110; Henry, **1**/15, 129, 134; Sybil, **1**/129, 134; Thos, **1**/67, 110, 310*; **3**/340*

Sandie *see* Sandy

Sands (Sandes), Cath, **1**/44, 125; Henry, **1**/6; John, **1**/118; Marg, **1**/6; Margery, **1**/118; Ralph, **1**/44, 125

Sandy (Sandie, Sandye), Anne, **1**/229; Geo, **1**/159; John, **1**/13, 34; Margery, **1**/13, 34; Mark, **2**/77*; Randolph, **1**/84; Wal, **1**/229; Wm, **1**/84, 159

Sanford *see* Sandford

Sare *see* Sayer

Sarson, Eleanor, **1**/399; Humph, **1**/399; p. 268

Saule (Sawle), Kath, **1**/507; Ric, **1**/507; Sarah, **1**/173; Wm, **1**/173, 332*, 461, 467

Saunders, Ant, **2**/135; Benj, **3**/10; Isobel, **2**/204; Joan, **1**/62, 71; John, **1**/62, 71; **2**/204; **3**/10, 103; Sarah, **2**/135; Thos, **1**/525; **3**/41*, 48*n*; Wm, **1**/85, 525; **3**/103; —, **3**/178*n*

Savage, Ant, **1**/143; **2**/41; Giles, **1**/373; Henry, **2**/40*n*, 41; John, **1**/143; **2**/85*; Ric, **1**/373

Savory, Edw, **2**/301; Joan, **3**/275; Mary, **2**/162; **3**/343; Rob, **3**/233, 302*n**, 303*, 343*; Thos, **3**/275; Wm, **2**/162*, 301, 354*; **3**/343

Sawcombe, Edm, **1**/43; Joan, **1**/308, 365, 441; John, **1**/70, 308, 365, 441; Rob, **3**/233, 303*, 343*; Thos, **1**/43, 70; **3**/275

Sawle *see* Saule

Sawyer, Jas, **1**/344; John, **1**/344

Sayer (Sare, Seare, Sere, Seyer, Sire, Syer, Syre), Anne, **2**/315; **3**/283; Dan, **2**/235, 315; **3**/283*, 354*; Jas, **2**/112, 292, 306, 308; **3**/99, 161*n*, 174*, 102, 208, 363; Joan, **2**/78; John, **1**/107, 227, 368*n*, 369, 489*n**, 493*; **2**/78; **3**/283, 363; p. 272; Marg, **2**/292, 308; **3**/99, 102, 174, 363; Ralph, **1**/107, 368*n*, 369; **2**/112; Sarah, **2**/306; Wm, **1**/227; widow, p. 269; —, **2**/235

Scanderight, Wal, **2**/352*

Scriven (Scryven), Alice, **1**/178; Henry, **2**/28; Jane, **1**/10, 20, 93; John, **1**/20, 404; **2**/28; p. 272; John, mayor, **1**/547, sheriff, **1**/321; Nic, **1**/10; Ric, **1**/20; Thos, **1**/10, 20, 93, 120, 178; Wm, **1**/10

Scrivener, Hugh, **1**/478; John, **1**/478

Scryven *see* Scriven

Scudamore, Eliz, **1**/249; Wm, **1**/249, 413*; **2**/245*; **3**/356*; p. 271; Wm, sheriff, **2**/247; —, **2**/245

Seaborne, Henry, **1**/481; John, **1**/481

Seaman, Edith, **2**/72; Marg, **1**/137, 209; Ric, **1**/36; Rob, **2**/72; Thos, **1**/36, 137, 179, 209; Wm, **2**/72*;

Dr, p. 267; —, p. 268; —, alderman, p. 268
Searche, Geo, **1**/69; John, **1**/69
Seare *see* Sayer
Sedgewick (Sedgewicke), John, **1**/24; Wm, **1**/24, 30*
Seizemore *see* Sisemore
Selwyn (Sellwine, Sellwyn, Selwin), Henry, **1**/418–19, 564*n*, 565; pp. xix, 270; Isobel, **1**/418–19; Martha, **2**/242, 362; **3**/26, 48, 70, 72, 198, 224, 292; Mary, **3**/359; Rob, **1**/110; Thos, **1**/110, 564*n*, 565; **2**/242, 362; **3**/26, 48, 70, 72, 102, 161*, 198, 224, 359; Wm, mayor, **3**/140; —, **3**/102, 161
Semys (Semigs, Senmigs), Thos, alderman, **1**/30, mayor, **1**/61; Wm, **1**/270; —, **1**/270
Senox *see* Sinnox
Sere *see* Sayer
Sermon, Ric, **3**/357*; Sam, **3**/388*; *and see* Surman
Sexstone, Anne, **3**/345; Clement, **3**/345
Sexty, John, **3**/350*, 353*; Susannah, **3**/350, 353; Wm, **3**/353
Seyer *see* Sayer
Seys, Serjeant, **2**/285*n*; p. xxiii
Seysmore *see* Sisemore
Shatford *see* Shotford
Shaw, Joan, **3**/306; John, **3**/306, 356; Wm, **3**/356
Shayle (Sheyle), Chris, **1**/202; Eliz, **1**/202; Thos, **2**/62*
Sheppard (Shepheard), Adoliza, **3**/356; Edm, **2**/91; Edw, **2**/101, 179, 194; p. 269; John, **2**/101, 117*n*, 331; **3**/72, 278, 356; Joseph, **2**/91; Sam, **1**/549, 577; **2**/331; Susannah, **3**/72; Thos, **1**/547*; **2**/179, 194; Wm, **1**/549, 577
Shere, Thos, **1**/121*
Sherington, Thos, **1**/209; *and see* Cherrington
Shervington (Shurvington), Isobel, **1**/43, 51, 79, 98; Thos, **1**/43, 51, 79, 98, 135, 147, 247; —, **1**/135, 147, 247
Shewell *see* Showell
Shewen, John, **1**/126*
Shewringe, Edm, p. 266
Sheyle *see* Shayle
Shill, Ant, **2**/156; John, **2**/156
Shingleton *see* Singleton
Shipton, Alice, **3**/38; Dan, **3**/108; Eliz, **1**/574; **3**/196, 234; John, **1**/574; **2**/66, 226, 325*, 341*; **3**/38, 66, 108*, 196, 234; p. 273; Sarah, **2**/66, 226, 341; Thos, **2**/341; —, **3**/66, 108
Shipway, Eleanor, **1**/258; Ric, **1**/258
Short, John, **3**/54; Wm, **3**/54
Shotford (Shatford), Anne, **1**/386; John, **1**/386*; Thos, **3**/381*n*
Shott, John, **1**/525; Philip, **1**/551; Thos, **1**/551; Wm, **1**/525
Showe, Roger, **1**/130*

Showell (Shewell, Showle), Hugh, **1**/125; John, **3**/47; Thos, **3**/47; p. 269; Wm, **1**/125
Shurvington *see* Shervington
Silly, Ric, **3**/397; Thos, **3**/397
Silvester, Thos, **2**/64*
Simmes (Symes, Symmes, Syms), Anne, **2**/33; Francis, **1**/372; **2**/324; John, **1**/324, 461, 473; Rob, **1**/461; **2**/33; Thos, **1**/372, 473, 553; **2**/324; Wm, **1**/324, 553
Simonds (Simon, Simondes, Simons) *see* Symons
Simpkins (Symkins), Eleanor, **1**/34, 83; John, **1**/34, 83
Singer (Synger), Felix, **1**/178; John, **1**/178; Thos, p. 266
Singleton (Shingleton), Anne, **2**/18, 296; Dorothy, **1**/31, 227; Frances, **1**/75, 84, 130, 190, 237, 249; **2**/16, 68; Francis, **2**/68; **3**/25, 145; Joan, **1**/426, 542; John, **1**/498; **2**/18, 296; John, sheriff, **2**/106, 231; Lawr, **1**/25, 190, 227, 274, 330, 426, 542; **2**/3, 70, 217; Lawr, alderman, **2**/33, 39, 287, mayor, **1**/579; **2**/1, 213, sheriff, **1**/459; Mary, **2**/3, 70, 217; Ric, p. 272; Sarah, **3**/25, 145; Thos, **1**/31, 75, 84; Wm, **1**/25, 34*, 75*, 84*, 130, 190*, 237, 249*, 498; **2**/16, 68*; Wm, alderman, **2**/151, mayor, **1**/497; **2**/33, 86, sheriff, **1**/279; —, **1**/274; **2**/3
Sinnox (Senox), Eleanor, **2**/236*n*; Isobel, **2**/237; John, **2**/236*n*, 237; Thos, **2**/237*
Sire *see* Sayer
Sisemore (Seizemore, Seysmore, Sysemore), Alice, **3**/330; Ant, **2**/239; Chas, **3**/272; Dennis, **3**/355; Eleanor, **3**/283; Joan, **3**/242, 355; John, **3**/242, 354*n*, 355*; p. 271; Sam, **3**/272; Thos, **2**/239; Wm, **3**/283, 336
Skelton, Francis, **2**/247; **3**/237; Ric, **2**/247; **3**/237
Skett, Benj, **1**/322; Roland, **1**/322
Skillern (Skillam, Skillerne, Skillum, Skyllarne), Eliz, **2**/63*n*; Isaac, **2**/83; John, **1**/168; **2**/106; Ric, **2**/18*, 63*n*, 243, 272; **3**/86*; Sarah, **2**/243, 272; Wm, **1**/168; **2**/83; **3**/74*n*, 86, 365; —, **3**/86
Skinner (Skynner), Anne, **1**/490; **2**/74; John, **2**/269*; **3**/144; Mary, **3**/260, 310, 345, 385; Rob, **1**/2, 490; **2**/141; Sam, **2**/141; **3**/260*; Stephen, **3**/234, 307; Thos, **3**/377; Wm, **1**/2; **3**/144, 224*, 234, 310, 345, 377, 385
Skyllarne *see* Skillern
Skynner *see* Skinner
Slaughter, Wm, **1**/96
Sleight, Ric, **3**/338*n*
Slicer (Sliser, Sulicer), Edw, **1**/363*–4; Eliz, **2**/189, 327, 336; Jas, **1**/364; **2**/189, 191, 327, 336
Sly (Slye), Mary, **3**/263, 289, 292; Wm, **3**/263, 289, 292

INDEX OF PERSONS

Smale *see* Small

Smaleman *see* Smalman

Small (Smale), Edw, **1**/157*; Nic, sheriff, **2**/247

Smallwood, Jane, **2**/139, 193, 333, 368; John, **2**/139, 193, 333*, 368; John, sheriff, **3**/198

Smalman (Smaleman), Joan, **1**/126; Jonicy, **1**/199; Ric, **1**/36, 126, 199

Smart (Smarte), Anne, **3**/159; Ant, **2**/293; **3**/159; Eleanor, **1**/410, 413; John, **1**/126*, 255, 410, 413; **2**/3, 265*; **3**/93*, 172*; Joseph, **2**/66; p. 270; Marg, **3**/62, 106; Mary, **3**/172; Ric, **1**/255; **2**/3, 66, 203*, 293, 367*; **3**/62, 106, 173; Susannah, **2**/367; Thos, **2**/367; **3**/173; Wm, **3**/172

Smith (Smithe, Smyth, Smythe), Alice, **1**/303; Anne, **1**/23, 32, 374*; Brice, **1**/453; Edw, **1**/168; Eleanor, **1**/143, 318; Eliz, **3**/204; Frances, **3**/366; Geo, **2**/63n, 64; Gervase, p. 267; Giles, **2**/2, 12, 214, 307; **3**/36, 55, 116, 143, 204, 323; Henry, **2**/202, 332; Hester, **1**/191, 197, 229, 276, 282; **2**/373; Humph, **3**/266; Jas, **3**/364*; Jane, **3**/203, 226, 325; Joan, **2**/217, 301; **3**/37, 266; John, **1**/32, 68, 92, 113, 136, 143, 318, 331, 374*, 392*, 408, 453, 510, 545, 555, 576; **2**/63n, 64, 111*, 240, 288; **3**/19, 36, 316n, 317*, 366; pp. 266, 271; Kath, **2**/76, 219, 287*; Marg, **1**/481, 490–1, 514; **2**/288; **3**/187; Matt, **1**/569; Maurice, **1**/356; **3**/324; Michael, **1**/113; **2**/367*; Nic, **2**/208; Peter, **2**/348; **3**/187; Ric, **1**/54, 65, 68, 74, 83–4, 93, 117–18, 122, 132, 137, 158, 169, 191, 197, 227, 229, 276, 282, 303, 324, 545; **2**/12, 202; Ric, mayor, **1**/245, 337, sheriff, **1**/141, 187; Rob, **1**/229, 364*, 435; **2**/363; **3**/37; Roger, **1**/134; Sam, **2**/363; Sarah, **1**/54, 65, 83–4, 117–18, 122, 132, 137, 158, 169; Susannah, **2**/291; **3**/29, 174, 246; Sybil, **2**/214, 307; **3**/55, 143, 323, 393; Thos, **1**/23, 68, 98, 136, 168, 229, 331, 381, 408, 435, 480*, 492, 569; **2**/217, 233, 301, 332, 363; **3**/19, 29, 37*, 141*, 203, 226, 313*, 325, 388*; Wal, **1**/576; **2**/2; Wm, **1**/134, 227, 356, 374, 481*, 490–2, 510, 514, 555, 577; **2**/5, 76, 208, 219, 233, 238*, 240, 287, 291, 348, 362n; **3**/29*, 74n, 116, 174, 246, 324; —, **1**/381, 577; **2**/5

Snead, Alice, **1**/31; Anne, **1**/32, 85; Bridget, **1**/177; Wm, **1**/32, 85, 177

Snell, Thos, mayor, **3**/391

Snowe, John, **1**/50*

Solas *see* Sollars

Sole *see* Soule

Sollars (Solas, Sollers), Edw, **3**/333n, 341; Francis, **1**/473; Jas, **3**/341; Ric, **1**/473

Solly, Edw, **1**/269; Wm, **1**/269; *and see* Sally

Soudley *see* Sowdley

Soule (Sole, Sowle), Andrew, **1**/315*; John, **2**/282; **3**/117; Thos, **3**/117; Wm, **2**/282; **3**/117*

Sowdley (Soudley), Eleanor, **2**/364; **3**/116, 158, 287–8; John, **2**/364; **3**/116*, 158, 287 *and n*, 288; p. xiv

Sowle *see* Soule

Sowtherne, Thos, **1**/112; Wm, **1**/112

Sparhawke *see* Sparrowhawke

Sparkes (Spark, Sparks), Abel, **1**/24, 50, 162; Anne, **3**/234, 282; Eleanor, **1**/24, 50, 162; Hester, **2**/162n; John, **1**/505; **2**/166; Ric, **1**/301, 505*; **2**/288; **3**/144, 234, 250n, 251, 282, 305*, 363*; p. xvii; Sarah, **3**/34, 48, 119, 211, 218, 294; Solomon, **3**/144; Thos, **1**/301, 399*; **2**/258*, 288, 374; **3**/34, 48, 119, 211, 218, 250n, 251, 294, 305, 347*; p. 273; Wm, **1**/401; **2**/162n, 166

Sparrow, Wm, **3**/317*

Sparrowhawk (Sparhawke, Sparrowhawke), Dorothy, **2**/288, 297, 345; Eleanor, **3**/101, 212; Eliz, **3**/56, 58; Joan, **1**/447; **2**/152, 174, 214, 223, 280, 310; Mary, **2**/253, 279, 313, 323, 348; **3**/28, 46, 49; Ric, **2**/337; **3**/92, 101, 212; Rob, **1**/351, 447; **2**/134*, 152, 174, 214, 223*, 280, 288, 297, 310, 337*, 345; **3**/56, 58, 239*; Thos, **1**/351; Wm, **2**/223, 253, 279, 313, 323, 348; **3**/28, 46, 49, 279*; —, **3**/92

Spencer, Beata, **3**/333; Edw, **2**/370; Giles, **3**/236, 288; Thos, **3**/236, 333; Wm, **2**/370; **3**/288

Spillman, Thos, **2**/333*

Springe, Eliz, **3**/120; Francis, **1**/527; **2**/276; **3**/120; Henry, **1**/72, 527; **2**/276; Isobel, **1**/301, 486; Lewis, **1**/72, 301, 486; **2**/326; —, **2**/326

Sprint, John, **1**/468; Zachariah, **1**/468

Stacie, John, **1**/47*

Stallard, Anselm, **1**/369, 415–16; **2**/2, 14; Dorothy, **1**/369, 415–16; Rob, **1**/21*; Thos, **2**/2, 14

Stanby, Thos, **1**/566

Staniford, Chas, **2**/180; Thos, **2**/180

Staple, Thos, **3**/72; Wm, **3**/72

Stapp (Stap), Sarah, **2**/58, 85, 229; Wm, **2**/58, 85, 229

Staunton, Rob, **2**/112; Wm, **2**/112

Staynar (Steyner), Cecily, **1**/106; Ric, **1**/53; Rob, **1**/106

Stayte (Steight), John, **2**/360; **3**/245*; Rob, **2**/360

Stedman (Steedman), Giles, **1**/258; John, **1**/499; Ric, **1**/498; Wm, **1**/258, 498–9

Steell, Sam, **3**/298; Stephen, **3**/298

Steephens (Steevens) *see* Stephens

Steight *see* Stayte

Stephens (Steephens, Steevens, Stevens) Alice, **1**/527, 579; **2**/13, 45, 54, 104–5, 108, 123, 154, 226, 258*, 265; Anne, **1**/365, 367, 404, 480, 532, 553; **2**/36, 56, 59, 81, 148, 172, 284; **3**/39;

INDEX OF PERSONS

Bridget, **2**/327; **3**/44; Chris, **1**/290; Edw, **1**/282; Frances, **3**/35, 94, 243*; Francis, **3**/312; Garnet, **3**/94; Geo, **1**/34, 91, 145, 168, 358; Henry, **1**/178, 506; **2**/36; **3**/396; Jas, **1**/328*, 365, 367, 404, 441*, 480, 506, 532, 553, 585; **2**/56, 59, 81, 148, 172, 284, 323; **3**/39, 74n, 199, 358; Jas, alderman, **2**/191, mayor, **2**/7, 56, 61, sheriff, **1**/517, 561; John, **1**/256, 290; **2**/156, 310, 327; **3**/12*, 44, 94, 243*, 333; Margery, **2**/252, 352; Mary, **3**/358; Matt, **1**/282; **2**/5, 163*, 213; Matt, mayor, **1**/328; Olive, **1**/91, 145, 168; Oliver, **1**/256, 555; p. 270; Paul, **3**/312; Philip, **3**/196; Ric, **1**/585; **2**/252, 352; Ric, sheriff, **2**/344; **3**/99; Rob, **1**/178, 373; Sam, **2**/273, 310; Thos, **1**/527, 557*, 579; **2**/13, 45, 54, 104–5, 108, 123, 154, 156, 213, 226, 258*, 260n, 265, 273, 310; **3**/35, 94*, 120, 196, 243*, 333, 369*; p. 272; Thos (*alias* White), **1**/574; Wm, **1**/373; **2**/2n, 5; **3**/25*, 48n*, 94, 109n, 120, 396; —, **2**/310

Stephenson (Stepherson), Anne (*alias* Cowles), **3**/72, 176; John, **3**/265; John (*alias* Cowles), **2**/121; **3**/72, 176, 279; Stephen, **3**/265; Stephen (*alias* Cowles), **2**/121; Wm (*alias* Cowles), **3**/16*, 279; *and see* Stevenson

Stevens *see* Stephens

Stevenson, W. H., pp. xxix–xxx; *and see* Stephenson

Stewart, Andrew, p. 267

Steyner *see* Staynar

Stiles (Styles), Jas, **3**/308*; Wm, **3**/270*

Stock (Stocke), Castle, **2**/274; Chris, **1**/546; Edw, **3**/26; John, **3**/372*; Thos, **1**/546; **3**/26; Wal, **2**/184; Wm, **2**/184, 274; *and see* Stookes

Stone, Henry, **1**/255; John, **2**/186*; **3**/24; Nic, **1**/255; Rob, **1**/255; **3**/24; Thos, **1**/255; Wm, **3**/160*

Stoneum, Nic, **1**/429; Thos, **1**/429

Stookes, Wal, **1**/133; Wm, **1**/133; *and see* Stock

Stowell, Mary, **3**/195; Wm, **1**/448*; **2**/322*; **3**/119, 195; —, **3**/119

Stratford, Ant, **1**/229; Arthur, **1**/267, 269, 419*; Marg, **1**/267, 269, 419; Thos, **1**/229; Wm, **1**/407n, 419

Strawford, Alice, **1**/82, 100; Joan, **1**/463; Wal, **1**/146, 463 ; —, **1**/146

Streete, Sam, **3**/281n

Stubbs, Thos, **1**/305; —, **1**/305

Sturmey (Sturmy, Sturmye), Blanche, **1**/434, 521; **2**/139; Dan, **1**/277; **2**/62*; Edm, **2**/139, 274n*, 279*; Edw, **1**/179, 434, 521; **2**/350; Eleanor, **1**/169, 182, 268, 427, 455; Eliz, **1**/485, 513; Geo, **1**/179, 529; Henry, **1**/277; **2**/350; Jas, **1**/529; John, **2**/47, 62, 213, 269; Mary, **2**/213, 269; Rob, **1**/34, 129, 169, 182, 268, 427, 455, 485, 513; **2**/100n, 102*; Sam, **3**/228n, 233*; Thos, **1**/13*, 34, 143, 293n; —, **1**/129, 143

Styles *see* Stiles

Suckley, Geof, **1**/486; Roland, **1**/486

Suffeild, Anne, **2**/51; Ant, **2**/51, 92, 350; **3**/54, 65; Henry, **1**/455, 467n; Hester, **3**/54, 65; Thos, **1**/455, 467n, 545*; **2**/51*, 92; p. 267; —, **2**/350

Sulaway, Wm, **2**/122*

Sulicer *see* Slicer

Summers (Sumers, Summer), Ant, **1**/522; Eleanor, **2**/285; **3**/162, 177; Eliz, **3**/396; Nat, **3**/177; Thos, **1**/522; **2**/285; **3**/92n, 162, 177*, 381, 396; —, **3**/92n

Surman, Geo, **1**/567; John, **1**/395, 449, 567, 585; Ric, **2**/169; Sybil, **1**/585; Thos, **1**/199, 395; **2**/169; Wm, **1**/199; *and see* Sermon

Sutor, John, **1**/430; Sam, **1**/430

Swaine (Swayn, Swayne), Edw, **1**/124; **2**/273, 363; **3**/160, 208*, 320*, 357; Eliz, **2**/273; Frances, **3**/323; Jane, **2**/363; **3**/160; Joan, **2**/26, 232; John, **2**/345; **3**/193n, 196, 238; Kenelm, **1**/351; Ric, **3**/208; Sam, **3**/331; Sarah, **2**/215; Thos, **3**/323, 385; p. 268; Wm, **1**/124; **2**/26, 215, 232; **3**/331, 357; p. 273; —, **2**/345; **3**/201n

Swett (Sweat, Sweate), Eliz, **2**/241; John, **2**/46; Ric, **2**/46, 241, 353; **3**/141, 201*; Thos, **3**/141, 143n; Ursula, **2**/353

Swift, John, **3**/102n

Syer *see* Sayer

Symes *see* Simmes

Symkins *see* Simpkins

Symmes *see* Simmes

Symons (Simon, Simondes, Simonds, Simons, Symmons, Symon, Symondes, Symonds), Anne, **1**/497; **2**/20; Chas, **2**/368; David, **3**/365*; Edw, **1**/280*, 304, 326, 330, 338, 527; **3**/223n, 226; p. 266; Eliz, **1**/280, 304, 326, 338; Emma, **2**/60; Francis, **1**/120; Henry, **3**/285n; Jas, **1**/68; Jane, **1**/120; Joan, **2**/37*, 142, 219, 318; **3**/129–30, 226; John, **1**/275, 346, 448*; **2**/20, 33, 60, 260n, 263, 276*, 368; **3**/102n, 104; Kath, **1**/480, 543; Lawr, **1**/280, 527; Nat, **1**/305, 399, 497, 537; p. 270; Nic, **1**/11; Ric, **1**/275*, 353*, 480, 537, 543; **2**/37*, 141n*, 142*, 219, 318; **3**/129–30; p. 270; Rob, **1**/275, 353, 385; Thos, **1**/11, 305, 399; Wm, **1**/68, 346; **2**/33, 260n, 263; **3**/104, 163n

Syms *see* Simmes

Synger *see* Singer

Syre *see* Sayer

Sysemore *see* Sisemore

Tackley (Tackey, Tacklyn, Tacly, Taklinge Tackley, Tacly), Eliz, **1**/326, 395, 409; Eliz (*alias* Besall, Bezell, Bussell), **1**/261, 275, 439; Thos, **1**/326, 395, 409; **3**/38*; Thos (*alias* Besall, Bezell, Bussell), **1**/261, 275, 439

Tailor (Tailer) *see* Taylor

Tainton *see* Taynton

Taklinge *see* Tackley

Tandy, John, **3**/121; Michael, **3**/121

Tanner, David, **3**/372*; Humph, **2**/310; Isaac, **3**/90; Roger, **1**/543*; Thos, **2**/310; Wm, **3**/90

Tarkinton, John, **2**/193; Joseph, **2**/193

Tarne, Leonard, **1**/70, 107; p. 271; Leonard, sheriff, **1**/399; Marg, **1**/70, 107, 198, 343; Miles, **1**/440; Sarah, **1**/440; Thos, **1**/198, 343

Tasker, Dinah, **2**/375

Tayloe, Thos, **1**/477*

Taylor (Tailer, Tailor, Tayler), Anne, **1**/190, 325, 331*; Ant, **1**/379, 481; Burral, **1**/39–40; Chris, **1**/39; Dorothy, **2**/121; Edith, **1**/142; Edw, **3**/365; Eleanor, **1**/414–16, 464, 533, 572, 576; **2**/41; Eliz, **1**/22, 382; Frances, **1**/29, 86, 107*; Geo, **1**/529, 543, 572, 576; **2**/41, 115, 126, 204, 324; **3**/39, 189*; p. 272; Geo, sheriff, **3**/12; Henry, **1**/157*; Humph, **1**/29, 37*, 86, 107*, 280; Jas, **1**/142, 467; Jasper, **2**/237; **3**/11, 25; Joan, **1**/108, 171, 349, 379, 442, 469, 476; **2**/115, 126, 204, 324; **3**/39; John, **1**/22, 39–40, 69*, 104, 107*, 190, 267, 276*, 287, 333, 372, 382, 417, 444, 465, 482, 550; **2**/41, 70, 237, 254*n*; **3**/11, 52*, 104, 366; p. 273; John, alderman, **1**/30; p. 265, justice, **1**/280, mayor, **1**/227; Kath, **1**/98, 100, 106, 172; Magdalen, **1**/514; Marg, **1**/467; Mary, **1**/417, 465, 482, 550; Matt, **3**/286; Nic, **1**/446; Philip, **3**/11, 366; Ric, **1**/25, 228, 267, 287, 333, 349, 379, 391, 414–16, 433, 442, 464, 469, 476, 505, 507, 529, 533, 585; **2**/40, 121, 268*, 285*n*; **3**/70, 286; Ric, sheriff, **2**/43; Rob, **2**/36*; **3**/388; Roger, **1**/444; Sam, **1**/433; **3**/196*n*; Thos, **1**/25, 98*, 100*, 119, 290, 325, 331*, 341, 379, 505, 513*n*, 514*; **3**/106*, 365, 388; Tim, **1**/108, 171; Ursula, **1**/119, 290; Wm, **1**/98, 100, 103*, 106, 172, 318*, 446, 481, 513*n*, 514; **2**/254*n*, 258*; **3**/69*n*, 70, 122*, 316*n*, 361*; Wm, mayor, **3**/347; widow, p. 269; —, **1**/280, 543, 585; **2**/40, 285*n*; **3**/11, 25, 104

Taynton (Tainton, Teinton, Teynton), Eleanor, **2**/294; **3**/30; Humph, **1**/91; Joan, **1**/170; John, **1**/25, 91; Michael, **1**/380; Ric, **1**/380; Thos, **1**/22, 170; **3**/30; p. 272; Toby, **3**/133; Wal, **1**/25; **2**/294*; **3**/30*

Teakle (Teeckle, Teekle, Teekell, Tickell, Tickle, Ticklee, Tikle), Joan, **1**/493; Kath, **1**/578; Nat, **1**/476*n*, 478; Ric, **1**/578; Sam, **1**/5, 337, 343, 400, 476*n*, 478*, 493, 574*n*, 578*; Wal, **1**/5; p. 265

Teinton *see* Taynton

Tench, Stephen, **2**/369*

Terrett, Henry, **1**/299; John, **1**/299; **2**/274, 281, 353; **3**/300; Ric, **3**/300; Sam, **2**/76; p. xxx; Thos, **2**/76, 274, 281, 353; p. xxx

Terry (Tirrey, Tirry), John, **1**/307; Mary, **1**/15, 49, 62, 123*; Ric, **1**/123, 212; Wm, **1**/15, 49, 62, 123*; —, **1**/212, 307

Tewe, Francis, **1**/306; John, **1**/306

Teynton *see* Taynton

Thackwell, Joseph, **2**/29; Thos, **2**/29

Thayer (Thayre, Theyer), Anne, **1**/355, 550; Giles, **1**/294*, 355, 433; **2**/23; Hugh, **1**/335; John, **2**/2*n*, 23; **3**/30; Rob, **1**/335; Thos, **1**/550; Wm, **3**/30

Thoare, John, **1**/48; Thos, **1**/48

Thomas, Abraham, **3**/108, 134*n*; Ant, **3**/9*; Arnold, **1**/162; Christiane, **1**/383; David, **2**/153; Dorothy, **2**/261; **3**/69; Geo, **2**/153; Giles, **2**/261; Griffith, **1**/162; Henry, **1**/420–1; **2**/26, 270; p. xxiv; Joan, **1**/96, 137, 228; **2**/26, 116; p. xxiv; John, **1**/96, 137, 198, 228, 316, 332; **2**/5*, 96, 363; **3**/48, 84*, 87*n*, 108, 134*n*, 175*n*, 193*n*, 216*n*, 217*, 323*n*; Jonathan, **2**/71, 116; **3**/48; Kath, **1**/374; Lewis, **1**/190; Marg, **1**/316, 332; **2**/363; Morgan, **1**/439; **3**/69; Ric, **2**/96; **3**/216*n*, 217; Roland, **1**/511; Thos, **1**/190, 238, 420–1, 511; **3**/17*; Wal, **1**/7; Wm, **1**/198, 374, 383, 439; **2**/71, 270; **3**/80*n*; *and see* Tomes

Thompson (Tompsin, Tomson, Tomsonne), Francis, **1**/567; p. 267; Ric, **2**/165*; Thos, **2**/222*; Wm, **1**/5, 564*n*, 567

Thornbury, Giles, p. 265

Thorne, Eliz, **1**/191; Giles, **1**/87; Joan, **1**/2*, 3, 6, 71, 76, 99, 158, 201, 307; John, **1**/2*, 3, 6, 71, 76, 87, 88, 99, 103*, 158, 191*, 201, 307; pp. xix, 267; John, justice, **1**/162, mayor, **1**/177, sheriff, **1**/79; John (*alias* Prentice), **1**/103; Ric, **1**/2; Roger, **1**/88; Sybil, **1**/103; Wm, **1**/191, 366*; —, p. 267

Thorpe, Anne, **3**/380; John, **3**/164; Ric, **3**/164

Tickle (Tickell, Ticklee, Tikle) *see* Teakle

Tiler (Tyler, Tylor), Alice, **1**/489; Anne, **2**/163; **3**/231, 247, 283, 308, 353; Edw, **3**/233, 248, 278, 343*; Eliz, **2**/264, 309; Jas, **1**/303*, 393, 523, 559, 575*; **2**/3, 118, 202, 342; **3**/228*n**; p. 270; John, **1**/489, 556*n*, 557*; **2**/109, 163, 259, 264, 309, 370; **3**/10, 31, 146*, 231, 242, 247, 283, 308, 353, 377; p. 267; Marg, **1**/523, 559, 575; **2**/3, 118; Mary, **2**/202, 342; **3**/278, 377; Ric, **1**/411*; Thos, **1**/489; Wal, **1**/33, 123; Wm, **1**/50*; —, **1**/123, 556*n*; **2**/370; **3**/10, 31

Till (Tyll), Alice, **1**/98, Dorothy, **2**/99; 245; Edw,

INDEX OF PERSONS

3/57; John, **1**/98; Mary, **3**/129, 354; Ric, **1**/98, 505; **2**/99, 245*, 369; **3**/57*, 129, 354; p. 271; Rob, **1**/98; Wm, **1**/437; —, **1**/505; **2**/369; **3**/57*
Tilleson, John, **2**/243*n*
Tilsley (Tylsley), Anne, **1**/370, 376–7, 384, 403, 406, 414, 426, 429–30, 445*, 448*, 449–50, 461; p. xxviii; John, **1**/86; p. xxviii; Philip, **1**/86, 370, 376–7, 384, 403, 406, 414, 426, 429–30, 445*, 448*, 449–50, 461; p. xxviii
Timbrell, Chris, **1**/551*
Tinsley, John, **2**/272; Wal, **2**/272
Tipper, Jas, **1**/581; Ric, **1**/581
Tippinge, Jas, **2**/232; Wm, **2**/232
Tirrett, John, **1**/81; Ric, **1**/81
Tirrey (Tirry) *see* Terry
Titcombe, John, **3**/14*
Tither (Tyther), Ant, **1**/316, 330; Eleanor, **1**/519; Edw, sheriff, **2**/291; **3**/51; Em, **2**/251; Marg, **1**/367, 380–1, 409, 463, 475, 495, 497, 506, 511, 525; Rob, **1**/316, 367, 380–1, 409, 463, 475, 495, 497, 506, 511, 519, 525; **2**/251; Rob, mayor, **2**/191, 231, sheriff, **1**/561; **2**/56; Thos, **1**/330
Togwell, Sybil, **1**/547; Wm, **1**/547*–8*
Tolson, Anne, **1**/14; John, **1**/14
Tomes (Tomas, Tombes, Toms), Chris, **1**/209; Dan, **3**/35; Eliz, **1**/553; **2**/158; John, **1**/212*, 246, 275, 414*–16*, 553; **2**/158; **3**/383; p. 273; John, sheriff, **2**/189; Marg, **1**/246, 275; Matt, **3**/35; Rob, p. 265; Wm, **1**/209; **3**/383; *and see* Thomas
Tomkins *see* Tompkins
Tomlingson, Chas, **1**/187; Nicholas, **1**/187
Tompkins (Tomkins), Abel, **1**/348; Eliz, **1**/122; John, **1**/122, 348; **2**/52*, 55*n*; Nic, **1**/119; Thos, **1**/119; Ursula, **2**/52; Wm, **1**/347*; **3**/118; Wm (*alias* Brymeyard), **2**/190; —, **2**/55*n*; **3**/118
Tompson (Tompsin) *see* Thompson
Toms *see* Tomes
Tomsonne *see* Thompson
Toney (Tony), Chas, **2**/301*n*, 304; **3**/370; Henry, **1**/360; Jas, **3**/370; John, **1**/360, 385; Thos, **1**/323*, 385; **2**/304
Tovey, Ric, **2**/226; Thos, **2**/226
Towey, Edw, **2**/67; Lawr, **2**/67
Townsend (Townesend, Townsende, Townshend), Chris, **1**/350, 467; **2**/81–2, 136; Edw, **1**/321, 350, 418; Eliz, **1**/467; **2**/67, 81; Geo, **1**/418; Giles, **3**/318*; Henry, **2**/79*n*, 82, 136; Humph, p. 266; Joan, **2**/49; John, **2**/4; Lawr, **1**/257; **2**/48*n*, 49; **3**/87; Perian, **1**/321; Ric, **1**/323; **2**/81; Thos, **1**/323; **2**/4, 48*n*, 49*; Wm, **1**/257; **2**/12*; **3**/87; widow, **2**/79*n*; —, **3**/211*n**
Travell, Rob, **1**/171; Wm, **1**/171; p. 272
Travis, John, **3**/99; Matt, **3**/99

Tray (Traye), Edw, **2**/139; Rob, **2**/139; p. 266
Tremeare (Tremere), Ant, **1**/82, 247; Marg, **1**/247; Stephen, **1**/82
Tricke, John, **1**/6; Wal, **1**/6
Trinder, Wm, **3**/83*
Trippet (Trippett), Chas, **1**/464; Thos, **1**/280, 324, 464; **2**/11; —, **1**/324; **2**/11
Trolley, John, **3**/242; Joseph, **3**/242, 266*n*
Trotman, Wm, **3**/35*
Trow (Trowe), John, **2**/314; **3**/190, 246, 367; Marg, **2**/314; **3**/190
Tucker, Henry, **2**/106*n*, 114; Thos, **2**/114, 362*, 364*n*
Tuckye, John, p. 273
Tuffley (Tufly), Chas, **2**/321; Kath, **2**/321; Nat, **1**/257; Wal, **1**/257
Tully, Ric, **1**/432; Thos, **1**/432; p. 272
Tunkes (Tunckes, Tuncks), Edw, **1**/95; John, **1**/41; Kath, **1**/41; Wm, **1**/95
Turbervile, Francis, **2**/326; John, **2**/326
Turbett, John, **3**/220*, 235, 276; Margery, **3**/235*; Rob, **2**/304*; Thos, **3**/108, 235*, 276, 345*; Wm, **3**/235; —, **3**/108
Turner, Anne, **3**/302, 386; Cuthbert, **1**/559*n*, 560; Edm (*alias* Barnard), **2**/274*n*, 275; Edw, **2**/60*, 63; Henry, **3**/164; Humph, **1**/513*n*; Joan, **1**/513; **2**/281, 342; John, **1**/513, 560; **2**/281*, 342*; **3**/17, 66, 158, 164, 275*, 306, 374*n*, 378; John (*alias* Barnard), **2**/275; Marg, **3**/306; Ralph, **3**/131; Ric, **3**/22*; Sam, **3**/131, 380*; Thos, **1**/513*, 559*n*; **2**/338*n**, 342*; **3**/66, 302, 386*; Wm, **2**/63, 281; **3**/17, 158, 378; —, **3**/64*n*
Tutley, John, **1**/396*n*
Twyninge, Jas, **1**/157; Ric, **1**/157
Tyler *see* Tiler
Tyll *see* Till
Tylor *see* Tiler
Tylsley *see* Tilsley
Tyther *see* Tither

Ufford, Dan, **1**/325; Jas, **1**/325
Uley, Arthur, **1**/211; John, **1**/211
Underhill, Frances, **3**/40, 148; Geo, **3**/207; Jacob, **2**/134*; Jas, **2**/369; **3**/40, 148, 207; —, **2**/369
Underwood, Ant, **3**/285; Chris, **3**/249; Mary, **3**/210; Ric, **2**/111*; **3**/210
Unwin, Rob, **2**/253; —, **2**/253; **3**/285

Vaiers (Vayers), Marg, **2**/67, 248; Thos, **2**/67, 248; p. 270
Vaisey (Vaisie) *see* Veysey
Varentur, Edm, **1**/100*
Varney, Edw, **1**/32; Tim, **1**/32

Varnham (Varnum), Gregory, **2**/255*; John, **2**/340; Wm, **2**/340
Vaughan (Vaughen), Aaron, **3**/29; Chas, **3**/392; David, **3**/211; Edw, **3**/252; Eliz, **3**/202; Isobel, **1**/489; Jas, **1**/34; **2**/175; John, **1**/63*; **3**/211; Joshua, **3**/110; Joyce, **3**/220; Judith, **2**/376; Marg, **1**/119; **3**/110, 146, 252, 297–8; Mary, **3**/29; Moses, **3**/202; Ric, **1**/34, 161, 256*, 489*, 578; **2**/109, 175; p. 266; Roland, **1**/119; Sam, **3**/228; Thos, **1**/489; **2**/129; **3**/29*, 109*n*, 110*, 146, 220, 228* *and n*, 297–8; Ursula, **2**/129; Wm, **1**/161; **3**/214*, 392; —, **2**/109
Vayers *see* Vaiers
Veisey *see* Veysey
Venn (Ven), Eliz, **1**/180, 189, 209; Henry, **2**/127; John, **1**/65, 180, 189; **2**/127; Ric, **1**/21*, 23, 168; Thos, **1**/23; Wm, **1**/65; —, **1**/168
Venton, John, **2**/291; Thos, **2**/291
Vernon, Geo, **3**/295; Henry, **3**/295
Veysey (Vaisey, Vaisie, Veisey, Veysee, Veysie), Dorothy, **3**/355, 367, 387; Jas, **1**/141; Marg, **2**/102, 161, 224, 297; **3**/10, 63, 177, 226, 260; Mary, **3**/347; Nat, **3**/295*n*, 355*, 367, 387*; Nic, **1**/141; Thos, **3**/16, 347, 386*n*, 387; Thos, sheriff, **3**/357; Wal, **2**/102, 161, 224, 297; **3**/10, 16, 63, 177, 226, 260; Wal, sheriff, **3**/115
Vice, Jonathan, **3**/380*
Viner (Vinar, Vyner, Vynor), Constance, **2**/251; Dan, **2**/175*; Eleanor, **2**/378; Henry, **1**/378; Humph, **2**/106; Joan, **2**/17; John, **3**/344; Mathias, **2**/17; Michael, **1**/494; Thos, **1**/494; **2**/99*, 378; Wm, **1**/378; **2**/106, 251; **3**/246*, 344
Voare, Chas, **2**/91*
Vosse, Eliz, **3**/188; Matt, **3**/188
Vyler, Henry, **1**/104; John, **1**/104
Vyner (Vynor) *see* Viner

Wade, John, p. 265
Wadley, John, **2**/327*; **3**/47, 287, 374*; p. 272; Ric, **1**/4; **3**/47; Thos, **1**/4; Wm, **3**/287
Wadman, Eliz, **2**/249, 275, 281, 348; **3**/41, 116, 122; Rog, **2**/104*, 249, 275, 281, 348; **3**/41, 116, 122
Wager, John, **1**/348; Ric, **1**/97, 107*; Rob, **1**/121, 181, 262, 348; Ursula, **1**/181, 262; —, **1**/121
Wagstaff (Wagestaff, Waggestaffe, Wagstaffe), Edw, **1**/261, 340, 406*; p. 266; Edw, sheriff, **1**/480, 559; John, **1**/406; p. 271; John, mayor, **3**/34, 184, 197*n*; Kath, **1**/261, 340, 406
Waite *see* Wayte
Walbridge (Walbeurge, Walbridg, Walburge), Anne, **1**/350; Eliz, **1**/170-1, 211; John, **1**/170, 171*, 182, 191, 211, 298; Ric, **1**/171, 298, 350; Simon, **1**/298
Waldin, Henry, **3**/325; Thos, **3**/325
Walker, Ant, **1**/211; **3**/121*, 135*n**, 268, 276, 344; Benj, **2**/355; Dan, **3**/295; Edw (*alias* Weaver), **1**/501; Francis, **2**/189; Jas, **2**/282; **3**/23, 90; Joan, **3**/295*n*; John, **1**/109, 282, 403; John (*alias* Weaver), **1**/501; Martha, **2**/282; **3**/23, 90; Mary, **3**/268, 344; Matt, **2**/189; Nic, **1**/376; Ralph, **2**/355; Ric, **1**/211, 376; **3**/295, 388*; Thos, **1**/109; Wm, **1**/340*, 403; —, **1**/282; **3**/295*n*
Walkley, Thos, **3**/69*
Wall (Walle), John, **1**/202; Ric, **2**/345*; Thos, **1**/202; Wm, **1**/31*; **2**/352*n*, 353*; **3**/263
Wallen, Francis, **3**/9; Thos, **3**/9
Wallington, Edw, **2**/84; Stephen, **2**/84
Wallis, John, **1**/145; Ralph, **1**/145
Walshe, Anne, **1**/37; Rob, **1**/37
Walter (Walters), Giles, p. 273; John, **1**/294*; **3**/349; Margery, **3**/349
Walton, John, sheriff, **1**/227
Wand, Wm, **2**/266; —, **2**/266
Wantner (Wantener, Wantnor), Abel, **1**/274; **2**/324; **3**/308, 379; Chas, **3**/379; Marg, **1**/96, 187, 311, 506, 554; Thos, **3**/308; Wm, **1**/96, 187, 274, 311, 554; **2**/324; family, p. xxxi
Waples, Henry, **1**/141; John, **1**/141
Ward (Warde), Ant, **1**/51; **2**/217*; Eliz, **1**/145, 168, 346; **3**/304, 350, 384; Geo, **3**/80, 250*n*; John, **2**/245; **3**/48*n*, 52, 80, 250*n*, 304, 350, 384*; Joseph, **1**/536; Mary, **1**/457; Nat, **1**/533; Philip, **1**/325, 457; **2**/117*n*; **3**/52; Rob, **2**/245; Thos, **1**/51; Wm, **1**/97*, 145, 168, 255, 325, 346, 533, 536
Warmington, John, **1**/483; Thos, **1**/483
Warne, Henry, **1**/108; John, **1**/108
Warneford, Wal, **3**/64; Wm, **3**/64
Warner (Warnor), Chas, **3**/263; Edw, **3**/263; Henry, **1**/146; Ric, **1**/146
Warwick, countess of *see* Rich, Susan
Warwick (Warwicke), Anne, **1**/500, 552; **2**/33, 82, 282; Wm, **1**/500, 552; **2**/33, 82, 282; p. 271; —, **3**/228*n*
Wasfield (Wasfeild, Wastfeild, Wastfield), Eliz, **3**/132, 145; Jane, **3**/296; John, **2**/14*, 150*, 318; **3**/20, 80, 132, 145; Nic, **2**/150; **3**/296; Rob, **3**/46; Wm, **3**/46; —, **2**/150, 318; **3**/20, 80
Washborne, Dan, **3**/266; John, **3**/296*, 363; Mary, **3**/266; Sam, **2**/166; **3**/363; Thos, **2**/166
Wastfeild (Wastfield) *see* Wasfeild
Waters (Watters), Andrew, **2**/154; John, **1**/431*; Thos, **2**/154
Waterson, Geof, **2**/271; Joan, **2**/271
Watkins (Watkin, Watkine), Anne, **1**/82; Geo, **1**/131, 229–30; Henry (Harry), **1**/65, 237; John,

INDEX OF PERSONS

1/103, 237; **2**/64, 210*; **3**/266; Mary, 1/147, 179; Maurice, 1/82; Peter, **3**/266, 278; Ric, 1/65, 147, 179; **2**/64; Rob, 1/230; Sam, **3**/278; Simon, 1/72; Thos, 1/131, 365*; Wal, 1/103 *and see* Gwatkin; Wm, 1/72, 229

Watson (Wattson), Humph, **2**/282*; John, **3**/176*; Matt, 1/30; Ric, 1/30

Watters *see* Waters

Watts (Wattes), Anne, 1/14; Edw, 1/198; Eliz, **3**/351; Herbert, 1/198; Jas, **3**/278; John, **3**/121, 278; John (*alias* Jones), **2**/305; Ric, **3**/41, 190; Ric (*alias* Jones), **2**/305; Rob, 1/14; **3**/311; Sarah, **3**/121; Thos, 1/113*, 493*; **3**/190, 351; Wm, **2**/299; **3**/41, 121*; —, **2**/299

Wattson *see* Watson

Way (Waye), John, **3**/224*, 346, 394; Susannah, **3**/346, 394; Wm, **2**/109*

Wayte (Waite, Wayt), Alice, 1/106; Henry, 1/188; Jas, 1/106; Ric, 1/188; Wm, **3**/122*

Weale, Eliz, 1/21, 122; Henry, 1/82; John, 1/413–14; Ric, 1/413–14; Thos, 1/21, 49, 82, 122; **3**/133*; Wal, 1/49

Weaver (Wevere), Anne, **3**/302, 372; Ant, **2**/108; Blanche, **2**/265; Edw, **2**/108; p. 266; Edw (*alias* Walker), 1/501; Francis, 1/131, 271*, 313, 331*; **2**/233*; Henry, **3**/261, 331, 398; Joan, 1/131; John (*alias* Walker), 1/501; Mary, **3**/379; Ric, **3**/222*, 261, 302, 304*, 372, 379; Sarah, **3**/331, 398; Thos, 1/22*, 313; **2**/52*, 55*n*, 199*, 265; **3**/58*; Wm, **2**/280*

Webb (Webbe), Anne, 1/132; **3**/332, 366, 375, 387; Ant, 1/288; Arthur, **3**/297; Edw, 1/470; Eliz, **3**/346; Geof, 1/201; Isobel, 1/85; Jane, **2**/298; **3**/82, 85, 245; John, 1/3, 85*, 132, 158*, 272, 341, 344, 383, 470, 512, 558, 574; **2**/101, 261, 298, 338*; **3**/82*, 85, 135, 245, 297, 375, 387*; pp. 265, 271; John, mayor, 1/441, 464; **3**/230, sheriff, 1/207; Leonard, 1/284; Peter, 1/284; Nic, 1/3, 80, 574; **3**/82; Nic, mayor, 1/561, **2**/69; **3**/385, sheriff, 1/391, 471; **2**/169; Ric, 1/23, 201, 288, 332; **3**/135, 262*n*, 346, 364; Ric, mayor, 1/3; Rob, 1/485*; Sam, **3**/277; Sergeant, 1/85, 558; Stephen, **3**/364; Thos, 1/13, 23, 80, 382, 485; **3**/277*, 311, 332, 366; p. 271; Thos, sheriff, **3**/306; Ursula, **2**/261; Wm, 1/132, 332, 382–3, 485, 508; **3**/277; p. 271; —, **3**/262*n*

Webley (Weblie, Webly, Weblye), Cath, 1/34; Geo, **3**/10; Giles, 1/398*, 529; **3**/177; p. 272; Henry, 1/561; John, **2**/185; Joseph, **3**/213*n*; Mary, 1/529; Ric, 1/561; **3**/32*; Rob, **2**/93*; Sam, p. 269; Thos, 1/34, 121*; **3**/10, 393*n*, 399*; p. 268*; Wm, **2**/185; **3**/177; pp. 268, 270; widow, **3**/393*n*; —, p. 268

Webster, John, 1/197; Wm, 1/197, 280

Wedge, Anne, 1/198

Weekes, Marg, 1/123, 200, 212; Wm, 1/123, 200, 212

Welch, Jas, **2**/224; John, 1/522*; Wm, **2**/224

Wellavise, Thos, **3**/122; Wm, **3**/122, 394*n*, 398*

Wells, Anne, **3**/297; John, **2**/88, 196, 328*, 357*; **3**/163*n*, 197*, 271, 297; Joseph, **3**/391; Mary, **3**/368, 390; Michael, **3**/391; Ric, **2**/88; **3**/196*n*, 197, 313, 368, 390; Sarah, **2**/196, 328

Welsteed (Wellsteede, Welstead, Welstedd, Welsteedd, Welsteede), Dan, 1/381; Eliz, **2**/14, 66, 96, 135, 217, 304, 341; **3**/57, 222; John, **2**/14, 66, 96*, 135, 217, 304, 341; **3**/57, 222; Thos, 1/381

Went, John, 1/117; Kath, 1/117

West, David, p. 266; John, 1/582; Mary, 1/582; Ric, 1/387*; Rob, **3**/18; Stephen, **3**/18

Wevere *see* Weaver

Weyman, Ambrose, **3**/240, 272, 299; D[an], witness, **3**/286; John, **3**/60, 311; Mary, **3**/272; —, **3**/60; *and see* Wyman

Wheeler (Wheelar, Whiller), Anne, 1/208, 282; E., p. 264; Francis, **2**/146; Henry, 1/162, 208, 282; pp. 265–6; Henry (*alias* Dowdswell), 1/419*; Jane, **2**/55; John, 1/147; Marg, 1/162; Sam, **3**/187; Thos, **3**/187, 213*n*, 281*; Wm, **2**/55, 146; —, 1/147

White (Whyte), Alice, 1/64, 207; Ant, 1/294*, 469*; **2**/241; **3**/201*; David, 1/208, 293, 353*, 393; Edith, 1/208, 293, 353; Giles, **2**/312; **3**/334; Hannah, **3**/280, 290, 326; Henry, 1/64, 207; Joan, **2**/1, 177, 182, 192, 258, 288, 313; **3**/27, 59, 67; John, 1/36, 45, 349, 574; **2**/147*, 276, 313; **3**/23, 230, 280, 290, 317, 326, 383*; John (*alias* Stephens), 1/574; Joseph (*alias* Wootton), **3**/26; Marg, 1/36, 45; **2**/241; Mary, **3**/383; Nat, **3**/353*; Rebecca, **3**/395; Ric, 1/347, 427*, 562; **2**/1*, 210, 312–13; **3**/67, 395; Sam, 1/562; **3**/81*; Sergeant, 1/393; **2**/1, 177, 182, 192, 258, 288; **3**/27, 59; p. 273; Sybil, **2**/147; Thos, 1/228*, 347, 349, 353, 393*, 568; **2**/313; p. xxix; Thos (*alias* Stephens), 1/574; Wm, 1/568; **2**/147, 276; **3**/23, 81, 334, 383; Wm (*alias* Wootton), **2**/300*; **3**/26; —, **2**/210; **3**/81

Whitefield (Whitfeild, Whitfeilde, Whitfield, Whitfielde, Whitfild), Alice, 1/11, 40, 92, 179, 267; Anne, **2**/311; Ant, **3**/197; Edm, **2**/65*; Edw, **2**/305; **3**/91, 201–2; p. 272; Hannah, **2**/48, 251; Jeremiah, **3**/197; Mary, **2**/305; **3**/91, 201–2; Ric, 1/11, 40, 92, 134, 179, 267, 451*; **2**/48, 251*, 311; —, 1/134

Whitehead (Whithead), David (*alias* Havard), 1/510–11; Thos, 1/118; Wm, 1/118; Wm (*alias* Havard), 1/510–11
Whithie (Whithe), John, 1/74*, 79*
Whitington *see* Whittington
Whitle, John, 2/100; Mary, 2/331, 364; 3/52; Sam, 2/100, 331, 364; 3/52
Whitmay, Geo, 1/143; Thos, 1/143
Whitorne *see* Whitton
Whitson, Joan, 1/544; John, 1/544; 2/118*; 3/64; —, 3/64
Whitter (Whittern, Whitterne) *see* Whitton
Whittingham (Whittingam), Abigail, 3/344; Alice, 2/18; Edw, 3/190, 344; Eliz, 3/190; Henry, 1/118; Jesse, 2/18; Joan, 1/298, 364; Ric, 1/118; Thos, 1/298, 364; 2/18*
Whittington (Whitington), Anne, 1/160, 181; 2/126; Hephzibah, 1/337; Ric, 1/171; Rob, 1/8, 160, 181, 333, 337, 520; Wm, 1/171, 520; 2/30, 126; —, 2/30
Whitton (Whitorne, Whitter, Whittern, Whitterne Whittorne), Anne, 1/148, 161, 177, 180, 317, 358; Eliz, 1/387; John, 1/67*, 68, 148, 161, 177, 180, 317, 358, 362, 387; 2/309; 3/66; Laur, 3/280*n*; Ric, 2/309; Wal, 1/460*
Whooper (Whoopper, Whoper, Whoppere), Anne, 1/331*; Jesse, 1/142, 315, 377; John, 1/74*, 142, 179, 256, 331*; —, 1/179, 315; *and see* Hooper
Whyte *see* White
Wickes, Marg, 1/188–9; Thos, 1/19; Wm, 1/19, 188–9 *and see* Weekes
Wiett, John, 1/24; Thos, 1/24; *and see* Hyett
Wiggett, Alice, 3/380; Sam, 3/191, 310, 380; Wm, 3/191
Wilcox (Wilcocks, Wilcoxe, Willcockes, Willcox, Willcoxe), Dan, 3/268; Jane, 1/248, 287, 333, 335; John, 1/134, 248, 287, 333, 335, 532; 3/219*, 231; John, sheriff, 3/217; Mary, 2/194; 3/219, 231; Thos, 1/532, 536*n*; 2/194; 3/268; Thos, mayor, 3/384, sheriff, 3/252; Wm, 1/134; 3/219
Wildboare, John, 1/387*
Wilkes (Wilks), John, 3/196; Susannah, 2/377
Wilkins, Eliz, 1/314, 338, 378, 423*, 490, 544; John, 1/25, 489*n*, 490; 3/68, 140; Mary, 3/68, 140, 308, 383; Matilda, 2/13, 41; Maudlin, 1/574; Nanfun, 2/110; Nic, 3/158; Ric, 1/109, 314, 338, 378, 423*, 450, 489*n*, 490*, 544, 574; 2/13, 41, 110*; 3/213*n*; Thos, 1/25, 109; 3/158; Wm, 3/198*; —, 1/450
Wilkinson *alias* Bevis, Jas 1/527*n*, 528; John, 1/527*n*, 528
Wilks *see* Wilkes

Willcockes (Willcox, Willcoxe) *see* Wilcox
Willes *see* Willis
Willetts (Willets, Willottes), Anne, 1/377, 394, 530, 537; Geo, 1/209, 377, 394, 528, 530, 537; Joan, 1/528; Rob, 1/209
Willey, Isobel, 3/135; Roger, 3/135
Williams, Anne, 3/253, 308, 338, 350; Ant, 2/81; 3/270; Chas, 3/135; David, 1/147, 407; Edw, 1/475; Eleanor, 1/532; 2/35, 166, 187, 234, 350; Elisha, 2/286*n*, 287; Eliz, 1/546; Evan, 1/532; Geo, 2/204*n*, 209; Griffith, 3/130; Henry, 1/103, 532; Hester, 2/317; 3/159; Hugh, 1/142; Isaac, 1/396, 532; 2/35, 166, 187, 234, 350*; Isaac, sheriff, 2/330; 3/206; Jas, 1/142, 405; 3/270; Jane, 1/559; 2/287; 3/15, 26, 73; Joan, 1/404; 2/95; John, 1/103, 404*–5*, 475, 528, 559*; 2/55*, 113, 209, 287*, 311; 3/15, 26, 53*n*, 130, 202*n*, 229, 243, 248, 280, 362*; pp. 271–3; Lewis, 1/528; Marg, 3/229, 362; Michael, 1/396, 546; Morgan, 1/159; p. xxiv; Nic, 2/95, 350*, 362*n*; 3/73, 135; p. 272; Philip, 1/405; Phyllis, 3/243; Ric, 1/318, 391, 424*; 2/81, 113, 302, 309, 327*; 3/62, 253, 308, 338*, 350, 362; p. 270; Rob, 1/407, 552; Thos, 1/71, 552, 559; 2/171*, 311; 3/371*–2*; Thos, clerk to the council, 2/309; Toby, 2/345; Wal, 2/187; Wm, 1/318; 2/187, 317, 345; 3/159, 248, 280; Wm (*alias* Baker), 2/292*; —, 2/302, 309; 3/62; *and see* Ap Gwillim; Gwilliam
Willins, Nic, 1/162; Philip, 1/312; Thos, 1/312
Willis (Willes, Wills), Chris, 2/159; Eliz, 3/389; Jas, 1/180, 443, 485; Jane, 1/485; Leonard, 1/111; Martha, 1/111; Ric, 1/180, 228; Sam, 2/159; 3/389; Thos, 1/228; 3/38; Wm, 3/38; *and see* Wilse
Willmetts *see* Willmott
Willmore, Wm, 1/463*
Willmott (Willmetts, Willmotts, Wilmott, Wilmotts), Arthur, 1/331 *and see* Chapman; John, 3/24; Lazarus, 3/87*n*; Mary, 2/197, 225; Ric, 1/555; Rob, 1/555; 2/53, 61, 197, 225, 326, 351; 3/24*, 91, 116, 118, 313*, 343, 364, 392; Sarah, 2/326; 3/24*, 91, 116, 118, 313, 343, 364; Thos, 2/351
Willottes *see* Willetts
Wills *see* Willis
Willse *see* Wilse
Willshire *see* Wiltshire
Willy *see* Wily
Wilmott (Wilmotts) *see* Willmott
Wilse (Willse), Anne, 3/120, 162, 259, 263; Giles, 2/267; 3/120, 162, 259*, 263; John, 2/35, 205, 215*; Joseph, 2/205; Thos, 2/35, 267; 3/259; *and see* Willis

INDEX OF PERSONS

Wilsheere (Wilsheire, Wilshere, Wilshier) *see* Wiltshire

Wilson (Willson), Chas, **2**/321; John, **2**/291*, 321; Ric, **1**/32; Sam, **1**/32

Wilton, Geo, **2**/170; Jas, **3**/209; Joseph, **2**/170; Morgan, **3**/209

Wiltshire (Willshire, Wilsheere, Wilsheire, Wilshere, Wilshier), John, **2**/104; **3**/374*n*; Lawr, **1**/3*, 15, 55, 77, 134, 158, 190*; **2**/244*; **3**/265*n*; Lawr, mayor, **1**/141, sheriff, **1**/29, 91; Sarah, **1**/3*, 15, 55, 77, 134, 158, 190; Rob, **1**/55; Stephen, **3**/364*n*; Thos, **2**/104; Wm, **1**/55, 158; —, **1**/158

Wily (Willy, Wyly), Jas, **2**/306; John, **3**/293; Martha, **3**/301, 361; Roger, **3**/293; Thos, **3**/301, 361; Wm, **2**/306

Winckworth, Jonas, **2**/143; John, **2**/143

Window (Windowe, Wyndow, Wyndowe), Anne, **1**/245, 327, 373, 385; Edw, **1**/146; Eliz, **3**/375; John, p. 265; Marg, **1**/493, 551; Ric, **1**/245, 327, 373, 385, 493, 551; **3**/280; Ric, sheriff, **1**/407; Wm, **3**/280, 372*n*, 373*, 375; —, **1**/146

Winiatt *see* Winniatt

Winnard, Ric, **2**/195; Thos, **2**/195

Winniatt (Winiatt, Winniat, Winniett, Wyneatt, Wyniat, Wyniatt, Wynniatt) Eliz, **3**/130, 160, 265, 275; Geo, **2**/277*; Henry, **1**/504; John, **1**/339, 504; **2**/16; **3**/382; Joseph, **1**/339; **3**/272*n*, 274; Ric, **2**/16; Stephen, **2**/261; Thos, **3**/130, 160, 265, 269, 274–5, 359; Wm, **2**/261

Winston, Alice, **3**/74; Eliz, **3**/70; Henry, **1**/503, 505; John, **1**/503, 505; **2**/197; **3**/70; Marg, **3**/358, 396; Thos, **2**/197, 250; **3**/358, 396; Wal, **2**/250; **3**/74

Wintle, Alice, **1**/453, 478, 545, 549; **2**/15, 75, 94, 196; Anne, **3**/330; Dan, **2**/355; Eliz, **2**/91; Henry, **1**/581*; **2**/291*, 355*; p. xxii; Jas, **3**/175*n*; John, **1**/315; **2**/15, 357; **3**/92*n*, 101*, 102*n*, 121*n*, 330; Little, **3**/102*n**; Mary, **2**/291, 355; Ric, **1**/315, 453, 478, 545, 549; **2**/15*, 75*, 94, 196, 263; **3**/121*n*; Rob, **3**/309*, 355; Sam, **2**/291; Sarah, **2**/357; Thos, **1**/555; **3**/39*n*; Wm, **1**/555; **2**/91; —, **2**/263

Winton, Humph, p. 272

Wise (Wyse), Denis, **1**/31, 160, 276, 352, 368, 463, 488, 557; **2**/31*, 64, 131*; Denis, alderman, **2**/7, 33, 58, 100*n*, 110, 131, 249; p. xxxi, mayor, **1**/559; **2**/120, 169; p. 264, sheriff, **1**/360; Eleanor, **1**/276; Hephzibah, **1**/368, 463, 488, 557; **2**/31, 64, 131; p. xxxi; Rob, **1**/31; p. xxxi; Thos, p. 265; Urian, **2**/31; p. xxxi

Witcombe, Anne, **1**/451; Edith, **1**/361; Eliz, **3**/393; John, **1**/337*, 358*, 451, 508; **2**/173*n*, 183*; Joseph, **1**/508; Ric, **3**/393; Sam, **3**/393*; Thos, **1**/161, 190, 285*, 295; **2**/97*, 179; Thos, sheriff, **2**/86, 214; Wm, **1**/161, 190, 285, 361, 574*n**, 579*; **2**/179

Withenbury (Wythenbury), Jas, **2**/275; **3**/71*; Joan, **2**/275; Sarah, **3**/343; Thos, **3**/343

Witherley *see* Wytherley

Witt, John, **3**/227; Ric, **3**/227; *and see* Witts

Wittar, Anne, **1**/63; John, **1**/63

Witts, Thos, **1**/318; Wm, **1**/318; *and see* Witt

Woadley (Wodley), John, **1**/161; **2**/312*, 336; Wm, **1**/161; **2**/336

Wodward *see* Woodward

Woggan *see* Woogan

Wolford *see* Woolford

Wolley *see* Woolley

Wolston, Godfrey, **2**/10; Henry, **2**/10

Wonnes, John, **1**/410; Thos, **1**/410

Wood (Woodd, Woode, Woods), Abraham, **3**/216*n*, 220; Bromley, **2**/141*n*; Chas, **1**/158; Eleanor, **3**/274, 324; Eliz, **1**/72, 249, 383, 429, 432; **2**/32; **3**/366; Geo, **2**/295*n*; **3**/24*; Giles, **1**/100; Hannah, **3**/172; Henry (*alias* Owen), **3**/10*; Isaac, **2**/210; **3**/20, 250; Jas, **1**/158, 249; **2**/256; **3**/172, 324; Jas, sheriff, **1**/480, 559; Jane, **2**/122, 191; Joan, **2**/141*n*; John, **1**/23, 54, 72, 245, 328, 383, 429, 432, 517, 533; **2**/20, 32*, 60, 184*, 210, 261; **3**/29, 74*n*, 82*, 108, 216*n*, 220*, 250, 366; p. 272; John, sheriff, **1**/547; Marg, **1**/533; **2**/184, 261; **3**/29, 82, 108; Mary, **1**/517; Ric, **1**/23, 100; **2**/256; Sam, **3**/143*n*; Thos, **2**/20, 60, 122, 191; **3**/20*; Wm, **1**/245; **2**/32; **3**/102*n*, 172*, 274*, 324; —, **3**/20

Woodcock (Woodcocke, Woodcoke), Anne, **1**/173; **2**/284*n*; Giles, **2**/286; Thos, **1**/142, 173; Wm, **1**/586*; **2**/284*n*, 286

Woodd (Woode, Woods) *see* Wood

Woodiatte *see* Woodyatt

Wooding (Wooddinge, Woodinge), John, **2**/69*; Marg, **3**/311; Susannah, **3**/115; Wm, **3**/17, 115, 304*, 311; —, **3**/17

Woodroffe, Francis, **3**/379; Wm, **3**/379

Woodward (Wodward, Woodwarde), Alice, **1**/326; Allen, **2**/316, 323*n*; Anne, **1**/541; **2**/40; Eliz, **1**/11, 35, 132, 138, 297, 419; **2**/219; **3**/102; Francis, **2**/6, 316; Gabriel, **1**/51, 119, 170, 228; Henry, **1**/171; Jas, **1**/4, 110, 534; Joan, **1**/119, 170, 228; John, **1**/65, 110, 171, 246*, 297, 326, 418, 443, 454, 464*, 535; **2**/6, 219, 279, 285, 372*–6*; **3**/18, 91, 102, 271*, 293*n*; pp. xxiii, 270; John, mayor, **2**/360, 362*n*, sheriff, **1**/408; Marg, **2**/285; **3**/18, 91; Mary, **3**/116; Ric, **1**/443, 531; **3**/109*n*, 116*; Sam, **2**/322; **3**/265*n*, 266*; Susannah, **2**/322; Thos, **1**/11, 35, 118, 132, 138, 297, 419; **2**/279; Wal, **1**/4; Wm, **1**/65, 118, 297, 308*, 531, 534–5, 541; **2**/40*; **3**/94*; —, **1**/454

INDEX OF PERSONS

Woodyatt (Woodiatte), Jas, **2**/166, 352; Ric, **2**/166; —, **2**/352

Woogan (Woggan), Anne, **2**/118; Thos, **2**/118, 143; *and see* Worgan

Wooles, John, **3**/106; Ric, **3**/147*; Thos, **3**/106

Woolford (Wolford), Arthur, **3**/146*n*, 148; Joan, **2**/289; **3**/30, 92, 148, 173; Ric, **3**/29*n*, 30; Thos, **2**/289; **3**/29*n*, 30*, 92, 148*, 173

Woolley (Wolley), Agnes, **1**/13; Eliz, **1**/396; Henry, **1**/396, 523; Jas, **2**/259; Ric, p. 268; Thos, **1**/13; **2**/259; p. 272; Wm, **1**/523; **3**/211*n*; —, **3**/211*n*, 244*n*

Woollwright, John, **2**/140; Wm, **2**/140

Woolvin, Thos, **3**/366*

Wootton (*alias* White), Joseph, **3**/26; Wm, **2**/300*; **3**/26

Worgan, John, **1**/168; Rob, **1**/168; *and see* Woogan

Workman (Workeman), Anne, **3**/347, 391; Ant, **3**/159*, 347, 391; Chas, **3**/103; John, **2**/309; Morgan, **3**/103; Ric, **2**/309

Worlocke, Guy, **2**/356*

Worme, Henry, **3**/371; Wm, **3**/371

Worrall, Henry, **3**/280*n*; Jas, **3**/366; Joshua, **3**/366

Wrench, Elias, **1**/314*

Wright, Anne, **2**/24; Edw, **3**/248; John, **2**/73, 321*; **3**/248; Ric, **2**/73; Rob, p. 267; Thos, **2**/24*; p. 269

Wyer, Francis, **1**/445; Leonard, **1**/445

Wyly *see* Wily

Wyman, Ambrose, **3**/58; Arthur, **1**/49; Henry, **1**/49; John, **1**/319*, 542; p. 273; Thos, **1**/542; **3**/58; *and see* Weyman

Wyndow (Wyndowe) *see* Window

Wyniat (Wyneatt, Wyniatt, Wynniatt) *see* Winniatt

Wyse *see* Wise

Wythenbury *see* Withenbury

Wytherley (Witherley), Eliz, **1**/189; Ric, **1**/189; Thos, **1**/85*, 189*, 211

Yarnold (Arnold, Yarnar, Yarnolde, Yearnold), Eleanor, **1**/7, 40, 121, 130, 172, 227, 275, 284; Francis, **1**/7, 40, 121, 130, 172, 227, 275, 284, 344–5, 417; Joan, **1**/344–5, 417; Rob, **2**/274*n*, 275; Sybil, **1**/398; Thos, **1**/7*, 398*; **2**/243*n*, 259*n*, 275; p. xxii; —, **2**/243*n*, 259*n*; *and see* Arnold

Yate (Yates, Yeate), Dan, **3**/27, 216, 219; Eliz, **2**/36, 87, 166, 293*b*; **3**/199; Francis, **1**/292, 333*, 394; **2**/240, 286–7, 299, 325, 347, 370; **3**/47, 74, 213, 279, 300; pp. xxvii–xxviii; Humph, **2**/361; **3**/27, 62, 219; Joan, **2**/240, 299, 325, 347, 370; **3**/47; John, **1**/394; **3**/142*n*, 163*; Josiah; **3**/62, 219; Mary, **3**/279, 300; Matt, **3**/199*; Ric, **1**/523; **3**/199*; Sam, **3**/213, 324, 399; Thos, **1**/523; **2**/36, 87, 166, 293*b*; **3**/199; Thos, mayor, **2**/330, sheriff, **2**/279; Wal, **2**/361; Wm, **1**/292; —, **2**/286; **3**/74

Yealfe *see* Yelfe

Yearnold *see* Yarnold

Yeate *see* Yate

Yeeding (Yeedinge), John, **2**/100; **3**/178*; Mary, **3**/178; Ric, **2**/100; Thos, **3**/178

Yelfe (Yealfe), Ezra, **3**/70; Ric, **1**/169; **3**/70; Thos, **1**/169

Yemans, Thos, **1**/95; Wm, **1**/95

Young (Yong, Yonge, Younge), Abel, **1**/328; Abraham, **3**/92; Chas, **3**/374*n*, 376; Henry, **3**/251; Jas, **2**/369; **3**/193*n*,, 211, 376; Joan, **3**/92, 211; John, **1**/11, 105, 314, 324, 330, 479; **2**/42, 49, 171*, 369; **3**/251; Joseph, **2**/132*, 160, 216*n*, 218*; **3**/364*n*; Kath (Cath), **1**/257*, 330; Marg, **1**/105; Marg (*alias* Meredith), **1**/141; Ric, **3**/160; Rob, **1**/324; **2**/42, 49; Sam, **3**/216*n*, 218; Thos, **1**/314, 479; **3**/144; Wal, **1**/45, 257*, 328, 330*; **3**/92*, 193*n*, 211*, 323*n*, 330*; Wm, **1**/11, 13*, 95; Wm (*alias* Meredith), **1**/141; —, **3**/144

INDEX OF PLACES

References to the calendar are to the volumes and pages of the MSS., which are given in the left-hand column of the calendar; references preceded by 'p.' or 'pp.' are to the pages of the introduction or the appendixes. An asterisk * indicates that the reference is to more than one occurrence of the name concerned. Places other than cities and major towns are in Gloucestershire unless attributed to another county. Hamlets and other minor places are indexed under the names of the parishes of which they were part except that, if there is no reference for the parish, the hamlet or minor place is entered in its own alphabetical position, with a cross-reference from the name of the parish in which it lay.

Abbey Dore *see* Dore
Abenhall, **3**/12, 252
Abergavenny (Mon), **1**/1, 54, 142, 432
Ablington, in Bibury, **3**/27
Acton [*unspecified*], **1**/294
Adlestrop, **1**/294
Alkington *see* Newport
Alstone (Glos) *see* Cheltenham
Alstone (Worcs), **1**/158
Alvescot (Oxon), **1**/510; **2**/10
Alveston, **1**/582
America *see* Barbados; Virginia
Ampney Crucis, **1**/23
Ampney, Down, **1**/11, 137, 267, 276, 460; **3**/101
Apperley *see* Deerhurst
Arle *see* Cheltenham
Arley, Upper (Staffs), **1**/16
Arlingham, **1**/25, 158, 443, 523; **2**/20; **3**/92, 199, 267, 279
Ashchurch, **1**/96; **2**/358; **3**/83, 374
Ashleworth, **1**/133, 202, 284, 344, 346, 351, 364, 539; **2**/117, 137, 165, 173, 218, 235, 264, 296, 298, 304; **3**/90, 287, 291, 382
Ashperton *see* Poppinger
Ashton Keynes (Wilts), **1**/148, 360, 434; **2**/367; **3**/66, 83, 93, 197, 249
 Leigh, **3**/122
Ashton [*unspecified*], **1**/41
Astley (Salop), **1**/315
Aston Ingham (Herefs), **3**/158, 288
Aston Somerville, **3**/245
Aston (Glos) [*unspecified*], **1**/277; **2**/130, 317
Aston (Herefs) [*unspecified*], **1**/159, 160, 170
Aston (Oxon) [*unspecified*], **1**/302
Auberrow, in Wellington (Herefs), **1**/4
Aust, in Henbury, **2**/264
Awre, **1**/464; **2**/11, 172, 191, 310; **3**/245, 285, 306
 Blakeney, **1**/123, 324; **2**/322
 Bledisloe, **3**/356
'Awsen' [Alstone, in Cheltenham?], **1**/346

Badgeworth, **1**/11, 46, 258, 272, 280, 292, 299, 311, 335, 338, 394, 446, 566; **2**/136, 145–6, 148, 228, 266, 272, 307, 340; **3**/45, 96, 102, 104, 131–2, 198, 213–14
 Bentham, **1**/135, 272, 316, 432; **2**/192; **3**/390
 Crickley, **1**/297, 533
 Witcombe, Little, **2**/92
 and see Shurdington
Badminton, Little *see* Hawkesbury
Badsey (Worcs), **1**/229, 268, 510
Bagendon, **1**/463, 571
Bampton (Oxon), **2**/235
Banbury (Oxon), **1**/568
Bankside (Surrey), **1**/107
Barbados, **1**/372–8; pp. xxiii, xxx
Barnwood, **1**/129, 273, 317, 363, 402, 498, 554, 568, 575; **2**/9, 19, 48, 68*, 86, 89, 120, 146, 173, 257–8, 267, 271, 364, 372; **3**/13, 66, 147, 172, 230, 268, 272
Barton Street, in Gloucester, **1**/13, 25, 125, 135, 147, 257, 279, 301, 343, 345, 392, 477, 520, 530, 538; **2**/4, 70, 83, 85, 95, 129, 135, 151*, 166, 174, 177, 210, 222, 227, 236–7, 244, 254 *and n*, 256, 270, 291, 304, 315, 337, 356–7, 366, 371; **3**/21, 59, 68, 87, 105, 230*, 354*, 363*, 369, 372–3, 376
'Batchfords Heath' [Besford Heath?] (Worcs), **2**/58
Bath, **1**/122
Bedfordshire, *see* Oakley; Westoning
Bengeworth (Worcs), **2**/192; **3**/296
Benington (Lincs), **2**/272
Bentham *see* Badgeworth
Berkeley, **1**/5, 69, 86, 114, 131–2, 136, 158, 255, 276, 352, 427, 449, 569; **2**/24, 27, 59, 82, 218; **3**/164, 213, 396
 Pedington, **1**/188–9
 Woodford, **3**/199
Berkshire *see* Eaton Hastings; Hungerford; Inglesham
Berrow (Worcs), **3**/364

321

Berry Hill *see* Dean, Forest of
Besford Heath *see* 'Batchfords Heath'
Bewdley (Worcs), **1**/16, 334, 350
Bibury *see* Ablington
Bicknor, English, **1**/64, 67, 76, 334, 462; **2**/153; **3**/260, 300
Bidford *see* Marlcliff
Birch, Little (Herefs), **2**/325
Birch, Much (Herefs), **2**/222, 240
Birdlip *see* Cowley
Birmingham, **1**/11
Birtsmorton (Worcs), **1**/30; **2**/29
Bishampton (Worcs), **1**/42
Bishop's Cleeve *see* Cleeve, Bishop's
Bishop's Norton *see* Norton (Glos)
Bishton, Old, in Tidenham *see* 'Buston'
Bisley, **1**/50, 142, 229, 268, 321, 350, 380, 407, 418, 531; **3**/89, 380, 398
   Througham, **1**/126; **2**/63
Blaisdon, **1**/121, 545; **3**/309
Blakeney *see* Awre
Bledington, **3**/38, 360, 392
Bledisloe *see* Awre
Bloxham (Oxon), **3**/210
Bloxwich (Staffs), **1**/319
Bockleton (Worcs), **2**/65
Boddington, **1**/69, 555; **2**/17, 128
   Haydon, **1**/305–6, 314, 376; **2**/215, 291; **3**/354
   Withy Bridge, **1**/4, 125, 272
Bosbury (Herefs), **1**/411
Bourton on the Hill, **1**/490, 514
Bourton on the Water, **1**/524; **2**/281
Bourton [*unspecified*] *see* Burton
Brampton Abbotts (Herefs), **3**/234, 366
Brecon, **2**/187
Breconshire *see* Brecon; Bronllys; Crickhowell; Talgarth; 'Wander'
Bredon (Worcs), **2**/304; **3**/235*
Brickhampton *see* Churchdown
Bridgnorth (Salop), **2**/269; **3**/145
Bridstow (Herefs), **1**/144; **2**/312; **3**/202
Brilley (Herefs), **1**/23
Brimpsfield, **1**/466, 473, 524, 547–8; **2**/180, 285; **3**/55, 297
Brinkworth (Wilts), **1**/64
Brislington (Som), **2**/222
Bristol, **1**/69, 111, 280, 325, 384, 500, 525; **2**/132, 171, 216, 268, 282, 363, 371, 376, 377*; **3**/13, 19, 61, 331; p. xiv
   apprenticeship in, pp. xvii; xix–xx
   merchants, p. xxiii
   municipal freedom pp. xi, xv
Brize Norton *see* Norton, Brize

Broadway (Worcs), **1**/553; **3**/54
Broadwell, **2**/202
Brockhampton, **1**/373
Brockworth, **1**/85, 87–8, 95, 103*, 431, 515; **2**/90, 93, 287, 335, 371, 376, 377*; **3**/231, 351
Bromsberrow, **1**/546, 586; **3**/24, 72, 84, 160, 289, 400
Bromsgrove (Worcs), **1**/342; **2**/294
Bronllys (Brecons), **3**/214
Brookthorpe, **1**/68, 173, 237, 315, 461, 474, 494; **2**/276
Broseley (Salop), **3**/217
Buckholt, the *see* Monmouth
Buckinghamshire *see* Hanslope
Buckland, **2**/354
Bullen *see* Ledbury
Bulley, **1**/159, 415–16, 479, 541, 587; **2**/139, 148, 178, 279; **3**/73, 143, 252
Bullinghope (Herefs), **1**/227
Burford (Oxon), **1**/124, 170, 298, 338
Burghill *see* Tillington
Burton [*unspecified*], **1**/566 *and see* Bourton
Bushley (Worcs), **1**/51, 157, 228; **3**/388
'Buston' [Old Bishton, in Tidenham?], **1**/99

Campden, Chipping, **2**/321
   Westington Park, **2**/320
Caple, Kings (Herefs), **1**/306
Cardiff, **1**/312, 442
Carew (Pembs), **2**/297
Carmarthen, **1**/262
Carmarthenshire *see* Carmarthen; 'Langdila'; Laugharne; Llangattock
Castle Eaton *see* Eaton, Castle
Cerney, North, **1**/118, 291; **2**/56, **3**/67
   Woodmancote, **2**/225
Cerney, South, **1**/340, 454; **3**/371
Chaceley (Worcs), **1**/499, 508; **2**/171, 184, 196, 214, 274; **3**/372
Chaddesley Corbett (Worcs), **1**/133
Charleton [*unspecified*], **1**/379, 460
Charlton (Worcs), **1**/507
Charlton Kings, **1**/38, 67, 144, 257, 329, 464, 469, 512; **2**/76, 124, 207, 253, 260, 339; **3**/22, 32, 122, 161, 178, 184, 248, 334, 353, 383, 389
Cheltenham, **1**/13, 34, 51, 53, 100, 172, 239, 256, 258, 279, 283, 333, 335, 354, 372, 384*, 412, 539; **2**/47, 62, 115, 135, 184, 195, 217, 231, 249, 265, 361; **3**/27*, 51, 55, 62, 73, 88, 101, 135, 159, 193, 219, 233, 270, 307, 313, 318, 333, 335, 388, 392, 395, 397; p. xxiv
   Alstone, **3**/30, 140, 313 *and see* 'Awsen'
   Arle, **1**/65; **2**/215
   Harthurstfield, **2**/106

INDEX OF PLACES

Cherington, **1**/12
Cheriton (Som), **2**/104
Cheshire *see* Haslington
Childswickham, **2**/336; **3**/80
Chippenham (Wilts), **1**/248
Chipping Campden *see* Campden, Chipping
Chipping Norton *see* Norton, Chipping
Churcham, **1**/111, 178, 276, 405, 568; **2**/91, 111, 190, 195, 234; **3**/47, 100, 195, 208, 217, 244, 290, 336
   Highnam, **1**/113, 328, 355; **2**/128, 153, 299; **3**/15, 312, 324
   Linton, **1**/127, 171, 558; **2**/207–9, 239; **3**/278, 367
   Over, **1**/76, 143, 160, 255–6, 287, 291, 359, 433, 455, 480; **2**/3, 66, 88, 146, 197, 335, 373; **3**/278, 322, 389; p. 265
Churchdown, **1**/25, 42, 71, 91, 95, 123, 288, 293, 306, 469, 481, 509, 581; **2**/17, 106, 175, 211, 213, 268, 277, 280, 377; **3**/32, 34*, 46, 315, 366
   Brickhampton, **1**/202
   Hucclecote, **1**/123, 298, 346, 494; **2**/45; **3**/38, 56, 352, 393
   Noke, **1**/298
   Parton, **1**/61, 429
Cirencester, **1**/32, 47, 63, 79, 87, 157, 177, 255, 281, 289, 311*, 327, 365, 377, 487, 534; **2**/8, 45, 64, 84, 149, 193, 196, 332; **3**/20, 312; p. xvii
Clearwell *see* Newland
Cleeve, Bishop's, **1**/168; **3**/74, 81, 172
   Gotherington, **1**/288
   Stoke Orchard, **1**/538
Cleeve (Herefs) *see* Ross
Cleeve [*unspecified*], **2**/180; **3**/175
Clodock *see* Longtown
Clunbury *see* 'Elumbery'
Coates, **1**/345
Coberley, **1**/331
Coleford *see* Newland
Colerne (Wilts), **1**/566
Colethrop *see* Haresfield
'Collwey' [Colwall?] (Herefs), **1**/33
Colwall (Herefs), **1**/24, 30 *and see* 'Collwey'
Combe St Nicholas (Som), **2**/283
Comberton (Worcs), **1**/132
Compton Wynyates (Warws), **1**/383
Cornwall, p. xxiv *and see* Crowan; Padstow; St Erme
Corse, **1**/178, 350, 441, 446, 552; **3**/51, 95, 263, 377
Corston *see* Malmesbury
Coulston (Wilts), **1**/576

Cowley, **1**/342, 547–8, 551, 573; **2**/61, 85, 147; **3**/83, 116
   Birdlip, **1**/480
'Crable' [Cradley?] (Worcs), **1**/31
Cradley (Herefs), **1**/45
Cradley (Worcs) *see* 'Crable'
Cranborne (Dorset), **2**/307
Cranham, **1**/126, 271; **2**/13, 46, 110, 170, 261; **3**/341, 349
Crickhowell (Brecons), **2**/116
Cricklade (Wilts), **1**/3; **2**/122
Cricklade St Sampsons, **2**/200
Crickley *see* Badgeworth
Croome, Hill (Worcs), **1**/157
Crowan (Cornwall), **1**/75
Crudwell (Wilts), **1**/574; **3**/62
Cwmcarn (Mon), **2**/153
Cwmyoy (Mon), **1**/405

Dean, Forest of, **1**/542
   Berry Hill, **2**/273
Deddington (Oxon), **2**/299
Deerhurst, **1**/322, 488; **2**/238
   Apperley, **1**/62, 159, 587; **2**/206
Deerhurst Walton, **1**/136; **2**/129
Denbighshire *see* Wrexham
'Dersum' [Dorstone?] (Herefs), **2**/373
Devon *see* Hole; Modbury; Tiverton
Dewchurch, Little (Herefs), **2**/220
Dewchurch, Much (Herefs), **2**/204
Didbrook, **1**/133, 352
Dixton (Mon), **1**/245
Dodderhill (Worcs), **1**/229
Donnington (Herefs), **1**/179; **2**/115
Dorchester (Dorset), **1**/478
Dorchester (Oxon), **3**/356
Dore (Herefs), **1**/21, 100
   Abbey Dore, **2**/372
Dorset *see* Cranborne; Dorchester; Manston
Dorstone *see* 'Dersum'
Dowdeswell, **3**/39
Drayton, Lower, in Penkridge (Staffs), **1**/95
Droitwich (Worcs), **3**/336
Dublin (Ireland), **3**/21
Dulas (Herefs), **2**/203
Dumbleton, **2**/166; **3**/270
Duntisbourne [*unspecified*], **3**/269
Dursley, **1**/300, 399, 433, 564; **2**/37, 309; **3**/134, 271, 294
Dymock, **1**/339, 376, 562; **2**/1, 16, 35, 62, 205–6, 276, 313, 356; **3**/14

Eardisley (Herefs), **2**/5

'East Harkeein' *see* 'Harkeein, East'
Eastcott, in Urchfont (Wilts), **1**/182; **2**/306
Eastington, **1**/112, 273, 324, 456
Eastnor (Herefs), **1**/40
'Eastwood' (Hants), **2**/138
Eaton, Castle (Wilts), **1**/509; **2**/180, 221
Eaton Hastings (Berks), **1**/304
Ebrington *see* Hidcote Boyce
Eckington (Worcs), **1**/109, 333, 567; **2**/59, 215
Eldersfield (Worcs), **1**/84, 148, 385, 447, 537, 565; **2**/191, 322, 374; **3**/20, 45, 247, 261 *and see* 'Elsfeild'
Elkstone, **1**/119; **2**/113 *and see* 'Elston'
Elmley Castle (Worcs), **1**/145
Elmore, **1**/21, 24, 272, 572; **2**/95, 313, 334; **3**/57, 305, 389
Elmstone Hardwicke, **2**/257, 360
  'parish of Elmstone', **2**/86
'Elsfeild' [Eldersfield, Worcs?], **1**/359
'Elston' [Elkstone?], **1**/465
Elterwalter (Westmld), **2**/18
'Elumbery' [Clunbury?] (Salop), **1**/238
English Bicknor *see* Bicknor, English
Epney, **1**/360, 375
Essex *see* Feering; Maldon; Wanstead
Evesham (Worcs), **1**/17, 42, 158, 430, 482; **2**/34, 340; **3**/176, 268
Evington *see* Leigh
Eynsham Ferry, in Eynsham (Oxon), **2**/375

Fairford, **1**/356
Farmington, **1**/49, 446, 471
Feering (Essex), **3**/325
Flaxley, **2**/46; **3**/62, 116
Flintshire *see* 'Scheviock'
Forden (Mont), **2**/6
Forthampton, **1**/496; **3**/141, 220
Framilode *see* Saul
Frampton Mansell, in Sapperton, **1**/81
Frampton on Severn, **1**/119; **2**/65, 134, 182, 306, 311, 352; **3**/70, 80, 100
Frampton [*unspecified*], **1**/177, 366
Freen Court *see* Sutton
Fretherne, **3**/395
Frocester, **1**/80, 277, 395; **2**/208, 224; **3**/179, 246
Frome (Som), **3**/383
  Frome Selwood, **3**/308

Ganarew (Herefs), **2**/228
Garsdon (Wilts), **1**/10
Garway (Herefs), **1**/141, 172
Glamorgan *see* Cardiff; Pendoylan; St Brides

Gloucester, *passim*
  bishop *see* Index of persons
  castle, **2**/62, 201; **3**/28
  Bluecoat Hospital and school, pp. xxii, 263
  churches: St John the Baptist, p. xxviii *n*; St Nicholas, p. 267
  Grey Friars, p. xx
  inns: the Bear, p. 265; the Bell, p. 266; the Boothall, pp. 265–6, 268*; unnamed, p. 265
  migration to, pp. xxiv–xxv
  Northgate, the, p. 266
  parishes: St Aldate, **2**/285*n*; **3**/381; p. xxvii; St Catherine, **1**/293; **2**/98; **3**/320, 368, 375, 382; pp. xxvii, 269; St Mary de Crypt, **2**/254*n*, 285*n*; St Mary de Lode, **1**/527; **2**/100, 131, 133; **3**/331, 344, 387, 397; p. xix; St Mary [*unspecified*], **2**/49; St Oswald, **1**/51; p. xxvii; St Owen, **1**/321; **3**/269
  quay, the, pp. 267–8
  siege, pp. xxiv, xxxi
  streets: Southgate St, **1**/101, 147, 158, 171, 412; **2**/161, 190; **3**/54, 91; p. 269; Lower Southgate St, **3**/196, 322, 358, 390; Westgate St, p. 267
  and see Barton Street; Hermitage; Kingsholm; Littleworth; Llanthony; Longford; Saintbridge; Sheephouse, Lower; Tuffley; Wotton
Godalming (Surrey), **1**/474
Golden Valley (Herefs), **1**/107
Gotherington *see* Cleeve, Bishop's
Gretton *see* Winchcombe
Guiting, Temple, **1**/541; **2**/7
  Kineton, **1**/543
Guiting Power, **3**/130
Gupshill *see* Tewkesbury

Hailes, **2**/10
Hailey, in Witney (Oxon), **1**/351
Halford (Worcs) [*recte* Warws?], **1**/10
Hampnett, **3**/35
Hampshire *see* 'Eastwood'; Shipton Bellinger; Southampton
Hampton (Salop) [*unspecified*], **3**/373
Hampton Lovett (Worcs), **1**/470; **2**/53
Hankerton (Wilts), **1**/277; **2**/109; **3**/253, 309, 350
Hanley Child (Worcs), **3**/267
Hanley (Worcs) [*unspecified*], **2**/54; **3**/386
Hannington (Wilts), **1**/431
Hanslope (Bucks), **1**/383
Hardwicke, **1**/117, 137, 169, 276, 347, 383, 401, 460, 485, 551, 585; **2**/106, 289, 348; **3**/322, 333, 353, 370
Harescombe, **1**/21, 170, 246, 269, 361, 407, 428, 506; **2**/27, 46, 281; **3**/290, 337

INDEX OF PLACES

Haresfield, **1**/146, 260, 337, 378, 381, 411, 527, 567, 570; **2**/149, 266, 296, 346; **3**/27, 189, 193, 221, 263, 277, 298, 310
   Colethrop, **1**/188
Harford *see* Naunton
'Harkeein, East' [East Harptree?] (Som), **1**/261
Harley (Salop), **1**/322
Harnhill, **1**/391
Harptree, East *see* 'Harkeein, East'
Harthurstfield *see* Cheltenham
Hartpury, **1**/32, 96, 122, 134, 203, 321, 382, 430, 450, 486*, 508, 526, 580, 584; **2**/12, 25*, 28, 61, 70, 138, 160, 239, 330; **3**/16, 55, 160, 319, 342, 344, 362
Hartwell (Northants), **1**/32
Hasfield, **1**/275*, 303, 365, 376, 417, 465, 468; **2**/21, 77, 194, 273–4, 312, 315, 318, 327, 336, 370; **3**/10, 26
Haslington [Ches?], **3**/212
Hatch, West (Som), **1**/197
Hatherley, Down, **1**/257, 461, 500; **2**/300; **3**/26, 37, 44, 278; p. xxvii
Hatherley, Up, **2**/267, 338; **3**/286
Hatherley [*unspecified*], **1**/110, 248; p. xxiv
Haughton (Lancs), **1**/94
Haverfordwest (Pembs), **1**/439
Hawkesbury, **1**/404
   Badminton, Little, **3**/360
Hawling, **3**/352
Haydon *see* Boddington
Hempsted, **1**/40, 44, 83, 121–2, 146, 160, 277, 282, 285, 327, 337, 345, 358, 364, 370, 372, 381, 402, 435, 444, 463, 553; **2**/161, 178, 266, 272, 313, 316, 324; **3**/122, 129, 140, 162–3, 209, 216, 312
Henbury *see* Aust
Hentland (Herefs), **1**/571
Hereford, **1**/481; **2**/226, 377; **3**/300*
   All Hallows, **2**/164
Herefordshire, p. xxiii *and see* Aston; Aston Ingham; Auberrow; Birch, Little; Birch, Much; Bosbury; Brampton Abbotts; Bridstow; Brilley; Bullinghope; Caple, Kings; 'Collwey'; Colwall; Cradley; 'Dersum'; Dewchurch, Little; Dewchurch, Much; Donnington; Dore; Dulas; Eardisley; Eastnor; Ganarew; Garway; Golden Valley; Hentland; Hereford; Holme Lacy; Hope, Sollers; Hope Mansell; Howton; Humber; Kington; Kinnersley; Lea; Ledbury; Leominster; Linton; Llancloudy; Longtown; Lyonshall; Marcle, Much; Marden; Mordiford; Newton, Welsh; 'Pitchersoken'; Poppinger; Pyon, Kings; Ross; St Devereux; Sapey, Upper; Snodhill; Stanford Bishop; Stretton Grandison; Sutton; Tarrington; Tillington; Upton Bishop; Walford; Wellington; Weston under Penyard; Weston [*unspecified*]; Whitchurch; Whitney; Withington; Woolhope; Wormsley
Hermitage, the, in Gloucester, **1**/45
Hidcote Boyce, in Ebrington, **1**/260
Highleadon, **1**/295, 334, 365, 372, 414; **3**/31
Highnam *see* Churcham
Hill, **1**/356; **2**/38, 240
Hill Croome *see* Croome, Hill
Hillsley, **1**/111
Hinton *see* Saniger
Hole (Devon) [*unspecified*], **1**/113, 177
Holme Lacy (Herefs), **3**/21
Hook Norton *see* Norton, Hook
Hope, Sollers (Herefs), **1**/480, 543
Hope Mansell (Herefs), **1**/147; **3**/67
Horsfield, **1**/260
Horsley, **2**/10
Howton (Herefs), **1**/356
Hucclecote *see* Churchdown
Hughley (Salop), **1**/135, 239
Humber (Herefs), **1**/484
Hungerford (Berks), **1**/116
Huntley, **1**/170, 469, 542, 567; **2**/17, 170, 176, 251, 293, 323; **3**/60, 141, 160, 212, 270, 299
Hutton (Westmld) [*unspecified*], **1**/343

Ilmington (Warws), **1**/161
Inglesham (Berks), **1**/391
Ipsley (Warws), **1**/551
Ireland, pp. xxii, xxiv *and see* Dublin; Kilmore; Londonderry
Itton (Mon), **2**/262, 268

Kellet, Over (Lancs), **1**/107, 146
Kemble, **1**/491
Kemerton, **1**/434, 517
Kempley, **1**/133, 504; **2**/361–2
Kempsford, **1**/230, 403
'Kerby Kendall' [Kirkby Lonsdale?] (Westmld), **1**/142
Kidderminster (Worcs), **2**/255
Kidlington (Oxon), **2**/189
Kilcot *see* Newent
Kilmore (Co. Monaghan, Ireland), **3**/32
Kineton *see* Guiting, Temple
Kings Caple *see* Caple, Kings
Kings Pyon *see* Pyon, Kings
King's Stanley *see* Stanley, King's
King's Sutton *see* Purston
Kingsdon (Som), **2**/51

Kingsholm, in Gloucester, **1**/7, 11, 307, 353; **2**/69, 83, 88, 105, 260, 262; **3**/84, 107, 357
Kingswood (Wilts), **1**/3; **3**/19
Kington (Herefs), **1**/107; **2**/352
Kinnersley (Herefs), **1**/532
Kirkby Lonsdale *see* 'Kerby Kendall'

Lambeth (Surrey), **1**/169
Lancashire *see* Haughton; Kellett, Over; Lancaster
Lancaster, **1**/36, 45; **2**/356
'Langdila' [Llandeilo, Carms?] **3**/265
Langford Budville (Som), **1**/31
Lassington, **1**/68, 87, 92, 108, 398; **3**/369
Laugharne (Carms), **1**/502
Laverton, **2**/351
Lavington, Market (Wilts), **3**/398
'Lay', **3**/314
Lea (Glos) [*unspecified*], **1**/572
Lea (Herefs), **1**/326, 395
Lea (Wilts), **1**/169, 279
Lechlade, **1**/517; **2**/53
Leckhampton, **1**/63, 482; **2**/330; **3**/204
Ledbury (Herefs), **1**/103, 134, 171, 344, 387; **2**/40, 114, 186, 235; **3**/145, 232, 253, 369
    Bullen, **2**/217
Leicestershire *see* Quorndon
Leigh, the (Glos), **1**/74, 80, 100, 112, 130–1, 274, 278, 283, 305, 387, 438, 461, 473; **2**/308; **3**/28, 58; p. xxiv
    Evington, **1**/402
Leigh (Wilts) *see* Ashton Keynes
Leominster (Herefs), **1**/98
Leonard Stanley *see* Stanley, Leonard
Levant, the, p. 261
Lew (Oxon), **1**/347
Lincolnshire *see* Benington; 'Scopby'
Linton (Glos) *see* Churcham
Linton (Herefs), **1**/177
Littledean, **1**/122, 131; **2**/227, 327, 351; **3**/292, 298
Littleton, Middle (Worcs), **2**/15
Littleworth, in Gloucester, **3**/247, 282, 334
Llancloudy, in Llangarron (Herefs), **2**/150
Llandeilo *see* 'Langdila'
Llandysilio (Mont), **1**/97
Llanfihangel (Mon) [*unspecified*], **1**/517
Llanfyllin (Mont), **3**/358
Llangarron *see* Llancloudy
Llangadog (Carms), **3**/242
Llangattock (Mon) [*unspecified*], **1**/335
Llanidloes (Mont), **2**/372
Llanvapley (Mon), **2**/374
Llanthony, in Gloucester, **3**/355
Llantrissant (Mon), **1**/70

Llanwenarth (Mon), **1**/65, 125, 147, 237
Llanyre (Radnors), **1**/14
London, **1**/138, 317, 327, 341*n*, 363, 545; **2**/67, 77, 117*n*, 123, 256, 283, 298, 322; **3**/37, 119, 277, 296, 341, 379, 394; pp. xxiv, 265
    alderman, pp. xx, 261
    citizen and haberdasher of, p. 261
    customs of, pp. xi, 262
    draper, p. xxiv
    mercers, p. xvii, xx
    visits to, p. xiv
    and see Bankside; Lambeth; Westminster
Londonderry (Ireland), **3**/363
Longborough, **2**/360
Longdon (Worcs), **1**/9; **3**/361
Longford, in Gloucester, **1**/12, 51, 55, 281, 332, 383, 470; **2**/108, 167, 340; **3**/47, 52, 80, 293, 304, 368
Longhope, **1**/6, 20, 105, 188, 315, 363–4, 449, 498, 519, 575; **2**/147, 224, 252, 341, 347, 351; **3**/91, 133, 158, 164, 174*, 203, 211, 218, 229, 248, 266, 325
Longney, **1**/5, 48, 108, 169, 367, 373, 433; **2**/21–2, 56, 112, 177, 337; **3**/70, 399
Longtown, in Clodock (Herefs), **1**/417; **3**/263
Low Countries *see* Netherlands
Lower Drayton *see* Drayton, Lower
Lower Sheephouse, *see* Sheephouse, Lower
Ludlow (Salop), **1**/359
Lydiard Millicent (Wilts), **1**/495, 497
Lydney, **2**/69; **3**/68
Lyonshall (Herefs), **1**/497, 508*, 547–8
Lypiatt [*unspecified*], **1**/104

Magdalens, the *see* Wotton: St Mary Magdalen's
Maisemore, **1**/71, 82, 86, 104, 188, 246, 249, 259, 275, 281, 294, 316, 319, 369, 385, 403, 486, 506, 534; **2**/10, 94, 97, 107, 113, 125, 192, 198, 239, 269, 283, 286, 324; **3**/13, 28, 36, 39, 57, 88–9, 130, 132, 192, 231, 242, 271, 282–3
Maldon (Essex), **2**/198
'Malechurch' (Radnors), **2**/129
Malmesbury (Wilts), **1**/104, 110, 333; **2**/216, 257, 261
    Corston, **2**/2
    Milbourne, **1**/120
Malswick *see* Newent
Malvern, Great (Worcs), **1**/170; **2**/26, 43, 232, 247
Manston (Dorset), **3**/63
Marcle, Much (Herefs), **1**/411, 550; **2**/185, 215; **3**/189, 371
Marden (Herefs), **1**/47, 97
Margarets, the *see* Wotton: St Margaret's
Marlcliff, in Bidford (Warws), **2**/12

INDEX OF PLACES

Market Lavington *see* Lavington, Market
Marlborough (Wilts), **1**/392; **2**/196
Marshfield, **1**/117–18
Mathon (Worcs), **1**/443
Matson, **1**/14, 327; **2**/185, 211, 240
Maugersbury, **2**/263
Mells (Som), **1**/75
Merionethshire *see* Penmaen
Milbourne *see* Malmesbury
Minchinhampton, **1**/79, 135, 160
Minehead *see* Periton
Minster Lovell (Oxon), **1**/506
Minsterworth, **1**/7, 9, 88, 107, 237, 259, 282, 298, 331, 349*, 368, 370, 380, 393, 507, 523, 576; **2**/16, 29, 33, 39, 76, 103, 109, 286, 292, 299, 317, 338, 350, 363; **3**/12, 16, 41, 45, 57, 61, 146–8, 176, 190, 248–9, 271, 273, 289, 304, 310, 318, 324, 361
Miserden, **1**/181, 250; **2**/292; **3**/64
Mitchel Troy *see* 'St Michael'
Mitcheldean, **1**/9, 29, 86, 403, 406, 448, 450, 485, 549, 577; **2**/16, 108, 115, 121, 135, 139, 155, 195, 265, 309, 354, 369–70; **3**/35, 45, 103, 162, 244, 251, 276, 348
Modbury (Devon), **2**/214
Monmouth, **1**/24–5, 407, 538; **3**/188
  Buckholt, the, **2**/204
Monmouthshire, p. xxiv *and see* Abergavenny; 'Combe Corran'; Cwmyoy; Dixton; Itton; Llanfihangel, Llangattock; Llanvapley; Llantrissant; Llanwenarth; Monmouth; Newquay, Penrhos; 'St Michael'; Skenfrith; 'Tarracleeve'; Tredunnock; Undy; Usk; Whitchurch
Montgomeryshire *see* Forden; Llanfyllin; Llandysilio; Llanidloes
Mordiford (Herefs), **2**/320
Moreton Valence, **1**/1, 291, 302, 349; **2**/332; p. 261
Morton *see* Thornbury
Morville (Salop), **1**/408

Nailsworth, **1**/160; **3**/198
Narberth (Pembs), **1**/172
Naunton, **1**/212; **2**/99, 128, 200, 308, 355, 363; **3**/15*, 213
  Harford, **1**/280
Netherlands (Low Countries), p. 267
New Radnor *see* Radnor, New
Newchurch (Radnors), **1**/72
Newent, **1**/20, 120, 409, 420, 441, 463, 524, 565; **2**/6–7, 11, 68, 89, 102, 241, 264, 279, 292, 321, 347, 352, 375; **3**/18, 23, 56, 61, 64, 90, 118, 120, 131*, 144*, 224, 234, 275, 308, 310–11, 345, 353, 382–3

Kilcot, **2**/74
Malswick, **3**/337
Newington Bagpath, **1**/560
Newland, **1**/161, 247; **2**/32, 374; **3**/93, 115, 227, 281
  Clearwell, **1**/228
  Coleford, **2**/242, 367; **3**/68, 132, 146–7, 159, 209, 222, 307, 337, 340, 391
Newnham, **1**/144, 207, 555; **2**/158, 161, 234, 251, 253, 259; **3**/43, 90, 190, 286
Newport, in Alkington, **2**/177
Newquay (Mon), **1**/475
Newton, Welsh (Herefs), **1**/43, 511; **3**/95
Nibley, North, **1**/179; **2**/103
Noke *see* Churchdown
Northamptonshire *see* Hartwell; Purston
Northleach, **1**/81, 145, 161; **3**/207
Norton (Glos), **1**/8, 43, 70, 83, 104; **2**/80, 112, 349*, 368, 373; **3**/32, 117
  Bishop's Norton, **3**/379
  Prior's Norton, **1**/136
Norton (Worcs), **1**/355
Norton, Bishop's *see* Norton (Glos)
Norton, Brize (Oxon), **1**/141
Norton, Chipping (Oxon), **2**/72
Norton, Hook (Oxon), **1**/97
Norton, Prior's *see* Norton (Glos)
Notgrove, **1**/109
Nottinghamshire *see* Skegby; 'Spurddonne'

Oakley (Beds), **1**/55
Oaksey (Wilts), **1**/582
Oddington, **1**/402, 472; **2**/13
Olveston, **2**/14, 50, 71, 150
Over *see* Churcham
Over Kellet *see* Kellet, Over
Oxenhall, **2**/247, 284; **3**/15, 219
Oxenton, **1**/485
Oxford, **1**/77; p. xxx
Oxfordshire *see* Alvescot; Aston; Bampton; Banbury; Bloxham; Burford; Deddington; Dorchester; Eynsham Ferry; Kidlington; Lew; Minster Lovell; Norton, Brize; Norton, Chipping; Norton, Hook; Oxford; Rollright; Witney; Woodstock
Oxlinch *see* Standish

Padstow (Cornwall), **1**/73
Paganhill *see* Stroud
Painswick, **1**/171, 179, 263, 268, 319, 327–8, 386, 399, 423, 425, 478, 529; **2**/12, 40, 107, 133, 170, 238, 245, 292, 293*, 377; **3**/18, 42, 46, 63, 103, 133–4, 203, 223, 254, 266, 278, 342, 371, 378, 389, 395

Parton *see* Churchdown
Pauntley, **1**/73
Pedington *see* Berkeley
Pembrokeshire *see* Carew; Haverfordwest; Narberth; St Davids
Pendock (Worcs), **3**/104, 106
Pendoylan (Glam), **1**/71, 162
Penkridge *see* Drayton, Lower
Penmaen (Merioneths), **1**/147
Penrhos (Mon), **1**/256, 290, 396
Pensham, in Pershore St Andrew (Worcs), **1**/353
Periton, in Minehead (Som), **3**/380
Pershore (Worcs), **1**/494; **2**/305; **3**/100, 350
   St Andrew, **2**/91 *and see* Pensham
Peterchurch *see* 'Pitchersoken'; Snodhill
Pinnock, **3**/345
Pitchcombe, **3**/133
'Pitchersoken' [Peterchurch soke?] (Herefs), **1**/10
Pontesbury (Salop), **2**/209
Poppinger, in Ashperton (Herefs), **2**/87
Prestbury, **1**/143, 337, 552–3, 557, 588; **2**/167, 169, 252, 355, 368; **3**/105
Preston, **3**/377
Prior's Norton *see* Norton (Glos)
Pucklechurch, **3**/316; p. xx
Purston, in King's Sutton (Northants), **1**/382
Purton (Wilts), **1**/404, 425
Pyon, Kings (Herefs), **1**/98, 100

Quedgeley, **1**/21, 96, 119, 307, 345, 358, 362, 453, 492; **2**/43, 119, 145, 159, 345; **3**/58, 204, 323, 370, 391
   Woolstrop, **2**/282; **3**/117*
Quinton, **2**/56, 285
Quorndon (Leics), **1**/71

Radnor, New (Radnors), **1**/131
Radnorshire *see* Llanyre; 'Malechurch'; Newchurch; Radnor, New
Randwick, **1**/179; **3**/21, 394
Redmarley D'Abitot (Worcs), **2**/297; **3**/44, 62
Redmarley (Worcs) [*unspecified*], **1**/284, 578; **3**/120
Rendcomb, **1**/94, 375, 561; **2**/349; **3**/264
Rissington, Great, **2**/364–5
Rissington, Little, **2**/137
Rissington [*unspecified*], **1**/587
Rockhampton, **1**/347
Rodborough, **1**/285; **2**/109; **3**/107
Rodley *see* Westbury
Rollright (Oxon) [*unspecified*], **2**/201
Ross (Herefs), **1**/108, 121, 146, 261, 284, 318, 325, 483, 544; **2**/4, 36, 44, 377; **3**/94, 199, 230, 232*, 283–4, 306, 314, 321
   Cleeve, **1**/76, 101
Ruardean, **1**/46, 298; **2**/37, 326; **3**/14, 28, 36, 260, 277, 325
   Wishanger, **3**/332
Rudford, **1**/136, 409; **2**/90, 339
Ryeford *see* Stonehouse

St Briavels, **1**/8, 352
St Brides (Glam), **1**/162
St Davids (Pembs), **1**/455, 458, 466
St Devereux (Herefs), **1**/83
St Catherine *see* Longford
St Erme (Cornwall), **2**/369
St John in Bedwardine (Worcs), **2**/345
St Margaret's Hospital *see* Wotton
St Mary Magdalen's Hospital *see* Wotton
'St Michael' [Mitchel Troy?] (Mon), **1**/63
Saintbridge, in Gloucester, **3**/382
Saintbury, **2**/14
Salisbury (Wilts), **2**/57
Sandhurst, **1**/4, 9, 35, 63, 86, 124*, 137, 145, 181, 187, 427; **2**/78, 160, 219, 250, 280, 307, 317, 347; **3**/29–30, 40, 74, 143–4, 158, 195, 317
Saniger, in Hinton, **2**/374
Sapey, Upper (Herefs), **1**/104
Sapperton *see* Frampton Mansell
Saul, **1**/445; **2**/253
   Framilode, **1**/389; **3**/292
'Scheviock' (Flints), **1**/91
'Scopby' [Sotby?] (Lincs), **1**/30
Sedgeberrow (Worcs), **1**/273
Sevenhampton, **1**/405
Severn Stoke *see* Stoke, Severn
Sheephouse, Lower, in Gloucester, **3**/385
Sheffield (Yorks WR), **3**/129
Shenington, **1**/339, 444; **2**/242
Sherborne, **1**/326; **2**/30; **3**/47
Sherston (Wilts), **2**/248
Shipton Bellinger (Hants), **1**/417
Shipton Moyne, **2**/152
Shipton Dovel, **2**/152
Shipton Solers, **1**/141; **3**/130
Shipton (Glos) [*unspecified*], **1**/368; **2**/301
Shrewsbury, **2**/158, 368
Shropshire *see* Astley, Bridgnorth; Broseley; 'Elumbery'; Hampton; Harley; Hughley; Ludlow; Morville; Pontesbury; Shrewsbury; Stow; Wellington
Shurdington, **3**/341
   Great Shurdington, **1**/323; **2**/241, 248*, 255, 312, 333; **3**/304
   Great Shurdington, in Badgeworth parish,

INDEX OF PLACES

1/330; **2**/163
Skegby (Notts), **1**/187
Skenfrith (Mon), **1**/465
Slaughter, Upper, **1**/569
Slaughter [*unspecified*], **1**/402, 456
Slimbridge, **1**/15, 267, 313, 461; **2**/18, 132, 140; **3**/92, 158, 321, 324, 331
Sneedham *see* Upton St Leonards
Snodhill, in Peterchurch (Herefs), **1**/180
Sollers Hope *see* Hope, Sollers
Somerford, Great (Wilts), **1**/84; **2**/143
Somerford (Wilts) [*unspecified*], **1**/487
Somerset, **1**/373 *and see* Bath; Brislington; Cheriton; Combe St Nicholas; Frome; 'Harkeein, East'; Hatch, West; Kingsdon; Langford Budville; Mells; Perriton; Ubley; Wellington; Wells; Worle; Wraxall
Sotby *see* 'Scopby'
Southampton (Hants), **1**/75
Southrop, **1**/118
Southwick *see* Tewkesbury
'Spurddone' (Notts), **1**/288
Staffordshire *see* Arley, Upper; Bloxwich; Drayton, Lower; Whitgreave
Standish, **1**/248, 324; **3**/88, 142, 147, 312
   Oxlinch, **3**/115
Stanford Bishop (Herefs), **2**/265
Stanley, King's, **1**/16, 113, 270; **2**/229, 257; **3**/89
Stanley, Leonard, **1**/5, 181, 295, 310, 510–11; **2**/242, 270*; **3**/81, 109, 235
Stanley Pontlarge, **3**/383
Stanley [*unspecified*], **1**/137, 146, 289, 340
Stanton, **1**/471; **3**/221
Stanway, **3**/214
Staunton (Worcs), **3**/16, 268
Staverton, **1**/21, 23, 32; **2**/216; **3**/161
Stoke, Severn (Worcs), **1**/318, 323
Stoke Orchard *see* Cleeve, Bishop's
Stonehouse, **1**/15, 67, 238
   Ryeford, **1**/328
Stourbridge (Worcs), **2**/377
Stow (Salop), **1**/313
Stow on the Wold, **1**/67; **2**/22; **3**/145
Stratford on Avon (Warws), **3**/270
Stretton Grandison (Herefs), **1**/343
Stroud, **1**/82, 135, 167–8, 181, 238, 310*, 318, 349, 367, 422, 456, 475, 492, 499; **2**/76, 136, 277, 351; **3**/107, 118, 133, 177, 216; pp. xxiv–xxv, xxx
   Paganhill, **2**/297; **3**/13, 279
Stroudwater, **3**/37
Suckley (Worcs), **1**/555
Sudeley, **2**/310

Surrey *see* Bankside; Godalming; Lambeth
Sutton (Herefs), **1**/119
   Freen Court, **1**/93
Sutton, King's *see* Purston
Swindon, **1**/14, 145
Syde, **1**/583

Talgarth (Brecons), **1**/7, 257
'Tarracleeve' (Mon), **1**/52
Tarrington (Herefs), **2**/110
Taynton, **1**/25, 34, 201, 338, 585; **2**/111, 370; **3**/17, 36, 48, 106, 289, 340, 374, 385
Teddington, **1**/249
Temple Guiting *see* Guiting, Temple
Tetbury, **1**/4, 346, 387, 562, 573; **2**/331
   Tetbury Upton, **1**/570; **3**/320
Tewkesbury, **1**/2, 5, 10, 22, 54, 112, 142, 170, 228*, 325, 354, 360, 426, 533, 536; **2**/19, 65, 67, 134, 148, 156–7, 228, 250, 269, 277, 279, 318, 321, 326, 346, 348, 369; **3**/19, 85, 190–1, 226, 343, 354–7; pp. xxiv, xxx, 264
   Gupshill **1**/81
   Southwick, **2**/226
Thornbury, **1**/457, 468
   Morton, **2**/119
Througham *see* Bisley
Tibberton, **1**/22, 324, 334, 457, 533; **2**/20, 47, 205, 223; **3**/41, 173, 263, 310
Tidenham *see* 'Buston'
Tillington, in Burghill (Herefs), **1**/99
Tirley, **1**/96, 103, 305, 308, 352–3, 435, 438, 483, 497, 526, 567; **2**/51, 59, 105, 169, 174, 210, 267, 315; **3**/122, 331, 357, 391
Tiverton (Devon), **1**/70
Tockenham Wick, in Tockenham (Wilts), **3**/364
Todenham, **1**/92, 299
Tortworth, **1**/12
Tredington, **1**/180
Tredunnock (Mon), **1**/159
Troy, Mitchel *see* 'St Michael'
Tuffley, in Gloucester, **1**/113, 245, 290, 344; **2**/152; **3**/22, 25, 344, 380, 387, 397
Turkdean, **1**/379, 481
Twigworth, **1**/44, 75, 83, 274, 423, 550; **2**/322
Twyning, **1**/22, 35, 117, 133–4, 293, 315; **2**/251; **3**/358, 395
Tytherington, **1**/483; **2**/104

Ubley (Som), **1**/335
Uckington, **1**/392; **2**/21, 66, 86
Uley, **3**/297
Undy (Mon), **1**/48
Upleadon, **1**/130, 256, 329; **2**/117; **3**/173, 175, 210

Upper Arley *see* Arley, Upper
Upper Sapey *see* Sapey, Upper
Upper Slaughter *see* Slaughter, Upper
Upton Bishop (Herefs), **1**/317; **3**/19, 39
Upton St Leonards, **1**/62, 167, 238, 261, 283, 307, 423, 458, 547; **2**/32, 36, 66, 83, 114, 178, 205, 225, 233, 254, 301, 346, 365; **3**/17*, 44, 236, 282, 291–2, 344, 382
    Sneedham, **1**/408
Upton [*unspecified*], **1**/15, 120, 173, 197, 297, 348
Urchfont *see* Eastcott
Usk (Mon), **1**/332; **2**/95

Vaynor *see* 'Wander'
Virginia, **2**/371, 376–8; pp. xxiii, xxx

Wales, p. xxiv
  South Wales, p. xxiii
  and see Abergavenny; Brecon; Bronllys; Cardiff; Carew; Carmarthen; 'Combe Corran'; Crickhowell; Cwmyoy; Dixton; Haverfordwest; Itton; 'Langdila'; Laugharne; 'Llanere'; Llanfihangel, Llangattock; Llanvapley; Llantrissant; Llanwenarth; 'Malechurch'; Monmouth; Narberth; Newchurch; Newquay, Pendoylan; 'Penmane'; Penrhos; Radnor, New; St Brides; St Davids; 'St Michael'; 'Scheviock'; Skenfrith; Talgarth; 'Tarracleeve'; Tredunnock; Undy; Usk; 'Wander'; Whitchurch
Walford (Herefs), **1**/179; **2**/121; **3**/132, 285
'Wander' [Vaynor?] (Brecons), **2**/375
Wanstead (Essex), **1**/109
Warwickshire *see* Birmingham; Compton Wynyates; Halford; Ilmington; Ipsley; Marlcliff; Stratford on Avon
Wellington (Herefs), **1**/68 *and see* Auberrow
Wellington (Salop), **3**/398
Wellington (Som), **3**/363
Wells (Som), **2**/67
Welsh Newton *see* Newton, Welsh
West Hatch *see* Hatch, West
Westbury [on Severn], **1**/26, 36, 62, 227, 314, 389, 414, 416, 437, 444, 479, 525, 529, 542, 551, 555, 581; **2**/81, 108, 208, 231, 291, 313, 327, 348, 353, 355; **3**/53, 106, 160, 274, 288, 346–7, 384
    Rodley, **3**/52, 103
Westend [*unspecified*], **1**/37, 109
Westerleigh, **1**/573
Westington Park *see* Campden, Chipping
Westminster, **3**/369

Westmorland, p. xxiv *and see* Elterwalter; Hutton; 'Kerby Kendall'
Weston under Penyard (Herefs), **1**/126; **2**/91, 237; **3**/11
Weston (Herefs) [*unspecified*], **1**/111
Westoning (Beds), **1**/85, 94
Whaddon, **1**/20, 98, 330, 332, 352, 388, 449, 457, 462, 464, 470, 519, 586; **2**/334, 370; **3**/107, 302
Wheatenhurst *see* Whitminster
Whitchurch (Herefs), **2**/218
Whitchurch (Mon), **1**/145
Whitgreave (Staffs), **1**/98
Whitminster, **1**/259
    Wheatenhurst, **3**/26, 208
Whitney (Herefs), **1**/285
Whittington, **1**/326
Willersey, **3**/366
Wiltshire *see* Ashton Keynes; Brinkworth; Chippenham; Colerne; Coulston; Cricklade; Crudwell; Eastcott; Eaton, Castle; Garsdon; Hankerton; Hannington; Kingswood; Lavington, Market; Lea; Leigh; Lydiard Millicent; Malmesbury; Marlborough; Oaksey; Purton; Salisbury; Sherston; Somerford; Tockenham Wick; Wootton Bassett
Winchcombe, **1**/65, 143, 341, 569; **2**/96, 181, 206, 363; **3**/16, 313, 319, 366
    Gretton, **2**/360
Winterbourne, **3**/282
Wishanger *see* Ruardean
Witcombe, Great, **1**/148, 349, 495, 525; **2**/197, 250; **3**/264
Witcombe, Little *see* Badgeworth
Witcombe [*unspecified*], **1**/503, 505*, 540
Withington (Glos), **1**/180; **2**/156, 243
Withington (Herefs), **2**/163, 262
Withy Bridge *see* Boddington
Witney *see* Hailey
Woodchester, **2**/256, 295; **3**/23, 72
Woodford *see* Berkeley
Woodmancote *see* Cerney, North
Woodstock (Oxon), **2**/213
Woolhope (Herefs), **1**/247
Woolstrop *see* Quedgeley
Wootton Bassett (Wilts), **1**/227
Worcester, **1**/269; **2**/70, 116, 302; **3**/58, 100, 102 *n*, 240*
Worcestershire, **1**/161 *and see* Alstone; 'Batchfords Heath'; Badsey; Bengeworth; Berrow; Bewdley; Birtsmorton; Bishampton; Bockleton; Bredon; Broadway; Bromsgrove; Bushley; Chaceley; Chaddesley Corbett; Charlton; Comberton; 'Crable'; Croome, Hill; Dodderhill;

INDEX OF PLACES

Droitwich; Eckington; Eldersfield; Evesham; Halford; Hampton Lovett; Hanley; Longdon; Malvern, Great; Mathon; Norton; Pendock; Pershore; Redmarley; St John in Bedwardine; Sedgeberrow; Staunton; Stoke, Severn; Stourbridge; Suckley; Worcester

Worle (Som), **1**/409

Wormington, **3**/349

Wormsley (Herefs), **1**/73, 79; **2**/256

Wotton, in Gloucester, **1**/64, 262, 274, 301; **2**/207, 252, 262, 339; **3**/35, 69, 331

St Margaret's Hospital (the Margarets), **2**/185, 282; **3**/9, 143, 317

St Mary Magdalen's Hospital (the Magdalens), **2**/154, 172, 185

Wotton under Edge, **1**/120, 318; **2**/9, 84, 135, 159, 236, 280, 288; **3**/10, 64

Wraxall (Som), **3**/69

Wrexham (Denbs), **3**/25, 46, 130

Yorkshire *see* Sheffield

INDEX OF TRADES, OCCUPATIONS AND RANKS
OF THE APPRENTICES AND THEIR PARENTS

References to the calendar are to the volumes and pages of the MSS., which are given in the left-hand column of the calendar; references preceded by 'p.' or 'pp.' are to the pages of the introduction or the appendixes. An asterisk * indicates that the reference is to more than one occurrence of the trade, occupation or rank concerned.

accounts, keeping of, **1**/382
alderman, **1**/31, 39, 391, 488, 574; **3**/85, 298, 335, 356; pp. xxv–xxvi
anchorsmith, **3**/377
apothecary, **1**/2, 8, 23, 80, 113, 145, 160, 181, 258, 289, 333, 337, 401, 461, 520*, 523, 578; **2**/15, 30, 36, 87, 90, 126, 137*, 142, 166, 171, 206, 225, 234*, 293*b*, 310, 339; **3**/15, 46*, 109*, 131*, 199*, 237, 246, 271*, 295, 312, 355, 365, 375, 391, 395; pp. xvi, xxv–xxvi

bagger, **1**/100
baker, **1**/12, 20, 24, 30, 36*, 43, 62, 64, 67*, 81–2, 98, 104, 109–10, 126, 129, 134, 138*, 146, 157, 159*, 160–1, 167, 169, 171–2, 177–8, 180*, 187, 199*, 228, 229*, 230, 237, 258–9, 263*, 267–8, 274, 279*, 283, 291, 294, 298, 307–8, 322, 326*, 330, 332–4, 340, 342, 344–5, 350*, 352, 354*–5*, 361, 363*, 364, 379–81, 386, 403, 410, 413, 415–16, 428, 433–4, 436*n*, 438–9, 456, 460*, 462, 470, 486, 489, 491, 494, 512, 517, 519, 523, 531, 534, 535*, 536*n*, 539, 545, 550–1, 553, 566–7, 571–2, 574*, 584; **2**/2, 5, 9*, 18*, 19, 23, 26, 32, 34, 39, 42, 46, 48*, 50*, 53, 59, 61, 67*, 74, 83, 107, 109, 111*, 112, 114*, 115, 117*, 127–8, 130*, 132, 138, 146, 150, 167, 169–70, 179*, 192, 198, 200–2, 207–8, 214, 225–6, 235, 244, 250–1, 253, 256, 264, 267*, 270*, 271, 274, 283, 292, 295, 299, 306–7, 311–12, 315, 320*, 322, 329*, 331–2, 334, 338*, 340, 348, 352, 353*, 360, 362, 364; **3**/10, 13*, 18–19, 21*, 23*, 26, 28*, 31, 40, 46–7, 55, 59, 67, 70–1, 73, 84, 95, 102, 103*, 104, 107*, 120, 130*, 133, 143, 146, 161–2, 172*, 175, 191–2, 196, 198, 203–4, 212–13, 220, 221*, 242, 244–5, 247, 253, 259*, 260–1, 263–4, 267, 273, 279–80, 282, 286, 288, 290, 301–2, 304*, 309, 312, 314*, 315, 319, 323*, 330–1, 336*, 337, 342*, 344–5, 351, 355, 360*, 361, 363*, 366, 369–70, 372–3, 374*, 377*–8*, 381, 386, 388–91, 395, 398–400;

pp. xiii, xvi, xxiv, xxvi, xxvii
barber, **1**/3, 11, 25, 32, 120*, 142, 298, 327, 350, 433, 529; **3**/70, 128, 246*, 268, 270, 289, 307, 316, 380; pp. xiii, xvi, 268
barber surgeon, **1**/41, 170, 171*, 182, 191, 211, 298, 358, 396, 430–1, 466–7, 473, 498, 523, 543, 545, 585; **2**/56, 63*, 67, 81*, 122*, 136, 139, 156, 193, 204, 244*, 254*, 262, 265, 268, 288, 310, 321, 324, 325, 327, 333*; **3**/39, 44–5, 60*, 95, 108, 117, 142*, 195–6, 214, 234, 236, 240, 242, 277–8, 283–4, 294, 314, 320–1, 336, 337*, 341, 348, 355*, 356, 364, 366, 379*, 387, 389; pp. xvi, xxvi–xxvii *and see* surgeon
basket maker, **1**/114, 450; **2**/284, 289; **3**/30*, 92, 148*, 173
beer brewer *see* brewer
bellfounder, **1**/420; **2**/31, 112; **3**/346*; pp. xvi, xxxi
blacksmith, **1**/10, 20, 24, 34, 45*, 47, 305, 365, 418–19, 441, 443, 447, 452*n*, 453*, 454, 497, 506*, 541, 559 *and n*, 570, 579*; **2**/4, 14, 40*, 49*, 52*, 58, 66, 70, 87, 96*, 135–6, 150, 158, 161, 163, 175, 177, 217, 222, 237*, 242, 248, 251–2, 260*, 265, 292, 304, 318*, 322, 341*, 355, 365, 366*; **3**/13, 52, 57, 80–1, 87, 93*, 105, 121, 132*, 145, 222, 225, 226*, 230, 233, 237*, 242, 244, 261, 266, 276–7, 280, 282, 296, 299, 300*, 303*, 306, 325, 330–2, 344, 349–50, 372, 379, 384*, 386; pp. xvi, xxi, xxiv *and see* farrier; smith
blackware man, **3**/92
bodicemaker, **1**/407, 428, 574; **2**/9, 19, 60*, 66, 71, 121*, 198, 226, 236, 238–9, 245, 294, 299, 325, 341*, 366; **3**/42, 45, 71–2, 84, 108, 128, 142, 144, 146, 176, 248, 265, 279, 294–5, 369*; p. xvi
bone lace weaver, **1**/305
bookseller, **3**/199 *and see* stationer
brazier, **1**/75, 168, 449, 584; **2**/159, 307, 314, 330; **3**/16, 40, 88, 134, 214, 244, 274, 276, 319, 361, 363, 399; pp. xvi, 265

INDEX OF TRADES, OCCUPATIONS AND RANKS

brewer (beer brewer), **1**/2*, 3, 6*, 51, 55, 71, 76, 99, 158–9, 162, 201, 257*, 261–2, 278, 291–2, 307, 332, 340, 346*, 387, 389, 406*, 411, 416*, 435, 438, 448, 501*, 534–5, 536 and n, 539, 547, 561, 570; **2**/36, 45, 53, 89, 106, 118, 120, 153, 181*, 219, 221, 229, 263, 272, 283*, 293, 311, 316, 320, 334, 344, 349*, 352–3, 361*; **3**/11*, 21, 24, 32, 58, 68, 102, 115, 196*, 323; pp. xvi, xix, xxvi, 266 *and see* maltster

bricklayer (brickmaker), **1**/318; **2**/95, 157, 215, 312; **3**/43, 270, 317, 333, 352*, 353, 356, 381, 384, 387, 392, 395, 398; p. xvi

broadweaver, **1**/4, 8, 10–11, 16, 33*, 35*, 37*, 48*, 52*, 65, 69, 104, 122, 129–30, 144, 173, 190, 200, 211, 229, 249, 260, 268–9, 273, 287*, 301, 334, 344, 366, 373, 378*, 387, 414, 441–2, 475, 491, 518*, 543, 545, 561, 294; **2**/82, 95, 99, 104, 177, 199, 215, 218, 220, 236, 369; **3**/19, 29, 45, 271, 279, 394, 395; pp. xvi, xxviii–xxix *and see* weaver

brushmaker, **3**/37, 108

burgess, **1**/518*

butcher, **1**/5, 8*, 15–16, 22*, 36, 63, 82, 92*, 100, 104–5, 131*–2*, 143, 146*, 158*, 169–70, 181, 200, 202, 210–11, 247, 255, 263, 268*, 271, 279*, 299, 313*, 318*, 322*, 331, 334, 338, 342, 360, 366*, 369–70, 387*, 402, 438, 446, 452*, 456, 463, 465, 498, 513*, 538, 559*; **2**/5, 16, 19, 33*, 52*, 69*, 73, 78, 90, 102, 111, 121, 129, 155, 174, 181*, 196*, 199, 217, 233, 246*, 248, 250–2, 259, 265, 272, 274–5, 281, 291, 302*, 309*, 314, 317, 321, 326*, 328, 330, 332, 342*, 355; **3**/20*, 21, 23, 41, 48, 49*, 55*, 65*, 69, 71, 73*, 74, 86–7, 92, 103–4, 109*, 140*, 142*, 147–8, 158–9, 161, 172, 175, 177*, 190, 210, 217, 224, 248–9, 259, 262, 263*, 264, 267–8, 271, 272*, 277, 279, 283*, 293, 302*, 303, 310, 312–14, 317–18, 324, 341, 344, 346*–7*, 353, 354*, 356, 358*, 364*, 368*, 371–2, 377*, 384–5, 391, 393–4, 397, 399; pp. xiii, xvi, xxvii

button maker, **2**/78, 99, 143, 201, 166, 184, 186, 209, 254, 261–2, 282, 300, 306–7, 316, 320–1, 352, 365; **3**/17, 23, 29, 49, 71, 82*, 90, 103, 108, 115, 190, 220*, 262, 287*, 301, 311*, 317, 348, 368, 373, 378; p. xvi *and see* leather-button maker

button-mould maker, **2**/305

capper, **1**/4*, 7, 65, 68, 119; p. xxv

cardmaker, **1**/2, 328, 394, 477, 504, 556; **2**/3*, 84, 151*, 316; **3**/105, 227*; p. xvi

carpenter, **1**/13, 20, 22, 34, 42–3, 124, 162, 208, 282, 290, 323–4, 374*, 393, 419*, 424, 437, 476, 497, 532, 587; **2**/50, 109, 145, 166, 180, 185, 262, 275, 282, 284, 286, 293*, 353, 356; **3**/20, 22*, 45, 54, 57, 59, 70–1, 94, 104, 110*, 122, 134, 145*, 147–8, 175–6, 187*, 209, 220, 225, 234, 244, 249, 263, 269*, 276, 281, 295, 309, 324, 343*, 352, 370, 378, 388*, 391, 398; p. xvi *and see* ship's carpenter

carpet weaver, **2**/276 *and see* weaver

carrier, **1**/325, 347; **2**/111, 132, 193, 236, 261, 283, 333*, 336; **3**/13, 162; p. xvi

carver, **3**/146, 297–8 *and see* stone carver

chandler, **1**/133, 143, 178, 228, 245, 249, 259, 273, 282, 299–300, 314, 324, 326–7, 334, 339*, 359–60, 373, 384, 385*, 400, 434, 444, 456*, 468–9, 473, 478, 483, 493*, 499, 501n, 523, 530, 550*, 551, 553–4; **2**/11, 12*, 18, 19*, 20, 42, 44, 47, 63, 66, 84–5, 89, 100, 103, 105, 121, 135, 139, 149*, 156, 173, 180, 200*, 218, 229, 238, 241, 243, 256, 293b, 300*, 304, 308–9, 325, 331*, 336, 338, 345*, 351, 354*; **3**/18, 29, 38, 42*–3*, 56–7, 59–60, 66*, 69, 86, 132, 135, 144, 267, 271, 293, 302; pp. xvi, xxvi–xxvii *and see* tallow chandler

chapman (petty chapman), **1**/86, 142, 301, 329, 511; **2**/45, 164, 347*; **3**/88

cheesemonger, **3**/350*, 353*

churchwarden, **1**/51

clerk (cleric), **1**/5, 32, 36, 46, 76, 87, 92, 112–13, 117–18, 119*, 121, 123–4, 137, 144, 160, 177, 179*, 258, 271, 277, 314, 339, 349, 356, 358, 360, 367, 375, 395, 399, 403, 405, 423, 434, 465–6, 468*, 494, 517, 569; **2**/43, 51, 65, 68, 80, 99, 124, 128, 163, 165–6, 173, 180, 205, 218, 222–3, 262, 293, 325, 365; **3**/51, 91, 95, 141, 189, 193, 214, 245, 253, 295, 297, 301, 308, 314, 323, 349, 363, 379, 395; pp. xxv–xxvi

clockmaker, **3**/363 *and see* watchmaker

cloth dresser, **2**/203

clothier, **1**/32, 66, 70, 77, 96, 119*, 122, 127, 134*, 136, 144, 146–7, 158*, 171, 182, 187, 190*, 197, 200, 212*, 228, 238, 248, 270, 281, 285*, 290, 300, 302, 318, 324, 333, 334*–5*, 341, 348–9, 361, 379, 395*, 407, 429, 448, 474–5, 477, 513n, 514*, 532, 573; **2**/38, 40, 109, 136, 148, 256–7, 317–18, 334, 339, 343*, 351; **3**/19, 37, 39, 69, 71*, 89*, 118, 133, 173, 198, 224, 234, 237, 240, 325, 360, 369, 380; pp. xi, xvi, xix, xxi, xxvi, 266, 268

clothmaker, **3**/133

clothworker, **1**/107, 452n, 453; **2**/135, 149, 369–70; **3**/21, 35, 107, 342

coachman, **2**/283

coalman, **3**/144; p. xxv

INDEX OF TRADES, OCCUPATIONS AND RANKS

coalminer (collier), **3**/68, 307, 340 *and see* miner

cobbler, **1**/108, 171; **2**/269n *and see* cordwainer; shoe mender; shoemaker

collar maker, **2**/273, 363; **3**/160, 208*, 228, 252, 316, 320, 365, 381; p. xvi

collier *see* coalminer

comber *see* wool comber

combmaker, **2**/44, 105, 215, 237, 285, 295, 337, 356*, 360; **3**/11, 18, 25, 31*, 43, 58, 64, 67, 81, 86, 91, 285*, 396; p. xvi *and see* jersey combmaker

cook, **1**/323, 330*, 348, 376, 383, 421–2, 455, 513*, 559n, 560, 564n, 567; **2**/51*, 96, 124, 151, 203, 281*, 342*; **3**/59; pp. xvi, 268

cooper, **1**/20, 64, 74, 85, 92, 103, 105, 106*, 111, 114, 121, 129, 141, 159–60, 170, 173, 189, 197, 207, 211, 239, 247, 258, 260, 261*, 280*, 294*, 301, 314–15, 322, 325, 342, 350, 353, 364, 369, 386*, 407, 411, 415–16, 418*, 465, 483, 495, 503, 505, 526, 539, 545, 547, 555, 560, 575, 581*; **2**/2*, 9, 14*, 38, 45, 103, 113, 137, 157, 178, 182, 190, 214*, 226*, 233*, 243, 255, 260*, 261, 274, 299, 302*, 309*, 314, 323, 349*, 365*; **3**/14, 36*, 47, 62, 80–1, 83, 93, 121–2, 129*, 134, 144, 147, 149, 163, 189*, 210, 218, 226, 236, 244, 253, 278, 303, 307–8, 316, 319*, 333, 338*, 350, 352, 356, 364*, 368, 391; pp. xvi–xvii, xxvii *and see* wine cooper

cordwainer, **1**/2, 4, 9, 11, 17, 26, 30*, 44, 46, 49*, 62, 65, 68–9, 88, 92*, 96, 97*, 103–5, 107, 108*, 110*, 112–13, 119, 123*, 124–6, 132, 133*–4*, 136–8, 142*, 145*, 146, 148*, 157, 158*, 160–1, 168, 171*, 173, 177, 179*, 181, 187*, 188, 197, 199*, 200–1, 208*, 209–10, 212*, 228, 237*, 238, 245*–6*, 255*–6*, 257, 259*, 267*, 271*, 272, 274*, 275–6, 280–3, 288, 290, 292*, 302, 305, 307–8, 310*, 312, 313*, 314, 315*–16*, 321, 323, 325*, 328, 331, 332*–3*, 341*, 343*, 346–7, 348*–50*, 352, 356, 358, 366, 368n, 369*, 370, 372–3, 375–6, 379, 384, 386*, 392*–4*, 396 *and n*, 397*, 399, 402, 403*, 404–7, 411–12, 419, 421, 422*, 423, 427*, 432–3, 438, 442, 444*, 445, 449*, 451*, 453*, 457*, 461, 464–5, 467*, 469–70, 473, 475–6, 478, 479*, 481, 485, 488, 490, 492, 494, 501 *and n*, 502*, 507, 513, 515, 517, 523*, 527n, 529*, 530, 540, 543, 545, 548, 549*, 551, 554*, 555–6, 557*, 559 *and n*, 560*, 562*–3*, 564* *and n*, 565*, 566, 569–71, 572*, 575–6*, 576–8, 581, 586*; **2**/1, 3*–5*, 7*, 11, 15*, 20–2, 24–5, 26*, 27–9, 39–40, 41*, 43*, 48–9, 54*, 65, 70, 72, 74, 75*–7*, 79, 80*–1*, 82, 88, 90, 92*, 93–4, 96–8, 100–1, 103, 105*, 107, 109*, 113, 115, 118, 124–5, 126*, 127, 136, 146, 159, 162, 163*, 165, 169, 172*, 175*, 177, 181, 182*–3*, 184, 192–5, 196*, 198, 201*, 202–3, 205, 209*–10*, 213*, 219, 224*, 227, 229, 231–2, 236, 240*–1*, 242, 244*, 245, 247*, 249*, 253–4, 258–9, 264, 276, 287, 315; **3**/42, 48n, 66, 69, 72, 119, 120*, 121, 142, 144, 147, 149, 159, 161*, 162–3, 174n, 179, 190, 194*, 196, 197*, 198–200, 201*, 203, 208–9, 212*, 213, 215–16, 217*, 219, 223*, 224, 228, 230*, 231, 233*, 234–5, 240, 242*, 247*, 248, 252, 254, 260, 265*–6*, 267, 271, 272*, 275, 278*, 279–80, 282*, 283–4, 290*–1*, 292, 297, 299*–300*, 302, 305*–6*, 308, 310–11, 313, 317, 319, 322, 326, 330*, 332, 333*, 348*, 353*, 357, 359–60, 365*, 367–8, 371–3, 378–9, 382*, 385, 386*, 390*, 392, 393*–4*; pp. xvi, xix–xx, xxvi–xxviii *and see* cobbler; currier; shoemaker

cotton weaver, **2**/279–81 *and see* weaver

coverlet weaver, **1**/126; **2**/348; **3**/335 *and see* weaver

currier, **1**/147, 541; **2**/7, 42, 46, 93, 125, 192, 195, 199, 262–4, 267, 269*, 271, 273*, 275*, 276, 279–80, 285*–6*, 287–8, 292, 293b, 294, 296*, 299–300, 305*, 308, 309*, 311, 313, 319*, 321–2, 324–5, 328*, 330, 331*, 335, 342, 344, 347*, 350, 356–7, 360–4, 368, 370*, 280, 304, 340; **3**/9–10, 13*–14*, 16, 18–20, 22–3, 25, 26*, 27, 28*, 30*, 31, 38, 43–4, 47–8, 52, 54–5, 58–66, 67*, 69–70, 72*, 73, 74*, 80*, 81, 88*, 89, 91, 92*, 94–5, 101*, 102, 104*, 106*, 109, 141, 146, 188, 194, 202, 211*, 233, 238–9, 280*, 290, 295, 320, 330, 345, 366, 371, 387; pp. xvi, xxvii, 269 *and see* cordwainer

cutler, **1**/6*, 31, 52–3, 64, 76, 92, 98, 126, 142, 159–60, 169, 178, 227, 239, 401*, 437, 454, 472*, 484, 489, 505, 522, 538, 543, 545, 556, 582*; **2**/27, 57, 69, 99, 153, 173*, 201, 222, 245*, 266, 268*, 281, 296–7, 335–6, 369; **3**/22, 57*, 63, 70, 103*, 104, 129*, 242, 264, 320, 321*, 354, 389; pp. xvi, xxvii, 268

distiller, **1**/540

doctor of medicine (doctor in physic), **1**/478; **2**/293; **3**/164 *and see* physician

draper, **1**/21, 33*, 35, 68, 121*, 123–4, 130, 135, 138, 158, 160, 230, 237, 247, 269, 274, 395*, 461; **2**/12, 16, 28, 37, 284; pp. xvi, xxi, xxiv–xxvi *and see* linen draper; woollen draper

dyer, **1**/49, 51, 79, 106, 111, 167*, 172*, 178*–9*, 180–1, 268, 483, 486; **2**/4, 9, 228, 245, 326; **3**/42, 281, 389; pp. xxix, 266

esquire, **1**/317, 368, 523, 549, 577; **3**/331; pp. xxv, 267–9

INDEX OF TRADES, OCCUPATIONS AND RANKS

farmer, **1**/122, 162, 237, 276, 328, 447, 455–6, 463, 465*, 466, 469, 471*, 473, 475, 480–2, 495,* 497*, 504, 509*, 524–5, 527–8, 533, 541–2, 547*, 549, 551, 554, 557, 565–6, 567*, 571, 573, 575, 576*, 577–8, 580, 582; **2**/3, 6, 18, 45, 53–5, 58, 76, 260, 261*, 268, 270*, 272, 273*, 277*, 279–85, 288, 291*, 292, 294, 296–7, 301, 304, 307–8, 310, 313, 315*, 317*, 318, 320, 324, 328, 332, 334, 337, 339, 341, 345, 348, 355–6, 361, 363–8; **3**/9*, 12*, 15–16, 17*–18*, 27*–8*, 30, 34, 35*, 38, 39*, 40, 41*, 44, 46, 48, 52*, 56, 61, 66, 68, 83*, 84, 91*, 95, 99, 100, 103, 115*, 117*, 120, 122, 131–2, 140–3, 147, 172, 174*, 178, 184, 203, 209–10, 213*, 216, 223, 253, 283, 286*, 287–8, 297, 315, 356, 361, 370; p. xxv *and see* husbandman; yeoman

farrier, **1**/305, 359, 364, 381, 548, 554; **2**/14, 67, 162*, 176, 248, 292, 298, 301, 310, 338*, 354; **3**/37, 64, 261, 266, 275, 396, 331, 340, 343*, 366, 398; pp. xvi, xxvii *and see* blacksmith; smith

fellmonger, **3**/104; p. xvi *and see* leatherseller

feltmaker, **1**/31, 108, 144*, 180, 189, 209, 260–1, 275, 280*, 295, 304, 312*, 326*, 330, 335, 338*, 344*, 349, 351, 395, 399–400, 408–9, 422, 429, 439*, 469–70, 481*, 486, 490, 491*, 502, 509–10, 514, 527, 534*, 536, 542, 558, 560, 567–8, 572–3; **2**/2, 5–6, 8, 10, 23, 44, 57, 58*, 75, 79*, 97, 101, 104, 106, 118, 127, 133, 140, 148, 155, 158, 161, 179, 183, 189*, 194, 202, 213, 215, 218*, 228, 251*, 253, 257, 259, 263–4, 272–3, 275, 277, 291, 295, 297–8, 301, 311*–12*, 318, 326, 335, 345, 346*, 348, 351, 353–4, 356, 360, 367*; **3**/16–17, 19, 28, 32, 44–5, 56, 66, 81, 83*, 84, 90, 93*–4*, 95, 106, 108, 110, 118*, 122, 143, 146–7, 173*, 176–7, 188*, 189, 190*, 197, 207, 209, 215*, 219, 222, 227*, 228, 236*, 241*, 246, 260, 269, 275, 293, 303*, 307, 312, 317*, 326, 331, 335, 343, 347, 357, 359, 368, 370, 378, 381, 383, 386*, 390, 398; pp. xvi, xxvii, 265, 266*, 267, 269

fisherman (fisher), **1**/44, 370; **2**/108, 335, 345; **3**/54, 361; p. xxv

fishhook maker, **2**/153; **3**/367 *and see* hook maker

fishmonger, **1**/106, 272, 363

flax dresser, **3**/388

fletcher, **1**/4, 6, 50

freemason, **1**/378*; **2**/265; **3**/49 *and see* mason; stone cutter

fuller (tucker), **1**/3, 16, 40, 45, 79, 179, 289, 310; **2**/37, 103, 257, 363; p. xxv

furrier, **2**/116, 262; **3**/206; p. xvi

gardener, **1**/34, 122, 160, 303; **2**/60, 161, 195, 210, 229, 262, 266, 271, 284, 341, 344, 378; **3**/18, 48, 63, 68, 84, 105, 121, 177, 191, 264, 280, 344, 371, 384, 356; p. xvi

garter weaver, **1**/305, 408, 447, 580*; **2**/19, 73–4, 104, 106, 115, 124, 134, 146, 152, 174, 214, 223*, 249*, 253, 274–5, 310, 337*; **3**/41, 193, 212; pp. xvi, xxiv *and see* weaver

gate keeper, p. 266

gentleman, **1**/3, 21, 23–4, 30–2, 35*, 40, 49, 70*, 81, 97, 99, 105, 120, 124, 131, 135, 141, 157–8, 167, 171, 187, 190, 212, 238, 245, 255, 262, 268, 274, 284, 290, 293, 297, 299, 302–4, 310, 316, 322, 329–30, 335, 337, 339*, 341, 343–5, 352, 359, 361, 372–3, 386*n*, 433*, 436*n*, 437, 442–3, 458–9, 463, 464*, 485–6, 498–9, 507, 516, 532, 540, 542, 544, 550, 552, 569, 577, 583*, 585–6, 588; **2**/10, 12, 16, 24, 28, 30, 32, 36, 47, 54, 62*, 67, 75, 87, 97, 101, 108, 116, 120, 126, 128–9, 138, 177, 185, 187, 198, 202, 204, 207, 210, 216–17, 227*, 228, 234, 237–8, 244, 250, 254*, 255, 259*, 265, 272, 288, 298, 304*, 310, 327, 338–9, 352–4; **3**/13, 15–16, 22, 32*, 43, 46–7, 62–4, 67, 73, 88, 92, 96, 102*, 106, 119, 132*, 133, 143, 145, 159–60, 173, 176, 179, 188–9, 192, 198–9, 210, 214, 216, 227, 232, 254, 296, 304, 311, 319, 332, 347, 349, 351, 355, 358, 361, 364, 366, 372–3, 375, 377, 383, 389, 391, 392*, 395, 399; pp. xxi, xxv–xxvi, xxxi, 265*, 266, 272*

gentleman of the bedchamber, p. 267

glass carrier, **1**/34

glass founder, **3**/313

glassmaker, **3**/87, 90, 110, 116, 118, 231*, 276, 295, 335, 365

glazier, **1**/97, 107*, 121, 167, 181, 262, 348*, 455, 522; **2**/46, 57, 120*, 241, 263, 280, 353, 366; **3**/31*, 40–1, 64, 141*, 201, 225, 315, 322, 324, 342, 356, 385; p. xvi

glover, **1**/2, 7–9, 15, 20, 21*, 22, 25, 32, 34, 36, 40, 46, 66*, 70, 74, 80, 82, 83*, 91, 95, 107, 112, 117, 120*, 121–2, 129–30, 132, 145, 168*, 169, 172–3, 178, 182, 189, 198*, 227, 228*, 245, 247, 255, 261, 268, 275, 284, 317–18, 335, 341*, 343–5, 352–3, 359, 364, 385, 398*, 402, 404, 409, 417, 425, 427, 434, 436*, 437, 440, 446, 449, 455*, 467, 480, 482, 485, 489*n*, 490, 509, 513, 515, 521, 527*n*, 528, 530, 536*n*, 537, 543–4, 568, 584*, 585; **2**/17, 20–1, 36, 37*, 47, 62, 65, 74, 94, 102, 118, 139, 141*–3*, 155, 193, 199, 208*, 213, 219, 225, 243, 268, 269*, 279*, 286*, 288, 291, 293*b*, 295–6, 318, 350, 352, 369; **3**/20, 23, 24*, 29*, 36*, 37, 42, 68, 104, 119, 129,

INDEX OF TRADES, OCCUPATIONS AND RANKS

glover (*cont.*)
130*, 149*, 158, 163*, 174, 191, 203, 226, 229, 246, 249, 260*, 261–2, 266, 276, 286*, 299, 310, 314, 325, 340, 346, 362*, 368, 380*, 396*, 397; pp. xiii, xvi, xxvi–xxvii

goldsmith, **1**/299, 403*; **3**/241*, 321; p. xi

grocer, **2**/116, 171, 206, 294*, 309, 316; **3**/30*, 51, 96, 133, 141, 179, 208, 213, 234, 276, 301*, 324, 340–2, 351, 370*, 372, 375, 389–90, 394, 399; pp. xvi, xxv–xxvii

gunsmith (gunmaker), **1**/20, 110, 275, 342*, 361, 364; **2**/62*, 114, 214, 242–3, 255*, 265, 289, 318; **3**/58, 61, 100, 175, 262, 306, 325, 358; p. xvi

haberdasher, **1**/1, 34, 61–2, 64, 85*, 91, 104–5, 111*, 112, 119, 134, 142, 145, 168, 178, 207, 210, 293, 298, 306, 312, 318, 322, 327, 362*, 406, 410, 458*, 499, 508, 524, 535, 540, 545, 555, 558, 563, 583; **2**/23, 55, 75, 91, 94, 124, 216, 229, 234, 272, 285, 361; **3**/26, 43, 47, 53*, 55, 132, 189, 232, 285, 331, 350, 366, 370, 389; pp. xiii, xvi, xxvi, 261 *and see* hatmaker; milliner

hatmaker, **1**/24 *and see* haberdasher; milliner

haulier, **2**/43, 331; **3**/9, 47, 201

heelmaker, **2**/293

hemp dresser, **3**/231

hive maker, **1**/190

hook maker, **1**/388* *and see* fishhook maker

hooper (hoopmaker), **1**/76, 87, 100, 404*; **2**/147; **3**/160

horn breaker, **3**/213, 349*

horn turner, **3**/262, 302

horner (horn maker), **1**/576; **3**/26, 36, 54, 80–1, 84, 86*, 143, 240, 311; p. xvi

hosier, **1**/5, 23–4, 34, 50, 82, 101, 162, 292, 428; **2**/71, 220, 264; **3**/71*, 100; p. xvi

hostler *see* ostler

husbandman, **1**/1–4, 7–8, 9*–12*, 13, 14*–15*, 20*, 22, 25*, 30, 33–4, 36, 38, 42–3, 46, 48, 51, 53, 55, 61–5, 68–70, 72*–3*, 76, 79, 80*, 82, 84, 92, 95*, 97–8, 104*, 107, 109*, 110, 112–13, 117–18, 119*, 120–2, 125*, 126, 132–3, 135, 141*, 142, 143*, 145*, 146–8, 157*–8*, 159–61, 168–9, 170*, 171, 172*, 173, 177–8, 181, 191, 203, 227*, 228–30, 237–8, 245–6, 249, 256–9, 261, 275*, 281, 285, 287, 290–1, 294, 297–8, 305, 307, 311, 314, 315*, 319, 322–3, 326*, 327, 329, 337, 340, 344, 347, 349–50, 352, 353*, 355*, 360–1, 363, 365, 367, 369, 372–3, 376*, 377, 379*, 380*, 381–2, 383*–4*, 386, 391, 393, 399, 403, 405, 408–12, 417, 420, 425, 431, 435*, 508*, 510, 514, 519, 525, 543, 548*, 585; **2**/7, 8, 12, 14, 21, 43, 61, 66*, 69–70, 73*, 76–7, 79, 83, 85, 89–90, 93*, 94–5, 97, 99, 100*, 102, 104–5, 106*, 110, 111*, 112, 113*, 115, 117, 119*, 120, 122–3, 125, 130, 133–5, 140, 146, 148*, 150–3, 155–7, 160, 166–7, 169, 170*, 173–5, 178*, 184, 189–90, 192, 194–5, 197, 200, 203–6, 208, 210, 211*, 213–15, 217–18, 219*, 220, 232–5, 238, 239*, 242, 249*, 250–2, 372*, 373–5; **3**/55, 69, 90, 107, 130, 143, 231*, 265–70, 275, 277, 278*; pp. xxiii, xxv, xxx, 261 *and see* farmer; yeoman

innkeeper (innholder), **1**/43, 160, 270, 326–7, 442, 467, 494, 512, 527n, 528, 572, 585; **2**/18, 24*, 33*, 34, 53, 58, 76, 85, 92, 124, 138, 164, 215, 229, 284, 296, 306, 308*, 324, 327–8, 362, 368; **3**/85*, 102, 141, 213, 225, 278–9, 294, 331, 334, 348, 365, 374*, 392; pp. xiii, xvi, xxvii, xxx, 265*

ironmonger, **1**/308, 404; **2**/65, 194*, 259*, 274, 325*; **3**/25, 145*, 159, 210, 223, 232, 272*, 292, 296–7, 339, 360*; pp. xi, xvi

jersey combmaker, **2**/236 *and see* combmaker

jersey comber, **2**/257, 358; **3**/116*; p. xvi

jersey spinner, **3**/178

joiner, **1**/34, 48, 62–3, 68, 72, 107, 120, 123*, 135, 179, 201, 202*, 229, 256*, 260, 276, 301, 346, 356, 362, 370, 386*, 396n, 405, 421, 424, 426, 434, 436, 460, 486–7, 489*, 513n, 537, 546, 578, 587; **2**/3, 65, 95, 109, 129–30, 147, 207, 215, 256, 273, 275, 299, 314*, 321, 323, 326*, 340, 348, 350*; **3**/25, 29*, 61*, 70, 73, 88, 93, 110*, 117*, 134–5, 146, 172*, 202, 214, 220, 228*, 250*, 267, 281, 297–8, 309, 318, 320, 334, 336, 353, 356, 368, 374, 392–3; pp. xiii, xvi, xix, xxvii, 266

knight, **2**/15; p. xxv

knitting, **2**/378

labourer, **1**/4, 10, 30, 32, 86, 101, 103, 121, 133, 145, 147*, 158–9, 169, 173, 178, 180, 261–2, 295, 301, 303, 330, 333, 335, 337, 343, 362, 366, 381, 393–4, 408, 411, 427, 429–30, 445, 450, 495, 505, 511, 520, 529, 531–2, 553, 581; **2**/12, 20, 24, 27, 38, 108, 153–4, 164, 176, 184, 193, 216, 271, 286, 337, 357, 364, 368, 376–7; **3**/14–15, 17, 22–3, 25, 35, 36*, 38, 53–4, 68, 90, 108, 118, 120, 164, 223, 224*, 225, 239–40, 243, 248*, 259, 261–2, 264, 266, 270, 280, 284, 289, 302, 308, 322, 333, 353, 360, 362–3, 370, 375, 386; pp. xvii, xxvii

lantern maker, **1**/255*, 260; **2**/26, 232; p. xvi

leather-button maker, **3**/51 *and see* button maker

INDEX OF TRADES, OCCUPATIONS AND RANKS

leatherseller, **2**/123 *and see* fellmonger
linen draper, **3**/86 *and see* draper
linen weaver, **1**/530 *and see* weaver
locksmith (lokyer), **1**/80, 340; **3**/20, 144

maltster (malt maker), **1**/69, 75, 104, 117*, 118, 123, 190, 314, 323, 342, 350, 354, 377, 391, 396, 426, 487, 512, 532, 553, 581; **2**/59, 72*, 148, 171–2, 247, 274, 281, 284, 288, 291, 323, 340, 353, 355, 367*, 378; **3**/19, 39, 59, 73, 85, 148, 191–2, 282, 296, 335, 351, 371, 375, 380, 390–1; p. xvi *and see* brewer
mariner, pp. 268–9 *and see* navigator; pilot; sailor; trowman
mason, **1**/35, 63, 161, 548, 560; **2**/10, 13, 49, 147, 172, 199, 226, 265, 279, 322; **3**/14, 26, 63, 207, 219, 334, 355, 395; pp. xvi, 267 *and see* freemason; stone cutter
mat maker, **2**/279
mercer, **1**/3*, 9, 10*, 13, 15*, 16, 20, 23, 25, 31*–2*, 33, 38*, 39–40, 42, 45*, 47*, 50*, 55*, 63*, 65, 67–8, 71, 76, 81*, 84–5, 95*, 101, 103, 109–10, 112*, 114, 118, 124*, 131–3, 135–6, 143–4, 147, 157*, 160–1, 167, 173, 177, 188, 203, 238*, 239, 248–9, 257, 260–2, 267, 270*, 272, 276, 277*, 280, 284, 295, 297, 302–3, 310–11, 324*, 327*, 329–30, 332, 335, 337–9, 341*, 342, 344, 345*, 346–7, 351*, 352, 356, 360, 368, 372*, 382*, 389, 391–2, 398–9, 401–2, 404, 413–17, 421, 422*, 431, 442, 446, 451*–2*, 458, 461, 463, 464*, 465–6, 468, 476–7, 482–3, 486–8, 492, 496, 501n, 507–8, 510, 512*, 513n, 515*, 527, 529, 533, 538, 549, 553, 557, 561–2, 565, 567, 571, 573–4, 576–7, 581, 583, 585, 586*; **2**/6, 11*, 16–17, 23, 31*, 32–3, 40, 51, 62*, 64, 75, 79*, 80, 86, 94, 97, 100–1, 119, 121, 128, 131*, 138, 143, 152, 158–9, 177, 180, 185, 204, 228, 231, 235, 242, 254, 257, 266, 295, 298, 301, 306, 313, 317, 327, 365–6; **3**/10*, 16–17, 40*, 51, 160, 162*, 164, 179*, 188, 215*, 216, 227, 268, 270, 274*, 277*, 311, 324*–5*, 332, 347, 366, 369, 377, 381, 383–4, 394, 397; pp. xi, xiii, xvi–xvii, xxi, xxv–xxvii, xxxi, 264
merchant, **1**/36, 45, 54, 69, 73, 134, 201, 239, 349, 387; **2**/165, 171, 216; **3**/21, 51, 53*, 67, 72, 82*, 85*, 89, 95, 102, 179, 198*, 219*, 245, 254, 335*, 352, 358, 363, 371, 372*–7*; pp. xvi, xxiii, xxv–xxvi, 267
merchant of the staple, p. 261
merchant tailor, **1**/207
metalman, **3**/358; pp. xiii, xxvii
miller, **1**/74, 85, 126, 132, 138, 281, 291, 331, 343, 401, 451, 502, 516; **2**/13, 70, 224, 231, 253, 267, 277, 311, 332, 354; **3**/27, 62, 109, 210, 235, 268, 373
milliner, **1**/137, 351, 367, 406, 435, 472, 482, 537; **2**/50, 71, 108, 133, 157*, 190, 220, 239; p. xvi *and see* haberdasher; hat maker
millwright, **2**/90
miner, **3**/146–7 *and see* coalminer
musician, **1**/258, 387*; **2**/147*, 304

nailer, **2**/81, 98, 201; **3**/292
narrow weaver, **1**/258; **2**/134, 137, 191, 196, 206, 209*, 220, 228, 248, 274, 295, 370; **3**/9*, 10, 122, 263, 299; p. xxix *and see* weaver
navigator, **2**/269 *and see* mariner; pilot; sailor; trowman
notary public, **1**/197

ostler (hostler), **1**/522; **3**/129
overseer of the poor, **3**/381–2

painter, **1**/315, 447, 516
painter stainer, **3**/74*
pargeter, **2**/154; **3**/243, 285*, 332–3, 348; p. 267 *and see* plasterer
pauper, **1**/313, 326, 329, 340, 341*, 351, 403, 472, 500, 540; **2**/20 *and see* son of the people
pavior, **2**/271*; **3**/322*
periwig maker, **3**/70, 128, 142, 246*; p. xvi
pewterer, **1**/7, 36, 41, 45, 84*, 86, 99, 107, 131, 207, 210, 270, 300, 304, 306*, 319, 321, 357*, 368, 396n, 397, 443, 549, 558; **2**/17, 23, 72, 108, 149, 159, 217, 263*, 298*, 300*, 301, 332*; **3**/16, 37, 40, 60, 87, 134, 163, 200, 221*, 245, 265, 291, 323, 350, 363; pp. xvi, xxvii
physician, **2**/312; **3**/94; p. xvi *and see* doctor of medicine
pilot, p. 268
pinmaker (pinner), **1**/157, 177, 260, 280, 298, 326, 328, 329*, 331, 365, 369–70, 373, 376–7, 396n, 403, 406, 414, 426, 429–30, 445*, 448*, 449–50, 461, 476, 494, 500, 515–16, 518, 527*, 528, 531, 534–5, 537, 542, 544, 549, 571, 579*; **2**/11, 13, 30, 34, 42, 45, 49, 53–4, 57*, 63*, 73, 81–2, 91, 94*, 95, 98*, 99, 100*, 101, 102*, 104, 105*, 107–8, 111–12, 118, 119*, 120, 123, 125–6, 127*, 132*, 133, 140, 141*, 142, 150*–1*, 154*–5*, 156–7, 162, 164–5, 174, 179, 184, 186*, 187, 191*, 195*, 197, 209–11, 222, 224, 225*, 226, 234, 249, 253, 258*, 260–1, 265, 268, 271, 273, 277, 280*, 282, 284, 286, 287*, 291, 293, 301, 305, 310, 314*, 322, 332, 333*, 334, 337, 339*, 341, 344, 347*, 354, 355*, 357, 363, 366, 369, 370*; **3**/9, 10*–11*, 12*, 17*, 19*–20*,

pinmaker (*cont.*)
21–2, 25, 34, 35*–6*, 37–8, 48, 53, 59, 62, 69, 85, 87–8, 94, 107, 115, 116*, 117–20, 122, 129–30, 131*, 135*, 144, 158, 159*, 160, 162–3, 173, 175*, 176–7, 178*, 190, 192, 194–5, 206, 216, 218*, 222*, 223, 236, 239, 243*, 246–7, 251*, 262, 265*, 267, 269–70, 274*–5*, 281*, 286, 289, 293, 297*, 305*, 307, 309, 315*, 320, 330*, 337, 338*, 345*, 357*, 358, 359*, 361*–2*, 367*, 368, 376*, 381–2, 383*, 385; pp. xvi, xviii, xxvii–xxviii

pipe maker, 3/207, 348, 390* *and see* tobacco-pipe maker

plasterer, 2/185, 211, 240, 293, 301, 305, 337; 3/115, 176, 193, 271, 323, 334*, 338, 365, 376*, 385, 386*; p. xvi

plumber, 1/435; 3/27

ropemaker (ropier), 1/5, 42, 103*, 108, 191, 337, 343, 357, 400, 404*, 476n, 478*, 493, 559, 578*; 2/235, 287*, 315; 3/15, 26, 30, 35, 100, 283*, 318, 354*, 359*, 363; p. xvi

rugmaker, 3/72, 107

saddler, 1/4, 11–12, 24–5, 30, 41*, 47, 53, 97, 109, 116, 136, 142, 148*, 157, 188, 207, 248, 256, 295*, 306, 324, 328, 346*–7*, 351, 382, 401, 430, 479*, 528*, 539, 546, 553, 555, 563*, 564; 2/8, 50*, 53, 106, 123, 197, 203, 225, 326; 3/23, 24*, 82*, 91, 145, 189, 230, 232, 252, 268, 285, 287, 313*, 321, 324, 339, 343, 364, 378, 380, 392; p. xvi

sailor (mariner), 1/11, 13, 24, 394, 500, 525; 2/156; 275 *and see* mariner; navigator; trowman

salter, 1/9, 12, 74, 170, 431, 532; 3/212*, 277

sawyer, 1/329; 2/197, 294, 314; 3/38, 336, 384

schoolmaster, 3/361

scrivener, 1/108; 2/232*, 252; 3/87, 295, 384, 399; p. xvi

sealmaker, 1/347, 431, 513n, 514*; 2/10

serge weaver, 2/283, 351; 3/100, 354, 378, 390*, 392, 393*; pp. xvi, xxviii–xxix *and see* weaver

sergeant in the army, p. 267

servant, pp. 265*–9*; covenanted, 1/52

shearman, 1/33, 38, 50, 65, 72, 79, 91, 97, 98*, 100, 137, 146, 148, 168, 172, 179–81, 208, 246*, 293, 353*, 393, 522; pp. xiii, xvi, xxix

shepherd, 1/169

ship's carpenter, 3/349 *and see* carpenter

ship turner, 2/351

shoe mender (shoe repairer), 1/259; 2/305, 344*, 357; 3/16, 90–1, 129, 173–4, 202*, 211, 233 *and see* cobbler

shoemaker, 1/4, 15, 40, 74*, 86, 99, 201–2, 337; 2/71, 85, 92; 3/298; pp. xi, xiii, xvi, xxvii *and see* cobbler; cordwainer

sievemaker (sievegar), 1/16*, 135, 302, 382, 399, 417, 454, 531, 564, 568, 575; 2/15*, 114, 160, 258, 288; 3/44, 83*, 218*; pp. xvi, 268

silkweaver, 1/1, 11, 48, 120, 130–1, 137, 144, 161, 173, 238–9, 291, 410–11, 436n, 437*, 454, 463, 476n, 478, 480, 492, 501*, 511, 518*, 522*, 530, 533, 536, 538, 568–9, 574, 578–9, 583; 2/2*, 47*, 72–3, 113, 124, 130*, 134*, 136, 145, 149, 161, 163, 167, 175, 207, 227, 233, 248, 250, 253, 255*, 257–8, 267, 268*, 269–71, 277, 279, 285–6, 288, 296, 297*, 305, 313, 317, 321, 322*–3*, 327, 334, 337, 340–1, 345–8, 350–1, 355–6, 362–3, 367*–9*; 3/15*, 19, 28, 34*, 37, 38*, 40*, 41, 46, 48, 49*, 52*, 53, 56, 58, 61, 63, 65*, 68, 92*, 94, 101*, 105, 107–8, 109*, 118, 119*, 122, 131, 133*, 141, 144*, 148*, 158*, 161–2, 164, 173, 176–8, 184, 193, 201–2, 204, 207, 208–9, 213, 216, 224, 228*, 239, 250, 261, 279, 284, 294*, 304*, 316, 338, 347–8, 357, 366–7, 369, 373, 379, 381, 389–90, 396; pp. xvi, xxv, xxvii–xix, 261 *and see* weaver

single woman, 3/218, 243 *and see* spinster

skinner, 1/53, 87–8, 100, 189, 327, 368, 459, 521; 2/83, 103, 106, 221; 3/65, 266, 354; p. xvi

smith, 1/12–13, 14*, 36, 43, 52, 70–1, 87, 92, 96, 101, 103*, 105, 118*, 119–20, 122, 131, 137*, 141*, 142, 168, 178–9, 182, 187, 190, 198, 209, 228, 258, 274, 277, 308, 311, 319, 323, 328–9, 338, 348, 388, 411, 462, 502, 568; 2/243, 338*, 340; 3/37, 268, 275, 298*, 304 *and see* anchorsmith; blacksmith; farrier; goldsmith; gunsmith; locksmith

soap boiler, 2/156; 3/209; p. xvi

soldier *see* sergeant

son of the people, 1/66 *and see* pauper

spinster (spinster sempstress), 1/248, 461, 500, 540; 2/372*–7*; pp. xxiii–xxiv *and see* single woman

spoon maker, 2/368

stationer, 1/3, 73, 77, 122, 179; 2/342*; 3/32; p. xvi *and see* bookseller

stone carver, 2/321–2, 349*; 3/71, 119*; p. xvi *and see* carver

stone cutter, 3/41, 178, 253*, 261, 379; p. xvi *and see* freemason; mason

surgeon (master surgeon), 1/16, 87, 138, 411; 2/45, 56, 363; 3/61, 94, 101* *and see* barber surgeon

tailor, 1/5, 23*, 24–5, 27*, 30–1, 32*, 33, 35, 43, 46*, 47, 51*, 63*, 68, 72, 79, 85*, 92, 94, 98*, 100, 104, 111, 124, 129, 135*, 146, 147*, 148,

INDEX OF TRADES, OCCUPATIONS AND RANKS

159*, 161, 170, 172–3, 177*, 179, 180*, 188, 198–9, 202, 209, 247*, 256–7, 262, 267*, 268, 269*, 279–80, 285, 288–90, 298, 313*, 317*, 324, 331*, 340*–1*, 349, 357–9, 362, 368, 374–5, 382, 388, 396, 400*, 403, 405*, 409, 413–14, 419*, 433, 436*, 438, 442, 443*, 446, 458–9, 462, 466–7, 468*, 471, 474*, 475–6, 479, 483–4, 489*, 498, 500*, 507*, 516, 521, 526*, 532*, 533, 535–6, 541*, 542, 546*, 547, 550, 557, 559n, 561*, 566, 567*, 568, 573, 576, 580, 582–3; **2**/3, 7*, 10, 18–19, 21, 22*, 25*, 35*, 38, 42*, 48, 51, 55*, 60*–1*, 69, 71*, 72, 75, 83, 84*, 85, 88*, 90, 101–2, 110*, 112, 113*–14*, 116*, 117, 125, 127, 129, 135, 138, 141*, 142–3, 145, 152, 160–1, 162*, 165–6, 178*, 179, 181–3, 186–7, 190, 193*, 194, 197–8, 205, 210, 213, 221–4, 226–7, 234*, 237, 239*, 242*, 243, 251, 255, 259, 260–1, 270–2, 282, 287*, 292, 293, 293b, 295–7, 298*–9*, 300, 306, 307*, 308, 311, 313, 317, 323*, 324, 327, 334*, 339, 345*–6*, 350*, 356, 362*, 365; **3**/10, 12, 18, 21–2, 30–2, 37*, 41, 45, 48, 52, 54*, 57, 60, 62, 63*, 64, 70, 86*, 87, 89, 90*, 94, 99–100, 102, 105–6, 131, 135*, 142*, 143, 148, 160*, 174*, 177, 188, 191, 193, 195, 196*, 199, 200*, 206*, 208*, 211, 222, 225–6, 229*, 232*, 235, 238*, 239, 241*, 242, 248, 250, 260–1, 263, 268, 272–3, 279–81, 289*, 291–4, 296, 298, 303, 306–7, 310*, 311–13, 316–17, 319, 322–5, 331, 332*, 335, 338, 339*, 341–2, 351*, 352, 355*, 357, 358*, 359, 363*, 365*, 367*, 369*, 373, 375*–6*, 384, 386*–8*, 391, 394, 396*–7*, 398–9; pp. xi, xiii, xvi, xxvi–xxvii, 266–7, 269 *and see* merchant tailor

tallow chandler, **3**/375 *and see* chandler

tanner, **1**/6, 16, 19*, 21, 29, 44, 54*, 65, 67, 69–2, 79, 83–4, 87, 96, 113, 117–18, 122*, 123, 125, 126*, 132–7, 143, 147*, 158–9, 161–2, 168–9, 171, 179–81, 187, 188*, 189, 191, 197*, 199–200, 212, 227, 229*, 245, 255, 263, 270, 272*, 276–7, 280–5, 293*, 294, 300–1, 311, 315–16, 318–19, 321, 324–5, 328*, 332, 339, 344, 353, 363–4, 365*, 367*, 375, 380–1, 383*, 388–9, 391, 399, 400, 402*, 404, 407–9, 420, 423, 425*, 429, 432*, 443, 445, 452*, 457*, 463, 472, 475, 478, 480–1, 482*, 485, 489n, 491, 493, 495*, 497*, 498, 503*, 506*, 508*, 509, 511, 517, 519*, 524*–5*, 526, 529, 533, 536 *and n*, 541, 544, 547*, 548, 552*, 555, 561–2, 569, 573*, 574, 582, 587*, 588; **2**/8–9, 13, 18, 22, 24, 27, 29*, 32, 39, 43–4, 55, 56*, 59–60, 65, 81, 83, 96–7, 107, 117–18, 122, 128, 133, 140, 148, 170–1, 177, 183, 185, 189, 191*, 192, 202, 204, 208, 235, 237, 247, 251, 266, 285, 293–4, 304, 306, 315, 327, 330, 332, 336, 364; **3**/11, 14, 16, 20, 23–4, 27*, 34–5, 38–9, 81*, 108, 115–16, 131, 172, 199, 235*, 237, 276, 288, 316, 345, 347*, 359, 375, 382*–3*, 395; pp. xiii, xvi, xxvi–xvii

thatcher, **2**/16

theology, professor of, **3**/193, 245

tiler, **1**/54, 318, 569*; **2**/38, 185, 211, 240, 293; **3**/88, 110, 115, 143, 188, 193, 276, 324, 333, 334*, 338, 376*, 385; p. xvi

tinplate worker, **3**/266

tobacco-pipe maker, **2**/93*, 137, 190, 222, 236, 245, 335, 336*; **3**/100, 106, 132, 178, 192, 237; p. xvi *and see* pipe maker

tobacconist, **2**/252, 352; **3**/143, 308; p. xvi

town clerk *see* Index of Subjects: clerk

toyman, **3**/394

trowman, **1**/118; **2**/172, 191, 258; **3**/217, 343; p. xxv, 268 *and see* mariner; navigator; sailor

trunkmaker, **1**/525

tucker *see* fuller

turner, **1**/6, 66, 100, 118, 124, 146, 210, 350, 472, 539, 570; **2**/11*, 44, 64*, 75, 89*, 105, 125–6, 199, 201, 215*–16*, 237, 256, 269, 324, 356*, 360, 364, 368–9; **3**/10*, 22, 25, 43, 46, 67, 161, 146, 298; p. xvi *and see* ship turner

turnmaker, **1**/575

upholsterer, **1**/167, 210, 246, 277, 549; **2**/165, 193; **3**/282, 392; p. xvi

victualler, **1**/2, 325, 407, 476, 521; **2**/41, 78, 85, 134, 142, 179, 204, 228, 261, 263, 270*, 276, 282, 315, 321, 355, 362; **3**/39, 52, 66, 73, 80, 121*, 159*, 188, 191, 269, 287, 315–16, 331, 333, 363; p. 267

vintner, **1**/11, 22, 106, 133, 141, 160, 179, 238, 256, 269, 331*, 441, 471, 484, 499–500, 552, 564; **2**/82, 111, 158, 229, 282, 309, 328, 347; **3**/51, 53, 67, 117, 134, 206, 252, 340, 282, 306; p. xvi

waggoner, **3**/374

watchmaker, **3**/321; p. 268 *and see* clockmaker

waterman, **1**/107

weaver, **1**/3*, 12–3, 14*, 15, 21*, 25–6, 50, 53, 55, 86–7, 94, 97, 99*, 105, 109, 110*, 111, 113*, 117, 119, 125, 130, 132–3, 135, 138*, 143, 161, 170–1, 181, 198, 211, 268, 271, 282, 289*, 292–3, 304*, 344–5, 347, 348*, 351, 360, 374, 379*, 381, 389, 397, 399, 402, 412, 435, 440, 454*, 477, 484, 487, 489n, 492*, 499, 502, 506, 509, 516, 521, 546, 562, 564, 577, 579; **2**/13, 117n, 148, 205, 231, 281, 325, 348; **3**/49, 65, 116, 211,

weaver (*cont.*)
218, 240, 251*, 277, 337, 363, 371, 377*, 398–9; pp. xi, xiii, xvi–xvii, xx, xxvi, xxviii–xxix *and see* broadweaver; carpet weaver; cotton weaver; coverlet weaver; garter weaver; linen weaver; narrow weaver; serge weaver; silk weaver

wheelwright (wheeler), **1**/412; **2**/185; **3**/282, 352, 358; p. 266

white-wire drawer, **3**/35

wine cooper, **2**/92 *and see* cooper

wiredrawer, **1**/8, 29, 37*, 44*, 73, 86*, 107*, 109, 121, 125*, 129, 143, 147, 209*, 211, 229, 262, 299, 314, 317, 325, 331, 338*, 347, 377–8, 394, 403, 423*, 450, 476n, 477*, 482, 489n, 490*, 499, 510–11, 520–1, 530, 537, 540, 543–4, 547*, 548, 551, 556, 570, 574; **2**/4, 8, 13, 35, 41*, 52, 58, 60–1, 68*, 84, 86, 98, 110, 129, 147, 156, 170, 172–4, 176*, 180, 187, 206, 209, 233, 259, 266, 268, 286*, 316*, 333, 360; **3**/12, 29*, 44, 68–9, 87, 95, 101, 120*, 135n, 140*, 163, 212, 270, 308, 315, 343, 359, 370, 383; p. xvi *and see* white-wire drawer

wool comber (comber), **2**/351, 364; **3**/39, 42, 56, 105, 118, 135, 158, 233, 236, 265, 273, 287, 288*, 311, 314, 332, 336, 344, 346*, 354, 366, 371, 393, 396; p. xvi *and see* worsted comber

woollen draper, **1**/22, 23*, 24–5, 31, 42, 49, 65–6, 75, 84, 94, 99, 181, 190*, 208, 227, 249*, 250, 269, 273, 288, 304, 317, 321, 330, 352, 354, 361, 413, 426, 457, 459, 507*, 542, 544; **2**/3, 58, 68, 70*, 91, 119–20, 136, 217, 221*, 232, 245*, 256; **3**/22, 270, 298, 356; p. xvi *and see* draper

worsted comber, **2**/331 *and see* wool comber

yeoman, **1**/4, 5*, 7*, 8, 9*, 10–13, 15, 21*, 22, 23*, 24–5, 34, 40–2, 44, 62, 65, 67*, 68, 71, 72*, 75, 76*, 80, 81*, 83*, 84, 85*, 86, 88, 94*, 95, 96*–8*, 99, 100*–1*, 103*, 104, 109, 116, 118, 126*, 127, 131–3, 134*, 135, 136*, 144*–5*, 147, 160*, 167–8, 170–3, 178*, 180, 188*, 189, 202, 228–30, 237, 239*, 246–7, 248*–9*, 250, 255, 256*–7*, 259, 260, 267*, 268–70, 272*–4*, 276*–7*, 278–9, 281–2, 283*–4*, 285, 288, 291–2, 293*, 294, 299–300, 302–3, 306*, 307–8, 311*, 313*, 314–15, 316*, 317, 319, 321–2, 326*, 327, 328*, 330*, 331, 332*–4*, 335, 338, 340, 343–4, 345*–6*, 347–8, 349*, 350, 351*–2*, 356–9, 362–3, 365, 368 *and* n, 370, 372–3, 375, 378, 382, 383*, 385*, 387, 389, 392, 396*, 398, 401, 402*, 404–5, 407*, 408, 414–16, 418, 423, 427–9, 430*, 431–2, 434, 438, 441, 444*, 445, 446*, 449, 453, 455–8, 460*–1*, 462–3, 464*, 466, 469*–70*, 472–4, 478, 479*, 480, 483, 485*–7*, 488, 490, 492, 493*, 494, 496, 498, 499*, 503, 504*, 506–7, 508*, 510*, 511–12, 515, 517*, 518–19, 523, 524*, 526, 527 *and* n, 531*, 533–4, 536–9, 543, 547–8, 550*–3*, 554, 555*, 557–8, 560–2, 565–6, 567*–8*, 569–71, 572*, 573, 582, 584*, 586, 587*; **2**/1–3, 5–7, 9–11, 12*, 14, 17*, 19, 20, 27, 35, 38–9, 48*, 56, 58, 59*, 61–3, 65–7, 69, 74*, 76, 78, 83, 86–7, 89, 91*, 103, 105, 107*, 109–10, 112–13, 115*, 117, 119, 121, 128–9, 133, 135, 137–9, 145, 146*, 149–50, 153, 159–61, 167, 169, 171, 174, 176, 178, 180, 182, 184, 192, 196–8, 200–3, 205–6, 207*, 208–9, 219, 221, 224, 225*, 226–7, 239*–41*, 247*–8*, 252–3, 255, 256*–7*, 258, 260, 262–3, 264*, 265, 266*–7*, 268, 272, 274, 276*, 280*, 282–3, 285, 291, 292*, 293b, 294–5, 297*, 298–301, 306*–7*, 311–12, 313*, 316–17, 320, 322, 324, 326–7, 330*, 334–5, 336*, 338*, 340*, 342, 346, 347*, 348, 349*, 350, 351*, 354, 358, 360*, 361–4, 367, 370*; **3**/12, 14*–16*, 17, 19, 21, 24–5, 26*, 27, 28*, 29–31, 32*, 34, 36–8, 40, 44*–5*, 46, 47*, 48, 54, 55*, 56, 57*–8*, 61–2, 64, 66–7, 70, 72, 74*, 80*, 82–3, 84*, 86, 89, 91, 93*, 100, 103–4, 106*, 107, 115, 116*, 117, 122, 130*, 133, 134*, 135, 140, 143–7, 158*, 160, 161*, 162–3, 172, 175*, 176, 189–90, 193, 199–200, 204, 207, 212, 214–15, 217–20, 221*, 222, 229–30, 232–5, 239, 244, 245*, 246–9, 251, 252*, 254, 260–1, 263*, 264, 271–4, 278, 285, 288, 289*–92*, 295, 299, 302, 304*, 310*, 312*, 313, 316–17, 320–1, 322*, 324*, 333–4, 336–7, 340, 341*, 342, 344, 345*, 346, 349*, 350–2, 353*, 354, 357, 364*, 366–73, 374*, 376, 379–80, 382*–3*, 384, 385*, 386, 388*, 389–93, 397–8, 400; pp. xxi, xxiv–xxv, 268–9 *and see* farmer; husbandman

SELECTIVE INDEX OF SUBJECTS

References to the calendar are to the volumes and pages of the MSS., which are given in the left-hand column of the calendar; references preceded by 'p.' or 'pp.' are to the pages of the introduction or the appendixes. An asterisk * indicates that the reference is to more than one occurrence.

ACTS AND STATUTES
 Artificers, 1563, pp. xi–xiii, xvii
 Poor Law, 1601, p. xii
 Settlement, 1691, p. xii
APPRENTICE
 age of, pp. xii, xvii–xviii, xxi–xxii
 allowed to learn 'any art or mystery', **1**/73
 assigned to new master, **1**/5, 31, 54, 85, 212, 227, 246, 280*, 342, 348, 389, 412, 418; **2**/9, 33, 39, 58, 61, 94, 100, 109, 176, 249, 280; **3**/161, 164, 179, 184, 195, 299, 310, 317, 326, 330, 347*, 355, 362, 367; pp. xix, xxxi *and see* Appendix V
  at apprentice's request or on his own action, **1**/98, 327; p. 264
  by or with consent of old master, **1**/80, 249, 261, 269, 295, 328, 330, 377 571; **2**/7, 41, 54, 81, 110, 151, 191; **3**/317, 357, 377, 386–7; p. xix
  by or with consent of mistress [master dead, or presumably so], **1**/401; **3**/31; **2**/287, 349; p. xix
  by order of [Quarter] Sessions, **1**/270; **2**/322; **3**/312; p. xix
  on death or departure of old master or mistress, **2**/37, 60, 110, 119–20, 131, 315; **3**/307, 385
  to new master in different trade, **1**/249; **2**/268, 284; **3**/31, 280
 at end of term, to have:
  according to customs of Gloucester, **1**/171
  instrument called a citherne, **1**/211
  money, pp. xviii–xx, xxiii
  no clothes, **2**/118
  nothing, **1**/116
  three suits of clothes, **2**/127, 149
  two suits of clothes, **1**/1, 19, 29, 64, 75–6, 87, 91, 109–10, 113*, 114, 116, 124*–6*, 129*–36*, 137–8, 141*, 167, 246, 291, 346, 355*–7*, 363–4, 365*, 366–7, 373–4, 375*–6*, 377, 393–5, 410, 411*, 443, 562, 578*; **2**/155, 256, 349
  two suits of clothes, for holidays and work, **1**/61; pp. xviii, 261
  two suits of clothes, one specified, **2**/256; p. xix
 bound a second time, to new master, **1**/375, 548; pp. xix, 274–6
 bound a second time, to old master, **1**/304, 379; pp. xix–xx
 bound to a parent, p. xxi
 death of, by drowning, **1**/405
 discharged, **1**/330, 547; **2**/164, 244, 268, 307, 309; **3**/36, 230, 313; pp. xx, xxxi, 264
  because over 27 when bound, **1**/481; p. xiv
 during term
  himself or parents to find clothes, food or other necessaries, **1**/246, 271, 571; **2**/9, 155, 349; p. xviii
  master to find clothes, food or other necessaries or money for clothes, **1**/116, 208, 246; **2**/150, 349; pp. xviii, 261–2
 fatherless, pp. xxi, xxv–xxvii
 female, **1**/248, 305; **2**/26, 372*–7*, 378; pp. xi, xxiii
 fraudulent, **2**/308; p. xiv
 freedom to be granted, **1**/31, 162, 328
 living not with mistress, **3**/26
 not bound by indenture, p. 268
 pauper, pp. xiii, xv, xxvii
 placed by or with agreement of chamber, mayor and aldermen or mayor and burgesses, **1**/351*, 406; **2**/184, 187
 placed by or with consent of parish officers, **1**/51; **3**/381–2
 service as covenanted servant at end of term, **1**/52
 service done for only a year, **2**/199
 service not done, **2**/308; because absent, **2**/39; because sick, **2**/270
 service other than in Gloucester, p. 265
 service with master before being bound, **3**/298, 313
 surname taken from father's forename, **1**/23, 71, 125, 147*, 159, 162, 172, 238, 417, 517; p. xxiv
 taken on improperly, **3**/ 24
 wages, **1**/92; **2**/134, 155
assizes, **2**/141*n*; p. xxi
books [an unexplained mention], **1**/129*n*
bucket money *see* firefighting

chamber, city, p. 269*; chamberlain, p. xv; accounts, p. 270
CHARITIES, pp. xii, xix–xxiv, xxxi, 263
  bond to repay in event of death, 1/501n; p. xii
  casting vote *see* mayor
  founder's kin, 1/357n
churchwardens, 1/51; pp. xiii, xxvii
city court, attorney in, p. 268
clerk of council (town clerk), 2/309; pp. xiii–xiv, xxii, 267; death of, 1/39
common council, 2/141n*, 308; 3/24, 26, 134; pp. xiii–xv, xx–xxi, 265
companies *see* guilds

death *see* apprentice; clerk; mayor
drainage *see* water supply

East India Company, p. xx

fee forgiven *see* mayor
firefighting: bucket money, pp. xiv, 270
fraternities *see* guilds
FREEDOM, MUNICIPAL, p. xiii
  admission, pp. 265–73
    at request of bishop, pp. 267–9; of chancellor, p. 267; of mayor, p. 266
    by apprenticeship, pp. xiv, xvi–xvii, 270–3; though master not a freeman, p. 269
    by patrimony, pp. xiv, xvi–xvii, 270–3
    of widows, p. xxvii
    on condition of public works, pp. 265*, 266, 267*–9*
    on marriage to freeman's or burgess's widow, daughter or grandchild, pp. 265, 266*–9*
    readmission after disfranchisement, pp. 265*, 266
  apprentice to be granted *see* apprentice
  master disfranchised or not a freeman *see* master
  not taken up, p. xv
  not to be granted, 1/481; 3/286
  privileges of, pp. xiii, xv

GUILDS (companies, fraternities), pp. xi–xii, xvii
  composition companies (bakers, barbers, butchers, glovers, haberdashers, innkeepers, joiners, mercers, metalmen, shearmen, tailors, tanners, weavers), pp. xiii, xv
  bakers, rules of, p. xiii
  barbers, p. 268
  cooks and innholders, 2/203
  dyers, p. 266
  mercers, master of, 1/31
  metalmen, rules of, p. xiii

  shoemakers, p. 267
  smiths and hammermen, p. 268
  tailors, pp. 266–7, 269

INDENTURES, pp. xi–xiv, xvii, 261–2
  cancelled (or delivered up), 2/74, 244, 251, 307, 309; 3/24, 26, 36, 207, 286, 313
  cancelled by being burnt, 2/164; p. xx
  enrolled (registered) by order of mayor and justices, 2/297
  enrolled (registered) long after being made, 2/46, 62, 87–8, 92, 108, 110*, 112, 151, 159, 192, 193*, 194, 199
  enrolled (registered) without fee, 1/358
  enrolled: language of entries, 2/76, 257; p. xxxi; exceptionally in English (before 1651, after 1660), 1/363, 443; 2/258 3/356
  lost, p. 268; lost and new ones made, 3/385
  made by master, 1/363
  made void, 2/220; registration void because in wrong mayoralty, 1/312*
  replaced by one for longer term *see* term
  text given in full, 1/1. 29, 39, 61
inns *see* Index of Places: Gloucester

MASTER
  disfranchised, 2/308; 3/134; p. xiv
  gone away, 2/131; p. xix
  having more than one apprentice, pp. xxvii–xxviii, xxxi
  incapable of keeping apprentice, 3/230
  not a burgess, 2/135
  not a freeman, 1/162, 395–6; 2/201, 237, 251; p. 269
  not living in the city, 3/230, 310, 331, 357
  sworn as a burgess, 2/184
  widow as, p. xxvii
MAYOR
  apprentice placed by, p. xxvii
  casting vote in applying charities, 2/25n, 141n; 3/311n, 393n; p. xxi
  death of, 1/1
  dinner for, p. 260
  fee payable to, p. xiv; fee forgiven, p. 272
  registration by, p. xiv

overseers of the poor, 3/381–2; p. xiii

plague, ordinances for preserving the city from, p. 265
PREMIUM, pp. xvii, xxi
  paid by kinsman, 1/505, p. xvii
  paid by mayor and burgesses, 2/323, 333, 352

recorder (of Gloucester), pp. xxiii, 267, 269

sheriff (of Gloucester), p. xiv
steward (of Gloucester), p. xiv
surname *see* apprentice

TERM, pp. xi, xiii, xvii–xviii
  not fulfilled, **3**/286

  replaced by longer one, **1**/304
  years remitted, **1**/31
town clerk *see* clerk of council
trained band, p. 267

wages *see* apprentice
water supply or drainage, pp. 265, 267
widow as master *see* freedom; master